INTERNATIONAL BUSINESS TAXATION

LAW IN CONTEXT

Editors: Robert Stevens (University of California, Santa Cruz)
William Twining (University College, London) and
Christopher McCrudden (Lincoln College, Oxford)

International Business Taxation

A Study in the Internationalization of Business Regulation

SOL PICCIOTTO

Professor of Law at the University of Lancaster

WEIDENFELD AND NICOLSON
London

Dedicated
with deepest love and gratitude
to
my parents, Murad and Rachel

George Weidenfeld and Nicolson Ltd
91 Clapham High Street, London SW4 7TA

ISBN 0 297 82106 7 cased
ISBN 0 297 82107 5 paperback

Photoset by Deltatype Ltd, Ellesmere Port, Cheshire
Printed in Great Britain by
Butler & Tanner Ltd, Frome and London

TABLE OF CHAPTERS

TABLE OF CONTENTS

ACKNOWLEDGEMENTS

The research for this book originated as part of a larger project on the co-ordination of jurisdiction to regulate international business, which is continuing. I am grateful to the Nuffield Foundation, the Research and Innovations Fund of the University of Warwick, and the Legal Research Institute of the School of Law, for grants which have assisted this research; as well as to the University of Warwick for study leave during which some of it was carried out.

I am grateful to many tax officials and specialists for their assistance and for taking time to explain and discuss their work and opinions on professional matters with me. Help of various kinds was given by far too many people to mention. Those who were kind enough to give time for interviews include: Peter Fawcett, Peter Harrison and P. H. Linfoot of the UK Inland Revenue; Mr Sweeting and Robert Tobin, Revenue Service Representatives of the US Internal Revenue Service; Arthur Kanakis, Sterling Jordan, Paul Rolli of the IRS; Mark Beams, Ann Fisher, and Stan Novack of the Office of International Tax Counsel of the US Treasury; Harrison Cohen of the US Congress Joint Tax Committee; John Venuti of Arthur Andersen and Robert Cole, of Cole, Corette (both formerly of the US Treasury); Jean-Louis Liénard and Jeffrey Owens of the OECD Fiscal Committee; Pietro Crescenzi of the European Commission; John Blair and Dick Esam of the International Department of the Confederation of British Industry; Mme Suzanne Vidal-Naquet of the Fiscal Commission of the International Chamber of Commerce; Mr Aramaki of the Japanese Ministry of Finance; Anne Mespelaere and Noel Horny, French Attachés Fiscaux; M. Froidevaux, legal adviser to the Trade Development Bank in Geneva; M. Luthi of the Swiss Federal Tax Office's international department; Frau Portner of the German Federal Ministry of Finance and Stefan Keller of the Federal Foreign Ministry.

Liz Anker and Jolyon Hall at the University of Warwick library have been helpful in tracking down obscure sources and keeping an eye open for interesting items; and I have also had much assistance from librarians at the Inland Revenue library, the Public Records Office and the Library of Congress. I would like to thank colleagues who have read, and provided helpful comments on drafts of parts of the book, especially Julio Faundez and Joe McCahery. Robin Murray first awakened my interest in the transfer price question and has long provided a source of lively stimulation. Many colleagues at the University of Warwick, especially in the School of Law and the Department of Sociology, have made it a congenial intellectual environment, despite the increasing pressures; while colleagues and friends at the Law Faculty of Nagoya University, especially Professors Kaino, Matsui and Taguchi, were extremely hospitable and helpful during part of my study leave. Hugo Radice, Robert Picciotto and Joe Jacob also provided hospitality and help during visits to the USA. Tim Green and Wiebina Heesterman have been unfailingly patient in unravelling wordprocessing problems, while Helen Beresford, Barbara Gray, Jill Watson and Margaret Wright have provided superbly efficient administrative support which has enabled me to keep on top of my teaching and administrative duties while continuing work on this book. Of course, responsibility for the arguments and views expressed in this book, as well as for the errors which undoubtedly remain, is wholly mine.

For helping to provide a domestic environment that was also intellectually stimulating, my deepest affection goes to my wife, Catherine Hoskyns, and our wonderful daughter, Anna; also to other short and long-stay visitors, especially Mark, Fiona and Pauline.

INTRODUCTION

The taxation of international business is a vital political and social issue, as well as raising many fascinating legal, political and economic questions. Taxation is the point of most direct interaction between government and citizens, the state and the economy. Yet the technical complexities of taxation often make informed debate difficult. This book aims to provide a survey of the development and operation of international business taxation which is sufficiently detailed to provide an adequate understanding of its complexities, yet analytical enough to bring out the important policy issues.

The international interaction of tax systems has been recognized since at least the First World War as an important element in international finance and investment. With the growth of state taxation of income, including business income or profits, each state had to adapt its tax measures to its international payments and investment flows. Conflicts and differential treatment between states led to pressures from business for the elimination of international double taxation. Although early hopes of a comprehensive multilateral agreement allocating jurisdiction to tax were soon dashed, a loose system for the co-ordination of tax jurisdiction was laboriously constructed.

This was composed of three related elements. First, national tax systems accepted, to a greater or lesser extent, some limitations on their scope of application. Second, a process of co-ordination by international agreement emerged, in the form of a network of bilateral tax treaties, based on model conventions, adapted to suit the political and economic circumstances of each pair of parties. The third element was the growth of a community of international fiscal specialists, composed of government officials, academic experts and business advisors or representatives. It was they who devised the model conventions, through lengthy discussion and analysis and countless meetings. They also negotiated the actual bilateral treaties based on the models, the experience of which in turn contributed to subsequent revisions of the models. Finally, the allocation to national tax jurisdictions of income derived from international business activities has depended, to a great extent, on bargaining processes also carried out by such specialists, on behalf of the state and of business.

These international tax arrangements were an important feature of the liberalized international system which stimulated the growth of international investment after the Second World War. This growth of international business, and especially of the largely internationally integrated corporate groups, or Transnational Corporations (TNCs), led to increasing pressures on the processes of international business regulation. In the field of taxation, the loose network of bilateral tax treaties proved a clumsy mechanism for co-ordinating tax jurisdiction. They defined and allocated rights to tax: broadly, the business profits of a company or permanent establishment could be taxed at source, while the returns on investment were primarily taxable by the country of residence of the owner or investor. This compromise concealed the disagreement between the major capital-exporting countries, especially Britain and the United States, and other countries which were mainly capital importers. The former claimed a residual right to tax the global income of their citizens or residents, subject only to a credit for foreign taxes paid or exemption of taxed income: in economic terms, this was to ensure equity in taxation of the returns from investment at home and abroad. Capital-importing countries on the other hand emphasized their right to exclusive jurisdiction over business carried out within their borders, whatever the source of finance or ownership.

This divergence was exacerbated as international investment became predominantly direct rather than portfolio investment, since internationally-integrated firms are able to borrow in the cheapest financial markets and retain a high proportion of earnings, in the most convenient location, rather than financing foreign investment from domestic earnings and repatriating all foreign profits. However, such firms were able to exploit the avoidance opportunities offered by the interaction of national tax laws and the inadequate co-ordination established by the international arrangements. Specifically, it was possible to defer taxation of investment returns by countries of residence, on foreign earnings retained abroad and not re-patriated; while maximizing costs charged to operating subsidiaries so as to reduce source taxation of business profits. An important element in such strategies was the development of facilities in convenient jurisdictions, some of which had already emerged as tax havens for individual and family wealth. This quickly became transformed by the related but even more important phenomenon, the offshore financial centre.

The problem of fair and effective taxation of international business was necessarily related to the increasing tensions within national tax systems. The growing burden of public finance has tended to fall primarily on the individual taxpayer, as states extended incentives to business investment, especially from abroad, and as international business in many industries reduced its effective tax rate by use of intermediary companies located in tax havens. While these arrangements had some legitimacy in relation to the retained earnings of genuinely international firms, they became increasingly available for others, including national businesses, as well as individual evaders and criminal organizations.

Thus, attention became focused on the possibilities for international avoidance and evasion available for those who could take advantage of transfer price manipulation, international financing and tax and secrecy havens. Since the countries of residence of international investors already claimed a residual jurisdiction to tax global earnings, their response was to strengthen their measures for taxation of unrepatriated retained earnings. However, such unilateral measures quickly ran into jurisdictional limitations, due to the lack of any internationally agreed criteria for defining and allocating the tax base of international business. The original debate about international double taxation had considered, and largely rejected, the possibility of a global approach, which would have required international agreement both on the principles for defining the tax base, as well as a formula for its apportionment. Instead, the tax treaty system had embodied the approach of separate assessment by national tax authorities; however, it was accepted that they could rectify accounts presented by a local branch or subsidiary if transactions between affiliates did not represent the terms that would have applied between independent parties operating at 'arm's length'. Such adjustments would represent effectively a case-by-case allocation of globally earned profits, and would require negotiation and agreement between the firm and the competent authorities of the countries involved. As the problems of international allocation became exacerbated, the questions of effectiveness and legitimacy of these arrangements came to the fore.

From the earliest discussions of international taxation, government officials had emphasized that measures to combat international tax avoidance and fraud must complement the provisions for prevention of double taxation. Business representatives were more ambivalent, and emphasized the need for freedom in international financial flows. Model conventions for administrative assistance between tax authorities, both in assessment and collection of taxes, were drawn up; but they were implemented only to a limited extent, generally by means of one or two simple articles in the treaties on avoidance of double taxation. These have nevertheless formed the basis for an increasingly elaborate system of administrative co-operation. The secretive and bureaucratic character of this administrative system has been the target of some criticism by business representatives. However, they have opposed proposals to rationalize and legitimate anti-avoidance measures, notably a new multilateral treaty for administrative assistance drafted within the framework of the OECD and the Council of Europe, which was opened for ratification in 1988.

The question of international equity was also raised by the controversy over Worldwide Unitary Taxation (WUT) which emerged from the end of the 1970s. This resulted from the application by some states of the United States, especially rapidly-growing states such as California, of their system of formula apportionment in a systematic way to the worldwide income of TNCs. Foreign-based TNCs, which had tried to establish a foothold in important US markets frequently at the expense of substantial local losses, complained that the levying of state income taxes on a proportion of their worldwide income was discriminatory. It was also alleged that such global approaches to allocation were contrary to the separate accounting and arm's length pricing principles embodied in the tax treaty system. This revived interest in the history of the international arrangements, which showed that separate accounting had never excluded the allocation of either profits or costs by some sort of formula method. The international adoption of a unitary approach was excluded in the early discussions because of the great difficulty anticipated in reaching agreement for uniformity, both in assessment methods as well as in the actual formula to be used. However, it had always been accepted that the allocation of profits and costs of internationally-integrated businesses, even on the basis of separate accounts, might be done by a formula method. Instead of an internationally-agreed general formula, this meant negotiations on a case-by-case basis. This was considered workable by most of the tax officials and business advisors who operated the system, who felt that specific technical solutions could be found, but an openly-agreed international scheme would be politically impossible. However, the growth of global business and the increasing complexity of its financing and tax planning arrangements have put increasing pressures on this system.

These pressures have combined with the concern about international avoidance to raise very directly the issues of international equity – where and how much international business should be taxed. It is these social and political issues that have long been buried in the technical intricacies of the international taxation system. I hope that this study will enable some of these issues to be brought into public debate and discussion. At the same time, it aims to provide a systematic introduction to the major issues of international taxation of business income or profits that will be of interest to students and teachers either in law, economics or political science. The study attempts to integrate perspectives from all these disciplines, and to make a contribution based on a specific study to a number of areas of social science theory, notably the historical development and changing character of the international state system and international legal relations, and the dynamics of international regulation of economic activities. I am very aware that the ambitious nature of my undertaking may lead specialists to feel that I have not adequately dealt with particular technicalities, while others may find parts of the book too detailed and technical. This is a small price to pay, I believe, for the rewards in increased understanding of the issues that come from a more integrated inter-disciplinary approach. To facilitate matters for a potentially varied reader-ship, I have provided introductory and concluding summaries in most chapters, as well as the outline in this Introduction.

Sol Picciotto   University of Warwick
6 June 1991

I
History and Principles

The taxation of business profits or income originates essentially from the early part of the twentieth century. As state revenue needs became increasingly significant with the growth of military and welfare spending, most industrial capitalist countries moved from reliance on a multiplicity of specific duties, in particular high customs tariffs, to general, direct taxes on income. The acceptance of direct taxes rests on their application, as far as possible equally, to income or revenues from all sources, including business profits. Since many businesses operated on global markets, this raised the question of the jurisdictional scope of taxation.

During the first half of this century, international business profits resulted mainly from foreign trade and portfolio investment abroad; concern therefore focused mainly on defining where profits from international sales were deemed to be earned, and where a company financed from abroad should be considered taxable. The question of export profits was broadly resolved by developing a distinction between manufacturing and merchanting profit, and allocating the latter to the importing state if the sale was attributable to a Permanent Establishment.

The problem of international investment was more difficult, and gave rise, as will be discussed in more detail below, to conflicts between the residence and source principles. The compromise arrangement which emerged consisted in restricting taxation at source to the business profits of a Permanent Establishment or subsidiary, while giving the country of residence of the lender the primary right to tax investment income. This formula was inappropriate or ambiguous in relation to the type of investment that came to dominate the post-1945 period: foreign direct investment by internationally-integrated Transnational Corporations (TNCs).

1. Global Business and International Taxation

The first TNCs had already emerged by 1914, resulting from the growth of world trade and investment, and the increased concentration of large-scale business institutionalized in the corporate form, in the period 1865–1914, from the end of the American Civil War to the outbreak of the First World War. However, long-term international investment at that time primarily took the form of loans, in particular the purchase of foreign, especially government, bonds. It has been estimated that of the total $44 billion of world long-term foreign investment stock in 1914, no more than one-third, or some $14 billion, could be classified as foreign direct investment (Dunning 1988, p. 72). Even this figure includes as investments involving 'control' many which were significantly different from subsequent international direct investments. British lenders concerned with the high risk of foreign enterprises used syndicated loans, for example to invest in US breweries in the 1890s (Buckley & Roberts 1982, pp. 53–6). A common pattern in mining was for a syndicate to secure a concession to be transferred to a company floated for the purpose, thus securing promotional profits as well as a major stake for the founders, as for example the purchase of the Rio Tinto concession from the Spanish government by the Matheson syndicate in 1873 (Harvey & Press 1990). Similarly, Cecil Rhodes raised finance from a syndicate headed by Rothschilds to enable the centralization and concentration of Kimberley diamond mining after 1875 under the control of De Beers Consolidated Mines; and Rhodes and Rudd again raised capital in the City of London for the development of gold mining, setting up Gold Fields of South Africa Ltd in 1887, and in 1893 Consolidated Gold Fields, to pioneer the mining finance house system, in which control of the company's affairs typically was divided between operational management on the spot and financial and investment decisions taken in London. These were the successes among some 8,400 companies promoted in London between 1870 and 1914 to manage mining investments abroad (Harvey & Press 1990).

A high proportion of foreign direct investment prior to the First World War was directed to minerals or raw materials production in specific foreign locations, and did not involve internationally-integrated activities. These were certainly the major characteristics of British international investments, which were dominant in that period: Britain accounted for three-quarters of all international capital movements up to 1990, and 40 per cent of the long-term investment stock in 1914 (Dunning, in Casson 1983). Indeed, by 1913 the UK's gross overseas assets were worth nearly twice its gross domestic product, and the gross income from abroad (including taxes paid in the UK by foreign residents) has been estimated at 9.6 per cent of GDP (Mathews, Feinstein & Odling-Smee 1982). Some 40 per cent of British investment was in railways, and a further 30 per cent was lent directly to governments.

Nevertheless, it was in the period 1890–1914 that the first TNCs were established, in the sense of international groups of companies with common ownership ties (Wilkins 1970; Buckley & Roberts 1982). However, the co-ordination of their activities was relatively undeveloped: they were indeed referred to at the time as 'international combines', and there was not always a clear distinction between an international firm and an international cartel (Franko 1976). In the 1920s there was a resumption of foreign direct investment, especially by US firms in some new manufacturing industries, notably automobile assembly. The crash of 1929 and the ensuing depression caused fundamental changes. Not only did it result in the virtual ending of new net international investments until after 1945, it caused changed attitudes which affected the prospects for their resumption. State policies, especially exchange controls, as well as the caution of investors, limited international capital movements. After 1946, new foreign investment was largely by major corporations, usually building on previous ties with specific foreign markets. Above all, this direct investment characteristically involved relatively little new outflow of funds: the investment frequently took the form of capitalization of assets such as patents and knowhow, with working capital raised locally, and subsequent expansion financed from retained earnings (Whichard 1981; Barlow & Wender 1955).

This investment growth was facilitated by tax treaties whose basic principles emerged before 1939 and which quickly spread after 1945. These treaties did not directly tackle the issue of allocation of the tax base of internationally-organized business among the various jurisdictions involved. Instead, they allocated rights to tax specific income flows: the country of source was essentially limited to taxing the business profits of a local branch or subsidiary, while the country of residence of the parent company or investor was entitled to tax its worldwide income from all sources, subject at least to a credit for valid source taxes. This was intended to ensure equality of taxation between investment at home and abroad; however, capital-importing countries and TNCs argued for primacy of source taxation, to ensure tax equality between businesses competing in the same markets regardless of the countries of origin of their owners (see Chapter 2 below).

This debate viewed investment as a flow of money-capital from a home to a host state: it was therefore already irrelevant to the growth of direct investment in the 1950s, which took place largely through reinvestment of retained earnings and foreign borrowing; and became even more inappropriate with the growth of global capital markets from the 1960s. TNCs pioneered the creative use of international company structures and offshore financial centres and tax havens for international tax avoidance. Thus, they were able to reduce (sometimes to zero) their marginal tax rates, at least on retained earnings (Chapters 5 and 6 below). This in turn tended to undermine the fairness and effectiveness of national taxation (Chapter 4 below). The tax authorities of the home countries of TNCs responded by measures attempting to claw back into tax the retained earnings of 'their' TNCs, initially with unilateral provisions which were later co-ordinated (Chapter 7 below). These have met with partial success, but have also encountered great technical and political difficulties, reflecting continued jurisdictional problems.

International arrangements for taxation of international business still assume that, subject to a reasonable right for source countries to tax genuine local business activities, the residual global profits belong to the 'home' country of the TNC; but there are no clear criteria for the international allocation of costs and profits between home and host countries (Chapter 8 below). More seriously, however, this assumption is becoming increasingly inappropriate as TNCs have become much more genuinely global, combining central strategic direction with a strong emphasis on localization and diversity, with complex managerial structures and channels aiming to combine decentralized responsibility and initiative with global planning (Bartlett & Ghoshal 1989). Shares in them have become internationally traded and owned; they often draw on several centres for design, research and development located in different countries in each major region; and even their top managements are becoming multinational. Businesses such as banks and stockbrokers involved in 24-hour trading on financial markets around the world have become especially global, and able to take advantage of even tiny price differences in different markets. While the international co-ordination of business taxation has come a long way, it seems still to lag significantly behind the degree of globalization developed by business itself.

2. The Rise of Business Taxation

The move towards direct taxation of income or revenue was a general trend, especially in the years during and following the First World War; but specific variations developed in different countries, in particular in the application of income or profits taxes to businesses and companies.

2.a Taxing Residents on Income from All Sources

A number of states have applied their income taxes to the income derived by their residents from all sources, even abroad, although sometimes this does not apply to income as it arises, but only when remitted to the country of residence. The definition of residence, already difficult for individuals, creates special problems in relation to business carried out by artificial entities such as companies; while the formation of international groups of companies raises the question of whether a company owning another should be treated as a mere shareholder, or whether the group could be treated as resident where the ultimate control is exercised.

(i) Britain and the Broad Residence Rule
Britain was distinctive, since it already had a general income tax, introduced

by Pitt and Addington during the Napoleonic Wars. Although this never produced more than about 15 per cent of government revenues during the nineteenth century, it was important in establishing a single general tax on every person's income from all sources. Increases during the Boer War led to pressures for a graduated rather than a flat-rate tax, and a super-tax was instituted in 1909 in Lloyd George's 'people's budget', entering into effect only after a constitutional conflict with the House of Lords. Between 1906 and 1918 the basic rate rose from one shilling to six shillings in the £ (i.e. from 5 per cent to 30 per cent), with a super-tax of 4/6 (a top rate of 55 per cent), and the total yield increased seventeen-fold (Sabine 1966).

Pitt's property and income tax of 1798 was levied

> upon all income arising from property in Great Britain belonging to any of His Majesty's subjects although not resident in Great Britain, and upon all income of every person residing in Great Britain, and of every body politick or corporate, or company, fraternity or society of persons, whether corporate or not corporate, in Great Britain, whether any such income . . . arise . . . in Great Britain or elsewhere [39 Geo. 3 c. 13, sec. II].

This broad applicability was repeated in Schedule D of Addington's Act of 1803, and again when income tax was reintroduced by Peel in 1842.[1] It therefore applied from the beginning to bodies corporate as well as individuals, so that when incorporation by registration was introduced after 1844, the joint-stock company became liable to tax on its income like any other 'person'. Not until 1915 were companies subjected to a special tax, the wartime Excess Profits duty, which was levied on top of income tax (and accounted for 25 per cent of tax revenue between 1915 and 1921). After 1937, companies were again subjected to a profits tax and then (in 1939) an excess profits tax, both levied on top of income tax; from 1947 the profits tax was levied with a differential between distributed and undistributed income (until 1958). Only in 1965 was a Corporation Tax introduced which actually replaced both income tax and profits tax.

The personal character of the income tax, and its early emergence, therefore established the principle of taxation of British residents on their worldwide income. The liberal principle of tax justice, which legitimized the general income tax, was thought to require that all those resident in the UK should be subject to the same tax regardless of the nature or source of their income.

However, when the possibility of incorporation began to be more widely used, in the last quarter of the nineteenth century, problems arose in relation to the liability to British tax of companies whose activities largely took place

---

[1] Schedule D contains the broadest definition of income chargeable to tax, and is the provision in relation to which the residence test has continued to be mainly relevant: for the important differences in assessment between case I and cases IV and V of Schedule D, see below. Repealed in 1816, the income tax was reintroduced as a limited measure in 1842, to supplement revenue lost through reduction of import duties.

abroad. In 1876 the issue was appealed to the Exchequer court, in two cases involving the Calcutta Jute Mills and the Cesena Sulphur mines. Both were companies incorporated in England but running operations in India and Italy respectively; each had executive directors resident at the site of the foreign operations, but a majority of directors in London, to whom regular reports were made. The judgment of Chief Baron Kelly showed an acute awareness that the cases involved 'the international law of the world'; but he considered that he had no alternative but to apply what he thought to be the clear principles laid down by the statutes. The court held that in each case, although the actual business of the company was abroad, it was under the control and disposition of a person (the company) whose governing body was in England, and it was therefore 'resident' in Britain and liable to tax there. Aware that many of the shareholders were foreign residents, and that therefore a majority of the earnings of the company belonged to individuals not living in Britain and therefore 'not within the jurisdiction of its laws', the court contented itself with the thought that if such foreigners chose to place their money in British companies, they 'must pay the cost of it'.[1]

However, it was made clear that the decisions were not based on the fact that the companies were formed in Britain, but that the real control, in the sense of the investment decisions, took place in London. This was confirmed by the House of Lords decision in the De Beers case (*De Beers v. Howe*, 1906). De Beers was a company formed under South African law; not only that, but the head office and all the mining activities of the company were at Kimberley, and the general meetings were held there. Nevertheless, the House of Lords held that 'the directors' meetings in London are the meetings where the real control is always exercised in practically all the important business of the company except the mining operations'. Hence, although the company was not a British 'person', it was resident in Britain and liable to British tax on its entire income wherever earned. Further, in *Bullock v. Unit Construction Co.* (1959), East African subsidiaries were held to be managed and controlled by their parent company in London and therefore resident in the UK, even though this was contrary to their articles of association.

The decisions on residence still left open the question of definition of the tax base since, although the British income tax was a single comprehensive tax, it required a return of income under a series of headings – five schedules each containing separate headings or 'cases'. On *which* income were UK-resident businesses liable? In particular, were they liable to tax on the trading profits of the foreign business or only on the investment returns? This distinction had important implications which were not fully clear either in legal principle or in the minds of the judges. Included in liability to tax under Schedule D were the profits of a trade carried on in the UK or elsewhere (case I of Schedule D), and

---

[1] Since the British income tax was considered to be a single tax, companies were permitted to deduct at source the tax due on dividends paid to shareholders and credit the amounts against their own liability: see section 3.b below.

the income from securities (case IV) or 'possessions' (case V) out of the UK. A UK resident could in principle be liable under case I for the profits of a trade carried on abroad; but the House of Lords in *Colquhoun v. Brooks* (1889) also gave the term 'possessions' in case V a broad interpretation, to include the interest of a UK resident in a business carried on abroad (because the case concerned a partnership which itself was resident abroad, although the sleeping partner was UK-resident). The distinction was significant, since under case I profits are taxable as they arise, while income under cases IV and V was taxable only when actually remitted to the UK; the importance of the distinction was reduced after 1914, when most overseas income was brought into tax on the 'arising' basis. However, if a UK company or UK shareholders set up a foreign-resident company to carry on the foreign business, the courts took the view that UK-resident shareholders did not own the business itself but only the shares in the company. Even a sole shareholder was considered to have only the right to a dividend (*Gramophone & Typewriter Ltd v. Stanley*, 1908), unless the foreign company was a mere agent of the British company (*Apthorpe v. Peter Schoenhofer*, 1899; see also *Kodak Ltd v. Clark*, 1902). The UK owners would thus be liable to tax only on the dividends declared by the foreign-resident company, and not on its business or trading profits, which could therefore be retained by the firm without liability to UK tax.

The tax commissioners were normally willing to find that a company operating a business abroad was liable to tax under case I if directors in the UK took the investment decisions. However, confusion seems to have been caused by the view taken in *Mitchell v. Egyptian Hotels* (1914), apparently based on a misunderstanding of *Colquhoun v. Brooks*, that case I only applied if part of the trade took place in the UK. Nevertheless, a majority of the judges in the Egyptian Hotels case were willing to hold that the same facts that showed a company to be resident in the UK established that part of its trade was in the UK. This was the basis of the view taken by the Inland Revenue, which in its evidence to the Royal Commission of 1953 stated that for a company to be chargeable under case I it must be resident in the UK (using the central management and control test) *and* have part of its trade in the UK; but that 'in practice the two tests coalesce'. Despite the fundamental confusion in the legal position, caused especially by the disagreements among the judges in the Court of Appeal and House of Lords in the Egyptian Hotels case, this important legal principle was not further clarified by test case or statute.[1]

Nevertheless, British investors in a foreign business could not escape potential liability to income tax on its trading profits unless the whole of its activities and all the management and control took place abroad. This could be arranged, however, and it was even possible for a company registered in Britain to be resident abroad. In *Egyptian Delta Land and Investment Co. Ltd v. Todd* (1929) a British company set up in 1904 to own and rent land in Egypt

---

[1] See the discussion in Sumption 1982, ch. 9, and the analysis by Sheridan 1990.

had in 1907 transferred the entire control of the business to Cairo, and appointed a new board whose members and secretary were all resident in Cairo, where its meetings were held and the books, shares register and company seal kept. To comply with the Companies Acts the registered office remained in London and a register of members and directors was kept there by a London agent paid by fee, but the House of Lords held that this did not constitute UK residence. Later, tax planners could set up foreign-resident companies to ensure that individuals resident in the UK could escape tax on the trading profits of a foreign business. Thus, the entertainer David Frost in 1967 set up a foreign partnership with a Bahamian company to exploit interests in television and film business outside the UK (mainly his participation in television programmes in the USA); the courts rejected the views of the Revenue that the company was a mere sham to avoid tax on Frost's global earnings as a professional – the company and partnership were properly managed and controlled in the Bahamas and their trade was wholly abroad.[1]

The decision in the Egyptian Delta Land case created a loophole which in a sense made Britain a tax haven: foreigners could set up companies in the UK, which would not be considered UK resident under British law because they were controlled from overseas, but might be shielded from some taxation at source because they were incorporated abroad. This possibility was ended by the Finance Act of 1988 (s.66), which provided that companies incorporated in the UK are resident for tax purposes in the UK. However, the control test still applies to companies incorporated outside the UK, as well as to unincorporated associations such as partnerships, and remains relevant for tax treaties.[2] This brings the UK substantially into line with many states (especially European Community members), which use both incorporation and place of management as tests of residence (Booth 1986, p. 169).

The test of 'central management and control' developed by the British courts has never been defined by statute, despite calls for such a definition by judges and by committees (Booth 1986, p. 25). In practice, the Inland Revenue has interpreted it to mean the place where the key strategic decisions of directors are taken, as against the 'passive' control exercised by shareholders (Simon 1983, D 101–111). This provided a basis, however shaky, for the British authorities to exercise some jurisdiction over the worldwide profits of multinational company groups (TNCs) controlled from the UK. In the 1970s, however, as the pace of internationalization accelerated, and TNCs evolved more complex patterns, the Revenue developed doubts as to the

---

[1] *Newstead v. Frost* (1980); until 1974 income derived by a UK resident person from the carrying on of a trade, profession or vocation abroad was taxable under case V only on remittance: ICTA 1970, s.122 (2)(b) repealed by FA 1974, s.23.

[2] In general, Britain's pre-1963 treaties use as the test of company residence 'central management and control', while more recent treaties use the OECD model's phrase 'place of effective management': see below.

effectiveness of the definition. In particular, the control test enabled companies to arrange financial or servicing functions in affiliates whose central management and control could be said to be located offshore, and thus reduce UK tax by deducting interest charges, management fees or insurance premiums from the UK trading profits of their related entities (dealt with in Chapters 5 and 6 below). In 1981, the Revenue published a consultative document favouring a move to the test of 'effective management', which had been used in tax treaties and had been thought to amount to much the same in practice as 'central management and control'. Criticism of these proposals led to their withdrawal. The Revenue restated its interpretation of the 'central management' test, while at the same time affirming that it now took the view that the 'effective management' principle used in many tax treaties (based on the OECD model treaty) involved a different test, and therefore by implication the UK would apply this different test where its tax treaties used the 'effective management' principle, at least for the purposes of the treaty.[1]

This is the chequered history to date of the principle of taxation of the worldwide profits of British-based companies, founded on the doctrine of control, viewed from the angle of the investor of capital. The original logic of the British approach flowed from the liberal principle that all British residents should be subject to the same income tax regardless of the source of their income. In view of Britain's position prior to 1914 as by far the largest source of global investment funds, it was not surprising that the Inland Revenue should wish to apply the income tax to all businesses whose investment decisions were taken in London, and this view was generally backed by the courts; although there was more uncertainty about whether liability should extend to trading profits if wholly earned abroad, rather than the investment returns or dividends actually paid. At the same time, foreign-based companies were liable to tax on income arising in the UK, including that arising from carrying on a trade or business there. This potential overlap with the jurisdiction of other countries does not seem initially to have caused any significant problems, no doubt because the British tax was low (until the Lloyd George budget and then the war), compliance was relatively lax, and similar taxes did not exist in other countries. In the case of foreign-based companies manufacturing abroad and selling in Britain, the Revenue developed the distinction between manufacturing and merchanting profit, and the tax was levied on the profits from the mercantile activity actually carried out in Britain.[2]

---

[1] Statement of Practice 6/83, replaced in an expanded form by SP 1/90; see Note in [1990] *British Tax Review* 139.
[2] Income Tax Act 1918, Rule 12 of All Schedules Rules, now Taxes Management Act 1970, ss.80–1, see Ch. 8, section 1.d below. See also *Firestone Tyre & Rubber v. Llewellin (I.T.)* (1957) for the reverse case, where contracts were concluded by a foreign parent outside the UK for the sale of tyres manufactured by its UK subsidiary: the foreign parent was held to be trading in the UK through its subsidiary as agent, since the essential element was not the place where the contract was concluded, but the manufacturing subsidiary's links with the foreign clients.

(ii) Germany: Residence Based on Management

Britain was both typical and exceptional in its approach to residence. Many countries which developed a broadly-based income tax applied it to all residents, including other capital-exporting countries such as Sweden and the Netherlands; but in the case of companies the preferred test of residence was the location of the 'seat of management', which placed less emphasis on ultimate financial control (Norr 1962). This test meant that parent companies were less likely to be liable to taxation on the business profits of their foreign subsidiaries.

Notably in Germany, the Corporate Tax Law introduced under the Reich in 1920 introduced the combined test of the 'seat' of a company,[1] or its place of top management.[2] However, in contrast with the British test of 'central management and control', the 'place of top management' test did not include control of investment decisions, but focused on actual business management. Thus, companies effectively managed from Germany but incorporated abroad (often to avoid high German tax rates on their foreign business) could be taxed in Germany on their business profits;[3] and the Tax Administration Law of 1934 explicitly provided that a foreign subsidiary whose business was integrated with that of its German parent company should be regarded as managed and therefore resident in Germany.[4] However, majority ownership was not necessarily top management, even if the majority shareholder was informed and consulted about important investment decisions.[5]

The rule 'required a complete financial and organizational integration', and the courts finally held that it meant that the parent company must itself be carrying on a business of the same type as that of its dependent 'organ' and with which it was integrated. In one case, for example, the parent company co-ordinated four subsidiaries operating railways: it supplied them with rolling stock, and generally managed their financial, legal, investment and administrative activities. Its operations were held to constitute representation of the group to the outside world, and thus of a different type from the actual business carried on by the affiliates themselves.[6] Thus, the German residence rule did not apply to a foreign holding company, and in practice became

---

[1] The seat is the registered head office, which for a company formed under German law must be somewhere in Germany.
[2] The tax statutes of the various German states preceding this law, dating back to the Prussian Income Tax Law of 1891 which established the liability of corporations to income tax, were based only on the company's seat: Weber-Fas 1968, p. 218.
[3] Weber-Fas 1968, p. 240, provides a translation of some of the main decisions of the German tax courts on this provision; see also Weber-Fas 1973. The *Organschaft* theory was originally developed to prevent the cascade effect of turnover tax being applied to sales between related companies, a common occurrence since merged businesses often remained separately incorporated because of a high tax on mergers: see Landwehrmann 1974, pp. 244–5, and the Shell decision of 1930, discussed in Chapter 8, section 1.e below.
[4] Steueranpassungsgesetz s.15, Reichsgesetzblatt 1934–I, p. 928.
[5] Reichsfinanzhof Decision III 135/39 of 11 July 1939, translated in Weber-Fas 1968, p. 246.
[6] Decision of the Reichsfinanzhof of 1 April 1941, I 290/40: [1942] Reichssteuerblatt, p. 947.

'essentially elective' (Landwehrmann 1974, p. 249). Following concern at the rapid growth in the use of foreign intermediary companies in the 1960s to shelter the income of foreign subsidiaries, Germany enacted an International Tax Law in 1972 permitting taxation of the receipts of certain types of foreign base companies as the deemed income of their German owners (see Chapters 5, 7 and 8 below).

Other countries with a residence-based income tax explicitly exempted business profits either if earned or sometimes only if taxed abroad. Generally, therefore, companies could avoid home country taxation of their foreign business profits, if necessary by interposing a holding company or ensuring top management was abroad. Even if they had to set up foreign subsidiaries to do so, they did not have to go to the great lengths of ensuring the foreign companies were controlled from abroad that were necessary under British law.

2.b Taxing the Profits of a Business Establishment: France

A different approach emerged in countries where taxation of business and commercial profits emerged as part of a schedular system, taxing income under a series of headings. In France, despite several attempts from 1871 onwards, the general income tax was not introduced until 1914, as a personal tax on the income of individuals. This was followed in 1917 by taxes on other types of revenue: commercial and industrial profits, agricultural profits, pensions and annuities and non-commercial professions, but these were considered as separate and parallel schedular taxes, or *impots cédulaires*. These were added to the old taxes on income from land and mines, and the tax on movable property (securities, loans or deposits). Not until 1948 were these separate schedular taxes replaced by a company tax.

Hence, under the French system, the income tax from the beginning applied only to individuals, while business activities were always taxed separately and according to the sources of the revenue. This separation of the taxation of individual income from the schedular taxes applying to specific types of revenue gave the latter a 'real' rather than a 'personal' character.[1] The old property taxes were considered as arising where the land, building or mine was situated. In the case of industrial or commercial profits, liability to tax arose in respect of profits made by an establishment situated in France, regardless of whether it was operated by a company or other business entity incorporated or resident in France. Equally, a French company was not liable to tax in respect of the profits of its establishments abroad. However, France did include in the income of companies and establishments the interest and dividends received on securities (considered to be movable property), whether the debtor was in

---

[1] Court 1985 discusses the influence of the French and continental European schedular taxes on the early tax treaties, as well as more recent policy.

France or abroad. Equally, the individual income tax was levied on the income of those domiciled in France regardless of its source.

The emphasis in French taxation on the revenue derived from an activity or from property (movable or immovable) thus focused on the place where the activity took place or the property was located, i.e. the source of the revenue, rather than the place of residence of the taxpayer. It therefore enabled a more differentiated approach to the question of tax jurisdiction, by using the concept of the earnings of an 'establishment'. Other systems also shared this approach, including Belgium, some Central European countries, Italy and other Mediterranean countries, and many in Latin America. In Belgium, the duty on persons carrying on a profession, trade or industry was held by the courts in 1902 to apply to the global income of a company carrying on business partly abroad. This immediately led to business pressures to exempt foreign-source income, and although this failed, the law was changed to reduce to half the duty on profits earned by foreign establishments (International Chamber of Commerce 1921). In general, however, countries with this type of schedular income tax emphasized taxation of income at source, so that companies were not taxed on the business profits of their foreign establishments. However, schedular income taxes encouraged manipulation between different types of source, and the lower yields meant greater reliance for public finance on indirect taxes. Tax reforms following the Second World War generally introduced an integrated income tax; although corporation and individual income taxes were generally kept separate, usually the tax paid by companies on the proportion of profits distributed as dividends could be at least partially imputed to shareholders as a credit against their personal income tax liability (see below section 3.b).

2.c The USA: the Foreign Tax Credit

In the United States, the constitutional limitation of the federal taxing power meant that no general revenue tax was possible until the 16th Amendment was ratified in 1913, although a 1909 'excise' tax on corporate profits had been held valid by the courts. The ratification of the 16th Amendment finally enabled federal taxation to switch from indirect to direct taxes, and a sharp reduction of import duties was accompanied by the introduction of a graduated individual income tax. The Revenue Act of 1917 introduced a tax on corporations of 6 per cent of net income, which was doubled a year later, plus an excess profits tax. This was a graduated tax on all business profits above a 'normal' rate of return; by 1918 US corporations were paying over $2.5 billion, amounting to over half of all federal taxes (which constituted in turn one-third of federal revenue). This led to a rapid growth of the Bureau of Inland Revenue, and the institutionalization of a technocratic bureaucracy with a high degree of discretion in enforcing tax law, in particular in determining what constituted 'excess profits'. Equally, the high corporate taxes turned the major corporations into tax resisters (Brownlee 1989, pp. 1617–18).

Both the individual and the corporate income tax in the US were based on citizenship: US citizens, and corporations formed under US laws, were taxed on their income from all sources worldwide. Companies formed under the laws of other countries were, however, only liable to tax on US-source income. Thus the place of management or control of a corporation was irrelevant under the US approach. Profits made abroad were therefore not liable to US tax if the business were carried out by a foreign-incorporated company, but all corporations formed in the US were subject to tax on their worldwide income, including dividends or other payments received from foreign affiliates. However, this was mitigated by the introduction into US law of a novel feature, the provision of a credit against US tax for the tax paid to a foreign country in respect of business carried on there (Revenue Act 1918, ss.222 and 238).

The foreign tax credit was introduced following complaints by American companies with branches abroad that high US taxes disadvantaged them in relation to local competitors. It seems to have been the suggestion of Professor Adams of Yale, at the time the economic advisor to the Treasury Department, who accepted the concept that a foreign country had the prior right to tax income arising from activities taking place there. A foreign tax could previously be deducted as an expense before arriving at taxable income. To allow it to be credited not only meant a greater reduction in US tax liability, it entailed an acknowledgement of the prior right of the foreign country to tax profits earned there at source.

However, in order to prevent liability to US taxes being pre-empted by other countries, this was quickly subjected to limitations, in the 1921 Revenue Act. The credit was amended to prevent it being used to offset tax on US-source income, by providing that it could not exceed, in relation to the US tax against which it was to be credited, the same proportion that the non-US income bore to US income. The extent to which foreign taxes may be credited has been subject to different limitations at various times: initially the credit was 'overall', allowing combination of all income from foreign jurisdictions; but in 1932 a 'per-country' limitation was introduced, so that the credit for taxes paid in each country could not exceed the US taxes due on income from that country (although some carry-back and carry-forward was allowed after 1958, and taxpayer election between the overall and per-country limit was allowed from 1961 to 1976).

The US Tax Reform Act of 1986 introduced a new combination of the per-country and overall limitation by establishing 'baskets of income' to separate high-taxed and low-taxed foreign income for credit purposes. Other countries which have introduced the foreign tax credit have also used a variety of approaches to limitation. Further, in the case of alien residents of the US, the 1921 Act provided that it was only allowable if their country offered US residents the same credit. However, the tax credit was extended by allowing taxes paid by US-owned foreign-incorporated subsidiaries to be credited against the tax of their US parent, in relation to dividend remittances from them (see further Chapter 5 below). Although the Netherlands had allowed a tax credit from 1892 for traders deriving income from its then colonies in the East Indies, the American measure seems to have been the first general unilateral foreign tax credit (Surrey 1956, p. 818).

3. The Campaign against International Double Taxation

The introduction of direct taxes on business income, and the rise in their rates after 1914, immediately brought home to businessmen the relative incidence of such taxes as a factor in their competitive position. To those involved in any form of international business, the interaction of national taxes became an immediate issue, and led to the identification of the problem of 'international double taxation'.

3.a Britain and Global Business

This was perhaps most acutely felt in Britain, due to the way taxation of residents had come to cover the worldwide income of all companies 'controlled' from Britain. As the rate of tax rose steeply in Britain, and other countries also introduced income taxes, globally-active businesses based in the UK quickly became conscious of their exposure to multiple taxation. Although there had been some complaints when an income tax was introduced in India in 1860 (which were renewed after other countries within the Empire did likewise in 1893), it was not until 1916 that a temporary provision for partial relief was introduced (UK Royal Commission 1919–20, Appendix 7c). The Board of Inland Revenue negotiated arrangements within the British Empire to allow the deduction from the rate of UK tax of the rate of Dominion or colonial tax on the same revenue, up to half of the UK tax rate, and these arrangements were embodied in the 1920 Finance Act (s.27). Nevertheless, despite strong pressure from business interests, the Revenue would not accept the exemption of foreign source income, nor even a credit along US lines. This view was approved by the report of the Royal Commission on Taxation of 1920.

Business pleaded for equality in the conditions of competition with foreign firms importing into the UK. The administrators responded that tax equity required the same treatment of the income of all UK residents no matter what its source. They acknowledged that a case could be made to relieve foreign investors in companies controlled from Britain, but this would depend on international arrangements to facilitate movements of capital, and require negotiation with the foreign countries of residence. The Revenue considered that the relief arrangements negotiated with the Dominions were justified because there was hardship in contributing twice for what could be considered to be the same purpose – 'the purposes of the British Empire'; with other countries there was no such shared purpose. In addition, the differences in national tax systems, as well as language and travel problems, would make the negotiation of international arrangements very difficult. Nevertheless, the Revenue conceded, it might become expedient to grant some relief, to obtain favourable treatment from, or avoid retaliation by, foreign countries. The Royal Commission suggested that such arrangements could perhaps be negotiated by a series of conferences, possibly under the auspices of the League of Nations.

To those involved in international business, the unfairness of overlapping taxation of the same income seemed plain, and the solution to the problem seemed quite simple. Sir William Vestey, the beef magnate, argued strongly in his evidence to the British Royal Commission that he should be put in a position of equality with his competitors. He singled out the Chicago Beef Trust, which paid virtually no UK tax on its large sales in Britain: not only did it escape UK income tax on its business profits by being based abroad, it also avoided tax on its sales in Britain by consigning its shipments f.o.b. to independent importers, so that its sales were considered not to take place in Britain.[1] The Vestey group had moved its headquarters to Argentina in 1915, to avoid being taxed at British wartime rates on its worldwide business, but Sir William expressed his preference to be based in London. He argued for a global approach to business taxation:

> In a business of this nature you cannot say how much is made in one country and how much is made in another. You kill an animal and the product of that animal is sold in 50 different countries. You cannot say how much is made in England and how much is made abroad. That is why I suggest that you should pay a turnover tax on what is brought into this country. . . . It is not my object to escape payment of tax. My object is to get equality of taxation with the foreigner, and nothing else.[2]

The process of lobbying on behalf of business was quickly internationalized, principally through the International Chamber of Commerce (the ICC), which was set up in Paris in 1920 (although its prehistory goes back to 1905). From its founding meeting the question of international double taxation was high on the ICC's agenda (as it has remained ever since), and it set up a committee which began its task with a simple faith that an evident wrong could be simply righted. As its chairman, Professor Suyling put it in the committee's report to the 2nd ICC Congress in Rome in 1923:

> If only the principle that the same income should only be taxed once is recognised, the difficulty is solved, or very nearly so. It only remains then to decide what constitutes the right of one country to tax the income of a taxpayer in preference to

---

[1] The Trust was of course subject to US taxes, but unlike the UK, these did not apply to subsidiaries formed abroad, e.g. in Argentina.
[2] UK Royal Commission on Income Tax 1920, Evidence, p. 452, Question 9460.

any other country. It does not seem probable that there would be any serious difference on the matter.

Support for action was given by a resolution passed at the International Financial Conference at Brussels in 1920, and the matter was referred to the Financial Committee of the League of Nations. Unfortunately, however, significant differences quickly became apparent, both as to what constitutes international double taxation, and how to prevent it.

3.b National and International Double Taxation

International double taxation is normally defined in the terms stated much later by the OECD Fiscal Committee:

> The imposition of comparable taxes in two (or more) states in respect of the same subject-matter and for identical periods [OECD 1963, para. 3].

This definition obviously hinges on the important word 'comparable'. As we have seen, there were significant differences between countries both in the way they taxed business profits, and in what they considered to be double taxation. The issue of international double taxation was therefore one aspect of the more general question of what constitutes double taxation.

Double taxation is a pejorative term for an elusive concept. Legal or juridical double taxation only occurs if the same tax is levied twice on the same legal person. This is rare, although more frequently different taxes are levied on the same income of one person: for instance, individual income normally bears both social security contributions and general income taxes. The problem is exacerbated by the interposition of fictitious legal persons, mainly the trust and the company. If an individual invests or runs a business through a company, and income tax is levied both on the company's profits and on that proportion of those profits paid to the individual as dividends, it could be said that the same stream of income has been taxed twice, although in the hands of different legal persons. This is referred to as economic double taxation, and there are different views as to whether it should be relieved, and if so, how.

A single income tax applied to both individuals and companies (as was the case in the UK from 1845 to 1965), most directly raises the question of economic double taxation. Hence, in the UK relief was given by allowing companies to deduct at source the income tax due on dividends paid to shareholders and credit the total sums against the tax due on the company's own profits. This approach essentially treats the company as a legal fiction, a mere conduit for investment. On the other hand, under the so-called 'classical approach', favoured until now by the USA, the Netherlands and other countries, the company is considered to be separate from the shareholders who invest in it, and therefore both individuals and corporations are separately taxed on their income. This means that distributed profits are taxed more heavily than those retained within the corporation. Systems which wholly or partially integrate individual and corporate income taxes aim to remove the incentive to retain profits within the company. The choice of alternatives is influenced by whether it is thought that investment decisions are more efficiently taken by the corporation or by its shareholders. When the UK adopted a separate corporation tax in 1965, it too adopted the 'classical' system, but it moved to the present system of partial integration through the Advanced Corporation Tax in 1973. Studies of possible integrated arrangements have been carried out within the US government to consider bringing the US system into line with other major countries. Canada moved away from the classical approach in 1949, and further towards integration in 1971.

However, other systems historically treated a business profits tax or a corporation income tax as a different tax from the personal income tax, so the issue of double taxation relief did not arise so directly. Many of the countries of continental Europe, such as France, had begun from the perspective that taxes on business or commerce were levied on the activity itself, and were separate from the taxes applied to income, including taxes on investment income. From this point of view, the tax on business profits should only be applied by the country where the business activity was actually located. On the other hand, it did not matter if a tax was also levied on the return on investments in that business, whether by the country of residence of the recipient or by the country where the business was actually carried on, since it was a separate tax.

Britain, however, applied its income tax both to the worldwide trading profits of companies considered to be resident in the UK, as well as to the profits from business carried on in the UK by foreign-owned companies. Countries with a separate tax on business profits logically thought it should be applied at the source, where that business was carried on. Britain and the US, which taxed companies, like other legal persons, on their income, favoured taxation based on residence, which meant that they could tax all those they defined as residents or citizens on their worldwide income or profits. Britain went furthest in espousing the view that income should be taxed by the country of residence of the investor. Coupled with the principle that the residence of a company, based on the test of central management and control, was the place where the investment decisions were taken, this meant that the profits of a business carried on abroad, whether through a branch or a foreign subsidiary, could be directly liable to UK income tax, even if not repatriated.

Since British companies obtained relief from their liability for UK income tax by deduction of the tax due on dividends paid to British shareholders, they were perhaps more sensitive to the double taxation issue. By the same token, this made it easier for the Inland Revenue to take a more relaxed attitude, at least to complaints by British residents that their foreign income had already been taxed abroad. Why should the British Revenue take the responsibility for an allowance in respect of tax paid to a foreign state, especially if that foreign state did not make any such allowance to its domestic taxpayers? The issue took on a different complexion as British international investment became more predominantly direct investment by companies, and especially once the separate corporation tax was introduced after 1965.

This divergence of ideological standpoint, between the residence and source principles of business taxation, to some extent reflected and reinforced national economic interests. As we have seen, Britain was by far the largest international lender in the period up to 1914, mostly in the form of fixed-interest portfolio investments, while countries such as France and Italy were net debtors. The United States was also a major source of international investment, although a higher proportion of this was direct investment by US corporations. Although US taxes covered the worldwide income or profits of US citizens and corporations, the foreign direct investments of US corporations were more leniently treated than those of the UK in two major respects. First, US taxes applied only to corporations formed under US law, or to the US trade or business of foreign-registered companies. Thus, by carrying out foreign business through subsidiaries formed abroad, no direct US taxes applied to those foreign profits. Second, a US corporation with earnings from a foreign branch could choose either to deduct foreign taxes paid from gross profits, or to credit them against the US taxes payable on that income (provided the tax credit did not exceed the proportion of foreign to US income). Furthermore, the foreign tax credit was also allowed in respect of dividends paid from foreign subsidiaries, which would form part of the US parent's taxable income: the foreign tax paid on the underlying foreign income could be credited, in proportion to the ratio of dividends repatriated to the gross foreign income. Thus, the foreign tax credit was designed to ensure that there was no tax disincentive for US foreign investment.

The question of what constitutes 'double taxation' is part of the broader issue of tax equity. In liberal theory taxation should apply equally to all legal persons, to create the least impediment to the working of market forces and the free decisions of economic actors. However, markets are themselves created and conditioned by state regulation (see Chapter 4 below). As the type and structure of economic activities become more complex, it becomes increasingly difficult to decide what constitutes 'equal' treatment. As states come under increasing pressure in resolving the political issues posed by the question of domestic equity, arrangements for maintaining international equity come under additional pressure (see below, Chapter 3). In particular, the method adopted by a state for dealing with the relationship of individual and corporate income taxation has important implications for international tax arrangements (see below, Chapter 2, section 2.d).

4. Origins of the Model Tax Treaties

The roots of the arrangements for the international co-ordination of taxation lie in the work done in the inter-war period, mainly through the League of

Nations. This produced the model bilateral tax treaty, which was an innovative method of co-ordinating the jurisdiction of states to tax international business. Furthermore, the model treaties drafted by the Fiscal Committee of the League embodied some of the basic principles and key terms which are still in use today.

4.a The Economists' Study and the Work of the Technical Experts

The Financial Committee of the League began by commissioning a study by four economists (Professors Bruins, Einaudi and Seligman, and Sir Joshua Stamp).[1] Their report of 1923 was something of a compromise. On the one hand, it put forward the basic principle that the 'modern' tax system is based on the ability to pay, which therefore favoured taxation by the country of residence; also, the exemption from tax at source of the income of non-residents would stimulate international investment. This argument seems to have been influenced by a British memorandum submitted to the committee, which had argued that taxation by the borrowing country of the return on investments (especially fixed-interest investments) would increase the cost of borrowing, since lenders would demand a higher pre-tax rate of return from which to pay the tax (PRO file IR40/8192; Herndon 1932). This could be said to beg the question of *which* state, source or residence, should have the right to tax international investments. On the other hand, the economists acknowledged that considerations of pure theory might have to yield to the practical needs of national budgets. In fact, their analysis of 'national allegiance' showed that international investments resulted in a division among different countries of the elements of allegiance which they identified, the most important factors being the source of the wealth created and the residence of its owner (League of Nations 1923; see also Carroll 1939).

The report therefore accepted that agreement on the allocation of jurisdiction to tax could not be reached on the basis of any simple general principle. Instead, it identified four possible methods of reconciling the different national approaches. First was a foreign tax credit such as that adopted by the US, which in principle conceded priority to the source country, while retaining a residual right for the country of residence. The converse approach would be for the source country to exempt non-residents. Third, an international agreement could establish the basis for a division of taxes between source and residence countries, as had been done by Britain with its dominions. Finally, also by international agreement, different types of tax could be assigned according to the primary economic allegiance of the income in question: hence, the source would have first claim to the profits of the business itself,

---

[1] For their individual views on the issues, in a more academic context, see Stamp 1921, pp. 117–29; Seligman 1926, 1927; Einaudi 1928.

while returns on investment, such as interest and dividends, could be treated as personal and taxed in the country of residence of the recipient.

Even prior to receiving the economists' study, the Financial Committee had set up a committee of Technical Experts (government tax officials), to study the technical aspects of the possible arrangements and make specific proposals. The increased urgency to produce practical proposals resulted from concern that the lack of internationally co-ordinated tax arrangements was contributing to international capital flight. Hence, the International Economic Conference in Genoa in 1922 had passed a resolution urging that tax evasion should be added to the problem of international double taxation under consideration by the League, although this had been approved subject to the condition that there should be no interference with the freedom of international markets or the principle of bank secrecy.

The Technical Experts began with representatives of seven European countries (Belgium, Czechoslovakia, France, Britain, Italy, the Netherlands and Switzerland), and their work resulted in a series of resolutions, submitted in their first report (League of Nations 1925). These were approved by the Financial Committee, although it also emphasized the 'disadvantages of placing any obstacles in the way of the international circulation of capital, which is one of the conditions of public prosperity and world economic reconstruction'. The group was enlarged to a Commission of twelve, later thirteen when the USA agreed to send a delegation (as observers, since the US was now not a member of the League). A second report was produced (League of Nations 1927), containing preliminary draft conventions based on the resolutions previously approved, and these conventions were put forward for consideration by a general meeting of governmental experts called by the League in Geneva in October 1928.

The reports of the Technical Experts built upon the economists' study, also following consultations with business representatives through the ICC. Once again, they expressed respect for the general principle of taxation of income by the country of residence, based on the personal link of the recipient. Equally, however, they considered that this principle was unlikely to gain general acceptance, even leaving aside the validity of the economic arguments made in its favour, due to the imbalances of international investment flows. Debtor countries were for the most part unwilling to give up jurisdiction to tax foreign investors, and especially the profits made by businesses owned or financed from abroad.

Indeed, although Britain, the main protagonist of this approach, did manage to agree a treaty with Eire in 1926 which exempted non-residents, this instance was unique. The principle of priority of the country of residence only gained acceptance in relation to one special type of business, that of shipping. Reciprocal agreements between the main trading nations during the 1920s provided that enterprises engaged in shipping should be taxed in their countries of residence; and this was later extended to aviation. Even so, shipowning countries were annoyed by taxes on cargoes sometimes levied by exporting countries, as happened between Britain and Australia in 1928 (PRO file IR40/7463), or half a century later between Japan and the USA (see *Japan Line v. County of Los Angeles*, 1979).

In the special case of international transport the convenience of the residence principle overcame its other drawbacks, principally the lack of reciprocity, and the ease of avoidance by the use of residences of convenience. Acceptance of the residence principle was facilitated by the fact that the maintenance of a national shipping fleet, and later a national airline, has been regarded as a national strategic and economic priority, and most states far from taxing them heavily have usually subsidized them; while taxation at source is possible through the opportunities for charges by ports on transport movements. More recently, however, renewed pressures have emerged for more taxation at source, especially by developing countries; this has been considered especially important for countries which have busy ports but no resident shipping lines. If international deregulation of air transport leads to similar imbalances a move towards more taxation at source may develop there also (Surrey 1978, p. 119; UN CTC 1988b, Ch. 5).

There was no alternative, therefore, but to find a way of reconciling the tax claims of both the country of source and that of residence. Initially, the international business lobby favoured the American idea of the foreign tax credit as the easiest means of reconciling the source and residence principles of taxation. It had two major attractions: it gave priority to the source country while simultaneously retaining residual rights for the country of residence; and it was a simple principle, which could even be implemented unilaterally.

However, this simplicity was deceptive, since a unilateral credit meant that the income of foreign branches and receipts from subsidiaries would always be taxed at the higher of the home or overseas rates. Business therefore complained that it provided an incentive to other countries to increase their tax rates. For these reasons, the US government reconsidered its reliance on a purely unilateral tax credit. Although the State Department had ceased US involvement with the League of Nations when the Senate refused to ratify US membership, it agreed to a suggestion from the Department of Commerce in 1926 to respond to an invitation to participate in the work of the Committee of Technical Experts (Carroll 1965).

The work of the Technical Experts had been dominated by Italy, France and other continental European states, since Britain was isolated both in favouring the residence principle and in having a single general tax on all types of income. Accordingly, the Technical Experts favoured allocation of taxes according to the categorization of sources of income (the fourth option identified in the economists' study), and they began by distinguishing between impersonal and personal taxes. This approach allowed a state which imposed schedular taxes of a 'real' character to tax not only the profits of a business carried out by an establishment located within its territory, but also payments for the carrying out of services within its borders, and even income from 'movable property' – i.e. the payment by a debtor of interest and dividends on securities. Personal taxes on the other hand should be levied only by the state of residence of a legal person, although it was conceded that they could be applied to the profits of a foreign-owned establishment.

When the USA joined the enlarged Technical Experts Committee in 1926, it reinforced the arguments for restriction of source taxes. The American aim, generally supported by big business, was, in return for conceding some taxation at source of foreign-owned business, to impose limits on the extent of source taxes. US officials 'perceived that the United States could through tax treaties retain jurisdiction over the entire taxable income of its citizens and corporations, yet on a reciprocal basis prevail upon the other Contracting State to give up a part of its tax with a view to encouraging business and investment' (Carroll 1965, p. 693). Accordingly, a compromise emerged, based on the fourth approach identified in the economists' study: the allocation to the source state of the right to tax business profits, and to the state of residence of priority to tax the returns on investment; combined with a foreign tax credit on American lines. The British representatives supported this approach, but strong reservations by the Treasury about its desirability prevented its implementation by the UK in the inter-war years (see section 4.c below).

4.b The 1928 Conference and the Model Treaties

The Technical Experts' second report put forward four preliminary draft conventions, the most important being Convention I, dealing with direct taxes. This was based on the distinction between impersonal taxes, allocated to the source country, and personal taxes, to be levied by the country of residence. Impersonal taxes were not only taxes on immovable property (taxable where the property was located), but also those on 'movable property'. This included both investments in the form of loans (public funds, bonds, loans and deposits – taxable in the state of residence of the debtor), as well as shares (taxable by the state where the real centre of management of the company is located). The state of residence of the owner of both immovable and movable property could also subject such income to personal income taxes; however, unless it also applied an impersonal tax to such income domestically, it should give a credit for the tax paid in the other contracting state. This was modified at the 1928 meeting to introduce a US-style limitation of the foreign tax credit: the credit could not exceed the amount representing the same proportion of the tax payable on the total income as the income taxable at source bore to total income.

During the 1928 meeting it became clear that the proposed draft on income taxes suited only states which accepted the distinction between personal and real taxes. Negotiations during the meeting therefore produced two further alternatives to this draft, for use when one or both states applied a single personal-type of tax on all kinds of income. Convention Ib prioritized taxation by the taxpayer's country of domicile (defined as the country of normal residence, or permanent home);[1] however, it permitted taxation at source of income from immovable property, and of the business profits of a permanent establishment, which should be allowed as a credit against the residence country tax. Convention Ic, on the other hand, gave the exclusive right to the source country to tax income from immovable property and the business profits of a permanent establishment; and although income from both loans and shares was in principle allocated to the country of the recipient, a tax at source by the debtor's country could continue, and double taxation should be relieved either by a credit in the recipient country, or by a refund from the debtor's state.[2]

All three versions entailed the abandonment of the approach urged by the UK that double taxation should be avoided by the exemption of non-residents; in particular they all conceded that a state could tax at source the business profits of a permanent establishment operated by a foreign company. However, the two new alternatives introduced important limitations to source taxation, especially of interest and dividend payments. It had become clear that a single collective agreement was impossible, once the idea of allocation of tax jurisdiction according to a general principle (such as residence) was rejected. Instead, the three variants of the Convention on Direct Taxes were to provide models for bilateral agreements between states, to be adapted by negotiation to the tax systems and economic relationships of each set of treaty partners, as appropriate according to their tax systems. In addition, the 1928 conference approved model treaties based on the other three drafts proposed by the Technical Experts: Convention II on Succession Duties, III on Administrative Assistance in Assessment, and IV on Assistance in the Collection of Taxes (League of Nations 1928).

Nevertheless, the three versions of the Direct Taxation model embodied agreement on some important basic principles. In particular, it was conceded that profits made by a foreign company could only be taxed at source if made through a Permanent Establishment situated within the territory. Agreement was also reached that the country of residence of an enterprise should be defined in terms of the real centre of management. Affiliated companies or subsidiaries were not to be treated as Permanent Establishments, but as separate entities. Although in many respects the concept of a Permanent Establishment was far from satisfactory, it became established as a key factor in the compromise over tax jurisdiction. For example, British income tax,

---

[1] The definition of fiscal domicile was substantially expanded in later treaties; since fiscal domicile has usually been defined in terms of residence, no distinction is normally made between state of domicile and state of residence in international tax law.
[2] League of Nations 1928; Carroll 1939. An interesting account was provided by J. G. Herndon, who was secretary of the US delegation: Herndon 1932.

which, as we have seen, asserted jurisdiction over the worldwide profits of resident companies, also applied to the local profits of foreign residents. In the early 1920s, the Inland Revenue began to tax foreign commodity traders if they sold on a regular basis through a broker or commission agent in the UK. Pressures through contacts in the League's Technical Experts committee led to the enactment of a power to exempt non-resident traders unless they had a fixed place of business, or used an agent who had authority to conclude contracts on their behalf, which contributed to the formulation and acceptance of the Permanent Establishment principle.[1]

The concept of the Permanent Establishment was the key to the compromise between the economic interests of creditor and debtor countries, as well as for an accommodation between the business tax systems of a personal character based on income and those of a real character based on sources of revenue. It established a separation between the taxation of business profits which could be attributed to a Permanent Establishment and taxed at source, and the taxation of investment profits, which could be treated as 'personal' income and taxed in the country of residence of the investor. It also offered a basis for accommodation between debtor and creditor countries: foreign-owned branches or subsidiaries could be taxed at source, provided this was limited to the business profits of a Permanent Establishment; while the home country could retain the right to tax its residents (including corporate groups) on their global income, although this should be subject to a credit or exemption for business profits taxed at source.

Although there was some agreement on basic principles, the 1928 meeting left specific aspects of the division of the international tax base for bilateral negotiation. Crucially, it left open two important questions: first, whether the source country could impose any tax on payments embodying a return on investments, notably interest and dividends. Second, where an enterprise had a Permanent Establishment in more than one state, the drafts merely provided that the competent administrations of the states concerned should come to an arrangement for the apportionment of profits between them. Thus, the 1928 draft conventions did not tackle the treatment of transactions between the branches or subsidiaries of a single enterprise; but this issue quickly came to the fore.

4.c The Fiscal Committee and Inter-War Treaties

On the recommendation of the 1928 intergovernmental meeting, the League set up a Fiscal Committee, which continued the work of the Technical Experts. Its membership of eight (later nine), plus an observer from the ICC, included nationals of states that were not members of the League, notably the United

---

[1] Finance Act 1930, 20 & 21 George V c. 28, s. 17. See Carroll 1965, p. 701, and discussions in the Reports of the Fiscal Committee, especially 6th and 7th sessions, reprinted in US Congress 1962a.

States; and in addition contact was maintained by correspondence with up to 40 further states (Carroll 1939, p. 27). Its main work consisted of continuing the effort to develop principles for the allocation of tax jurisdiction between states. However, this inevitably led also to discussions and comparative studies of tax systems themselves. Thus, the inter-war period was one in which determined attempts were made to achieve a basis for the coordination of taxes applicable to international business. Much progress was made on the technical aspects in the meetings of fiscal experts coordinated through the League. However, the arrangements that were agreed required the conclusion of bilateral agreements based on the accommodation of mutual interests, and the international political climate was not very propitious for the implementation of such solutions.

This work produced a modest but significant beginning in the lifetime of the League. Between 1920 and 1939 almost 60 general treaties were concluded for he avoidance of double taxation of income and property, although there were any more agreements on specific tax matters, notably shipping as mentioned ove. The general double tax treaties that were concluded were almost tirely bilateral, and between continental European states (Carroll 1939, pendix II). Only one general multilateral tax treaty was concluded: that of exempting automobiles registered in one member state from tax in her if entering temporarily.

significant obstacle was the attitude of the British government, especially reasury, which saw no reason to give up its claim to tax British residents eir worldwide income. Logically, this implied that double taxation be avoided by exempting non-residents from taxes at source: yet as we en, apart from the special case of shipping, the only agreement in which nciple was embodied was that between the UK and Eire in 1926. The Treasury justified the primacy of the residence principle by pointing to hat in practice interest payments, whether on short-term deposits or ational loans such as government or municipal bonds or company s, were not normally taxed at source. The problem really arose in companies doing business, or 'trading', in more than one country, individuals owning shares in foreign companies. On this, the ok the firm view that it could see no reason to sacrifice a penny of rder to stimulate British and German firms to set up business in countries, or to encourage individuals to speculate in buying s. On the contrary, double taxation was a welcome deterrent to s. A key memorandum stating these arguments was produced for r of the Exchequer in 1933 by Sir Richard Hopkins,[1] and it was d by the Treasury to block any change of policy.

The Treasury succeeded in ensuring that its view dominated British policy throughout the 1930s. Although the Inland Revenue produced a draft treaty based on version Ib of the 1928 models, and negotiations were attempted in the 1930s with Italy, Switzerland, Germany, the Netherlands and France (PRO file IR40/8192), no treaty was concluded. The Imperial arrangement negotiated after 1916 (see section 3.a above) became increasingly ineffective as new taxes were passed which were not covered by it, especially by the Dominions. While the British Treasury felt that it was being generous in giving up half the tax on the returns on British imperial investments, the colonies and Dominions increasingly resented the British insistence on its right to tax the returns on activities taking place within their territories. Due to the differences of view, the matter was not even raised at Imperial conference after British proposals to revise the arrangements were rejected in 1930 a 1933 (PRO file IR40/5263). Pressure from British firms with foreign bran or subsidiaries, exerted for example by the British section of the ICC stonewalled by the Treasury right up to 1944 (PRO file IR40/7463).

Only France, which had been influential in the drafting of the models of 1928, succeeded in negotiating treaties based on them, w (1930), Belgium (1931), USA (1932), Germany (1934), Sweden (Switzerland (1937), and a draft UK–French treaty was on th signature in 1939. In addition to the 1932 treaty with France, States concluded only one other general double tax treaty, wi 1938.

The reason for the French success in negotiating treati instructive. Under French law, companies were taxed n industrial and commercial profits (like any business) but a earned on their securities. This 'impôt sur le revenu des valeu dated back to a law of 29 June 1872 (one of the older ir dating the revenue taxes instituted in 1917), applied France: in the case of foreign companies doing busines issue shares in France, it applied by reference to the pr the business located in France. However, since fore also be liable to income tax in their countries of resid double taxation. Furthermore, the companies were their dividends represented by their assets in Fra made in France. Although the French authorities tax an 'arbitrary' character, they argued tha determine the contribution made by the Fren business as a whole (League of Nations 1 declared themselves willing to agree recip countries to eliminate any double liability provided a strong inducement to other co

However, as we have seen in the previ the allocation of tax rights, which was al put forward by the League's Technical Experts, allowed the source country the right to tax income from 'movable property' (shares and other rights). Furthermore, the French were not willing to limit their taxation of a local branch or subsidiary to its declared business profits, which they suspected might be kept low even though the firm as a whole made a high profit. They therefore insisted on the principle of source taxation as a 'deemed dividend' of profits 'diverted' abroad to the parent (see Chapter 8, section 1.b below). The Franco–US treaty agreed in 1932 provided some limitations on the application to US corporations of the French tax on income from securities; but it also empowered both states to make such adjustments to the declared profits of a permanent establishment as may be necessary to show the exact profits, as well as to include in the taxable profits of an affiliate any profits 'diverted' by conditions different from those which would be made with a third enterprise.[1] However, the French did not ratify the treaty until 1935, after the US Congress had enacted a provision permitting retaliation by doubling the tax rate on citizens or companies of countries imposing discriminatory or extraterritorial taxes.[2] The French treaties therefore strengthened the need for a study of the tax treatment of intra-enterprise transactions.

5. Allocation of the Income of Transnational Enterprises

The Fiscal Committee of the League carried out an extended study of the allocation of business income of transnational companies, leading to a model Convention. As we have seen, the 1928 drafts established that taxation at source should be limited to the profits of a Permanent Establishment, but in the case of a business with Permanent Establishments in more than one country it left open the question of how the profits were to be allocated between the establishments. The same problem of allocation arose when the foreign business was organized through a subsidiary or affiliated company. However, this was less clearly recognized, since each affiliate was treated as a separate legal person. This meant that assessment had to begin from the accounts of the affiliate; but equally that tax assessors could use their existing powers of assessment to deal with a suspected 'diversion' of income by means of 'distorted' pricing between related affiliates.

5.a The Carroll Report and the Problem of the Transfer Price

Funded by a $90,000 grant from the Rockefeller Foundation, the Fiscal Committee commissioned a detailed study of the taxation of transnational

[1] A similar clause was also part of the French treaties of 1931 with Belgium and Italy: see Tixier & Gest 1985, p. 355.
[2] This continued in existence as s.891 Internal Revenue Code; see Carroll, in Bischel 1978.

enterprises. This resulted in a five-volume report of over 1,200 pages, comprising parallel studies of the treatment of this problem in 27 different systems (League of Nations 1932, 1933). The studies were written by national experts, usually tax officials, and the inquiry was co-ordinated by Mitchell B. Carroll, who had succeeded Professor Adams as the expert representing the US on the Fiscal Committee. Carroll had originally been sent to participate in the League's work as the US Commerce Department's specialist on European legal and tax matters; it was apparently he who had persuaded the State Department not to rely solely on the unilateral tax credit. For the allocation study, he visited 35 countries, meeting both tax officials and business contacts made through the help of the ICC.

The Carroll report established the basis for the subsequent treatment of the allocation problem, which remained largely unquestioned until half a century later, when the dispute over worldwide unitary taxation stimulated a re-examination of the issues (see especially Langbein 1986 and Chapters 8 and 9 below). Carroll himself subsequently practised as a lawyer with Coudert Brothers in New York, and in 1938 he helped to found the International Fiscal Association, of which he became the long-serving first President.

The analytical report, which Carroll himself wrote, saw the roots of the problem of allocation as lying in the increasingly complex structure of international businesses, which raised the question of the basis for 'transfer pricing' between their various parts. Carroll therefore identified, probably for the first time as a policy question, one of the key issues posed for national regulators by the internationalization of business organization, as well as the consequences for the companies themselves of their exposure to multiple regulation.

Since his analysis strikingly foreshadowed some of the discussions which were to take place several decades later, it is worth quoting at length:

> Tax collectors complain that sometimes enterprises take the rate of tax in various countries into consideration, and fix the transfer price from the factory to the selling establishment at so high a figure as to show little or no profit in the books of the sales branch. Through the arbitrary fixation of inter-establishment billing prices or charges for interest, royalties, services, etc., profits can be shifted from place to place, the purpose frequently being to transfer them to the country with a low rate of tax or no income-tax at all. . . . The tax official in each country where there is an establishment has at his immediate disposal only the accounts (if any) of the local establishment, and it is necessary for him to ascertain whether or not they reflect the true profit attributable to that establishment. . . . This entails, in some cases, allotting to it the capital normally required to carry on its activities, and, in every case, billing to it or making charges at the same rates as it would to an outsider. Unfortunately, however, the local establishment is not so treated by the great majority of enterprises, and the tax inspector finds it necessary to adjust the accounts after securing whatever additional information is available, or to make an assessment on an empirical or fractional basis. Cases arise where the taxpayer has tried meticulously to allot profits in a fair way between the various establishments,

but the authorities of the several countries are of a different opinion as to their share of the taxable income. . . . When all the assessments are added together, the enterprise finds that it has paid tax on much more than 100 per cent of its net income. Incidentally, it has had to argue with the authorities of each country in regard to the amount of profit allocable thereto, and possibly has had to produce copies or extracts of its head office accounts in order that the authorities of each country may examine the local accounts in the light thereof. This all requires expenditure of time and money on the part of the taxpayer as well as that of the tax-collector. [League of Nations 1933, vol. IV, pp. 12–13.]

Carroll found that three approaches were possible in allocating business profits: (i) separate accounting; (ii) empirical methods; and (iii) fractional apportionment. Each had its advantages and disadvantages, and they were usually employed in combination by tax authorities. Most tax systems required a declaration of income by the taxpayer, which in the case of businesses generally involved a balance sheet and profit-and-loss account. Although these were required to be an accurate and just reflection of the business, few tax systems prescribed the form of accounts or laid down criteria for the allocation of income between related businesses.

Most systems attempted, as far as possible, to determine the income of a local branch, establishment or affiliate on the basis of separate accounts. However, all states adopting this as the primary approach also insisted on verifying whether such accounts (if available) were a true reflection of the activities of the establishment. This verification usually relied on comparing the accounts with those of similar but independent businesses, in addition to examining the accounts of the parent or related business to ascertain the breakdown of income and costs between them.

If it proved impossible by such means to establish adequate separate accounts, most systems would fall back on the empirical method. This entailed assuming that the local establishment made the same percentage profit either as the enterprise as a whole, or as others in a similar line of business, and assessing its taxable profit merely by applying the relevant percentage, either to its turnover or to some other factor, such as capital employed.

An important advocate of the separate accounting approach was the British Inland Revenue. Nevertheless, its report conceded difficulty in ascertaining separate UK profits, in particular for goods manufactured abroad and imported for sale by a related establishment. In such cases, and as a check in general, the validity of the accounts was tested by empirical methods. It emphasized the importance of having a clear picture of the course of the interlocking transactions, and attempting to establish by negotiation a reasonable basis, for example for the invoicing of goods. This might be by reference to the price of similar goods to an unrelated buyer; or if there were none or the goods were of a specialist kind, by taking the UK sale price and allowing a merchanting profit. The UK report estimated that some 55 per cent of total cases were settled on the basis of separate accounts, usually after negotiation. However, it emphasized that 'the fact that the revenue authorities have the alternative of basing profits on a percentage of turnover prevents the taxpayer taking up an unreasonable attitude' (League of Nations 1932, p. 191). In some 20 per cent of cases the proportion of turnover method would be resorted to, and in a further 25 per cent the proportion of another appropriate factor, e.g. an assets basis for banks, premiums for insurance companies, freight for shipping and train-mileage for railways.

In a small number of tax systems, however, fractional apportionment was either the primary or the only basis of allocation. This was especially the case for Spain, which in 1920 had abandoned assessment on the basis of book-keeping, since many local branches of foreign companies showed little or no profit. The Spanish report argued strongly for its system as the only fair and practicable one. It reasoned that this was the only system which could ensure that no enterprise was taxed at more than 100 per cent of its profits. Furthermore, this approach maintained the liberty of the enterprise, since it did not entail attempting to control hundreds of costs, often in remote countries, which would result in the substitution of arbitrary prices and taxation on the basis of largely imaginary accounts. Under the Spanish system, any branch or affiliate forming a unity with a foreign company had its profits allocated not by any fixed principles laid down by law, but by principles determined by a committee of experts, or 'jury', subject to the taxpayer's right to appeal to the Council of Ministers. Nevertheless, where separate accounts were maintained, the jury would pay regard to them in determining the criteria for allocation.

Several other systems also used fractional apportionment as the primary method, notably France whose tax on income from securities (discussed above) applied to the proportion of assets represented by the local branch; and it was also common within federal systems, being used in particular by Swiss cantons, and by a number of states of the United States. In addition, it had been established as the basis of apportionment between former members of the Austro-Hungarian empire, in Austrian treaties with Hungary and Czechoslovakia.

Carroll considered that the allocation problem arose mainly in relation to the taxation by a host country (to use terminology that has become familiar subsequently) of the local branch of a foreign-owned company. He assumed that a home country taxing an enterprise with overseas branches could assert at least residual jurisdiction over its worldwide profits (League of Nations 1933, p. 15). He also treated allocation between affiliated companies separately from relations between branches of the same company. Inter-affiliate pricing was considered to create the possibility of 'diversion of profits' if the transactions were not 'carried on at arm's length' (p. 109). National tax laws provided several different means of dealing with such 'diversion of profits' – Carroll identified five. However, these were not different methods of calculating an adjustment of profit, but rather slightly different legal theories justifying it. For example, a British provision of 1915 allowed a local affiliate to be taxed as the agent of a foreign company for profit diverted to the latter; in Germany on the other hand, the tax administration had taken the view that it could assess the foreign company directly, if it formed a single economic unity with the local affiliate, and this had been upheld by the Reichsfinanzhof in 1928 and 1930; whereas in France, diverted profits could be taxed as deemed dividends (see Chapter 8, section 1 below). The methods of calculating the 'true' income of a local subsidiary were in practice the same as in the case of a branch (i.e. empirical or fractional methods could be used, if only as a check). Nevertheless, Carroll seemed to assume that, since the problem was seen as 'diversion of income', rectification must be by substitution of market for manipulated prices.

5.b The 1935 Allocation Convention

On the basis of the Carroll report a draft Convention was drawn up in 1933, which the Fiscal Committee sent to states for comment. After consultation, it was decided to publish the revised text as a model for bilateral treaties, rather than calling a conference to attempt its multilateral adoption. Therefore, this treaty was never approved by a formal intergovernmental meeting, nor used on its own as the basis for bilateral treaties. Nevertheless, its provisions were later incorporated into bilateral treaties and eventually into the model conventions which succeeded the 1928 models, and they remain important today.

The Draft Convention for the Allocation of Business Income between States for the Purposes of Taxation (League of Nations 1935) followed on from the 1928 Conventions, laying down the principle that an enterprise domiciled in one contracting state should be taxed in the other only on profits attributable to a Permanent Establishment. Where an enterprise had establishments in more than one state, it specified that there should be attributed to each 'the net business income which it might be expected to derive if it were an independent enterprise engaged in the same or similar activities under the same or similar conditions'. With some rewording, this still remains the essence of the 'arm's length' approach required by Article 7 of the current UN and OECD model tax treaties.

The 1935 draft further specified that the arm's length approach should in principle be implemented by establishing separate accounts, if necessary by rectifying 'to re-establish the prices or remunerations entered in the books at the value which would prevail between independent persons dealing at arm's length'. If no accounts are produced, or if they cannot be rectified, or with the agreement of the taxpayer, the business income of the establishment might be determined by applying a percentage to the turnover comparable to that of enterprises in a similar line of business. If both of these methods failed, the income might be computed by applying to the total income of the enterprise as a whole 'coefficients based on a comparison of gross receipts, assets, number of hours worked or other appropriate factors, provided such factors be so selected as to ensure results approaching as closely as possible to those which would be reflected by a separate accounting'. These provisions were incorporated into the basic model double taxation treaty finalized by the League, and included in revised form in Article 7 of the OECD and then the UN model. Although the 'percentage of turnover' method is now no longer explicitly referred to in Article 7, it is discussed in the OECD Commentary, and accepted as one way of establishing an 'arm's length' profit. Article 7(4) does still permit allocation 'on the basis of an apportionment of the total profits of the enterprise to its various parts', although only where this approach has been customary in that state, and only if the outcome of an apportionment is in accordance with the arm's length principle.

However, although the draft allocation convention allowed fractional apportionment as an alternative method, this applied only between separate Permanent Establishments *of the same enterprise*. It did not apply to the treatment of separate but related enterprises, i.e. subsidiaries. It had already been established in the 1928 Conventions that a subsidiary should not necessarily be treated as a Permanent Establishment. Instead, the 1935 Convention provided that, where enterprises were 'owned or controlled by the same interests' and were consequently not independent entities, their accounts could be adjusted to take account of the diversion of any item of profit or loss from one to the other.

This formulation seemed to reject any possibility of treating affiliates as part of a single entity, and appeared to establish a rather narrow version of the 'arm's length' principle in relation to inter-affiliate dealings. Yet this method of organization of international business was already frequent, and was to become the central feature of the financial structure of transnational corporations. These provisions of the 1935 Convention also substantially survive, in Article 9 of the OECD model, dealing with the adjustment of accounts between associated enterprises. The separate treatment of allocation between Permanent Establishments and between associated enterprises, and the lack of any explicit reference in Article 9 to the use of customary apportionment methods as a back-up, still have implications today.[1]

5.c Limitations of the Carroll Report and of the League Approach

The Carroll report argued that, on the basis of existing administrative practice, separate accounting was the preferred method of allocation, although verification by recourse to other methods (empirical methods and fractional apportionment) was necessary when accounts did not reflect a fair

[1] See Langbein 1986, pp. 636–7, and Chapter 8 below.

allocation (pp. 88–9). This has been criticized as confusing two distinct matters: separate accounts, and the use of the arm's length criterion. Separate accounts as the starting point of an assessment does not necessarily require the use of the separate enterprise or arm's length criterion for the allocation of income or expenses (Langbein 1986, p. 632).

This was not, however, merely a conceptual confusion on Carroll's part, nor deliberate proselytism 'to make the world safe from fractional apportionment' (Langbein 1986, p. 638). Carroll's conclusions flowed from the assumptions on which his study was based. His study, as we have seen, began by identifying the two facets of the problem as being (i) the manipulation of transfer prices to minimize or avoid taxes, and (ii) the exposure of international businesses to overlapping taxation. The assumption that transfer pricing is only a problem if there is a deliberate manipulation of prices leads to the conclusion that the aim of allocation should be to re-establish the 'true' profits of that part of the business which is within the tax authority's jurisdiction.

An alternative approach would have accepted that for a globally-integrated firm there is no 'true' profit for its parts, as Sir William Vestey had acknowledged (see section 3.a above). On this approach, the need would be to develop criteria for a fair allocation of profit between the constituent parts. Such criteria would assess the contribution made by each part to the total profits, rather than trying to treat the parts of the business as if they were independent businesses. Those tax authorities which started from separate accounts were clearly well aware of the limitations of such accounts, and also that they could not be checked solely by reference to alternative 'normal' pricing. For example, the British Inland Revenue stated that separate accounts could only be used as the basis in about half their cases, and then only because there was the threat in reserve of an assessment based on percentage of turnover. On the other hand, the principle of fractional apportionment could be shown to have clear advantages, as argued in the Spanish report, and shown by the experience of federal systems. Since it entailed treating the accounts of a globally integrated enterprise as a single unity, it avoided the many problems and administrative difficulties involved in attempting to construct arm's length relationships where none existed. It could not seem irrational from the business point of view: indeed, it was the very principle that had been put forward by Sir William Vestey in 1919.

The apportionment method had, however, major and overriding disadvantages. It required acceptance of a uniform rate of profit for the constituent parts of an integrated international business; and it posed the problem of how to ensure uniformity of application by different tax authorities. Uniformity of application of apportionment would entail, first, general agreement on the formula to be applied for the apportionment. The draft allocation convention of 1935 referred generally to 'coefficients based on a comparison of gross receipts, assets, number of hours worked, or other appropriate factors', without laying down the weight to be attached to each factor. The Spanish experience showed that differences in the characteristics of different industries, or even between different firms, made it difficult to apply a single formula uniformly; there, the formula had to be fixed in each case by a jury. No doubt divergences of economic interest between countries would have made it even more difficult to achieve general international agreement on a formula, or on a procedure for deciding cases, just as differences between capital-importing and capital-exporting countries had led to divergence between the source and residence principles.

More seriously, however, the apportionment principle could be said to require also a uniform approach to the computing of the total profit of the enterprise as a whole. This raised the question of uniformity of accounting principles. Here again, it was not merely a technical matter, but involved a common approach to questions of fiscal policy, in particular the central question of the treatment of the relationship between capital and revenue as embodied in rules such as those governing the depreciation of assets and allowances for investments, for example in machinery or research and development. Finally, acceptance of a uniform rate of profit meant that a national tax authority (particularly if it started from separate national accounts) would have to accept that profits apparently earned within its jurisdiction might be reduced by losses sustained elsewhere. Of course, the converse could also occur.

Significantly, separate accounting and the arm's length criterion were favoured not only by the lawyer Carroll, but also by Ralph C. Jones, a Yale professor of accounting, whose report on the accounting aspects of allocation was printed as Volume V of the study. Jones posed at the outset the clear alternatives of general apportionment and separate accounting, and firmly recommended the latter.

> Even if a uniform fraction were adopted, methods of computing net income would vary so widely as to cause some double taxation. Moreover, it is quite inconceivable that legislative and administrative authorities will generally permit income earned within their jurisdictions to be reduced by losses sustained elsewhere. [League of Nations 1933–IV, p. 8.]

However, both Jones and Carroll recognized the limitations of separate accounting, since not all items of income and expenditure can be allocated to a specific source. Particular problems are caused by items of general overhead, especially the expenses of the real centre of management, as well as the financing of capital items benefiting the enterprise as a whole. Carroll's report showed widespread use of the proportionate allocation of such expenses based on various formulae. Jones insisted that this was fundamentally different from the general apportionment method, since such specific apportionments were 'with a view to attributing to each the income it would earn if it were an independent enterprise, but not in accordance with the relative importance of different establishments' (p. 8).

Nevertheless, it is plain that the separate accounting/arm's length approach does not resolve the question of the basis of apportionment, but *converts it into a series of determinations in relation to specific items of income or expenditure.* Furthermore, the arm's length principle does not provide a clear and uniform measure. The Carroll report recognized that arm's length did not always entail the independent-dealer criterion, but could be satisfied by prices based on remuneration for services (see Langbein 1986, p. 636).

The position was summed up by the German report, which stated that fractional apportionment was not only the ideal method, but one that would in practice be used in the numerous cases where 'separate assessment' was not feasible. Hence, national fiscal authorities would need to give each other reciprocal assistance to facilitate allocation and to develop agreed general principles, which might take the form of defined allocation percentages (League of Nations 1932, p. 122). This anticipated that what could perhaps not be resolved by a global agreement on a system of general apportionment would have to be negotiated piecemeal over a longer period (see Chapter 8 below). If general apportionment could not be established because of the difficulties of ensuring uniformity, separate accounting and arm's length would nevertheless require international co-ordination to implement case-by-case special apportionments.

6. Conclusion

We have seen that the establishment as a major means of state finance of taxes on income and profits, in the first two decades of the twentieth century, raised questions of fairness or equity, both at the national and international levels. Nationally, the issues of proportionality or fairness of application could be resolved through the state political mechanism. It is notable, however, that although broad principles, such as higher rates of tax or 'super-tax' on higher incomes, were debated through relatively open and representative political processes, the specifics of their application, especially to business and corporate income, became embedded in technical and bureaucratic processes of administrative regulation. Although these processes could attempt to ensure a degree of fairness nationally, the wide involvement of firms in international trade and investment meant that some international co-ordination was required to ensure the equalization of global conditions of competition.

Ideally, it was thought, this could best be achieved by agreement on general principles allocating jurisdiction to tax between the various states involved in different types of international economic activity. However, this quickly proved impossible, since the issues of fairness within each state in taxation of incomes and profits were influenced by the characteristics of its international economic relations. Thus, Britain taxed all types of income in the hands of the recipient, and its major role in world trade and international lending reinforced the view that all its residents should be taxed on all income from anywhere in the world. Although domestically a refund was paid to companies of the tax on that proportion of their profits paid as dividends and therefore taxed again in the hands of shareholders, there seemed no reason to make such a refund to foreign companies. This was particularly so since other countries applied separate taxes to business profits and to personal income. For other countries, especially in continental Europe, fairness consisted in taxing the earnings from all types of assets, including shares and loans or debt-claims, where the assets were located; not surprisingly, these countries were largely net importers of capital. Hence, the different perspectives of national states on tax principles were exacerbated by considerations of national economic interest.

Nevertheless, significant progress was made in agreeing on the form and many of the principles of a model bilateral treaty; but the approach it embodied entailed the reciprocal bargaining of tax rights, which would tend to reinforce the preoccupation with national interests. More seriously, the allocation between national states of different tax rights made it difficult to treat an internationally-organized enterprise as a single unity, since this would require agreement at the international level on issues which were already hard to resolve nationally (the definition of the tax base of a business) as well as on general principles for the allocation of the enterprise's tax base among the various countries in which it operated. Thus, the question of inter-state equity in the allocation of income from international business was avoided; or, rather, it was postponed, since the enforcement by states of the different rights to tax internationally-generated income would inevitably lead to specific problems and eventually to more general conflicts.

By preferring to treat internationally-organized businesses as separate national entities on the basis of separate accounting, the main national tax administrations avoided opening up the discussion of the broader policy matters. They therefore preserved their own roles as technical administrators of a fiscal system whose underlying policy bases were determined and legitimated by largely national political processes. Significantly, the Fiscal Committee could be regarded as one of the quiet and unsung successes of the League, achieving an unusual degree of agreement and even action during a period otherwise marked by increasing economic national and political conflict. This was due in no small measure to its having treated international taxation as an essentially technical matter.

Such an approach also had disadvantages, since it meant that agreements reached in the international forum could be difficult to implement nationally. For example, J. G. Herndon, who was secretary to the US delegation at the 1928 meeting, refers to the failure of the attempt in 1930 to enact a version of the draft convention on direct taxation into US law, to facilitate exemption of dividend payments from withholding tax at source. He attributed this failure to the lack of substantial public opinion in the US in support of the proposal, since its aims had not been publicized. It would have been to the benefit of the US, since the income of American residents from foreign investment in 1927 was some $900m, while the outward flow was only $275m; but the Treasury Department's Bill failed for lack of time, as the Ways and Means Committee was busy with the tariff reform, an issue with greater domestic political resonance (Herndon 1932).

However, perhaps the most important outcome of the inter-war years was to begin to create a community of international tax specialists. The decade of discussions which produced the drafts agreed at the 1928 meeting had resulted from many meetings and discussions of the issues. The governmental representatives on the Committee of Technical Experts had consulted closely with business representatives nominated by the ICC's double taxation committee. They were also influenced by the experience of negotiation of bilateral treaties by some states, mainly those of Central Europe. There were increasing regular contacts of fiscal specialists, whether government officials, academics or business representatives or advisors. Frequently, individuals combined more than one role, or moved from one to another. This began to generate a community within which ideas and perspectives as well as economic advantage could be traded. It was these direct contacts between specialists which filled the gap created by the difficulties of resolving by any general global principles the issues of international allocation of the tax base of international business.

2
The Tax Treaty System

The key legal mechanism for the co-ordination of states' jurisdiction to tax international business has been the bilateral tax treaty. By accepting that the internationally agreed texts of 1928 and 1935 would not be treated as a multilateral treaty but as a model for bilateral agreements, the foundation was established for a highly flexible system. The basic text of the model could be adapted to the particular circumstances of each pair of partner states, while in turn the adaptations made in bilateral negotiations could feed back into future, multilaterally agreed models. The reports of the international committees responsible for drafting the models came to be a common point of reference for national courts in helping to interpret the treaty texts.

On the other hand, while the flexibility of the system has facilitated its growth, it has resulted in an uneven patchwork of great complexity. The reliance on bilateral agreements results in bargaining which tends to focus on the trading of national benefits, rather than the establishment of an equitable and effective international regime. Thus, state negotiators will be concerned with the relative net revenue gains, and this produces an incentive for states to design national taxes applying to foreign investors, mainly withholding taxes on dividends and other payments, which act as a bargaining counter for treaty negotiations. The revenue consideration may be offset for some states by the desire to attract foreign investment; but such states may be in a weak position to press their claim to jurisdiction if their interest is in offering tax holidays or other benefits to foreign investors.

The unevenness and porosity of the treaty network undermine its regulatory effectiveness. The lack of any clear criteria of international tax equity has encouraged and legitimized international tax planning and avoidance, which have been facilitated in turn by the inducements offered by states anxious to attract investment or financial business. This has consequently led to a process of continual renegotiation of treaties, as the economically stronger countries seek to block loopholes in the treaty network, especially those which allow unintended beneficiaries to take advantage of treaty provisions by 'treaty-shopping'. The increased international mobility of capital has also made it increasingly important to ensure international co-ordination of tax systems, but the process of inter-state negotiation is slow and ponderous, resulting in continual problems of disjunction with domestic tax changes and reforms.

1. Postwar Development of the Bilateral Treaty Network

A turning-point in the development of international tax arrangements was the successful negotiation of a US–UK treaty in 1944–5. The agreement reached by these two powerful states, each with its own network of international relations, was the key to the development of the postwar system of tax treaties.

1.a The US–UK Treaty Negotiation

In the wartime context of the Atlantic Charter and the planning of a liberalized postwar world economy, the British Treasury was manoeuvred into modifying its views and accepting a treaty based on a foreign tax credit. It seems that the British Foreign Office, in particular the then Second Legal Advisor, Eric Beckett, played a key role, mobilizing pressures from commercial interests and support from the Board of Trade (see PRO file FO371/38589). The general theme of the arguments made by business groups was that it was no longer possible to penetrate foreign markets purely through exports, and the operation of foreign branches or subsidiaries had been made extremely difficult by the absence of double taxation treaties and the imposition by countries such as France and the US of high taxes on remittances, which were then liable to UK taxation.

In 1944 the British Chamber of Commerce in Paris, temporarily resident in London, wrote to Anthony Eden pointing out that the postwar resumption of British trade with France would require a tax treaty, since double taxation had become a serious prewar problem (PRO file FO371/41963). At the same time, British firms operating in the US (such as Linen Thread, Spratts Dog Biscuits and J. & P. Coats) also wrote to the Foreign Office, continuing pressures made in the 1930s, pointing out that the absence of any US–UK treaty had led to the reduction of profits remitted by British-owned subsidiaries in the US, while their American competitors benefited from the foreign tax credit. British subsidiaries in the US were said to have been obliged to have recourse to 'unsatisfactory expedients such as invoicing goods at higher prices to the subsidiary or leaving profits to accumulate in the US', because of high US taxes on profit remittances. The Foreign Office was advised that British firms with major US subsidiaries (thought to number 57) had taken legal advice about ways used to circumvent this. 'One method is to fix a maximum invoice price here at such a level that the American branch makes no profit. This meant showing two prices on the invoice, but even so the American customs accept the lower price to the ultimate purchaser' (PRO file FO371/38588). However, such expedients were clearly unsatisfactory.

A 1944 memorandum sent to the Treasury from the British Chamber of Commerce in the US, pointed out that the problem of international double taxation had increased with high wartime tax rates, which were unlikely to decline quickly after the war. It argued that Britain was no longer a net creditor, and should acknowledge that the attempt to make the foreigner pay for international double taxation through higher prices had failed. The costs had been borne by the trader, and there had been 'a steady drift of British oversea [sic] business into oversea operations and a migration of the management overseas'. It argued for the exemption of foreign profit from UK tax until distributed in the UK to a UK resident (PRO file FO371/38588).

It was probably with the encouragement of the Foreign Office that the American government took the initiative, proposing in January 1944 a treaty based on the recently-concluded US-Canadian and US–Swedish treaties. This was followed up with a visit to London in April 1944 of a technical team, which hoped to return with an initialled agreement. The British Foreign Office skilfully eased the way, channelling the representations from British firms and chambers of commerce, to overcome the reservations of the Treasury and the Inland Revenue.[1]

Treasury caution was expressed in the argument that American investment in Britain would have to be controlled after the war, and that the growth of British subsidiaries abroad should not be allowed to substitute overseas production for exports from Britain. In reply, the Foreign Office pointed out that since US firms already benefited from the unilateral foreign tax credit, the US proposal on double taxation was essentially a political one, in the context of the Atlantic Charter. In place of *ad hoc* responses to complaints from British business, there was a clear case for a comprehensive policy, which should include revision of the Dominion arrangements. The Inland Revenue took the view that new arrangements should be agreed, since international double taxation led to evasion. However, an agreement with the US should be carefully negotiated, since it would inevitably establish a baseline for future treaties. Reciprocal enforcement of taxes should therefore be omitted, and the exchange of information should be limited, as in the UK–Irish treaty, to information necessary for the enforcement of the treaty. Although both reciprocal enforcement and mutual assistance might be justifiable between the US and the UK, they would not be desirable with other countries with which the traffic would be mostly one-way.

On this basis, Sir Cornelius Gregg was able to negotiate a final draft in

[1] Following a meeting with the Inland Revenue in 1944, Eric Beckett wrote that congratulations were due to the Foreign Office, as he doubted that any progress would have been made on the tax treaty had the Office not mobilized the Board of Trade and commercial interests: PRO file FO371/38589.

Washington between November 1944 and January 1945. While final details were being agreed, approval by the War Cabinet was held up by last-minute doubts about the exchange of information provisions. These were expressed by the Minister of Information, who claimed that overseas investors would move money out of the City, fearing breach of banker–client confidentiality. These fears were allayed by a report from the Chancellor of the Exchequer that the Bank of England was strongly in favour of the treaty, and that in confidential discussions bankers had also given their support, pointing out that safeguards had been made for confidentiality in the limited information exchange provision (PRO file FO371/44585).

The conclusion of this treaty was a crucial step, since it brought into alignment the US, whose policies would clearly be crucial to the postwar investment and trading system, and the UK, which still retained a major international trading and financial position. As a result, Britain adopted the foreign tax credit: the 1945 Finance (No. 2) Act provided for a credit for recognized taxes paid in treaty countries (on a country-by-country basis) against the tax that would be due on the total income calculated under UK rules, up to the maximum UK tax that would have been payable on the foreign income.

Thus, both these key international actors began negotiating their postwar international tax arrangements on a similar basis (Gregg 1947). By 1948 some 66 general agreements on income and property taxes, or on the taxation of industrial and commercial enterprises, had been concluded; by 1951 120 were in force with 30 more under negotiation. By far the majority were concluded by Britain and the United States, although several European countries also negotiated some among themselves.

The largest number resulted from Britain's renegotiation of the Dominion arrangements: by 1951 general bilateral treaties had been concluded with five Dominions and 36 dependencies. Agreements were also quickly made with several European countries, as well as other countries with which Britain had links such as Israel and Burma. In addition, the UK encouraged or negotiated treaties between British dependencies or ex-dependencies (e.g. Ghana–Nigeria, India–Pakistan), and wherever possible extended to the dependencies agreements made with other countries.[1] To encourage the negotiation of agreements, a unilateral relief was introduced by Britain in 1950, allowing a tax credit for income from non-treaty countries, but with a limit of three-quarters of the UK tax in the case of Commonwealth countries, and one-half for profits made elsewhere. Designed to provide a bargaining counter in negotiations, this limit was abolished in 1953 following the first report of the Royal Commission on the Taxation of Profits and Income (UK Royal Commission 1953).

---

[1] The extension to dependencies of tax treaties by Britain, as well as by some other countries such as the Netherlands and Belgium, later caused problems when those countries became independent and some came to be used as tax havens: see Chapter 6 below.

1.b International Oil Taxation

The spread of tax treaties during this period was an important element in foreign economic policy, establishing a basis for the rapid growth of direct foreign investment and of transnational corporations, especially American firms setting up businesses in Europe. In establishing the regulatory framework for this process, there were often complex interactions between officials of different government departments, internally and internationally, as well as with the advisors and managers of the major transnational companies. An interesting illustration of this is provided by the changes in international oil company taxation at this time.

Renewed postwar exploration in the Middle East had led to the discovery of vast new oilfields in the Gulf states, notably Kuwait and Saudi Arabia, and by 1949 the oil companies, with US State Department support, began negotiating new concession agreements. These were based on the 'Aramco formula', which had originated in the concession negotiated with Venezuela in 1942, and the merits of which had been pointed out to Middle East governments by a Venezuelan delegation in 1949. In place of a per-barrel royalty, the new arrangement provided for a mixture of royalties and profits taxes based on 'posted prices'.

The posted price was the transfer price for crude oil from the production companies to the downstream refiners; since most international oil was controlled by the vertically-integrated oil majors, the posted price was a largely notional price. The combination of royalties and profits taxes was supposed to amount to a 50–50 split of profits between government and companies, at the oil production stage. The level of production profits mainly depended on the posted price, but although the producer companies sometimes pressed for improvement of the 50–50 proportion, attention was not focused on how posted prices were fixed until they were reduced by the oil companies in the late 1950s to stimulate demand from independent purchasers. The oil-exporting countries reacted strongly to the resultant fall in their revenues, and this led to the formation of OPEC in 1960 (Odell 1986, p. 21).

A major advantage for the oil companies of the Aramco formula was that, whereas royalties were merely deductible from gross profits as an expense, the profits taxes could be credited dollar for dollar against the taxes payable by the oil companies to their home states, provided that they were accepted as income taxes qualifying for the foreign tax credit. Hence, the extra revenue payable to the host governments of the producing states would be funded in effect by the oil companies' home states. The new tax laws in Saudi Arabia had been drawn up by oil company advisors, with State Department support, to facilitate their approval as eligible for tax credit.[1] A similar law for Kuwait required British

---

[1] A British official minuted a meeting of 21.7.52 with Mr Barthelow, an oil company advisor, formerly of the US State Department, who was said to have authored the Saudi and Kuwaiti laws and was drafting that of Bahrain: PRO file FO371/4236, p. 179.

government approval, as the Protecting Power.

Despite State Department support, these arrangements were viewed with suspicion by the US Treasury and the IRS, which regarded them as a means of funnelling subsidies to the Middle Eastern governments without the need for the approval of Congress. The British Exchequer was if anything more alarmed, since it was even more dependent on taxation of overseas profits for revenue. The extent of potential losses if the arrangement were emulated, not only for oil but other minerals concessions, could be enormous: in relation to Kuwait alone, the losses to the British Exchequer were estimated at £6m per year at the existing levels of output.

Following informal contacts between British and American Revenue officials on the occasion of a UN Fiscal Commission meeting, the US Treasury wrote formally in October 1951 asking whether the British had yet formed a view on the oil tax credit. The British Treasury wrote a persuasive note for a Cabinet committee arguing that there was no case for the taxpayer, rather than the cash-rich oil companies, to subsidize Middle Eastern governments to ensure their stability. The oil state host governments themselves could have no special interest in the way they obtained their revenues (whether by a general company profits tax or a specific oil tax) but only in the amounts. The proposed Kuwaiti tax, for example, could hardly be said to qualify for credit as a general income or profits tax, since it had been specially devised and tailored to the costs of the oil concessions and applied to only a handful of companies; provided the British government took a firm line on disallowing the oil states' tax for credit, it was in the Americans' interests to follow suit.

However, both the Foreign Office and the Ministry of Fuel and Power took a different view. It was not merely a matter of not hampering the British oil companies in their competition with the Americans for new concessions. Both the British government and the oil companies were reliant on US support in relation to world oil arrangements: for example, in trying to re-establish British interests in Iran after the nationalization of the Anglo-Iranian Oil Company. Furthermore, following the sterling crisis of 1949, the British government had asked for co-operation from the American oil companies in measures to reduce the dollar costs of oil. Although they had not been able to agree to a proposal to reduce oil imports by their British subsidiaries by substituting sterling-area oil, they had rearranged their sales so that their UK companies would show disproportionate profits: it was estimated that in the case of Caltex alone this would produce £4.5m additional tax revenue, as well as the beneficial dollar inflows. Continued co-operation with such arrangements would clearly be endangered if the companies should hear that the British government was opposing the 'tax route' for boosting oil state revenues. Foreign Office objections and procrastination prevented any response at all being sent to the American Treasury's enquiry. In due course, the oil taxes were approved in the US for credit, and the British Inland Revenue was obliged to follow suit. (See PRO files T236/4234–4239.)

This episode is a good illustration of the complex geopolitical strategic issues that could be raised by international tax questions. Although the oil industry is a special case, it is a very important one. Occurring in the early days of development of the tax treaty network, this example clearly shows that the taxation of transnational companies involved a transnational politics: divisions within national governments, and alliances between parallel departments of different governments, with the advisors and consultants of TNCs, often themselves former state officials, playing a ubiquitous role. In such a situation, it was perhaps not surprising that the Foreign Office officials and transnational company representatives proved more adept at international manoeuvring, and formed a sort of alliance, which in the event defeated the Treasury and Revenue departments (cf. Cox 1981, Picciotto 1991).

However, the allowability of upstream oil taxes for tax credit downstream became built in to the politics and economics of the oil industry. Once the principle was conceded, it was very hard to take away or even limit. Thus, when the North Sea oilfields were first opened up, the British Department of Trade and Industry apparently did not realize until the late 1960s that there would be little if any British tax revenue under the existing tax system, since foreign tax credits could largely wipe out profits on the North Sea fields (UK House of Commons 1971–2, esp. p. 275). Parliamentary pressure led to the complex 'ring fence' system for North Sea oil taxation.

In the US, there has been continual criticism of what some consider to be the concealed subsidization by the American taxpayer of the oil producer states (Engler 1961; Odell 1986, pp. 35–6). This led to some renewed attempts to deny allowability of foreign oil production taxes for credit, for instance when Indonesia introduced production-sharing arrangements in 1976, and again in 1979 for Saudi Arabia's participation-oil arrangements. The oil companies have defeated these attempts only by adroit international manoeuvres and determined lobbying. According to one account, Indonesia asked the US IRS to draw up a tax that would be allowable for credit in the US; although the IRS refused, the same result was produced by US law firms producing versions which were submitted to the IRS and amended until an acceptable one was found (Kingson 1981, p. 1265). Nevertheless, restrictions on allowability against non-oil income were approved by Congress in 1975 and 1976. Reporting to Congress following further reform proposals, the US Comptroller-General took the view that the credit was not a suitable energy policy instrument; this report pointed out that 75 per cent of the total foreign tax credit was claimed by the oil industry, an average of $15–17 billion annually in 1974–6, 95 per cent of which was claimed by the twelve largest oil firms (US General Accounting Office 1980). Although Congress has continued to snipe at the credit, the oil industry's lobbying power has protected it from complete withdrawal of the advantage.

1.c International Investment and Tax Equity or Neutrality

Despite the spread of bilateral treaties, the postwar period saw considerable disagreement and uncertainty about the principles on which international tax arrangements should be based. Although bilateral treaties were quickly developing into an extensive network, there were still considerable unevenness of coverage and variations of substance which reflected the divergences and lack of clarity in aims. As we have seen in the previous chapter, pressures from business for measures to prevent international double taxation had achieved limited results in the period between the wars. In particular, the UK, with extensive income from foreign lending and exports of goods and services, had been concerned to maintain equality of taxation of its residents on income from all sources, and reluctant to give up tax revenue on income from abroad. However, capital-importing countries were reluctant to exempt non-residents from taxation on locally-earned business income, or even on returns on local investments such as interest and dividends. These differences of perspective on equity for taxpayers were inter-woven with the issue of inter-state equity: the principles adopted for the allocation of tax rights could significantly affect state revenues since some states were predominantly net importers and others net exporters of investment capital.

The US–UK treaty, and the introduction by the UK of the foreign tax credit, had established a common position for these two states, which dominated the world economy, especially in foreign investments. They both maintained the overriding, ultimate right of the home state to tax the income of its residents from overseas business. However, they conceded that the host state had the prior claim to tax the business profits attributable to a Permanent Establishment, and this tax should be credited against the tax levied by the home state on the total global profits. Taxes at source on investment income, such as interest on loans or dividends on shares, should be minimal or zero. In this way, although the host country could tax the business profits made through a fixed local base, the free international flow of investments would not be hampered by high source taxes on foreign-owned business or on remittances. At the same time, home countries could maintain the same level of taxation on all their residents, whether their investments were made and profits came from at home or abroad.

This allocation of tax rights, however, did not directly establish any principles of equity in the allocation of the tax base of international business between states, or inter-state equity. It therefore made it very hard, if not impossible, to reconcile equity from the point of view of both the home and the host states. In the postwar climate of concern to encourage international investment (while not damaging domestic investment), this question was posed as the problem of reconciling tax equity from the point of view of capital-export and capital-import. From the point of view of a capital-importing host country tax equity between those active in the same market requires that their tax burden should be the same regardless of the country of origin of the investor. From the point of view of a home country, equity means equal tax treatment of domestic and foreign profits, to ensure that capital is not diverted from domestic to foreign investment, and residents do not escape taxation by making their investments abroad. Economists often go beyond the question of tax equity and speak of neutrality, in the sense that a tax system which affects different investment decisions in an equal way should produce the least distortion and therefore the most efficiency in the allocation of economic resources. However, the concept of neutrality depends on the abstractions derived for the purposes of economic theory. In practice it must be considered in relation to the characteristics of different types of investment and the definition of taxable income or the tax base: in particular, direct investment differs from other capital movements, and the taxation of company profits is not equivalent to taxation of other returns on capital (Alworth 1988, pp. 30–2).[1]

Capital-export equity favours residence-based taxation, while capital-import equity favours source-based taxation. The main capital-exporting countries, the US and the UK, had only conceded primacy of taxation at source for business profits: they still retained the right to tax the returns from foreign investment, subject only to a credit for allowable foreign taxes. This residual overall right to tax investment returns meant that the foreign investor paid the higher of the home or host country tax rates. The strongest argument of the capital-exporting countries was that the unilateral abandonment of their jurisdiction to tax overseas investment would not lead to fairness in international taxation. Competition to attract inward investment would mean exemptions and tax holidays or ineffective taxation at source; in such a situation, exemption of foreign-source profits by residence countries would mean inefficient international allocation of investment, and inequitable international taxation. Certainly, the countries of origin of investment at that time had generally higher and more effective business taxes than the capital-hungry countries which were willing to offer tax privileges to attract investment. On the other hand, both capital-importing countries and international investors combined to argue that the stimulation of international investment was needed to establish the foundations of growth in the postwar world economy, and this required the exemption of foreign investment profits from residence taxation.

These arguments were debated in the 1950s in particular in the US and the UK (see Chapter 5 below). The US debate clarified that the citizenship basis of US taxation meant that only individual citizens and corporations formed in the US were directly liable to US taxes on foreign investment profits. For the bulk of foreign investment, which took the form of foreign direct investment

---

[1] For these reasons I prefer the concept of equity or fairness. On the other hand, to an economist, the notion of fairness is imprecise, and merely means what is acceptable to government, or according to 'arbitrary political judgment': Devereux & Pearson 1989, p. 16.

channelled through subsidiaries incorporated abroad, US taxation only applied to profits remitted to the US parent, and could therefore be deferred if profits were retained abroad. In practice, the US system allowed *both* exemption of retained foreign earnings *and* a credit in respect of that proportion of the tax paid on the repatriated profits. Thus, the credit approach could be very similar in practice to exemption. Countries which exempt foreign source business profits may tax as income in the hands of the parent company the net profit repatriated as dividends, or other payments such as fees and royalties. Furthermore, they may take into account the foreign income in determining the tax rate applicable to the remaining income (exemption with progression).

In the UK, the taxation of overseas profits had been a matter of some political sensitivity since the rejection by the Royal Commission report in 1920 of the pressures to modify it. The Annual Reports of the Commissioners of Inland Revenue from 1925 carried figures on the foreign investment income taxed in the UK, although no estimate was possible of the proportion of the trading profits of UK residents attributable to overseas business. Following renewed pressures from business, the matter was given extended consideration by the Radcliffe Commission (the Royal Commission on Taxation) in 1953–5. Its final report stressed that the taxation of overseas income was not a purely domestic matter, but must be considered 'in the light of the taxing systems and principles of other countries and of any generally accepted understandings as to taxing jurisdiction that can be said to have international recognition' (para. 633). The argument for exemption of overseas earnings carried great weight, but there was insufficient consensus in the Commission to concede it completely and immediately. It recommended instead the compromise proposal of exemption of the undistributed earnings of 'overseas trade corporations', defined in the ensuing legislation in 1956 essentially as UK resident companies trading wholly overseas. These provisions were in force until the enactment of the Corporation Tax in 1965.[1]

Thus, both Britain and the US were only willing to concede the argument for exemption, if at all, for foreign business profits produced by direct investment abroad. The overriding problem was that the international tax arrangements, negotiated between 1918 and 1948, provided an inadequate basis for discussion or negotiation of international equity. Both the procedures and principles of the arrangements assumed bilateral bargaining of national interest based on reciprocity. There had been a virtual abandonment of any attempt to agree multilateral conventions, even for mutual assistance, so that the basic procedure was the negotiation of bilateral treaties based as far as possible on an internationally-agreed model draft. This procedure inevitably gave the major role to the internationally-dominant countries; yet they have

[1] For a discussion of the international aspects of the post-1965 corporation tax and a discussion of tax neutrality and tax bias, from a fairly abstract economic viewpoint, see Bracewell-Milnes 1971.

been obliged to rely either on finding an actual reciprocity of interest or ideology with potential treaty partners, or some other inducement or pressures.

The substantive provisions of the model drafts reinforced this approach of reciprocal bargaining of national interest. They assumed that host country primary jurisdiction was confined to the business profits of a locally-incorporated company or a Permanent Establishment, so the bargaining essentially focused on the limitation of the withholding taxes charged on the remittance of dividends, interest, fees and royalties. It certainly became increasingly clear that national approaches to equity, combined with bilateral international bargaining, provided an inadequate basis for a tax framework that could be both fair and neutral in relation to international investment. From the point of view of internationally-mobile capital, equity could not be assured by unilateral or bilateral state measures. Greater uniformity and international equity in taxation of international business must be sought through broader international agreement. Unfortunately, attempts to develop a comprehensive international approach to business taxation achieved only a limited success, as will be seen in the next section.

2. The Role of International Organizations

As a counterpoint to the continuing and expanding process of bilateral negotiation of tax treaties, international organizations have played an important part in the postwar period. They have primarily provided a forum for merging multiple bilateral positions into multilaterally-agreed provisions in model treaties, which in turn have formed the basis for bilateral negotiations. Also, the specialist committee reports, including their commentaries on the model conventions, have been an important expression of agreed opinion, which have considerable influence and indeed legal effect in the interpretation of agreements. Finally, the meetings of committees and working parties of such organizations have served as important occasions for national administrators to develop closer working relationships, a common ideology and even a certain camaraderie.

An attempt to continue and develop the work of the League's Fiscal Committee was initially made in the immediate postwar period within the framework of the United Nations, by setting up a Fiscal Commission under the Economic and Social Council. It soon proved impossible however, in the political atmosphere of the Cold War and decolonization, to achieve any agreement on the underlying policy issues. In the event, it was the OECD, a more limited grouping of developed capitalist countries, that provided the main forum for multilateral discussion and negotiation, both of model treaties and of tax matters generally. Subsequently, the UN, by setting up a group of experts, played some part in broadening the discussion, and in particular incorporating the developing country viewpoint. In addition, an increasing role has been played both by regional organizations and groupings, as well as more informal arrangements, to develop closer co-ordination in tax matters.

2.a The Mexico and London Drafts and the UN Fiscal Commission

The work of the League's Fiscal Committee had been continued during the war by its officials, from a base in the United States, at Princeton University. From there they organized western hemisphere Regional Tax Conferences in Mexico City, which brought into its work the Latin American countries, none of which had attended the 1928 meeting, and which the US considered 'would be interested in industrial and commercial expansion when the war was over' (Carroll 1965, p. 707). These meetings considered and re-evaluated not only the League of Nations drafts, but also the main prewar bilateral treaties, which had been concluded mainly between continental European states. The meetings were dominated by capital-importing states, not only the Latin Americans but also Canada, which had argued for a strengthening of source taxation in negotiations for the tax treaty with the United States concluded in 1942. In other respects, the policy of the US and its experience in negotiating bilateral treaties was influential.

The Mexico meetings resulted in the amalgamation of the 1928 and 1935 conventions into a single draft Model Bilateral Convention for the Prevention of the Double Taxation of Income, referred to as the Mexico draft of 1943. However, the matter was reconsidered by the Fiscal Committee when it reconvened for its Tenth Session in London in 1946. This produced a new draft, which included property and wealth taxation, but also amended the Mexico version in several crucial respects. Rather than replace the Mexico draft, the two were published together, with a commentary. The London and Mexico models also contained revised versions of the 1928 drafts on Succession taxes, and a draft which combined into one the 1928 conventions on Administrative Assistance in Assessment and in Collection of taxes. The publication of these three draft model conventions (League of Nations 1946) was the Fiscal Committee's legacy to the international fiscal community. It provided the technical basis for the postwar growth of international fiscal co-ordination, while at the same time revealing significant disagreement on basic principles.

The divergence between the Mexico and London drafts reopened the split between the source and residence principles of international taxation. The Mexico draft explicitly stated the primacy of the right to tax business income at source. It provided that all income should be taxable 'only in the State where the business or activity is carried out', although this did not apply to 'isolated or occasional transactions . . . without . . . a permanent establishment'. It also laid down that payments of interest, dividends and royalties should be taxable at source, i.e. in the state of the payer. Although the state of domicile was allowed to tax worldwide income, it was required to grant a credit in respect of all source taxes levied according to the principles laid down in the convention. The source principle was even extended so far as to say that, in the case of the export of raw materials, the entire income resulting from sales at world market prices was to be considered as realized in the exporting country.

In contrast, the London draft reasserted the principles developed in the prewar League models, in particular the limitation of taxation at source to the income produced by a Permanent Establishment. The criteria for determining what constitutes a Permanent Establishment were contained in a Protocol (which was in fact identical in both drafts). The basic definition was an installation or fixed place of business of a productive character. It therefore excluded ancillary activities such as warehousing or research laboratories; and a line was drawn between an independent agent or broker, which was excluded, while a duly accredited agent with power to enter contracts on behalf of the enterprise was included as a Permanent Establishment. The London draft made interest taxable at the domicile of the recipient. Although dividends were taxable at the domicile of the paying company, they were to be exempt from tax if paid to a controlling company (i.e. from a subsidiary to a parent). On the other hand, patent royalties could only be taxed in the country of exploitation of the patent if they were paid to a related company.

Although they disagreed on the primacy of source or resident taxation, the Mexico and London drafts did not reopen the debate between arm's length and global apportionment. The provisions for allocation of income were the same in the two drafts, and merely incorporated the provisions of the 1935 allocation convention as a Protocol. The Commentary justified the separate accounting/arm's length approach as necessary to give equality or 'national treatment' for foreign-owned branches, and to limit taxation to a strictly territorial scope without reference to results or data outside the country concerned (League of Nations 1946, p. 18). However, it also pointed out that the retention of fractional apportionment, even if only in third place after separate accounting and percentage of turnover, did not exclude its use: in particular, it might be a necessary means of achieving the aims of separate accounting in allocating items of expenses that must necessarily be proportionately allocated, such as head office expenses (ibid. p. 21). The Protocol also preserved the different treatment of related enterprises in the 1935 Convention: affiliates were excluded from the definition of permanent enterprise, and inter-affiliate pricing must be on the 'independent enterprise' basis, although subject to adjustment where profits have been 'diverted' (ibid., Protocol, Art VII).

The League's Fiscal Committee had hoped to be reborn under the aegis of the United Nations, and to continue its work, notably by reconciling the divergences between the Mexico and London drafts. Continuity seemed a real possibility when the UN's Economic and Social Council in 1946–7 set up a Financial and Fiscal Commission, consisting of fifteen experts chosen by member states, and this Commission began with an ambitious programme in which international tax matters figured as a major item. However, its deliberations proved much more politicized than was the case under the League, largely because its broader membership now also included developing countries and the Soviet bloc. With Cold War hostility added to the differences of perspective between developing and developed countries, as well as between Anglo-Saxon and continental European countries, the problem of international taxation could not be treated as a purely technical one.

This diversity of perspectives led to debates at the main sessions of the Commission in 1951 and 1953 that were often heated, according to Mitchell Carroll, now present as an observer on behalf of the US National Association of Manufacturers (Carroll 1951, 1953). By majority, the Commission refused to support a proposal from the International Civil Aviation Organization for taxation of air transport enterprises by their countries of domicile. A general resolution was approved favouring the avoidance of double taxation by means of treaties, and stating that countries seeking to attract capital need not offer favourable tax treatment, but that the main burden of relief from double taxation should be on the home country. While this established the prior right to tax of the source or host country, no agreement could be reached on whether this was an exclusive right. The exemption of foreign income from taxation in the home country was favoured by the LDCs, by international business itself, and by some governmental bodies concerned with international investment, such as the International Development Advisory Board (IDAB) set up by President Truman's Act for International Development. With the Soviet bloc countries abstaining on this issue, a Cuban resolution for exemption of the income derived from a foreign Permanent Establishment failed to gain acceptance. In reply to the IDAB's Rockefeller Report 'Partners in Progress', which supported tax exemption of foreign investment income, the US Treasury representative on the UN Commission defended the foreign tax credit as neutral between home and foreign investment, and argued that exemption would lead to competition to lower taxes by capital-seeking countries and undermine a sound and equitable tax system (see section 1.c above, and Chapter 5 below).

Since international financial matters were now primarily dealt with by the International Monetary Fund and the World Bank (IBRD), and consensus on the main principles of the international tax system seemed impossible to attain, the UN's Fiscal Commission seemed to have little role, and ceased to meet after 1954. Its secretariat continued purely technical work, such as the establishment of a fiscal documentation centre and continuing the compilation of tax treaties begun under the League. The UN's most successful activity in this period was the provision of technical assistance to LDCs in developing their tax systems; but this came under the wing of the Technical Assistance

Board and not the Fiscal Commission (UN 1954, Chrétien 1954). In 1965, the International Monetary Fund set up its Fiscal Affairs Department largely to provide fiscal advice to developing countries, and much technical assistance has also been provided by the foreign tax assistance staff of the US IRS, funded by US AID (Oldman & Surrey 1972).

2.b The OECD Fiscal Affairs Committee

It could not have been very surprising that agreement on the basic principles of international jurisdiction to tax was hard to reach between the developed capitalist countries on the one hand, and either developing countries or the Soviet bloc on the other. Since neither of the latter were exporters of capital, there was no direct basis of reciprocity for the allocation of jurisdiction to tax. On the other hand, between the capitalist developed countries themselves, although there were many imbalances in the extent and type of capital flows, there was at least some mutuality.

In this situation, it was not surprising that the mantle of the League's Fiscal Committee was picked up by the Organization for Economic Co-Operation and Development (OECD). It was the predecessor organization of the OECD, the OEEC (Organization for European Economic Co-operation), which in 1955 resumed consideration of the double tax treaty system. This was initiated by some European countries, such as Switzerland, concerned to remove tax constraints on international capital movements. It also resulted from pressures by the international business lobby, articulated once again mainly by the International Chamber of Commerce. The ICC had in the postwar period maintained its active interest in the problems of international taxation; while it was heartened by the adoption by countries such as Britain of the foreign tax credit, and by the rapid spread of double tax treaties, it was concerned by their increasing diversity and the consequent unevenness in the international tax regime. A resolution was passed at its Tokyo Congress, inviting the OEEC to consider the possibility of a multilateral double tax convention to facilitate international investment.

In 1956 the OEEC set up a Fiscal Committee, and in 1958 gave the Committee the task of preparing a new draft convention for the avoidance of double taxation of income and capital, together with proposals for implementation. The intention was to facilitate the increasing economic interdependence and co-operation of the developed countries by harmonizing as far as possible their systems of business taxation. The primary aim of the OEEC, and later the OECD, was to facilitate international investment, so its natural starting point was the London model treaty. No radical new approach was attempted. The Committee contented itself with working through the established model articles, taking into account the practice of states in the bilateral treaties they had concluded since the London draft. It aimed to work towards uniformity, by publishing agreed versions of the articles, together with commentaries to harmonize their interpretation. At the same time, there was a need to encourage the more widespread adoption of the model treaty, especially by the more 'peripheral' members of the organization, such as Ireland, Spain, Greece, Iceland, Portugal and Turkey, as well as by the financial entrepôt states such as Switzerland and Luxembourg. The aims of universality and uniformity diverged, and inevitably the Committee found itself formulating drafts which allowed, or even facilitated, variations to take into account the different perspectives and practices of national tax systems. The slow progress made by bilateral negotiation, in which each concession was subjected to bargaining, exasperated the ICC, which called for unilateral implementation of tax credit or exemption arrangements and the negotiation of a multilateral convention. The Fiscal Committee in reply pointed out that unilateralism was impossible, but it promised to pursue the grail of multilateralism (OECD 1963, pp. 26–9).

In 1963, the organization (which had become the OECD in 1961) published its draft Double Taxation Convention on Income and Capital, together with Commentaries, which were quite extensive especially on the most important articles. The Committee's Report stressed the importance of these Commentaries in the elaboration of international fiscal law, since they had been drafted and agreed unanimously by the government-nominated experts, in contrast to the Commentaries in the League's drafts which had been prepared by the Secretariat. Although they were not designed to form part of any treaties based on the Model, they were intended to assist in their interpretation, especially in the event of disputes (OECD 1963, p. 18). It was envisaged that they would do so as part of the drafting history or *travaux préparatoires* of each treaty. Indeed, where provisions agreed in the OECD Committee have led to changes in national tax law, the OECD Commentaries are an important souce of national legal interpretation also. Even in the UK, whose courts do not even refer to parliamentary history as a guide to statutory interpretation, the OECD Commentaries are regarded as an essential guide to interpretation.[1] Bearing this in mind, member states have been careful to request the inclusion in the Commentaries, where appropriate, both of their 'interpretations' (often of the commentary as well as of the model treaty language), and of their 'reservations', where they are unable to accept a provision in the model.

Although the 1963 OECD model was largely based on the work of the League, especially the London draft, it embodied some significant refinements. Although essentially technical and detailed, these consisted of some attempts to modify the international tax regime to take into account the new forms of international business that were developing with the rapid growth of international trade and foreign investment. In particular, the postwar growth of foreign direct investment had led, as has already been mentioned, to the

---

[1] *Fothergill v. Monarch Airlines* (1981), *Sun Life Assurance of Canada v. Pearson* (1984).

maturing of the Transnational Corporation (TNC), operating a globally integrated business through a network of subsidiaries and affiliates. This made it more than ever vital to agree on principles for the treatment of inter-affiliate transactions.

The OECD model reaffirmed the basic principles of the London draft, such as the concept of the Permanent Establishment (PE) and the arm's length rule. However, the former was refined by providing that the source country could tax only the income *attributable* to the PE. This entailed rejecting the 'force of attraction' principle, by which all income from within a country is attributed to a PE located in it, and requiring instead the separate treatment of different sources of income from within the country. Thus, a foreign enterprise doing business through a PE could also make unrelated investments, such as buying shares in or licensing technology to other companies, without having the income from them automatically attributed to the income of the PE.

The growth of TNCs also made it essential to resolve the problem of jurisdiction to tax inter-affiliate payments: interest, dividends and royalties. As we have seen in Chapter 1, this had already in the inter-war period proved to be the most difficult area in which to reconcile the conflicting tax systems and economic interests of states. Now the best solution that could be found was to develop the concept of the withholding tax. This had already been used in the London draft in relation to the taxation of interest payments by the debtor's state. The Committee came up with a 'package deal' limiting taxation at source to agreed maxima for interest (10 per cent), dividends (15 per cent, but 5 per cent if paid to a company owning at least 25 per cent of the shares of the payer), and royalties (taxable only in the recipient state). However, these provisions were subject to many reservations by states, and are commonly a main focus of bargaining in tax treaty negotiations, with consequent variations in the levels set by bilateral treaties.

The work of the OECD Fiscal Committee greatly stimulated the spread of bilateral double tax treaties among OECD members, which had already begun in the postwar period following the publication of the League models. Whereas between 1920 and 1939 fewer than 60 general tax treaties were concluded among all countries, by 1955 when the OECD began work on the subject, there were already 70 such treaties in force among developed countries alone. Between 1958, which saw the publication of the first Report of the Fiscal Committee, and July 1963 when it issued the entire draft Double Taxation Convention on Income and Capital, 23 bilateral conventions had been concluded and eight revised, among OECD members. By the end of the first twenty years of work of the OECD Fiscal Committee a network of 179 such bilateral treaties had been agreed among OECD members, and by 1985 this figure was 202 (OECD 1977, Lienard 1985). Among the main international investing countries the network was virtually complete.[1]

---

[1] For a survey of the provisions and operation of these treaties, focusing on UK law, see Davies 1985.

2.c Developing Countries and the UN Group of Experts

By the time of the publication of the 1963 OECD model, the number of independent states had begun to grow rapidly, with the achievement of political independence by many colonial territories, especially in Africa and Asia. Although some attempt was made by the developed countries (DCs) to extend the tax treaty network to these underdeveloped or less-developed countries (LDCs), these efforts met with relatively little success.

The different attitude of the LDCs as capital-importing countries to the allocation of tax jurisdiction had been demonstrated in the meetings which led to the Mexico draft. Not only did the LDCs themselves consider the standard tax treaty model inappropriate to their needs, the policies of the DCs towards them were contradictory. While the Revenue and Treasury authorities considered it important to maintain the right to tax returns on capital invested abroad, other policy considerations favoured the encouragement of the economic development of LDCs and the minimization of taxation on investments in them. As we have seen, this point of view was pressed not only by the capital-importing countries themselves, but by groups representing foreign investors and traders. They found sympathetic ears in ministries of foreign affairs, who were sometimes able to persuade the Treasury and Revenue authorities to accept special concessions, such as the US concession in 1942 to western hemisphere trading corporations, emulated in 1956 by Britain with its Overseas Trade Corporations.

Following pressures from British business, the Radcliffe Commission also recommended in 1953 that credits for overseas tax could in appropriate cases be agreed to extend to tax 'spared' by developing countries to attract capital.[1] Perhaps unsurprisingly, the Treasury and Inland Revenue were not happy with the idea of giving a credit for taxes that had not actually been paid; but associations representing business continued to pressurize a reluctant Treasury, via the Foreign and Colonial Office, to give effect to this recommendation (PRO file IR40/12668). These pressures, as well as the work of the UN discussed below, did have some result: as some UK tax treaties with Commonwealth countries were renegotiated in the 1960s and 1970s, they have in appropriate cases included a British credit for taxes 'deemed paid' but spared under pioneer industry relief or other investment incentives (e.g. UK–Barbados 1970, UK–Ghana 1977).

Nevertheless, the general inappropriateness of the tax treaty system for LDCs (see Irish 1974) was reflected in the paucity of treaties negotiated with them, apart from those negotiated on their behalf in the immediate postwar period by their colonial mother-countries, especially Britain. For example, by 1970 Ghana had been party to only eight general double tax treaties, all made by the United Kingdom on her behalf prior to independence in 1957. Only

[1] Tax sparing or tax holidays entail special tax exemptions for new investors, usually during the first few years that an enterprise is established.

two, those with the UK and Nigeria, related to countries with which there were significant financial or commercial dealings. Her lack of interest in negotiating such treaties was attributed to the lack of reciprocity involved in the existing tax treaty model, since it restricted the right to tax at source. While this benefited residents of the treaty countries deriving income from Ghana, there were few Ghanaian residents deriving income from those countries, and in any case Ghanaian tax was levied only on income received in Ghana (UN 1973, p. 147).

In order to examine the special problems of tax treaties between developed and developing countries, the UN Secretary-General set up an Ad Hoc Group of Experts, in response to a resolution of the UN's Economic and Social Council of 4 August 1967. This group conducted meetings and issued seven reports between 1967 and 1978. Its work resulted in the publication of the Guidelines for Tax Treaties between Developed and Developing Countries (UN 1974), a Manual for Negotiation of Tax Treaties between Developed and Developing Countries (UN 1979) and a Model Treaty (UN 1980).

However, the UN Guidelines did not make any new departure in the approach to tax treaties. They took as their starting point the 1963 OECD draft, and merely noted the differing views expressed by experts from developed and developing countries on some of the points of principle. Amendments or modifications to the OECD model were agreed on some dozen points; in several cases there was a failure to agree. Neither the Guidelines, the Manual nor the Model Treaty could be said to challenge the basic principles of the OECD model. Although the report of the UN experts stressed the primacy of taxation at source, this was not expressed in any general principle comparable to Art. IV(1) of the Mexico model. But the UN Guidelines and Model Treaty did enlarge the scope of source taxation, mainly by broadening the definition of a Permanent Establishment; it also allowed an option for taxation of the operating profits of international shipping in proportion to freight receipts by a state with which contacts are more than casual.[1]

A firmer stand on the principle of taxation at source has been taken by the Latin American countries. This has been embodied in Decision 40 of the Cartagena Agreement (Andean Pact) of November 1971, which established both a multilateral arrangement between the members and a model treaty for application with other countries. A similar approach was developed for the broader Latin American grouping covered by LAFTA, the Latin American Free Trade Area, based on the discussions of three meetings of a group of experts.[2] However, their emphasis on the source principle has in some ways

---

[1] For a detailed comparison stressing the departures made by the UN version, see Surrey 1978b. The UN group of experts has continued to meet at intervals and issue reports, focusing on co-operation in tax matters, the contents of which have continued to follow fairly closely the issues raised by the reports of the OECD Committee.
[2] The definition of source was somewhat refined following the LAFTA meetings: see Ramon Valdes Costa, in CIAT 1978, p. 25ff.; see also Atchabahian 1975.

made it harder for Latin American countries to combat tax avoidance. Following the Shoup mission in 1960, Venezuela and other countries accepted that foreign income could be included in the computation of a resident's tax liability, to combat capital flight (Valdes Costa, in CIAT 1978, p. 93). The Andean model contains no provisions on transfer pricing, and since it is not acceptable to most capital-exporting countries, the Latin American states have been slow to develop a treaty network which could provide them with administrative co-operation from other countries. Notably, despite extensive investment and trade between the USA and Latin America, the US has no treaty with any major Latin American country. This is due not only to the latter's insistence on the source principle, but also to the US Congress's rejection of the tax sparing credit, despite continued pressure from the foreign trade lobby (Hufbauer et al. 1988).

However, the pressing need of developing countries for foreign investment has led many of them to a more active negotiation of tax treaties. Thus, a number of developing and newly industrializing countries, some of which already had some treaty links, have been drawn into an ever-wider treaty network, for example the Philippines, Sri Lanka, South Korea, Thailand and Egypt. Some developing countries began to conclude treaties among themselves – e.g. India–Tanzania in 1981, Korea–Malaysia 1983, Indonesia–Thailand 1982. At the same time, some developed countries became willing to make concessions to agree treaties with them. Thus, the tax sparing credit has been accepted by many OECD countries, other than the US: one study showed nineteen developed countries had agreed such a provision, while 38 developing countries had benefited from the concession in one or more treaties (Amico 1989). Some developed countries have also accepted a strengthening of source taxation in other respects too: notably by expanding the definition of Permanent Establishment, to include, for example, building sites or oil rigs in operation for less than a year. This benefits not only developing countries – many developed countries also now have offshore oil drilling activities; indeed, the treatment as PEs of oil rigs in place for over 30 days was agreed in a 1979 Protocol to the US–UK treaty.

Some treaties between new partners have departed completely from the model direct tax treaty. For instance, the treaty between France and Saudi Arabia of 1983 applied only to physical and not legal persons, favoured passive investments, and covered death duties as well as income tax. As one commentator stated, it 'seems less in the nature of a tax treaty than in the nature of an investment treaty whereby the French government is trying to attract . . . certain types of Saudi investments' (Juillard, in Allen & Ward 1985, p. 32).

The broadening of the treaty network has also included East European countries, which became concerned to encourage investment from abroad following their economic reforms. From 1972 most of them rapidly developed quite an extensive treaty network, initiated by the 1972 treaty between Poland

and West Germany, and three treaties negotiated by Romania in 1973. The USSR–US treaty of 1973 showed the political acceptability of such arrangements, although its terms were somewhat limited. Several of the East European countries now have over fifteen treaties each (Romania, Hungary, Poland and Czechoslovakia), while the others have eight to ten (USSR, Bulgaria, GDR: see Easson 1989, p. 523). Also, China negotiated a series of treaties in the 1980s, following the economic reforms initiated there from 1979. Until recently, these countries have had a special regime for foreign investors, with an emphasis on joint ventures and controls on the repatriation of profits in hard currency, so there has not been the same concern with ensuring adequate source taxation as in developing country treaty negotiations; paradoxically, their opening to the market will require greater caution in the negotiation of the terms of tax treaties.

These developments certainly began to break up the log-jam created by the postwar divergence over the reconciliation of source and residence taxation. The treaty network has spread to an extent that, although by no means universal, is very extensive. Nevertheless, the broadening of the net also revealed weaknesses in its structure.

2.d International Co-ordination and Tax Treaty Negotiation

We have seen that, from the beginnings of the application of direct taxation to business income or profits, representatives of international business pleaded for the co-ordination of taxation to ensure global equality of competition. National tax systems took account, to varying extents and in various ways, of the need to limit national taxation of international business to those profits which could in some sense be regarded as falling within national tax jurisdiction, as framed by the liberal approach of the classical international law of jurisdiction, which interpreted state sovereignty as permitting a state to exercise jurisdiction according to any principle it preferred, provided this did not infringe any positive rule of international law (see further Chapter 11 below). Thus, even Britain based its extensive claims to tax on the principle of territoriality:

> The Income Tax Acts . . . impose a territorial limit, either that from which the taxable income is derived must be situated in the UK, or the person whose income is to be taxed must be resident there [Lord Herschell, in *Colquhoun v. Brooks*, 1889, p. 499].

Thus, a tax jurisdiction which claims to be territorial can produce extensive overlapping taxation, since it may be used to justify taxation both of business profits at source and of residents on their worldwide income. However, countries can virtually eliminate juridical double taxation unilaterally, either by exempting residents on foreign profits earned through a Permanent Establishment, or by granting a credit for equivalent foreign taxes paid.

Nevertheless, as the US had found in the 1920s, it is inadequate to rely purely on unilateral national measures to co-ordinate taxation of international business. The business lobby in particular realized that the unilateral foreign tax credit not only fails to guarantee co-ordination, but has the crucial disadvantage that it creates an incentive for countries to raise their taxes, especially on investors from abroad, since it is not the investor but the foreign treasury that absorbs an increase in source taxes provided they can be credited against home tax liability. This led to the attempts through the League of Nations to reach a comprehensive agreement allocating tax jurisdiction, aimed at limiting taxation at source. Unfortunately, divergences between national approaches to business taxation, as well as conflicting interests due to imbalances in ownership of international investments, made a comprehensive multilateral solution impossible. The substitute device, the negotiation of bilateral treaties based on an agreed model, was not immediately effective, but spread rapidly in the immediate postwar years, and provided at least an adequate basis for the rapid growth of international investment. However, the emergence of a world of flexible and rapidly-mobile international investment has placed a very heavy burden on the bilateral tax treaty as the principal means for establishing a framework for the co-ordination of international business taxation.

The bilateral treaty offers a number of advantages and apparently easy solutions to the problems of co-ordination. It appears adaptable to the particular circumstances and relationship of each pair of treaty partners, and to allow each state to retain sovereignty over its own internal tax arrangements. However, these advantages are to some extent illusory. First, definite parameters for negotiation are established by the constraints of the overall treaty network: for example, a treaty term or provision which may be appropriate for a particular partner may nevertheless be avoided for fear that others may request it.[1] Thus, we saw that the UK Inland Revenue was reluctant to concede a broad information exchange provision in the 1945 treaty with the US, because it might set a precedent for other countries, with whom such an exchange would be less beneficial. Secondly, not only is the power of a state to decide its own tax system inevitably constrained by the global nature of economic activity, but also the patterns of international tax arrangements themselves establish constraints. Certainly, a sovereign legislature can alter domestic tax arrangements, which may result in significant changes to the effects of already-agreed treaty provisions; it may even override treaty obligations to do so. However, such actions will produce inevitable protest and perhaps retaliation from its treaty partners.[2] In reality, the

[1] In some cases treaties are accompanied by protocols formally undertaking not to agree better terms with another state without granting the same terms to the treaty partner (most-favoured-nation clause): Vann 1991, p. 110.
[2] See Chapter 11 below for the dispute between the US and its European treaty partners over 'treaty overrides'.

international context imposes significant constraints on the state's apparently sovereign powers of taxation.

However, no global forum has emerged within which issues of international tax policy and co-ordination can be discussed. At the very least, the effective operation of the treaty system requires a multilateral forum for discussion of its dynamics, focusing on the model treaty terms and commentary. Although the OECD Committee has been authoritative, its role has been confined, both by its limited membership, and by its being composed only of government officials, and the consequently secretive and arcane character of its deliberations.

Furthermore, the model treaty which emerged from the international discussion initiated after the First World War, also offers some misleadingly facile solutions to the problems of international co-ordination. As we have seen, the specialists who studied the question in the 1930s shrank from the attempt to develop agreed principles for the definition and allocation of the tax base of internationally-organized business. Thus, the model bilateral treaty makes no attempt at an agreed definition of taxable income, nor at any criteria for division of that taxable capacity. Instead, it concentrates on the classification and assignment of taxation rights, according to types of tax and the relationship of the state to the taxpayer (Rosenbloom & Langbein 1981, p. 366). This approach avoided the necessity for what would have been a far-reaching harmonization of the principles of definition of the business tax base.

Most importantly, it means that tax treaty negotiations are not simply concerned with principles for the division of revenue between national authorities. The relationship of a pair of potential treaty partners is certainly structured by the extent to which each is or may be an importer or exporter of capital to the other. However, national treasuries must weigh two conflicting interests: on the one hand in ensuring adequate revenue from effective and fair taxation; and on the other, in providing sufficient inducements for, or at least no obstacles to, capital investment. Thus, although the conflict between the residence and source principles of taxation reflects the different perspectives of predominantly capital-importing and capital-exporting countries, it is not simply a struggle to maximize tax revenues at source or at residence. On the contrary, as we have seen, countries which stress the source principle may wish to exercise the prior jurisdiction it gives them by granting tax sparing concessions. Equally, some countries which stress the predominant right of residence taxation may exercise that right by exempting foreign-source income. However, the fact that the bilateral tax treaty model focuses on the definition and assignment of rights to tax and not directly on the principles for division of revenue, does not mean that mutual revenue considerations are absent. Rather, since the process of negotiation of bilateral tax treaties focuses on the reciprocal bargaining of taxation rights, the negotiators must balance the interest in revenue with that in influencing investment flows. Paradoxically, although the treaty negotiation may appear to focus on the revenue benefits to each party, agreement is more likely to be reached by mutual concessions intended to facilitate investment flows.

In the model treaty, there is a delicate balance in the allocation of taxation rights. The original League studies, as we have seen, stressed that the country of residence of the international investor had the strongest links and best claims to the investor's taxable capacity, and taxation at source would increase the cost of borrowing and impede international capital movements. However, it was impossible to deny the right of a state to tax activities actually taking place within it. Hence, in the OECD model treaty virtually all the exclusive rights to tax are given to the state of residence (OECD 1977, p. 146 para. 6). The source state is given an unlimited right to tax only a few types of income: in particular, income from immovable property. However, the treaty allows that certain types of revenue flows may be taxed by other than the residence state, principally the state of source. In most cases, the permissive right to tax at source is subject to limitations. Thus, the right to tax business profits is given exclusively to the state of residence, except for the source state's permissive right to tax the profits attributable to a Permanent Establishment situated in that state (Article 8.1). The imposition of withholding taxes on dividends, interest, and fees and royalties at source is of course subject to limits, which must be agreed. However, the principle of source taxation was conceded, and where a permissible tax is levied at source, the state of residence must accept the obligation to relieve the double taxation which might result, either by exempting that income from tax, or by allowing a credit for the source country tax.

This allocation of tax jurisdiction is primarily aimed at relieving juridical double taxation. The extent to which international double taxation in the broader sense, referred to as 'economic', is relieved depends on the view taken in each contracting state on what constitutes economic double taxation and how to relieve it (see Chapter 1, section 3.b above). The treaty principles work best if states accept the 'classical' view that the tax on company profits is separate from that on shareholder income and creates no double taxation. Essentially, the treaty allocates the corporate tax on business profits (if earned through a Permanent Establishment) to the state of source, while the income tax is allocated to the state of residence of the shareholder (subject to credit for a permitted withholding tax). However, this distinction is upset if states move towards the integration of corporate and individual income taxation (OECD 1977, pp. 97–103). A fully-integrated system, such as applied in the UK until 1965,[1] poses less problem since it operates merely to reduce the tax on the corporation by the amount of the credit in respect of the tax payable by the shareholders. The difficulty came when states began to move towards partially-integrated systems based on imputation, or a credit to the shareholder in respect of the tax paid by the company.

---

[1] With the exception of profits tax.

The issue came to the fore in 1965, when France introduced its '*précompte*' at the same time that its treaty with the US was being renegotiated. Under an imputation system, the basic corporation tax is likely to be higher, to attain the same level of revenue once imputation credit has been given to the shareholders. This in turn means that if the bargaining in the bilateral treaty focuses on balanced reciprocal reduction of withholding taxes, the imputation country will gain, since it has levied a higher corporation tax, unless it concedes an imputation tax credit to non-resident shareholders. Some suspected the change in the French tax to be aimed at improving its bargaining position with the US (see Kingson 1981, p. 1194); nevertheless, the US–French treaty signed in 1967 did concede an imputation tax credit to US portfolio investors in French companies. Similarly, following the change in the UK to the Advanced Corporation Tax system after 1973, the UK granted an imputation credit under its new treaty with the US, both to portfolio investors and also partially to direct investors.[1] However, other countries which introduced such partial integration (Germany, Canada) have not given imputation credits to investors from countries operating the classical system, i.e. the US (Kingson 1981, pp. 1194–1261; Easson 1989, pp. 503–10; Ault 1978). Thus, ironically, the movement to mitigate economic double taxation at national level by integrating the corporate and personal income taxes has exacerbated the problem of international double taxation.

From the point of view of the country of residence of the shareholder in a country operating the classical system such as the US, it may be argued that the failure to give an imputation credit to investors from abroad is discriminatory (Kingson 1981, p. 1199); on the other hand, the source country is not obliged to relieve the shareholder in respect of an income tax which is levied by the country of residence. The fact that some countries have nevertheless been willing to grant such a credit is due to their interest in attracting foreign investment. Yet a good economic argument can be made that to provide reciprocal imputation tax credits would merely promote cross-flows of investment at substantial revenue costs to both countries (Musgrave 1978, discussed in Kingson 1981, pp. 1222–6).

From this brief account it can be seen that the bilateral tax treaty is a rather crude method for achieving harmony between tax systems. The increasing sophistication of forms of financing of capital investment poses continually new issues for tax authorities in attempting to ensure national and international tax equity. In the 1980s these issues have included, notably, the tax treatment of foreign exchange gains and losses (OECD 1988), the capitalization and deductibility of brand-names and goodwill, the treatment of various types of loan capital particularly in debt-financed acquisitions and buy-outs,

---

[1] Most UK treaties provide for a tax credit on dividends from UK companies less a 15 per cent withholding tax to foreign portfolio investors, and a 50 per cent credit less a 5 per cent withholding tax on dividends paid to a foreign company with 10 per cent or more of the voting power of the paying company: see Simon 1983, F. 215 for full details.

and the tax treatment of provision by commercial banks against risky sovereign debt. The international liberalization of capital movements makes it more urgent to ensure harmonization of such decisions about the tax treatment of investment. Yet it is virtually impossible for this to take place through the periodic renegotiation of a network of several hundred bilateral tax treaties. In the absence of adequate international harmonization, national authorities are too often faced by the dilemma that domestic measures to ensure fair taxation of income from capital create the risk of capital outflow, unless their measures are emulated by competing states.[1] This indicates a need for a much more developed process of international harmonization of business taxation than is possible through the system of bilateral tax treaties.

[1] For a discussion of the various ways in which taxation may affect capital flows see IMF 1990, ch. VI.

3
The International Tax System at the Crossroads

It is now over a century since it first became clear that the taxation of business income by national states must take place within an international framework. It also became apparent fairly early that unilateral national provisions, such as the exemption of foreign income or the foreign tax credit, could not by themselves adequately accommodate national taxation to the international revenue flows generated by trade and investment. Although early hopes of a comprehensive multilateral arrangement among states to co-ordinate income taxation were soon dashed, a serviceable technical solution was found, in the form of the model tax treaty which could be negotiated with suitable modifications on a bilateral basis between states. Although little progress was made on this in the 1930s, the network of bilateral double tax treaties grew rapidly after 1945, and greatly facilitated the rapid internationalization of trade and investment in the postwar period.

Nevertheless, the system has fallen far short of being the global or comprehensive one which many have repeatedly hoped could be created. The greatest pressures for global harmonization have come from international businessmen, traders and investors, pleading for equality in the conditions of competition and the elimination of international double taxation. Tax administrators have been sceptical of the possibility of anything more than rough justice in taxation, and have naturally been more concerned with effectiveness and the prevention of international tax avoidance. Conceding, however, that inequity and multiple taxation stimulate avoidance, they joined in the elaboration of the treaty system. The starting point for the negotiation of international tax arrangements was therefore equality of treatment for businesses based in different countries but engaged in international trade and/or production. However, national negotiators, especially representatives from finance ministries, were more concerned with the effect on international investment flows and the equitable allocation of tax revenues between states.

1. The Interaction of National and International Equity

A global approach would have required these issues to be tackled head on, as was shown by the analysis in the Carroll report of the fractional apportionment method (see Chapter 1 above). Fractional apportionment would need international agreement both on the general basis for the establishment of the integrated accounts of a global business, as well as on the formula for the fractional apportionment of the overall profit. This would require the global enterprise to accept an obligation to report on its worldwide business to every national tax administration. For their part, national authorities would have to accept an allocation of tax revenue to them that was not only determined by the agreed formula, but also depended on the profitability of the enterprise as a whole. A country would be obliged under this method to accept that no tax would be due to it from an enterprise making a loss globally, even if it considered that the local branch was operating profitably (see Chapter 1, section 5 above).

Clearly, therefore, legitimation for the global approach would have to be established at the international level. However, the legitimacy of direct taxes on income rested on the principle of equality of treatment of taxpayers, which was rooted in the national state. Furthermore, and perhaps more seriously, such a process of international legitimation would have to be based on a new approach to equity. The Carroll report showed that the experience of the fractional apportionment method, in particular in Spain, was that neither the determination of the global accounts nor the fractional apportionment could be carried out on the basis of general principles or a single formula. The particular characteristics of different industries, as well as of different firms, would require a case-by-case evaluation, which was carried out in the Spanish system by a jury. This in turn would have undermined the principle of equality of taxpayers embedded in national tax systems.

The majority opinion of those experts participating in the Carroll study therefore favoured separate accounting, despite the major difficulties it entailed, because the immediate establishment of a global approach and fractional apportionment posed too many problems. The German report summed the matter up by arguing that although a global approach was an unattainable ideal, a nationally-based system should work towards it:

> It may be said that the method of fractional apportionment (*Verteilung*) is preferable, both from the viewpoint of fairness, which is identical with just taxation, and from the viewpoint of diminishing as much as possible double taxation. This method will always be of importance in practice because, in numerous cases, the separate assessment of income will not be possible. Unquestionably the ideal, and therefore perhaps the unattainable, goal would be to determine the total profits of the entire enterprise on the basis of uniform law and to divide the total profits on agreed principles. . . . In international intercourse, a uniform determination of total profits is not possible, in view of the fact that there is no harmony between the tax

legislation of the various countries. It would be possible for each interested State, however, even in carrying out its own internal law, to determine the total profits in accordance with rules of assessment applicable in its case. The adoption of some system of reciprocal fiscal assistance might considerably lessen the difficulty of determining the total profits. . . . An agreement regarding the principles of allocation would remain essential. Certain principles of allocation might be evolved in practical experience . . . but they would probably have to be different for the various categories of enterprises and . . . experience might lead to the establishment of certain well-defined allocation percentages (*Teilungsquoten*). [League of Nations 1933–III, p. 122.]

However, the separate accounting method which was embodied in the international treaty system attempted to reinforce the principle of taxpayer equality by establishing the international principle of non-discrimination between national and foreign-owned firms. This notion of taxpayer equality requires the disaggregation of the global unity of the international business, and the separate treatment of its separately incorporated subsidiaries or permanent establishments located in each country. However, this approach does not resolve but postpones the problem of inter-state allocation. Each state must have the power to scrutinize and if necessary rectify the arm's length accounts. If such rectification is actively pursued by national tax authorities, it will result in renewed problems of double taxation, unless the basis of such rectification is internationally agreed. This results in case-by-case negotiations involving national tax authorities and firms, as well as attempts to evolve general principles based on experience. As the discussion in subsequent chapters of this book will show, this has been the pattern of emergence of an increasingly internationalized system of tax administration in the past two decades, which resembles that prognosticated by the German report of 1933 quoted above.

It could be that international businessmen would also favour the ideal of a global unitary approach, in order to establish a uniform and manifestly fair application and allocation of taxation: this was certainly the view expressed by Sir William Vestey as early as 1919, in the comments quoted above (Chapter 1, section 3.a). In practice, however, they have generally opposed such an approach, on the grounds that the unlikelihood of broad international agreement on basic principles would exacerbate rather than resolve the problem of multiple taxation. This viewpoint was again forcibly expressed in the campaign led by major European TNCs in the 1980s against Worldwide Unitary Taxation by state tax authorities in the USA, which will be discussed in Chapter 9 below. Instead, global business has preferred to find an accommodation with the system based on separate accounting, which with its multiplicity of perspectives and arrangements continually generates overlap and conflict.

What can clearly be seen, however, is that this accommodation rests on the emergence of international tax planning, which enables internationally-organized business to minimize its exposure to tax by taking advantage of the interaction of national tax systems, as well as differences between bilateral tax agreements. In particular, as will be discussed in the next two chapters, the TNC has been able to use the network of double tax treaties, as well as the creation of captive state entities as tax havens, in order largely to avoid taxation of retained earnings. This is an example of the more general paradox, that the development of nationalism and national regulation does not retard but in some respects stimulates the growth of internationally-organized business, especially TNCs. Globally-organized firms are able to take advantage of differences in national regulation and loopholes in international regulatory co-ordination, and therefore have preferred to oppose and even hinder the development of adequate globally-oriented international systems of business regulation or control.

However, it has become increasingly clear in recent years that a new approach is needed to tackle the problem of international business taxation. International tax planning, especially by the exploitation of the tax treaty system and of tax havens, has greatly undermined both the effectiveness as well as the legitimacy of the international tax arrangements. As we have seen, these arrangements essentially rest on a compromise which limits taxation at source to the business profits of a Permanent Establishment or subsidiary, while giving the country of ultimate residence jurisdiction to tax repatriated investment income. The use of the offshore haven not only allows retained earnings to be accumulated without being taxed, it also permits reduction of taxable business profits by charges for services or overhead costs (management costs, research and development, insurance, finance) which can be made payable to a conveniently located subsidiary. Such arrangements have become increasingly common not only for TNCs but even for nationally-based businesses, which can reduce their taxable profits by using, for example, 'captive' offshore insurance companies. This has led to increased efforts by the main capitalist countries to claw back into taxation profits accumulated in tax havens. National measures against tax haven subsidiaries, defined in various ways as Controlled Foreign Corporations (CFCs), have been combined with a drive to improve mutual assistance between tax authorities and develop a co-ordinated approach to the taxation of global business.

The generalization of national measures against CFCs has weakened the cogency of the argument made by international business at home, that such provisions undermine their position in foreign markets *vis-à-vis* competitors.[1] However, TNCs have been on stronger ground in attacking the validity of the assertion of jurisdiction by their home country over their foreign profits. This has led to complex provisions in the measures against CFCs to avoid taxation of profits that could validly be said to have been earned abroad, and these complexities inevitably create further loopholes (to be discussed in more detail

[1] See, for example, Board of Inland Revenue 1982, para. 14; Deutscher Bundestag 1986.

in Chapter 7 below). The underlying difficulty is still that of finding an effective and legitimate way to divide nationally a profit that has been created by global activities. Although increased international administrative co-ordination can try to deal with the symptoms of this problem, it is unable to resolve the fundamental cause (see Chapter 10).

2. The International Crisis of Tax Legitimacy

The increasing crisis of international business taxation has interacted with a growing crisis of tax legitimacy in the developed capitalist countries since the mid-1970s. Both could be said to be rooted in the recurring difficulty of establishing fairness and efficiency in the taxation of income derived from different revenue flows.[1]

At the same time, underdeveloped countries have also suffered from chronic fiscal problems, due in no small part to the facilities provided by the international financial system for both foreign investors and part of the local bourgeoisie to ensure their minimal exposure to taxation. The facilities for sheltering wealth developed by the offshore tax havens and financial centres are an important factor in the capital flight which is a major contributor to the debt crisis of the underdeveloped countries (Lessard & Williamson 1987). Individual income taxes account for a significantly lower proportion both of GDP and of tax revenue in underdeveloped compared to developed countries; and although revenue from corporate taxation by contrast is often propor-tionately much higher, this is mainly the case in countries where a few prominent companies are engaged in important oil or mineral exports (Tanzi, in Newbery & Stern 1987, pp. 224–6).

Finally, the increased market-orientation of previously centrally-planned economies has led them to introduce or lay greater stress on income taxation. Here again crucial questions of equity and efficiency are raised, in particular, the relative burden to be placed on individual incomes and corporate profits: a sharp increase in personal taxation would be extremely unpopular, as well as restraining consumer demand, while it is feared that nascent entrepreneurship could be fettered by excessive taxation of business income (Newcity 1990).

2.a The Movement for Tax Reform

By the 1970s, in the industrialized countries, the postwar Keynesian compromise began to break down as inflation and other factors made the burden of taxation fall increasingly on personal income taxation of low and middle-income wage-earners. At the same time, business, especially manufac-turing and mining industry, made increasingly skilful use of investment

[1] For a discussion of fairness, efficiency and legitimacy, see Chapter 4 below.

incentives and privileges obtained through lobbying, as well as tax planning devices, to minimize its tax payments. In the US in particular, corporate taxes declined as a proportion of federal government receipts from 26.5 per cent in 1950 to only 6.2 per cent in 1983, while individual income taxes increased from 39.9 per cent to 48.1.[1]

In most developed countries, the share of revenue from corporate taxation remained relatively stable in the two decades 1965–85, while the burden of increased state spending fell increasingly on personal income taxation and social security contributions (OECD 1987b, p. 64). This laid the basis for populist campaigns to reduce personal taxation. At the same time, there was concern that corporate tax avoidance, based largely on the use of tax allowances which have a different effect on different companies and industries, was producing inefficiencies in the allocation of investments.

These factors undermined the broad acceptance of the fairness of income taxes, which during the twentieth century had become the mainstay of government revenues in developed countries, especially since the Second World War when their collection had been facilitated by deduction of personal income tax at source. It seemed increasingly difficult to reconcile vertical equity (progressive rates on higher incomes) with horizontal equity (equal treatment of incomes from different sources). Although there were some calls for corporate taxation to be abolished altogether (e.g. Auerbach 1983), there were also attacks on the 'corporate freeloaders', directed at the elimination of corporate tax shelters, especially depreciation allowances (Citizens for Tax Justice 1985). This view was not confined to anti-business circles: President Reagan's Treasury Secretary, Donald Regan, recounts how he shocked the President into initiating tax reform in 1983 by revealing that General Electric and 57 other big corporations paid less taxes than his own secretary (Regan 1988, p. 194).

Major attempts to restore the legitimacy of income taxes were therefore made in a number of capitalist countries, especially the US and the UK. In several of the main capitalist countries, reductions in the top rates of personal and corporate taxes have been combined with the elimination of privileges and exemptions and attempts at more effective enforcement. It is certainly very attractive in principle to combine a broadening and simplification of the tax base, by ending tax privileges and shelters, with a reduction in top rates of tax, while at the same time making a determined attack on avoidance. However, there is little evidence yet to support the views of some right-wing economists that lower tax rates in themselves would produce increased revenues by encouraging entrepreneurship. Rather, the broadening of the tax base has been used to combine reductions of top rates with populist reductions in basic rates of personal tax. Certainly, the British reforms of corporation tax in 1984, involving the abolition of stock relief and reduction in capital allowances, as

---

[1] US Congress 1984; note however that state corporate income taxes have grown at a faster rate than other state taxes: Musgrave, in McLure 1984, p. 229, and Chapter 9 below.

well as measures to tax the retained earnings of Controlled Foreign Corporations in tax havens, contributed to the inflows of revenue which financed the cuts in top rates, and significant cuts in the basic rates of both personal and company tax (Devereux 1987). Not only did the reductions in top rates lead to political criticisms of handouts to the rich, they also focused attention on the regressive nature of other important taxes, such as national insurance contributions, and the ill-fated Poll Tax. At the same time, many argued that the attack on tax shelters was not being vigorously pursued.

Although the US Tax Reform Act of 1986 was a comprehensive package, it was criticized as replacing one set of distortions by another. Although the attractions of a radical reform enabled a sharp break away from the trend of annual tax bills handing out benefits to favoured constituencies, the pressures of the political process inevitably meant that reform was bought at the price of a myriad of exclusions and concessions (Birnbaum & Murray 1987). The Act certainly produced a thicker tax code and a vast increase of workload for tax consultants.

Such reforms have aimed to maintain or restore the contributions of direct taxes to national revenues. At the same time, the increasing pressures on direct taxes on incomes have led both to their supplementation by a wider range of taxes (especially turnover taxes) and to a reconsideration of the role and basis of income tax. Many economists have advocated a shift to expenditure or consumption rather than income as the tax base. By measuring spending rather than disposable income, it would encourage savings and investment (Kaldor 1980), but although an expenditure tax has been tried in India and Sri Lanka it was repealed in both countries; such a change would create significant problems of international co-ordination if carried out unilaterally (Meade 1978).

Some economists have also advocated a radical switch to a consumption basis for the corporate income tax, by exempting interest and dividend income and allowing full deduction of all business purchases but not allowing deduction of interest payments as an expense; this might reduce inequity, by bringing the effective tax rate on domestic capital to the rate *de facto* applied to international investment, but even its advocates accept that a unilateral move in this direction would be impossible (Bird 1988, p. 296).

Some governments have attempted to reduce the burden of personal income taxation by increasing indirect taxes, such as turnover taxes or value-added taxes. In some countries, notably France, indirect taxes and social security contributions have historically made a proportionately much greater contribution to national revenues than direct taxes on income. However, while such taxes are efficient to collect and can take some of the pressure off income tax, they are regressive and can be politically difficult to implement or increase beyond a certain point. Popular resistance created continuing political crises over the attempts to introduce VAT in Japan; the US still has no national sales tax; and there is strong resistance in Britain to further increases in the scope of VAT in line with European norms. Canada followed New Zealand in introducing a broad-based value-added tax on sales from 1991, but although it was praised by tax experts it aroused considerable political opposition. For developing countries, the World Bank has advocated the increased use of user charges to bolster state revenue and investment in infrastructure services (IBRD 1988, p. 81), but argues that tax reform must consider the interaction of a range of commodity and income taxes (ibid., p. 86). In general, although consumption-based taxes have been making an important contribution to state revenues, their regressive nature makes it unlikely that they could replace taxes on income.

Although these attempts to restore the legitimacy and effectiveness of taxation have been carried out by national governments responding essentially to domestic fiscal and political pressures, they have taken place as part of a worldwide debate. Changes in taxation, especially major changes by the dominant states in the system, inevitably exert a pull on other states, because of the high mobility of capital (Razin & Slemrod 1990). They also have significant implications for the international co-ordination of taxation. Above all, a determined attack on avoidance, if it is to take place, must be internationally co-ordinated, since the opportunities for international avoidance form such a serious obstacle to effective national tax enforcement.

Certainly, the attempts to re-legitimize income taxation in Britain and the USA included new measures aimed at ensuring taxation of a 'fair' share of the income of global businesses. Although the US Tax Reform Act did not change the basic approach to international taxation, it included many provisions drawing back income into the US tax net. These included:

(i) the 'super-royalty' concept, allowing revaluation of intangibles transferred internationally to reflect the income earned by the transferee (see Chapter 8 below);
(ii) the 'separate basket' modification to the foreign tax credit (see Chapter 1 above) which, although it did not replace the overall tax credit with a per-country limitation as had been threatened at one point, required increased itemization;
(iii) a new tax on the profits of US branches of foreign corporations (see Chapter 5, section 2.b below);
(iv) ending the deductibility of interest on acquisition expenses of dual-resident corporations against the income of related US corporations.

These measures entailed unilateral reallocations by the US of global income into the US tax net. This unilateralism involved the overriding of existing treaty obligations, which led to protests by the USA's treaty partners (see Chapter 11 below). The continued attack by the IRS on tax havens also led to complaints against US unilateralism. Thus, in the absence of adequate international criteria for the allocation of income between states, national attempts to re-establish fairness in income taxation have increased international conflicts.

The international co-ordination of indirect taxes should be simpler, in technical terms at least. The system introduced in France in the mid-1950s of a Value-Added Tax on turnover based on the destination principle provided the basis for the adoption of the VAT as the fiscal base of the EEC (Easson 1980). Although the abolition of EC frontier controls and the completion of the internal market was thought to require a switch from the destination to the origin principle, criticisms of the theoretical solution of moving to an origin basis led to arguments for the more practical solution of moving tax borders to account books (Cnossen 1983). Administrators have also preferred the view that a common internal market does not require harmonization of consumption taxes but only abolition of border controls, so that the problem is rendered technical instead of political.[1] Certainly, the difficulties of obtaining political approval for the greater degree of harmonization needed to move to the origin principle obliged the Commission to retreat from the blueprint proposed in 1987, and it is being treated, at least in a transitional period up to the end of 1996, as a problem of collection, to be solved by a clearing-house mechanism. However, the result is 'a patchwork of provisions' (Terra & Kajus 1990, p. 318) which appear to rely greatly on improved administrative co-operation, and still leave important issues unresolved, notably the criteria for treatment as a single taxable person of undertakings within a linked group (ibid., p. 319). There are significant parallels with direct taxation, where the difficulties of harmonization have also led to greater reliance on co-ordination and administrative co-operation. Harmonization, rather than co-ordination, would require a closer alignment of VAT rates which, although a relatively easy matter technically, has run into greater political opposition, since taxes on spending become deeply rooted in socio-political patterns which are locally and nationally based.

2.b European Community Harmonization

The major impetus for a more fundamental attempt at tax harmonization results from the programme for completion of the EC Internal Market by 1992. This has enabled the revival of initiatives by the Commission that had been allowed to become virtually dormant, including those for the co-ordination and harmonization of direct taxes on business. The Commission had been quite active in the 1960s in making proposals for harmonization of taxes on business and income from capital, but the initiatives flagged in the 1970s (Easson 1980); and although a directive was approved in 1977 for mutual assistance in tax matters even this received only lukewarm support in practice from national tax administrators (see Chapter 10 below). However, fresh work was begun after 1979, when the Parliament deferred a decision on the 1975 Commission proposal for a system of company taxation based on partial imputation and banded tax rates (European Commission 1975), and

[1] Peter Jefferson Smith of the UK Customs and Excise, in Gammie & Robinson 1989, p. 33.

invited the Commission to work on harmonization of the business tax base. This renewed activity led to a proposed directive on the carry-over of the losses of undertakings (COM 84(404); see Andel, in Cnossen 1987).

The Commission became more ambitious once the target of 1992 was set by the adoption of the White Paper on the Completion of the Internal Market, and the Single European Act accelerated the political processes, although tax matters still require unanimity in the Council of Ministers.[1] Compared to the harmonization of VAT, which was already causing considerable conflict, business tax harmonization would be even more far-reaching; but a strong economic case could be made out for a considerable degree of co-ordination, if not full harmonization, of corporate taxation (Devereux & Pearson 1989; Gammie & Robinson 1989). The Commission produced proposals for the alignment of the rates of corporation or business taxes, as well as draft principles for harmonization of the business tax base circulated and quite widely publicized in 1988. Harmonization of the definition of taxable profits would entail acceptance that member states could no longer provide for investment incentives via the tax base – although grants and credits could be given by other means, to the extent permitted under the procedure for approval of state aids (Articles 92–3 of the Rome Treaty).

Other important aspects of the proposal included allowing a five-year period for the writing-off of goodwill, which would have a significant effect on company acquisitions especially in the service sector. An important role in the implementation and development of the process of harmonization of the tax base of business was envisaged for an Advisory Committee made up of national representatives and Commission officials. There was some scepticism that rapid progress could be made on such ambitious proposals, even with the political impetus given by the 1992 target. To maintain the momentum, Mme Scrivener, the Commissioner responsible for taxation, in December 1990 appointed a working group under Dutch former Finance Minister Onno Ruding, to report on the degree to which corporate taxation distorts the internal market, and whether Community action should focus on harmoniza-tion of the tax base or of tax rates. Both politicians and academic economists differ in their evaluations of the degree of direct-tax harmonization necessary to liberalize the movement of capital. This is important not only in relation to

---

[1] The primary aim of the Treaty of Rome was to establish the Common Market and the free movement of goods, so in addition to the removal of tariffs it included specific provisions for taxes on products (Articles 95–9 Rome Treaty); however, the removal of exchange controls and other direct restrictions on the free movement of capital was not reinforced by any specific Community competence in relation to direct taxation. Instead, Article 220 of the Rome Treaty urges that the abolition of double taxation within the Community be taken up 'so far as is necessary', by negotiation between the member states, which restricts the role of EC institutions in this field. It was for this reason that the arbitration of double taxation claims resulting from transfer price adjustments was dealt with by a Convention between the Member States and not a Directive, as originally proposed by the Commission, thus removing its enforcement from the purview of Community institutions (see below, and Chapter 10, section 3.a.iii).

direct corporate taxation, but also corporate–personal tax integration, i.e. the tax treatment of dividends.[1]

In the meantime, significant progress was being made on establishing a European tax regime for groups of related companies. In mid-1990 agreement was reached on three long-standing proposals, which entailed benefits for cross-European groups of companies, and might pave the way for similar provisions applying beyond Europe. Agreement in the form of a treaty established an arbitration procedure for double taxation claims resulting from adjustments of transfer prices (EC 1990c; see Chapter 10 below); a Directive for a common system of taxation for mergers or acquisitions between different member states prohibited member states from taxing gains or preventing carry-over of losses (EC Council 1990a). A further Directive on dividend payments from subsidiaries to parent companies within the Community required member states to exempt from withholding tax dividend payments made directly by a subsidiary to a parent company, if both companies are resident in a member state and the parent owns at least 25 per cent of the capital of the subsidiary, while requiring the state of the parent to exempt such distributed profits from tax or allow a credit for the related corporation tax paid at source (EC Council 1990b).

Following this success, two further proposals for Directives were issued at the end of 1990: first, to extend the exemption from withholding tax also to interest and royalties paid directly by a subsidiary to a parent, defined in the same way as in relation to dividend withholding taxes (EC Commission 1991a). A second, more far-reaching proposal, would permit the offsetting of profits and losses between members of a corporate group within the Community, in this case where 75 per cent of the capital and a majority of the voting rights is owned by the parent (EC Commission 1991b). Mme Scrivener also referred to the Ruding group the more radical possibility of consolidation of tax accounts of groups of companies within the Community.

Perhaps significantly, the progress made towards liberalization has not been matched by agreement on measures to prevent avoidance and evasion. This was illustrated by the controversy over a relatively limited proposal, linked to the liberalization of capital movements within the Community, which was put forward in 1989 (European Commission 1989), for a minimum 15 per cent withholding tax on income from bank deposits, shares and bonds held by Community residents in other EC states. Motivated by pressure, especially from the French government, to prevent tax evasion which might ensue from the lifting of exchange controls, it was nevertheless opposed by the financial centres, Luxembourg and the UK. The Commission saw this as a minimalist proposal to extend taxation of bank and bond interest at source to all European Community residents, which would entail little administrative burden, since there was already some provision for source taxation of interest

[1] Compare, for example, the respective contributions of Musgrave and Bird in Cnossen 1987. See also Devereux & Pearson 1989.

in all member states except Luxembourg, Germany and Greece. Germany had attempted to come into line by introducing a withholding tax on all interest payments from January 1989, but this lasted only until July, and was cancelled by the new government coalition, following an outflow of capital estimated at DM60 billion, mainly to Luxembourg. In principle, this failure should strengthen the case for a harmonized EC withholding tax which Luxembourg would also be obliged to apply. However, since the Commission's proposal did not apply to Eurobonds, it raised the threat of capital flight to non-EC financial centres, while the idea that the withholding tax could be extended worldwide was described as 'little more than a pious hope' (UK House of Lords 1989, p. 10). Since deduction at source is applied by most countries to employment income and dividends, and often also to interest payments to residents, it would seem both logical and equitable to extend it to interest payments to non-residents.[1] However, the existence of international capital markets, and especially of offshore financial centres and tax havens, makes it difficult to apply source taxation of interest payments to non-residents without a comprehensive international arrangement for enforcement (see Frank in Council of Europe 1981, 100–1). Indeed, Britain and the US introduced exemption from withholding tax for payments to non-residents of quoted Eurobonds in 1984 in order to compete with the offshore financial centres (see Chapter 7, section 3(ii) below). Hence it was not surprising that the EC's withholding tax proposal was shelved, although a related proposal to improve information exchange did obtain support.[2]

In taxation, as in other areas, the impetus and processes for seeking harmonization within the European Community are a significant force in the world system, since European harmonization can act as a catalyst for broader global agreement. Conversely, some matters (such as the imposition of a tax at source on interest payments to non-residents (discussed above), cannot be dealt with purely within the European framework. Europe also provides a barometer for the storms that harmonization proposals are likely to provoke. Issues which cannot be resolved within the framework of relatively common culture and interests, as well as the supranational structures, of the EC are unlikely to make much progress on the world stage. In this perspective, it is significant that fundamental issues of business tax harmonization have finally come on to the European agenda; but equally notable that so far the targets are minimalist, and may remain so. The British government in particular has

---

[1] This point was made by the EC's Economic and Social Committee in its comments on the withholding tax proposal: EC Economic and Social Committee 1989.
[2] This provided that, where the tax authorities of a member state show that a 'significant' transfer of funds has taken place without an appropriate tax declaration, the requested state would be required to obtain and provide information about the funds, even if its own administrative procedures do not allow such information to be obtained for its own tax enforcement purposes: COM(89)60 Final; Official Journal 1989/C141 p. 7. Despite the public support it obtained, this proposal had still not been approved by the end of 1990. Chapter 10 below deals in more detail with administrative assistance in tax enforcement.

taken the view that market forces are more effective in producing regulatory convergence than co-ordinated state action;[1] but market forces tend to result in competition to reduce regulation or offer exemptions, which would reduce tax revenues and not necessarily end distortions. A survey of British companies showed a near-unanimous view in favour of the creation of a uniform tax base and a band of tax rates in the EC (Devereux & Pearson 1989, p. 72). The move towards abolition of withholding taxes on intra-group payments should pave the way towards taxation of corporate groups on their EC operations based on consolidated accounts; but the EC member states would still be faced with choosing between negotiating concessions of sovereignty and tax rights between residence and source jurisdictions, or taking the leap to either European unitary taxation based on formula apportionment or a single European corporation tax.[2]

The measures for completion of the internal market, especially the liberalization of capital movements, will also have significant implications for the tax treaties of EC members with other countries. For example, limitation of benefits provisions in recent US treaties, such as the US–German treaty signed in 1989, in certain circumstances deny treaty benefits to third-country shareholders, such as partners in a German joint-venture company (see Chapter 7, section 3.a below). The logical trend should be towards the increasing alignment of the terms of EC member states' tax treaties with third countries, co-ordination of treaty negotiation and of their interpretation and application by the competent authorities, and eventually the joint negotiation of tax treaties by the EC states. Since taxation is one of the most jealously guarded of sovereign powers, this evolution may be a slow one.

Conclusion

To summarize, it seems that taxation of corporate or business profits will remain a significant element of state finance in most developed capitalist countries, in developing countries and, increasingly, in the former state socialist countries. The search for an adequate, globally-oriented system to co-ordinate business taxation is therefore unavoidable. Yet the debate on fundamental issues has just begun, and the political processes for publicizing the debate and considering solutions are virtually non-existent.

[1] This view was expressed in relation to taxation by J. Isaac, Deputy Chairman of the Board of Inland Revenue: Gammie & Robinson 1989, p. 28.
[2] Devereux & Pearson (1989) canvass the options (ch. 4); although they see the strong advantages of the single European company tax, they exclude it as involving too much surrender of sovereignty; the advantage of the unitary approach would be outweighed by administrative costs so long as tax systems differed, but there would be pressure to harmonize them due to the absence of capital-export neutrality. McLure (1989) argues that increased economic integration will make it harder to attribute geographical source to income and force states to grasp the nettle of a unitary approach.

4
International Tax Avoidance

The first three chapters of this book focused on the way that the international tax system developed as a result of multiple, related policy initiatives by different national states, as well as international negotiation and compromise between states. It is crucial to recognize, however, that an important part was also played by initiatives taken by taxpayers themselves, in particular the major international corporations and their advisors.

Indeed, as has already been pointed out (Chapter 3, section 1 above), the emergence of international tax planning attempted to resolve some of the problems caused by the failure to agree international principles of tax equity or effective arrangements for the allocation of tax jurisdiction. International tax planning emerged within a process of bargaining and negotiation between specialist consultants and the tax officials of the main capitalist countries, and this process has essentially reinforced the international tax arrangements, based largely on national equity and bilateral treaties, to which both private consultants and government officials have become increasingly committed. However, the increasingly widespread availability of access to the mechanisms of international tax avoidance, as well as the increasing complexity of the arrangements for allocating international income and expense in the absence of internationally-agreed principles and criteria, have put the international tax system under increasing strain. This will be discussed in detail in the following chapters. A necessary first step, taken in this chapter, is the analysis of the dynamics of taxation as a process of economic regulation, focusing on the problem of avoidance.

1. The Legal Regulation of Economic Relations

Taxation, like any type of economic regulation, must be seen not merely as a series of more or less functional decisions by the state and its officials, but as a dynamic and in many ways contradictory *process*. Business taxation, in particular, is a process primarily of negotiation between tax officials and corporate managers and advisors. The officials, usually structured in a hierarchic bureaucracy, have the important advantage of access to state power: they can order an audit, issue an assessment to tax, publish regulations and statements of practice, or resort to the courts or legislature to clarify or amend the law. Recourse either to legal adjudication or legislative intervention depends not only on technical legal issues such as the interpretation of statute or the logic of case-law, but a variety of other factors. These, which may be referred to as the cultural elements in a legal/administrative process, include the social backgrounds and relationships of the actors, general social attitudes including moral and political considerations, as well as more immediate questions such as the resources of time, people and skills which the parties might reasonably make available.

The greater resources which they can apply give businesses, especially the largest corporations, a considerable advantage over state administrators: not only can they devote more people and time to tax planning, they can also pay salaries which in most countries ensure that the best tax inspectors often become corporate tax consultants. Most important, tax planning gives the business taxpayer a power of initiative which means that the tax gatherer is responding after the event. On the other hand, tax officials generally have very broad powers to disallow claims which can reverse these advantages by putting the taxpayer very much on the defensive. Not all taxpayers are able or willing to divert substantial resources from their actual business to tax planning; and a system that allows too free a rein to such planning undermines equity as well as wasting resources.

Studies of the process of legal regulation tend to separate consideration of the social factors or 'context' from any analysis of the legal concepts or rules themselves. Thus, 'socio-legal studies' focus on the extra-legal factors, the relations of economic or social power that influence the way in which the legal process 'really' works (law-in-action as against the law-in-the-books); while the economic analysis of law applies techniques of neo-classical economics to evaluate the efficiency of legal rules. For these approaches, the legal rules themselves are a given, and the nature of legal reasoning is an external and normally unproblematic question.

On the other hand, jurists who focus on the legal rules tend to adopt a functionalist view of legal reasoning, which may be rationalist or anti-rationalist. Rationalism is the stance of legal positivism. In traditional positivism, legal reasoning is accepted as a process of inductive-deductive logic, consisting of applying rules to 'facts', thus combining legal with sociological positivism; the same fact–value dichotomy holds where, especially in common-law systems, rules are not only formulated by statute or code but also emerge inductively, by comparing and distinguishing decisions in previous similar fact-situations. In more modern versions of legal positivism, legal reasoning and the development of legal principles are celebrated as a self-reproducing system, whose character and links with the social system result from historical constitutive moments; this allows for a more elaborate historical explanation of the social origins of law, but the sphere of the social and the sphere of law are still seen as essentially separate and autonomous.

Positivism is rationalist, in that it emphasizes the inner logic of the rules and concepts themselves: legal reasoning is a craft, consisting either of choosing, applying and adapting rules that best fit the 'facts' (in the blunt pragmatism especially of British legal positivism), or teasing out and fashioning principles that can make an elegant or functional system. Equally functionalist are the various perspectives that emphasize that the process of application, interpretation and development of rules is not driven by the inner logic of the rules themselves, but by 'external' social factors. These include many types of legal realism, policy-oriented functionalism, and structuralist Marxism. In reaction to rationalism, post-modern approaches seek to deconstruct the concepts wielded by lawyers, as essentially ideological constructs; but seeking to avoid functionalism they fall into an anti-rationalist view that stresses the radical indeterminacy of rules.

What is needed is a social theory of law itself, which can theorize the historical development of forms of regulation, including specific legal principles and their application, as a social process. This section deals briefly with the contradictions and dynamics of taxation as a mode of economic regulation in capitalist or market-economy societies, before going on to consider tax avoidance and, specifically, its international dimension.

1.a Liberal Forms and their Limits

The form of state regulation which most closely corresponds to a fully developed market-economy society is liberal regulation. Liberal forms of regulation require the maximum freedom for social actors to engage in economic transactions, within a framework of fixed and settled laws which enable them to choose and plan their transactions. Law enforcement is indirect, relying primarily on voluntary compliance, supplemented by inducements, or *post facto* sanctions on detected law-breaking. Pure liberalism requires a radical separation of legal form and economic substance. Laws must be addressed to the generality of legal subjects, without distinction as to their social or economic position.

The processes of legal regulation of economic relations are therefore essentially structured by markets and competition. The regulators, on behalf of the state, enforce the laws and seek to implement and develop policy, while the economic actors whose activities are regulated are free to choose and adapt their transactions. They may comply with or breach the law. More importantly, their actions may influence the patterns of development of legal relations as much as do the measures taken by regulators. The ways in which they modify the legal form or economic substance of their transactions might clearly frustrate the spirit of the law or the intentions of the legislators, and so lead to retaliation. Not uncommonly however, a whole new legal-economic landscape might be opened up, posing new problems for the regulator and the legislator. It was not envisaged, for example, by Senator Sherman, when steering the Anti-Trust legislation through Congress in 1890 to outlaw agreements restricting competition, that it might be a contributory factor in the great merger movement from 1897 (see Lamoreaux 1985). Nor did the drafters of the English companies legislation of 1844–62 envisage that the protection of limited liability would be used extensively by private companies or even sole traders: and it was after this had become a widespread practice, and against significant judicial opposition, that the House of Lords sanctioned the sole-trader company in the famous *Salomon* case (Ireland 1984). Thus, the legal forms devised by professionals for economic actors, using the facilitative structures of private law, make a significant contribution to the dynamics of a regulatory system (McBarnet 1984).

However, liberal forms have never and could never exist in a pure form. First, some element of public regulation is needed to create, establish and maintain the terms of trading on markets. Markets cannot exist without state regulation, since the state is essential to the creation and guaranteeing of the property rights that are traded. The creation of property rights is another way of saying that social relations are structured so that they are mediated by commodity exchange. Since it is the state, or public bodies generally, that govern those social relationships, state action crucially determines the terms of trading on markets. In that sense markets are never 'free'and state regulation, including taxation, cannot be purely 'neutral'.

Hence, state intervention is essential, both historically and continually, in order to help define and delimit legitimate property rights: from the enclosures of common land to the compulsory purchase of land for roads, the granting of oil prospecting or land development rights, or the outlawing of the use of confidential price-sensitive information when trading in securities. The sale of property rights or economic privileges was historically an important source of state revenues, and continues to be so today to varying extents, quite importantly for example in oil-producing states. Such state action can create wealth for specific individuals or groups, or deprive them of it, so it is frequently discriminatory. The easiest category to discriminate against is the foreigner, and the characteristic of the mercantile state, in which state revenue is raised mainly by charging for economic privileges, is the use of tariffs or duties especially on imports.

Secondly, liberal forms are continually undermined by the operation of markets and competition. They seek generally to maintain equality in the conditions of competition, and this is in the general interest of all economic actors. However, the pressures of competition continually drive those actors to seek advantage over their competitors. Indeed, competition is best thought of not as a state of equal conditions between economic rivals, but a process of equalization which creates differentiation due to the continual pressures on each actor to seek out and defend special advantages. In the economic arena, this drives firms to seek production, marketing or managerial advantages. In the political-legal arena, they seek regulatory advantages: finding and exploiting loopholes in the regulations, obtaining special treatment by the regulators, or modifying transactions to bypass the regulations. Since the process of competition itself leads to economic inequalities, it also creates political demands for state intervention to redress inequality, as well as undermining the general and non-discriminatory characteristics of liberal forms. It becomes impractical as well as politically difficult or unethical to enforce the same laws in the same way in relation to small and big business, or the ordinary wage-earner and the very rich. Even in relation to the social treatment of individuals, laws are introduced to bring about and maintain equal treatment: politically-motivated and often contradictory attempts to use discrimination to secure substantive equal treatment. To resolve these problems, pure liberalism gives way to welfare liberalism. This entails a limited movement away from pure legal formalism, and even accepts an element of discrimination, on political or social grounds, to re-establish an adequate substantive social basis for formal equality to operate. However, the political system can become overloaded by claims for special treatment by special-interest groups.

As liberal forms of regulation become undermined, they are supplemented by more direct, selective and interventionist forms. Thus, for example, the need for generally-applicable rules for widely diverse legal subjects and social situations can lead to vagueness and lack of specificity, and can undermine fairness and predictability: this may be referred to as the problem of indeterminacy. Thus, general rules operated within a liberal-legal framework tend to be supplemented or replaced by administrative regulation by bureaucracies. These characteristically entail powers for officials to take administrative decisions on a selective basis; frequently, this is done on the basis of much more specific and detailed rule-systems. Such detailed rules may be formalized as subsidiary legislation or regulations; or, frequently, they may remain informal, either as administrative guidelines or even more informal rules of practice. In particular, in relation to economic and business regulation, the emergence of the large corporation leads to an important role for bureaucratic-administrative negotiation and bargaining, since the size and the frequent diversity of the corporation's assets and investments makes its decisions directly social ones. Bureaucratic-administrative regulation does not supplant, but significantly modifies liberal regulation. While it is more explicit about the substantive content of rules than liberal forms which strive for neutrality, it raises new problems of fairness and the control of discretion.

1.b Fairness, Efficiency and Legitimacy in Taxation

State taxation begins from the primary purpose of raising money for the treasury. In that sense, it always involves a political choice which affects differently specific individuals or groups, i.e. a collective decision to deprive some of wealth for the benefit of others or for the common good. However, in a society where market relations are dominant, the dominant considerations are those of liberalism: that the tax burden should fall equally on all and that its enforcement should interfere as little as possible with private economic activity. These were classically expressed in Adam Smith's four canons of taxation: equality, certainty, convenience and economy.[1]

The very notion of equality, however, is clearly problematic, since it involves attempting to treat as equal legal subjects social actors who may be economically quite unequal. Smith's general notion was that citizens should contribute to the treasury in proportion to the revenues they enjoy under the protection of the state. His principle therefore favoured the direct taxation of the incomes of all citizens, rather than specific levies such as stamp duties or window-tax, which were unrelated to ability to pay. Yet even the single uniform rate of income tax which applied in Britain during the nineteenth century (although only to a relatively small minority) was much resented and evaded. As the scope of the income tax grew in the twentieth century, the question of proportionality came to the fore. The principle of equality gave no clear guidance in relation to the two main issues which arose as the income tax became a mass tax: the threshold of taxable income, and the progressivity of tax rates. The principle of ability to pay and the view that a uniform rate bears unfairly on those with middle and low incomes justifies progressively higher rates on higher bands of income, sometimes referred to as 'vertical' as against 'horizontal' equity; those favouring the 'free' operation of markets prefer a uniform percentage rate on incomes.[2] The introduction of progressive rates has resulted historically from fierce political debates and, usually, wartime emergency; and high rates on high wealth have been denounced as confiscatory. Most recently, in the 1980s, high marginal rates have been attacked as a major cause of tax avoidance and evasion (IEA 1979). Meanwhile, the acceptance of income tax as a mass tax has turned debate about the threshold to one about the 'poverty trap'.

The question of equal treatment, or equity, also arises in relation to the economic efficiency of taxation. In principle, efficiency requires the optimal allocation of resources, and therefore tax neutrality – the incidence of taxation should as far as possible be equal in relation to the alternative choices available to economic actors. For some, this can justify the use of taxes by the state for

[1] *Wealth of Nations*, Book IV, Ch. II, Part II.
[2] Musgrave & Musgrave 1984, chapter 11, discuss the various views of political philosophers and economists.

raising finance for general social purposes and redistribution. For others, efficiency can only be assured by the private transactions of economic actors through the market, hence the state is always an obstacle.

Whether from the perspective of fairness or efficiency, the major difficulty in ensuring the equal incidence of income taxation is the treatment of income from different sources. Should the same rates apply to the wage-earner and the rentier? Should business or corporate profits be treated as income and taxed on the same principles as individual income, so that the sole trader, the partnership and the company are taxed in the same way? Is there a clear and valid distinction between income and capital gain? Underlying all these questions is the definition of income itself, the tax base, which is at the heart of the operation of direct taxes. It is also at the heart of the problem of avoidance.

Taxation is not an abstract exercise in political or economic philosophy, but a practical matter of raising state finance for the public good. The overriding aim is therefore effectiveness, which must be predicted, based on estimations of the patterns of compliance, non-compliance and avoidance. It is in this sense that the question of *legitimacy* is central to the evaluation of taxation, as well as other types of legal regulation of economic activity. Legitimacy in this sense combines the interrelated issues of equity and effectiveness. To the extent that a regulatory system lacks fairness it fails in political acceptability, and will also tend to fail in effectiveness as enforcement becomes difficult and non-compliance grows. Equally, a system which has problems of enforceability and therefore of effectiveness will tend to lose political acceptability.

2. Taxation of Revenues and Opportunities for Avoidance

Studies of enforcement and regulation as a social process have normally focused on compliance and non-compliance, leading to debates about the legitimacy of regulatory agencies seeking negotiated solutions rather than strict enforcement of the law. This assumes that the content of the law is unproblematic, a positivist fixed quantity, whereas on closer examination neither compliance nor non-compliance are as straightforward as they may superficially seem to be.[1] More can be learned about the dynamic of regulatory processes by analysing the often large grey area in the middle: avoidance. In relation to taxation, the accepted terminology in English distinguishes between the reduction of tax liability by illegal means, referred to as evasion,

---

[1] For a study of taxpayer compliance, focusing on individual taxpayers, see Smith & Kinsey 1987: the study emphasizes the problematic aspects of compliance (for example, according to US IRS data, 8 per cent of tax-return filers overpay), and the 'complexity' of the regulations means that much non-compliance may be unintentional, or due to inertia or indifference. However, as with other socio-legal studies of regulatory enforcement, although the law is acknowledged to be often 'complex' and full of 'loopholes', its actual content is deemed to be ascertainable. This contrasts sharply with the rule-scepticism of radical realism, critical legal studies and post-modern approaches to law.

and the attempt to do so by lawful means, avoidance. In French, direct unlawfulness is straightforwardly described as tax fraud, the rest is '*évasion fiscale*'. However, international usage has now accepted the distinction between evasion, which is clearly illegal, and avoidance, which uses legal means, but might in some circumstances be invalid or unlawful.

The category of unlawful avoidance has grown in importance, as regulators have been unwilling or unable to pursue evasion. This has been due to a combination of the social factors involved in pursuing the stigmatization as criminals of respectable people, and the legal problems especially in proving intent in relation to economic transactions. Revenue authorities therefore normally prefer to settle cases on the basis of the recovery of the unpaid taxes, plus a penalty if possible. Very few cases are dealt with by criminal prosecution, although some may be selected, to produce an 'in terrorem' effect. Individuals in the public eye seem prone to such targeting, as shown by the prosecutions in the UK of Lester Piggott the jockey (successful) and Ken Dodd the comedian (unsuccessful), and in the US of the Hemsleys, prominent hotel proprietors (partly successful).

Both the line between valid and unlawful avoidance, and that between avoidance and evasion may be difficult to establish. For example, a taxpayer may have grounds, based on professional advice, for arguing that a particular transaction has produced no taxable revenue, and therefore need not be reported. Such failure to report would be evasion if the transaction were shown to be taxable and the taxpayer to have deliberately withheld information; it would be valid avoidance if the transaction were indeed held not taxable; and it would be invalid avoidance if taxable but the taxpayer were accepted as having honestly believed there was no obligation to reveal it. This typical situation also reveals the difficulty in such a context of proving the intent necessary to establish evasion, and the importance of the role of the professional advisor.

The form taken by avoidance reflects and responds to the forms of the regulation being avoided. In general, avoidance of legal regulation of economic activities is rooted in the divergence between the legal form and the economic substance of transactions – the possibility for an economic actor of achieving substantially the same economic result by formally different legal means. This possibility enables an economic actor or legal person to avoid a legal transaction to which penalties are attached, yet achieve substantially the same result, by means of another legal path to which these penalties have not formally been given. The possibility of avoidance therefore poses an inherent problem, since the effectiveness of the regulatory system depends on a degree of reliability in the predictions of behaviour on which it is based.

Both the opportunity and the motive for avoidance are minimized to the extent that regulation can rely on the same legal rule applied universally. So, if the same rate of tax were applied to all revenues of all persons in a tax universe the system would be the most robust or impervious to avoidance. If the same rate of tax applied to earned income, investment income and capital gains, no tax reduction could be achieved by legal devices attempting to divert a revenue flow from one to another of these channels.

As we have seen, however, economic inequalities and the effects of competition make it impossible to achieve equality of regulation by treating all legal subjects alike. Regulatory systems are therefore subject to contradictory pressures. On the one hand, the extension of formal equal treatment to the widest possible universe of legal persons creates the most robust system, from the point of view of technical enforcement. On the other hand, substantive or economic equality, and political notions of fairness, frequently require distinctions to be made between different categories of legal person. Attempts to achieve such substantive equal treatment can be undermined, however, if differences in treatment can be avoided by exploiting the separation between formal legal categories and their economic substance.

Avoidance is therefore not simply an opportunistic activity, and the opportunities for it do not arise equally; rather, it develops symbiotically with the mode of regulation. This also explains why both the toleration of a certain degree of avoidance, as well as the development of anti-avoidance measures, are political questions.

In relation to revenue taxation, therefore, the problems of avoidance centre on two main points. First, the existence of different tax rates for different types of revenue (income from different sources, such as employment, investment or business; capital gains; gifts; inheritance); and second, differences in treatment of different categories of legal persons. Avoidance revolves around either the transfer of revenue to a lower-taxed person or of expenses to one who is more highly taxed; or the manipulation of transactions so that a benefit is received in a form or at a time that attracts less tax.

Generally, such manipulation centres crucially on the dividing line between income and capital (Kay 1979; Bracewell-Milnes 1980, p. 24). Avoidance opportunities are therefore much less in relation to individual employment income than for either business income or income from capital (Kay 1979). For the employed taxpayer, there is a close correlation between receipts and income: opportunities for avoidance are limited to fringe benefits, payments in kind and deferred benefits such as pensions. In contrast, in relation to business or investment the relationship between receipts and income is much more tenuous: there may be income but no clear receipt, or it may be unclear whether a receipt is of income or capital. Allowable expenses are a broader category and again harder to define precisely for business than for employment. The distinction between investment and consumption is harder to establish and easier to manipulate. Finally, it is easier to manipulate the direction or timing of business or investment revenues by use of fictitious legal persons (trusts or companies).

3. The Economics, Politics and Morality of Avoidance

Avoidance rests upon the choice or creation of transactions that are valid in formal legal terms. In pure liberal principle, this formal validity is sufficient: if the transactions chosen by taxpayers are valid but considered undesirable by the regulator, then the latter must seek legislative approval for a (non-retrospective) change in the rules. This formalistic approach can undermine legitimacy by reducing the system to a ritualistic game, in which the elaborate avoidance schemes of the taxpayer are countered by anti-avoidance measures. To satisfy the liberal requirement of certainty in the law, these should be specific counter-measures; but this results in complex and technical provisions which tax officials process through an uncomprehending legislature, producing 'large bodies of complex, unsystematic and almost incomprehensible tax statutes' (Rotterdam IFS 1979, p. 346). The alternative is to adopt the 'shotgun' approach of broadly drafted anti-avoidance principles; but these give officials a wide discretion, and they may be interpreted narrowly or unpredictably by courts. Hence, broad anti-avoidance rules are often supplemented by informal or semi-formal guidelines. In practice, both these approaches usually involve processes of consultation and negotiation between state officials and specialist bodies and pressure-groups of professionals, mainly lawyers and accountants. This negotiation of enforcement takes place within a structure of rules combining broad standards and specific guidelines; and the legal status of such rules not only differs between different political and social systems, but in each case is itself subject to some negotiation and change.

The toleration of avoidance is criticized on the grounds that opportunities for avoidance are unequal, and the avoidance/anti-avoidance game is wasteful of resources (Kay 1979). In reply, the classical liberal justification is based on the freedom of individuals to plan their affairs and dispose of their assets subject only to declared law. In the tax field, this has been expressed in well-known legal dicta, such as Lord Atkin's statement in *Inland Revenue Commissioners v. Duke of Westminster*, the *locus classicus* of English law on tax avoidance schemes:

> I do not use the word device in any sinister sense; for it has to be recognised that the subject, whether poor and humble or wealthy and noble, has the legal right so to dispose of his capital and income as to attract upon himself the least amount of tax. The only function of a court of law is to determine the legal result of his dispositions so far as they affect tax. [1936, p. 8.]

Fundamentalist economic liberals go further and proclaim tax avoidance to be not a vice but a virtue, a blow against the tyranny of egalitarianism (Shenfield 1968, p. 35), and a safety-valve which liberates wealth from unproductive state uses to productive private ones (Bracewell-Milnes, in IEA 1979). This argument is taken even further, to demonstrate that measures against avoidance and even evasion may be against the economic interest of the fisc itself, by inhibiting economic activity, or diverting it from channels which generate fiscal benefits (e.g. paid employment and the cash economy) to others outside its net, such as the subsistence household economy (Bracewell-Milnes 1980, Appendix).

3.a The Business Purpose Rule

The pure liberal approach may be modified to invalidate sham transactions. However, given that economic actors are free to choose the form of their transactions, there is no objective basis for categorizing any particular form as a complete sham; although it may be done on the basis of an evaluation of the subjective factors of motive. Hence, the focus is normally on transactions which may be regarded as 'artificial', based on the criterion of legitimate business or economic purpose. This remains a modification rather than an abandonment of the liberal approach. Certainly, some have argued that the adoption of a substance-over-form approach undermines the requirements of certainty and predictability which are the basic requirements of a liberal system. However, this assumes that formal rules can be defined by reference to conditions which are entirely factual or objectively determinable. Even in the case of facilitative private law rules which regulate transactions between legal subjects *inter se* this is often impossible, and formally realizable rules are replaced or supplemented by less precise standards (good faith, foreseeability, reasonableness etc.).[1] In the case of rules imposing burdens or granting benefits as a consequence of specified transactions (normally the case with tax rules), the preference that legal subjects should be free to choose the form of their transactions contradicts the priority of formalism. Indeed, a tax code which attempts to rely only on specific and formal rules is likely to be so often amended as to become a minefield rather than a field of fair play for taxpayers and the fisc. Hence, the business purpose rule has been defended on the grounds that with such a general backstop 'statutory safeguards need not be provided every time an ingenious taxpayer or his adviser thinks he sees a way to manipulate statutory language in a manner foreign to the purpose of the provision' (Surrey 1969, p. 694).

In fact, the modification introduced by a business purpose requirement may

[1] For a fuller discussion see Kennedy 1976 and Kelman 1987, chapter 1. Kennedy's argument links the choice between broad standards and specific rules to a broad difference in political vision between altruism (= standards) and individualism (= rules). Kelman prefers to regard this as a general cultural connection rather than a predictive or causal link, and stresses that in specific controversies both these approaches, as well as intermediary positions, 'uncomfortably coexist'; although he explores their interaction, he still seems to agree broadly with Kennedy's view that they express competing visions. In my view, it is necessary to go further and explore the interaction of rules and standards, which generally exist in combination in the regulatory systems of advanced capitalist society, although their different combinations in different societies and contexts reflect differences in political culture and social relations more generally.

be hard to spot. For example, a dictum which is quoted even more often than that of Lord Atkin above, is the statement of Lord Clyde:

> No man in this country is under the smallest obligation, moral or other, so to arrange his legal relations to his business or to his property as to enable the Inland Revenue to put the largest possible shovel into his stores [*Ayrshire Pullman Motor Services & Ritchie v. I.R.C.*, 1929, p. 763].

At about the same time, an even more famous American judge, Learned Hand, made an apparently very similar statement:

> Anyone may so arrange his affairs that his taxes will be as low as possible; he is not bound to choose that pattern which will best pay the Treasury; there is not even a patriotic duty to increase one's taxes [*Helvering v. Gregory* 1934, p. 810].

Indeed, statements to this effect proliferate in tax court decisions everywhere. However, Learned Hand's dictum in *Gregory* was part of a seminal judgment which established the 'business purpose' rule in American law. In his view, the 'choice' which was permitted was between transactions which each have a business or economic purpose; given such a choice, it is legitimate to select the most tax-efficient one. This draws a distinction between transactions which have a valid business purpose, and those which are artificially designed merely to avoid tax; or, even more extreme, purely sham transactions.

This introduction of a business purpose criterion was not clarified until much later in British law. British judges have been reluctant to develop a general business purpose rule, but they have been more willing to try to develop criteria to single out the 'unacceptable' tax planning industry. It took indeed more than half a century for a general rule similar to that in *Helvering v. Gregory* to be approved in Britain, in *Ramsay v. IRC* (1982), and *Furniss v. Dawson* (1984) (see Millett 1986; Tiley 1987, 1988). The court decisions were the final battle in a protracted war initiated by the Revenue against the sale of off-the-peg tax schemes in the 1970s, especially through the Rossminster group (Tutt 1985). These decisions caused a considerable stir; but in the event it seems to have been limited to the 'step-transaction' rule. This is that intermediate steps in a chain of pre-ordained transactions may be disregarded, or the entire chain treated as a single act, if the steps were evidently designed to produce a result which if directly carried out would have attracted tax.[1]

On the other hand, the US courts have gone beyond the business purpose rule and adopted a more general substance-over-form approach. However, the difference in approach can be traced to differences in the role of courts and their relationship to the legislature, as well as to wider political and social factors (see Tiley 1987, 1988). In particular, under the British parliamentary system the Inland Revenue can normally be sure that its proposals will be

---

[1] *Craven v. White; IRC v. Bowater Property; Baylis v. Gregory* (1989); there remains some disagreement among the judges as to what constitutes a 'pre-ordained' series of transactions.

enacted, provided it can satisfy the Treasury and the Chancellor of the need to block a loophole (Stopforth 1987), as well as overcoming the technical and political arguments put up by tax specialists during the pre-legislative consultation process, which has become increasingly important. This leads to more specific and statute-based anti-avoidance rules. Thus, a more specific business purpose rule has been embodied in a number of legislative anti-avoidance provisions, where tax consequences are deemed to flow from certain artificial transactions unless the taxpayer can show a valid business purpose other than reduction of tax liability. This is the principle used for example in the provisions against the use of overseas trusts or companies to shelter private income (now s.739 ICTA 1988; see Chapter 5 below).

3.b General Statutory Anti-Avoidance Rules

Other common-law countries have longer involvement with general anti-avoidance rules, notably Australia and New Zealand, which have also given British judges (hearing cases on appeal to the Privy Council) some experience of their interpretation. The original very broad provisions[1] merely laid down that any contract, agreement or arrangement should be 'absolutely void' in so far as it had the 'purpose or effect' of in any way directly or indirectly altering, relieving or defeating any income tax liability or preventing the operation of the statute in any respect. Not surprisingly, the criterion of the 'purpose or effect' of the arrangement was held to be not the subjective motive of the taxpayer but an objective 'predicate' test:

> [Y]ou . . . must be able to predicate – by looking at the overt acts by which it was implemented – that it was implemented in that particular way so as to avoid tax. If you cannot so predicate but have to acknowledge that the transactions are capable of explanation by reference to ordinary business or family dealing without necessarily being labelled as a means to avoid tax then the arrangement does not come within the section. [Lord Denning in *Newton v. Commr. of Taxation* [1958] 2 All E.R. 759 P.C., at p. 765.]

The importance of the word 'necessarily' was emphasized in a later case:

> If a bona fide transaction can be carried through in two ways, one involving less liability to tax than the other, the . . . transaction [cannot be declared] wholly or partly void merely because the way involving less tax is chosen [Lord Donovan, in *Mangin v. IRC*, 1971, p. 751].

Indeed, in *C.I.R. v. Challenge Corp.*, Lord Templeman went even further and, citing the *Duke of Westminster* case with approval, argued that there is no

---

[1] For a history of the provisions, originating in New Zealand's Land Tax Act 1878 and included in its first income tax statute of 1891, see *Mangin v. Inland Revenue Commr.* (1971); the most recent versions were, in Australia s.260 of the Income Tax Assessment Act 1936, replaced by Part IVA of the Income Tax Assessment Act in effect from 28 May 1981; and in

avoidance in the case of tax 'mitigation', that is to say where the tax advantage comes from a reduction of income or the incurring of an expenditure (1987, p. 167); but it is not yet clear whether this view will gain more general acceptance.[1]

The later versions of these provisions laid down that the section applied even if there is a valid business purpose, provided the tax avoidance purpose is more than merely incidental. Also, quite importantly, they empowered the Commissioner to intervene to restructure the transaction so as to counteract the tax advantage. This meant both that an invalid transaction is not necessarily 'annihilated' (which might have equally bad consequences for the revenue); but also that, unless the tax authorities do invoke the section, the transactions will be undisturbed.[2] Hence, a general statutory anti-avoidance provision of the shotgun (or blunderbuss) type also operates mainly as a threat to wholesale or unwary avoidance, but will not pose any real danger to careful tax planning. Where the tax authorities are given powers to restructure transactions which might be considered artificial, they are given a basis for negotiation with the taxpayer's advisors, which helps to entrench the function of tax planning, although within the limits of acceptability set by the negotiations with state officials.

3.c Abuse of Legal Forms

In civil law systems, there is the same ambivalence. Most have a concept of 'abuse of rights' in private law, either embodied in the Civil Code or developed jurisprudentially. However, there has been some reluctance to apply the doctrine in relation to taxation, although this has occurred in some countries in the modified form of '*fraude à la loi*', either jurisprudentially or in the Tax Code. The taxpayer is considered to have the right to arrange her affairs in the way that is most advantageous to her, but this right must not be 'abused' by the concealment of the economic reality of a transaction by use of legal forms.

Thus, in France the principle of abuse of rights has been explicitly enacted in the Tax Code (Art. L64 of the Book of Fiscal Procedures), but it does not prevent the taxpayer from choosing an optimal tax route from among alternative legal forms for a transaction, and the administration must prove both the intention to avoid tax and the artificiality of the form chosen (Tixier & Gest 1985, p. 414). In Belgium, the courts have refused to apply the doctrine to taxation, but have more recently been willing on occasion to disregard 'sham'

New Zealand s. 108 of the Land and Income Tax Act of 1954, replaced by s.99 of the IncomeTax Act 1976.
[1] New Zealand's Commissioner of Inland Revenue issued a statement to clarify enforcement of s.99 following the *Challenge* decision: see (1990) 44 *Bulletin of International Fiscal Documentation* 288 and A. M. C. Smith (1991).
[2] For a comparison of the New Zealand and Australian provisions with the rule newly enacted in Singapore, as well as the Hong Kong provisions, see Liang 1989.

transactions used for tax avoidance. Sweden has not applied the abuse of rights principle, but enacted a statutory anti-avoidance provision in 1981. On the other hand, Switzerland has both a well-developed general principle authorizing an economic approach, as well as specific legislative provisions, in particular a 1962 decree against the improper use of tax treaties. Substantially similar are the Dutch principle of '*fraus legis*', and the German rule on 'abuse of forms and structures of the civil law'.[1]

3.d Tax Planning

In effect, while the 'business purpose' rule combats crude artificial avoidance schemes, it authorizes tax planning. Professional tax planning is generally able to establish a pattern of legitimate business activity which optimizes tax payments from the taxpayer's viewpoint. If a company's new investment may be financed in a number of different ways, is it not reasonable to choose the most tax-efficient? And how can the relative importance of the tax factor be judged? If the criterion of 'purpose' slides into the subjectivity of 'motive', legitimacy is threatened: the validity of a transaction cannot depend on the state of mind of the citizen.[2] Hence, the business purpose test tends to outlaw only the most 'weird and wonderful' schemes, which might not even stand up to rigorous technical scrutiny (Millett 1986). Nevertheless, it introduces into the law a terrain that must be contested, since a transaction might be required to have a demonstrably valid purpose, beyond its purely formal legal validity.

This contest is in terms of the interrelated elements of economics, politics and morality. These factors are not normally directly invoked, but are embedded in the process of legal reasoning, the application of the general principles of law to the 'facts' of a case, whether this is done by legal advisors evaluating the validity of a proposed strategy, or by an adjudicating tribunal. It is by this process that the formal requirements of abstract legal principles are applied to the substance of actual social and economic transactions to determine their acceptability (Tiley 1988).[3] Nevertheless, this normally takes

[1] Section 6 of the Steueranpassungsgesetz, later modified in section 42 of the 1977 Abgabenordnung. See generally Avery Jones 1974; International Fiscal Association 1983; Rotterdam IFS 1979; Ward et al. 1985.

[2] Thus, the British Court of Appeal has recently recommended a 'balancing test' to decide whether the transaction was a commercial one in a fiscally advantageous form, or was entered into essentially for fiscal purposes but under the guise of a commercial transaction; the test should be an objective one, but subjective evidence of motive might be relevant: *Stokes v. Ensign Tankers (Leasing) Ltd* (1991).

[3] It should be clear from my argument that I do not consider that law is a self-contained and self-referential body of rules, as claimed by the traditional positivists such as Austin and Hart, or, subject apparently to more complex mediations, by the newer ones such as Luhmann and Teubner. This does not mean, however, that it is either a mechanism manipulated in class interests, as suggested by some crude versions of Marxism, or consisting of radically indeterminate concepts which leave scope for arbitrary interpretation, as suggested by some critical legal scholars (see the survey and critique by Kelman 1987). My stance is that the forms taken by legal rules result from the more general forms of social relations, autonomized

place within the same broadly liberal assumptions embedded in legal formalism.

In evaluating the economic value of a transaction in liberal terms, the question is whether the economic transaction in the form chosen by the taxpayer is a 'normal' one, since the business purpose rule assumes that a transaction which could take place by a 'normal' route is diverted to an artificial one. However, strict limits can be imposed on this by the pure liberal argument that it is more beneficial to allow a transaction to take place even in a form which avoids tax, if the alternative is that it might not take place at all. This assumes that economic actors may be seen as having a range of possibilities open to them, including refraining from activity, or choosing to undertake such activity in a sphere beyond the reach of the fisc (such as the household economy, or a foreign jurisdiction). If the decision to undertake the activity is based on a calculation which assumed a tax-efficient route, it is difficult to conclude that tax-avoidance is the dominant or exclusive purpose. This argument can be taken further in the fundamentalist liberal direction mentioned earlier. This denies the right of the state to challenge the economic actor's choice of transactions. High rates of tax, in particular, can be said to inhibit activity which could generate a larger tax base; and it has even been argued that, paradoxically, measures against both evasion and avoidance can result in a reduction of state revenues (Bracewell-Milnes 1980). This perspective essentially assumes that private transactions are more beneficial to the economy as a whole than activities funded, organized or stimulated by state finance. However, not all adjudicators accept this view of the economic desirability of private transactions.

The political validity of a tax avoidance transaction is normally expressed as depending on whether it conforms to the spirit of the law. Hence, it is not only the intention of the taxpayer, but also that of the legislator which is relevant. This is the problem of 'loopholes' in the law. To the tax official, the taxpayer may only validly make a choice which reduces tax liability if the legislator intended to allow that choice. In this view, tax reduction is limited to explicit tax incentives or disincentives – for example, choosing not to smoke cigarettes, or deciding to invest in a development area for which a tax incentive has been provided. As the OECD's Fiscal Committee rather frankly put it: 'governments tend to take an operational approach towards tax avoidance to cover those forms of tax minimization which are unacceptable to governments' (OECD 1987a–I, p. 8). This can clearly be criticized as 'Tax avoidance is what the fisc says it is, without the application of legal tests' (Bracewell-Milnes 1980, p. 18). However, the regulatory net cannot be infinitely stretched – or

by a historical process of abstraction; in particular, in capitalist societies based on generalized commodity production and market relations, law mediates the relationships of economic subjects, subject to the permeating authority of the state: see Picciotto 1979. The interpretation and application of legal concepts is, therefore, also a social process, institutionally autonomized, but also part of the social whole, and in which economic and political ideologies play a part.

again legitimacy would be threatened. The law enforcer must consider, first whether a new pattern of activity may be tolerated; this is frequently the subject of negotiation, which might result in adaptation or modification. If the activity is considered unacceptable, a decision must be made whether to proceed against it under existing legal provisions, or to seek approval for legislative amendments.[1]

The morality of transactions is often ringingly said to be quite irrelevant to their legal validity. In practice, however, the impossibility of deciding these issues of validity in purely formal legal terms inevitably raises ethical or moral issues. Most commonly, the form it takes is the requirement of openness or frankness. The taxpayer who has laid out the transactions without secrecy or any element of deceit is more likely to gain the approval both of the official and the judge. Since tax planning strategies are developed in consultation between the managers of a business and its professional advisors, considerations of professional ethics in the giving of advice also play an important part. These entail balancing the professional's duty to produce the most economical result for the client against the more general obligation to ensure that accounting and taxation regulatory systems operate fairly for all, and perhaps even in the interests of society.[2]

In broad terms, therefore, the three principles on which the validity of tax avoidance rests may be summarized as follows:

   i the existence of a valid economic or business purpose;
  ii compliance with both the letter and, broadly speaking, the spirit of the law;
 iii openness, or at least lack of excessive secrecy.

These criteria may be identified both in the advice of tax planners (see e.g. Freeman & Kirchner 1945), as well as statements by officials or policy-makers (see e.g. OECD 1987a, p. 9).

4. International Investment and Tax Avoidance

International tax avoidance results from the same factors as national avoidance, but is qualitatively and quantitatively different in scale. We have seen that the opportunities for avoidance result from the problems of equity inherent in a liberal regulatory process such as direct taxation of incomes. In a system consisting of many overlapping jurisdictions, the problem of equity is

---

[1] Normally such amendments take effect prospectively; but it is not unknown for the government side to take advantage of its access to the legislative process to introduce a 'clarification' in the law which may affect pending cases: for an example, see Capon in Fordham CLI 1976, p. 104 and Chapter 8 below.
[2] See Cooper 1980 for an entertaining elaboration of the professional's dilemma, and Cooper 1985 for an analysis of the main forms of income tax avoidance, and their effects, under US law.

magnified. To the extent that freedom of movement of individuals, commodities and funds between jurisdictions is permitted and possible, problems of international equity will arise. Immediately, this involves reconciling equity in the capital-importing or source jurisdiction with equity in the capital-exporting or residence jurisdiction. In addition, where internationally-integrated activities are concerned, the jurisdictions themselves may have competing claims to a fair allocation of taxable capacity. At the same time, the existence of multiple, often inconsistent, national approaches to tax equity will create magnified opportunities for avoidance. Problems of co-ordination in enforcement will also magnify the possibilities of successful evasion.

International avoidance has therefore resulted from the interaction of tax systems and the unevenness left by the methods found to accommodate and co-ordinate them. It has been defined very generally as 'the reduction of tax liability through the movement or non-movement of persons or funds across tax boundaries by legal methods' (Wisselink, in Rotterdam IFS 1979, p. 29). The opportunities for such avoidance result from differences between tax jurisdictions, mainly in relation to:

(i) the scope of taxation (definitions of residence and source, treatment of foreign earnings);
(ii) the distinction between capital and revenue, and the categorization of types of revenue;
(iii) the tax treatment and rates of tax applied to various legal persons and categories of revenue or capital.

International avoidance may be prevented by the prohibition or control of movements of persons or funds, or countered by disallowing or disregarding such movements for taxation purposes. International business necessarily generates international movements of persons and funds. International tax planning entails organizing international business transactions in legal forms which involve the optimal tax liability consistent with maximizing the overall return.

As we have seen in previous chapters, from the point of view of international business, the problem is that international transactions involve a greater likelihood of exposure to multiple taxation. Hence, the continuing demand of the business lobby has been for relief from 'international double taxation'. During the first half of this century, multiple taxation resulted mainly from international trade and portfolio investment; concern therefore focused mainly on defining where profits from foreign sales were deemed to be earned, and where a company financed from abroad should be considered taxable. The question of export profits was broadly resolved by developing the distinction between manufacturing and merchanting profit, and allocating the latter to the importing state if the sale was attributable to a Permanent Establishment.

The problem of international investment was more difficult, and gave rise, as we have seen, to conflicts between the residence and source principles. The compromise arrangement embodied in tax treaties restricted taxation at source to the business profits of a Permanent Establishment or subsidiary, while giving the country of residence of the lender the primary right to tax investment income. This formula was inappropriate or ambiguous in relation to foreign direct investment by internationally-integrated TNCs, which were increasingly able to take a global view on both the sources and the application of their funds.

In the postwar period, as already mentioned, the major international creditor countries, the US and the UK, continued to claim the right to tax the worldwide profits of their TNCs, subject to a credit for foreign taxes paid. International business argued that the foreign tax credit was inequitable: it meant that profits earned abroad always paid the higher of the home or host country rates of tax; and if the home rate were higher, the investor did not compete on equal terms in the host country market. The Treasuries of the US and the UK argued that the tax credit offered equality of treatment between investment at home and overseas: to exempt foreign income would provide an incentive to overseas investment, as well as encouraging competition among states to attract capital by offering tax reductions. In any case, since most capital-exporting countries taxed repatriated foreign earnings, foreign investors were not disadvantaged against each other. However, since the new pattern of foreign direct investment could take place with relatively little outflow of funds, this debate had an element of shadow-boxing. The large global corporate groups were transnational, in the sense of having an identifiable national origin and corporate base, while their investment capital came initially mainly from foreign profits and then increasingly from global capital markets. The underlying problem was the equitable international allocation of the tax base generated by business activities in several countries which were internationally co-ordinated by a single firm. However, this issue was not addressed in any international forum for more than two decades.

Instead, an international tax avoidance industry emerged. Its primary initial aim was to secure the minimization of taxes on the retained earnings of TNCs. Defenders or apologists argue that international tax avoidance has legitimately focused on averaging international tax rates, or reducing them as far as possible to the lowest rather than highest rates (Bracewell-Milnes 1980). In their view, international tax avoidance or planning is a legitimate response to the inequity of the foreign tax credit, which offers only capital-export neutrality, and imposes tax at the higher of the home and host country rates. However, tax planning has ensured that many international businesses are able to benefit from considerable reductions in average tax rates, using devices which have minimized taxable business profits at source, while routing payments through convenient channels to low-tax countries or tax havens. Furthermore, the tax planning industry, as it developed in sophistication, has become available not only to relatively legitimate international business, but also to activities that were much less legitimate and even less international.

In a sense, international avoidance has helped to reduce the distortions produced by the disharmony in international tax arrangements, for the TNC itself is able to structure its global financial flows so as greatly to reduce or eliminate the effects of these distortions on its investment decisions. However, both national and international equity have been increasingly undermined by the exploitation of international avoidance opportunities by TNCs to reduce the cost of capital to them, especially by using the offshore-based international financial system (see Chapter 6 below, and Bird 1988, Alworth 1988).

With the initial growth of international avoidance, the issue of international equity was first treated as a problem of international avoidance of national taxes. The next chapter will trace the tensions in the policies of the two main capital-exporting countries, the US and the UK, towards the taxation of foreign investment and the problem of avoidance. It was only as the limits of unilateral approaches became clear that an international debate about avoidance emerged, and attempts have been made to co-ordinate action at the international level. These moves towards co-ordination, however, once again revived doubts about the adequacy of the international arrangements, as well as the fundamental question of international equity.

5
The Dilemma of Deferral

International tax avoidance, as was argued in the previous chapter, resulted generally from the limitations of the solutions offered by international tax arrangements to the problems of effective and equitable taxation of internationally-organized business. These limitations came increasingly to the fore as international investment more dominantly took the form of direct investment; and the problems were most acute for the tax systems of the US and the UK, the two main sources of foreign direct investment. The TNCs, which were the vehicle for this direct investment, developed sophisticated techniques essentially to exploit the deferral of taxation on retained earnings. These techniques built on devices pioneered between the wars to shelter family wealth and their increased use by TNCs consolidated the international tax avoidance industry.

This chapter will consider mainly the British and US taxation of foreign direct investment, and the different ways in which they influenced and reacted to the problem of taxation of the retained earnings of TNCs. The problem was posed slightly differently for each country according to the structure of its taxation of international business, and the responses of national authorities were also different, although made with an awareness of the international context and of the measures introduced by other states. In both Britain and the US, as we have seen, when direct taxation was first introduced it applied in broad terms to the income from all sources worldwide of all legal persons considered to be within its ambit. However, Britain, the first to develop an income tax, applied it to residents, while the US law applied to citizens. This difference came to take on an increasing significance with the increased importance of international direct investment through foreign-incorporated subsidiaries. This created opportunities for avoidance of US taxation on retained earnings by channelling them into foreign-incorporated subsidiaries, and led the US to enact the first provisions for taxation of Controlled Foreign Subsidiaries (CFCs). Under British law, even a foreign-incorporated subsidiary could be liable to British tax on its business profits if it was controlled from the UK, although from 1956 to 1965 British-resident companies trading wholly abroad were exempt on their retained profits. After 1965, the British authorities used administrative powers controlling the transfer of residence abroad to try to impose limits on the volume of retained earnings in foreign subsidiaries of British TNCs. The growing international interpenetration of capital, however, eventually called into question both the unilateralism of the US approach, and the direct administrative controls of the UK.

1. The UK: Controls over the Transfer of Residence

We have seen in Chapter 1 that from very early on, British tax jurisdiction came to be asserted over the profits of any firm whose central management and control was in the UK. This meant that a UK company could not easily escape British tax on its foreign business merely by incorporating a subsidiary abroad.[1] However, it was possible for British-based international businesses to transfer abroad the place from which they were managed and controlled.

Rising tax rates after 1909, combined with court decisions confirming the extent of the control rule, led to some company emigrations, and the Royal Commission of 1918–20 heard that this was likely to continue (Evidence, para. 8282). For example, the American Thread Company had been held in 1911–13 to be resident in Britain because its affairs were controlled by meetings held in England of a committee of directors representing its majority shareholder, English Sewing Cotton. Consequently, the arrangement was changed so that its affairs were managed in the USA (*Bradbury v. English Sewing Cotton*, 1923). Tax rates came down only slowly in the 1920s and rose again in the 1930s, which encouraged further emigration, not only of businesses but of individual wealth. In 1920, for example, *The Times* reported the sale to Chilean interests of nitrate companies, due apparently to the prospects of higher dividend payments once their trading profits were not liable to UK tax (2 March 1920, p. 23a).

It was considered difficult to make legitimate complaint against the transfer of central management and control from the UK to a foreign country where the substantial business of a company was actually carried on. However, there was greater concern that wealthy individuals or families could find the means

---

[1] As discussed in Chapter 1, the Revenue considered that the same factors that tended to show that a company was controlled from and therefore resident in the UK also tended to show that its trade was sufficiently based in the UK to be taxed on its business profits directly under case I of Schedule D; but where a company was managed completely outside the UK, with no actual exercise by the UK shareholders of their powers of control, unless the foreign company could be considered a mere sham or agent of the UK shareholders, the latter would be liable only on its declared dividends.

to transfer control of their capital abroad, while themselves remaining in Britain and retaining rights to enjoy the proceeds in a non-taxable form.

1.a The Islands

In particular, attention was drawn to the increasing use of the Channel Islands (and the potential of the Isle of Man) for avoidance of British tax. The Inland Revenue had found, following publicity given to the case of Sir Robert Houston, that considerable numbers of large private investment companies had been formed in Jersey and Guernsey, whose shareholders and directors appeared to be mainly nominees. Although the precise nature of the evasions they concealed were not known to the Revenue, some had been traced to British residents. Apart from illegal evasion, they could be used for avoidance if British residents transferred assets to them, allowed their capital to accumulate, and enjoyed the proceeds by means not taxable in the UK, such as loans or capital repayments.

Both the Channel Islands, which were originally part of the Duchy of Normandy, and the Isle of Man, which was purchased by the Crown from the Dukes of Atholl in 1765 to end its use for smuggling, are dependencies under the Crown: they are British islands, although not part of the United Kingdom. Their special position based on royal grants is respected by the UK Parliament, which can legislate for them but does not do so without prior consultation and, normally, agreement. They have fiscal autonomy, and although the UK government represents them in international affairs and can conclude treaties on their behalf, by constitutional convention it does so only with their agreement.[1] The issue of the use of the islands for avoidance of British taxes was taken up in negotiations initiated in 1923 for a fiscal contribution towards 'the expenses of Empire'. The island parliaments objected to annual payments, but offered a one-off contribution to the costs of the war.

In 1927, Sir John Anderson, on behalf of the British government, agreed not to press the matter of fiscal payments over the Channel Islanders' objections, but asked for co-operation in dealing with the use of the Channel Islands by British subjects for tax avoidance. His letter was accompanied by an Inland Revenue Memorandum, which found its way into the local press.[2] The Revenue's proposals were comprehensive, and included measures to restrict company formation in the islands to those carrying on bona fide business there

---

[1] See the Report of the Royal Commission on the Constitution 1973, Cmnd 5460, Part XI. Although the Islands pressed for a formal declaration that it would be unconstitutional for the UK to bind them internationally or legislate internally without their consent, this was resisted by the Royal Commission, which pointed out that the UK is responsible for the territories under international law and must therefore have the ultimate legal power. The Islands are not part of the European Community and maintain their own customs regimes as well as separate tax systems.

[2] The text is reproduced in Johns 1983, p. 85.

and beneficially owned by native islanders, as well as provisions to apply British income tax and super-tax to persons transferring their residence there from Britain.

These proposals would have entailed changes in British law to tax the income of persons who transferred their residence abroad. Furthermore, effective enforcement would require the assistance of the island authorities, both to supply information and, more importantly, to collect the taxes. Under pressure, the islands' bailiffs agreed to such measures, provided they were not unique, but were capable of applying throughout the Empire (Pocock 1975, pp. 64–7). A clause providing for reciprocal enforcement of revenue judgments within the British Empire was slipped into the Administration of Justice Bill of 1928. However, it quickly drew the attention of the business lobby, especially shipowners, who expressed the concern that it would reciprocally oblige the UK to enforce foreign taxes which might be unacceptable, such as Australian taxes on shipping cargoes. In fear of losing the whole Bill, the Law Officers dropped the clause. At this stage, the Inland Revenue saw no point in introducing controls on the transfer of residence abroad without arrangements for co-operation in assessment and collection, which seemed unlikely to be obtainable, so this proposal was not reintroduced (PRO file IR40/7463).

1.b Family Trusts: the Vestey Cases

It nevertheless was considered important to take action against persons who continued to be resident in Britain, while transferring their wealth abroad in ways which allowed them to continue effectively to enjoy it. This could be done not only through low-tax jurisdictions, such as Jersey, but also by forming private companies in countries which did not tax income from abroad. The Finance Acts of 1936 and 1938 therefore enacted provisions which for half a century were a legal battleground, in which complex and sweeping legislative provisions and the ingenious devices which have been attempted to circumvent them have led to some strange interpretations by the courts, and occasional legislative amendment. The aim and scope of the provisions[1] were indicated by the section's preamble, stating that it was enacted:

> for the purpose of preventing the avoiding by individuals ordinarily resident in the United Kingdom of liability to income tax by means of transfer of assets by virtue or in consequence whereof, either alone or in conjunction with associated operations, income becomes payable to persons resident or domiciled out of the United Kingdom.

The objective was therefore quite specific – to prevent a UK resident from continuing to enjoy income by transferring assets to a foreign company or trust and receiving from it loans, capital payments or other benefits. However, the

[1] Originally the Finance Act 1936 s.18, later ICTA 1970 s.478, and then ICTA 1988 ss.739–46.

terms of the provision were widely drafted, especially the notion of 'power to enjoy' income derived by the UK resident as a result of the asset transfer. To be fully effective against any possible circumvention, the provisions aimed to include any beneficiaries and to tax the whole of the income sheltered (potentially including all the income of the transferee whether or not derived from the transferred assets), even if not actually paid over to the resident beneficiary. This gave the Revenue very broad powers, and has been denounced as a 'preposterous state of affairs' which could only be made tolerable by its exercise of 'discretion as to whom, and how and how much income to assess', a discretion so wide as to amount to a 'suspension of the rule of law' (Sumption 1982, pp. 116, 138).

Nevertheless, gaps were found in the Revenue's armoury, especially by the Vestey family trusts, which gained two spectacular victories over the provisions, after occupying lawyers and courts at intervals for decades. As mentioned above (Chapter 1, section 2), the Vestey brothers had left the UK in 1915 so that their meat business should not be taxable on its worldwide profits in the UK. William Vestey stated in his evidence to the Royal Commission that while his tax position in Argentina suited him admirably, he would prefer to come back to Britain to live, work and die. He also wrote to the Prime Minister, Lloyd George, in 1919, stating that if the brothers could be assured that they would pay only the same rate of tax as the American Beef Trust paid on similar business, they would immediately return. Failing to receive such assurances, they took legal advice from 1919 to 1921, as a result of which they established a family trust in Paris. Returning to London, they leased all their properties, cattle lands and freezing works in various countries to a UK company, Union Cold Storage, stipulating that the rents should be payable to the Paris trustees. By various deeds they provided for funds from the trust income to be used for the benefit of their family members (but not themselves); but the trust deed also gave them power to give directions to the trustees as to the investment of the trust fund in any way whatever, although subject to such directions the trustees were given unrestricted powers.

Following the death of Lord William Vestey, the Inland Revenue assessed his executors and his brother Edmund for the years 1937–41 for a total of £4 million, in respect of the receipts of the Paris trust. These assessments were upheld until the case reached the House of Lords in 1949. Evershed, L.J. in the Court of Appeal considered that the power to give the trustees directions gave the brothers effective control over the revenues produced from the assets, and that this was a benefit which amounted to a power to enjoy income (*Vestey's Executors v. IRC*, 1949, p. 69). The House of Lords disagreed, on the grounds that under English trust law the trust funds were to be applied for the benefit of the beneficiaries; the brothers' power to give directions gave them no more than a right to direct the trustees to give them a loan on commercial terms, which would not amount to a payment or application of the income for their benefit as contemplated by the statute (Lord Simonds, p. 83, Lord Reid, p.

121). In any case, the power to direct the investments was given to them jointly, while the statute referred plainly to the power to enjoy only of an individual.[1] Thirty years later the Vestey trust gained an even more decisive victory when the House of Lords confined the scope of the anti-avoidance provisions of the statute to the actual transferor and not other beneficiaries (*Vestey v. IRC*, 1979). Although the position was substantially restored legislatively in 1981[2] the liability of beneficiaries other than transferors became limited to the benefits actually received and not the entire income from the transferred assets (Sumption 1982, ch. 7).

These provisions were aimed at private wealth rather than business income or profits. Although some arrangements might involve both, as in the cases of wealthy families such as the Vesteys, the 1949 decision by the House of Lords that the power to direct trustees as to foreign investments did not fall within the section meant that these provisions had little application to the control of foreign business.[3] Individuals such as the Vesteys could live in the UK and direct the investments of companies abroad, provided they obtained no personal benefits themselves, and provided that the actual exercise of corporate control (in particular the holding of board meetings) took place abroad.

1.c Companies: Controls over Foreign Subsidiaries

It was not until 1951 that powers were introduced governing the transfer abroad of control over a company's business. These powers were described as 'an exceptional and no doubt temporary requirement' by the Royal Commission's report in 1955 (para. 641). They perhaps might have been abolished when provisions were enacted in 1956, also on the recommendation of the Royal Commission, for exemption from UK tax of the undistributed earnings of British-resident Overseas Trade Corporations. However, when this exemption was ended with the introduction of corporation tax in 1965, powers to control the manipulation of company residence became even more necessary. The original provisions remained, virtually unchanged, in the anti-avoidance armoury until 1988, and an important vestige remains still.[4]

Through the control of transfers abroad of company residence, the Revenue attempted to regulate the use by British-owned business of foreign-resident affiliated companies. The 1951 provisions required a company to obtain prior Treasury permission not only to transfer its residence abroad, but also to transfer any part of its trade or business to a non-resident; also, most importantly, permission was needed for a company to cause or permit any

---

[1] This loophole was partly blocked by the Finance Act 1969 s.33.
[2] Finance Act 1981 ss.45–6, now ICTA 1988 ss.739–41.
[3] It applied rather to individuals who wished to be resident in the UK while receiving income from investments in a foreign business: e.g. *Latilla v. IRC* (1943).
[4] ICTA 1970 s.482; what remains is now ICTA 1988 s.765.

non-resident company over which it had control to issue any shares or debentures, or for it to transfer any shares or debentures to a non-resident company. Since 'debenture' has been given a very wide meaning by the courts, encompassing any specific debt acknowledged in written terms, this last requirement was very sweeping, especially when considered in conjunction with the necessary Bank of England approval under the Exchange Control Act 1947. However, these very broad requirements were limited by general exemptions granted by means of General Consents (five in all). The administration of applications for special consent was carried out by a department headed by a Chief Inspector (Company Residence). Applications, except in straightforward cases, were referred to an outside Advisory Panel, sitting in private (although allowing the attendance of the applicant's repesentatives), whose task was to weigh the advantages to the applicant against the prospective loss of revenue and foreign exchange, and to recommend to the Chancellor whether it would be in the national interest for permission to be granted (Simon 1983–, para. D4.119).

These powers were used to try to regulate the form taken by the foreign operations of British-based company groups or TNCs for tax purposes and negotiate an acceptable rate of taxable remittances. Foreign-owned companies were given a general exemption, if set up in the UK after 1951 to carry on business. General exemption was also given for the issuing of shares or debentures by a company formed after 1951 in a Commonwealth country for the purpose of starting and carrying on a new industrial activity there (GC no. 4); as well as for the issue of shares by a non-resident company directly to a UK resident company (GC no. 2). Plainly, the major concern of the Revenue was to control the use of intermediary non-resident companies by British-owned TNCs to avoid UK tax on retained foreign profits. Applications for consent could be granted subject to conditions or undertakings; and it appears that a common condition was to require the repatriation as dividends of a specified proportion of the profits accumulated overseas, such as 50–60 per cent (see Simon 1983–, para. D4, p. 112; Ashton 1981, p. 119). The administrative and discretionary nature of the procedure gave some scope for flexibility in negotiating the proportion of overseas earnings to be taxable as investment income in the UK according to the circumstances of the company; although equally, the secrecy of the procedure may create doubts as to whether that discretion was exercised either properly or fairly.

In addition, the requirement of consent was designed to prevent the use of transfers of residence purely for tax avoidance. However, the technicalities of the section offered significant avoidance opportunities: for example an 'off-the-shelf' company which had no trade or business could start a UK branch and later become non-resident without consent; and such a company could also be set up by a directly-owned non-resident subsidiary of a UK company (Dewhurst 1984). The criminal sanctions imposed by the section required a significant element of intent, so that company directors or their advisors could not be convicted without evidence to disprove that they honestly believed no breach was involved. In fact, it seems that no prosecution was brought in the near four decades of life of the provision (Dewhurst 1984); and the Keith Committee expressed surprise at finding a criminal sanction for a tax avoidance provision, and recommended that the penalty be made a civil one (UK, Keith Committee 1983, p. 158).

The requirement of consent for transfer of residence abroad was therefore essentially an administrative measure which provided the basis for private, indeed secretive, negotiations between the Revenue and British-owned TNCs. This apparently satisfied both parties. Whether for this or other reasons, the issues of national or international equity of British taxation of the returns from foreign direct investment did not arouse any significant public or political debate for more than two decades after 1955.

1.d Modification of the Residence Rule

A variety of factors from the mid-1970s led to measures intended to bring British principles of taxation of foreign investment earnings more into line with those of other countries. These factors included the re-emergence of the international debate on taxation of international investments, focusing on matters such as the transfer pricing policies of TNCs (to be dealt with in Chapter 8).

A major factor was the policy of liberalization of controls on international capital movements initiated by the Thatcher government's ending of all exchange controls in 1979. The abolition of exchange controls could not easily be reconciled with the continuation of the requirement of prior permission for the transfer of company residence abroad, and for raising capital through a foreign subsidiary. At the same time, membership of the European Community made it legally doubtful whether the Treasury could withhold permission for a company to transfer its residence to another EC country, even if this might be a step towards transfer outside the EC altogether.[1] To block this potential loophole, the Finance Act of 1988 (s.105) provided that a company transferring its residence abroad without Treasury consent should be deemed to have disposed of and immediately reacquired its assets, thus rendering it liable to capital gains tax. With this provision in place, the requirement of consent for transfer of company residence abroad could be ended. However, permission is still needed for the issue of shares or debentures by a foreign subsidiary which, as we have seen, is used to control the use of foreign subsidiary structures by British TNCs.[2]

[1] Although the Revenue eventually won the test case in 1988 in the European Court of Justice: *Reg. v. H.M. Treasury & CIR ex parte Daily Mail and General Trust PLC* (1988).
[2] This remains in ICTA 1988 s.765. However, the liberalization of capital movements within the EC means that transactions falling within EEC Directive 88/361 are exempt from this requirement, although they must be reported to the Inland Revenue within six months: Movement of Capital (Required Information) Regulations, S.I. 1990/671.

More broadly, however, it was clear that the residence rule was increasingly hard to operate, especially without the discretion given by the procedure for requesting consent. The traditional test of residence, based on the place where the effective investment decisions were taken, was limited to 'oversight and passive management'. This was generally taken to mean the place where the key board meetings were held: it could therefore be easy to manipulate, since on this narrow view it would be easy to exclude foreign subsidiaries from the British tax net merely by holding board meetings abroad. More seriously, this could also be done for companies with substantial business in the UK, thus avoiding liability to advance corporation tax, as well as corporation tax on overseas business and investment income and realized capital gains. Conversely, board meetings could be held in the UK if it was advantageous to import the losses of unprofitable subsidiaries via the group relief provisions.

On the other hand, a broad approach to residence, which would not rely only on the location of board meetings, might not be upheld in the courts. Although it would suit the Revenue to include in principle all unremitted income of foreign subsidiaries, this could widen the net too far, including, for example, foreign subsidiaries of non-British TNCs with regional headquarters in the UK. The position was further complicated by tax treaties, since in cases where a company is treated as resident by both treaty partners, the treaty definition of residence applies. However, Britain's treaties have followed two models: the older model in the postwar treaties defined residence as where the business was 'managed and controlled', while later treaties used the test in the OECD model, of 'place of effective management'. Although for a while the UK view was that the two terms were synonymous, the Revenue subsequently accepted that in the light of interpretations in other OECD countries, a difference existed.[1]

Proposals were therefore put forward in 1981 to enact for the first time into British law a statutory definition of company residence. The preferred criterion of the Revenue was the place where 'the management of the company's business as a whole was conducted'. Not surprisingly, this was attacked as too vague and broad. A Working Party set up by the Institute for Fiscal Studies found some of the criticisms of the proposals unfounded, and supported the arguments for a statutory definition; but it found that the best approach was to build upon the principle of 'effective management' (Institute for Fiscal Studies 1982). As a stopgap, the Revenue issued a Statement of Practice (6/83) to define the test. It also pressed ahead with its related proposals to tax the deemed foreign income of Controlled Foreign Corporations (CFCs), enacted in 1984, thus bringing the UK broadly into line with most other OECD countries (see Chapter 7 below). Finally, the Finance Act 1988 provided (s.66) that any company incorporated in the UK is deemed resident there for tax purposes.[2]

---

[1] See OECD 1977, p. 57; Statement of Practice 6/83, reissued as amended as SP 1/90.
[2] With transitional provisions for a company which became non-resident with Treasury consent, Schedule 7.

However, the test of central management and control has not yet been replaced, and could therefore still be applied to British-controlled companies registered abroad. This residual provision (modified for treaty countries, as mentioned above), as well as the requirement of approval for the issue of debentures by foreign subsidiaries, remain as a fall-back for the Revenue: thus, for example, foreign companies formed for investment in UK real estate may be treated as UK resident (Yerbury 1991, p. 33). However, taxation of unrepatriated earnings from foreign investment is now dealt with primarily under the CFC provisions (discussed in Chapter 7 below).

2. The US: Tax Deferral on Retained Foreign Earnings

The US income tax applied from the start both to all income from US sources, and also to the income of US citizens from all sources worldwide. Although this was based on a similar principle of tax equity to Britain's, it differed significantly, in that taxation of income from all sources applied not to residents but to US citizens. This became crucial in the case of companies, since it covered only corporations formed under US law; companies formed under foreign law were not regarded as subject to US tax, even if they were wholly-owned subsidiaries of US corporations.

2.a Individuals

Taxation of US citizens on their worldwide income has given the American authorities a wide personal jurisdiction over US citizens wherever they may be resident. Thus, the IRS officers who are attached to many American embassies are importantly concerned with the tax returns of US citizens living abroad (as well as dealing administratively with the allocation of income of international businesses: see Chapter 10 below). Liability to US tax on worldwide income is mitigated by allowing foreign tax paid to be credited, so that in effect US citizens and corporations are expected to pay the higher of the US or the foreign tax. In addition, individuals resident abroad have since 1926 been allowed an exemption for foreign earned income.[1]

2.b Foreign Corporations

US taxation of a corporation formed abroad is limited to income 'effectively connected with the conduct of a trade or business within the United States'. Although a foreign corporation doing business in the US through a branch is subject to corporate tax on its 'effectively connected' income, distributions of

[1] Apart from an experiment between 1978 and 1981 with a system of deductions for foreign 'excess living costs', this has continued in force, with various complex safeguards (Owens 1980, Pt. III s.vi).

after-tax profits to its head office are normally free of tax. However, if the 'effectively connected' income averages more than 50 per cent over a three-year period, the US has applied a withholding tax on the dividends paid by the company, and on interest paid to its foreign creditors, either at the full 30 per cent rate or at the treaty rate applicable under any treaty with the company's country of residence. But it is easy to see that this tax is difficult to collect, since it is levied on payments made abroad by foreign companies. Thus, it became convenient in some circumstances for foreign companies to do business in the US through a branch, especially if the company could be formed in a convenient jurisdiction. This led to the provisions in the 1986 Tax Reform Act for the US branch tax, a withholding tax on the 'dividend equivalent amount' of after-tax profits of a US branch of a foreign company. Since this was specific to foreign companies it could be said to conflict with the non-discrimination provisions of tax treaties, so this 'treaty override' entailed negotiation of specific protocols with US treaty partners (see Chapter 11 below).

Since foreign corporations are not subject to US tax on their foreign income, wealthy Americans appreciated, from an early date, that they could limit US taxation on their foreign investment income if their foreign assets could be transferred to companies formed abroad. Legislation against such 'foreign personal holding companies' was enacted in 1934, to apply the highest rate of US tax of 70 per cent on undistributed passive investment income of a foreign corporation qualifying as the personal holding company of a US citizen. In 1937, new provisions taxed the US shareholder in a foreign personal holding company directly on the undistributed income. To justify these measures, evidence was given by the Treasury to a joint Congressional committee on Tax Evasion and Avoidance, set up at the request of President Roosevelt, which showed a growth in holding companies set up by Americans in the Bahamas (64 companies set up in 1935–6), Panama, Newfoundland and other low-tax jurisdictions.

2.c US Corporations: Foreign Branches and Subsidiaries

The exclusion from US taxation of subsidiaries formed abroad, combined with the foreign tax credit, offered US corporations some choice in the forms through which their foreign business could take place. A foreign branch is not treated as a separate entity for tax purposes; its income therefore forms part of the taxable income of the US corporation and it may claim the same allowances and deductions. This made foreign branch operations useful for a period in extractive industries, especially oil, to take advantage of the generous percentage depletion allowances permitted under US law.

The foreign branch may credit its allowable foreign income taxes directly against the US taxes due from the corporation as a whole. A major problem has been to decide when a foreign tax is an 'income tax' allowable for credit. This can lead to complex interactions and negotiations, as shown in the international political and economic manoeuvres in the postwar period when oil-producing countries moved from a royalty to a profits-tax system (discussed in Chapter 2, section 1.b above). Even greater complexities arose in the 1970s and 1980s under some of the production-sharing arrangements for oil then introduced, in deciding which of the producer country levies should be regarded as deductible costs and which as income taxes eligible for credit (Gifford & Owens 1982, III, pp. 37–41). Numerous other types of tax levied, especially by developing countries, on foreign-owned companies have also raised this problem. In economic terms, it is difficult to establish any adequate rationale for distinguishing between foreign sales taxes or royalties, which at most may be allowable as an expense in computing profit, and taxes on profits which can be credited dollar for dollar against US taxes due (Surrey 1956, pp. 819–25; Tillinghast 1979, pp. 264–70).

For most purposes, US corporations have organized foreign business through subsidiaries formed abroad, since companies formed abroad are not liable to US taxes at all on business profits earned abroad. The rule that taxes apply to the entire income of US citizens and entities formed under US law, which was apparently enacted from basic principle or political instinct in 1913, became an increasingly important policy decision as US foreign investment grew (Surrey 1956, p. 827). Dividends remitted to the US parent are subject to US taxes, but the parent may credit against them the foreign income tax paid on the underlying income, i.e. the proportion of foreign income taxes paid which the dividend represents of the total profits before tax. Thus, earnings retained abroad in a foreign subsidiary are not liable to US tax, until repatriated as dividends: in that sense, the US tax is 'deferred'. These tax considerations have helped to encourage the characteristic form of US foreign investment: direct investment by US corporations through a network of foreign subsidiaries.

The foreign subsidiary has been preferred even over tax privileged status offered for certain types of corporation. In particular, the status of a Western Hemisphere Trade Corporation, enacted in 1942, gave an entitlement to a lower corporation tax rate of 38 per cent for a US corporation doing 95 per cent of its business outside the US, in the western hemisphere. This had a curious history. The intention was to exempt from wartime excess profits taxes and surtax US firms operating abroad, on the grounds that these high taxes were aimed at domestic industries profiteering from wartime conditions. Also, complaints had been made about the high US wartime tax rates by several US corporations with operations in Bolivia, Argentina and Central America. It was apparently not realized that the formula used in drafting, referring to income derived from the active conduct of a trade or business outside the US, could also include export sales (Surrey 1956, pp. 832–8). In practice, the WHTC form was less advantageous for foreign operations than using a foreign subsidiary (UN 1953, p. 24); on the other hand, it became widely used for US exports. By 1954, a Congressional Committee proposing other revisions in the tax code stated that 'although the [WHTC] . . . provisions produce some anomalous results, it has retained the provisions in order to avoid any disturbances at the present time to established channels of trade' (Surrey 1956, p. 838).

Indeed, in 1971, President Nixon and the Congress went further, and granted special tax status for US corporations qualifying as Domestic International Sales Corporations (DISCs). This allowed deferral of US taxes for approximately half of the profits channelled to a DISC. However, specially generous interaffiliate pricing rules allowed transfer of a higher proportion of profits from manufacturing to export, so that in practice a high proportion of the income of corporations with exports was freed from US tax, even if returned for reinvestment in the USA. Critics pointed out that the DISC was merely a tax subsidy to some of the largest US corporations, having at best a small incremental effect on exports. The subsidy was costing $1.5 billion by 1976, and only 59 corporations accounted for over half of the total net income of all DISCs (Surrey, Pechman & McDaniel, in Gifford & Owens 1982, III, p. 516). The DISC provisions were condemned as an export subsidy by the GATT, but not repealed until the Tax Reform Act of 1984. Their replacement, the Foreign Sales Corporation (FSC) allowed exemption from tax at corporate level for foreign trade income derived from foreign presence and economic activity of a foreign subsidiary organized in a qualifying foreign country. Qualifying countries were essentially those willing to provide information exchange satisfactory to the IRS.[1]

2.d The Deferral Debate

After 1945, the US definitively surpassed Britain as the dominant world economic power and source of international investment. This led to considerable debate in the postwar period about the US role and responsibility in stimulating foreign investment for economic development. Hence, pressures were renewed for the liberalization of the foreign tax credit, or the extension of total exemption to foreign earned income. From 1945 to 1959 a series of official and semi-official reports and studies examined the foreign investment policy question, including the issue of tax incentives or disincentives. Although some, such as the IDAB's Rockefeller Report 'Partners in Progress' of 1951, went as far as to recommend US tax exemption of income from new foreign investments, other studies did not favour exemption. Proposals for exemption put to Congress by the Eisenhower administration in various forms in 1953–4 were rejected.

On close examination, little grounds could be found in principle or policy for tax incentives for US foreign investment. Data collected by the Department of Commerce and the IRS showed that US foreign investment was highly

[1] The UK has not qualified for FSC status: see Chapter 10 below.

concentrated in relatively few firms. Of the more than half a million corporations making tax returns in 1949, only 2,200 or 0.4 per cent had foreign investments; 442 of these controlled 93 per cent of the foreign investment stock, 62 of which had 71 per cent, and the ten biggest had 40 per cent (Barlow & Wender 1955, ch. 2). Encouragement of foreign investment by a wider group of the largest corporations did not require exemption from US tax liability. The corporations' cautious attitude to foreign investment risk meant that, especially in manufacturing, foreign subsidiaries were set up with a low initial dollar investment from the parent: working capital was provided often from loans raised abroad, while further expansion was financed from retained earnings. Equity capital was often minimal, and the book value of foreign subsidiaries low in comparison to their earnings, since parent companies preferred to make loans, because interest payments were tax-deductible at source, and less likely to be blocked by foreign exchange controls.

Given this pattern, US tax liability was no real disincentive to the expansion of foreign direct investment. Tax deferral already gave a great incentive, not only to retain earnings in the firm rather than distribute them as dividends, but also to reinvest foreign earnings abroad, since reinvestment in the US (e.g. by loans to the parent) might make the returns on such investment liable to US taxes. Thus, deferral of US taxation on retained foreign earnings reinforced the separation practised by US corporations between the financing of domestic and foreign investment.

Paradoxically, a move towards full exemption of foreign business income would have had most effect on profits from exports rather than investment. The profit on foreign sales of goods manufactured in the US is divided between manufacturing and export profits, and export profits are considered to be earned abroad if title to the goods passes abroad. The inclusion of such export profits earned abroad in an exemption for foreign earnings would have greatly added to the revenue loss from exemption to the Treasury, as well as creating difficulties of definition, and posing starkly the problem of inequity to the US taxpayer. This created a significant obstacle to the exemption proposals (see Barlow & Wender 1955, ch. 16).

The debate therefore became centred on the extent to which tax deferral itself was legitimate or desirable. Proposals to give explicit legitimacy to deferral were made by academic analysts (Barlow & Wender 1955, ch. 19), as well as in a bill placed before Congress by Congressman Boggs (HR 5 of 1959–60: see Tax Institute 1960). These provided for a special class of 'foreign business corporations', whose income from foreign operations would not be subject to US tax until distributed in the US.

The extension of explicit legitimacy for tax deferral would have extended its scope both explicitly and, more importantly, by implication. For example, an anti-avoidance provision enacted in 1932 required IRS approval for a transfer of assets to a foreign corporation if such transfer might be considered part of a plan for avoidance of US taxes. The Treasury and the Revenue had taken the position that setting up foreign business in such a way as to enable tax deferral could come within this section; but the legitimation of deferral via a 'foreign business corporation' would prevent such administrative rulings endangering the systematization of tax deferral.[1]

The delimitation of the extent to which deferral was legitimate had become important, since the rapid growth of US foreign direct investment during the 1950s had led to the development of foreign subsidiary structures to exploit the interaction of the US and foreign tax systems, as well as the tax treaty network. Essentially, these structures enabled earnings from foreign operating subsidiaries to be routed, often through a conduit company, to a holding company in a low-tax jurisdiction, or tax haven. This minimized tax at source on foreign retained earnings, and made them available for investment in any new foreign operation (see Chapter 6 below). It also enabled the marshalling and averaging of the tax credits available from the various operating subsidiaries, to be applied to that part of the profits eventually repatriated. Since the tax-paid credit could be carried forward, it acted as an interest-free loan to the US corporation. A few corporations had already established such holding companies before the war, but during the 1950s such structures became more widespread. Their relative merits were openly canvassed, often in terms not only of the technicalities involved, but also the degree of respectability.[2]

In 1961 the Kennedy administration recommended the ending of the deferral privilege. Opponents of his proposal pointed out that it would make the US unique in taxing profits earned by US-owned companies abroad as they accrued.[3] However, the deferral debate was given a new impetus by a growing concern about the US balance of payments, which had registered significant deficits in 1958 and 1959.

2.e The Controlled Foreign Corporation and Subpart F

The Kennedy administration's proposal faced a barrage of criticism in Congress, and business lobbyists and academics testified to its committees that foreign direct investment was an important factor in US exports, and that to end deferral would harm the competitive position of American TNCs in world markets (US Congress 1962). Rather than end deferral, Congress concentrated on what was considered to be its abuse, the accumulation of earnings in tax-haven holding companies. It therefore enacted Subpart F of

[1] The non-recognition of asset transfer provision became s.367 of the Tax Code; after 1976, in place of advanced decision that the IRS was satisfied that there was no tax avoidance purpose, Congress substituted a clearance procedure appealable to the Tax Court.
[2] See Tax Institute 1960, pp. 211–12, for a discussion comparing a Bahamas–Curacao (now Netherlands Antilles) set-up as more respectable than one based on Panama or Liberia.
[3] The UK, the other major capital exporting country, had asserted a broad jurisdiction to tax any company controlled from the UK; as discussed in the previous section, it had from 1956 provided for exemption for the undistributed earnings of British-resident Overseas Trade Corporations, but this was ended in 1965.

the tax code, which taxes US shareholders of foreign companies falling within the definition of a Controlled Foreign Corporation (CFC), on their share of certain categories of undistributed profits.

A CFC is defined as a foreign corporation over 50 per cent of whose voting power is owned by US persons, each of whom owns directly or indirectly over 10 per cent. The income which is taxed on a current basis includes: (i) 'foreign base company sales income', essentially income from sales or purchases of personal property (goods), either to or from a related person (affiliate), if neither the manufacture nor the use of the goods take place in the country of incorporation of the CFC; (ii) 'foreign base company service income' derived from rendering commercial, industrial or other services to a related person outside the country of incorporation of the CFC; (iii) 'foreign personal holding company income', which is passive investment income such as interest, dividends or royalties; but such income is excluded if produced from the conduct of a business, for example interest or fees from the conduct of a banking or financial business, or royalties earned from the conduct of a business by the CFC. Included, however, is income from the insurance of US risks.

Originally, the 1962 Act excluded from Subpart F any income derived from international shipping and aircraft operations; and it also provided that some otherwise taxable Subpart F income could remain sheltered if reinvested in a developing country. In 1975, the developing country reinvestment provision was repealed, while the exclusion of shipping and aircraft profits was limited to those reinvested in such activities. Furthermore, in 1976, Congress added two new categories of income taxable as Subpart F income: income earned from participating or co-operating in an international boycott (aimed at US corporations complying with the Arab boycott of Israel), and foreign bribe payments.

The Subpart F provisions had a dual effect. On the one hand, they targeted some types of retained foreign earnings of American TNCs which should be immediately liable to US tax. Under the US approach, any CFC whose income is 70 per cent or more of the type defined by Subpart F is taxed on its entire income as if it were a US corporation. If its Subpart F income is 10 per cent or less, it could be disregarded. Where the Subpart F income is between 10 per cent and 70 per cent, only the actual Subpart F income is taxed on a current basis.

At the same time, however, the enactment of Subpart F *legitimized tax deferral* on retained earnings which did not fall within or could be channelled outside those categories. Nevertheless, this was an implicit legitimacy, not an explicit one, as would have resulted from the proposals for deferral for US Foreign Business Corporations. Subpart F did not end the deferral debate, but had the effect of converting subsequent proposals to end deferral into bargaining over modifications of Subpart F, between the various factions and pressure groups active in the legislative process.

As we have seen, initially in the 1950s, in the context of a generous approach to the US supply of investment for a capital-hungry world, the pressure was to exempt foreign income. This resulted instead in focusing attention on the non-taxation of US-owned foreign subsidiaries, especially with the emergence of US balance of payments problems in the late 1950s. By the 1970s, the dominant concern became the 'export' of US jobs by transfer of investments abroad, and the growing competitiveness of Japan and of export-oriented newly industrializing countries. Nevertheless, the principle of deferral, subject to Subpart F taxation of CFC income, survived. A Congressional vote to end deferral in 1975 resulted only in the modifications to Subpart F of 1975 and 1976 already mentioned. President Carter in 1978 expressed an intention to end deferral, but it came to nothing. Although the Treasury department again included ending deferral among the radical proposals for tax reform initially proposed under the Reagan presidency, it did not survive into the sweeping Tax Reform Act of 1986.

This outcome resulted not simply from powerful lobbying, but from the recognition that the internationalization of capital had made it impossible for the US to achieve efficient taxation of TNCs unilaterally. Taxation of international capital was no longer merely a matter of equal treatment of inward or outward investment, but now concerned the cost of capital to and the allocation of investment by internationally-integrated firms. US-based TNCs could structure and time the flows of payments from foreign affiliates so as to minimize their net (post-foreign tax credit) US tax liability on overseas earnings, although this entailed significant administrative costs.[1] More importantly, economic analysis of the effects on investment decisions and the cost of capital provided strong support for the ending of deferral (Alworth 1988). Nevertheless, it was difficult to end deferral unilaterally and without related measures. Studies published by the Treasury argued that the ending of deferral could not be considered in isolation from the lower effective tax rates on domestic corporate investment, resulting from the various preferential provisions that narrowed the tax base. The ending of these preferences, coupled with the reduction of the nominal tax rate, provided an opportunity to increase effective US taxation of foreign investment. Nevertheless, to do so by unilaterally imposing US taxation on the consolidated worldwide operations of US TNCs, it was argued, would create an incentive for foreign countries to increase taxation of US-controlled subsidiaries, and hence reduce the US

---

[1] A detailed study of the repatriation of dividends, as well as interest, rent and royalties, in 1984 from over 12,000 US CFCs to 453 parents showed that 84 per cent of CFCs paid no dividends at all, and concluded that 'many firms are able to take advantage of intrafirm financial transactions and their abilities to time repatriations in order to reduce their US tax liabilities. That is, the combination of the credit system and deferral can diminish substantially the revenue raised by the United States from the taxation of overseas operations of US multinationals. . . . The present US system of taxing multinationals' income may be raising little US tax revenue, while stimulating a host of tax-motivated financial transactions' (Hines & Hubbard 1989, pp. 33–4).

revenue gains (due to the foreign tax credit). At the same time, higher US taxes on CFCs would, it was predicted, lead to a cumulative loss of competitiveness which also would produce a net reduction rather than an increase in US tax revenue from foreign income (Hufbauer & Foster 1977). Hence, it was not surprising that the Reagan tax reforms did not involve ending deferral; but they did include a number of measures drawing back foreign income into the US tax net, such as the 'super-royalty', and generally increasing pressure for adequate policing of intra-firm payment flows (see Chapters 3, section 2 above and 8 below). However, the necessity for a more international approach to the whole question had by now become increasingly obvious.

3. The Limits of Unilateral Measures

As we have seen in this chapter, Britain and the US, historically the main capital-exporting countries, both responded early, but by unilateral measures, to the emergence of international avoidance; the form which it took and the issues raised for each country reflected its approach to the taxation of foreign earnings. Not only were the initial responses unilateral, they were frequently insular. While both countries accepted that the growth of foreign investment should be encouraged, their fiscal and balance of payments concerns, as well as pressures for equity for domestic taxpayers, required efforts to try to claw back into taxation at least a proportion of foreign retained earnings. Both countries tried to ensure this by strengthening their rules on taxation of residents. In addition, the US IRS began to tighten up its administration of the arm's length rule regulating transfer prices (to be considered in Chapter 8 below).

What was largely lacking in the long US debate about taxation of foreign investment was an international perspective. Yet deferral, especially its exploitation through subsidiary holding companies, base companies, and tax havens, had starkly revealed the limitations of the international tax system. As we have seen, the international arrangements had given the source country the right to tax business profits, and the country of residence of the investor jurisdiction over investment profits. At the same time, the allocation of income between related enterprises of the same transnational firm was to be done as far as possible on the basis of the Arm's Length principle rather than a worldwide unitary approach based on formula apportionment. International tax avoidance had exploited this approach. TNCs could earn high profits from foreign operations based on technology and know-how which had already covered their costs in the home market. Yet they could also minimize liability to tax at source on those foreign profits by allocating the maximum deductible expenses to their foreign operating subsidiaries. At the same time, by maximizing the profits accumulated in or through low-tax country subsidiaries, they minimized their exposure to taxation in their own home countries of residence.

However, these unilateral approaches offered only partial solutions. They were largely ineffective in stemming the growth of international avoidance, which developed illegal evasion in its wake. They were also inadequate as solutions to the national problems. These limitations were inherent in what were essentially unilateral national approaches to the international problem of allocation of jurisdiction to tax internationally-integrated business. Both countries attempted to exert control over the deployment of foreign subsidiaries so as to include in taxation by the country of ultimate residence a proportion of foreign retained earnings. Yet there were no adequate criteria to justify the allocation of such income in this way.

For example, the inclusion in US taxation under Subpart F of foreign base company sales and service income assumed that such income concealed investment income, which the US was entitled to tax, rather than business profits, which would be properly attributable to the foreign source country. It might be acceptable to apply US taxes to foreign sales of goods manufactured in the US channelled via a Bermuda sales subsidiary; but where the German manufacturing subsidiary of a US TNC channels its sales via a Swiss sales affiliate, is it not German rather than US taxes which are being avoided? Furthermore, what if the US corporation is itself owned by a British or French company? (see Tillinghast 1979, pp. 262–3; Park 1978, pp. 1631–3).

The unilateralism of Subpart F also limited its efficacy from the US point of view, since it excluded profits earned from the active conduct of a foreign trade or business. This exclusion was necessary once it was decided to target only the abuse of deferral, yet it left a wide scope for continued exploitation. Manufacturing companies could engage in partial assembly or processing in the CFC's base country: this led to litigation (*Dave Fischbein Manufacturing Co. v. Commissioner*, 1972) and to detailed IRS rules. Much more seriously, financial and banking business could be channelled through such a foreign base country in ways which made it very hard to establish that no active business was really being carried on there (see Chapter 7 below).

For these reasons, neither the breadth of the UK residence rule, nor the early enactment of the US rules against CFCs, succeeded in stemming international tax avoidance. The use or abuse of tax havens continued to grow rapidly in the 1960s and 1970s, and became of increasing concern to the Revenue authorities of several of the main capitalist countries. Evidence on the extent of use of tax havens was gathered for the US Treasury and the IRS and published in a report by Richard A. Gordon, the Special Counsel for International Taxation, in 1981 (the Gordon Report, US Treasury 1981). More discreetly, the British Inland Revenue did not publish the special survey it carried out at about the same time, but some of the information gathered was given in its 1982 proposals on Taxation of International Business, which led to the enactment of UK provisions on CFCs (see Chapter 7 below).

By this time, a number of countries had enacted some provisions against foreign tax havens or tax shelters. In particular, Germany had also found its rules on company residence ineffective against tax-haven intermediary companies (see Chapter 1, section 2.a above), and after attempting to deal with the problem administratively, enacted a comprehensive Foreign Tax Law of 1972, modelled on the US Subpart F provisions (see Chapter 7, section 1.a below). As the enforcement of these measures came under consideration, the limits of unilateralism became apparent, and the OECD Fiscal Committee undertook a series of studies on international avoidance and tax havens. This brought the governmental authorities into conflict with representatives of international business, who resented the increasing slur of illegitimacy being cast on international arrangements which they had developed in order to overcome what they regarded as the inadequacies of the international tax system. Yet government and business representatives were still equally reluctant to open the Pandora's box which both considered had been firmly padlocked by the historically-developed principles of international taxation. Nevertheless, these principles – separate accounting and arm's length pricing – were proving increasingly inadequate to resolve the questions of international equity raised by the allocation of the tax base of internationally-operating business.

6
Tax Havens and International Finance

The problem of international taxation has always been closely linked to that of international capital flows. We have seen that it was in order to encourage inward investment that capital importing countries were persuaded to tax at source only the business profits attributable to a Permanent Establishment or subsidiary, and to restrict their withholding taxes on outgoing dividends, interest, royalties and fees. The capital exporting countries, principally the US and UK, while claiming jurisdiction to tax repatriated income, developed the use of the foreign tax credit to ensure tax equity between home and overseas investment returns. This assumed that international investment flows were essentially portfolio investments: that the investor chose whether to place money at home or abroad, and brought home the returns on foreign investment. Some countries went further and exempted residents from tax on income from foreign investments. While this in principle conceded the primary right to tax to the source country, tax concessions to attract investment and low or no withholding taxes on investment returns could significantly reduce the tax rate on foreign investments if channelled through convenient intermediaries.

As foreign investment became dominated by the direct investment of TNCs, the distinction between business profits taxable at source and investment profits taxable in the home country of the investor became harder to maintain. Policy-makers became increasingly aware that a TNC carrying on business through a foreign subsidiary, especially one that is 100 per cent owned, has considerable flexibility in determining its capital and cost structures (Lessard 1979). This gives it considerable control over the proportion of earnings declared as business profits of the subsidiary, from which dividends may be paid to the group, and the amounts payable to related companies as interest on loans, or fees or royalties for services. Since such payments may normally be deducted from gross profits before taxation, the TNC could minimize business profits taxable at source.

At the same time, by choosing the forms and routes taken by payments from foreign operating subsidiaries, TNCs could also minimize their liability to taxes on investment returns. In particular, as profits from foreign investment grew, TNCs increasingly took advantage of tax deferral, by accumulating investment returns offshore ready for reinvestment rather than returning them to be taxed at home. Hence, the foreign tax credit became ineffective as a means of ensuring equity between returns on domestic and foreign investment. The argument for complete exemption of foreign profits from taxation by the country of residence of the owner was lost in the 1950s, in the US and the UK, but became a debate about the permissible limits of deferral of taxation on earnings retained abroad (discussed in the previous chapter). Deferral of home country taxes on earnings retained abroad encouraged TNCs to expand their foreign operations primarily through retained earnings and foreign borrowings. This pattern became tolerated, although the authorities in the countries of origin of the TNCs attempted to impose limits on the proportion of global profits which could be spirited into low-tax limbo.

An important factor in the ability of TNCs to minimize their international tax exposure has been the role they have played in international capital markets. In turn, however, the growth of these markets has stimulated others to seek the advantages of low-tax borrowing and lending. The TNCs, as international businesses, could with some degree of legitimacy organize their activities to reduce their average overall tax rate, by basing some (especially financial) operations in low-tax countries. This was not so for nationally-based businesses or investors. Yet, as international capital markets have grown, facilities have been developed which make it increasingly tempting for a much wider range of those with access to or need for capital to overstep the often hazy boundary between avoidance and evasion. This temptation is all the greater since the facilities and procedures involved have been pioneered for the benefit of the world's major corporations and banks, and under the protection of the respectability they afford.

Already in the 1950s, companies expanding abroad had begun to set up intermediary subsidiary companies as conduits or bases for financing foreign operations (Gibbons 1956). As was mentioned in the previous chapter, tax avoidance by the use of convenient foreign jurisdictions had already emerged in the 1920s and 1930s, mainly to shelter private family fortunes. Thus, for Britain the Channel Islands and the Isle of Man, for the US the Bahamas and Panama, and in continental Europe the statelets of Liechtenstein and Monaco as well as the banking centres Switzerland and Luxembourg, had already become tax shelters. New locations began to offer themselves in the postwar period: the Netherlands Antilles, which had the advantage of tax treaties extended to it by its colonial mother-country Holland, announced low tax rates specifically designed to attract holding companies in January 1953.[1]

[1] See notes in the Bulletin for International Fiscal Documentation 1953, pp. 7 and 21.

Other former colonial dependencies tried to follow suit, as their rulers saw that attracting financial business could prove lucrative; although the prospects of offshore status providing a basis for economic development were more remote, since brass-plate companies are not great generators of employment. A link with a large metropolitan country provided a good basis, not only because of the possible applicability of tax treaties, but also other advantages to attract investors – a familiar language and legal system, and association with a hard currency.

The use of intermediary companies located in such tax havens was initially somewhat discreet, due to the uncertainties in the laws of home countries such as Britain and the US on taxation of foreign retained earnings, and the discretionary nature of much of its administration (discussed in the previous chapter). Subsequently, international tax avoidance arrangements became much more generalized, publicly available and discussed, due to a great extent to the emergence of the offshore financial centre.

1. Offshore Finance

In the 1960s the tax haven became overshadowed by the related but much more important phenomenon: the 'offshore' financial centre. This came about as the taxation inducements for TNCs to finance expansion abroad from foreign retained earnings were reinforced by balance of payments controls designed to limit the outflow of investment capital. The combination of these factors led to the emergence of international financial markets, in which offshore centres have played an important role. The emergence of a 'deregulated' arena of international finance was tolerated and in many respects encouraged by the main monetary authorities. However, they have subsequently experienced difficulties in taming the monster they helped to create, as unsupervised financial centres facilitated concealment both of outright criminal activities, as well as of a wide variety of semi-respectable transactions. The subsequent relaxation of protectionist controls in the major centres has attracted some business back to them; while the development of international co-ordination of supervision by central banks and other regulators has established a degree of security for investors in offshore markets. However, the continued availability of locations offering the combination of secrecy and low or no taxes still poses problems for regulators.

1.a The Growth of Deregulated Offshore Sectors

In the broadest sense, an 'offshore' financial transaction consists of a deposit, loan, or other monetary obligation denominated in a currency other than that of the country in which the transaction takes place. Thus, a Eurodollar deposit is a deposit denominated in dollars, made outside the United States. A very discreet Eurodollar market had originated in the late 1940s with dollar deposits by the Chinese and Soviet communist governments in European banks. It began to grow a decade later, after the introduction of currency convertibility in many countries meant that first non-residents and then residents were permitted to hold foreign currencies.

However, the major growth in international financial markets was in the 1960s, and resulted from the increasing restrictions on access to domestic capital markets for foreign investment. The major impetus to the growth of the Eurodollar market was given by President Kennedy's Interest Equalization Tax (IET) of 1963, designed to stop the outflow of American portfolio investments due to higher European interest rates. Then, measures were taken by surplus countries to limit the inflow of capital from lenders. Thus, West Germany imposed a 25 per cent 'coupon' or withholding tax in 1965 on lending by non-residents to residents: this, combined with bank controls on the volume of Deutschmark (DM) bond issues, created an indirectly regulated market for DM bonds, both foreign bonds (issued by German banks for foreign borrowers) and Eurobonds (strictly speaking, those where foreign banks are included in the issuing syndicates).[1] Further, the US supplemented the IET from 1965 by the Voluntary Foreign Credit Restraint Program, and later the Foreign Direct Investment Program which was compulsory from 1968: these were aimed at ensuring that large US corporations with foreign activities maintained positive payments balances. The result was that US TNCs largely borrowed abroad to finance their foreign expansion, especially in Europe.

At the same time, changes in banking conditions encouraged US banks to set up branches abroad to compete for funds. US interest rates had long been kept low by domestic controls – the Federal Reserve's Regulation Q prohibited interest payments on US domestic deposits of less than 30 days and imposed limitations on interest rates for longer deposits. As interest rates rose after 1956, corporate treasurers sought a return from short-term balances, and the banks invented Certificates of Deposit (CDs), but these also became subject to controls in the credit crisis of 1966. This encouraged banks to bid abroad for funds, and corporations with internationally flexible funds to keep them out of the US, often in foreign branches of US banks. The effect of these measures was:

> [L]ittle else than to remove a large part of the American money and capital markets offshore where, having discovered many advantages (like lower taxes and freedom from officially imposed reserve requirements), much of the markets have remained [Mendlesohn 1980, p. 34].

---

[1] These arrangements changed with the West German liberalization after 1984, when the 25 per cent coupon was replaced by a 10 per cent withholding tax on all DM instruments; effective from 1 January 1988, this, however, lasted only a few months – see Chapter 3, section 2 above.

Hence, international financial markets grew as a result of restrictions by the US on borrowing in US markets by foreigners or by US TNCs for foreign investment. At the same time, converse restrictions by other countries, such as Germany and Switzerland, had the same effect, by limiting access by non-residents to their domestic capital markets. These restrictions were accompanied by an increasing willingness of national authorities to allow first non-residents, and then residents (sometimes subject to limitations), both to hold foreign currencies, and then to lend such foreign currency savings to 'foreign' borrowers.

The emergence of international financial markets could hardly be said to have been planned or even deliberate. Nevertheless, the toleration or acceptance by the main capitalist countries of 'offshore' financial markets served a function during the transitional period of rapid growth of inter-national business in the 1960s and 1970s. Offshore finance grew in the shadow of related domestic monetary and financial systems, and enabled monetary and banking controls to be operated with a differentiation between purely domestic and internationally-oriented financial transactions. The offshore markets could not be directly regulated, but the authorities controlling the major international currencies had powers of indirect control. However, these have been limited by the extent of the offshore centres' needs for external support, and the interest of the onshore centres in maintaining semi-autonomous and partially-controlled centres in preference to the growth of centres which might be harder to control. For these reasons, monetary authorities not only accepted limits on their control over the rapidly growing offshore financial markets, but usually agreed that their financial oversight should not be co-ordinated with the Revenue's attempts to control tax avoidance (see section 1.c below).

In any event, the mushrooming growth of offshore centres could not easily be controlled. In the 1950s only seven US banks had foreign branches, and they registered a slow growth, from 105 foreign branches in 1954 to 124 by 1960. By 1965 the total had jumped to 180; a decade later there were 732 foreign branches owned by as many as 125 US parent banks, and a large proportion of these were in 'offshore' centres. London was the first growth point for Eurodollar and international financial activities, and by 1965 accounted for 10 per cent of US overseas bank branches and over 45 per cent of their deposits. Thereafter, however, the most spectacular growth took place in centres which were more definitely 'offshore', especially small jurisdictions in the Caribbean, such as the Bahamas, the Netherlands Antilles, the Cayman Islands and Panama. These were countries whose proximity to the US made them convenient intermediaries for the massive investment flows into and out of the US, and which offered tax as well as banking and monetary advantages.

Studies done for the US Treasury's Gordon Report show that international bank deposits in tax haven areas were $10.6 billion in 1968, half held by non-banks and half by banks; a decade later non-bank international deposits in tax havens had grown nearly seventeen times, while bank-owned international

Table 1 *International Bank Deposits in Tax Havens 1968–78 (US$ billions)*

Year	Held by non-banks W. Hem.	Total	Both banks & non-banks W. Hem.	Total
1968	0.3	5.3	1.5	10.6
1969	1.3	8.4	4.8	17.8
1970	2.0	11.8	7.5	26.1
1971	2.7	16.1	15.4	40.2
1972	3.9	17.6	23.5	60.2
1973	5.6	23.5	35.4	88.3
1974	10.6	36.7	55.2	130.6
1975	13.9	41.8	77.9	170.5
1976	18.7	50.7	112.0	234.1
1977	28.2	70.5	131.8	296.9
1978	31.5	88.7	159.5	384.9

International bank deposits are foreign and local currency deposits owned by non-residents and foreign currency deposits owned by residents.

Tax havens covered are: *Western Hemisphere*: Bahamas, Bermuda, Caribbean residual, Cayman Islands, Neths. Antilles, Panama; *Others*: Bahrain, Hong Kong, Luxembourg, Singapore and Switzerland.

Source: IRS study published in Gordon report, US Treasury 1981, p. 41.

deposits had grown thirty times (see Table 1). The Gordon Report studies also showed that offshore centres, defined as those with deposit banks' foreign assets exceeding a proportion necessary for trade (based on an average of other countries), were generally located in jurisdictions which could be defined as tax havens.[1]

International financial markets consist of overlapping and interrelated layers. All the main national capital markets also have an international sector. As a minimum, they permit non-residents (and usually residents also) to hold foreign-currency deposits, known as Eurocurrency deposits, which usually take the form of Certificates of Deposit with a minimum denomination of $0.5 million. Although some countries have imposed restrictions on the issue of foreign bonds in domestic markets, most allow considerable freedom for both residents and non-residents to invest in foreign-dominated (Eurodollar) bonds.[2] Central to the attractiveness of international capital markets is their

[1] They included Belgium/Luxembourg, whose financial statistics are combined, and the UK, which includes the Channel Islands and the Isle of Man (as well as the extensive international sector of the City of London which in some senses is 'offshore'); and France, whose excess foreign assets are explicable by other reasons: US Tax Haven Study Group 1981, p. 6.
[2] To avoid the requirements for registration with the Securities and Exchange Commission, most Eurocommercial paper is certified as not offered or sold in the US or to US nationals; however, the latter are permitted to participate in the secondary market, i.e. purchase bonds even if they have not been registered with the SEC, provided they have been 'seasoned' usually for at least 90 days: see Bowe 1988, p. 116. Widespread holdings by US institutions of Netherlands Antilles bonds created difficulties when the US denounced its tax treaty with the Netherlands Antilles: see Chapter 7, section 3(ii) below.

freedom from regulation, including taxation. Since such lending is effectively free both from tax and from bank reserve requirements, it is at the same time cheap for borrowers (thus reducing their capital costs), as well as producing a higher real rate of return for lenders. Complete freedom from regulation only exists in the fully-fledged offshore centres, which are both tax and banking havens. It is the existence of these havens that ensures the continuation of a deregulated environment, and induces the authorities of the central capitalist countries to maintain or even expand their own semi-regulated 'offshore' sectors.

1.b The Inducements and Temptations of Offshore Finance

The main tax advantage of international financial instruments (mainly Eurocurrency bonds) is that there is no withholding tax levied at source on interest or principal repayments. This is an important requirement, despite the fact that much investment in these markets is by state or official institutions which are in any case not liable to tax, and by TNCs, which can credit such source taxes against their home country tax liability. The main motive for basing the issue of international securities in jurisdictions which do not levy withholding taxes is to increase their attractiveness for private investors. Although these investors are liable to tax on such earnings, and should in principle declare this income for taxation in their countries of residence, it is commonly accepted that in very many cases this does not occur. Thus tax avoidance colludes with outright evasion. Evasion is further facilitated by the issuing of most Eurobonds in bearer form; and by the fact that a large volume of the investments in these markets is handled by major Swiss banks. They offer private clients managed external discretionary accounts: investments are made by the bank, which can claim reduction or exemption from withholding tax, but the risk is borne by the client. It is commonly estimated that half of all Eurobonds are held by individuals, whose motives are a combination of the security offered by a hard-currency investment in a high-rated borrower, as well as tax evasion (Mendelsohn 1980, p. 174; Gallant 1988, pp. 48–9).

An offshore centre must have a degree of physical convenience and adequate communications facilities; given these, any jurisdiction can try to encourage offshore banking business. This is done by separating bank activities aimed at non-residents from those of residents, and granting the offshore banking sector a special regime. This means a combination of the following:

(i) no reserve requirements in respect of banking activities for non-residents;
(ii) exemption of the banks within this sector, as well as non-residents (both individuals and foreign-owned companies), from any foreign exchange controls which might apply to local bank business and residents;
(iii) legal protection of the confidentiality of bank records, and of information about

clients' affairs held by lawyers and accountants, preferably by criminal penalties;

(iv) other company and commercial law provisions giving wider protection of the secrecy of financial and commercial transactions: for example, permitting company shares to be unregistered or issued to bearer, and imposing minimal annual reporting obligations on companies (usually under special provisions for 'international business companies').

Depending on the extent of such facilities, there are degrees to which a centre may be considered 'offshore'. For example, most countries' laws require banking confidentiality; but in certain circumstances this may be overridden by law. The extent of banking secrecy in law depends on the degree of protection given to confidentiality in relation to inquiries by enforcement agencies relating to suspected criminal offences, or regulatory evasion or avoidance, especially by foreign agencies in relation to infringements of tax or financial market regulations (see Chapter 10, section 2 below).

The term 'offshore financial centre' may also be limited to centres in which such banking business may be, and almost entirely is, carried out purely on paper by 'shell' branches or subsidiaries. For example, the Cayman Islands in 1989 was the world's fifth largest banking centre (after the UK, Japan, the US and France) in terms of deposits, but the vast bulk of these were nominal paper (or rather electrically recorded) transactions: of over 500 banks licensed by Cayman only 70 had any physical presence on the islands other than a name-plate, and only eight actually carried out local business.[1] The business supposedly carried out by a Cayman Islands branch or subsidiary of a New York bank is entirely handled by the New York staff, and merely notionally 'booked' to the Cayman Islands entity. In contrast, London is a major financial centre where those banks engaged primarily or entirely in offshore business offer a range of services, primarily handled by staff physically located there, although these services are usually 'wholesale' financial services rather than actual 'retail' commercial banking. In either case, however, the link of an offshore transaction with the particular jurisdiction is optional: offshore markets 'need have no fixed geographic location, and today could almost be viewed as existing in the telecommunications infrastructure' (US Congress 1987, p. 87).

Many countries have offered such facilities to attract international financial business, although not all have succeeded in doing so. The need for a basic infrastructure, including sufficient legal and financial specialists, and a sufficient level of business to justify it, can make it hard for a new centre to become established. However, fashions can change, especially if political developments create uncertainty in an established competitor: for example,

[1] UK Gallagher Report 1990, p. 90; *Financial Times* 25 October 1990. The Cayman Islands was developed as a tax haven from 1965, apparently with the approval of the British colonial authorities: see UK Foreign and Commonwealth Office 1972, p. 15, and Chapter 10, section 2.a(ii) below.

the crisis created in Panama in 1988 by the US indictment of General Noriega for narcotics offences, and the subsequent US sanctions against and then invasion of Panama, caused an outflow to Caribbean havens.[1] Essentially, the major variations that determine the characteristics of individual havens depend on the willingness of its authorities to allow the use of their protected offshore sector to avoid or evade other countries' laws, including their taxes.

Public discussion of these matters shows a certain ambivalence. On the one hand, international banking facilities and capital markets are frequently spoken and written of with great approbation, as providing an efficient source of low-cost capital for international investment. On the other hand, there has been increasing concern that these facilities have facilitated tax evasion and capital flight, especially from countries such as many in Latin America with severe foreign debt problems (Lessard & Williamson 1987). Furthermore, as these facilities became well established and easily accessible, their use became increasingly widespread, not only for tax evasion and avoidance, but also to conceal sources of funds (money laundering) from a wide range of illegal or semi-legal activities, and facilitate their investment.[2]

1.c Respectability and Supervision

We have seen that many countries can be said to have a deregulated or offshore sector, but there are important differences in degree, depending on the extent and type of regulation of financial transactions and institutions. Indeed, the separation between international and domestic capital markets has become greatly reduced with the ending or subversion of many restrictions on access to domestic capital markets during the 1980s. At the same time, some of the major countries with important financial markets have themselves permitted or encouraged the growth of a semi-offshore sector to attract funds from non-residents. In particular, the UK has continued to foster the City of London as a financial centre, and added to its attractiveness for Eurocurrency bond flotations by allowing payments of interest on quoted Eurodollar bonds to non-residents free of tax since 1984; the US introduced a similar exemption at the same time, as part of a concerted effort to reduce the attractiveness of the less regulated locations further offshore (see Chapter 7, section 3.b below). Further, there are other developed countries where the financial and banking sector is more entrenched culturally and more important to the national economy: in Europe, Switzerland and Luxembourg; while in the Far East, Hong Kong has perhaps moved into this category. The remaining centres are

[1] Registration of International Business Companies in the British Virgin Islands jumped to 2,000 in 1987, and 7,000 in 1988, making a total of 13,000 by the end of 1988; while in Montserrat it was the growth of offshore banks that was phenomenal, numbering over 340 by the end of 1988 (UK Gallagher Report 1990, pp. 49, 101), but leading to a major fraud investigation and withdrawal of most of these licences: see below.
[2] See US President's Commission 1984; US Congress 1983a, 1983b; Blum 1984; Naylor 1987; Walter 1985.

small countries with a narrow economic base, where the financial sector has grown, often under the initial impetus of a small group of professionals and interested parties, but with the necessary encouragement from the government, aiming to provide a primary source of national income. All these centres offer different attractions and advantages, but also different degrees of security and of respectability.

(i) Problems of Supervision

The main global financial centres are concerned to ensure (a) that financial markets are supervised sufficiently to prevent fraud and bankruptcy which might trigger a broader financial crisis; and (b) that unsupervised financial institutions and facilities are not used as a cloak for crime, or more generally for regulatory avoidance. Initial steps were taken through the Basle Committee of Bank Supervisors, which established a 'concordat' in 1975 (revised in 1983) allocating responsibility for, and co-ordinating through information exchange, the prudential supervision of international banks; the Committee later made an important step towards harmonization of bank regulation through its agreement on capital adequacy standards. This minimal co-ordination still required pressure on the mushrooming offshore centres to improve their standards of supervision. Some part has been played by semi-formal international groupings, notably the Offshore Group of Banking Supervisors and the Commission of Latin American and Caribbean Banking Supervisory and Inspection Organizations. At the same time, the US authorities in particular have maintained various types of pressure, both directly on the offshore centres themselves, and indirectly by urging countries such as the UK and the Netherlands to use their influence in their dependencies and former dependent territories to improve local supervision and develop international liaison. In relation to the concealment of crime, increasing concern during the 1980s culminated in an agreement at the economic summit of the Group of Seven in 1989 to combat money-laundering by establishing obligations on banks to vet their clients, and strengthen international procedures for criminal judicial assistance (see Chapter 10, section 2.a below, and Intriago 1991).

The development of such supervision has, however, been an uneven and patchy process, for a variety of reasons. Financiers and professionals active in the provision of these services are, to different degrees, resistant to close supervision or regulation; and they can form powerful lobbies, not only in countries such as Switzerland and the UK where the financial sector is economically important, but even in countries such as the US and Germany where the authorities have been more conscious of the problems of evasion and avoidance. Also, although these states have considerable power in relation to the tiny countries which offer the most deregulated services, this power is limited by two main factors. First, although the presence of a deregulated financial services sector based largely on brass-plate companies would not be an adequate basis for the development of any more than the smallest economy, it can make a major difference to a small statelet with a few thousand inhabitants,[1] especially to the professionals and state officials who primarily benefit. Second, the regulatory authorities face the constant problem that if they tighten control too much over those jurisdictions where they have the most power, transactions and institutions will remove themselves to locations which would be harder to control.

Indeed, as we have seen, offshore centres have typically emerged in countries which have been or remain dependent territories, not sovereign states in international law. Their colonial past created some of the advantages they offer, such as the language, legal system and a hard currency link. These connections also give the mother country authorities some powers of control: those countries that are still dependencies are usually internally self-governing, but the metropolitan power normally appoints a governor and conducts their foreign affairs. The frequently byzantine and personalized politics of such statelets and the fragility of their economies gives the powerful states some influence, especially through the giving or withholding of aid, or even direct political or military intervention, as occurred in Panama. However, it may be hard to use these powers to interfere with domestic policies, and the cost of aid may be a burden which the metropolis wishes to reduce, so the development of a financial sector may be hard to resist. The difficulties that the US has faced in inducing changes to the business and banking system in Panama, even after the invasion which ousted General Noriega, demonstrate the extent of the problem.[2]

The overarching issue in the process of development of international financial regulation has been respectability. Success in establishing and maintaining an international financial centre depends on mastering the contradictory process of offering investors both concealment and security. Offshore centres have therefore been vulnerable to pressures to regulate the use of their offshore facilities, in order to control badly-run or fraudulent institutions, and prevent use of their facilities for concealment of criminal-source funds. However, the volume of such funds, especially from narcotics, is such that the weak governmental structures in some havens may be undermined by corruption, sometimes at the highest levels. Attempts by a US Senate subcommittee to quantify the volume of illicit funds using offshore facilities produced estimates ranging between $9 and $50 billion, showing that, while many billions are involved, precise estimation is impossible (US Congress 1983a, pp. 15–16). At the same time, the growth of a largely unregulated international financial sector has facilitated activities ranging

---

[1] For figures on the contributions of this sector to the economies of British dependencies in the Caribbean, see UK Gallagher Report 1990.
[2] The US and Panama were reported to be on the verge of signing a treaty, after a year of heated argument, which would give US investigators access to bank account information on

from clear fraud to behaviour which is more borderline, and in relation to which it has been difficult to clarify national standards, let alone develop an international consensus. A notable example of the latter has been insider dealing in stocks and shares, which became an increasing problem in the 1980s with the growing sophistication and internationalization of securities markets, leading most major countries to tighten up their laws, as well as attempt to develop co-operative enforcement arrangements, especially with banking centres such as Switzerland. At the same time, the availability of sophisticated channels for secret financial transfers and asset ownership has attracted a variety of social institutions for purposes sometimes combining high finance and politics. Thus, the Vatican Bank (the IOR – Instituto per le Opere di Religione) became involved first with Michele Sindona and then Roberto Calvi in a network of offshore deals which resulted in the Ambrosiano Bank collapse (Naylor 1987); Britain's National Union of Mineworkers attempted to keep its money from sequestration by taking it offshore during the major miners' strike (see *Clarke v. Heathfield*, 1985); and US President Reagan's National Security Office transferred funds through Swiss banks from the illegal sale of arms to Iran for the use of the Nicaraguan *contras*.

The US authorities have been particularly active, perhaps because they have felt most threatened by the growth of evasion and avoidance, in trying to expose and prosecute the involvement of financial institutions in illegal or semi-legal activities. Thus, they have acted against the facilitation of transfer of illicit funds abroad, involving violations of the US Bank Secrecy Act, by the Chemical Bank (US President's Commission 1984, p. 48) and the Bank of Boston (US Senate 1985a); and the involvement of brokers E. F. Hutton with Mafia leaders and money laundering (Walter 1985, pp. 132–3).

Such incidents culminated in criminal charges against two subsidiaries of the Luxembourg-registered Bank of Credit and Commerce International (BCCI) and prosecution of several of its senior officials, for complicity in the use of the bank in Miami, Panama and London by alleged launderers of narcotics money, including General Noriega of Panama; the bank pleaded guilty in January 1990 resulting in forfeiture of $15m. These prosecutions contributed to major losses for 1989, leading to negotiations for the extensive restructuring of the bank, under the eyes of a committee of central bank regulators from Luxembourg, the UK and other countries which had been monitoring its affairs since 1987.[1] However, this was pre-empted by an unprecedented action taken to put the bank into liquidation, taken jointly by the Bank of England and other bank regulators in July 1991; although, significantly, the consultations prior to this action excluded the Central Bank

customers suspected of money-laundering; although the US had pressed for tax evasion to be included, this had been resisted by Panamanian banks: *Financial Times*, 5 April 1991.
[1] See in particular the press reports by Mike Weiss 'The Florida Sting' in the *Sunday Correspondent*, 8 July 1990, and by Richard Donkin and Victor Mallett, 'Chastened Retreat to Mid-East Roots', in the *Financial Times*, 11 June 1990.

of the United Arab Emirates and the majority owners of the bank, the Government and the Sheikh of Abu Dhabi. This drastic action was explained to have been necessary due to evidence finally uncovered by the auditors that the bank had systematically allowed or encouraged its facilities to be used for widespread frauds, many of them involving tax evasion of an international character.

(ii) Dilemmas of UK Policy Towards Havens

The British authorities in particular have had an ambiguous and difficult relationship with the various dependencies which have offered themselves as financial centres. The Isle of Man and the Channel Islands, as has already been mentioned (Chapter 5 above), emerged early as tax havens for British citizens wishing to avoid UK-resident status. After 1960, their development as offshore financial centres, to be joined by Gibraltar, took place within the Sterling Area and under Bank of England supervision. Even after the end of exchange control in 1979, the islands continued to co-operate with the Bank of England on a voluntary basis. The interest of both sides was to foster a specific role for the British offshore centres, in conjunction with the development of the City of London as a financial entrepôt. It was nevertheless understood that any oversight carried out by the Bank of England was not co-ordinated with the Inland Revenue, despite the evident advantage that the Revenue would gain from information pooling (Johns 1983, p. 98). Most of the agreements between 1947 and 1952 between the UK and virtually all British dependencies, including the 1952 arrangements with Jersey, Guernsey and the Isle of Man, remain in force and provide for information exchange between the tax authorities. However, they extend only to information which each authority collects for its own tax purposes (see Chapter 10 below), which would not apply to non-residents at whom offshore facilities are aimed. Hence, the Revenue is only able to obtain very limited information relevant to UK tax evasion through formal legal channels, even from British banks with branches in the islands.[1]

The rapid growth and increasing use made of offshore financial institutions subject to minimal supervision has inevitably led to difficulties. The collapse of the Savings and Investment Bank in the Isle of Man in 1982 led to a tightening up of banking supervision there, under a Bank of England official seconded to the island; but the lack of co-ordination with other British authorities was revealed by the Barlow Clowes collapse in 1988: although Mr Peter Clowes was refused permission to buy two banks in the Isle of Man, Barlow Clowes International established a base in Gibraltar and his operations were relicensed by the Department of Industry in the UK shortly before he absconded, leaving behind evidence of fraud and another clutch of disappointed investors (UK Parliamentary Commissioner 1989). Following the

---

[1] *R. v. Grossman* (1981), which involved cheques deposited in the Savings and Investment Bank before its collapse, and cleared through an account the S.I.B. maintained with Barclays Bank: see Chapter 10, section 2.a(i) below.

Barlow Clowes affair, the British government commissioned a report into the financial sectors of its remaining Caribbean dependencies (UK Gallagher Report 1990). Apparently independently of this inquiry, the discovery of irregularities in Montserrat led to the setting up of a Task Force including detectives from the Fraud Squad of Scotland Yard, co-operating with US law enforcement agencies. One bank appeared to have been defrauding small investors in the US; while much of the growth of B-class banks seemed to have been due to the active promotion of Montserrat bank licences in the US, with the collaboration of professionals and officials in Montserrat, and administrative laxity in relation to the granting of bank licences and continued supervision. These investigations led to the reduction of banking licences from over 340 in 1989 to fewer than 100 a year later (UK Gallagher Report 1990, pp. 105–7). Changes were made to the island's constitution, to remove responsibility for the offshore banking sector from the locally elected administration to the British-appointed Governor, although another provision giving the Governor overriding powers to enact legislation was withdrawn after threats of secession.[1]

British government policy appears to have accepted or even encouraged the development of offshore financial business in such territories, and to aim at improving supervision of the financial sector so as to provide security for investors and to avoid gross scandals (UK Gallagher Report 1990). The existence of such centres with links to sterling and the UK is regarded as helpful to London's own position as a financial centre; while stringent supervision of centres with which the Bank of England and the Department of Trade and Industry have established a *modus vivendi* might drive business further offshore to centres which would be harder to supervise. The British authorities can offer the inducement of designated status under the UK financial services legislation to territories willing to strengthen supervision of their financial sector; but this would be negated by any moves to reduce the tax advantages of such centres. Although many of these territories are still British dependencies in international law, they are internally self-governing, and even the power to conduct their external affairs which is nominally retained by the British government cannot effectively be exercised without consultation.[2]

[1] *Financial Times*, 7 Dec. 1989; 5 Jan. 1990, 3 March 1990. See the Montserrat Constitution Order, S.I. 2401/1989.

[2] The remaining British territories in the Caribbean are Anguilla, Bermuda, British Virgin Islands, Cayman Islands, Montserrat and the Turks and Caicos Islands. The Cayman and Turks and Caicos Islands were ruled as part of Jamaica, from 1863 and 1873 respectively, until 1959. The Federation of the West Indies, established in 1957, had a high degree of self-government, including delegated authority from the UK, over its own external affairs. Following its dissolution in 1962, the main islands became independent (Barbados in 1966, Jamaica in 1962, and Trinidad and Tobago in 1962); other Caribbean territories (Antigua, Dominica, Grenada, St Lucia, St Vincent and St Christopher-Nevis-Anguilla) were given the status of Associated States under the West Indies Act 1967, with the UK agreeing to consultation in the exercise of its reserved powers over external affairs and defence (see Report of the Windward Islands Constitutional Conference 1966, CMND 3021); all these became independent by 1981, except for Anguilla which, following its secession from St Christopher-Nevis, again became a dependency. Other dependencies in the region also became independent: the Bahamas in 1973 and Belize in 1981.

Thus, although the UK may have formal power to take measures to end the attractiveness of some of these centres for tax avoidance, for example by signing tax information exchange treaties[1] on behalf of dependencies, this would be regarded as a blow to their offshore financial business which could undermine the economic viability of many of the island statelets and create political instability. It remains to be seen, however, whether the attempt to separate 'respectable' from criminal financial transactions can be successful. The temptations offered by enormous movements of funds shrouded in secrecy are great and almost inevitably engender corruption, while there are few general economic benefits for the majority of the population.

Thus, British government efforts have concentrated on improving supervision and attempting to curb the use of offshore financial facilities for criminal purposes (see Chapter 10, section 2.a below). Paradoxically, by reducing the possibility of fraud and improving security, these measures have facilitated the use of offshore centres for tax evasion and avoidance, which is increasingly their main *raison d'être*. The occasional collapse of an offshore financial intermediary might indeed be the best deterrent to tax evasion, although it also hurts other investors. The provisions introduced to improve supervision, which include some co-operation with the international supervisory authorities, have only been acceptable provided they clearly exclude the investigation of tax avoidance and evasion.

The continued and even growing use of these facilities in increasingly sophisticated but relatively legitimate ways, not only by TNCs but many businesses and individuals, has exacerbated the problems of tax authorities in allocating the profits of international business. Offshore centres have increasingly offered not only the possibility of formation of intermediary 'letter-box' companies, but of offshore financial subsidiaries, or subsidiaries providing services such as insurance, purchasing or marketing, or licensing of intellectual property rights and know-how, which could be said to be more than merely nominal activities. The proliferation of such devices made it increasingly difficult for national tax authorities to assert jurisdiction over a fair proportion of the internationally-generated profits, especially on the basis of unilateral enforcement and the arm's length approach. Both the use of tax havens for international avoidance and the question of transfer pricing increasingly became matters of public concern, frequently associated in the public mind with the less salubrious scandals hitting the headlines.

2. Tax Havens

International tax avoidance is made possible by the existence of different national approaches to equity in the taxation of international activities, and

[1] Discussed in more detail in Chapter 10.

the absence of any comprehensive international approach to equity. Therefore, the broadest definition of a tax haven would include any country whose tax laws interact with those of another so as to make it possible to produce a reduction of tax liability in that other country. By such a definition virtually any country might be a 'haven' in relation to another. Tax havens are therefore more narrowly defined as countries which offer themselves or are generally recognized as havens: this is referred to in the Gordon Report as the 'reputation' test (US Treasury 1981, p. 14). The OECD report on tax havens refers to the 'classical tax havens' – jurisdictions making themselves available for avoidance of tax which would otherwise be payable in relatively high tax countries, usually by attracting income from activities carried on outside the tax haven (OECD 1987a–I, para. 10). The attitude of these reports is to stigmatize the havens: the Gordon Report's reputation test is referred to as the 'smell' test, and the implication clearly is that it is a bad smell.

One reply to this view is that the problem lies not with the havens' (lack of) regulations, but in the inappropriate, ineffective or unfair character of the regulations being avoided. Thus, Luigi Einaudi, who was one of the economists who authored the report for the League of Nations in 1923, later argued that haven states put pressure on others whose taxes are badly administered to make their taxation fairer (Einaudi 1928, pp. 35–6). It is claimed that in many or even most cases, the laws of the haven jurisdictions were not, historically, deliberately designed with international avoidance in mind: this has been argued, for example, on behalf of the Channel Islands (Powell, in Avery Jones 1974). This argument is somewhat disinguous, since undoubtedly such countries were sought out and their laws and facilities exploited; and they have generally been maintained, advertised, and further developed for these purposes, often with the active encouragement of their state authorities. There are examples of the laws of such offshore havens being deliberately amended or adapted to attain or retain their attractiveness as offshore centres. A well-known case is the trusts law of the Cayman Islands, which was deliberately adapted in 1967, reputedly on the advice of a British tax lawyer, to deprive trust beneficiaries of any legal right of action, thus avoiding the 'power to enjoy' provisions in the British anti-avoidance measures on family trusts (discussed in Chapter 5, section 1 above); in riposte, the British statute was further amended in 1969 to provide that a beneficiary had a 'power to enjoy' even if it is not legally enforceable. On a later occasion, the Cayman Islands reinforced its bank secrecy law by enacting a Confidential Relationships (Preservation) law in 1976, as a response to the Miami District court decision in *US v. Field*.[1] International tax consultants frequently offer, or are called upon, for help in designing the legal and administrative facilities of small offshore jurisdictions, with the intention of attracting the registration of intermediary companies and the development of offshore financial business

---

[1] *In re Grand Jury Proceedings, US v. Field* (1976), see Chapter 10, section 2.a(ii) below.

(see e.g. US Senate 1983, p. 11). Although havens have also been under pressure to tighten up the supervision of their financial sectors, as we have seen in the previous section, this has made them more attractive for tax avoidance and even evasion.

Defenders of havens must therefore fall back on legitimizing havens by attacking the tax system which gives rise to them. Sometimes this is done straightforwardly from the perspective that all taxes are evil and therefore any means of legitimate avoidance (but not illegal evasion, of course) is justified (e.g. Langer 1988, ch. 1). The very term 'haven' is used to conjure positive images, sometimes reinforced by equivalents in other languages – 'oasis' in German, 'paradise' in French (Chambost 1989). The more sophisticated versions of this approach point to the defects in the arrangements for prevention of international double taxation, which from the point of view of international capital were remedied by the devices they pioneered.

This view accurately indicates that it is not merely a matter of delinquent countries, but a systemic problem. As advisors and consultants discovered and exploited havens, state authorities had to decide how far they were willing to tolerate or encourage their use. The arguments for tax exemption of foreign-source income were widely accepted; and even those countries, such as the US and UK, which maintained the residence principle (based on capital-export equity), still allowed tax deferral, within limits which they tried to control. Countries such as Switzerland or Luxembourg were willing to tolerate or even encourage the use of their laws, exempting foreign-source income and imposing no withholding tax on interest or other payment outflows. This was hardly surprising in view of the social and economic importance of banking and finance to these countries. Others, such as the Netherlands and later Singapore, fostered provisions which would encourage the setting up of holding companies to act as regional headquarters of TNCs in their jurisdictions. However, when the increased sophistication of international avoidance began seriously to undermine tax equity and effectiveness, they later came under pressure at least to limit the more blatant devices.

At the same time, centres with fewer advantages to attract financial business have usually been more willing to overstep the bounds of propriety; in some cases, they had already been used as convenient financial bolt-holes for those involved in organized crime: e.g. Panama and the Cayman Islands. The more 'respectable' havens such as Switzerland have justified themselves, both by the arguments about international equity, and by pointing to the more extensive facilities offered by the 'delinquents' whose activities would be harder to control. Delinquent countries may be less vulnerable to pressures from the powerful than might be supposed: they may have few other opportunities for economic development, and their state structures may be too weak to resist corruption (US Congress 1983a, Pt. V, pp. 45–95).

Such havens can be used both for deliberate evasion and for grey-area avoidance, of taxes and other laws. The key to international avoidance of business taxes is the use of intermediary companies and trusts. This enables a taxpayer to channel revenue through an intermediary legal person and thereby save tax by changing the character of the eventual benefit to the ultimate recipient. The location of the intermediary in a specially-chosen jurisdiction lends an entirely new dimension to a chain of transactions: like two closely-marked football players passing the ball to a third one who is unmarked, it can create major gaps in the defences of tax authorities. For an individual (or family), or a firm doing business nationally, the use of such a foreign intermediary company is more likely to be classified as either tax evasion or illegitimate avoidance.

The TNC, however, since it is composed of an international network of affiliated companies, can much more legitimately structure this network so as to optimize the total tax burden of the TNC as a whole. It is important to stress that these strategies optimize, rather than minimize, tax liability, since it is necessary to bear in mind the transaction costs of complex arrangements, including their effect on the firm's management structure, as well as the risk that they might be disallowed or fail in some way. Nevertheless, international competition puts considerable pressure on a firm to establish a corporate structure which minimizes its tax exposure.

Avoidance strategies can be broken down into four main options:

(a) channelling interaffiliate payments, especially dividends, through intermediary companies formed in countries chosen so as to minimize both withholding taxes at source and taxation of foreign income payments on receipt;

(b) reducing the taxable business profits of an operating affiliate, by allocating costs such as R & D and interest on loans, or charges for services such as insurance or distribution, to be paid to an intermediary in a low-tax country;

(c) raising finance from international capital markets on beneficial terms due to the tax avoidance and evasion possibilities; or

(d) marshalling the TNC's income from all sources to make best use of tax benefits, e.g. by ensuring sufficient income is derived from sources outside its country of residence to make full use of available tax credits.

Tax havens may be divided into three broad categories. The main havens are those which have no or very low taxes on all corporate or business income. An intermediary 'base' company formed in such a jurisdiction can freely engage in a variety of activities on behalf of the corporate group; the charges it makes to affiliates can reduce their tax liability, while accruing profits to itself which are subject only to the haven's no/low-tax regime. However, most such countries (Base-Havens) do not benefit from participation in the network of double tax treaties, so they are not suitable locations for holding companies, since payments of dividends, interest and fees to them would be subject to high withholding taxes at source.[1] The second category of haven consists of

[1] Some low-tax havens did, for historical reasons, benefit from some treaties, but these have in most cases been cancelled or modified in recent years: see Chapter 7 below.

countries with conventional tax systems and benefiting from double tax treaties, but which levy no or little tax on receipts of foreign-source or passive investment income (Treaty-Havens). Since they often have some double tax treaties, they can be used as locations for intermediary 'conduit' companies, which receive dividends and other payments, having paid low withholding taxes at source due to the treaty, and usually transmitting them on to a base company in a low-tax country. Finally, a large number of countries offer particular tax incentives or benefits, which may sometimes be exploited for a particular international tax advantage.

Attempts have been made by some countries to define and even list tax havens, usually in anti-haven legislation, if it is based on a locational rather than a transactional approach (see Chapter 7 below). Thus, the Japanese measures define as a haven a country which levies tax at less than half the Japanese corporate tax rate, and authorize the Ministry of Finance to designate a definitive 'blacklist'. The French law refers to countries with tax rates less than two-thirds that of France, while the German refers to 30 per cent and the UK 50 per cent of their respective company tax rates. The French and German lists are administrative 'grey lists', for guidance and not legally binding; while the UK publishes a 'white list' of exempt countries, with a second, much longer, list of conditionally exempt countries (i.e. the exemption excludes corporations benefiting from specified tax incentives). No official list is published by the US, but several government departments maintain internal lists, including the IRS in its tax audit guidelines (see PSI Staff Study, US Congress 1983a, pp. 10–11; Caccamise 1988, p. 555).

These official lists provide an authoritative guide to tax havens; but they are not entirely reliable, since they are infrequently revised. Also, the designation tends to focus on havens which for geographical or other reasons are favoured by the designating country's residents; and it may be cautious, since official designation of a haven can be a politically delicate act (see Table 2 and Arnold 1985, 1986). These factors account for variations between lists published by each country, as well as differences from lists sometimes compiled by specialists or academics (e.g. Wisselink in Rotterdam IFS 1979; Rappako 1987, pp. 34–5). The various tax planning encyclopaedia prepared by specialist tax advisors, on the other hand, give a comprehensive examination of very many countries according to the particular advantages they offer (Chambost 1989; Diamond & Diamond 1974–; Langer 1988; Saunders 1990–; Spitz 1990–).

3. Intermediary Company Strategies

As already indicated, a single tax haven location is unlikely to possess all the desirable attributes for an intermediary company: it is therefore common for a firm conducting international operations to make use of a network of

Table 2 *Tax Havens*

(1) Countries Taxing All Income at Low Rate

Haven		Listed by		
ANDORRA	Japan	France	Germany	
ANGUILLA	Japan			
BAHAMAS	Japan	France	Germany	USA
BAHRAIN	Japan	France	Germany	USA
BERMUDA	Japan	France	Germany	USA
BRIT CHANNEL IS	Japan	France	Germany	USA
BRIT VIRGIN IS	Japan	France		USA
CAYMAN IS	Japan	France	Germany	USA
DJIBOUTI	Japan			
HONG KONG	Japan	France	Germany	USA
ISLE OF MAN	Japan	France	Germany	USA
LIECHTENSTEIN	Japan	France	Germany	USA
MACAO	Japan			
MALDIVES	Japan			
MONACO	Japan	France	Germany	USA
NAURU	Japan	France		USA
NEW CALEDONIA	Japan			
TURKS & CAICOS IS	Japan	France	Germany	USA
VANUATA/NEW HEBRIDES	Japan	France	Germany	USA

(2) Countries Taxing Foreign Source or Certain Other Income at Low Rate

Haven		Listed by		
ANTIGUA	Japan	France	Germany	USA
ARUBA	Japan	France	Germany	USA
BARBADOS	Japan	France	Germany	USA
COOK IS	Japan			USA
COSTA RICA	Japan	France		USA
CYPRUS	Japan			
GRENADA	Japan	France		USA
GIBRALTAR	Japan	France	Germany	USA
JAMAICA	Japan	France	Germany	
LIBERIA	Japan	France	Germany	USA
LUXEMBOURG	Japan	France	Germany	USA
MALTA	Japan			
MONTSERRAT	Japan	France		
NETHS ANTILLES	Japan	France	Germany	USA
PANAMA	Japan	France	Germany	USA
SEYCHELLES	Japan			
SOLOMON IS	Japan			
ST HELENA	Japan	France	Germany	
ST KITTS/NEVIS	Japan			USA
ST VINCENT	Japan	France	Germany	USA
SWITZERLAND	Japan	France	Germany	USA
URUGUAY	Japan	France	Germany	

(3) Other Countries Sometimes Listed

Haven	Listed by		
ANGOLA	France	Germany	
AUSTRIA			USA
BELIZE			USA
CAMPIONE	France	Germany	
FRENCH POLYNESIA	France		
GILBERT & ELLICE IS	France	Germany	
IRELAND			USA
KIRIBATI	France		
KUWAIT	France		
LEBANON	France		
NETHERLANDS			USA
SINGAPORE			USA
TONGA	France	Germany	
VENEZUELA	France	Germany	

NOTES. The table is based on the designated countries listed under the anti-tax haven legislation of Japan, France and Germany; the UK announcement designates exempt and conditionally exempt countries, so the UK non-exempt countries are not given, although no country listed above is unconditionally exempt under the UK lists (except Venezuela).

The first two parts of the table are based on the Japanese black list, which is legally binding: first published in a Ministry of Finance announcement in 1978 with 27 listed countries, a further 6 were added in 1979: see Arnold 1985, Appendix, and OECD 1987–1, fn 13. An announcement in 1989 added a further 9 countries and withdrew one.

The French list is an administrative list which is not legally binding, but in practice is conclusive: see Arnold 1985, pp. 288, 300, 364.

The German list is also an administrative list, which was published in 1974 and has not been revised: Arnold 1985, p. 300.

The US list is not directly linked with the anti-haven legislation (subpart F), but is given for guidance only, as a non-exhaustive list, in the IRS Manual Handbook: edition of 30/6/89, PART IV – Audit and Investigation, Exhibit 500–8.

intermediary companies.[1] In particular, a classical haven is unlikely to benefit from participation in tax treaties. Intermediary companies may therefore be broadly categorized as either base or conduit companies. The conduit company focuses on minimization of source-country withholding taxes on investment income: so it is located in a country with relevant tax treaties which also exempts or puts a low tax on receipts of passive investment income. Such income can then be transmitted to the base company. The base company is formed in a classical haven, whose low/no-tax regime allows it to carry out a number of functions on behalf of the group, reducing the tax liabilities of affiliates in high-tax countries, while profits channelled to the base company are subject only to the no/low-tax regime.[2]

International tax planning concerns itself largely with devising the best

[1] For a discussion of various intermediary company structures see Saunders 1990–, ch. 2.
[2] The base-conduit distinction is made in the OECD tax havens report, OECD 1987a–I, although sometimes confusingly: e.g. OECD 1987a–I paras 28–9.

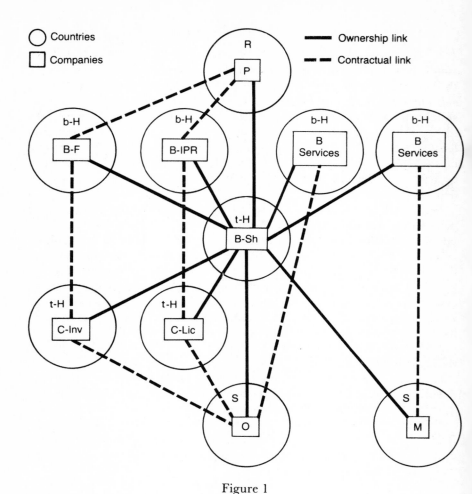

Figure 1

combinations of conduit and base companies, and the most favourable forms, as well as routes, to be taken by investments and the consequent revenue flows (see Figure 1). Broadly, the parent (P) in country of residence (R) sets up tax haven intermediary companies, to carry out tasks of asset administration, and/or the provision of services to the Operating Companies (O), or Marketing/Sales Companies (M); this is normally done through Base (B) and Conduit (C) companies located in appropriate Havens (base-Havens b-H, or treaty-Havens, t-H: see Figure 1). The assets held by the various Base Companies are made available, for suitable charges, either directly or through Conduit companies to the Operating or Marketing companies. The charges should maximize the costs that can be attributable to O and M, and deducted from their gross profits (hence reducing source taxation of business profits), while minimizing withholding taxes levied by S, as well as residence taxation of the investment returns in the hands of C or B.

A base company carrying out asset administration is often called a holding company, since it holds the assets created by the group or transferred to it by the Parent. The main Holding company which owns the shares of the foreign subsidiaries of the group (B-Sh) would be established in a country which has a suitable network of treaties, to minimize withholding taxes at source on the dividends, and which itself exempts receipts of overseas dividend income from local taxation. Other holding companies may be set up to hold different types of assets, in particular B-IPR for intellectual property rights (patents, copyrights, trademarks and other rights); and B-F for financial assets such as debentures or loans.

B-F could be located in a classical haven which exempts all interest payments to non-residents and has no treaties with their countries of residence under which information about the payments could be obtained; or it could be in a state which levies no withholding tax on Eurobond issues, for the more limited purpose of Eurobond flotation. However, loans from B-F to the Operating subsidiaries may have to be channelled through an investment conduit in a treaty-Haven (C-Inv), to ensure deductibility and minimum withholding tax liability for O's interest payments. C-Inv might charge O interest at say 12 per cent (with a low or reduced withholding tax), while paying a rate of 11.5 per cent to B-F, thus paying tax in C only on a fraction of the interest payments (OECD 1987a–III, para. 5). Alternatively, B-F might enter into a 'back-to-back' arrangement with a bank, whereby in return for a deposit by B-F, the bank makes the loan to O, at a slightly higher rate (the 'turn'). Other methods of financing group subsidiaries can also be used, such as the leasing of assets, also utilizing conduits in suitable locations. Similarly, B-IPR will be located in a classical base-Haven, and will normally license rights via a treaty-Haven conduit (C-Lic), to ensure reduced withholding taxes at source.

The other major type of function of a base company is the provision of services: shipping/transportation; marketing/wholesaling; insurance; and central management services, including accounting and legal work. Such Services intermediary companies will also be located in suitable low-tax base-Havens; they will not normally need to benefit from tax treaties, since payments to them will be for services rendered to O and M, but they will have to be carefully structured in relation to R to avoid anti-haven legislation (discussed in Chapter 7).

The rapid growth in the use of such structures from the late 1950s was subsequently documented by various inquiries made by the authorities of TNC home countries. A memorandum by the German and French tax administrations published in 1974[1] cited official figures showing 3,500 companies in Luxembourg benefiting from holding company privileges, while Switzerland had some 10,000 and Liechtenstein 20,000; moreover most of

[1] 14 *European Taxation*, Pt. 4, p. 136.

these were letter-box companies, since they were registered at a handful of addresses (20 for Luxembourg, about 500 for Switzerland, 40 for Liechtenstein), mostly those of banks or lawyers. Similar figures were given in a European Commission document on tax arrangements for holding companies in the EEC.[1]

Over a decade later figures given by the German Finance Ministry in a parliamentary written reply showed a continued growth: in 1986, the estimated numbers of German-owned companies in relevant havens were: Bahamas 221, Channel Islands 101, Isle of Man 14, Cayman Islands 70, Liechtenstein and Switzerland (combined) 12,200, Luxembourg 4,200, Monaco 55,[2] Netherlands Antilles 167, Panama 608 (Deutscher Bundestag 1986, p. 4). These figures were given as part of a lengthy response to 70 questions posed by a group of Opposition members of parliament; the official reply indicated some of the statistical estimation difficulties, as well as the limits of official information due to the confidentiality of negotiations with taxpayers. The British Inland Revenue conducted a survey in 1982 of UK-owned TNCs, and some indications of the results were given: between 130 company groups, some 220 non-resident companies were identified as likely to have the object of reducing UK tax: 35 were captive insurance companies (with total undistributed profits of £108m) and 50 equity holding companies (UK Board of Inland Revenue 1982, pp. 15–16).

The US studies, published in the Gordon Report (US Treasury 1981) and the report on Caribbean Basin tax havens (US Treasury 1984), showed that the numbers of corporations formed in tax havens are highly disproportionate in relation both to the populations and to the economic activities of these countries. It estimated an average of 55.1 corporations per 100,000 population in tax havens, as compared to 1.2 per 100,000 in other countries in 1979; a disparity which had grown when compared to the 1970 figures of 32.9 and 0.9 respectively (US Treasury 1981, p. 34). While the ratio of foreign assets to merchandise exports averaged 1.34 in the world in 1982, the ratio for the Bahamas was estimated at 36.42, Bermuda at 108.33 and Panama 114.3 (US Treasury 1984, also given in OECD 1987a–I, Table 1). Figures in the Gordon Report, reproduced and supplemented in the OECD report, showed direct investment flows and stock in tax haven countries which were both a significant element of the total, and highly disproportionate to the actual economic activity of the havens.

The concern over use of tax havens which emerged first in the 1970s could be said to have been part of the more general political reaction to the rapid growth

---

[1] COM(73) 1008, published in Avery Jones 1974, p. 109.
[2] The use of Monaco as a base-haven was severely restricted by its treaty with France of 18 May 1963, which required Monaco to tax all entities having more than 25 per cent of their turnover outside Monaco; nevertheless, corporations organized elsewhere but administered from Monaco are liable only to a tax on a proportion of office expenses (Langer 1988–, pp. 57–8).

of TNCs during the 1960s. However, the onset of recession and the emergence of neo-liberal governments in key countries (Reagan in the US, Thatcher in the UK, Kohl in Germany, as well as the continuing reign of the LDP in Japan) brought a strong reaction to this political thrust by the end of the 1970s. It is notable that, nevertheless, renewed concern was expressed about havens in the 1980s, in more official and rather sober terms. Some of the causes of this were discussed in Chapter 3 above: even pro-business governments must concern themselves with both tax justice and efficiency if their political and ideological base is populist and neo-liberal.

Tax legitimacy had become increasingly threatened as the use of tax haven devices seemed to have gone far beyond the exploitation of tax deferral by TNCs. The location of service activities and finance in low-tax havens could effectively produce a significant reduction in their overall global tax liability for many companies. Furthermore, this could be done irrespective of any international business in which such a company might or might not be engaged. Thus, a 'captive' insurance company could charge premiums not only for the international business of a TNC, but also for its home business; and such an affiliate could be set up by a company which had no significant international activity. At the same time, concern about tax havens intersected with increasing concern about the use of offshore financial facilities, which also seemed to be spreading far beyond 'respectable' business (as discussed in section 1 above). Thus, US Internal Revenue Commissioner Egger, in testimony to a Congressional Committee, stated that the IRS criminal investigations branch had identified 707 cases between 1977 and 1982 involving foreign countries, totalling over $2.6 billion unreported income, 53 per cent from legal and 47 per cent from illegal sources (US Congress 1983b, p. 266).

Finally, an important feature of the official studies of the 1980s, especially those reported through the OECD, was the attempt to develop a common attitude and approach to combating the tax haven phenomenon. This had become increasingly necessary as the anti-avoidance measures brought in and enforced by various countries began to intersect and affect others.

7
Anti-Haven Measures

In response to the growing use of tax havens and international intermediary companies, tax authorities have activated general anti-avoidance provisions, as well as enacting more specific provisions aimed at international tax shelters. Most countries have some general legal provisions against tax avoidance, whether developed by case-law in the courts or enacted in legislation. Such anti-avoidance rules consist of 'substance over form' provisions, often based on the test of 'business purpose'; or provisions against the 'abuse of law'. However, as the discussion in Chapter 4 has shown, such rules introduce economic, political and moral factors which are weighed, if only implicitly, in determining tax liability. Also, reliance on a general rule entails a wide discretion for the administrative authorities, an uncertain outcome for court cases, and the lack of definite and precise criteria to distinguish valid from invalid avoidance arrangements. For these reasons they are frequently supplemented or replaced by more detailed and specific rules. These can take a variety of forms, ranging from specific provisions in statute or subsidiary legislation, to much more informal administrative guidelines or practices.

General anti-avoidance rules may be relied upon by tax administrators either to disregard an intermediary company as a mere sham or, more often, to rectify for tax purposes the transaction between the intermediary and the taxpayer. Some countries, for example the Netherlands, still prefer to rely on such general principles, supplemented to some extent by rules of guidance or administrative directions. However, due to the strength of the principle of separate legal personality of a company, it is often difficult for an intermediary company to be treated as a mere sham, except in blatant cases. For example, in the US, in a case where the taxpayer, a resident alien, had completely failed to keep books clearly reflecting his income, the Tax Court agreed to disregard foreign corporations set up by him and to treat moneys received by them as received for the taxpayer's use and benefit, which entitled the revenue to compute his income (*Factor v. CIR*, 1960).

More frequently, either judicial or statutory principles may allow the disregard of specific transactions, or the reattribution of payments or income, if an 'artificial' entity has been interposed.[1] Thus, in *Johannson v. US* (1964) the federal courts refused to accept that the Swedish heavyweight boxer Ingemar Johannson was exempt from US taxes on the earnings of his bouts with Floyd Patterson, holding that the Swiss company specially set up to receive those earnings 'had no legitimate business purpose, but was a device used . . . so as to escape taxation by the US', and the company could not be regarded as a bona fide Swiss resident (although accepted as such by the Swiss authorities) so as to benefit from exemption under the US–Swiss treaty. In practice, however, a general substance-over-form or business purpose rule is an uncertain and often inequitable means of regulating professionally developed and properly organized international tax planning.

More commonly, therefore, general anti-avoidance rules of the 'shotgun' type have been supplemented by specific provisions in relation to particular problems, especially the use of artificial intermediary legal persons (trusts or companies), and the treatment of transactions between related companies. The more general anti-avoidance provisions have remained as a threat, and may still be used in some circumstances: for example, to prevent avoidance of source taxation, by disallowing as a deduction, or treating as a 'deemed dividend', payments made to a related company in a low-tax country. However, the use of offshore base companies for avoidance of residence taxation, by taking advantage of tax deferral to accumulate retained earnings, has been countered in most of the developed countries by specific measures deeming the ultimate shareholder to be liable for tax on the earnings of so-called Controlled Foreign Corporations (CFCs). These anti-CFC provisions have raised issues of tax jurisdiction, since they entail taxation of foreign non-resident companies merely on the basis of their ultimate ownership and/or other close connection with the taxing state. They have therefore had to be carefully circumscribed, limiting their effectiveness.

This chapter will focus first on the growth of residence taxation of base companies defined as CFCs, and the exploration of its limits, and then go on to consider the interaction of anti-haven measures with tax treaties, leading to a discussion of the increasing use of various limitation of benefits provisions to counter the avoidance of source taxation by conduit companies.[2] The related question of interaffiliate pricing or transfer pricing will be covered in the next chapter.

---

[1] See generally International Fiscal Association 1989, esp. p. 32.
[2] Other more specific anti-avoidance measures are not dealt with here: for example, provisions to ensure taxation of income from entertainment and sporting activities for which payments may be made to non-resident 'rent-a-star' companies: see OECD 1987c–II, especially paras. 54–9; the UK provisions were enacted in 1986 and are now in ICTA 1988, ss.555–8.

1. Controlled Foreign Corporations

As we have seen in Chapter 5, Britain attempted to deal with the problem of the use of intermediary companies to maximize tax deferral by applying a broad rule of company residence, combined with administrative measures (based on the requirement of permission for transfer of assets abroad or for raising finance through foreign intermediary companies), which enabled the Revenue to agree specific arrangements with individual companies for taxation of a proportion of retained earnings. The US authorities also were prepared to use general anti-avoidance provisions on the transfer of assets abroad to establish some control over deferral (see Chapter 5, section 2.d above), but this was overtaken by the emergence of the general debate over deferral, resulting in the Subpart F legislation against Controlled Foreign Corporations.[1] This approach, entailing more specificity in the definition of how far the retained earnings of a TNC could legitimately be taxed by the home country, proved influential, and similar provisions were enacted by the main developed countries over the ensuing two decades.

1.a The Spread of Anti-CFC Provisions

Other countries such as Germany, applied the slightly narrower test of residence based on the location of top management; this did not include co-ordination and financial functions, and was therefore more easily avoided than the UK's rules by setting up holding companies (Chapter 1, section 2.a(ii) above). Following the enactment of the US CFC provisions, the West German authorities methodically began to study the problem, and to develop a similar approach. The government produced a report on international avoidance (the *Steueroasenbericht* or Tax Oases report) in 1964, in response to a parliamentary request of 1962 (German Government 1964). Initially, the government tried to act on the basis of administrative measures, in a decree of 1965 based on the general tax avoidance provisions of the Tax Administration law.[2] However, the general trend of court decisions was to restrict the scope of these general anti-avoidance provisions. Although a decision of the Bundesfinanzhof in one case allowed income received by Swiss investment companies to be treated as fiduciary income attributable to their German

---

[1] The development of these and other US measures in the 1960s against international avoidance owed much to Stanley S. Surrey, who had come from the International Program in Taxation of the Harvard Law School to be Assistant Treasury Secretary for Tax Policy from 1961 to 1969, and whose influence on US tax policy, and international tax arrangements generally, continued until well into the 1970s.

[2] Steueranpassungsgesetz ss.5, 6 and 11, now codified in the Abgabenordnung ss.39, 41 and 42. These general provisions allow a transaction to be treated as a sham in certain circumstances, restrict the abuse of legal forms, and empower the attribution of income to other than the formal owner where property is owned or income received on behalf of another (so-called Treuhand relationships).

shareholders, an earlier case of 1968 held that a letter-box base company could not be regarded as a sham; subsequent decisions in 1974–6 supported this view (Huiskamp, in Rotterdam IFS 1978, pp. 309–12; Rappako 1987, pp. 169–74). Since the 1965 Tax Havens decree was an administrative measure which depended on these statutory rules, its effectiveness was doubtful. New legislation was necessary, and the administration published a comprehensive legislative memorandum in 1970 which, after consultation with interested parties, formed the basis of the Foreign Tax Law (Aussensteuergesetz: AStG) which came into force from 1 January 1972.

Similar legislation has also been enacted by the other main OECD countries. Canada brought in provisions on Foreign Accrual Property Income (FAPI) in the 1972 tax reform which came into effect in 1976. Japan introduced a Special Tax Measures Law in 1978 which included the designation of tax havens and the requirement for Japanese owners of subsidiaries in designated havens to report the subsidiary's undistributed income. France enacted legislation on tax haven companies in 1980,[1] and the UK enacted its CFC provisions in 1984.[2] New Zealand and Australia enacted anti-CFC legislation in 1988 and 1989. Other countries have applied general anti-avoidance provisions to tax haven intermediary companies, while considering enacting specific legislation, for example Finland and Sweden (Rappako 1987, pp. 208–9).

Although these measures differ in detail, their broad approach is similar. Their effect is to deem residents who are shareholders of a tax haven company to be liable to tax in certain circumstances on the income of that company, even if the income is not distributed or paid over. They therefore involve a further extension of residence taxation, which in a sense is 'extraterritorial'. This opens them to the criticism that an excessive tax jurisdiction is being claimed (Park 1978; see Chapter 11, section 1 below). Government proposals for anti-CFC measures certainly resulted in strong campaigns by industrial and financial pressure groups in most countries; and in some cases, notably Japan and the UK, this resulted in a softening of the proposals. It is notable, however that, even during the 1980s which has generally been a period of international liberalization, the business lobby has been unable to prevent measures to tax foreign retained earnings. Although anti-CFC measures may in principle involve a major extension of the jurisdictional claims of home countries to residence taxation, it is difficult for a designated haven to object that its tax base is being unfairly appropriated, if the haven itself is largely exempting that income from tax. Furthermore, the fact that similar measures were being introduced by most of the main capitalist countries made it hard to argue that international competitiveness would be damaged. Equally, it meant that the overlapping of jurisdiction involved in anti-haven measures did not lead to the sort of jurisdictional conflicts which occurred with other

---

[1] This became Article 209b of the Code Général des Impôts.
[2] OECD 1987a–I, paras. 62–4, 99–114 and Annex II, Arnold 1985, and Arnold 1986.

'extraterritorial' regulation of international business (see Chapter 11 below and Picciotto 1983). However, in this case the jurisdictional question focused on the scope and application of tax treaties (to be discussed in the next section). It is significant, also, that in formulating anti-CFC measures, states were sensitive to the question of the effective limits of their jurisdiction, and this has been harmonized to some extent through the OECD Committee.

1.b Defining CFC Income

Important limits have been imposed on taxation of CFCs, flowing from the very basis of tax jurisdiction. Since the residence country is essentially asserting its own jurisdiction over a proportion of the tax base generated by an internationally operating business, it must use clear and acceptable criteria if it is to avoid conflict with other countries. Such criteria must establish definitions (i) of the income which is claimed to be liable to tax, and (ii) of the relationship of resident taxpayers to that income, essentially based on their 'control' over the CFC.

(i) The Income Liable to Tax

Two approaches have been used in the definition of the 'tainted' income. The US, and later Canada, adopted a 'transactional' or 'shopping' approach, by defining certain types of activity as tainted, and therefore asserting the right to tax only the income from such activities. Such income is essentially passive investment income and foreign base company sales and service income (see Chapter 5, section 2 above). This approach does not require any definition of a tax haven nor listing of recognized havens. The alternative approach specifies that all the income of certain subsidiaries resident in countries where they benefit from a low-tax regime is taxable. This is the 'locational' or 'designated jurisdiction' approach, adopted by Japan, France and the UK (Arnold 1985; Arnold 1986, pp. 432–44; OECD 1987a–I, para. 63). However, this approach also provides exemption for companies with certain types of income; while the 'transactional' approach may also exclude a foreign subsidiary not substantially used for a tax avoidance purpose (which is determined by comparing the tax rates involved). Thus, the two approaches reach a substantially similar result (Arnold 1985); indeed, the German method combines elements of both.

Both approaches essentially use two basic concepts, differently combined: (a) location in a 'low-tax' country: i.e. that substantially less tax is paid in the company's country of residence than would be paid in the designating country; and (b) receipt of 'passive income': i.e. income which is earned without carrying out any substantial activity in the country of residence.

In defining a low-tax jurisdiction, the easiest method is to compare nominal tax rates. This is somewhat crude, since the nominal rate may be considerably different from the actual effective rate, because some countries are much more generous than others in the deductions they allow to arrive at taxable income;

but it is administratively complex to calculate and compare annually the effective rates. Thus, Japan relies on a comparison of nominal tax rates to produce its definitive blacklist of tax havens. France and Germany, on the other hand, publish haven lists which are for guidance only ('grey' lists), and can be more flexible – France appears to rely largely on nominal tax rates, while Germany takes into account the effective rate (see Chapter 6, section 3 above, and Arnold 1985, pp. 288–90).

The most sophisticated approach, perhaps because it was enacted later, is that of the UK, which compares the actual tax paid by the target company in its country of residence with what would be paid under UK tax rules. This principle is the broadest and most effective; in fact, the British legislation[1] makes no reference to designated havens, and thus recognizes that in principle any country may be a haven in relation to another (see Chapter 6, section 2 above). However, the provisions are subject to an overriding 'motive' test; and in response to pressures for more precision to assist tax planners, the Inland Revenue announced an informal 'white list' of countries presumed not to be havens.[2] However, to be exempt a company must not only be resident in one of these presumed exempt high-tax countries, but also must be deriving at least 90 per cent of its income from doing business in that country; otherwise, a comparison must be made of the actual tax paid, and if it is not at least 50 per cent of what would have been paid under UK tax law, the company may be a CFC.

The UK legislation is very comprehensive, and in principle gives the Revenue very broad powers, and discretion in deciding whether to invoke them, which is done by Direction. However, its potential scope is checked by several exemptions and an overriding statutory exclusion. A company is exempt if (i) it has an 'acceptable distribution policy' – essentially, if it distributes at least half of the proportion of profits to which the UK shareholders are entitled (90 per cent for a non-trading company); or, (ii) it is genuinely carrying on business (other than 'investment business') in its country of residence and is effectively managed there; or, (iii) it is publicly quoted (elaborately defined in Schedule 25 III); or (iv) it has chargeable profits of less than £20,000 in the accounting period. The overriding exclusion for 'motive' allows exemption where the reduction in taxation was minimal or not a main purpose of the transactions; or where it was not one of the main reasons for the CFC's existence to achieve a reduction in UK tax by diversion of profits from the UK.[3]

---

[1] Finance Act 1984 ss.82–91 and Schedules 16–18; now ICTA 1988 ss.747–56 and Schedules 24–6.

[2] This is based on an extra-statutory concession exempting companies operating in countries accepted by the Revenue not to be havens, which it was estimated would exempt 90 per cent of non-resident subsidiaries (Simon 1983–, D4.131). The list designates 48 countries unconditionally, and a further 29 provided the subsidiary does not benefit from defined tax privileges (Simon 1983–, D4.141).

[3] That is, where it is reasonable to suppose that but for the existence of the CFC a UK resident would have received all or a substantial part of its income and consequently have had a higher UK tax liability: s.748(3) and Schedule 25IV.

These tests give the targeted taxpayer a legal basis for objection against an unreasonable application of the Revenue's powers; but there is no provision for a remedy against the generous treatment of one taxpayer in relation to another (Deutsch 1985, p. 8). Perhaps the aim, and certainly the effect, of this legislation was as much to discourage the use of some types of tax haven intermediary company as to raise revenue. The provisions included a power to require relevant books, accounts and documents to be produced by any UK company which appears to be the controlling company of a foreign subsidiary which may be a CFC, and it was reported that the Revenue promptly wrote to UK multinational groups asking for lists of their non-resident controlled subsidiaries and copies of their accounts (Deutsch 1985, p. 8, and Chapter 10 below).

The second step in defining the tainted income is the characterization of passive income not earned by carrying out a genuine activity in the country of residence. Normally, passive income includes that resulting from carrying out a holding company function: e.g. what is described in the British rules as 'investment business' – holding securities, patents or copyrights; leasing; dealing in securities (other than as a broker); or making investments for related companies.[1] However, it is more difficult to define if the income results, at least formally, from carrying on a business, whether it is manufacturing, wholesale buying/selling, or services, including construction, design or research, and financial services such as banking and insurance. Under the US Subpart F, detailed regulations have been made to try to distinguish substantial foreign manufacturing from a notional assembly operation. Most countries regard income from service activities as tainted if the activity is carried out for a related company outside the CFC's country of residence; in the case of countries using the locational rather than the transactional approach, where more than a certain proportion is carried out for related companies. However, there are many types of activity, in services, or construction, or offshore drilling, which require a minimal physical base, while specialists and equipment which need not be located at that base are despatched to various global locations as needed; provided at least a significant proportion of their business is done with unrelated clients, such services and the costs of associated personnel can be channelled through a tax haven subsidiary which may be considered as having an 'active' business (US Treasury 1981, pp. 79–84).

(ii) Control and Residence

The second main limb of the definition of a CFC is the connection with taxpayers resident in the designating jurisdiction, and the relationship of the CFC itself with the privileged tax regime or low-tax haven. The basis of imposing liability to tax on the undistributed income of a CFC is that it is

[1] ICTA 1988, Schedule 25 s.9.

'controlled' by residents of the tax country; it is necessary to use a broad definition of control, to minimize potential loopholes, but most CFC laws specify that at least 50 per cent of the shares in the CFC must be held by resident taxpayers in the taxing country. As the OECD report states, 'Minimum ownership formulae vary and one of the main problems is apparently how to counter strategies used by taxpayers to avoid these criteria' (OECD 1987a–I, para. 63). The definition of the connection between the CFC and the haven poses special problems under the locational or designated jurisdiction approach (Arnold 1985, p. 365), since a company may benefit from low taxation by separating its country of incorporation from that of residence; or by carrying out its intermediary company activities through a branch. Thus, a company incorporated in the UK (which is not designated as a haven by countries using the locational approach such as Japan and France) could have been managed in a haven where its intermediary business was carried on: this loophole was closed when the UK changed its residence rule to include all UK-incorporated companies (see Chapter 1 above). Equally, a French company could carry on its intermediary activities through a branch in a haven, which would not be taxed under French law which exempts foreign income earned through a foreign Permanent Establishment. This must be dealt with both by a broad connection principle, and a provision such as that in the UK's informal exemption, that a high proportion of the company's business (in that case 90 per cent) must be done in the exempt country.

1.c The Effectiveness of Anti-CFC Measures

The complexities of CFC measures have certainly made them a fruitful source of revenue for lawyers and accountants, but in practice much less for governments, as can be seen from the figures that some countries have released. Thus, the German figures show that both the total amounts recovered and the average recovery per case are relatively low. The amounts collected under the AStG (Table 3, column 3) are less than 1 per cent of the total revenues from Germany's corporation taxes.[1] This may partly be due to cases being dealt with on other grounds, or not being dealt with at all: the German authorities reported to the OECD Committee that only 15–25 per cent of suspected cases had been audited (OECD 1987a–I para. 102). The Japanese government reported that in 1983 428 firms had filed returns under the anti-haven law in respect of 1,914 subsidiaries in seventeen designated havens, which resulted in additional income liable to tax of Y31.4 billion; also, 386 audits between July 1983 and June 1984 had revealed errors in 49 cases, resulting in additional taxable income of Y3.4 billion (ibid.). This combined total of Y35 billion once again is tiny: less than one-half of one per cent of Japan's revenue from corporation tax.[2] For the UK, the tax yield from CFC

[1] Taken from OECD Revenue Statistics.
[2] The figure for revenues from corporation tax is given in Japan, Ministry of Finance 1985, p. 299.

Table 3 *Tax Revenues Recovered under German CFC Rules (AStG ss.7–14)*

Year	Cases (No.)	Total amounts (Million DM)	Average per case (Million DM)
1972	99	25.953	.262
1973	492	50.455	.103
1974	449	35.543	.79
1975	439	34.089	.78
1976	461	20.757	.45
1977	477	23.310	.49
1978	509	41.483	.82
1979	443	11.111	.25
1980	358	14.634	.41
1981	553	59.382	.11
1982	496	28.232	.57
1983	394	29.833	.76

Totals may not correspond due to rounding. Compiled from Deutscher Bundestag 1986, p. 7.

cases dealt with by the International Division of the Inland Revenue was £12.5m in 1987–9.[1]

Thus, it is likely that the main effect of CFC legislation has been to induce firms to reorganize their offshore subsidiary structures. This may have resulted in the repatriation of a higher proportion of retained foreign earnings; but to a significant extent companies have been able to avoid the CFC rules. The US experience after two decades of operation of Subpart F, detailed in the Gordon Report, was that the use of tax haven intermediary companies by US corporations had continued to grow (US Treasury 1981, pp. 39–40). It may also be the case that CFC legislation, by bringing the retained earnings of some foreign subsidiaries into the tax net, will have pushed some offshore activities more clearly over the line from doubtful avoidance to illegal evasion.

Equally, however, some practices which fall outside CFC rules have been legitimized. In particular, activities which can be said to be genuine trading activities of a tax haven company cannot easily be included in the CFC net. This includes businesses such as construction, shipping and offshore drilling, as mentioned above. Above all, CFC measures find it hard to deal with financial services, such as banking and insurance, carried out by 'captive' subsidiaries, which are in many cases regulated by specific rules under the CFC laws; but under these rules services such as banking or insurance are generally considered to produce 'passive' income only if they are provided in respect of the home-country business of the shareholder or related companies. This excludes services provided for foreign operations, which can be charged to operating companies and reduce taxable business profits at source (unless the source country disallows deduction of such payments if made to a tax haven affiliate). Furthermore, if a

[1] Given in UK Board of Inland Revenue 1988, vol. 3, though it is not clear whether this is from cases investigated or the total yield from all CFCs.

significant proportion of such services is provided to unrelated third parties, for example by using pooling arrangements, then the 'captive' could be regarded as carrying on an independent insurance or banking business, and therefore fall outside the CFC net (US Treasury 1981, p. 89).

Furthermore, parent companies may derive direct benefit, by 'secondary sheltering' of tax-exempt income. The simplest method is for the subsidiary carrying on the CFC-exempt business in a low-tax country to make loans to the parent, or to other affiliates. Such an 'upstream loan' is not taxed as income to the recipient (as a dividend would be), and indeed the interest payments on the 'loan' are normally tax deductible by the 'borrower'. This was described as 'a rather naive and straightforward form of tax avoidance' by the OECD Fiscal Committee (OECD 1987a–II, para. 72); but although some countries such as the US have provisions to tax such loans in some circumstances, others have found it more difficult to counteract. In the UK, the Revenue was forced to withdraw its proposals on upstream loans, following criticism, especially that it would interfere with the carrying out of the central treasury function of multinational company groups based in the UK, which might therefore move this function, and the important associated investments, elsewhere (IFS 1982, p. 31).

2. Anti-Avoidance and Tax Treaties

The development of measures against tax havens and intermediary companies has important international implications. Such measures necessarily entail the interaction of laws and jurisdictions of the states involved, and of domestic tax laws and treaty provisions.

We have seen that, although both the use of general anti-avoidance provisions and the enactment of specific measures against CFCs have been done by countries under their own national laws, they have exercised their sovereignty with some caution, aware of the difficult issues of tax jurisdiction involved. The jurisdiction issue was most immediately expressed by objections from taxpayer groups (see Chapter 11, section 1 for a further discussion of tax jurisdiction). Consequently, the measures have been carefully defined, as we have seen: first, to establish an effective connection with the taxing country based on the residence of the shareholders controlling the CFC; and secondly, to target income which but for the interposition of the intermediary company would have accrued to its shareholders.

Not surprisingly, these measures have also raised a number of issues for negotiation between states. Since international tax arrangements are based on the network of bilateral tax treaties, these issues have focused on the negotiation or application of tax treaty provisions. Countries taking measures against international avoidance must consider carefully the implications of such measures both for their existing treaties, and for the possibility of concluding further treaties. It may be that targeting a country as a haven and applying unilateral measures to tax intermediary companies resident there, would preclude the possibility of a more co-operative relationship with the putative haven, based on a treaty or other arrangement. Alternatively, the development of national measures can occur in parallel with negotiations with a haven country, aimed at inducing it to change its own laws to limit its use as a haven, as well as to agree suitable treaty arrangements.

Thus, for example, at the time of the German Tax Havens study initiated in 1962, the concern in both West Germany and France over the growth of holding companies created pressure on Switzerland to limit the use of Swiss law for both base and conduit companies, and to negotiate new tax treaties with anti-avoidance provisions. The Swiss government went some way to meeting these concerns, by issuing a Decree in 1962 on improper use of tax treaties based on the principle of 'abus de droit' (Switzerland 1962), followed by administrative regulations which limited the exemption from federal tax for foreign-source income to defined non-abusive situations. However, this did not affect cantonal taxes, and the Swiss tax on a base or conduit company with foreign income from a treaty country remained effectively only 5 per cent. Eventually, treaties were signed with France (1966) and Germany (1971) which incorporated anti-abuse provisions based on the 1962 Swiss decree. The treaties went further, however, and excluded from relief on withholding taxes for interest and royalties (but not dividends) any Swiss company with substantial non-resident participation, unless it is subject to cantonal profits taxes.[1] Thus, the treaty negotiations and the domestic legislative processes in both sets of countries mutually influenced each other; although the overall process cannot be said to have been a harmonious one, nor to have produced results which adequately satisfied any of the parties.

On the international plane, this process has shown up the limitations of the bilateral treaty network, which bears the burden of attempts to co-ordinate different national approaches to equity in the taxation of international business (see Chapter 1, section 4 above). We have seen that a degree of reciprocal advantage is necessary for two countries to negotiate such an agreement. A small country with an underdeveloped economy, exporting no capital, and perhaps having little prospect of attracting inward investment, may prefer to have no treaties. Hence, it may be tempted to become an offshore financial centre and a tax haven. Other countries, such as Switzerland or Luxembourg, have some well-developed industries including some major global TNCs, but also have a substantial banking and financial services sector. These countries have been willing to conclude treaties, but have argued strongly for provisions which put minimal restraint on international capital movements. In their own way, they too became tax havens. Even the UK, which seeks to preserve the City of London as a financial centre, has refrained from measures such as provisions against upstream loans for that reason.

[1] See Knechtle 1979, pp. 119–22; OECD 1987s–III, Annex II, citing Article 23 of the German–Swiss treaty. Note that this article also explicitly permits the parties to take their own measures against abuse of tax relief on withholding taxes.

In the simplified model of international avoidance using intermediary companies outlined in Chapter 6, section 4, we saw that a parent company in the residence country can use holding company or service company subsidiaries in base-havens, as well as conduits in treaty-havens, as intermediaries for activities carried out by operating subsidiaries in source countries (see Diagram 1). Some havens may fulfil both base and conduit functions, but it is convenient to separate the two functions analytically. Thus, measures against international avoidance take the form of anti-base provisions and anti-conduit provisions. In both these cases, the enacting country must consider not only the compatibility of the measures with existing tax treaties, but their implications for revisions which may be desired or new treaties which could be negotiated. Thus, the anti-avoidance measures must be either broadly, or even specifically, acceptable as legitimate by a range of actual or potential treaty partners.

This was recognized by the OECD Fiscal Committee, when it examined the tax treaty implications of anti-avoidance measures (OECD 1987a–II and 1987a–III). The Committee had to contend with the view, expressed by Switzerland, that anti-avoidance measures were contrary to the existing OECD model treaty, and therefore cannot be enforced without agreement with treaty partners and specific incorporation in treaties (OECD 1987a–II, paras. 95–7). The Swiss view was that, since tax treaties define and allocate rights to tax, a residence country cannot use anti-avoidance rules to tax the undistributed income of a base company validly incorporated in a treaty-partner state, unless the treaty specifically recognizes the applicability of those rules. The large majority of OECD members took the contrary view, that national anti-avoidance rules were not incompatible with the spirit of the OECD model treaty (ibid., para. 40). However, especially in the case of specific anti-avoidance measures (such as taxation of CFCs), the Committee considered that counteracting measures should conform to some general principles. Although no clear-cut rules could easily be laid down, the Committee concluded:

> An international consensus should be established, to which States newly introducing counteracting measures might refer. In this respect, the OECD Committee on Fiscal Affairs . . . would . . . appear to constitute the appropriate forum for the discussion of such policy issues [ibid., para. 48].

This view means at least that a state wishing to take anti-avoidance measures under its own domestic law may go ahead and do so. However, such measures should comply with the broad international consensus of acceptability referred to by the Committee. In addition, they must be tailored to the specific provisions of tax treaties, either in existence or to be negotiated. We will consider compatibility both with general principles and specific provisions, in relation first to anti-base and then to anti-conduit measures.

2.a Anti-Base Provisions

Intermediary base companies do not directly take advantage of the relief from double taxation provided by treaties, but exploit the possibilities for deferral offered by the limits on the tax jurisdiction of the country of residence. Hence, a base company may be set up in a country which has no tax treaties. Nevertheless, anti-base measures have implications for the residence state's tax treaties with third countries: either with a source country, or another residence state. In addition, some countries with existing treaties may be tempted to develop offshore business and become base-havens also; or a residence state may wish to try to conclude a treaty with a base-haven, and in such cases it is important that its anti-base provisions be defensible and compatible with negotiable variations of the model treaty.

The legitimacy of taxation of base company income focuses on two arguments: (i) that base companies formed in the haven are being used to shelter investment income which has no valid connection with the haven; and (ii) that they are used not only for illegitimate avoidance but also illegal evasion: they may conceal either income which is fraudulently evading tax, or which has been illegally earned, perhaps from narcotic drug smuggling or other forms of organized crime (or both). The two arguments overlap, since the authorities in the taxing countries argue that by offering facilities for the illegitimate concealment of income from taxation, havens are encouraging illegality and turning themselves into shelters for criminals. On the other hand, havens try to keep the two issues separate: they defend the legitimacy of international tax avoidance in the name of freedom of movement of capital, and try to draw a strict line between such avoidance and tax fraud. This debate is most intense in relation to the attempt to develop international co-operation in tax enforcement, which will be considered below (Chapter 10). The point to be noted here is that the states asserting jurisdiction to tax foreign retained income of their residents must do so on a basis that can generally be accepted as valid, if they are to secure co-operation and avoid a variety of difficulties.

Three broad principles emerged from the OECD Committee's report which considered anti-base measures. Generally, anti-avoidance measures should be used only 'to maintain equity and neutrality of national tax laws in an international environment'. Therefore, (i) they should target only income that is genuinely passive income, and should not extend to 'activities such as production, normal rendering of services or trading by companies engaged in real industrial or commercial activity'; (ii) they should be aimed at base companies benefiting from low tax privileges and 'not be applied to countries in which taxation is comparable to that of the country of residence of the taxpayer' (ibid., para. 47); (iii) the counteracting measures should not normally treat the base company as non-existent (ibid., para. 34). These three principles generally reflect the limits which countries enacting anti-CFC rules have accepted. In particular, the bar against treating as non-existent a company validly created under the laws of another country coincides, as we have seen, with the view often taken by the authorities and courts in the countries enforcing anti-avoidance measures.

The particular legal form taken by the anti-avoidance measures may, however, have considerable implications. Although R cannot ignore the existence of B, it might treat B as a resident of R (and therefore directly liable to R's taxes); but if there is a treaty between R and H, the place of residence would have to be established under the treaty rule of residence: the OECD model (Article 4.3) lays down that in cases of conflict the principle of 'place of effective management' must be applied. Furthermore, if the anti-avoidance provisions of R take the form of treating B as a resident of R, this would entail giving B the right to protection and benefits under a treaty (if one exists) between R and S, since under such a treaty residence normally depends on the law of R. This is important, since although B may have been established in a country without treaties, it is much more likely that there would be a treaty between R and S, and the benefits might be considerable (reduced withholding taxes on payments from O to B, and a credit in R for taxes paid to S).

These implications can be avoided, however, since usually the specific measures against CFCs do not treat the CFC as resident in R, but merely deem its income to be attributable to its controlling shareholder(s) P. Nevertheless, the view taken by most OECD members is that where R has taxed income derived from country S in the hands of P, R should allow a credit for taxes paid to S, in order to 'comply with the spirit of international law by seeking to avoid double taxation' (ibid., para. 57). However, if R adopts the approach of attribution of B's income to P, it does not entitle B to the benefits conceded by S under any treaty with R; furthermore, S is not likely to take a generous view and concede any adjustments (ibid., para. 59).

Finally, questions of compatibility and co-ordination may arise between two residence countries which each enforce anti-base measures, since conflicting jurisdictional claims may arise. For example, as mentioned in Chapter 5, section 3 above, if a US parent company shelters the sales of its German manufacturing subsidiary in a Swiss base company, both US and German anti-avoidance provisions may be used to bring the profits retained in the Swiss affiliate within their respective tax nets. In such a situation, there is likely to be a bilateral treaty in force between the two residence countries, but the view of those countries with CFC provisions is that, in the absence of any specific clause in this treaty, both are entitled to apply their measures to the base company (OECD 1987b, para. 65). However, the taxpayer may ask for elimination of the double taxation thus generated, under the competent authority mutual agreement provisions of the treaty (Arts. 9(2) and 25; see Chapter 10 section 3 below).

However, these provisions were not designed to deal with this problem, and are not adequate to do so. If both residence countries treat the intermediary B as a resident, then it would be directly subject to double taxation, and since B has been treated as a resident it could invoke the mutual agreement procedure (Article 25). As we have seen however, most CFC laws tax the shareholder companies resident in R on income deemed to arise to them from B. In such circumstances, the mutual agreement procedure of Article 25(1) would not apply; a related procedure for competent authorities to consult over pricing between related enterprises is provided for in Article 9(2), but a number of states do not accept this article, and in any case it deals with the adjustments of transfer prices in transactions between associated enterprises. Nevertheless, the arrangements for simultaneous examination of related companies, which have been set up by a number of the main OECD countries, could include consideration of adjustments between two residence countries (see further Chapter 10, section 2.c below). The possibility of using the corresponding adjustment procedure in such cases is alluded to in the OECD Base Companies report (OECD 1987a–II, paras. 39, 65–6); but the report recommends that the matter be dealt with by the inclusion of specific clauses in treaties, such as the one between Canada and West Germany, which requires the state of which the 'controlling shareholder' is resident to give credit for the anti-base tax of the other state (ibid., para. 66). This gives priority to the residence country of a regional parent, and residual rights to the ultimate parent's country of residence.

2.b Anti-Conduit Provisions

Conduit companies, as we have seen, are set up in countries which have a convenient network of tax treaties, to take advantage of the reduced withholding taxes on payments of dividends, interest, fees and royalties which treaties provide. Since the conduit is not the ultimate recipient of such income, but has merely been established in country T-H to take advantage of treaty benefits, this device is regarded as 'treaty shopping'. From the point of view of the source country, it entails an improper advantage being taken by third parties of treaty benefits which were intended to be granted to bona fide residents of the treaty partner state (Rosenbloom & Langbein 1981, pp. 396–7; Rosenbloom 1983).

(i) Denial of Benefits under Tax Treaties

Denial of treaty benefits to companies resident in treaty countries necessarily entails an interaction between any measures taken under the domestic law of S and the provisions of the treaty between S and T-H. Tax treaties are normally incorporated directly or indirectly into national law; so if S wishes to deny a treaty benefit to a resident, O, it would entail changing domestic law explicitly to override the treaty provisions (see Chapter 11, section 2 below). However, relief can be denied to O if C can be considered not a valid beneficiary of the treaty. As with anti-base provisions, S cannot normally ignore the existence of C if it is a company validly formed under the laws of T-H; however, S may consider that C is not entitled to treaty benefits because it is not a bona fide resident of T-H or not the genuine recipient of the payments entitled to exemption. This may be justified by the provision of Article 4.1 of the model treaty, which excludes from the term 'resident of the Contracting State' any person 'liable to tax in that state in respect only of income from sources in that state or capital situated therein'. However, it seems that this provision was introduced in the 1977 model for a limited purpose, since the Commentary gives the example of diplomatic personnel; it would be a very far-reaching exclusion to deny treaty benefits to all residents of countries which tax only domestic source income (OECD 1987a–III, para. 14).

It does seem, however, that the question of the abuse of treaty limitations on withholding tax by conduit arrangements was raised in the drafting of the 1977 OECD model. Articles 10, 11 and 12, which deal with restrictions on source taxation of dividends, interest and royalties, each specifically state that the reduced withholding tax only applies 'if the recipient is the beneficial owner of the dividends'. The Commentary indicates that this excludes cases where 'an agent or nominee is interposed between the beneficiary and the payer'. The exclusion seems intended to apply, for example, to holdings of shares or bonds by Swiss banks on a nominee basis for clients. However, the OECD model provides no further assistance: the Commentary merely adds that 'States which wish to make this more explicit are free to do so during bilateral negotiations'. As the 1987 Report comments, 'Opinions may differ as to whether the absence of an overall solution to the conduit problem was at the time a serious flaw in the 1977 OECD Model' (OECD 1987a–III, para. 16).

This failure or flaw can be traced, once again, to the disagreements about international tax equity and the limited nature of the solutions inherent in the bilateral treaty model. We have seen that withholding taxes on payments to non-residents, and their limitation on a reciprocal basis by treaty, were the key to reconciling residence and source taxation (Chapter 2 above). From the point of view of the source country, withholding taxes ensure capital-import equity: i.e. that investors from abroad are not taxed more lightly than domestic investors and taxpayers. Thus, even the US has had a withholding tax on all payments to non-residents since 1936 (initially at 10 per cent, and since the war at a flat rate of 30 per cent). However, the tax treaties which were negotiated in the immediate postwar period between the main capitalist countries limited withholding tax rates to low or zero rates, on a reciprocal basis, with the aim of encouraging international investment flows. The OECD model recommended a maximum of 15 per cent for dividends – or 5 per cent if paid to an affiliate – 10 per cent for interest, and zero for royalties. In fact, many states have agreed lower rates: the US, for instance, negotiated an exemption for interest paid to residents of many of its treaty partner states, in order to attract private investment into the US.

However, some countries which signed treaties agreeing low or zero withholding tax rates did not apply any significant taxes themselves to such foreign-source income: notably Switzerland and Luxembourg. Both they, and other countries which wished to encourage financial business, such as the Netherlands, allowed or facilitated the setting up of holding companies, which could take advantage of the 'participation exemption' for dividends received from an affiliate. Then, as we have seen, the expansion of offshore finance during the 1960s spread to other countries, which had even more incentive to become tax havens. Some of these were former colonies, and inherited tax treaties which had been extended to them by agreement between their mother country and the treaty partner. Thus, the USA in 1955 had agreed to the extension of its treaty with the Netherlands to the Netherlands Antilles; and in 1958 the US–UK treaty of 1945 was extended to twenty British overseas territories. These included several in the Caribbean, such as the British Virgin Islands and Barbados, which later adjusted their internal laws to take advantage of the treaties, to attract holding companies which could perform a base and/or conduit function in relation to the US (US Treasury 1981, pp. 149–52).[1]

Nevertheless, the wording of the treaty provisions based on articles 4 and 10–12 of the OECD model certainly provided support for any source state wishing to deny treaty benefits to Conduit companies. This could be done unilaterally, simply by refusing treaty relief and applying the full withholding tax in suspect cases. Such action was upheld by the US Tax Court in a case (*Aiken Industries Inc. v. Commr.*, 1971) in which promissory notes of a US company to a Bahamian affiliate were transferred to a newly formed Honduran affiliate in exchange for its own notes bearing the same interest rate. The court held that the Bahamian company was not entitled to treaty relief since it was not the 'recipient' of the interest. On the other hand, as we have already seen, courts may be reluctant to ignore the existence as a separate entity of the Conduit (*Perry R. Bass v. Commr.*, 1968), and especially in cases where the conduit receives dividends, it is hard to treat it as a mere nominee if it has no legal obligation to pass on revenue received to a beneficial owner.

---

[1] The full list of British territories benefiting from the extension to them of the US treaty was Aden, Antigua, Barbados, British Honduras, British Virgin Islands, Cyprus, Dominica, the Falkland Islands, Gambia, Grenada, Jamaica, Montserrat, Nigeria, Rhodesia and Nyasaland, St Christopher, Nevis and Anguilla, St Lucia, St Vincent, Seychelles, Sierra Leone and Trinidad and Tobago: see US–UK Exchange of Notes of 19 August 1957 and 3 December 1958; the US ended these extensions by notice taking effect from 1984: see section 3.b below. In addition to the US, Denmark, Norway, Sweden and Switzerland also accepted the extension of their tax treaty with the UK to British dependent and associated states. The list of territories covered in each case was similar but not identical to that of the US, but these extensions established some treaty links which offered avoidance opportunities, e.g. Switzerland–British Virgin Islands: Davies 1985, pp. 221–2. Although the UK's newer tax treaties do not normally contain a territorial extension article, those previous extensions have been expressly retained, and depending on the state succession practice adopted by each territory, might also continue in force after such a territory attained independence. Britain also accepted the extension of its treaties to the dependent territories of other states: in particular the UK–Netherlands Exchange of Notes of 13 and 29 July 1955 extending to the Netherlands Antilles the treaty of 1948; replaced by the Exchange of Notes of 24 July 1970 extending the new UK–Netherlands treaty of 1967; this was abrogated in respect of the Netherlands Antilles by the UK in 1989, see below. The only other extensions accepted by the UK have been UK–Denmark (to the Faroe Islands); and UK–South Africa (to Namibia): Davies 1985, p. 222.

Another example is where an insurance premium is exempt from excise tax because it is paid to a resident in a treaty country, but the risk is reinsured (perhaps on a pooled basis) with a company in a low-tax non-treaty state.

Furthermore, there are considerable administrative difficulties involved in distinguishing a conduit from a genuine recipient. The Gordon Report stated: 'In 1979 only about 75 Form 1042s (the form which must be filed by a United States person making a payment to a foreign person) were audited. . . . The IRS simply is not in a position to audit tax haven holding or insurance companies claiming treaty benefits to determine whether they are eligible for those benefits' (p. 165). Also, effective administration is likely to require assistance from the treaty-haven, since conduits are likely to be set up under laws which allow companies to conceal their beneficial ownership, by using shares issued to bearer. Such assistance would obviously depend on whether the treaty partner government is willing, or even able under its own laws, to obtain information about beneficial ownership, and to supply it under the treaty's exchange of information provisions, which may therefore require renegotiation (US Treasury 1981, p. 164, and Chapter 10 below).

(ii) Treaty Benefits and Investment Flows

Although it is possible for a source state to take unilateral action to restrict or deny treaty benefits, to be effective such measures should be specific and targeted in relation to each treaty-partner. They must take into account not only the tax laws of that country, but also its regulation of foreign exchange, banking and financial markets generally, and the pattern of investments between it and the source state. For these reasons, anti-conduit measures have become increasingly specific, and have been negotiated between treaty-partners, aiming at agreed provisions to combat abusive treaty shopping. A number of issues are involved in considering what constitutes 'abuse' in this context. Reduced or low withholding taxes on payments to non-residents aim to encourage inward investment, and this desire conflicts with the objective of ensuring that such foreign investors bear a fair tax burden, or capital-import equity (US Treasury 1981, p. 152). Thus, the US IRS as late as the mid-1970s was issuing administrative rulings permitting the use of Netherlands Antilles holding companies as conduits for investment into the United States, for example in real estate; as well as for the issuing of Eurobonds by financial intermediaries of TNCs. Between 1965 and 1973 some ten billion dollars' worth of Eurobonds were issued by US TNCs through Netherlands Antilles' intermediaries, with the encouragement of the US Treasury (Langer 1978, p. 741).

However, the availability of low withholding taxes gave a considerable inducement to foreigners not resident in US treaty partner states, to take advantage of conduit arrangements to route their investment into the US. Thus, by 1978 about one-third of the approximately $22 billion worth of stocks in US companies owned by non-residents were held in Switzerland, 90 per cent of them by Swiss banks on a nominee basis (Langer 1978, p. 742; US Treasury 1981, Table 1, p. 177). The US suggested to its treaty partners a certification system with arrangements for the balance of the tax to be collected and refunded where the recipient was found to be a nominee. Although some, such as the Swiss authorities, were willing to try, the sheer volume of transactions created considerable administrative difficulties.[1] Other countries would not do so, often because their own laws made it impossible to trace owners of bearer shares or beneficiaries of nominee accounts.[2] This in effect meant that loan capital for an investment in the US was substantially cheaper if channelled through such a foreign conduit; not surprisingly this created a temptation for US residents to use the same means to evade US taxes (Karzon 1983). Thus, international avoidance undermines tax legitimacy and stimulates more flagrant evasion.

3. Combating Treaty Shopping

For these reasons, attempts have been made to insert anti-treaty shopping clauses in tax treaties, which restrict relief from withholding taxes to bona fide residents of the treaty partner state.

3.a Limitation of Benefits Clauses

A variety of provisions have been developed to attempt to restrict treaty benefits (low withholding taxes or other exemptions) to those considered genuinely entitled to them.[3] An early limitation provision was contained in the US–UK treaty of 1945, which reduced the withholding tax for dividends to 15 per cent, with a further reduction to 5 per cent when paid to a controlling company; however, the latter reduction was not to apply if the relationship between the two companies was 'arranged or maintained primarily with the intention of securing such a reduced rate'. A similar clause was included in a number of US treaties in the 1950s, but it was not effectively activated until 1979 (Rosenbloom 1983, pp. 780–1). It clearly suffers from the flaws of any general anti-avoidance rule, relying on the subjective test of 'intention' and giving administrators a broad discretion. Hence, subsequent provisions have attempted to be more specific; but to avoid restricting benefits unduly, they have also introduced both 'safe harbour' exceptions and an overriding power for administrators to grant benefits in appropriate cases.

The first specific exclusions targeted investment and holding companies: this type of so-called 'exclusion' provision has commonly been included in

---

[1] Figures on amounts of additional tax collected by treaty partners under these arrangements were given by the IRS, see US Congress 1983b, p. 280 (see Chapter 10, section 4.b(ii) below).
[2] See testimony of R. Egger and D. Kanakis of the IRS, in US Congress 1984b.
[3] For a history and analysis of the provisions in US treaties, see Rosenbloom 1983.

treaties with Luxembourg, for example its treaty with the US of 1962, excluding holding companies formed under a specified Luxembourg law. To avoid the difficulties which may be created when the specified law is changed, a reference is normally added extending the exclusion to any similar laws subsequently enacted. A broader version of the 'exclusion' provision applies more generally to a company which in its country of residence is either tax-exempt or not subject to tax at the usual rate on corporate profits. This can create difficulties, since tax exemption may be granted for a variety of reasons which that country considers valid, whether to charitable entities and pension funds, or to intermediary companies given a participation exemption. This tax-status-related exclusion clause has therefore often been combined with the requirement that such a company is excluded only if owned substantially (e.g. 25 per cent or more) by third-country residents: the so-called 'look-through' requirement.[1] There remained, however, the problem that the low-tax or special-tax regime requirement entailed a judgment by the source country as to the level of taxation to be applied by its treaty partner.[2]

Since the main target of limitation of benefits clauses is the conduit, attention has been given to refining the definition of 'look-through', and combining it with 'safe harbour' exceptions. Usually, treaties specify that no more than a minimum percentage, e.g. 25 per cent or 50 per cent, of the capital of the recipient must be owned either by non-residents of the haven, or by residents of either contracting party. If applied alone, this would be a drastic measure, as it would discourage even bona fide foreign investment in the treaty-haven. Thus, a 'safe harbour' is normally provided, allowing a company to be eligible for relief if its shares are listed on an approved stock exchange. However, it is possible to obtain such a listing even though only a very small proportion of the conduit company's shares (even less than 5 per cent) is actually offered to the public, and some conduits have apparently obtained such a quotation. Thus, it is common to require 'substantial and regular' trading in the principal class of shares in the company on a recognized exchange (this is the formula used in US treaties, such as New Zealand, Bermuda, Germany). An additional exception can be given by a 'bona fide' proviso: i.e. that treaty benefits can still be accorded if the company is not used principally for the purpose of obtaining treaty benefits (see below).

The main problem with both 'exclusion' and 'look-through' is that they do not deal with arrangements where the recipient is not subject to any special tax regime, and may even be owned locally, but passes receipts through to a third entity by deductible payments which leave it with a low or nil tax liability in its

[1] For example, Article 16 of the US–UK Treaty of 1975.
[2] This may make it difficult for the source country to set any more than a low threshold for 'normal' taxation: e.g., the 1963 Protocol to the US–Netherlands Antilles agreement excluded from the limitation of withholding taxes on dividends, interest and royalties any corporation eligible for special tax concessions then available 'or to substantially similar benefits'; but it was apparently agreed during the negotiations that a new 15 per cent tax if enacted would be sufficient: see Rosenbloom 1983, p. 783.

country of residence. These are 'stepping stone' conduits or back-to-back financing arrangements (see Chapter 6, section 4 above). Under such an arrangement a bank in the treaty-haven, or a conduit company owned by local attorneys or other serviceable individuals, lends money to affiliate O in country S at a market rate, say 12 per cent, while borrowing from O's related finance-company H-F, at a rate which is only slightly lower, say 11.5 per cent. Thus the stepping-stone conduit pays tax in T-H, although only on the low profits produced by the half per cent rate differential. The location of the stepping-stone must ensure that no withholding tax is levied on its payments to H-F, so they may be routed through a second conduit C-2.

To defeat such arrangements, it is necessary to combine 'look-through' with a 'prohibited payment' or 'base-erosion' provision. This requires that not more than a specified proportion (say 50 per cent) of the income received from the source state should be used to satisfy claims by third-country residents. Thus, in the German–Swiss treaty Article 23.1(c) specifies that no more than 50 per cent of receipts may be used to satisfy claims of non-residents (cited in OECD 1987a–III, Annex II). However, the base-erosion requirement may be ineffective if the income is passed on in the form of a loan, or even a dividend. Some states have been reluctant to accept such a clause however (Oliva 1984, p. 321), since it can pose problems of definition which lead to difficulties of administration.[1] Anti-conduit provisions therefore may include a power for the competent authorities to agree that an exemption may be granted.

A general objection which can be made to all these requirements is that by creating obstacles hindering claims to tax treaty relief, they can deter investment from third countries. The UN Ad Hoc Group of Experts particularly pointed out the disadvantages to developing countries, and suggested that there should be a presumption that bona fide recipients can claim treaty benefits (UN 1988c, pp. 15–16). Although the OECD countries are reluctant to accept such a general presumption, they have recognized the problem by trying to develop a variety of tests of bona fides.

In particular, an 'activity test' can be used, allowing the recipient to establish bona fides by the relatively objective criterion of showing that the income was incidental to or derived from the carrying on of a trade or business. This test was included in the US protocol with Belgium in 1988 and in the treaties signed by the US in 1989 with both India and Germany. However, there is concern that this provision may provide a loophole for holding companies or co-ordination centres: hence, it usually excludes investment business except for a bank or insurance company. The 'active trade or business' requirement also involves difficult judgments in relation to complex international company groups, especially conglomerates and joint ventures, so it may need to be further refined: thus, the US–German treaty of 1989

---

[1] See e.g., US–Bermuda treaty of 1986, Art. 4.3(b) and Exchange of Notes, Point 2.

included a memorandum of understanding giving examples to clarify the provision, and stating that as the parties gained experience in administering it, further understandings and interpretations would be published.[1] The MOU also mentions that account will be taken of the views of the tax authorities of other states, especially European Community members. This is important in view of the objection made by some EC states to the anti-shopping provisions of the branch taxes introduced by the 1986 US Tax Reform Act, that they are inappropriate to the complex capital structures of some European firms, a trend which is likely to increase with the liberalization of movement of capital in the EC (see Chapter 11, section 2.b(ii) below). The US is reluctant to grant derivative benefits to third-country owners, as it regards each treaty as a package (Terr 1989, p. 526): for example, dividends paid to a German-French-Belgian joint venture company established in Germany are eligible for reduced withholding taxes only to the extent that the German, French and Belgian owners are eligible under their respective treaties (US–German treaty MOU, example VI). Hence, the US treaties with EC members should eventually either be aligned, or replaced by a single US–EC treaty.

All these measures allowing the source state to deny treaty benefits involve complex judgments by source state tax officials of the activities and nature of companies resident in the treaty-partner. So it is increasingly common for anti-abuse provisions to include a requirement of consultation between the treaty partners' competent authorities over the denial of treaty benefits, and a right of access to the competent authority by a taxpayer wishing to challenge denial of the benefit. The limitation of benefits provisions have therefore opened up a new area requiring closer international co-ordination of tax administration (see Chapter 10 below).

The precise combination of provisions which it may be appropriate to include in a particular treaty must be carefully considered, in the light of the interaction of the tax laws of the parties and the investment flows between them. Consideration should be given to whether limitation of benefits should target only companies, or other entities such as trusts and even partnerships, and perhaps individuals also. Further, the limitation may apply only to payments of dividends, interest and royalties, or may extend to all treaty benefits (Rosenbloom 1983, pp. 810–16). On the other hand, it may be preferable for a specific benefit to be subject to specific limitation: for example, the US–France protocol of 1978 exempting French insurers from the US insurance excise tax does not apply to the extent that the insurer reinsures with a person not entitled to the same exemption. A stringent limitation provision may not be necessary if the treaty benefits are relatively slight, i.e. if the restriction of source taxation is not significant, and the treaty-partner is not known as a treaty-haven. However, it must be remembered that conditions

---

[1] See Terr 1989, pp. 526–30 for an analysis of the examples appended to the treaty; he concludes that they tend to favour integrated businesses and functionally vertical structures.

may change, and that investors may find a way of taking advantage of the most unlikely loopholes.

3.b Renegotiation or Termination of Treaties with Havens

Arrangements for dealing with treaty shopping entail detailed negotiations between the source and recipient country over the interaction not only of their tax laws, but of other provisions, such as company and banking laws and practice. From one point of view, it is quite legitimate for the source country to ensure that the recipients of investment profits in a treaty country genuinely fall within the category of those entitled to withholding tax relief. On another view, such negotiations entail pressure to 'rewrite the tax law of a foreign country which desires to attract foreign investment through tax benefits', or in more extreme terms are 'no more than a civilised version of gunboat diplomacy' (Oliva 1984, p. 299).

On the other hand, it is not the state which is trying to enforce its tax which necessarily possesses all the gunboats. In fact, the US, which above all countries might be accused of economic gunboat diplomacy, has not had a very easy time in its attempts to renegotiate treaties to eliminate treaty shopping. US negotiators were already aware in the 1960s of the potential for abuse of treaty benefits in countries offering special tax regimes for foreign-owned holding companies. A clause excluding withholding tax relief for holding companies was included in a number of treaties, such as the 1962 treaty with Luxembourg, and a treaty with Brazil signed in 1967 which never went into effect. However, such a specific exclusion provision has only a limited effectiveness, as mentioned above; nevertheless, it was still the basis for the anti-treaty shopping provision in the US Model treaty published in 1977.

The increasing concern with abuse forced a reconsideration, and negotiations were opened with several countries (Switzerland, the British Virgin Islands and the Netherlands Antilles) to revise and tighten up the anti-shopping provision (Rosenbloom & Langbein 1981, p. 397). Although a new treaty was signed with the British Virgin Islands in February 1981, its anti-shopping clause was based on the 1977 US Model's provision for exclusion of holding companies, and it quickly became apparent that this alone would prevent US ratification of the BVI treaty, which would require Senate approval. The US Treasury published a much tighter anti-shopping model clause in June 1981 (followed in December 1981 by a further, slightly relaxed amended version). The Senate Foreign Relations Committee made it plain that it would insist on an acceptable version of this clause in all treaties: thus, ratification of a proposed treaty with Argentina, which contained no anti-shopping clause (the US negotiators had not requested one, not believing Argentina to be a tax haven), was conditioned by the Senate on inclusion of such a clause (Oliva 1984). The BVI and Argentina treaties remain unratified a decade later.

The concern of the US to restrict the use of treaties by 'unintended beneficiaries' has also required the renegotiation of long-standing treaties, which has not proved easy. A new standard was set with the negotiation of the Protocols to the French and Belgian treaties in 1988, and the new German–US treaty signed in 1989 (Terr 1989; Olmstead & De Jean 1989). The real test would be faced in the renegotiation with the Netherlands, which has long provided a convenient location for the 'Dutch mixer' conduit holding companies, taking advantage of the complete exemption of dividend receipts to repatriate foreign income, and also used as a convenient route for direct investment into the US (Langer 1988, pp. 73–8; Bennett 1991).

It also quickly became obvious that any haven which had an existing treaty had no inducement to agree a revision with a more stringent anti-shopping provision. Therefore, the Gordon Report recommended termination of existing tax haven treaties, especially those with British territories and the Netherlands Antilles, describing them as 'an affront to sound tax administration, existing only to be abused' (US Treasury 1981, p. 170). Consequently, in June 1983, the United States gave notice of termination of the treaties with British possessions, as well as those with former Belgian territories (Burundi, Rwanda, Zaire), to take effect from 1 January 1984. The treaties with the Dutch former colonies of Netherlands Antilles and Aruba (which had formerly been part of the Antilles) were not terminated at this stage, but in July 1984 Revenue Rulings were issued which sought to curtail their use for Eurobond flotation, at least prospectively. This announcement was co-ordinated with a similar statement by the UK Inland Revenue.

However, it proved more difficult to put new treaties in place with these countries. The programme seemed to start well, when Barbados became the first British former colony to sign both a double tax treaty and an agreement for mutual assistance in tax matters, at the end of 1984. This was aimed mainly at preventing third-country residents from making use for their US business of the favourable tax regime established by Barbados for so-called 'international business companies' to try to develop offshore financial business, based on several advantages possessed by Barbados, including the tax treaties which had been extended to it by the UK. Thus, the anti-abuse provision excluded from the treaty benefits any company less than 50 per cent owned by residents of either Barbados or the US, or if a substantial part of its income was used to meet liabilities to third-country residents (other than US citizens). This provision was reinforced by the treaty for mutual assistance, under which Barbados agreed to supply information necessary to enforce US tax laws, including information from banks (see Chapter 10 below). On this basis, the treaty was approved by the US Senate for ratification,[1] and came into force in 1986.

Unfortunately, however, the anti-abuse provision in the Barbados treaty,

[1] See statement of Ronald A. Pearlman before Senate Committee on Foreign Relations, 30 July 1985.

by defining specific exclusions from treaty benefits, also created a potential 'safe harbour' for other types of offshore business which could take advantage of the treaty. Specifically, since the anti-abuse clause did not apply to companies more than 50 per cent owned by residents of Barbados *or the US*, it opened up the possibility of some US-owned business moving offshore. In principle, this would be combated by the Subpart F provisions; but, as we have seen, these can be avoided to some extent, especially in respect of financial business such as insurance unconnected with the US, or carried out for an unrelated party (which may be done by 'pools'). Even if a company is subject to Subpart F, this can still represent a substantial tax advantage (US Treasury 1981, pp. 86–90). The advantages given by the treaty were confirmed by Finance Minister Haynes of Barbados, who was quoted as saying that Barbados would aim to use the excise tax exemption to attract insurance business and by offering 'one-stop-shopping' would try to broaden its offshore financial business.[1]

The Barbados treaty not only meant encouragement for some US insurance business to move offshore, it also created a competitive advantage for Barbados against Bermuda, which had been the main home for insurance and reinsurance companies seeking tax and offshore financial benefits. It may be that this was the intention of the US treaty negotiators; certainly, some tax specialists had advocated the extension of treaty benefits to several centres, thus creating competition between them, in return for agreements to end secrecy provisions to enable some policing (e.g. testimony by Marshall Langer, in US Congress 1983b, pp. 205–7).

Both countries were put on the same footing when a treaty was signed with Bermuda in 1986 on taxation of insurance enterprises and mutual assistance in tax matters, which gave exemption also for Bermuda-based insurance business, subject to similar limitations in respect of third-country bene-ficiaries. This time, however, the unease of the US Congress at this policy was expressed in a letter written to Treasury Secretary Baker by Congressman Rostenkowski, Democratic Chairman of the House Ways and Means Committee, opposing the Bermuda treaty.[2] Baker's response stressed the 'unique circumstances' of the US relationship with Bermuda, due to the national security interests – a US naval and air base covers 10 per cent of Bermudan land mass. Baker pointed to the economic damage to Bermuda caused by the loss of insurance business to Barbados, due to its recent treaty; also that the anti-abuse provision prevented any treaty benefits to companies owned by third-country residents, and that US owners of Bermudan insurance companies would be liable to tax under Subpart F for their share of income from insurance of related parties.

---

[1] Tax Notes 1986, vol. 33, pp. 22–5.
[2] Letter of 15 July 1986, Tax Notes 1986, vol. 29, p. 302: although the House Committee has no formal role in treaty ratification, it is the initiator of domestic tax changes, which could be used to nullify treaty benefits.

However, the Senate Foreign Relations Committee was only partially reassured by this response, and finally approved the Bermuda treaty for ratification in September 1988 only with reservations. These were that the exemption on the US excise tax on insurance premiums would apply only to Bermudan companies subject to taxation under Subpart F; and the exemption would in any case end from 1 January 1990. These conditions were tied to an undertaking by the Treasury department to renegotiate the treaty with Barbados, to end the exemption from insurance excise tax from 1990. Thus, the offshore insurance business of Bermuda would be put on a footing of competitive equality with Barbados, but by taking away from both countries the concessions made by the treaty negotiators. Although the Bermuda treaty was ratified on this basis at the end of 1988, it was possible that if they lost considerable offshore business, both Bermuda and Barbados would withdraw from the treaties; even if the treaties remained in force, co-operation under the mutual assistance provisions would be hindered (see Chapter 10 below). Not only was opinion in Barbados angered by Congress's overriding of their agreement, but this made it harder to negotiate with others.

The same dilemma was revealed in US relations over this same period with Aruba and the Netherlands Antilles. In August 1986, after several years of negotiation, treaties were finally signed with these former Dutch colonies. Like the Barbados and Bermuda treaties, these obliged the havens to provide mutual assistance in tax matters, which would require amendment of their secrecy laws, and curtailed – but did not completely eliminate – the treaty-shopping possibilities of the offshore countries. In the case of the Netherlands Antilles and Aruba, the treaty sought to end the privileged tax treatment of Eurodollar borrowing based there (for flotations after July 1984, the date of the new IRS Rulings mentioned above); but excluded from the treaty-shopping clause both international mutual funds and qualified real estate companies. Again, therefore, this embodied a bargain whereby the havens accepted co-operation with the US authorities and curtailment of their wide-ranging treaty-shopping possibilities, in exchange for a more restrained but secure specialization. Instead of a tax avoidance 'supermarket', exposed to the risk of US retaliation, they would become up-market 'boutiques', each with its own financial lines on offer (Davidson 1986).

This compromise seemed unlikely to satisfy any of the parties standing behind the negotiators. The US Congress was unhappy with the legitimation of treaty-shopping behind the safe-harbours of the limited anti-abuse clauses, considering that the 'boutique' approach to treaty shopping would merely redistribute offshore business, rather than close it down. Having agreed concessions with some countries, it would seem impossible to deny others some similar advantages. Also, these negotiations coincided with the enormous and complex bargaining within the US surrounding tax reform: to give some tax advantage to US-owned offshore business such as insurance or real-estate investment would not only undermine the drive for fairness in US taxes, it would also reduce the revenue available to allow the reduction in the top tax rates which alone could provide the political basis for the domestic tax reform.

For their part, the Netherlands Antilles and Arbua were reluctant to give up the Eurobond interest exemption, and did not take the necessary steps to amend their internal law to permit ratification of the treaties agreed in 1986. Thus, on 29 June 1987 the US notified them of the termination of their treaties with the US, with effect from 1 January 1988. However, this announcement had a devastating effect on the Eurobond market. The cancellation of the treaty affected all Eurobonds issued in the Netherlands Antilles, and not only those issued since 1984; such bonds normally included a clause allowing early redemption in case of any change in the tax situation, and this would allow the borrowers to refinance at the lower rates now prevailing in the markets. The resultant sharp fall in prices of Netherlands Antilles bonds threatened considerable losses to the bondholders, many of which turned out to be US institutions. As a result, less than two weeks later, on 10 July, the US authorities were forced to retreat, and modify the notice of termination, stating that Article 8 of the treaties, which exempts interest paid by US persons to residents and corporations of Aruba and the Antilles, would continue in force.[1]

Nevertheless, the treaty benefits had effectively been ended by the IRS Rulings of July 1984, matched by a similar statement by the British Inland Revenue (mentioned above); when the British terminated their treaty with the Netherlands Antilles with effect from April 1989, there was no major market reaction, since the UK measures did not apply to payments made to service quoted Eurobonds issued before 26 July 1984 (Finance Act 1989, s.116). The ending of exemption of interest meant that payments *to* finance companies in the Netherlands Antilles could be subject to withholding tax at source if made from the US or the UK direct to the Netherlands Antilles. However, payments could still be made via a Dutch holding company, since the Netherlands has no withholding tax on interest payments and its 1986 treaty with the Netherlands Antilles provided for a low withholding tax on dividend payments.

A more potent measure against Netherlands Antilles bonds was the move by the US and the UK in 1984 to join the offshore centres instead of trying to beat them, by giving US borrowers direct access to the Eurocurrency markets in London and Luxembourg, without the necessity of a Netherlands Antilles intermediary. The UK enacted legislation in 1984 which allowed payment without any withholding tax deduction of interest on quoted Eurobonds held in a recognized clearing system, subject to the proviso that the paying agent prove to the Revenue that the beneficial owner is not resident in the UK. This offered an inducement to companies to move their Eurobond flotations to London, where they might be more effectively policed, as concerns tax evasion

[1] Although it was unclear whether the US could withdraw from the treaty while unilaterally leaving part of it in force; the treaty partners eventually accepted this partial revocation.

by UK residents, while non-residents are offered secrecy. However, UK-resident companies are still permitted to pay interest gross to a Netherlands Antilles subsidiary for the purpose of servicing quoted Eurobonds.[1] At the same time, the US coupled its repeal in 1984 of the withholding tax on interest on domestic bonds bought by foreigners with a provision for 'special registered' status under which, provided the investment house certifies that the interest is paid to a non-resident, the identity of the bondholder is not revealed to the US Treasury. This gave the bondholders some of the advantages of bearer status, while protecting the US against evasion of its taxes (I. Walter, in Lessard & Williamson 1987, p. 118). Thus, in order to gain more control over international capital markets and ensure enforcement of their own laws, these states are offering arrangements which in effect facilitate evasion of the laws of other countries. However, the Netherlands Antilles has been obliged to begin to reconcile itself to becoming a non-treaty haven.

To induce actual and potential havens, especially in the Caribbean, to enter into agreements with comprehensive anti-avoidance provisions, the US offered other benefits which might replace their offshore financial business. For countries accepting agreements for assistance in tax matters, the US offered: deductibility for US taxpayers of convention expenses (to boost tourism); eligibility as a base for Foreign Sales Corporations (FSCs); and the possibility of investments from tax-free earnings of companies accumulated in Puerto Rican banks.[2]

In addition to these, a range of other inducements were put forward under the Caribbean Basin Initiative (CBI), established under the Caribbean Basin Economic Recovery Act of 1983, including duty-free entry of certain goods (with important exclusions such as textiles and clothing, footwear and canned tuna). These additional advantages were conditioned on a country meeting seven mandatory and eleven discretionary criteria (US Dept. of Commerce, CBI Guidebook, 1988). Assistance with combating tax avoidance is not itself a condition of eligibility for CBI status, but co-operation in the US anti-narcotic drugs drive is, and may involve similar requirements – essentially, a treaty for exchange of information and legal assistance, and changes in domestic laws to limit bank and company secrecy. However, this may be limited to the criminal context, as with the treaty negotiated in 1986 by the UK with the US on behalf of the Cayman Islands.[3] Havens are usually more willing to grant legal assistance of this sort in relation to criminal matters,

---

[1] The exemption for quoted Eurobonds is now ICTA 1988, s.124; the exemption of payments to a Netherlands Antilles subsidiary applies only if it is 90 per cent owned by a company resident in the UK which is not a 51 per cent subsidiary of a non-UK resident: Finance Act 1989 s.116.

[2] Referred to as 'qualified possession source investment income' or QPSII funds.

[3] This excludes tax matters except for tax fraud in relation to the proceeds of crime: Article 19(3)(e), see Chapter 10 below; the treaty was finally ratified in 1990 and is to extend also to Anguilla, the BVI, Montserrat, and the Turks and Caicos Islands.

perhaps including tax fraud; but the US authorities aim to obtain co-operation against tax avoidance. Hence, the tax benefits (convention deductibility, FSC status, and access to QPSII funds) are on offer only in exchange for tax enforcement assistance.

The combination of the stick of withdrawal of tax treaty benefits, and the carrots of these inducements, had persuaded eight countries to enter into Tax Information Exchange Agreements with the US Treasury by September 1990.[1] Surprisingly however, even some of the long-term treaty partners of the US, notably the UK, were listed as ineligible for benefits such as FSC status, due to limitations on their tax assistance provisions.[2] Many countries still prefer to have no tax treaty with the US, and to try to attract investment independently through favourable tax arrangements, which from the point of view of US tax officials essentially entail encouraging international tax avoidance. Critics of the US programme argued that it asked too much for too little, and that a broader approach including fostering educational, cultural and technological development and interaction should be negotiated, in lieu of the unilateral carrot-and-stick approach (Zagaris 1989). On the other hand, the UK still maintained agreements with many of its dependencies and former dependencies, which had been concluded in the 1947–52 period,[3] but the provisions on information exchange are limited by the British view that they cover only information available to each tax authority for enforcement of its own law (see Chapter 10 below). Although Britain is responsible for the foreign affairs of many of these territories, and could enter into tax information treaties on their behalf,[4] in practice this might produce no improvement in co-operation and could instead provoke secession.

---

[1] Barbados, Bermuda, Dominica, Dominican Republic, Grenada, Jamaica, Mexico and Trinidad and Tobago; agreements signed with Costa Rica, Peru and St Lucia still required them to enact domestic legislation to authorize the supply of information. See US Treasury announcement, Tax Notes, 3 September 1990.

[2] The Inland Revenue takes the view that assistance can only be provided if there is a UK tax interest: see further Chapter 10 below.

[3] Some treaties had been terminated by the territories concerned: e.g. the Seychelles in 1982, and Dominica, St Lucia and St Vincent-Grenadines all in 1986; while the UK terminated its arrangement with the British Virgin Islands in 1971: see Table in Simon 1983–, vol. F.

[4] For example, if the UK ratified the OECD/Council of Europe multilateral assistance convention, it could be applied to UK overseas territories (Article 29); in practice this could not be done without the prior agreement of the government of the territory concerned: see Chapter 6, section 1.c above.

8
The Transfer Price Problem

Fair taxation by national states of an internationally-organized business requires an equitable allocation between the various jurisdictions of the tax base of the business. This entails the attribution to the various parts of the business operating in different states not only of the profits but also, most importantly, of the costs for which each is responsible.

TNCs do not consist of a series of separate unrelated businesses carried out in different countries; rather, each TNC is a single organization operating related activities. There are nevertheless many variations between TNCs in the degree of integration of their operations, depending both on the characteristics of the businesses and the history and growth of the particular firm. These factors, as well as the firm's management style, result in various methods of reconciling centralization of strategic direction with decentralization of direct operational functions. The pricing of internal transfers between the various profit-centres within the firm is therefore an important aspect of the firm's own strategic management. For national states, including the tax authorities, these internal transfer prices[1] have become an increasingly important factor, as the internal transfers within TNCs, of tangible and intangible goods, services and finance, have become a major element in international trade and payments. Intra-firm transactions account for over 30 per cent of the exports of leading countries such as Japan, the UK and the US, and are especially significant in high-technology industries such as chemicals, machinery and transport equipment (UN 1988a, p. 93; UN 1978).

Although the pricing of internal transfers was identified very early as a key

---

[1] I refer to the 'transfer price problem' to emphasize the inherent issue posed by the setting of prices in transactions between related entities. The term 'transfer pricing' commonly carries the additional connotation of the use of manipulation of such prices to transfer funds so as to avoid foreign exchange controls, minimize taxation, etc. This use of the term assumes that there is an obvious 'correct' price, and any deviation is a manipulation or abuse. As I explain in the text, it is this mistaken starting-point that has been at the root of many of the difficulties in analysing the problem.

problem for the taxation of international business, it was not until the 1970s that it came squarely on to the international agenda. The reasons both for its long concealment and its reappearance have already been indicated in previous chapters. The approach adopted in the League of Nations period emphasized that the starting-point for the national tax administrator must be the separate accounts of the particular subsidiary or branch; however, these could be rectified, preferably using the arm's length criterion. This solution resulted from the perception of the problem as being the manipulation of prices by the firm in order to minimize taxation or avoid double taxation (see Chapter 1, section 5 above). By adjusting the accounts of local affiliates using the arm's length criterion, the underlying issue of the basis of allocation was avoided, since the enterprises could deal with each national authority on the basis of separate accounts, negotiating whatever adjustments might be necessary on a practical basis, case by case.

It was only following the rapid growth of TNCs in the postwar period (in absolute, although less so in relative terms) that the more active use of powers to rectify accounts brought to the fore once more the underlying issue of international allocation. It became increasingly plain that the problem was not merely that firms could avoid tax by fixing prices which were other than the 'true' ones; the underlying issue was the need to establish criteria to determine a fair allocation of costs and profits. The arm's length criterion assumed that this question could be resolved 'naturally', by reference to market prices set for comparable transactions between unrelated parties. As we will see in detail in this chapter, however, transactions that are strictly comparable are hard to find, and such a procedure can be complex and difficult. In practice, administrators have resorted to an arm's length *profit* criterion, comparing the profitability of the entity with that of comparable independent firms. While this approach was authorized as a fall-back technique or a check on the validity of price adjustments, it has come to be increasingly relied upon as a primary method, especially in the absence of comparable transactions. Furthermore, profit-comparison has tended to become profit-split, since tax authorities are naturally concerned that the local entity should show a reasonable proportion of the total profits of the enterprise as a whole.

Nevertheless, the starting-point of separate accounts and the independent enterprise criterion means that there is no effective measure for the fair allocation of the overall profit. Yet economic theory strongly suggests that the existence of TNCs is rooted in the additional returns, or synergy profits, which can be earned by such an integrated organization. In the absence of criteria for the equitable division of the tax base of such integrated firms, the problem has been resolved in practice by administrative or bureaucratic processes of bargaining, both between firms' representatives and national officials, and between officials of different countries.

1. Separate Accounts and the Arm's Length Fiction

The separate legal personality of an incorporated company poses recurrent problems for business regulation, not least for the administration of direct taxes on income or profits. From the earliest days of direct taxation, tax administrators and legislators were reluctant to allow parent and subsidiary companies to be treated in the same way as independent entities for tax purposes, since related companies have the power to structure transactions between them so as to reduce the overall tax liability of the group. Hence, measures quickly emerged in tax codes, administrative regulations or court decisions, to prevent such avoidance. Two approaches are possible in this context: to require consolidation of the accounts of companies under common ownership; or to adjust accounts between related companies.

1.a The US: From Consolidation to Adjustment of Related Company Accounts

In the US from 1917, affiliated corporations were required to file a consolidated return.[1] The courts supported the logic of consolidation:

> The purpose of requiring consolidated returns was . . . to impose the war profits tax upon the true net income and invested capital of what was, in practical effect, a single business enterprise, even though conducted by means of more than one corporation. Primarily, the consolidated return was to preclude the reduction of the total tax payable by the business, viewed as a unit, by redistribution of income or capital among the component corporations by means of inter-company transactions. [*Burnet, CIR v. Aluminum Goods Manuf. Corp.*, 1932, p. 547.]

However, consolidation required the elimination of all inter-affiliate transactions, and the inclusion as income of the proceeds of sales only once made outside the group. It was particularly difficult to consolidate the income of foreign affiliates not doing business in the US, which were not liable to US tax.

For these reasons the emphasis shifted to ensuring correct taxation of related corporations by adjusting the accounts between them if necessary. Initially, Congress authorized the Revenue to prepare consolidated returns for businesses under common control only where necessary to compute their 'correct' tax liability (Revenue Act 1921 s.240(d)). This was revised in s.45 of

[1] Articles 77 and 78 of Regulation 41 made by the Commissioner of Inland Revenue under the Revenue Act 1917, for the wartime excess profits tax, required information to be filed on all inter-company relationships, and provided that this tax could be levied on the consolidated returns of affiliated corporations. This was confirmed by the Revenue Act 1918 s.240, which extended consolidation to the corporation income tax. Some anomalies were caused by the application of corporation income tax in 1917/1918 to separate companies, while requiring consolidation of affiliated companies' accounts for the excess profits tax. See *Aluminum Co. of America v. US* (1932).

the 1928 Act, which instead gave a very broad power to adjust accounts of related corporations.[1] The House Ways and Means Committee identified the problem as being that 'subsidiary corporations, particularly foreign subsidiaries, are sometimes employed to "milk" the parent corporation, or otherwise improperly manipulate the financial accounts of the parent company'. The intention of s.45 was therefore to provide the powers 'necessary in order to prevent evasion (by the shifting of profits, the making of fictitious sales, and other methods frequently adopted for the purpose of "milking"), and in order clearly to reflect their true tax liability'.[2]

Section 45 of the 1928 Act, later enacted with minor changes as s.482 of the Tax Code, has remained in force since that time:[3]

> In any case of two or more [add: organizations,] trades or businesses (whether or not incorporated, whether or not organized in the United States and whether or not affiliated) owned or controlled directly or indirectly by the same interests, the Commissioner [subst.: Secretary or his delegate] is authorized to [subst.: may] distribute, apportion, or allocate gross income, deductions [add: credits or allowances] between or among such [add: organizations,] trades or businesses, if he determines that such distribution, apportionment or allocation is necessary in order to prevent evasion of taxes or clearly to reflect the income of any of such [add: organizations,] trades or businesses.

The omission in the 1928 wording of any reference to the consolidation of accounts underlined the separate taxability of members of a group under common control, while giving the Revenue very broad powers to adjust accounts. The breadth of the Revenue's discretion was confirmed by court decisions. The power was held to apply to prevent any avoidance or reduction of tax liability, and not only to criminal tax evasion: *Asiatic Petroleum v. CIR* (1935). This case resulted from a manoeuvre by Royal Dutch Shell to transfer profit out of the US through the sale by Asiatic, a Delaware corporation, of the stock of a subsidiary at cost to its Dutch affiliate Bataafsche, which resold at a profit back to another US affiliate. The courts rejected a determined legal onslaught on s.45, including the claim that it was an unconstitutional deprivation of property without due process of law. Another landmark decision held that the Revenue is entitled to make any adjustments necessary and proper 'clearly to reflect the income', even to transactions having a sound

---

[1] The House Ways and Means Committee, which initiates revenue bills, considered that consolidation was too favourable to corporations, and especially that foreign affiliates, whose income could not be consolidated, could be used for tax avoidance. The House therefore eliminated consolidation altogether from the 1928 Finance Bill; but it was restored by the Senate Finance Committee, although only for domestic corporations within an affiliated group. However, the reference to consolidation was dropped from the anti-avoidance provision (s.240), which was enacted in broader language as s.45 of the 1928 Act.

[2] Report 350, 67th Congress, 1st session, p. 14, cited in *Asiatic Petroleum Ltd (Delaware) v. CIR* (1935); see below.

[3] Some minor subsequent amendments are indicated in square brackets: for the much more important amendment of 1986 introducing the 'commensurate with income' standard, see section 3.f below.

motivation not primarily related to tax saving (*Central Cuba Sugar Co. v. CIR*, 1952).

1.b France: Taxing Profits Transferred to a Foreign Parent

While the American authorities were concerned about subsidiaries, especially those formed abroad, being used to milk parent companies, some European countries identified the reverse problem: that local foreign-owned companies might be 'dummies', formed to comply with protectionist commercial requirements or preferences, but transferring their profits to the parent. The most radical approach was taken by the French Treasury, which considered that it could impose the tax on income from securities ('impôt sur le revenu des valeurs mobilières'), on the proportion of the dividends distributed by a foreign parent company represented by the value of its holdings in the French branch or subsidiary in relation to its total assets. This was resented by foreign investors and their governments as being both extraterritorial and double taxation. The French rejected these arguments, since French companies were also subject to taxation both on their commercial profits and on the dividends paid to their owners. Although France agreed to mitigate any double taxation by concluding bilateral treaties, the resulting half-dozen treaties generally preserved the French right to tax both the profits of the French establishment and a 'deemed dividend' represented by any diverted profits (see Chapter 1, section 4 above; Carroll 1939, p. 49; League of Nations, 1933, p. 115).

Thus, the French tax treaties concluded in 1931 with Belgium and Italy and in 1932 with the USA included a provision empowering each state to reallocate any profits or losses transferred between related enterprises due to their relationship being conducted in conditions other than those which would apply between independent enterprises. The French authorities therefore refocused on the 'diverted profits' which should be reattributed to the local subsidiary. Hence, a very general provision was enacted in 1933 empowering such diverted profits to be restored to the accounts of the local subsidiary.[1] The 1933 provision remains in almost exactly the same wording as s.57 of the Code General des Impôts:

> In assessing the income tax due by undertakings which are controlled by or which control enterprises established outside France, the income which is indirectly transferred to the latter, either by increasing or decreasing purchase or sale prices, or by any other means, shall be restored to the trading results shown in the accounts.

---

[1] Loi du 31 mai 1933, art. 76; codified in art. 20, Decree of 20 July 1934: Recueil Dalloz Périodique et Critique 1934, p. 172.

The same procedure is followed with respect to undertakings which are controlled by an enterprise or a group of enterprises also controlling undertakings located outside France.

The condition of control or dependence is not required when the beneficiary of a transfer is established in a country or a territory with privileged tax status as defined in Article 238–A para.2 of this Code (added by Finance Act 1982 Art. 90–II).

Should specific data not be available for making the adjustments provided in the foregoing paragraph, the taxable profits shall be determined by comparison with the profits of similar undertakings normally managed.

1.c The League of Nations and Arm's Length

The international discussions in the League of Nations reaffirmed the principle of the adjustment of the accounts of local affiliates, based on the criterion of independent enterprises dealing at arm's length. The 1935 draft Convention on allocation provided that where, between companies owned or controlled by the same interests, there were commercial or financial relations different from those which would have been made between independent enterprises, any 'diverted' item of profit or loss must be re-attributed (1935 Allocation Convention Art. VI, see Chapter 1, section 5 above).

However, the League studies were primarily concerned with the problem of branches of the same company; and agreement was reached that a branch, provided it fell within the definition of a Permanent Establishment, should be taxed on the basis of separate accounts and the criterion of 'independent persons dealing at arm's length'. Thus, Article III of the 1935 Convention, dealing with Permanent Establishments, was much more detailed than Article VI, on enterprises under common control: the phrase 'dealing at arm's length' was used only in Article III. Significantly, Article III permitted as a fall-back the 'percentage of turnover' method, and even the allocation of the total income on the basis of 'coefficients'. No doubt it was easier to accept that these profit-apportionment methods could be used in the case of a single company which already had consolidated accounts, than to permit or require consolidation for separate but related companies.

Both provisions have been incorporated into subsequent model treaties: Article III, substantially modified, is still the basis for Article 7 of the OECD and UN models, while Article VI remains in virtually identical wording in Article 9 of the models. Article 7(2) requires the attribution to a Permanent Establishment of 'the profits which it might be expected to make if it were a distinct and separate enterprise engaged in the same or similar activities under the same or similar conditions and dealing wholly independently with the enterprise of which it is a Permanent Establishment'. Although the article itself no longer refers to the 'percentage of turnover' method, it is still accepted as a fall-back method, and discussed as such in the Commentary to the OECD model (para. 23). This can still be important, especially for financial firms such as banks and insurance companies, which often operate abroad through branches.[1] In this connection, a disagreement has arisen about the 'percentage of turnover' method. The OECD Committee's report on taxation of multinational banking indicated that while the majority of the committee's members considered that the 'appropriate coefficients' required a comparison with other similar enterprises in the same country, Japan and the United States considered that industry standards could be used which might be international (OECD 1984–II, paras. 64–7). While historically the provision intended national comparisons, a good case can be made that this would not be adequate today for a global activity such as banking (see section 3.a below). Article 7(4) of the models still allows a global apportionment method to be used for Permanent Establishments, although only where this has been used traditionally and only if 'the results are in accordance with the principles' of the article.[2] Article 9 of the model treaties is the key provision for taxation of international company groups; yet although its wording is obscure the OECD 1977 Commentary provided virtually no elucidation, merely stating 'It is evidently appropriate that adjustments should be sanctioned in such circumstances and this paragraph [Art. 9 para. 1] seems to call for little comment.' Nevertheless, the US by reservation stated its belief that 'this Article should apply to all related persons, not just an enterprise of one contracting state and a related enterprise of the other contracting state, and that it should apply to "income deductions, credits or allowances", not just to "profits" '. To ensure this, the US model treaty includes a third paragraph which permits application of provisions of national law for any adjustments necessary clearly to reflect the income of any related persons.

1.d The UK: Profit Split and Arm's Length

The League provisions were also substantially influenced by British rules, which dated back to 1915. These aimed to prevent avoidance of high wartime taxes by foreign companies trading in the UK through branches or subsidiaries.[3] Hence, the 1915 Finance Act provided that a foreign non-resident person doing business through a local branch or agent could be taxed in

[1] Thus, the UK has since 1915 taxed foreign life assurance companies doing business in the UK on the basis of the proportion of the UK to world premiums applied to their world income from investments, less a deduction in the same proportion for management expenses. Although this method has been held to be contrary to the basic arm's length provision of Article 7(2) of the model treaty (*Ostime v. Australian Mutual Provident Society*, 1960), it was considered to be preserved by the proviso in Article 7(4), especially when interpreted in accordance with paragraph 24 of the OECD Commentary: *Sun Life Assurance Co. of Canada v. Pearson* (1984).
[2] The OECD Committee, in the Multinational Banking Enterprises report, stressed that the 'global apportionment' approach permitted in Article 7(4) was for use in exceptional cases only, and as a subsidiary method; it should not be confused with the separate enterprise standard laid down as the norm in both Articles 7 and 9. The majority of the Committee deduced from this that it is inappropriate to allocate the global costs of a firm by formula in attributing expenses, specifically, in deciding the true costs of interest to a multinational bank: OECD 1984–II, para. 69, and section 3.c(iii) below.
[3] Since a foreign subsidiary of a UK parent company could be treated as resident and taxable

its name; similarly, where the foreign non-resident was doing business with a UK resident and 'owing to the close connection and . . .,to the substantial control exercised by the non-resident over the resident', business was carried on between the two in such a way as to produce to the resident person a profit lower than that which might be expected, the non-resident person should be chargeable to tax in the name of the resident person as agent.[1] Whether operating through a local branch, agent or subsidiary, the foreign parent could be assessed using the same rule: if the 'true amount' of the profits made by the foreign parent could not be 'readily ascertained', the non-resident parent could be charged to tax on the basis of a percentage of the turnover of the business of the parent done through the UK entity (Rule 8).[2] Thus, there was a broad power to raise an assessment based on the foreign parent's profits, and the problem of enforcement jurisdiction was evaded by treating the local subsidiary as an agent.

These measures were undoubtedly taken in response to moves by foreign companies to minimize their exposure to UK tax. For example, the Gillette company of Boston set up a UK subsidiary in 1908, but then wound it up in 1912 and transferred its UK business to a separate subsidiary in Massachusetts, which as a non-resident of the UK would have been taxable only on its UK business. In 1915 Gillette went further, ceased to trade directly in the UK, and instead licensed its UK business to a new company set up by its former UK managing director. Nevertheless, the Revenue tried to treat the new UK company as 'under the control' of Gillette in Boston, although their link was only contractual; but this was firmly rejected by the High Court as 'arbitrary taxation gone mad'. (*Gillette Safety Razor Co. v. Commrs. of Inland Revenue*, 1920).

Thus, from 1918 the Revenue had broad powers to adjust the profits of local branches or subsidiaries of foreign firms. This approach was re-evaluated after 1945, when the UK adopted the League of Nations' London model as the basis for negotiating bilateral treaties (see Chapter 2, section 1.a above). In 1951 a new statutory provision was enacted to deal with international interaffiliate transactions.[3] This applied to any two bodies of persons under common

in the UK (see Chapter 1, section 2 above), it was presumably thought unnecessary to deal with that case.

[1] Finance (No. 2) Act 1915 s.31(3)(4)(5); re-enacted in Income Tax Act 1918, All Schedules Rules 7–9. In Australia a similar section was enacted in 1922, which became s.136 of the Income Tax Act, applying to international transactions until 1981. Since this was fairly easily avoided by interposing a second Australian company to hold the shares of both the resident and non-resident company, it was replaced by the more comprehensive provisions of Division 13 of the Income Tax Assessment Act 1982.

[2] A modification was introduced in 1918 for sales of goods manufactured abroad by the parent: the tax charge could be limited to 'the profits which might reasonably be expected to have been earned by a merchant or . . . retailer': Rule 12, All Schedules Rules, Income Tax Act 1918, now TMA 1970 s. 81. This was the concept of 'merchanting profit', see League of Nations 1932, pp. 191–4.

[3] Finance Act 1951 s.37, re-enacted as Income Tax Act 1952 s.469, replacing Rule 7 of the 1918 Rules. The section was introduced when it was realized that s.51 of the Finance (No. 2) Act 1945, which provided for the conclusion of tax treaties, was insufficient to empower the adjustment of accounts between related entities, although there was considerable suspicion of it as a 'socialist' measure: House of Commons debates (1950–1), vol. 488, cols. 2454–66, vol. 489, cols. 2071–98, esp. col. 2076.

control, replacing the previous rule allowing a non-resident to be treated as doing business through a local branch or agent where the close connection produced less than ordinary profits to the resident; but the remaining rules dealing with a non-resident doing business in the UK through a branch or agent continued in force; and in such cases, the 'percentage of turnover' method, with the proviso for a 'merchanting profit' for resales of foreign manufactures, still apply today.[1]

In contrast, the provisions on related entities are concerned not with the overall profit but the pricing of specific transactions. The powers they give the Revenue are limited to the adjustment of the price of any transaction if it is fixed at less or more than 'the price which it might have been expected to fetch if the parties to the transaction had been independent persons dealing at arm's length'. In such circumstances a price adjustment can be made, by direction of the Board of Inland Revenue, to ensure that 'the like consequences shall ensue as would have ensued' if the transaction had been 'a transaction between independent persons dealing at arm's length'. The power to adjust does not apply if the beneficiary is resident and doing business in the UK: that is, if an undervalued sale results in a lower deduction to a UK-resident buyer, or an over-valued sale increases the profits of a UK-resident seller.[2] The section has remained essentially the same since 1951.[3] Significant amendments in 1975 clarified the 'common control' criterion, and added broad powers to require information, including information from foreign subsidiaries if owned 51 per cent or more by a UK resident company.[4] In addition, the Oil Taxation Act of 1975, which brought in a special Petroleum Revenue Tax for oil extraction and exploitation, introduced a specific definition of arm's length pricing for such activities.[5] Interestingly, this specifically provides that it shall be assumed in determining the arm's length price that both buyer and seller should secure 'reasonable profit from transactions of the same kind carried out on similar terms over a reasonable period' (ICTA 1988, s.771(6)(a)).

---

[1] Rules, 8, 9 and 12 of the 1918 General Rules are substantially re-enacted in the Taxes Management Act 1970 ss.80–1. In some circumstances a subsidiary in the UK may be treated as the agent of its parent so that some of the parent's business may be considered to be carried on in the UK: *Firestone Tyre & Rubber Co. v. Llewellin* (1957).

[2] However, the courts have held, partly on the analogy of this provision, that sales at undervalue between two related resident companies are not sales in the course of trade, so can be credited at market value: see *Sharkey v. Wernher* (1955) and *Petrotim Securities v. Ayres* (1963). Resident companies, on the other hand, may benefit from exemption of tax on inter-affiliate payments and from group relief on trading losses of affiliates.

[3] ICTA 1970 s.485; now with revised drafting ss.770 and 773 ICTA 1988.

[4] Finance Act 1975 s.17. The section had previously defined as bodies under common control two companies either of whom controlled the other or both of whom were controlled by 'some other person'; in response apparently to a dispute with a taxpayer, the 1975 amendment specified 'for the removal of doubt' that this included control by other 'persons' in the plural; this measure was regarded as tantamount to unfair retrospective legislation by the lawyers involved in the pending dispute: see Capon in Fordham Corporate Law Institute 1976, p. 104.

[5] OTA 1975 ss.13–21, Schedule 9, now ICTA 1988 s.771; and see *Reg. v. A-G ex parte ICI* (1985).

These powers to adjust the prices of specific transactions are much more precise than the broad power in the 1918 rules to tax the 'true profit' of a foreign parent, or for that matter the sweeping provisions of the American s.482 allowing allocation or apportionment of any income or deductions. In practice, however, the US powers have been exercised within the framework of specific regulations (to be considered below) and a system in which recourse to adjudication is more frequent. By contrast, the British authorities prefer to deal by discreet negotiations and private settlement with the taxpayer. Notably, in the 40-year life of the British 'arm's length' provision, there has been only one litigated case under it, and indeed it appears that there have been very few instances of a formal direction by the Board to effect a price adjustment.[1] Essentially, the confidential negotiations between the Revenue and the taxpayers' professional advisors have been carried out 'under the umbrella' of the powers given by the section.[2] Nevertheless, officials may feel constrained by the lack of any administrative rules and their vulnerability to expensive and time-consuming court proceedings. This may explain the remark of a senior Revenue official, on the face of it rather surprising, that in the UK transfer pricing is 'not an administrative matter' but subject to control by the Special Commissioners and the Courts (Hunter, in Competent Authorities 1986, p. 593).

1.e Germany: Organic Unity and Profit Split

In German law also, provisions were enacted in the inter-war period to deal

---

[1] The requirement of a Direction was introduced during the passage of the provision in 1951, following criticisms that the power would entail excessive administrative interference in the pricing decisions of companies: House of Commons debates 1950–1, vol. 489, col. 2094. It has been claimed that no record is kept of such directions: Hansard 1983–4 vol. 52, p. 222. The only reported case is *Commrs. of I.R. v. Lithgows Ltd* (1960), in which the Scottish Court of Session upheld a decision of the Special Commissioners, rejecting a Revenue view that there was common control where a majority of the shares of two companies were held by trusts for members of the same family (different heirs of Sir James Lithgow), with almost but not exactly the same trustees.

[2] This phrase was used by an Inland Revenue official directly concerned with transfer pricing adjustments, in interview; see also Rouse in Fordham CLI 1976. In the case of pricing between related entities in the UK and a treaty country, the much broader provisions of the treaty articles apply, at least to adjustments relieving persons from UK taxation. Under s.788(3) ICTA 1988, any arrangements for relief of double taxation have effect over other legislation, *inter alia*, for determining the income or chargeable gains (i) of non-residents and their UK establishments; (ii) of UK residents having 'special relationships' with non-residents. This would allow adjustments as provided for in the relevant tax treaty, i.e. to profits and not just prices, and not only where there is legal control but any 'participation' direct or indirect by one person in both entities. It is not clear, however, whether this can create a charge to tax (Davies 1985, para. 14.04): since s.788 provides for the enforcement of arrangements for 'relief from double taxation', it empowers the Revenue to adjust income so as to relieve a person from UK taxation; but it does not appear to permit a unilateral adjustment of income by the UK, even in terms allowed by the treaty, unless the adjustment were agreed by the treaty-partner. Hence, a charge to UK tax must be created by an adjustment to a price, not to income or profit.

with inter-affiliate transactions; however, these proved inadequate and were replaced by new legislation in 1972. The high corporate tax rate in the 1920s was an incentive for local subsidiaries of foreign companies to establish pricing arrangements which minimized German tax liability. To combat this, the income and corporate tax laws of 1925 made two provisions. Where a foreign enterprise (which would not be fully subject to German tax) operated a business through a branch establishment, the income of the local establishment could be assessed by comparison with similar businesses or on the basis of a normal return on the capital employed (s.34). In the case of a separately incorporated company (which would be fully subject to German tax), if, as a result of a special relationship, there was a 'clear disparity' in the profits achieved by the German entity by comparison with the normal profit levels in such business, its taxable profit could be fixed at the level of the return normal in that type of business domestically (s.33).[1] However, the latter provision applied only if one company directly owned at least one-quarter of the shares of the other, so it could easily be avoided by interposing an intermediary.

This problem came before the Tax Appeal Court (the Reichsfinanzhof) in the famous *Shell* case in 1930.[2] The Rhenania company, an affiliate of Shell which imported and refined oil and marketed petroleum products in Germany, had shown a loss in 1925 but had been assessed to tax on the basis of a normal rate of return on assets of 14 per cent. The court accepted that on a strict construction of the 1925 legislation, s.34 seemed intended to apply where there was no legally separate company, while s.33 only authorized an assessment based on estimated profits where there was a direct ownership relationship, as well as proof of abnormally low profits. These provisions were, however, the first venture by the legislature into a difficult terrain, and should not be interpreted so narrowly as to be easily avoided. Thus, the court was willing to agree that a locally incorporated subsidiary could qualify as the 'branch establishment' of the foreign enterprise under s.34. This could be so if they formed an 'organic unity' (*Organschaft*). However, the 'organic unity' concept, originally developed to prevent the 'cascade' effect of turnover tax being applied to sales between related firms, required a very close relationship such that the dependent enterprise was totally controlled managerially by its parent;[3] and it was not clear that the relationship between the Rhenania company and Shell was of this type. The court considered that account had to be taken of the development of large global enterprises, in relation to which a looser concept of unity was applicable: it could include related entities under common control if their separate parts could not be adequately understood as autonomous units but whose position in the economy as a whole could only be explained by reference to the combined enterprise. In such circumstances,

---

[1] Einkommensteuergesetz 1925, ss.33 and 34 (Reichsgesetzblatt 1925–I, p. 196); Körperschaftssteuergesetz 1925 s.13 (ibid., p. 211).

[2] Judgment of 30 January 1930, IA 226/29, [1930], Reichssteuerblatt p. 148, No. 220.

[3] See Chapter 1, section 2.a(ii) above.

instead of the full liability to tax of the German company based on its own accounts, it could be treated as a branch and the tax liability would be on the proportion of the parent's profits attributable to the subsidiary.

A few months later, the same court went further and held, in the *Citroën* judgment, that where 'organic unity' could be shown, the profit attributable to the business in Germany must be proportionate, and they could therefore be computed as a fraction of the income of the whole enterprise.[1] In that case, the German subsidiary assembled automobiles using engines and components supplied from France; and the French parent also supplied the capital and some of the skills. In such circumstances, even if the German company's books appeared to be in order, it should be proved that intra-firm prices produced a proportionate profit, for example by showing sales of engines at the same prices in similar quantities to independent entities (p. 758). Otherwise, the income attributable to the German business should be estimated as a proportion of the total. The UK Inland Revenue advised the Foreign Office in 1931 that there were no grounds for objection to these decisions, since the same principles applied under British law (PRO file IR40/5674).

However, the effectiveness of these provisions was largely undermined, especially in the period 1950–70, by a number of doubts, uncertainties and loopholes. First, the organic unity concept was based on the principle of managerial integration, and could easily be avoided by the interposition of a holding company (Chapter 1, section 2.a(ii) above). Also, once Germany entered into tax treaties, it was held that the treaty provisions on company residence would override this rule (Landwehrmann 1974, p. 250). In practice, the 'organic unity' theory could be used to the benefit of the taxpayer, and was rarely used to its disadvantage.[2] Furthermore, doubts were cast by jurists on the validity of the organic unity theory under international law (and thus, under the German Constitution), since it involved an assertion of jurisdiction over foreign companies (Weber-Fas 1968, pp. 184–6).[3] Thus, when the avoidance of tax by the use of intermediary companies and tax havens became an issue in the early 1960s, the tax authorities sought initially to establish administrative rules under the general anti-avoidance provisions of the tax law (see Chapter 7, section 1.a above). When this also proved to provide an uncertain legal foundation, the government finally enacted the Aussensteuergesetz (Foreign Tax Law) of 1972. Section 1 of this law gives a broad power, similar to those in the French and US provisions, to adjust the

---

[1] Judgment of 16 September 1930, IA 129/30, [1930] Reichssteuerblatt p. 757, No. 937.

[2] Landwehrmann 1974, p. 251; but see the 1963 decision cited in the next footnote.

[3] However, in 1963 the Bundesfinanzhof upheld a decision by the tax Commissioner that a 99 per cent owned Japanese subsidiary of Schering could be treated as its organ and thus resident in Germany (Judgment of 18 December 1963, [1964] BStBl III 253; an English translation is provided in Weber-Fas 1968, p. 249); the Court held that 'there is no single test for what constitutes sufficient contact to establish tax jurisdiction', so the German Organschaft theory was not contrary to international law and was thus valid under the German constitution. Note that this was prior to the German–Japanese treaty.

income of a taxpayer if it has been reduced due to non-arm's length transactions with a related entity.

1.f Other National Provisions

Some other countries also made some attempts to deal with the problem in the 1930s. Thus, Belgium enacted a provision in 1938 to allow profits of foreign related enterprises to be taken into account in assessing a company to Belgium tax; this was originally aimed at Luxembourg holding companies, and was amended in 1962 and 1973 (Wisselink, in Rotterdam IFS 1978, pp. 87–9). Japan, on the other hand, perhaps because its companies did not venture into foreign direct investment until much later, did not enact a transfer pricing law until 1986. Other countries have also slowly introduced either specific legal provisions or administrative regulations based on the arm's length rule. Thus, in Brazil a law of 1964 combating tax avoidance by family enterprises was amended in 1977 and 1983 to apply to pricing between related legal entities, in seven types of defined transactions (Leite 1991). While the general principle that accounts must fairly reflect a firm's business activities is accepted in one form or another everywhere, specific legal and administrative measures for the evaluation of transfer prices have been surprisingly slow to develop.[1]

1.g The Advantages of Adjustment

Thus, the generally agreed approach has been to start from the separate accounts of separate branches and subsidiaries of an international corporate group, while providing powers to the revenue authorities to adjust those accounts as necessary to reflect the true profit. In the case of separately incorporated entities, inter-affiliate transactions must be judged by the test of independent entities dealing at arm's length. If such transactions have been conducted on a non-arm's length basis, the tax authorities have a broad power to adjust the accounts; although the British provisions are somewhat narrower in specifying adjustments to prices of specific transactions rather than adjustments to income and costs generally. In the case of branches the treaty provisions still allow adjustment of profits using 'percentage of turnover' or other methods, provided that substantially the same result is reached.

The adjustment of separate accounts undoubtedly had advantages over attempting to consolidate the accounts of related companies. First, it is possible to use a much broader definition of 'common control' for a power to adjust than would be possible for consolidation, which must be based on the related company being wholly or at least majority owned. This is not to underestimate the difficulties of defining 'common control' and of enforcing

---

[1] A brief general report was compiled on approaches used in taxation of TNCs based on a questionnaire to tax administrations in 34 Commonwealth countries: Commonwealth Secretariat (n.d., 1987?).

the principle effectively against determined avoidance. For example, intrafirm loans can be routed through an independent third party by using a parent company guarantee, or 'back-to-back' loans (see section 3 below). In some countries, notably the UK and Japan, the definition looks to formal legal powers of control, and may be easily avoided, as can be seen in the British court decision that related family trusts are not under common control if even one trustee is different (*Commrs. of I.R. v. Lithgows Ltd*, 1960). Other laws have a broader definition of common control, including any powers of influence: thus, the German rules of 1983 include connection through 'special channels of influence' (*besondere Einflussmöglichkeiten*) and through 'identity of interests' (1983 Rules, para. 1.3.2, see Rädler & Jacob 1984, p. 10).

Second, the adjustment of accounts of a local affiliate can be done by a national tax authority without proceeding to what would amount to a full examination of the entire group to eliminate all internal transactions; and without delaying the taxation of a profit made on an inter-affiliate sale until the final profit is realized by a sale outside the group.

The difficulty with adjustment of accounts lies in establishing criteria for the adjustment. Since the problem was identified as being the 'diversion' of profits, the intention was to establish the 'normal' profit, and it seemed natural to define this as the profit which would have been made had the parties been truly independent (Surrey 1978, p. 414). This was all that was meant, initially, by the arm's length criterion. There is considerable evidence that what the revenue authorities sought in practice was a fair allocation of the total profit to the local affiliate. This is evident from the various national reports for the League of Nations study: notably, the British Inland Revenue, which strongly favoured adjustment of accounts, stated that only 55 per cent of cases were settled on the basis of separate accounts, and even then, the agreement of the taxpayer to adjustments was greatly facilitated by the availability of the alternative method, assessment based on a percentage of turnover (League of Nations 1932, p. 191; see Chapter 1, section 5 above). As we have seen, those countries which had already enacted national laws had created powers to adjust the profits of local branches and subsidiaries. For example, the French transfer pricing law of 1933 cited above, specifically provided that price adjustments could be checked by comparing the profits of the local affiliate with those of 'similar undertakings normally managed'.

If the aim of individual tax authorities was to ensure a reasonable profit allocation to the local affiliate, it was nevertheless important in the international context that this be done by adjusting the prices of specific transactions. The reason is plain: a reallocation of 'diverted' profit from one affiliate to another will lead to double taxation unless the adjustment of accounts by one tax authority can be followed by a corresponding adjustment acceptable to the other. It appears more legitimate if this is done by an adjustment of prices for specific transactions than by a profit split. In most cases, indeed, the company can merely adjust its internal accounts in some suitable manner. Since most such adjustments take place as part of informal negotiations with tax examiners in one country, the firm may find a way to adjust the related company's accounts informally, perhaps even without any need for negotiations with the authorities in the related country.[1] On the other hand, if it were explicitly accepted that the aim was to ensure taxation of a 'fair' proportion of the profit by each national tax authority, it would require explicit international agreement on the definition and allocation of the tax base of the company group. Instead of opening up this broad question, the arm's length criterion served the purpose of confining the allocation issue to a case-by-case negotiation of specific pricing by individual companies.

2. Elaborating the Arm's Length Principle

It was not until the 1960s that the problem of transfer pricing began to surface again in public discussion. Despite the broad powers which many states gave their tax authorities in the 1920s and 1930s, international businesses did make use of transfer price manipulations to transfer profits internationally, not least in order to avoid what they considered unfair or double taxation. For example, British firms with subsidiaries in the US stated, when pressing the government for a tax treaty in 1944, that high US taxes on dividends had forced them to repatriate profits by 'unsatisfactory expedients such as invoicing goods at higher prices' (see Chapter 2, section 1 above). The spread of the network of bilateral tax treaties helped to stimulate the rapid postwar internationalization of business, especially of American TNCs. As has been recounted in previous chapters, the rapid growth of foreign direct investment reawakened discussion of the fairness of international tax arrangements. Business groups and capital-importing countries argued for home country exemption of foreign profits, but the main capital-exporting countries, in particular the USA and the UK, would only concede a limited deferral of tax on foreign retained earnings. An international tax planning industry emerged to assist international business to maximize tax deferral, which led to the exploitation of the opportunities for tax avoidance and arbitrage.

2.a The US Regulations of 1968

It was in this climate that there was a renewal of concern about the possibilities for tax avoidance offered by transfer price manipulation. This was felt first and most strongly by the US, whose firms were the most active in expanding abroad. Also, since US tax law exempted foreign subsidiaries (while under British law companies managed and controlled from the UK could be considered resident and taxable there) US TNCs could more easily escape all US tax on foreign retained earnings (see Chapter 5 above). Thus, when the

---

[1] This is the likely explanation for the puzzle noted by US officials, of a substantial 'gap' between potential and actual Corresponding Adjustment cases: Coates & Kanakis, in Competent Authorities 1986, p. 602. It is likely that in many cases where the US authorities have effected a s.482 adjustment, the firm is able to adjust its related company accounts either without reference to the foreign authorities concerned, or by private agreement with them.

US Congress rejected the proposals of President Kennedy's administration in 1962 to end tax deferral for foreign subsidiaries, it nevertheless gave strong support for more active enforcement of controls over transfer pricing. Indeed, the House approved an amendment to section 482 which would have allowed formula apportionment of taxable income between affiliates unless the taxpayer could show arm's length transfer prices for tangible property based on comparable market transactions; also, income could not be allocated to any foreign affiliate whose facilities were 'grossly inadequate for its business outside the United States'. Although these proposals were omitted from the final bill, the reason given was that section 482 already provided sufficiently strong powers to allocate income and deductions; and the Treasury was urged to explore new guidelines and regulations to ensure this.[1]

In fact, the IRS had already responded to the concern to ensure adequate taxation of the foreign earnings of US TNCs, by initiating an international enforcement programme in 1961 reactivating s.482 (Bischel 1973, p. 492). Thus, for example, the advertising agency Young & Rubicam was subjected to a s.482 adjustment for having understated its US income in 1960 by failing to charge its overseas subsidiaries for management and administrative services performed by the parent; however, the adjustment was eventually overturned by the courts, on the grounds that the Revenue could not show that specific managerial services had been performed for specific subsidiaries (*Young & Rubicam v. US*, 1969). Exposed to the increasing use by tax examiners of the wide powers of the section, taxpayers themselves were pressing for new regulations to ensure more uniformity (Tillinghast 1979, p. 271).

The s.482 regulations were finally approved in 1968, and provided the basis for the US IRS's monitoring of transfer pricing for two decades without substantial changes, although dissatisfaction with them was continually expressed on all sides.[2] These regulations defined five categories of related party transactions, and specified rules to be used in determining appropriate pricing for each category. The five categories were: loans or advances; the performance of services; the use of tangible property (i.e. leasing); the transfer or use of intangible property (i.e. rights to technology and know-how); and the transfer of tangible property.[3]

---

[1] See US Treasury 1988, p. 9, and reports cited therein.

[2] The initial draft regulations of 1965 were withdrawn following widespread comments, and a revised draft of 1966 was finally approved in 1968. Proposed changes drafted in 1971 were not implemented, apparently on the grounds noted by a 1978 memorandum, that they would benefit large firms at the expense of small business, and 'condone the non-arm's length pricing of inter-corporate transactions': US General Accounting Office 1981, pp. 48–9. Yet the Gordon Report in 1981 again recommended a study of the regulations with a view to revisions to reduce uncertainty and subjectivity: US Treasury 1981, pp. 129–32.

[3] Income Tax Regulations, Code of Federal Regulations, para. 1–482; referred to hereafter as ITR. The related regulations for allocating the costs or deductions of a single corporation between domestic and foreign source income, although originally proposed as a package with the s.482 regulations, were not finally adopted until 1977: 'The relationship between the two sets of regulations is not easy to grasp and may well be inharmonious': Surrey 1978a, p. 451. This relationship was subsequently changed in some significant respects by the Tax Reform Act 1986, adding s.864(e) to the Tax Code, and by the regulations enacted under it.

The regulations specify, for each category of transaction, that the primary test should be the Comparable Uncontrolled Price (CUP): the amount that was charged or would have been charged in independent transactions with or between unrelated parties dealing at arm's length. Relevant circumstances should be taken into account in determining comparability for particular transactions: for example, for loans, the period of the loan, any security, the credit standing of the borrower and prevailing interest rates; for leasing, the type and condition of the property and its investment and maintenance costs.

Despite the emphasis on the primacy of the CUP, the regulations offered alternatives for each type of transaction. A 'safe harbour' was defined for three types of transaction, loans, services and leasing: as long as the supplier is not in the business of providing such services to unrelated parties, the arm's length price is specifically defined. For loans, the 'safe harbour' interest rate was originally 4–6 per cent; it was occasionally changed as rates rose, but this procedure was criticized as too slow (US GAO 1981, p. 15) and eventually, in 1988, the safe harbour rate was defined in relation to Federal rates, which are specified monthly (US Treasury 1988, p. 74). For services and leasing, the 'safe harbour' was defined on the basis of a cost formula; but the leasing safe harbour option was removed in 1988.

In the case of intangibles (intellectual property and know-how), no specific alternative was provided for CUP, but the regulations listed a dozen factors that should be taken into account in fixing an arm's length price (ITR 1–482–2–d–2–iii). Finally, for the pricing of tangibles (goods), the regulations provided a four-tier hierarchy of methods: first, CUP; then, Resale Price Minus an appropriate profit mark-up; third, Cost of Production Plus an appropriate profit mark-up; and only where none of these methods can reasonably be applied may 'fourth methods' be used – i.e. 'some appropriate method of pricing other than those described . . . or variations on such methods' (ITR 1–482–2–e–1–iii).

By attempting to control the broad discretion in s.482 to adjust related company accounts, the 1968 Regulations significantly transformed the Arm's Length rule. Instead of treating Arm's Length as a general principle for ensuring that the allocation of overall profits and costs between related companies was broadly fair, the US approach set out on the steep slope of attempting to define rules for the pricing of specific transactions. At the same time, the US authorities were keenly aware that such rules should not be unilaterally established, but must as far as possible be internationally agreed. Professor Stanley Surrey, the influential US Treasury Assistant Secretary, recognized the international implications of US transfer price adjustments. He and his colleagues were active in international meetings, both of professional bodies (e.g. Surrey & Tillinghast 1971) and intergovernmental organizations (Langbein 1986, pp. 647–8).

2.b International Concern about Transfer Price Manipulation

Nevertheless, the continuing efforts at defining internationally agreed principles for pricing intrafirm transactions have had relatively little success. The starting point was the Arm's Length principle based on separate accounts since, as pointed out above, the leading states had by the 1930s adopted price adjustments based on arm's length rather than try to establish internationally-agreed criteria for allocation.[1] However, the general arm's length principle had been used as a means of ensuring a 'fair' profit allocation, and administrators certainly used profit comparisons as a check. The problem was that by embarking on a system based on detailed rules to be applied to individual transactions the US was introducing a degree of specificity on which it was very difficult to obtain international agreement. In the 1970s, pressure to reach international agreement on transfer pricing rules became increasingly intense. Yet, although report after report reaffirmed the importance of the arm's length principle, there was a complete failure to reach any agreement on specific pricing rules.

Initially, the transfer pricing issue was not treated as a matter of great urgency, although it appears that the OECD Fiscal Committee, at the request of the US, set up a working group as early as 1965 to examine the problem. However, by the 1970s the power of 'the multinationals' was becoming a highly politicized issue. Of particular concern was the ability of TNCs to move both short-term liquid funds and longer-term investment capital between countries and currencies, partly by the adjustment of payment terms between affiliates. In this period of transition from the fixed exchange rate system to floating rates, the TNCs' primary need was to minimize their exposure to currency fluctuations; and the devices they used, such as 'leads and lags' in intrafirm international payments, in turn contributed to currency instability. The issues merged into a generalized debate about the power of international capital *vis-à-vis* the state. Not only did a leading academic economist announce that 'the national state is just about through as an economic unit' (Kindleberger 1969, p. 207), the Governor of the Bank of England in a published speech referred to public concern about whether the power of multinational enterprises 'is such as to represent a significant reduction in the sovereignty of the host government' and discussed in detail their effects on national economic policy-making (Governor of the Bank of England 1973).

Some of this generalized concern was brought to a head by the *cause célèbre* of Hoffmann La Roche. A report by the British Monopolies Commission in 1973 revealed that Roche UK was paying grossly inflated prices to its Swiss affiliate for the active ingredients for drugs to be packaged for sale; these drugs were

---

[1] This was therefore not a US campaign to 'export' the arm's length criterion, as argued by Langbein 1986; indeed, as Langbein acknowledged, Surrey in his published writings accepted some of the limitations of arm's length and kept open the possibility of other approaches.

librium and valium, wonderful new non-barbiturate tranquillizers, sold on prescription and therefore mostly paid for by the National Health Service. Roche's transfer price was £370 a kilo for librium and £922 for valium, while the same active ingredients could be obtained from small companies in Italy (where Roche's patents were not protected) for £9 and £20 per kilo respectively. The company told the Monopolies Commission that its pricing policy for drugs was based on what the market would bear in each country, although in the UK the price was negotiated with the government under the then-voluntary price regulation scheme for pharmaceuticals. The British subsidiary's accounts showed direct payments to its parent company for overheads, especially for the heavy research programme in its Swiss and US laboratories. These were determined by what the Inland Revenue would allow by comparison with similar UK pharmaceutical firms – about 12 per cent of sales. But Roche's UK business was concentrated on a few, highly-profitable items – tranquillizers and vitamins. Thus, Roche argued that it was not fair to look at the profitability of individual drugs, especially such highly successful ones as librium and valium, since these must finance the company's overall research effort. However, it refused to provide the Commission with data on its worldwide activities (UK Monopolies Commission 1973). The dispute was eventually settled by the payment of an agreed sum to the NHS; but the case led to investigations in many other countries of Roche's pricing policies. It is not publicly known whether the Inland Revenue had itself taken any action on Roche's transfer prices under its own powers, or did so subsequently. However, the case undoubtedly created political pressures in Britain and other countries to set up a more active policing of transfer pricing. The British Inland Revenue in 1976 established a special central unit within the Technical Division to train and advise inspectors on international transfer pricing questions.

The concern about the power of multinational enterprise became sufficiently politicized for the United Nations to become involved, and eventually led to the establishment of the UN Centre on Transnational Corporations. In practice, however, the UN has proceeded very cautiously. The first major study, the Report of the Group of Eminent Persons to study the impact of multinational corporations on development and on international relations, was notably conservative on international tax questions. It rejected, in a few brief sentences, the idea of allocation of worldwide profits for taxation based on an agreed formula, but provided no new ideas to resolve the problems of transfer pricing or tax avoidance, merely urging further work by the Group of Experts on Tax Treaties (UN 1974a, pp. 91–4). This body had already produced its guidelines for tax treaty negotiation, but in subsequent meetings in 1976 and 1978 it considered transfer price adjustment issues, in the context of the competent authority mutual agreement procedures.

At the same time, the OECD Fiscal Affairs Committee had accelerated its consideration of the question, having been pressed to do so by the OECD

Council, which had adopted a Declaration and Decisions on International Investment and Multinational Enterprise in 1976. Appended to these were the OECD Guidelines for Multinational Enterprises, which *inter alia* urged multinationals to 'refrain from making use of the particular facilities available to them, such as transfer pricing which does not conform to an arm's length standard, for modifying in ways contrary to national laws the tax base on which members of the group are assessed'. The more detailed examination of the matter by the Committee on Fiscal Affairs resulted in the celebrated 1979 report on Transfer Pricing and Multinational Enterprises.

The OECD Committee and the UN Group of Experts, working at the same time and with overlapping membership, produced similar conclusions. Their reports were written in a context not only of generalized political concern about transfer pricing, but also of specific pressures generated for tax officials by the issue of Worldwide Unitary Taxation, brought to a head by the dispute over Article 9(4) of the draft US–UK treaty (see Chapter 9, section 4 below). Both reports generally confirmed the primacy of the Arm's Length principle and supported the general approach embodied in the US regulations of 1968. This entailed attempting to elaborate more specific criteria to be used in evaluating the pricing of specific transactions of various kinds. Thus, they confirmed the Comparable Uncontrolled Price as the most appropriate and in theory the easiest method, but they specified further that, in view of practical difficulties, the alternatives of Resale Price Minus or Cost Plus might be useful (in the OECD Report these were stated as general alternative methods, not only for tangibles as in the US regulations). Finally, it was conceded that 'the complexities of real life business situations' might create difficulties requiring a combination of these methods, or other methods still, to be used (OECD 1979, para. 13). Nevertheless, proposals for a radical reformulation of the approach by moving away from arm's length to 'so-called global or direct methods of profit allocation, or towards fixing transfer prices by reference to predetermined formulae for allocating profits between affiliates' were firmly rejected (OECD 1979, para. 14). Significantly, however, even the OECD report remarked that this did not mean that 'in seeking to arrive at the arm's length price in a range of transactions, some regard to the total profits of the relevant MNE may not be helpful, as a check on the assessment of the arm's length price' (ibid.).

The 1979 OECD report in particular established a general international consensus that the transfer pricing question ought to be taken seriously, and that arm's length should be the guiding principle for dealing with it. However, the report did not take the form of a new model treaty, nor even a commentary on the relevant provisions of the existing model; the OECD Council simply adopted a recommendation that member states take into account the considerations and methods set out in the report when reviewing and if necessary adjusting transfer prices.

A variety of methods have been used in adopting the principles of the

OECD report in the laws and practice of member states. Some countries, for example the Netherlands, continued to rely on general anti-avoidance rules, based on the principle that business profits must fairly reflect the substance of transactions, while publicizing their general support for the OECD report.[1] Others found the report lacking in specificity, and enacted detailed regulations. Thus, the West German authorities had used a semi-official handbook as the basis for enforcement of the general Arm's Length adjustment rule enacted in section 1 of the Aussensteuergesetz of 1972 (Strobl 1974); but, finding the OECD report inadequate, they issued detailed regulations in 1983.[2] These regulations attempted to provide detailed and specific rules: those parts which interpreted the existing statute were considered binding on the administration, but other parts were considered to be essentially for guidance and therefore binding in the aim to be achieved and not the specific methods indicated (Höppner 1983, pp. 211, 213–15). The Italian Ministry of Finance also preferred to issue its own detailed guidelines.[3]

In Japan the legislature had initiated consideration of the question in 1977, but a specific law was not passed until 1986: it was phrased in very general terms, and the administrative regulations subsequently approved were little more specific. The UK has avoided elaborating any regulations, and the outline 'guidance notes' issued in 1980 referred only in the most general terms to methods:

> In ascertaining an arm's length price the Inland Revenue will often look for evidence of prices in similar transactions between parties who are in fact operating at arm's length. They may however find it more useful in some circumstances to start with the re-sale price of the goods or services etc. and arrive at the arm's length purchase price by deducting an appropriate mark-up. They may find it more convenient on the other hand to start with the cost of goods or services and arrive at the arm's length price by adding an appropriate mark-up. But they will in practice use any method which seems likely to produce a satisfactory result. They will be guided in their search for an arm's length price by the considerations set out in the OECD Report on Multinationals and Transfer Pricing. [UK Board of Inland Revenue 1980.]

Despite the general agreement on the arm's length approach, neither the international studies and reports nor the development of national practice and rules have succeeded in establishing agreed common criteria, still less common rules. The apparent widespread agreement on the Arm's Length approach has contrasted starkly with the indeterminacy about the actual content of the arm's length rules. The reaffirmation of Arm's Length appears

[1] However, the Dutch Ministry of Finance issued a circular letter containing administrative guidelines on 25 April 1985, following the subsequent OECD report of 1984 on some more specific transfer pricing issues.
[2] Bundessteuerblatt 1983, Part I, p. 218; English and French language versions and a useful glossary of German tax terms are provided in Rädler & Jacob 1984.
[3] Italy, Ministry of Finance 1980. Materials on national transfer pricing rules and practices are most usefully collected in International Bureau of Fiscal Documentation 1987–.

to be more than ever necessary in order to avoid the political difficulties that would be caused by opening up the question of an international basis of allocation of the tax base of TNCs. Thus, a German Finance Ministry official has stressed that the administrative adjustment of transfer pricing would be redolent of 'planned economy and sterile bureaucracy' if it were not firmly based on the principle that 'Even members of a group of enterprises are supposed to act in their pricing like participants of a free market' (Höppner 1983, p. 212).

Yet it is clear that many of the underlying issues have not been resolved. To be sure, overt conflict has been averted and *ad hoc* solutions have been found, largely through the rapid development of procedures for administrative co-operation and co-ordination (to be discussed in Chapter 10 below). Nevertheless, at least one official who has been continually involved has stated that he has feared for two decades that there might be a 'general open clash between tax authorities in the field of arm's length pricing' (Menck in Competent Authorities 1986, p. 585).

Indeed further public conflict emerged as the 1990s opened with renewed attacks in the US Congress on taxation of TNCs. Hitherto, the Congress had been primarily concerned with the problem of US TNCs taking advantage of deferral to minimize their US tax liability. This led to a modification of the cornerstone of the US transfer pricing regime, s.482 (the first substantial change in nearly 60 years since its enactment), made by the 1986 Tax Reform Act; which was followed by proposals in a Treasury White Paper of 1988 for significant modifications in the administration of the section (to be discussed in detail in section 3.f below). While this was still under consideration, however, there was increasing concern about the rapid growth in foreign direct investment into the US, especially by Japanese firms (US Congress 1990a). Fuelling a general political concern about 'unfair competition', a staff study for the Oversight Subcommittee of the House Ways and Means committee in July 1990 highlighted figures showing that 25 Pacific-rim and eleven European-based multinationals with more than $35 billion in retail sales in the US in 1986 paid little or no income tax while handling billions of dollars distributing foreign-made products in the US for their foreign parents. It was stated that the 36 companies accomplished this through 'inflated pricing of goods purchased from the foreign parent, or the performance of functions not properly compensated for by the foreign parents'. Senior IRS officials confirmed that close attention was being paid to foreign-owned firms, which generally showed a lower rate of return on assets, and of net income on gross receipts, than US-controlled domestic corporations; although Treasury officials advised a strengthening of enforcement of existing laws rather than any new initiatives, warning that actions must 'withstand the test of fairness and must adhere to international standards if US businesses are to continue to enjoy the benefits of co-operative relationships between the fiscal authorities of other countries'.[1] Lobbies on behalf of foreign investors argued strongly that

[1] Report in the *Financial Times*, 27 July 1990.

many factors could account for profitability differences, such as high start-up costs in the US market.

Attempting to defuse political pressures, the Chancellor of the Exchequer John Major wrote to the Treasury Secretary Nicholas Brady proposing a joint multilateral study of tax avoidance by multinationals, an offer which Brady gratefully accepted, along with a similar German proposal.[1] What was most striking was that neither the efforts by the US over three decades to develop an effective transfer price regime for US foreign direct investments, nor the work in international bodies, especially the OECD, since 1975, were regarded as providing an adequate answer to US political concerns about the adequacy of taxation of inward direct investment.

3. The Indeterminacy of Arm's Length

The administration of transfer pricing rules under the Arm's Length principle has faced two basic difficulties. First, it entails a focus on specific transactions; and second, it relies on finding comparable transactions between unrelated parties. Underlying these is the basic problem that Arm's Length depends on treating related companies as if they were unrelated. The essential advantages of a corporate group are that fixed costs can be jointly shared, and that a successfully integrated firm generates synergy profits, or additional returns attributable to the organization as a whole rather than any particular unit. The Arm's Length approach based on transactional analysis entails attempting to dissect this unity.

3.a Arm's Length Price or Arm's Length Profit

The arm's length principle essentially requires adjustments to be made to the pricing of specific transactions rather than performing a global profit allocation. Nevertheless, both tax administrators and courts have used the profit split produced by price adjustment as an important factor either in validating price adjustments, or even to decide what the adjustment should be. Some have justified this by arguing that arm's length merely requires affiliates to be treated as separate entities, and their assessment to begin from separate accounts, and that the approach is not vitiated by using profit-split as a check (Hunter, in Competent Authorities 1986, p. 594).

(i) Identification of Specific Transactions
The US regulations of 1968 were the first to establish a detailed approach to the identification of specific intrafirm transactions in which one affiliate is the supplier of something to another. However, a supplier-receiver relationship

---

[1] Letter of 29 August, printed in Tax Notes of 10 September 1990.

may be hard to define among related companies sharing factor inputs. It appears most clearly in the sale of tangibles, since there is a clear transfer of a physical item. The supply of tangibles for use (leasing) may also appear to be a clear bilateral transaction, although there may frequently be shared use. A loan may also appear to be a clearly bilateral relationship, but the common case of a parent company guarantee for a subsidiary's borrowing is not easy to classify. Most problems are caused by services and intangibles, which commonly consist of activities carried out for the joint benefit of all or many of the companies in a corporate group. Thus, the US s.482 rules provide detailed definitions to identify the 'renderer' of services, the 'developer' of know-how, and the beneficiary or recipient of each.

Further, a relationship which appears to involve a straightforward bilateral relationship may require more detailed analysis to define the various transactions involved. Thus, one relationship may involve two or more transactions: a sale of tangibles such as the active ingredient for a drug often involves a simultaneous transfer of intangibles, the rights to the patents embodied in it. Therefore, 'unbundling' the different transaction elements may be important. Equally, a transaction may be reciprocal: a patent licence will commonly include a grant-back clause for development patents, which must be dealt with by provisions for set-offs.

(ii) Profit-Split: Criterion or Check?

As the limitations of the transactional approach in the US regulations have become more apparent, the use of profit-split has gained ground. Initially, there was uncertainty as to its validity: in *Du Pont v. US*, the trial judge stated critically that 'the regulation approach seems to rule out net profit as a relevant consideration in the determination of an arm's length price, this despite Congress' encouragement to the contrary'.[1] However, the appeals court in the same case approved 'consideration of net profits in appraising the realism of prices charged' (*Du Pont v. US*, 1979, p. 456). This seemed to make sense of the prior cases: in *Lufkin Foundry* (1972) the use of profit-split by the Tax Court had been overturned on appeal, on the ground that there had been no attempt first to find an arm's length price; while in *Pittsburgh Plate Glass Industries Inc.* (1970) a profit-split analysis was used in support of the adjustment produced by a comparable. Finally, the courts went a stage further in *Eli Lilly v. Commissioner* (1988), in accepting an allocation based on profit-split, after attempts to fix arm's length prices had failed due to non-existence of comparables.[2] A study of all the s.482 cases in the courts between 1962 and

---

[1] Judge Willi, in *Du Pont v. US*, cited in US Treasury 1988 p. 34.
[2] In the meantime, Congress had enacted a new Tax Code provision, in response to this case, specifying that corporations with affiliates in US possessions (i.e. Puerto Rico) earning income from intangibles must divide the income, either under a cost-sharing method, or on the basis of a 50–50 profit split: Tax Equity and Fiscal Responsibility Act 1982 s.213(a), adding section 936(h) to the Tax Code; see below.

1980 – 22 cases – also confirmed the importance of profit-split (Donnelly 1986). The position thus reached in the US was that profit-split is important as a check on the reasonableness of adjustments to transaction prices; and it could also be used in its own right where adjustment based on arm's length is not possible.

In practice, in most countries, it is more likely to be the taxpayer that relies on the arm's length price criterion, by pointing to a market price which should be accepted as comparable; while the main point of reference for the tax authorities will be the profit which the price produces. Although this means primarily a comparison with the profits of other similar undertakings, inevitably there will also be some consideration of the internal profit-split within the TNC. Thus, the French law of 1933 (see section 1.b above) already provided that, in the absence of specific data to establish an arm's length price, the assessment may be done by comparison with the profits of similar undertakings normally managed. Similarly, the Japanese law of 1986 states that if a company does not provide the information necessary to calculate the arm's length price, the local tax office may calculate a price based on the gross margin ratio on sales or some other appropriate ratio of a similar company in the same line of business. A senior Japanese official has also indicated that profit-split is likely to be used by administrators as a check on the 'reasonableness' of a price adjustment (Competent Authorities 1986, p. 591). Equally, the German law of 1972 (s.1(3), as amended in 1976) allows, in the absence of other appropriate criteria, an assessment based on the return on invested capital, or margin on turnover, which could be expected under normal circumstances. The 1983 German regulations also specify that it is legitimate to compare the business results of the taxpayer, its related companies, and other similar companies, either as a check on or an alternative to other methods of establishing arm's length prices.[1]

Although the UK statutory provisions only permit adjustments to the pricing of specific transactions, in practice the profit-split produced is a major factor, and a senior official has accepted that a formula approach 'may well have a role to play in a final settlement based on economic reality' (Hunter, in Competent Authorities 1986, p. 594). An English court has held that the arm's length rule in a treaty provision based on Article 7(2) of the OECD model does not require 'the substitution for every transaction between the branch and the main enterprise of the transaction that would have been entered into if the branch and the main enterprise had been carrying on wholly separate businesses', but 'permits a method of ascertaining the profit to be attributed to the branch which is one which might have been agreed between the branch

---

[1] Sections 2.4.5 and 2.4.6, and Höppner 1983, p. 222. Cf. also Saunders 1989, p. 253, who states that the German criteria 'basically require the German tax administration to consider that every company must make an adequate return on capital employed or a gross profit which is compatible with that of its competitors'.

and the main enterprise if the branch had been an independent enterprise' (Vinelott, J. in *Sun Life Assurance Co. of Canada v. Pearson*, 1984, p. 507). Nevertheless, the basic statutory provisions (ICTA 1988, s.770) are much more specific than the treaty wording in requiring adjustments to pricing of transactions, and might cause some difficulty for the Inland Revenue if a case were to come to court.

However, profit-split is considered to be appropriate only as a guide and not as a criterion in itself. The difficulty is that, if it is not based on any rigorous evaluation of the consolidated accounts of the group of related companies, it is no more than a rough check on the profitability of the local subsidiary in relation to the group and in comparison with other similar firms. There may frequently be good reasons for significant divergence. A TNC might limit its operations in particular markets to highly profitable lines, or may have superior technology, which should produce much higher profits than local firms. Conversely, a foreign-owned subsidiary may experience difficulty in establishing itself in a new market, or may for other good reasons register repeated losses, in contrast with the group's more profitable operations elsewhere.

Furthermore, the use of profit comparisons has caused disagreements among national authorities. As we have seen, it has long been accepted, at least for a branch or other Permanent Establishment, that where separate accounts based on comparable market prices for specific transactions are not available, the profits could be calculated by comparison with similar independent firms, using percentage of turnover or other appropriate coefficients. Historically, this clearly meant comparison with similar enterprises located in the same country; but in the case of multinational banks, which frequently operate through foreign branches, Japan and the United States have taken the view that it is more appropriate today to use global coefficients or criteria (see section 1 above, and OECD 1984–II, paras. 64–70).

Finally, there is official agreement generally that the 'separate enterprise' approach must be kept distinct from the unitary method, which if it has any formal validity is considered at most an exceptional and subsidiary method applicable only to Permanent Establishments. So long as this remains the official position, it is hard to find any formal justification for the use of 'profit-split' in the sense of an evaluation of the profitability of a particular affiliate in relation to that of its corporate group as a whole. It is possible to argue that the separate enterprise criterion laid down in Article 9 of the model treaties does not require 'arm's length prices' for specific transactions, but an 'arm's length profit' for the affiliate, since it states in very general terms that where conditions between related enterprises differ from the separate enterprise standard, the profits which would otherwise have accrued may be restored and taxed accordingly. This justified the OECD Committee in treating the question of thin capitalization as a transfer pricing matter (OECD 1987c–I discussed below, section 3.c(i)). Significantly, however, the German authorities expressed a reservation to that report's reasoning, on the grounds that it was based on 'the notion of an "arm's length profit", rather than on the generally accepted notion of an "arm's length price" ' (ibid., p. 36 fn. 2). This demonstrates a reluctance to move away from the apparent security of specific price adjustments towards profit comparisons. The argument that the relevant profit comparison must be with global industry averages, because local firms are not comparable, made by Japan and the US in relation to banking, may be made for other businesses. In such cases, the 'arm's length profit' criterion might become a very loose approximation for a global profit allocation; and this the tax administrators certainly wish to avoid.

Thus, national laws, administrative regulations, court decisions and official practice all emphasize that profit-split is an ancillary criterion, and the primary approach must be to discover market prices charged by independent parties dealing at arm's length.

3.b Tangibles: The Search for Comparables

The US regulations, in particular, explicitly specify the Comparable Uncontrolled Price as the primary method and touchstone for pricing each category of transaction. The search for comparables has been fiercest in relation to tangible sales, since they are the most clearly bilateral transactions; moreover, the primary alternative method, Resale Price Minus, also depends on discovering unrelated parties in comparable circumstances: 'the vital prerequisite for applying the resale price method is the existence of substantially comparable uncontrolled resellers' (*DuPont v. US*, 1979, p. 450).

(i) The US Experience

More than 20 years of experience of administering the US regulations has shown that in a large proportion of cases where TNC pricing is examined no comparables can be found. This has been shown quantitatively by half a dozen studies of s.482 allocation cases. The Treasury's own report of 1973 revealed that of a total of 174 adjustments to the pricing of tangibles only 36, or 20 per cent, were on the basis of CUP (see Tables 4 and 5). This proportion was confirmed by academic studies based on questionnaires sent to companies (US Conference Board 1972; Burns 1980). Criticism of the arm's length method reached a peak when the General Accounting Office (GAO) published a report to the Congress in 1981, which concluded:

> Because of the structure of the modern business world, IRS can seldom find an arm's length price on which to base adjustments but must instead construct a price. As a result, corporate taxpayers cannot be certain how income on inter-corporate transactions that cross national borders will be adjusted and the enforcement process is difficult and time-consuming for both IRS and taxpayers. ... We recommend that the Secretary of the Treasury initiate a study to identify and

Table 4 *Methods Used in s.482 Price Adjustments for Tangibles*

Study	Method used (%)			
	CUP	Resale Minus	Cost Plus	Other
1. Treasury 1973	20	11	27	40
2. Conf. Bd. 1972	28	13	23	36
3. Burns 1980	24	14	30	32
4. GAO 1981	15	14	26	47
5. IRS 1984	41	7	7	45
6. IRS 1987	31	18	37	14

Source: US Treasury 1988, p. 22, derived from the following: 1. US Treasury 1973 (reprinted in Murray 1981 308). 2. US Conference Board report no. 555 1972. 3. Burns 1980. 4. US General Accounting Office 1981, ch. 4. 5. US IRS 1984. 6. US Treasury 1988, Appendix A, p. 8.

Table 5 *Official Studies of s.482 Adjustments*

	Treas. 1973		GAO 1981		IRS 1984	
No. of Corps. or Case files			519		823	
Files with potential adjs.	871					
Corps. for which adjs. made			200			
Transactions for which adjs. considered	1706				3080	
Adjs. made	886		403		2306	
Adjs. agreed	520				1335	
Value of adjs. in $m	662		277		4377	
TANGIBLES:						
Value in $m	313		124		2632	
Potential Adjs.	591				589	
Adjs. made	174		34		339	
of which agreed	91				127	
METHODS USED:	No.	%	No.	%	No.	%
CUP	36	20	5	15	139	41
RM	19	11	4	14	24	7
CP	48	27	9	26	22	7
Other	71	40	16	47	154	45

Sources: as for Table 4, lines 1, 4 and 5. The 1973 study was based on returns for which audit was completed in 1968 and 1969; the 1981 study cases closed in 1978 and 1979; and the 1984 study those closed in 1980 and 1981.

evaluate the feasibility of ways to allocate income under s.482, including formula apportionment, which would lessen the present uncertainty and administrative burden created by the existing regulations. [US GAO 1981, p. 54.]

The IRS and Treasury strongly countered the conclusions of the GAO report, and the figures on which they were based. There was certainly some basis for attacking the validity of the GAO's extraordinarily low figure of 15 per cent for adjustments based on CUP, since the total of 34 adjustments to the pricing of tangibles was not a large statistical sample. But what was surprising was that as few as 34 adjustments had been made to tangibles pricing, in a programme of audit including all TNCs with assets over $250m, in which over 500 international examiners' reports were completed over a two-year period. In contrast, many more adjustments were made to the pricing of loans, services and rents – 274 of the 403 adjustments; but they were almost all (240 or 87 per cent) made using safe haven rules. However, these accounted for only $60.4m by value, compared to the $277m produced by only 34 adjustments to tangibles pricing. The clear implication is that verification of tangibles pricing, since safe haven rules could not be used, consumed more time and expertise; but equally, it could produce more significant adjustments.

The IRS claim that pricing adjustments for tangibles were based on CUP in over 40 per cent and perhaps as many as 50 per cent of cases was subsequently supported by its own comprehensive study published in 1984, based on cases closed in the two years following those covered by the GAO study. Nevertheless, even this still showed that adjustments were more often made by 'other' methods than by using the CUP. The most striking factor was the sharp increase in the number of adjustments made: although the number of case files only increased from 519 to 823 (1.6 times), the overall number of adjustments increased nearly six-fold, with a total value over fifteen times as large; while for tangibles, adjustments increased ten times in number and over twenty times by value (Table 5). Clearly, the IRS had taken to heart the admonitions to improve enforcement of s.482, including the GAO's recommendation to use economists in all major cases not involving safe harbours (US Treasury 1988, p. 25). In fact, the Treasury changed tack, and the 1988 White Paper no longer attempted to defend previous practice, but proposed a new approach to pricing, the Basic Arm's Length Return Method (see below).

The statistical evidence is a significant indication that there are serious difficulties in establishing arm's length prices on the basis of comparables. The evaluation of detailed qualitative factors, as well as the effect of quantity on price, make it very difficult if not impossible to establish with certainty the comparability of similar items sold by third parties, and even of the same item sold by the same firm to third parties. Above all, few tax authorities have the time or expertise for this process. Even the USA has had difficulty in allocating resources commensurate with the growing scale of the problem: the total number of international examiners grew from 150 in 1977 to 505 in 1988, but this was merely keeping pace with the growth of US companies abroad, and the even more rapid expansion of foreign-owned businesses in the US (Woodard 1988).

(ii) The Administrative Burden of Scrutiny

Whether for political reasons or merely through lack of resources, other countries have put much less effort, even comparatively, into the scrutiny of transfer prices. In the UK, the transfer pricing unit of the Board of Inland Revenue[1] was reported in 1984 to have seven staff, only one of whom was a qualified accountant. Nevertheless, this unit was said to have been responsible for transfer price adjustments to profits 'of the order of £200m' in the decade 1974–84; while in the single year 1987–8 settlements of transfer pricing cases gave an immediate tax yield of £71m, and Controlled Foreign Company cases £12.5m.[2] In Germany the federal system means that tax assessment and collection is done by the Länder, of which only Bavaria has inspectors with specialized training, although co-ordination is ensured by a Federal Finance Office with some 70 auditors of whom about ten specialize in international matters.[3] However, due to differences in the administration of tax enforcement, direct international comparisons of the resources and effectiveness of departments responsible for transfer price adjustments are hard to make.

Developing countries in particular have recognized that it is crucial to establish some monitoring especially of import prices paid, not only on related company purchases, and not only for tax reasons but even more importantly to safeguard valuable foreign exchange. The establishment of a government monitoring unit, although expensive, is likely to be highly cost-effective, as was shown by countries such as Greece in the late 1970s (Ganiatsos 1981; UN 1978a); however, this type of unit is likely to be vulnerable to political pressures, especially in a period of liberalization and encouragement of foreign investors.

---

[1] At that time, Technical Division 2B; subsequently, a single International Division has been created, including both policy and technical work, and the transfer pricing unit is now International 5B: see UK Board of Inland Revenue 1988.
[2] The figures for staffing in 1984 and yield 1974–84 are from a ministerial answer to a parliamentary question, Hansard 1983–4, vol. 52, p. 222; that for 1987–8 is given in the Management Plan of the International Division, published in UK Board of Inland Revenue 1988, vol. 3. The latter document remarks: 'With regard to transfer pricing and Controlled Foreign Company casework the investigations handled on the Section are generally into major multinationals and are complex and specialised, often taking up to 5 years to complete with an uncertain outcome. It is also possible that some Transfer Pricing cases may finally reach the Special Commissioners over the next three years, dependent on the resources of the Solicitors Office to offer advice etc. The result is that yield fluctuates year by year, cannot be meaningfully forecast, and bears no relationship to the staffing resources put into them' (ibid., 9.9). It should be borne in mind that some tax districts, notably those covering the City of London, and the special Oil Taxation Office, deal directly with many cases, and have considerable expertise of their own, so that the central unit is mainly concerned with training, advice and international liaison, and is directly concerned only with major or difficult cases.
[3] Information from German Ministry of Finance, April 1987.

In the 1980s, as the problems of sovereign debt and shortage of foreign exchange have come more to the fore, many states have preferred to employ private firms to provide pre-shipment inspection services. This approach has been subject to political and other criticisms, but in view especially of the currency and capital flight problems of developing countries, it has become well established. Such a system can greatly facilitate the practical task of tax authorities. The need for confidentiality need not prevent information gathered for the purposes of one branch of government, such as customs or the Central Bank being used by another, and although there must be some limitations on tax authorities divulging information from tax examinations, exchange of information between government branches, subject to safeguards, is essential for efficient administration. For example, import prices declared to customs may differ from those returned to tax authorities, since the incentive to inflate invoices to reduce taxable profits or transfer funds abroad may conflict with the desire to reduce import duties.[1]

3.c Safe Harbours and Intrafirm Financial Flows

Some of the difficulties involved in establishing comparables may be avoided by the use of safe harbours. Safe harbours have two major advantages: they are easy to administer; and if they can be internationally agreed, they can ensure that an arm's length adjustment by one state will be automatically compensated by a corresponding adjustment by the other to prevent economic double taxation. However, a safe harbour is only possible for standardized transactions taking place in competitive markets. In such conditions, it may be possible to define a reasonably precise rule; but there is still the issue of whether such a rule should be inflexible, or merely create a rebuttable presumption. Fairness may require that the taxpayer be allowed to demonstrate that a price charged complies with the arm's length criterion even though it is outside the safe harbour. But from the point of view of the government this 'would serve only to reduce tax liability', since taxpayers would normally choose to rebut the presumption if it would be advantageous (US Treasury 1988, p. 73), although administrative costs must also be borne in mind. To allow both the taxpayer and the revenue to rebut the presumption would create uncertainty and defeat the purpose of the safe harbour. Although some administrations do use a 'rule-of-thumb', usually of an informal type, in some situations, this can hardly qualify as a safe harbour.

Loans are relatively standardized transactions taking place in highly competitive markets, and would therefore seem suitable for a safe harbour approach. For international lending, however, this means deciding which

---

[1] In the UK, the Keith Committee on Revenue enforcement powers recommended increased information exchange between the Inland Revenue and other government branches, especially the Customs and Excise, which is responsible not only for import duties but also for excise taxes including VAT.

market should provide the reference point. It has proved difficult to settle this in terms of principle, largely because there is an inevitable divergence of perspective between the source country, which is concerned to ensure that high interest rates on inter-affiliate loans are not used to reduce the taxable business profits of the local subsidiary, and the parent's country of residence, which will seek a full return on loans of capital. The UN Group of Experts went furthest, in specifying that the focus should be on the creditor, and therefore interest should be based on the creditor's borrowing capacity and the interest rate either in its own country or on the relevant capital market (Surrey 1978b, p. 161). This reflected the viewpoint of developing countries as capital importers; they would be reluctant to allow deduction of the higher rates of interest that would be likely to prevail in their domestic markets, since foreign investors would benefit from lower rates in the international financial markets. The OECD report was however much more circumspect: it merely listed the criteria to be taken into account in determining what would be a comparable loan, and in relation to the appropriate interest rate it could only conclude that 'no straightforward principle presents itself which would win general acceptance, and it would depend on the facts of the particular case' (OECD 1979, para. 200). The US is the only major country which formally uses safe harbour interest rates (which only since 1988 have been pegged to a realistic rate, published monthly).

However, the home states of TNCs have had to accept that these firms borrow in the cheapest markets, usually offshore, to finance their foreign subsidiaries. The home country revenue authorities have therefore shifted their attention from the rate of interest charged on inter-affiliate loans to ensuring that the capital structure of foreign subsidiaries realistically reflects the parent's investment. Highly complex arrangements can be devised for financing international operations, and tax considerations are an important element. A key factor is that interest is treated, in most cases, as an expense which is deductible from business profits. Furthermore, tax treaties usually reduce withholding tax at source on interest to a low level, often zero. It is also possible to route such payments through a conduit company to a base holding company in a tax haven, thus ensuring that the profits are not taxed at all (see Chapter 6 above).

(i) Thin Capitalization
Primarily for this reason, a TNC determining the capital structure of a subsidiary is likely to favour a high ratio of debt to equity; also because inter-affiliate interest payments may be more flexible and easier to repatriate than declarations of dividend. There may also be advantages in using forms of hybrid financing, such as convertible bonds or participating loans, which might be deductible for tax purposes while being treated as share capital from an accounting point of view. Under some circumstances a hybrid instrument might be treated as debt in the payor's country (so that the service payments

are deductible interest, although they may be subject to withholding tax) but as equity in the recipient state (so that they are dividends and qualify for a foreign tax credit).

However, the tax authorities may challenge such arrangements as being disguised equity contributions, or 'thin capitalization'. This entails the rejection by the source country of the company's categorization of the nature of its investment, usually by disallowing deductibility of some or all of the interest, and perhaps also by recategorizing some of the payments as dividends and taxing them accordingly.

Although a state is free to take such action unilaterally under its own laws, it clearly raises international issues. A refusal to allow interest deductions for foreign-owned firms may be seen as an impediment to international investment. The model double tax treaties do not specifically deal with the matter, but several of the treaty provisions offer a possible basis for a state to object to a treaty partner disallowing deduction of an interest payment, or reattributing such a payment as a dividend. Such a disagreement would fall to be resolved under the mutual agreement procedures of the treaty (Article 25 of the Models, see Chapter 10, section 3 below).

The thin capitalization issue has been addressed in general terms by the OECD Committee, which published a report favouring its treatment as a transfer pricing question under Article 9 of the model treaties.[1] The argument for this is that, unless a state's action is justifiable under Article 9, it may be contrary to Article 24(5), which requires non-discrimination between local and foreign-owned companies as regards deductibility of interests, royalties and other payments. However, if the thin capitalization rules apply equally to locally-owned companies, there is no discrimination and Article 24(5) does not apply.[2] In fact, there is nothing in the tax treaty models requiring a state to allow the deductibility of interest. If a state goes further than disallowing an interest deduction and reattributes a payment as a dividend, it might fall foul of Article 10, which limits source taxation of dividends to those defined as such in Article 10(3):

> income from shares . . ., not being debt-claims, participating in profits, as well as income from other corporate rights which is subjected to the same tax treatment as income from shares by the law of the State of which the company making the distribution is resident.

A minority of the OECD Committee considered that the exclusion of 'debt-claims' overrides the general inclusion of 'other corporate rights', and precludes reattribution of interest as dividends; but the majority considered that in appropriate cases reattribution was permitted; and it was generally

[1] OECD 1987c–I, following up the brief discussion of the problem in the 1979 report, paras. 182–91.
[2] Nevertheless, France has explicitly reserved the right to apply its domestic law on deductibility of interest notwithstanding Article 24: OECD 1987c–I, para. 66.

agreed that the ambiguity should be cleared up in later versions of the treaty or its commentary.[1]

If thin capitalization rules are treated as transfer price adjustments permitted under Article 9, rather than a valid exercise of the source country's unilateral jurisdiction, then the implication is that they must comply with the arm's length criterion. Nevertheless, some OECD member states apparently took the view that Article 9 could be read as being 'illustrative' rather than 'restrictive' (OECD 1987c–I, para. 49) in this context. However, the general view of the Committee has been that Article 9 is definitive, in requiring transfer price adjustments to conform to arm's length, and the general consensus here also was that 'thin capitalization rules ought not normally to increase the taxable profits . . . to any amount greater than the arm's length profit' (ibid., para. 49). However, Germany entered a reservation to the report's use of the concept 'arm's length profit', rather than the more specific principle of the arm's length price, and pointed out that 'the consensus regarding the actual application of the arm's length principle is extremely vague and precarious' (ibid., p. 36).

Once again, however, the problem faced by the Committee has been whether to opt for a fixed rule, with the merit of certainty and predictability, or a flexible approach, which can respond to the particular circumstances of each case. A majority took the view that a fixed capitalization ratio would be inconsistent with the arm's length requirement, unless it merely created a presumption which the taxpayer could rebut; and the report also urged that if a ratio is adopted, it should be fixed as high as possible, to minimize the number of taxpayers who would be obliged to take on the burden of disproving the presumption (ibid., para. 79). Clearly, this type of safe harbour would have the disadvantages for the Revenue identified by the US Treasury and mentioned above.

On the other hand, the Committee recognized the wide discretionary scope of the case-by-case approach. Although much comparative information is available to tax authorities about company financing, a company can normally choose its capital structure from a wide range of options depending on the specific conditions. Furthermore, it may not be appropriate to ask what level of debt an independent third party, such as a bank, would have allowed a company, since such a party would not have available to it the amount of information which a parent would have about its own subsidiary (ibid., para. 76). Thus, the Committee could come to no better conclusion than that the judgments of tax authorities and courts should be consistent and based on evidence of transactions between independent persons, applied in a reasonable manner (para. 78). In practice however, it seems that revenue authorities do operate defined ratios as an informal guide, to avoid the uncertainty of a

[1] OECD 1987c–I, paras. 56–60. The protocol to the France–US treaty signed in 1988 included a provision widening the definition of dividends to include any income treated as income from shares by the country of residence of the distributing company.

case-by-case approach, as well as the time-consuming process of individual evaluations.[1] However, the validity of Revenue challenges to related-company thin capitalization based on analogies to third-party 'arm's length' situations has been directly challenged by the increased use by many companies of leveraged recapitalizations, which have made it very hard to define a 'normal' capital structure (Briffett 1990).

Thus, the weapons available to revenue authorities are at best cumbersome, in relation to the complexity of financing devices open to companies produced by the fertile minds of the highly-paid accountancy and law firms. For example, the power to adjust related company financial transactions may be circumvented by channelling the loan through an unrelated company, back-to-back with a loan to it from a non-resident affiliate. Further advantages can be gained by using dual-resident companies, whose accounts can be consolidated with those of related firms in two jurisdictions, thus allowing a 'double dip', or deduction of the same interest twice.[2] These are merely some of the simpler schemes devised by the international tax specialists. The complexity of financing arrangements makes it very difficult for the authorities to operate effectively with precise rules; but it is equally hard to apply broad anti-avoidance provisions without accusations of arbitrariness.

Once a particular form of financing has become established, a move against it by one state results in objections from the business lobbies that they are being unfairly treated and their competitiveness will suffer. Thus, the growth of debt-financed company acquisitions (LBOs – leveraged buy-outs), many of them from abroad, led the US Congress to enact provisions in 1989 to limit deductibility of interest paid to related parties. These rules against 'earnings stripping' provide for non-deductibility of 'excess interest' paid to a related person if the recipient does not pay US tax on such income, and the payor corporation has a debt ratio over 1.5 to 1 and 'excess interest expense' (interest payments above a certain proportion of income) (Mentz, Carlisle & Nevas 1990). Business lobbies on behalf of overseas investors objected that this denial of interest deduction entailed a unilateral override of tax treaties (see Chapter 11 below). On the other hand, the US measures at least have the merit of providing a specific statutory rule.

A comprehensive solution would require an internationally co-ordinated approach. This could take the form of international agreement on more precise thin capitalization rules, although the increased complexity of company financing would make such rules arbitrary in operation, and probably discriminatory as between domestic and international transactions. A more radical approach would entail a joint move to end the deductibility of interest altogether, which might be coupled with an appropriate reduction in marginal

[1] Thus, the UK Inland Revenue has been widely stated to operate an informal safe harbour debt-equity ratio of one-to-one, as well as a rule of thumb that pre-tax profits should be at least three times the interest expense: see Tomsett 1989, p. 143.

[2] This is being combated by provisions against dual residence.

corporate tax rates (Bird 1988). While this has been considered by individual countries (for example, by the US Treasury in the course of the Reagan tax reforms) a concerted decision might be difficult to achieve.

(ii) Global Trading and Transfer Parking

Special difficulties have increasingly arisen in dealing with the allocation of gains and losses of firms which are transnational financial intermediaries (investment houses, both banks and stockbrokers) operating in the key financial markets around the world. In principle, their activities can be dealt with according to the traditional separate enterprise approach, by attributing the profit from each transaction to the branch or subsidiary making the sale, unless it is considered to be a dependent agent for the parent or head office and therefore entitled only to a commission similar to the 'merchanting profit' of a wholesaler. However, the growing complexity of multiple operations in different global markets, exploiting the possibilities of arbitrage and of market scope by trading assets continuously on an almost 24-hour per day basis, have undermined the effectiveness of the separate enterprise approach. Global trading offers considerable advantages of hedging and arbitrage (exploiting even small price differences in different markets) as well as access to a wider client base. An important element is regulatory arbitrage: exploiting differences in the regulatory treatment of transactions between markets. This includes not only or primarily tax treatment, but also various monetary and banking controls and prudential requirements, such as capital adequacy and liquidity rules, prohibitions of maturity mismatching and limits on foreign exchange exposure.

A direct means of regulatory arbitrage is for global finance houses to exploit the possibilities of internal intrafirm trading by the 'transfer parking' of transactions such as loans and foreign exchange positions. The use of transfer parking became publicized by investigations into the activities of New York's Citibank, following allegations made by an employee in 1977, which were revealed in a court case for unfair dismissal, and were followed up by investigations by the SEC and a US Congressional Subcommittee.[1] Parking entails transferring a loan or foreign exchange position to a related branch or subsidiary, either by booking it directly to the related entity, or by undertaking an offsetting transaction, sometimes returning it also by a 'round-trip' or 'back-to-back' procedure.

In the highly competitive money markets, a margin of a fraction of one per cent determines profit or loss, and structuring transactions to minimize the costs of regulatory compliance may become a necessity. Thus, Citibank in Paris registered a foreign exchange loss by instructing New York to direct the Nassau 'branch' (merely a separate set of books in New York) to buy $6m at

---

[1] The material is usefully summarized by Bartlett 1981, and in Dale 1984, Appendix 2, 'Citibank's "Rinky Dink Deals": A Case Study in Regulatory Arbitrage'.

FFr 4.7275, and then to resell the dollars to the New York and Brussels branches, for resale back to Paris, at FFr 4.7375. This reduced the taxable profits in Paris, and although the Nassau branch profits were taxable profits in the US, the bank's excess foreign tax credits still made it worthwhile. In such cases, where there is evidence that the sale and repurchase were simultaneous, it might be possible to establish tax evasion. In the absence of such proof, the validity of this type of transaction could depend on whether the sales were within prevailing market ranges, and whether they were booked in a low-tax centre in anticipation of profit, or retrospectively once it was known that a profit and not a loss had been achieved (Bartlett 1981).

Citibank's transactions were also part of more complex arrangements whereby the Paris office could avoid French tax on foreign exchange profits, converting them into lower-taxed interest income, by swapping a deposit in a low-interest currency for a high-interest currency which was placed with a related branch, giving Paris a loss on foreign exchange (from the forward discount on the high-interest currency), but interest earnings (from the interest rate spread between the two currencies) (Dale 1984, p. 201). The potential tax advantages of linking interest rate and currency swaps have been summarized as follows: 'Of course, with careful construction . . . there are opportunities for linking swaps to high interest borrowings of a soft currency with resulting benefits, such as the creation of tax-free gains and a capital gains tax loss, all in a fully hedged situation' (Selter, Godfrey & Atkinson 1990).

Tax authorities are not powerless against such manoeuvres: they can reattribute a profit transferred by the rebooking of a transaction; or more radically, can reattribute all the profits made by an offshore office, on the grounds that it is effectively managed from the local branch. This step was indeed taken by the German authorities in relation to business booked to the Nassau unit of Citibank based in Frankfurt (Dale 1984, p. 199). However, they face major enforcement problems due to the sheer number of deals and the dispersed nature of financial markets. These markets are dominated by a network of major participants, so that the rates quoted in the multiplicity of bilateral deals result in a prevailing price range; but there is no single market and no universally recognized market rate.[1] As Edwards, the dismissed Citibank employee, pointed out: 'In order to get a full picture of a Citibank inter-bank transaction, it is necessary to examine its individual components at all branches involved. The chances of random sampling in several Citibank branches producing a single complete parking transaction are almost non-existent' (cited in Barlett 1981, p. 110). Neither bank regulators nor tax authorities have the resources for continuous monitoring of such transactions on a worldwide scale. Ominously, Dale concludes that such activities 'far from being confined to Citibank, are endemic to multinational banking' (Dale 1984, p. 204).

---

[1] Report of Citibank's Audit Committee, prepared by the law firm Shearman and Sterling and accountants Peat, Marwick and Mitchell, cited in Bartlett 1981, p. 111.

Not surprisingly, it has been difficult for the national authorities to develop their own approaches to taxation of the profits from global financial trading, let alone establish agreed principles. The OECD Committee published one short study on taxation of foreign exchange gains and losses, which dealt only with gains or losses made incidentally in the course of a business which is not normally that of dealing in currencies, and even that report was described as a preliminary step in a rapidly developing field (OECD 1988, para. 5). On the treatment of currency swaps, the report was confined to a bare description (para. 70), not mentioning intrafirm swaps, and stating that 'The tax treatment of payments under instruments of these types is, in general, still being developed, and it is not yet, therefore, possible to comment on it very informatively' (ibid., para. 71).

In the meantime, the possibility of wide divergences in tax treatment created significant uncertainty. In response to a request from the US IRS studies were published by specialists, both in private practice and in the government service (Plambeck 1990; Ernst & Young 1991), which disagreed as to the appropriateness of formula apportionment. However, whether an apportionment or a separate entity approach is adopted, it would require detailed agreement between the major taxing authorities on the characterization of transactions and the attribution of gains and losses between the elements of a global trading team based in different offices. The official position of national tax authorities, and the view expressed by a consultant's report for the Institute of International Bankers, was suspicious of 'arbitrary' allocaton by formula, and preferred profit-attribution by identification of the functions carried out and risks assumed by each party (Ernst & Young 1991); but others argued that the formula approach would make more economic sense, by acknowledging that the profits of a globally-traded book of assets result from the synergy of the team as a whole (Plambeck 1990). A formula approach would require prior agreement between the various parties, which critics argued would be hard to achieve, but was put forward in its favour as being administratively simpler; while administration of a pricing system based on the separate entity approach would itself be facilitated if an advanced ruling agreement could be reached.

(iii) Proportionate Allocation of Financing Costs
Transfer parking is primarily a problem in relation to banks and other financial enterprises. However, many manufacturing TNCs are also major financial institutions in their own right. They are also of necessity active in foreign exchange markets, and the definition and allocation of their tax base will be significantly affected by the approach under national tax rules to currency conversion and foreign exchange gains and losses (OECD 1988). This is therefore another area where a concerted and co-ordinated approach by the major tax authorities is urgently required, to remove the inducement to firms to reduce their costs by international tax avoidance and arbitrage.

A different approach to intrafirm finance would be to allow or require deduction based on the average cost of external borrowing for the firm as a whole. This position has been taken in the US rules which require allocation of interest expense of a single corporation between its domestic and foreign activities according to the ratio of domestic to foreign assets (Internal Revenue Code, s.864). This applies especially to banking, since transnational banks do much of their foreign business through branches. Moreover, the Tax Reform Act 1986 extended this to consolidated corporate groups, including multi-national groups falling within a defined affiliation rule. This rule was fixed by the IRS in temporary regulations at 80 per cent ownership. It was soon after revealed that the Ford Motor group had decided to reorganize its financial, insurance and leasing subsidiaries to be owned through a new holding company, 25 per cent of the shares of which would be placed with institutional investors, so that the Ford ownership would fall below the 80 per cent threshold.[1]

However, the apportionment of interest expense has been criticized and rejected by a majority of the OECD Committee, which took the view that both a foreign branch and a subsidiary should be permitted to deduct the interest actually charged on inter-affiliate or parent company loans, provided the rate is arm's length (OECD 1984–II, especially paras. 58–62). Both Japan and the US took the view, opposed by the majority of the OECD members, that Article 7 of the model treaty permits but does not require deductibility of the interest charged between bank branches and the head office. Japan only allows deduction of the actual inter-branch interest charged if the source of the funds can be traced and documented; but since this is not normally possible, the interest cost allowed is normally a reasonable estimate based on prevailing rates. The US approach takes the view that money is fungible – or at least money of the same currency. Foreign bank branches in the US are permitted to deduct interest based on the original source of funds only if that original price is the price of Eurodollar borrowing; otherwise, a 'currency pools' method is used, which takes the average cost of borrowing for the corporation as a whole in that currency. This is defended as fairer and simpler, since 'a bank's receipts and payments of interest may be regarded as all flowing into and out of one common pool' (ibid., para. 59). However, the Committee took the view that it was not simpler to operate, since the detailed calculation of the cost of borrowings would be complex. More importantly, it disregards the specific role of the particular branch, which might not be typical of the bank as a whole, and might result in different costs, and thus in higher (or lower) earnings.

The broader problem is the anomaly entailed in apportioning or attributing costs on the basis of an average of the whole enterprise, while still purporting to tax the branch on a separate enterprise basis. In that respect, the question of

[1] *Tax Notes*, 30 October 1989, p. 531.

the cost of money to a banking firm is part of the larger problem of allocation of joint costs.

3.d Central Services: Joint Costs and Mutual Benefits

A matter which has long been the subject of conflicting views between the home and host countries of TNCs is the allocation of charges in respect of central management and service costs. Indeed, the model treaties still include a provision, inherited from the League drafts, specifying that allowance must be made in the calculation of the business profits of a Permanent Establishment for 'executive and general administrative expenses' incurred on its behalf (Article 7(3)). However, the UN model explicitly limits the deduction to 'actual expenses' in respect of management or other services or the use of patent or other rights; in contrast, the USA prefers to include in its treaties a specific reference to the deductibility in calculating branch profits of a 'reasonable allocation' of research and development as well as other expenses incurred for the purposes of the enterprise as a whole.

For separately incorporated subsidiaries, there is no explicit international provision for dealing with such central service costs, but the starting point is the 'separate enterprise' standard of Article 9. Nevertheless, it has been accepted that some of the general overhead costs of a multinational company group are incurred on behalf of the group as a whole, in respect of services provided to its members. The group may be structured so that such central services are provided either by the parent company, or by a regional centre for affiliates in that region, or by specific service centres such as distribution and marketing centres, a captive insurance company, or research laboratories. Such services may be administrative, for example planning and co-ordination budgetary control, accounting and legal services, and computing; they may relate to staff matters such as recruitment and training; or they may relate to production in a broad sense, covering joint purchasing, distribution and marketing services (including advertising), and research and development, including the administration and protection of intellectual property rights.

From the point of view of TNCs, these represent costs which must be deductible somewhere against gross profits, and they consider that tax authorities should not interfere with any reasonable arrangement for sharing or allocating them. The tax authorities for their part fear that a TNC may allocate such costs 'in order to obtain a tax advantage or to neutralize a tax disadvantage' (OECD 1984–III, para. 7); and they are unwilling to accept unreservedly the principle that all such expenses must be deductible somewhere.[1]

In principle, therefore, the attribution of such costs must be justified in

---

[1] For example, costs connected with exempt income may not be deductible – OECD 1984–III para. 18.

terms of the arm's length criterion. This raises two separate but interrelated questions: whether a charge can be justified, and what it should be. In principle, a charge can be justified only if the recipient can be shown to have derived a benefit. This 'benefit test' is most easily satisfied if the charge is made directly for specific service transactions, on a fee-for-service basis. Preferably, such a fee should be verifiable as arm's length by comparison with the cost of similar services from unrelated suppliers: for example, legal services could be billed at an hourly rate, which could be compared with the rate for comparable services from independent law firms.[1]

In practice, however, direct fee-for-service charging is frequently difficult. The main reason is that central services often do not benefit one affiliate exclusively. This is obviously the case for services carried out for the joint benefit of all or several affiliates, for example an international advertising campaign. Indeed, it could be argued that even if on one occasion a specific service is carried out for a particular recipient, there may well be a subsequent benefit to others if knowledge or expertise is thereby acquired. Furthermore, the benefit may be indirect and/or non-specific: it is common, for example, to pay a retainer to ensure the availability of some types of professional or specialized services, which may in the event not be required. Thus, it may be very difficult or impossible to evaluate the proportion of the benefit attributable to a particular affiliate; or to do so might require disproportionate administration costs.

It is therefore common for central service costs to be charged by an 'indirect' method apportioning the costs. Most tax authorities have been obliged to accept this, although some only do so if direct charging is impossible, and an actual benefit can be shown. On the other hand, the US rules mandate US parent companies to make a cost-apportionment to foreign affiliates for joint costs wherever there is a mutual benefit, based on the relative benefits. Apportionment of costs may be done by (i) cost-sharing, based on the estimated share in the benefits of each affiliate; in the case of production-related services, this may be done by a mark-up on the price of goods sold; or (ii) 'cost-funding', by contributions from each affiliate based, for example, on gross turnover (sometimes known as the 'fixed-key' method).

The difficulty is that these methods essentially entail allocation of costs by formula, which runs counter to the arm's length approach. Nevertheless, following the 1979 OECD report the business lobby groups pressed for acceptance of cost contribution arrangements. In its more detailed report of 1984, the OECD Committee went some way towards accepting the arguments of TNCs for these indirect methods, although several countries still had significant reservations, particularly to cost-funding, where the charges may be unrelated to the benefit received. This report accepted that even though

---

[1] This is likely to mean the comparable rate in the country of the recipient rather than of the provider, since deductibility is decided by the source country.

cost-sharing does not correspond to arrangements applied between unrelated parties, it may nevertheless be justified by the 'special situation of MNEs' (OECD 1984–III, para. 63). It laid down principles, described as non-exhaustive, which would facilitate the acceptance of a cost-sharing arrange-ment: it should be established in advance by a clearly formulated and binding contract, covering all affiliates which might be expected to benefit, observed consistently over several years and modified as soon as there is any relevant alteration in the activities of group members; the costs should be established by accepted accounting principles, and should entitle contributors to receive those services without any other payment (OECD 1984–III, para. 67).

This goes some way towards accepting the proportionate allocation of joint costs within an international company group. However, many countries, especially those which have been mainly recipients of direct investment, are still very restrictive in their allowance of deduction for joint costs. The German rules permit cost-sharing contracts, but they are quite strict in requiring proof of actual services performed, although where the volume fluctuates over several years an average charge may be appropriate (Rule 6.2.3). They also exclude a large category of costs coming within the 'shareholder costs' of the parent company. This concept has proved controversial. The OECD Committee distinguished between a loose and decentralized firm where the role of the parent may be that of monitoring its investments, and an integrated and more centralized TNC. In the latter case, the managerial and co-ordination activities of the parent could be regarded as generating 'extra profits' which accrue primarily to the subsidiaries and only indirectly to the parent, and therefore should be shared as a joint cost. Some OECD members, however, rejected this, and the issue was left to be dealt with bilaterally (OECD 1984–III, paras. 33–43).

Finally, there is the question of whether a service charge can include a profit element. The OECD Committee concluded that a profit mark-up is always appropriate in some cases, particularly where the provider is specially established to perform such services, or is particularly capable of them and they are especially beneficial to the recipient. When a direct fee-for-service is charged based on market prices, the charge will presumably include a profit element, unless the provider is operating below capacity. However, when the charge is indirect and based on cost-sharing, it is argued that since there is no risk, a profit element is inappropriate. This is the position taken in the German rules, but they permit an allowance for the cost of capital invested.

3.e Intangibles and Synergy Profits

The category of intangibles covers a very broad range of assets, related both to production and to marketing, and generally originating from knowledge, information or skills. They may be legally recognized as forms of property, such as patents, copyrights, designs and trademarks; or they may be other types of legally protected rights, such as confidential data and business know-how, which are independent of the services of a particular individual and therefore belong to the enterprise.[1] Intangibles are especially important to TNCs, whose pre-eminence is often due to technological advances, product differentiation, market positioning or distinctive managerial methods.

The transfer of rights to intangibles has two aspects: a payment for their value, and the acquisition of an asset which can generate an income stream. Therefore, such transfers are especially sensitive, since they can have a major effect on the distribution of the profits of a TNC. As with interest and central service charges, the source country will be concerned to ensure that royalties or fees payable for intangibles do not excessively reduce taxable business profits. Some countries, notably in Latin America, do not allow deductibility of royalties paid abroad, but this is only possible if the recipient is not a national of a treaty state, since the model treaties require non-discrimination. However, all countries frequently monitor carefully the extent and level of payments made for use of intellectual property rights, especially if made to low-tax countries: for example, Germany collects data on such payments especially to Switzerland and Liechtenstein, and maintains files for comparative purposes (Germany, Bundestag 1986, pp. 14–15). At the same time, the home country of a TNC will wish to ensure an adequate contribution or return from its foreign affiliates for the use of such assets. In addition, an intangible may be transferred to a subsidiary located in a country with a convenient tax regime: indeed, many countries offer specific incentives to try to attract high-technology investments. This can be hard for the home country of a TNC to counter through anti-base company or CFC measures: since the base-country affiliate will be carrying out a genuine manufacturing or service activity, it is hard to classify its profits as 'passive income' (see Chapter 7, section 2 above).[2] Therefore, the question will often be whether the price paid for the intangible fairly reflects its value in relation to the profits it helps to generate.

Although an intangible is often a specific identifiable property right, its particular nature as intellectual, scientific or artistic property gives it peculiar cost and profit characteristics. The essential problem is uncertainty and risk. It is necessary to make large up-front investments for basic scientific research and other creative activity such as design, or of even larger sums for applying these ideas to production or marketing, while no definite, measurable gains can be anticipated. Thus,

> At each stage in the R & D process, the final commercial benefits to be derived remain uncertain . . . and the degree of risk involved makes it difficult to estimate benefits from the outlays made which, in the event that some R & D projects prove successful commercially, will only materialise in the future. Moreover, MNEs will

---

[1] See the definition in the US Tax Code, s.936(h)(3)(b).
[2] Indeed, a special problem has been posed for the US by US corporations transferring intangibles to subsidiaries in Puerto Rico, to take advantage of tax incentives enacted by the US itself for possessions corporations.

understandably seek to recoup the cost of financing unsuccessful research from the results of successful research. [OECD 1979, para. 80.]

These characteristics create significant difficulties in establishing an arm's length price for an intangible. First, it can be especially difficult to establish an arm's length price based on a comparable, since the value of intangibles frequently lies in their difference or even uniqueness. Nevertheless, some authorities accept that the best that can be done is to evaluate the appropriateness of the terms of a transfer of intangibles in a general way, by comparison with similar transactions in the same industry, and perhaps using as a check the profit produced for the transferee over a period of time. Thus, the Italian Ministry of Finance in 1980 provided, for certainty and speed of administration, 'safe harbour' guidelines for patent royalties, of up to 2 per cent of sales (provided there is a prior written contract, and evidence of actual benefit); over 2 per cent and up to 5 per cent could be acceptable for special factors (originality, obsolescence, exclusivity etc.); and over 5 per cent of sales only in exceptional circumstances such as the high technological level of the industry (Italy, Ministry of Finance 1980). This type of approach offers an easily administrable rule, but may prove inflexible.

Where an adequate comparable cannot be found, it is difficult to fix an arm's length price based on cost, since 'the actual open market price of intangible property is not related in a consistent manner to the costs involved in developing it' (OECD 1979, para. 100). The OECD report therefore concluded that cost can at best provide some guidance as to the lower limit of a price.

Alternatively, some TNCs have used cost-contribution arrangements, under which affiliates pay a share of the direct and indirect costs of a research programme based on the proportionate benefit they are expected to derive, in exchange for rights in the intangibles that are produced. These arrangements are similar to the cost-sharing or cost-funding methods used for central services discussed above; and they raise, even more acutely, the same questions: is there a clear benefit for the recipient, and does the method used to fix the contribution fairly reflect the expected benefit. The 1979 OECD report pointed out that 'such arrangements might open up opportunities for profit transfers disguised as deductions for costs', and stressed the 'need for a strict interpretation of the notion of real benefit' to ensure that participants only pay for expenditure which is really in their interests (OECD 1979, para. 115).

The German rules allow cost-contribution contracts for research, on the same conditions as for central administrative services: they should be based on a clear prior contract, distributing actual identifiable direct and indirect costs by a recognized accounting method, in exchange for rights to the intangibles produced without any supplementary payments, and making an apportionment of costs based on the benefits anticipated (Section 7 of the 1983 rules). The US regulations of 1968 also allowed cost-sharing agreements, provided they are in writing, and reflect a good faith effort by participants to bear their proportion of costs and risks on an arm's length basis (regulation 1–482–2(d)(4)).[1] The 1988 White Paper conceded that cost-sharing could still be acceptable after the enactment of the 'commensurate with income' requirement by Congress (see below), but only under strict conditions. In particular, the sharing of costs should not be confined to single products (which might enable a foreign subsidiary to benefit from a high-profit item without paying for lower-profit or unsuccessful research), but should normally be based on product areas defined at least by three-digit SIC (Standard Industrial Classification) code; although either taxpayer or IRS could show that a narrower or broader agreement is more appropriate (US Treasury 1988, chapters 12 and 13).

Thus, the problems involved in establishing arm's length prices for specific intrafirm transactions are at their most intractable when it comes to intangibles. Intangibles are likely to be distinct if not unique, throwing into doubt the validity of comparisons with similar items, if any are available on the market. Pricing based on costs is extremely difficult, since they are essentially joint cost factors with uncertain outcomes, so that either fixing a price based on cost, or allocating cost contributions in relation to anticipated benefit, is likely to be arbitrary.

Above all, intangibles most clearly raise the problem of the allocation of profits from synergy: the additional profits generated for an integrated firm by reason of its features as an organization, and not attributable specifically to any of its parts. Like joint costs, synergy profits cut to the heart of the separate enterprise approach to the taxation of international company groups, since such profits by definition cannot be attributed to one particular affiliate. Both problems also entail the politicization of the transfer pricing question, since the issue posed is the allocation of profit rather than its attribution. If a country accepts deductibility of payments from a local operating subsidiary of a TNC for intangibles owned or developed elsewhere, it will be allowing a deduction from gross profits, or essentially a tax subsidy, for research based abroad. Furthermore, countries compete in offering tax advantages for high-technology operations, and a TNC may transfer rights to intangibles to a subsidiary located in a country with an advantageous tax regime, so that the TNC benefits from lower taxation of the additional monopoly profit. Thus for example, the German authorities have been particularly vigilant in scrutinizing technology royalties and licence fees paid to foreign related companies, especially to those located in Switzerland and Liechtenstein (German Bundestag 1986, p. 14).

---

[1] These criteria were expressed in much more general terms than the draft regulations proposed in 1966, which had put forward detailed rules: 31 Fed. Reg. 10394.

3.f The Commensurate with Income Standard and the US White Paper

The experience of these difficulties led to proposals by the US authorities in 1988 for a new approach. As has already been mentioned, there is a long history of political concern about the effectiveness of US taxation of US-based TNCs. Specifically, when Congress attacked tax deferral with the Subpart F provisions in 1962, it considered proposals to require formula apportionment if a TNC could not prove comparable arm's length transfer prices; these were withdrawn following administration assurances that the desired result could be obtained by increased enforcement of s.482. Nevertheless, there has been continuing debate about the effectiveness of enforcement of the section and of the 1968 regulations, which reached a peak with the GAO report of 1981. Although the IRS responded vigorously to those criticisms, both the IRS and the Treasury were aware of underlying problems with the arm's length method.

These concerns resulted in a provision in the mammoth Tax Reform Act of 1986 amending s.482, the first substantial amendment of that section since 1928. This provision, popularly referred to as the 'super-royalty', added the following final sentence to the section:

> In the case of any transfer (or license) of intangible property (within the meaning of s.936(h)(3)(B)), the income with respect to such transfer or license shall be commensurate with the income attributable to the intangible.

At the same time, Congress referred to continuing unresolved difficulties with s.482, and asked for a comprehensive study of inter-company pricing rules giving careful consideration to whether the existing regulations should be amended. The result was a bulky discussion document issued by the Treasury and IRS in October 1988: 'A Study of Intercompany Pricing'.

This study identified two major problems in the enforcement of s.482. First was the difficulty of obtaining adequate information to evaluate pricing, leading to long delays in closing cases. It argued that the burden was on taxpayers to document established pricing policies, but evidence from IRS examiners showed that most firms sought to justify the prices charged only when challenged, and by reference to whatever method most closely approximated to those prices.[1] The main problem, to which the bulk of the study was addressed, was the pricing of intangibles. Although this, and especially the problem of 'high profit intangibles', was the explicit focus, the

[1] The study urged a more aggressive use of administrative summons procedures by examiners (see Chapter 10, section 2.a below). It also pointed to the need for special scrutiny of the growing volume of direct investment into the US, in view of evidence of substantially lower profit levels being reported for foreign-owned TNCs (US Treasury 1988, p. 15). Although this point was given less attention initially than the remaining major parts of the report, the issue of the apparently low tax liability of foreign investors in the US later came to the fore, as mentioned in section 2.b above.

study had far-reaching implications, since the pricing of intangibles relates closely to charging for central services generally, and is also often 'bundled' in the price of tangibles. Hence, the question of intangibles is central to the structure of intrafirm relationships.

The White Paper articulated the implications of the 'commensurate with income' requirement inserted by Congress into s.482, while arguing that it is compatible with the arm's length standard. To do so, it put forward a new pricing method, based on rate of return, called the Basic Arm's Length Return Method (quickly labelled BALRM or the 'ballroom' method), and severely circumscribed the application of other methods.

(i) Restriction of the CUP Method

As to comparables, the study argued that the CUP method can only be relied upon if an 'exact comparable' can be found. An exact comparable would be a transaction transferring the same intangible to an unrelated party. Since such transfers are usually exclusive, it need not be in respect of the same market. However, there must be substantial comparability both of external factors (overall size of the market, degree of competition, collateral or continuing relationships), and of internal factors (the terms of the contract). An 'inexact comparable', involving a similar intangible, may be useful to provide comparative information, but cannot be the sole basis to determine pricing. It can only be relied upon if 'the differences between it and the related party transaction can be reflected by a reasonable number of adjustments that have definite and ascertainable effects on the terms of the arrangement' (US Treasury 1988, p. 91). The study was especially critical of reliance on industry standards or averages.

This would severely restrict the use of the CUP method. The White Paper stated that comparability would be easy to demonstrate in cases of widely available technology such as pocket calculators, digital watches or microwave ovens. But such technology is unlikely to be transferred within an integrated TNC unless it has distinct properties: for example, ball-point pen technology is widely available, but a company such as Parker Pen still commands premium prices based on unique intangibles. Thus, in a case following the White Paper but decided under the pre-1986 law, the Tax Court took the view that non-exclusive licences to soft contact lens manufacturing technology, granted by Bausch & Lomb to its production subsidiary in Ireland, could be evaluated on the basis of comparables, and rejected the IRS view that the unrelated party prices were not fully comparable because of the lower volumes involved (*Bausch & Lomb v. Commr.*, 1989).[1]

These examples also demonstrate that the 'exact comparability' requirement applies to sales of tangibles which embody an intangible. If components, ingredients or subassemblies embody design or production technology, or

[1] This decision was upheld by the 2nd Circuit Court of Appeals on 14 May 1991.

marketing intangibles such as brand identification, the requirement that a comparable be 'exact' will reduce the application of the CUP method for tangibles also.

(ii) Periodic Adjustments

The commensurate with income requirement also entails that the return for a transfer of an intangible must normally be subject to periodic adjustment, to reflect the actual profit earned from it. The study defends this as compatible with arm's length, citing evidence that unrelated parties also renegotiate terms, either on the basis of explicit clauses providing for renegotiation or by using termination clauses to do so.[1] Hence, payments fixed by reference to either exact or inexact comparables must be reviewed, and adjusted if there has been a significant unforeseen change in profitability due to subsequent events. However, periodic adjustment can be avoided if the taxpayer can point to an exactly comparable arrangement which does not permit adjustment (US Treasury 1988, p. 64).

(iii) The Arm's Length Return Method

The study put great reliance on the proposed new 'arm's length return' method, which should be used if there is no exact comparable (and to adjust a price based on an inexact comparable). This identifies the assets and factors of production employed by each related party, and allocates to them a 'market' rate of return. The first step is a functional analysis, breaking down the activities carried out by the parties into their component functions; next, those functions with measurable assets or production factors can be assigned a market rate of return on the value of those assets. The residual profit is then normally assigned to the parent company, since it is considered to be attributable to the non-measurable intangible assets. The reasoning is that many of the functions carried out by affiliated companies are also carried out by unrelated firms, and information will be available about their normal rates of return on measurable factors (plant, labour, equipment, working capital and routine know-how). In that sense, this is an arm's length method, since it is attributing profits based on those of comparable firms in the industry. It therefore resembles the profit comparison approaches based on 'empirical' methods or the use of 'coefficients', long permitted in international practice for Permanent Establishments, and also practised by several countries in relation to subsidiaries, as a fall-back if evidence based on market transactions is not available (as discussed earlier in this chapter).

---

[1] Appendix D of the White Paper provides a 'very preliminary' analysis of unrelated party licence agreements obtained from the files of the Securities and Exchange Commission, and a literature review, to show that licensors seek to secure a risk-free return commensurate with actual profitability. But the study concedes that the Congressional enactment of the commensurate with income requirement was a legislative rejection of the tax court decision in *French v. Commr.* (1973), which held that a long-term fixed-rate royalty agreement could not be adjusted under s.482 to take into account subsequent unforeseen events.

The major difficulty with the BALRM, however, is the way it separates 'measurable' factors, to which a normal rate of return is assigned, and then assumes that the residual profit is attributable to the parent company. This was immediately criticized by some tax specialists as an attempt by the IRS to treat foreign subsidiaries as 'contract manufacturers', despite tax court decisions rejecting such a result (Fuller 1988). It certainly seems that the rate of return method proposed in the White Paper has grown out of the analyses by IRS economists of company accounts in s.482 cases, using a 'profit-split' first to support a price adjustment and finally, in the *Eli Lilly* case, as the basis for the adjustment.

In *Eli Lilly*, the Circuit Court upheld the Tax Court's 'profit-split' methodology, which 'divides combined revenues based on an *ad hoc* assessment of the contributions of the assets and activities of the commonly controlled enterprises' (*Eli Lilly v. Commr.*, 1988, p. 871). However, in that case, on the view taken by the courts *both* the related parties owned some intangibles. Lilly had set up a manufacturing subsidiary in Puerto Rico, to which it had transferred valuable drug patents in exchange for stock, while retaining the US marketing intangibles (trade names etc.). The IRS challenged the transfer, on the ground that if the parties had been unrelated the transferor would have required payments for the continuing research and development programme; this would have meant treating the Puerto Rico subsidiary as a contract manufacturer. The courts, however, accepted that the stock transfer was valuable consideration, and judged that Eli Lilly's high profits from the US sales of the drug, based on its US marketing intangibles, provided sufficient funding of the research effort. But the Tax Court first re-evaluated the costs attributable to each party and allocated an appropriate rate of return on those costs (including a return to the US parent of 100 per cent on marketing costs); and then adjusted the profit split on the residual profit to a ratio of 45–55 (Lilly had allowed 40–60), reflecting its view of the relative contributions of Lilly US's marketing intangibles and Lilly PR's production intangibles.[1]

Hence, although the US courts have not yet accepted a profit-split which treats a foreign subsidiary as a mere contract manufacturer, this is because they have accepted that the subsidiary validly owned some intangibles (see also *Searle v. Commr.*, 1987). The White Paper argued that the profit-splits accepted by the courts in previous cases were arbitrary or had 'no discernible rationale', and this was the reason for developing a 'careful functional

---

[1] The Circuit Court upheld all the Tax Court's adjustments except a charge to Lilly P. R. for research and development expenses, which it considered incompatible with the acceptance of the patents-for-stock transfer: ibid., p. 871. In response to the Lilly case s.936(h) was added to the Tax Code in 1982, so that possessions corporations must split the revenue from intangibles at least 50–50 with their US parent. The 1986 Tax Reform Act, in adding the commensurate with income requirement to s.482, also amended s.367(d)(2) so that recognition of a transfer of intangibles is conditional on payments 'commensurate with the income attributable to the intangible'.

analysis' (US Treasury 1988, p. 39), i.e. the BALRM method. The difficulty is that functional analysis is only precise in relation to 'measurable' factors. If there are synergy profits, functional analysis cannot provide a precise allocation.

This the White Paper accepts, in its discussion of what it calls the 'profit-split addition to the basic arm's length return method'. It countenances that, where a large TNC has foreign subsidiaries that perform complex functions, take significant risks and own significant assets, it would be appropriate to divide the 'residual' or synergy profits according to the relative value of the intangibles contributed or risks assumed by the parties. It is conceded that 'it is easier to state this principle than to describe in detail how it is to be applied in practice', and that 'splitting the intangible income in such cases will be largely a matter of judgment' (US Treasury 1988, p. 101). This is perhaps a concession to the US's main treaty partners, some of which may be reluctant to accept an approach which allocates the entirety of the synergy profits of US TNCs to the parent company.[1]

Thus, the full rigour of the BALRM may be confined to subsidiaries with high-profit intangibles in convenient low-tax locations, such as Ireland or Singapore, or operating subsidiaries in relatively small markets. In principle, the application of the BALRM should also limit US taxation of foreign-owned TNCs (Carlson, Fogarasi & Gordon 1988), and this is becoming more significant as the growth of direct investment into the USA continues to even out the previous imbalance. However, this would depend on the willingness of the US authorities to accept that foreign-owned subsidiaries in the US do not own significant intangibles. It is more likely that due to the size and complexity of the US market, foreign-owned companies would be regarded as substantially distinct operations from their parents, thus justifying an allocation to them of an appropriate proportion of the residual profits. Equally, the other main OECD countries may also argue that there is a difference between major TNC affiliates with substantial operations and their own independent know-how, and smaller subsidiaries operating in restricted markets, or carrying out specific functions of a 'contract manufacturer' kind.

The rate of return method based on functional analysis represents a significant retreat from the attempt to adjust prices of individual transactions mainly by finding comparables. It may be that the identification of functions will provide a more precise and flexible basis for evaluating profit than other 'empirical' methods that have been used, such as gross margin on sales. It also makes it explicit that, at least in the case of integrated, research-based TNCs, there is likely to be a significant element of 'residual' profit attributable to the organization as such, which must either be assigned to the parent, or allocated among the main affiliates according to some measure of their contributions to

---

[1] The official foreign government responses to the White Paper were confidential and not published, although many of the relevant officials have expressed their personal views in symposia: see e.g. De Hosson (ed.) 1989.

the innovations and risks of the organization. But it does not resolve many of the problems which historically made the tax authorities fight shy of explicitly adopting a profit-split method. Hence, it is not much help in evaluating the profit-split between the related parties: by focusing on 'measurable' functions, it merely assumes that synergy profits accrue to the ultimate parent.

Due to their broader political and economic implications, there is likely to be continued reluctance to tackle these questions explicitly and publicly, and a continuing insistence that the normal and primary test of transfer prices is that of independent parties dealing at arm's length. Indeed, the White Paper was fiercely criticized by the Taxation Commission of the International Chamber of Commerce, as entailing 'fundamental deviations from the arm's length principle'. Professor Wolfgang Ritter, responding to the White Paper on behalf of that Commission, wrote that the basic arm's length return method:

> is nothing but another form of unitary taxation, now recognized by the US Federal Authorities, as a result of the international outcry which it provoked, to be unfair. BALRM analysis does exactly what unitary taxation does: instead of looking at the actual prices charged between related entities, it looks at the total profits earned by a number of entities and divides them up by reference to criteria determined by academic economists with no experience of the real business world. [Ritter, in De Hosson 1989, p. 73.]

4. Transfer Prices in Theory and Practice

The detailed analysis in the previous sections has shown the difficulties faced in applying the arm's length criterion. The initial adoption of the arm's length principle followed from the fear that any attempt to reach international agreement on general principles to define and allocate the tax base of internationally-integrated businesses would fail. Instead, it was hoped that the issues could be resolved either 'naturally', by using market prices, or by case-by-case agreement or direct negotiation between tax authorities. Reliance on market prices has provided at best a partial solution, principally because experience has shown that the criterion of comparable uncontrolled prices is an inadequate one. In a high proportion of cases, the internal transactions of an integrated firm are not comparable with those of independent firms. Furthermore, effective verification of prices by reference to comparables requires a sophisticated administrative bureaucracy, which must grow in proportion to the importance of TNCs in the economy. Although safe-harbour or bright-line rules may facilitate administration (e.g. the Italian rules on royalty payments, or the rules-of-thumb sometimes used for thin capitalization) they have not been generally adopted: if binding they are inflexible, and if presumptive they are uncertain (see section 3.c above). Significantly, it was the largest state, the US, which made the most determined efforts to operationalize the arm's length criterion based on comparables, and which has been forced to develop alternatives.

4.a Cost-Sharing and Profit-Split

It was, however, always accepted that the arm's length principle need not and could not rely exclusively on finding comparable market prices. Its essence was that taxation of the business profits of a branch or affilitate must begin from the separate accounts of that entity and proceed by adjusting specific transaction prices, to produce the result which would have obtained if the entity had been independent. This entails (i) analysing the intrafirm relationships so as to identify and correctly characterize specific transactions, and (ii) establishing criteria for pricing (in the absence of market comparables) which conform with the independent enterprise test. The difficulty of identification of specific transactions which can be priced is most acute in relation to joint and fixed cost items. This has led to a trend towards the proportionate allocation of such costs; while the problem of finding an independent enterprise criterion for pricing has led to the use of an arm's length profit standard.

We have considered above the problems involved in 'unbundling' relationships and characterizing transactions in terms of supplier-purchaser. We have also seen that pricing in the absence of comparables leads to serious problems in determining the allocation of costs. It is very difficult to allocate the joint costs and overheads of an integrated firm according to the specific benefit derived by each unit. This has led to the acceptance, in varying degrees, of 'formula' methods of allocating joint costs: in particular, the averaging of interest expense (required by the US and Japan, but not accepted by others, see section 3.c(iii) above); and cost-sharing for central services (more generally accepted, but subject to strict conditions, see section 3.d above), as well as cost-contribution for research (section 3.e above). Significantly, it is representatives of business who have pressed for acceptance of proportionate sharing of costs, although they are generally hostile to a formula approach to taxation. However, while some national authorities require the proportional allocation of some items of cost, others are unwilling to accept such an allocation without proof of specific benefit, and the principle has been rejected by a majority for some items, notably interest expense.

Reliance on an arm's length profit standard has resulted, in practice, from the problems of defining criteria for arm's length prices in the absence of comparables. Both in their administrative rules or guidelines, and as part of enforcement practice, the national authorities have relied extensively on comparison of the profits declared by the local entity with those of similar firms normally managed. This method has been justified not as a primary means of allocating profits, but as a check on the acceptability of price adjustments. Also, in principle it consists not in dividing the global profit of the firm as a whole, but in estimating, based on the value of assets or the volume of business, whether the profit of the local branch or subsidiary is in line with the levels of profit made by similar independent businesses. This is similar to the 'empirical' method which was given limited formal authority in the international model treaties.[1] Even this test has led to disagreements, specifically as to whether the comparison should be with global industry standards or those of other local firms (section 1.c above). More fundamentally, the profit comparison approach entails a shift from the arm's length pricing rule to an arm's length profit standard, which is controversial. Thus, when the majority of the members of the OECD Committee agreed to treat thin capitalization as a transfer pricing problem, Germany objected in principle on the grounds that the arm's length principle mean's arm's length prices and not arm's length profits (section 3.c(i) above).

For a number of reasons, however, profit-comparison tends to become profit-split. Inevitably, a profit-comparison will also be made between the profits made by the local entity and those of the related companies with which it deals. Further, since profit comparison is used when there are no substantially comparable independent-party transactions, it is likely that there will be no substantially comparable firms either. In such circumstances, the experience with the US rules has shown that the resale-minus, cost-plus and other alternative methods to CUP tend to result in profit-split. This is because the application of this type of cost analysis to an integrated TNC often does not result in one precise price, but a range or continuum. Applying microeconomic marginal analysis tends to produce a significant gap between the marginal price which will induce the producing affiliate to supply, and the price at which the marketing affiliate can make a profitable resale. Hence, both tax examiners and courts tend to 'split the difference' and adjust the price so that a 'reasonable' profit-split is produced.[2] Finally, to the extent that it is difficult or impossible to define specific transactions and adjust prices on the basis of market comparables, profit-split becomes not a fall-back but a principal method (accepted by the US courts in *Eli Lilly*: see section 3.a above).

This is implicitly recognized by the US White Paper proposals. The White Paper's Basic Arm's Length Return Method attempted to establish a more precise and detailed methodology for separate accounting in the absence of comparables, by the identification of factors of production and allocation to them of an appropriate rate of return. This is an attempt to make a cost-plus and profit-comparison approach work, by arguing that as long as there is functional comparability, it does not matter if there is no exact comparability of products. However, the authors of the White Paper were also clearly aware that this process might result in some very disproportionate profit-splits between the parent and its foreign subsidiary, since the BALRM method assumes that the additional profits from synergy are attributable to the parent.

---

[1] Allocation by 'percentage of turnover' for branches was accepted as a fall-back method: see section 1.c and Chapter 1, section 5.b above.

[2] This point has been particularly stressed by Langbein: see Langbein 1986, p. 658; Langbein 1989, p. 1395.

Hence, its concession that in some cases it may be appropriate for the 'residual' profit to be apportioned in some appropriate manner. Unfortunately, here the methodology failed, and no criterion could be proposed on which to base this profit-split: it must be fixed *ad hoc* by agreement among the parties concerned.

The move towards acceptance of proportional allocation of joint costs and the use of an arm's length profit standard are practical attempts to adapt the arm's length principle to the realities of the intrafirm relationships of an integrated TNC. While they still begin from separate accounts, they address the question of criteria for allocation of costs and profits of the firm as a whole. However, proportional allocation of costs, as we have seen, is controversial and remains anomalous without a global approach to profit allocation. On the other hand, profit-comparison based on return to assets or other methods may merely identify large residual profits, for the allocation of which no criteria have been suggested.

The arm's length approach attempts to maintain tax neutrality and equity in the allocation of international investment: by treating members of a group in the same way as unrelated companies, their tax burden should be the same and markets would not be distorted by taxation. The validity of this approach, however, depends on the economic rationale for the existence and development of international firms, and the internal pricing policies adopted by the firms themselves.

4.b Economic Theory and Business Practice

Until relatively recently, economic theory did not concern itself specifically with the phenomenon of the transnational corporation. International economic relations were treated as relations between national economies based on states, and consisting essentially of trade and investment and the corresponding international payments. Trade theory assumed immobile production factors (labour and capital), perfect competition, free access to technology, and no barriers to exports; it was complemented by international investment theory which accepted the existence of trade barriers and the mobility of capital as a factor of production, explained as the response to differences in price (interest rates) and resource endowments. Only from the late 1950s did international economists begin to try to explain the actual patterns of international business, increasingly dominated by TNCs. They began to accept that 'production factors' are much more diverse, and can vary significantly in quality (e.g. labour skills); also, that markets are imperfect, and enterprises can protect monopolistic advantages, especially in production technology and product specialization.[1]

Hence, the existence of TNCs could be explained as the exploitation, on an

[1] For a survey of the development of the debates see generally Dunning 1988, chapter 1.

international scale, of combinations of assets and locations which entail a competitive advantage. Initially, the focus was on firm-specific advantages of industrial organization, protected by entry barriers, which gave foreign firms a monopolistic position compared with local firms (Hymer 1960/1976), or technological advantages deriving from their control over the diffusion of new products (Vernon 1966). More recently the emphasis has been on analysing the advantages of the organizational form, under the influence of institutional and transaction cost economics, which has tried to refine the analysis of the dynamics of the firm. Rejecting the basic assumptions of the neo-classical paradigm based on the rational choice of the pure individual with perfect information, in favour of behaviourist and interactional models which emphasize bounded rationality and the important social roles of informal and formal organization, institutional economics analyses the characteristics of knowledge and its role in optimal decision-making, and argues that inter-nalization of transactions within the firm may be more efficient in dealing with uncertainty, risk and opportunism. Hence, the growth of the firm into the multidivisional corporation, the conglomerate and the TNC results not so much from economies of scale in production (which could be realized through contracting), but from the advantages of the organizational form, both in controlling and applying technological innovation and in taking strategic capital investment decisions (Williamson 1985, ch. 11).

Finally, writers have emphasized the advantages of spreading risks through international diversification (Rugman 1979). In particular, TNCs can benefit from the spreading of financial risks and the internalization of the manage-ment of arbitrage opportunities arising from diversity of currency exchange rates, financial markets and regulatory regimes (Lessard 1979). Important among these is of course taxation. This indicates that due to competitive pressure TNCs will seek the most favourable means of structuring their internal financial and other transactions to take advantage of regulatory differences and the inadequacies of regulatory co-ordination.

Two main conclusions can be derived from these analyses. First, TNCs exist to a great extent because of the competitive advantages they can derive from internalizing markets (Rugman 1982). The economies derived from internalization may be considered to result either from reduction of produc-tion costs, whether through economies of scale (increased production volume of one item reducing its incremental or marginal cost) or economies of scope (reducing the marginal cost of different items which can share joint factors); or from reducing transaction costs, by sharing and managing the costs and risks of appropriation of knowledge through research, design and managerial and other professional services, and other advantages of co-ordinated organiza-tion. Both the production cost and transaction cost perspectives emphasize that an integrated entity benefits from synergy profits, or additional returns attributable to oligopolistic advantages and the organizational form. Second, the advantages they gain from internalization, which would not be available to independent parties contracting through markets, entail the active management of internal transactions for the optimal benefit of the organization as a whole. This is particularly the case for regulatory arbitrage.

It is this feature of strategic management of internal transactions that clearly emerges from the more specific theoretical and empirical studies of transfer pricing. Authors have stressed that a company's internal pricing systems must respond to a variety of aims and constraints in relation to both its internal structure and goals as well as the external environment (Plasschaert 1980). It was not until the 1920s that large firms were forced to move away from centralized management structures to encourage decentralization and allow vertical integration through divisionalization (Chandler 1962, p. 44). This entailed, at least for the large bureaucratic firms, notably DuPont and General Motors, the 'development of financial instruments which made it possible to establish decentralization with co-ordinated control' (Sloan 1965, p. 119). Such a financial system must reconcile the often conflicting requirements of measuring performance and providing incentives for managers of cost-centres. In order to establish criteria to judge return on capital invested for each cost-centre, the internal costing structure depends crucially, in modern large-scale manufacturing, on assumptions about volume. Sloan emphasized that the key to the control system developed by General Motors in the 1920s was the establishment of the standard volume concept, enabling the firm to ride out short-term market fluctuations (Sloan 1965, pp. 142–8).

When, somewhat later, economists came to study the problem, they treated it as one in marginal analysis, and argued that unless perfect markets exist (when market prices should be used) internal pricing should be based on marginal cost price (Hirschleifer 1956, 1957). This has been cogently criticized from a business management perspective, however, as focusing on profit maximization on the basis of highly restrictive assumptions. By assuming that the operating divisions have no joint or common costs either for technology or marketing and that fixed costs are sunk, it omits the crucial element of business strategy, which entails choices and motivation (Eccles 1985). In practice, more recent surveys of business practice show that firms rarely use marginal cost, opportunity cost (mathematically programmed) or even standard variable cost prices. Where a cost-based price is used, it is full production cost, frequently with an allowance for profit also; furthermore, although cost-based prices are used less for international than domestic transfers, full-cost plus profit is more frequent internationally (Tang 1981, esp. pp. 141–2). When asked to rank the importance of factors affecting transfer pricing strategies, firms predictably place overall profit to the company first, while the competitive position and the performance evaluation of foreign subsidiaries were very important; also highly placed factors were restrictions on repatriation of profits or dividends, the need to maintain adequate cash flows, and devaluation and revaluation, as well as differentials in income tax rates and income tax legislation between countries (Tang 1981, p. 144).

Hence, the internal transfer pricing policies of TNCs are defined by an evaluation of the various strategic factors affecting the firm, of which exploitation of opportunities for financial, foreign exchange and tax arbitrage, within the constraints set by rule enforcement by state authorities, are among the most important external factors. Thus, there are likely to be significant tensions between the policies of the firms in setting prices and the criteria to be used by the tax authorities in determining which policies are acceptable. It is not clear that the independent enterprise standard is the best starting-point for such regulatory criteria, since it cuts across the firm's own strategic perspective, and is therefore likely to exacerbate such tensions. As we have seen, it is where the authorities have moved towards acceptance of proportional allocation of costs that there has been most harmony with company strategies. When it comes to the allocation of profits, although there has been apparent general agreement in principle on the separate enterprise standard, its application in practice has tended to heighten conflict, both between firms and regulators, as well as between national authorities among themselves.

Indeed, as the microeconomic methods applied to evaluation of transfer pricing by tax authorities have become more sophisticated, so they have increased these conflicts. As has been shown above, the marginal analysis assumptions of conventional microeconomics ignore the central factors of oligopolistic markets and organizational advantage; hence, their application will tend to result in the identification of a large item of residual profit (Witte & Chipty 1990). The firm's own internal pricing strategy must take into account how to allocate this residual profit, balancing managerial incentives, performance evaluation, regulatory compliance and avoidance and other factors. However, neither managerial nor microeconomic theories can provide criteria for its inter-jurisdictional allocation. The separate enterprise approach assumes in principle that, provided at least that foreign subsidiaries and branches show a reasonable return on assets or turnover, the synergy profits should be attributable to the parent. Langbein has argued that a transaction costs approach, as opposed to one emphasizing production costs, would negate this assumption, since the returns to organization would be seen more clearly as returns to the organization as a whole (Langbein 1989). However, transaction cost analysis does not produce any better theoretical basis for inter-jurisdictional allocation, although it may be a better rationale for defining when a firm should be treated as unitary (see McLure 1984, p. 103, and Chapter 9, section 2 below). Indeed, Langbein concludes that the transactional analysis perspective, emphasizing that economies of integration result from management of risk, suggests an inter-jurisdictional allocation based on a fractional system, 'employing fractions designed in accordance with a general understanding of the economic processes which produce and preserve the tax base' (Langbein 1989, p. 1410). However, beyond stating that these fractions should be multilaterally agreed, he is not able to suggest how transactional analysis might produce appropriate allocation criteria. In principle, it is not clear that the microeconomics of transactional analysis provides any better basis than that of production cost for proposing criteria for inter-jurisdictional allocation.

5. Conclusion

The arm's length standard resulted from the prioritization of national equity concerns over international equity. Inevitably, however, variations between national solutions to equity issues create differences which exacerbate the problem of international equity. In relation to international revenue flows, as we have seen in earlier chapters, this led to conflicts between the source and residence principles, partly accommodated through the bilateral treaty system with its allocation of tax rights, limitation of withholding taxes and reciprocal agreements on exemption or credit for foreign taxes. However, it is this very loosely co-ordinated treaty system which the internationally integrated firm has been able to exploit through international avoidance, mainly by means of tax haven intermediary companies (Chapter 6 above). The primary concern of anti-haven measures was to reinforce national equity by bringing back into taxation residents' income sheltered in havens: though by straining the treaty provisions, such as those defining residence, they raised inter-state equity issues. The stricter enforcement of transfer pricing rules, which was the other arm of the attack on international avoidance, has also resulted in highlighting the problem of inter-state allocation. In the absence of any general principles governing such allocation, the burden of solving the inter-state allocation issues has fallen on the administrative arrangements for co-ordination of tax enforcement.

From an equity point of view, the outcome can hardly be considered satisfactory:

> At best, the result in developed countries is to turn the taxation of multinational enterprises into a game of bargaining and negotiation. At worst, the result in some developing countries is to leave the amount of tax paid up to either the conscience of the company or the arbitrary decision of the authorities. [Bird 1988, p. 294.]

It is possible to put forward principles which may be applied by state authorities in such firm-by-firm bargaining over intrafirm pricing. For example, Robin Murray has argued that, from an under-developed country viewpoint, foreign TNCs should be allowed to recover only their global marginal costs plus a normal rate of return, which would mean pricing imported intermediates at marginal costs (or dumping prices) and exported primary products such that the raw material rent is appropriated by the owners of the land, usually the state (Murray 1981, pp. 167–70). However, he also stresses the power relationship involved in such bargaining, expressed administratively in the firm's control over the relevant information, and politically in the restraints which may be imposed on state officials, both resulting from the economic power of multinationals (ibid., p. 172). One might add that a key aspect of this power is the global strategic perspective of the TNC, which poses ultimate limits on the powers of state officials and the national state, in the absence of effective processes of international administrative and political co-ordination. Paradoxically, however, from the viewpoint of individual firms it is precisely this lack of co-ordination that underlies the 'arbitrariness' of national bargaining.[1]

The processes of administrative co-ordination will be considered in detail in Chapter 10. However, first we must consider the dispute over worldwide unitary taxation, which revived interest in the possibility that formula apportionment might produce a more satisfactory global basis for international business taxation.

---

[1] Hence the frequent pleas on behalf of business for stability and fairness in the criteria for determining the international tax base: see e.g. Milton, in McLure (ed.) 1984, p. 183, who points out that although taxpayers are often accused of manipulating transactions to reduce tax, governments also manipulate the criteria for defining the tax base to increase their tax take.

9
The Worldwide Unitary Taxation Controversy

During the 1970s an increasingly publicized dispute developed over what has been referred to as Worldwide Unitary Taxation (WUT). The dispute arose over the application by a number of American state jurisdictions of their system of formulary apportionment of the taxable income of a unitary business to the combined worldwide activities of TNCs doing business within the state. Attempts to prevent the widening application of this approach developed into a worldwide campaign, led by non-American, in particular British, TNCs doing business in the US. Although this campaign obtained support from the American Federal as well as most other national governments, and eventually succeeded in checking the application of unitary taxation to worldwide income, at the same time it focused attention on the problem of allocation of the income of globally integrated businesses. This in turn led to increased scrutiny of the effectiveness of enforcement of the arm's length pricing principles under the separate accounting approach, and stimulated renewed efforts by the US Internal Revenue Service to justify and develop its systems of audit of TNC accounts, as discussed in the previous chapter. It also encouraged the IRS to take the lead in pressing for further development of the international arrangements for co-ordination of the taxation of international business. Despite the widespread criticism of WUT, it became clear that a formula approach would be a necessary element of an improved system of international taxation.

1. Formula Apportionment in the USA

Formula apportionment had originated as a means of allocating taxes of cross-jurisdictional business within the USA. In the *State Railroad Tax Cases* (1875), the US Supreme Court upheld the validity of an Illinois state railroad tax of 1872 which was levied on the value of buildings, track, rolling stock and other property within the state, apportioned as to each county, city or town according to the proportion of the length of track within that locality in relation to the total length of track of that railroad. In the early years of the twentieth century, as states began to levy income taxes or franchise taxes on business profits, the principle of apportionment became commonly used to allocate the income of a multi-state business or corporation.

1.a Constitutionality

In 1920, in a landmark judgment by Brandeis J. (*Underwood Typewriter v. Chamberlain*), the Supreme Court held that such an allocation was not unconstitutional under the Commerce or Due Process clauses, since there was nothing to show that it was arbitrary or produced an unreasonable result. In 1924 the Court also approved formula apportionment applied to a foreign corporation importing beer brewed in Britain for sale in New York (*Bass, Ratcliffe & Gretton Ltd v. State Tax Commission*, 1924). New York's business franchise tax originating in 1909 was levied at 3 per cent of net income; corporations which earned some of their income from outside the state paid according to the proportion of the value of assets located in the state. This was upheld as valid in the *Bass* beer case, despite the fact that under the federal income tax rules the British company had no US income assessable to tax; the court agreed that manufacturing and selling ale constituted a unitary business, and the allocation of profits by New York was legitimate.

Within the federal framework, formula apportionment posed two questions: how far the approach of different states should be harmonized, and whether this was the task of the courts or the Congress. The courts were sometimes willing to strike down an allocation if it could be shown to be arbitrary or irrational. In *Hans Rees' Sons v. N. Carolina* (1930), the Supreme Court stated that 'evidence may always be received which tends to show that a State has applied a method which, albeit fair on its face, operates so as to reach profits which are in no just sense attributable to transactions within its jurisdiction' (p. 134). There, a company manufacturing belting in North Carolina and selling in many states from warehouses and a sales base in New York, showed that its profit was in three separate components: that from buying hides on the markets; that from manufacturing (which it assessed at the difference between tanning done by independent contractors and tanning done in its own plant); and that from sales. The Court agreed that although 'the ultimate gain is derived from the entire business', nevertheless the activities conducted in different jurisdictions did not form 'component parts of a single unit'. However, in *Butler Bros. v. McColgan* (1942), the Court stressed that 'One who attacks a formula of apportionment carries a distinct burden of showing by "clear and cogent evidence" that it results in extraterritorial values being taxed' (p. 507, *per* Douglas, J.).

The spread of state corporate taxation, and divergences between the approaches of different states, led to a flood of court cases. These came to a head in two cases which reached the Supreme Court in 1959.[1] By this time, 35 states had direct net income taxes on corporations, and there had been over 300 cases reaching the stage of full-dress opinions in the Supreme Court. The *Northwestern Portland Cement* case of 1959 squarely put the issue to the Court, whether a corporation engaged in 'exclusively inter-state commerce' could be subject to state income tax at all. Frankfurter J., in particular, stated the robust view that the Commerce clause of the Constitution precluded the states from taxing a corporation 'on income related to the state by virtue of activities within it when such activities are exclusively a part of the process of doing inter-state commerce'. However, a six–three majority of the Court held that a non-discriminatory and fairly apportioned state tax on inter-state corporate income was constitutional.

While there has been a continuing split in the Supreme Court between those holding restrictionist and expansionist views of state powers, the Court has tried to hold consistently to the principle that state taxation 'must bear a rational relationship, both on its face and in its application, to property values connected with the taxing state'.[2] In the *Norfolk & Western Railway* case (1968), the Court rejected Missouri's treatment as unitary of the profits of two different railroads which had not been operationally integrated but acquired by the same company for diversification. However, this principle falls short of giving the Court the role of ensuring the full harmonization of the approaches of different states, a role which the majority of Justices has felt is reserved for the Congress, although the Court has not been averse to giving Congress a push. Following the *Northwestern Portland Cement* case, the Congress did succeed in passing an Act[3] which prohibited states from taxing a corporation present within the state only through sales, solicited and filled entirely from outside the state. Despite further continual threats of and attempts at Congressional action, no comprehensive federal legislation has yet reached the statute book.

1.b Harmonization of State Formula Apportionment

In the meantime, the states have attempted themselves to harmonize their activities. The Uniform Division of Income for Tax Purposes Act (UDITPA), drafted in 1957 by the National Conference of Commissioners on Uniform State Laws, was adopted as Article IV of a Multi-state Tax Compact in 1966. The Compact established the Multi-state Tax Commission with the power to formulate regulations and develop practice to ensure optimal harmonization in the application of UDITPA. UDITPA laid down a three-factor formula based on tangible property, payroll and sales, and its acceptance by many states from the 1960s, with the explicit aim of heading off federal legislation,

[1] *Northwestern Portland Cement Co. v. Minnesota*; *T. V. Williams v. Stockham Valves* (1959).
[2] Fortas, J., in *Norfolk & Western Rly Co. v. Missouri State Tax Commission* (1968).
[3] Public Law 86–272 of 1959.

established widespread harmonization in the allocation of the profits of a unitary business. By 1982 over 23 states had adopted UDITPA, there were nineteen full and eleven associate members of the Compact, and the Multi-state Tax Commission was carrying out audits of multi-state firms on behalf of its member states.[1]

Divergences between states arise in particular in relation to (i) the formula used, and (ii) the criteria for determining whether a business is unitary. As regards the formula, some states specify in the taxing statute the formula to be used, while others merely require a fair apportionment, which is left to be decided by commissioners, on the basis of regulations, which frequently give the taxpayer the right to object and propose an alternative. Divergences arise in particular between states which are the home of manufacture and the primarily agricultural states where manufactured products are sold. UDITPA gives the taxpayer the right to elect the application of the three-factor formula, which aims to provide a balance of these competing interests. However, the Supreme Court has refused to put pressure on states to fall in line with the three-factor formula. Thus, in *Moorman Manufacturing Co. v. Bair* (1978), an Illinois animal feed corporation had 20 per cent of its sales in Iowa; assessments using a single-factor formula based on sales were upheld as valid by a six–three majority of the Supreme Court. Iowa's formula conflicted with that of Moorman's home state, Illinois, which had adopted UDITPA and its three-factor formula, but the judgment of Stevens, J., while conceding that the single-factor formula was imprecise, nevertheless held that neither the Due Process nor the Commerce clauses of the Constitution required the elimination of all double taxation. A strong dissenting judgment by Powell, J. stressed that it was the duty of the Court to establish a balance between the interests and rights of the several states, and that the single-factor formula effectively acted as a tariff on goods imported from manufacturing states.

What constitutes a unitary business has, however, proved to be the more difficult problem. Under UDITPA, the three-factor allocation formula applies only to 'business income'. The first step is therefore to distinguish non-business income from business income, which is defined as:

> . . . income arising from transactions and activity in the regular course of the taxpayer's trade or business and includes income from tangible and intangible property if the acquisition, management and disposition of the property constitute integral parts of the taxpayer's trade or business operations.

Non-business income is allocated not by the formula but according to geographical source. Thus, rent from real property unconnected with the business is allocated to the state where the property is located; patent and

---

[1] An attempt to invalidate the formation of the Compact as an unconstitutional compact or treaty among the states was rejected by the Supreme Court in *US Steel v. Multistate Tax Commission* (1978). For an example of a joint audit of a TNC carried out by the Commission, see *ASARCO v. Idaho State Tax Commission* (1982).

copyright royalties unconnected with the carrying on of the business are allocated to the state where those rights are utilized.

Secondly, a corporation may engage in different lines of business, which may or may not be regarded as unitary. Here the UDITPA does not help, and it is left to the courts to determine what constitutes a unitary business. On the whole, little difficulty is caused by vertically-integrated activities carried out by a single corporation in several states. R & D, purchasing, manufacturing, financing and marketing activities of a single corporation in relation to a single product line are normally highly integrated (although this was, exceptionally, found not to be so in the *Hans Rees* case). More problematic has been the situation where similarly vertically-integrated activities were carried out by separate but affiliated corporations registered in different states. In a case involving the auto manufacturer Studebaker (*Studebaker Corp. v. Gilchrist*, 1926), it was revealed that Studebaker's Indian manufacturing affiliate showed substantial profits, while the prices it charged to its sales subsidiaries produced losses or minimal profits for them. The New York Court of Appeals held invalid an attempt by New York to tax on the basis of the consolidated accounts of the group filed for federal tax purposes. Where an out-of-state corporation operated in New York through a branch, the profits could be allocated, as was decided in the *Bass* beer case. Where it operated through a group of subsidiaries, the New York tax statute gave the power to adjust intragroup prices to ensure that their relationship was 'as liberal and just as it would be if the subsidiary were a stranger' (Cardozo, J., at p. 71). However, since the Indiana subsidiary was not doing business in New York, it was not subject to New York tax at all. The Tax Commission had erred in neither attempting to adjust the intrafirm prices, nor even apportioning the profits shown by the consolidated return.

This posed a real problem, since many vertically-integrated firms could use a network of subsidiary companies to ensure that most profits appeared in low-tax states. To overcome this, several states began to apply formula apportionment to the taxable profits of an entire unitary business, taking account of the assets and activities of related corporations engaged in that same business. This could not be done by means of a consolidated return, since a state could not subject to its jurisdiction corporations not registered or doing business within the state, even if one of the affiliates of a corporate group was so present. Instead, they required the affiliate which was within the state to file a *combined report* covering all affiliated corporations engaged in the same unitary business, giving the information necessary to compute the combined profit and to apportion according to the formula. In computing the combined profit, the important step was to eliminate from the total gross receipts and expenses of the entire unitary business the effects of all inter-affiliate transactions relating to the unitary business. This made it irrelevant to investigate whether inter-affiliate pricing had been used to shift profits. Hence, taxation of a corporate group on a unitary basis by individual states is an alternative to joint taxation by states based on a single consolidated return.

However, combined reporting made it even more vital to establish criteria for what constituted a unitary business. The courts developed the three unities test, approved by the Supreme Court in *Butler Brothers. v. McColgan* (1942). These were the unity of ownership, of operation and of management. Unity of ownership and management do not normally cause much difficulty; it is operational unity that is harder to define. In *Butler Brothers*, the unity of operation was held to be satisfied for a distribution company whose purchasing was centralized; the court held that the loss shown on a separate accounting basis on sales from the wholesale warehouse in California unfairly disregarded the benefit from bulk purchasing created by the extra volume of California sales.

Nevertheless, it appears that state tax authorities were relatively selective in requiring the submission of a combined report, and confined its use to situations where it seemed that the separate accounts might not fairly reflect profitability. This selectivity also meant that, despite the early decision in the *Bass* case approving the application of the formula approach to foreign companies, the question of the application of combined reporting on a worldwide basis did not become important until the mid-1960s.

2. State Unitary Taxes Applied to Worldwide Income

Worldwide unitary taxation did not emerge from any deliberate policy on the part of state tax authorities, but as a result of the developing momentum of the unitary tax approach being applied to an increasingly internationalized business environment. A key element has been the developments in California. This state had pioneered combined reporting in the 1930s, to prevent motion picture companies siphoning off profits to their distribution subsidiaries in low-tax jurisdictions, especially in neighbouring Nevada. The three unities test developed by the California courts, was approved by the Supreme Court in the *Butler Brothers* case mentioned above, and California's system of combined reporting for affiliated corporations was approved by the California courts in *Edison California Stores v. McColgan* (1947). The policy of California's Franchise Tax Board had nevertheless been to require a combined report only where it seemed necessary.

A significant change took place following the decisions of the California Supreme Court in 1963 in two cases involving oil companies.[1] The cases concerned oil drilled in California and sold at the well-head to independent third parties; since their non-Californian drilling was less profitable, it was the companies who wanted all their US oil business to be treated as unitary, over the objections of the Franchise Tax Board (FTB). The Court rejected the FTB view that unity of operations existed only where the operations were

[1] *Superior Oil v. Franchise Tax Board* (1963); *Honolulu Oil v. Franchise Tax Board* (1963).

'necessary and essential' to each other; unity existed wherever operations 'contributed to or were dependent on' each other. The 'necessary and essential' test had proved most difficult to apply to horizontally-integrated firms, especially those with diversified businesses or conglomerates.

The 1963 decisions, as well as California's adoption of UDITPA in 1966, established combined reporting as a requirement in that state. The court decisions, in particular, 'gave taxpayers the unequivocal right to require combination when it benefited them and made the audit staff even more aware of the foreign combination issue' (Miller in McLure (ed.) 1984, p. 139). The state tax authorities needed little further incentive to try to replenish or increase state revenues by the active use of the unitary approach. While some, primarily American, firms found they could reduce their state tax assessments through unitary combination by setting off losses made outside California, other companies acquiring or setting up businesses in California would be subject to much higher local taxes based on worldwide profits. Since formula apportionment had been approved when applied to the domestic and foreign business of a foreign corporation as early as 1924 in the *Bass* case, there seemed no legal obstacle to its application to either American or non-American TNCs, on their global activities.[1]

In the late 1960s and early 1970s therefore, TNCs doing business in California began suddenly to find themselves required to complete a combined report covering their worldwide operations. This meant in many cases considerable additional effort, since the combined report differed from the consolidated accounts which the parent company would normally prepare. Separate profit and loss statements were required for each affiliate engaged in unitary business – but with factors such as amortization calculated according to US rules (whereas the accounts of affiliates or subsidiaries would normally comply with the requirements of its country of registration or residence). Further computation was necessary to convert net income to unitary business income subject to apportionment. Finally, figures were to be supplied for the property, payroll and sales, within and outside California, of each affiliate, for the calculation of the formula.[2] Firms which failed or refused fully to comply were subject to a tax penalty and a notice of tax payable based on the state tax

---

[1] The California courts had already held that the statute applied both to inter-state and foreign commerce in 1935, and this had been confirmed by legislative amendment in 1939: see Miller, in McLure (ed.) 1984, p. 138.

[2] The high cost of compliance was emphasized by the California courts which struck down combined reporting as unconstitutional: in *Barclays Bank v. Franchise Tax Board* (1990), the California Court of Appeals pointed out that the Barclays group consisted of over 220 subsidiaries operating in some 60 countries, but only three of these did business in the United States, and only 1.5 per cent of the income generated by the Barclays group worldwide in 1977 could be attributed to California; yet it would cost millions of dollars for Barclays to establish and maintain the global system necessary literally to comply with California's tax method: estimates ranged from $6.4 million to $7.7 million to establish the system, and from $2 million to $3.8 million a year to maintain it. However, the Tax Board argued that regulations

authorities' best estimate. These were in many cases for very large sums, especially significant since state and local taxes constitute a high proportion of the tax bill in the US.

As with domestic formula apportionment, the most difficult issue has been deciding what constitutes a unitary business. Even supporters of the unitary approach concede that this judgment can become very subjective. It has been difficult to establish clear criteria to decide whether activities involving different product lines or services, under the same overall ownership and central management, are sufficiently distinct operationally to escape being treated as unitary. In two cases involving oil companies, the Supreme Court had little difficulty in holding the oil business is unitary. In *Exxon v. Wisconsin Dept. of Revenue* (1980), although Exxon showed that its global organization was structured in three major divisions, and that only marketing and no exploration, production or refining took place in Wisconsin, a unanimous Court upheld the Wisconsin Department of Revenue's assessments; these showed a $4.5m profit over a three-year period when the Wisconsin subsidiary was treated as unitary, rather than the losses showed by the separate accounts filed by Exxon. In *Mobil Oil v. Vermont* (1980) the Court, with only one dissent, ruled that dividend income from overseas affiliates could be included as apportionable business income by any US state where an American TNC is taxable; the state of incorporation of the US parent does not have exclusive power to tax its overseas income.[1]

Outside the oil business, however, there was less certainty. Thus, in two cases in 1982, the Court by majority held that foreign affiliates were not operated as a unitary business with their US parents, even though they were in a similar line of business, because that business was not operated as an integrated whole. In *ASARCO v. Idaho State Tax Commission* (1962), a non-ferrous metal mining, smelting and refining company received dividends, interest on loans and capital gains in respect of substantial equity holdings in foreign mining companies. Although one such affiliate was essentially controlled by ASARCO and was rightly treated as operationally integrated, the Court held that the others were operationally autonomous, and should be treated as mere investments. A similar decision was given in respect of the Woolworth company's dividend income from its overseas affiliates, which were found to have 'little functional integration' with the parent, despite

permitted approximations to be used which could be readily ascertained from data in the published accounts.

[1] Vermont does not have combined reporting; where this is used the net income of all unitary affiliates is combined, which eliminates intrafirm dividends, at least from affiliates with which there is unity of ownership, i.e. effective control. It is still necessary, however, to consider whether dividends received from minority shareholdings, such as Mobil's 10 per cent share in Aramco, are apportionable as 'business income', or should be treated as non-business or investment income. It should be noted that Mobil did not deny in this case that its business was unitary, but argued that foreign dividend income should be taxed only by the state where the parent was incorporated. See Harley 1981, pp. 365–7.

managerial links and frequent communication with the parent, which had to approve major financial decisions (*Woolworth v. New Mexico*, 1982).

In *Container Corporation* (1983), however, the Court majority went the other way. It agreed with the California Supreme Court's view that where an investment is in a subsidiary which is in the same line of business, there is a presumption that it is likely to be unitary, since the aim is likely to be a better use of the parent's resources. Evidence of directives from the parent on professionalism, profitability and ethical practices was sufficient to confirm that the business was unitary. Significantly, the Court rejected a proposed 'bright line rule' that a substantial flow of goods was the test of operational unity; although this might be a reasonable and workable rule, it was not constitutionally mandated – the constitutional requirement was a flow of value, not goods. The 'bright line' approach had been put forward as an objective test which would require substantial interdependent basic operations between companies under common control (Hellerstein 1982). The difficulty lies in deciding what are 'basic' operations: Jerome Hellerstein excludes central service functions, including intellectual property management and even finance, so that the essential requirement seems to be a flow of goods. McLure has suggested that a transactional analysis perspective is more appropriate for analysing interdependency (McLure in McLure (ed.) 1984, ch. 3), but concedes that this increases indeterminacy (ibid., p. 112). It may be that the only way to ensure uniformity in deciding when a business is unitary is procedurally, by establishing a single, multi-representative body to take this decision (Harley 1981, p. 354).

These Supreme Court decisions were the tip of an iceberg of litigation which had been generated by the growing use of WUT by an increasing number of states. For example, the *Mobil* and *Exxon* cases were the eventual outcome of taxes levied by a number of states in the wake of the oil crisis of 1973–4. The sharp increases in prices of petroleum products which followed the measures taken by OPEC had an immediate impact on consumers, who found it hard to understand how the major oil TNCs could declare increased profits, based on the increased profitability of their exploration and production activities in the new world of dearer oil, while at the same time the higher product prices resulted in reduced sales and lower profits, or losses, for oil product marketing companies. Taxpayers were not sympathetic when the local marketing subsidiaries of the oil majors, which themselves were declaring large profits overall, declared a loss in the state. Nor were legislators sympathetic to the argument that such firms should not be taxed as unitary businesses, when the same corporations were resisting anti-trust investigations and proposals for divestiture of some of their business, on the grounds that they were more efficient because they were highly integrated.[1]

---

[1] Harley 1981, p. 399, fn. 94, citing Senate Judiciary Committee hearings, The Petroleum Industry (1976) 94th Congress 1st session, and a speech by Senator Kennedy (1978) 124 Cong. Rec. S.9434–5.

Hence, at a time of increasing international competitiveness, many foreign TNCs which had with difficulty established themselves in the important US markets, found their state tax assessments abruptly and unpredictably increased by substantial sums; this especially angered firms such as Barclays and Alcan, whose ventures into the US had been unfortunate and had sustained repeated heavy losses. However, in this period of intensifying pressure on state treasuries, and taxpayer revolts leading to moves to reduce personal taxation (where, again, the lead was taken in California), there was not much sympathy for the problems of large, especially foreign-owned corporations. The two main steps that they could take to attempt a reversal of WUT were to lobby government and to appeal cases through the courts.

3. The Constitutionality of Worldwide Combination

In the courts, companies had initially to face the reluctance of the judicial branch to limit the rights of the states. The Supreme Court in the 1980s has upheld the view of its predecessors that the Constitution does not require it to limit state powers of taxation, provided the state does not 'tax value earned beyond its borders'. In *Container Corp. of America v. Franchise Tax Board* (1983), the Court by a majority of five–three upheld the basic principles of California's worldwide combined reporting and formula apportionment as applied to an American TNC.

However, in addition to the other constitutional issues discussed in section 1 above, worldwide combination required an examination of whether WUT applied by the states impaired the federal government's exclusive powers to deal with foreign affairs and regulate international commerce. In *Japan Line v. County of Los Angeles* (1979), the Court did indeed invalidate a property tax applied to cargo containers, on the ground that by international agreement both containers and ships are subject to property taxes only in their home ports. Thus the taxation of containers by Los Angeles both created an enhanced risk of multiple taxation (the Japan Line's containers were apparently taxed also in Japan), as well as impairing federal uniformity in an area where it was essential, the regulation of international commerce.

In *Container Corporation*, however, the Court held that these considerations did not invalidate WUT when applied to net corporate income, principally because it found that there was no clear international arrangement that avoided double taxation of such income. Whereas in *Japan Line* the alternative to the state tax was a clear international rule allocating taxes on ships and containers to one state, the Court found that the alternative to WUT of corporate income was geographical allocation based on the arm's length rule, which merely produced a series of national reallocations of income based on potentially conflicting views of the arm's length criterion. As Brennan, J. put it

Allocating income among various tax jurisdictions bears some resemblance . . . to slicing a shadow. In the absence of a central coordinating authority, absolute consistency, even among tax authorities whose basic approach is quite similar, may just be too much to ask.

Since, in addition, no government *amicus curiae* brief had been filed to support the argument of interference with foreign relations, unconstitutionality had not been established.

The *Container Corporation* case still left open the question of whether unconstitutionality under the foreign relations clause would apply with more force to a non-American TNC. An even stronger case could be made if it could be shown that WUT directly violates international agreements. Aside from tax treaties, some argued that WUT infringes the 'national treatment' clauses of commercial treaties, some of which explicitly prohibit any taxation of business income 'in excess of that reasonably allocable or apportionable' to the territory. The modern US programme of negotiation of treaties of Friendship, Commerce and Navigation had indeed originated in the inter-war period, from US concern about discriminatory measures against foreign-owned companies, including French taxation of an allocated portion of dividend distributions by the foreign parents of branches or subsidiaries in France, regarded as 'extraterritorial' taxation by other countries (see Chapter 1, section 4.c above, and Granwell et al. 1986, p. 742). The non-discrimination provisions of commercial treaties are broader than those of tax treaties and, most importantly, they do not exclude state or local taxation. It may nevertheless be difficult to show that WUT specifically discriminates against non-American companies. Furthermore, the foreign parent company of a US subsidiary may have difficulty in establishing that it has a right of action, or 'standing', separate from the subsidiary itself (*Shell NV v. Graves*, 1983; Note 1984).

Ironically, then, it seemed that if WUT were to be judicially held unconstitutional, it would not be under the Commerce clause on the grounds of the potentiality of formula apportionment for inconsistencies of application, but as an interference with the federal government's conduct of foreign affairs due to its conflict with the arm's length standard established internationally. An important procedural obstacle was overcome when Alcan and ICI managed to persuade the 7th Circuit Court of Appeals that they had standing; but their case was initially confined to the state courts by the decision of the Supreme Court that the action was barred from the federal courts under the Tax Injunction Act, since an adequate remedy existed in state courts (*Franchise Tax Board of California v. Alcan Aluminum et al.*, 1990). This confidence was borne out when the California courts did decide that the California tax was unconstitutional, both as applied to a US TNC (*Colgate–Palmolive v. Franchise Tax Board* (1988) and to a foreign firm (*Barclays Bank International v. Franchise Tax Board*, 1990). California's WUT would finally perish, it seemed, by a judicial determination of unconstitutionality in its own State Supreme Court.

4. The Political Campaign against WUT

In addition to action through the courts, TNCs began to take up the question of WUT through national and international trade associations and chambers of commerce, and other forms of lobbying. At first, this was done discreetly: large corporations prefer to explain a reasonable case directly to a responsible official than to create a public row, which can be counter-productive. Non-American TNCs took up the matter with their home governments or tax administrations. These in turn raised it with the relevant US government officials with whom they came into contact. Officials of the US federal government were on the whole sympathetic, although considering themselves relatively powerless in a situation which concerned state prerogatives.

An opportunity to attempt some action against WUT arose in 1974, in the negotiation of a new US–UK double taxation treaty on income tax. The American federal government had initiated discussions for a new agreement to replace the historic treaty of 1945, due to the British introduction of a new system of taxation of corporate dividends in 1973. Abandoning the 'classical' system, Britain's new Advanced Corporation Tax increased the tax on corporate profits to 52 per cent, but allowed shareholders a refund equivalent to the basic rate of income tax payable on their dividends. This created a problem for non-resident shareholders, especially foreign companies with British subsidiaries.[1] Negotiations soon produced the draft of an agreement which allowed such US parents to recover half the ACT paid, while British firms with US affiliates benefited from reduction of the withholding tax on dividends from 15 to 5 per cent. At the same time, the negotiators took the opportunity to bring the treaty in line with new formulations that had been introduced in tax treaties since 1945.

However, one exceptional provision was included at the request of the British: in Article 9, which incorporated the arm's length principle of the OECD model, there was added a clause (4) explicitly stating that the arm's length method must be applied also in the case of taxation by political subdivisions of the Contracting States (treaties normally cover only federal taxes). If the treaty were ratified, and unless and until this provision were ruled unconstitutional by the US courts, it could prevent any American state from applying WUT to a British TNC. This provision survived the discreet consultations held by both sets of negotiators with specialists and interested persons, and the treaty was signed on 31 December 1975. In January 1977 the treaty was approved by the House of Commons. However, its ratification by the US required the 'advice and consent' of the Senate, which proved to be no smooth passage. In June 1978, two years after it was sent to the Senate, that body gave it its consent, but subject to a reservation tabled by Senator Church,

---

[1] For a discussion of the problems posed by integrated corporate-personal tax systems for tax treaties see Chapter 2, section 2 above.

the Foreign Relations Committee Chairman, eliminating Article 9(4): although his reservation had itself failed to gain approval either in the Committee or the full Senate, the treaty failed by five votes to gain the necessary two-thirds majority, until the reservation was resurrected.[1]

Instead of providing a discreet means of nipping in the bud the threat of WUT, Article 9(4) contributed to the growing controversy in the US over the unitary approach and the taxation of TNCs. In June 1979, 40 British TNCs set up the Unitary Tax Campaign (UTC) as a lobbying grouping. However, since the US–UK treaty contained valuable benefits for both British and American TNCs, nobody gained from the delay in ratification; so despite protests from the UTC, the British government and the House of Commons accepted the exclusion of Article 9(4), and the treaty finally came into effect in March 1980.

In place of the treaty approach, which might have prevented the application of WUT but only to British firms, the opponents of unitary taxation once again revived attempts at federal legislation, which once again ran into controversy. Not only did Senator Matthias' Interstate Taxation Bill of 1979 fail, but the House Ways and Means Committee commissioned a study by the Comptroller General on the taxation of TNCs. When this appeared in 1981, it was critical of the federal tax authorities' efforts in international taxation, and recommended that they study alternatives to the arm's length approach (US GAO 1981, discussed in Chapter 8 above).

The federal government was itself caught up in the contradictions of the issue. Although President Reagan had obtained political support from many sectors of big business, his own right-radical populism had matured in California, the home of the personal tax revolt and of WUT. The continuing political steam behind unitary taxation was shown by the growing number of states which had adopted or were moving towards it. By 1984, all 45 states which levied a corporate income tax applied formula apportionment to corporations conducting inter-state business; about half of these also applied it to the combined income of multi-company firms operating inter-state through subsidiaries; and about half of those using the 'combined' method required the inclusion of foreign subsidiaries involved in the same unitary business (US Treasury 1984a, p. 1). The Reagan government's efforts to reduce federal spending involved a New Federalism programme, which transferred many spending obligations to the states, and therefore fuelled their increasing interest in WUT as a source of revenue. The President rejected the advice of his Cabinet Council of Economic Affairs to support the Congressional legislative initiatives to curb WUT, and resisted pressures from the UTC and others to intervene with an *amicus curiae* brief in the Supreme Court's consideration of the *Container Corporation* case, discussed above.[2]   At the same

---

[1] The treaty therefore entered into force as modified by a protocol of 15 March 1979 which removed the reference to taxation by political subdivisions from Article 9(4), which remains in this emasculated form.

[2] See Freud & Tyler 'Mr Reagan's Taxing Problem', *Financial Times*, 1 November 1983.

time, the US was coming under political pressures from its closest allies; the issue was no longer one for technical discussions among officials, but an item on the agenda of summit meetings. Finally, President Reagan set up a high-level Worldwide Unitary Taxation Working Group under Treasury Secretary Regan, immediately before the visit to Washington in September 1983 by Mrs Thatcher, who had written to Mr Reagan protesting against unitary taxation and was expected to raise it with him in person.[1]

The Regan Working Group was immediately deluged with submissions from large corporations and other interested parties, and set up a Task Force to conduct hearings, sift the options, and try to come up with proposals which could satisfy the varied membership of the Group, which included representatives of WUT states and the Multistate Tax Commission, as well the Chief Executives of IBM, Ford, Exxon and other American corporations. Despite its best efforts, the Task Force could not come up with an agreed report for President Reagan to take to the London Economic Summit of June 1984. Here the President was berated by his allies, especially the British, not only over WUT but a wide range of assertions of regulatory powers by US bodies over TNCs and international business generally, such as the rows over the Laker case and over the US embargo against supply to the Soviet Union of equipment for the Siberia–Europe natural gas pipeline. Unilateral assertions by US regulatory bodies of jurisdiction over such different aspects of international business had led to complaints of 'extraterritoriality', and to political interventions at the highest levels in attempts to develop processes for the co-ordination of regulatory jurisdiction (Picciotto 1983).

When the Regan report did emerge in August 1984, it contained agreement in principle on, but disagreement on the actual method for, the introduction by states of the option of 'water's edge' unitary combination. 'Water's edge' would limit unitary combination to US business, both for US and foreign firms; however, the worldwide combined approach could be used if separate accounting (between their US and foreign business) resulted in tax evasion, or failed clearly to reflect income, or if the company failed to comply with disclosure requirements. In exchange for agreeing to move away from WUT, the states obtained a promise of federal assistance with taxation of corporations, especially TNCs. The IRS agreed to put more resources into auditing international business, and to help states with disclosure from corporations, including making available to states information received from treaty partners under the information exchange arrangements of double tax treaties (see Chapter 10 below).

No agreed way could be found, however, of reconciling the 'water's edge' rule with the other agreed requirement, that state tax policy should maintain equality of conditions of competition between US TNCs, foreign TNCs, and purely US firms. The difficulty centred on two specific problems: (i) the

---

[1] *Financial Times*, 24 September 1983.

treatment of 80/20 corporations (US firms with 80 per cent of their business abroad); and (ii) the right of states to include income received from abroad in the US taxable base.[1]

The lobbyists gave a cautious welcome to the Regan report's 'water's edge' proposals, and continued political pressure, as well as well-publicized threats by foreign TNCs to disinvest from unitary tax states, gradually led to a move towards the water's edge option. The disinvestment threat was privately conceded to be an empty one, since California's booming economy is calculated to be the eighth largest in the world. Perhaps more effective was the retaliatory amendment which the UTC had succeeded in inserting, through backbench action, into the UK Finance Act of 1985 (s.54).[2] This provision allowed the withdrawal of Advanced Corporation Tax refunds on dividend payments from the British subsidiaries of US parent corporations in unitary tax states. This was a very serious threat which, if implemented, would mean a breach of the US–UK tax treaty, and it produced several bills in Congress for counter-retaliation, and proud assertions of refusal to 'bow to the British'; but it may also have persuaded US TNCs, some of which had been lukewarm in their opposition to WUT since it hurt their foreign competitors far more than them, to add their voice to the protest. Nevertheless, the tabling of Administration-supported bills in Congress to block state use of WUT persuaded the dwindling number of WUT states to take action which would pre-empt federal legislation.

California, which was the most important state due to its booming economy, finally enacted legislation in September 1986, offering corporate taxpayers a 'water's edge election', but on stiff conditions. Companies opting out of worldwide unitary taxation would be locked in to that choice for ten years ahead, would have to accept comprehensive disclosure, and to pay a fee into a special Fund.[3] 80/20 corporations would be included in US combined income, as would receipts from overseas subsidiaries, although with a 75 per cent exclusion.

Reactions to the Californian legislation were mixed. It was hailed as a victory by some of the anti-unitary lobby, especially the foreign TNCs, and welcomed by the British government, which announced that retaliatory action would not now be taken (although the power to do so would remain). However, American TNCs objected that the inclusion of part of the income received from abroad was discriminatory as between US and foreign TNCs, and therefore failed to meet the Working Group's requirement of competitive

[1] For differing inside accounts of the Working Group, see Dexter 1985 and Mattson 1986.
[2] Proposals for such a measure had previously been resisted by the Government, which hoped to make headway through direct inter-governmental approaches.
[3] The fee would be thirty-thousandths of one per cent of its total of property, payroll and sales in California; reducible to a minimum of one-thousandth of one per cent by the amount spent in the state on new plant, facilities or employment: Senate Bill No. 85, Cap. 660, section 25115. The 'domestic disclosure spreadsheet' requires details of the activities of all, including non-US, related firms, and of the apportionment percentages reported to other US states.

fairness. A comment by the former Treasury official who had directed the Working Group's studies argued that on basic principle income received from abroad should be excluded under the 'water's edge' criterion, but equally no deduction should be allowed for interest payments on debt financing for foreign subsidiaries: state taxes are source-based, as opposed to federal taxes which are based on residence but allow a full foreign tax credit (McLure 1986a, 1986b). The fee requirement was also criticized as 'a ransom', but despite these reservations the Reagan administration withdrew the threat of federal legislation. California's Franchise Tax Board expected only some 350 of the estimated 1,000 TNCs in the state to take the water's edge option, due largely to the fee and the ten-year requirement. The California legislature enacted an amendment in 1988 relaxing the conditions for a water's edge election, including reducing the period of election to five years, but the lobby continued to press for a more satisfactory version of 'water's edge', both in California and in other states.[1]

Nevertheless, WUT was far from dead. It was clear that if state corporate taxation based on separate US accounts were to be effective, there would have to be a significant increase in the enforcement effort. State authorities complained that their examiners lacked expertise and information, and bodies such as the MTC had inadequate resources to carry out joint audits on their behalf. However, information exchange arrangements between states were increasing. The IRS also agreed to play its part, and announced in early 1987 a 25 per cent increase of the examiners assigned to international tax returns, both for non-resident US citizens as well as TNCs; but the increase has merely kept pace with the growth of foreign investment into the US (Woodard 1988). The IRS undertaking to supply states with information on TNCs obtained under tax treaties would require changes to the treaties, and although some treaty partners were said to have indicated a willingness to consider this, it would inevitably be a slow process, and dependent on abandonment by states of WUT (see Chapter 10 below). Enforcement based on separate accounts not only requires more audit resources, it necessitates detailed regulations on various aspects of intrafirm pricing, which need frequent revision, as well as international co-ordination, as we have seen in the previous chapter. The further study of s.482 enforcement which had been recommended by the GAO Report of 1981 and mandated by the Tax Reform Act of 1986 was carried out, and resulted in the controversial 'white paper' of 1988. The attack on the 'myth of arm's length' by advocates of WUT (see especially Langbein 1986) had achieved some effect: even the strongest advocates of separate accounts began to stress that the arm's length criterion is only a means of establishing true or fair accounts (e.g. Hunter in Competent Authorities 1986). In the view of some academic commentators, the unitary approach could have continuing, and perhaps increasing, validity and usefulness (McLure 1984 and 1989).

---

[1] For a summary of WUT in California see Plant, Miller & Crawford 1989.

5. The Global Apportionment Alternative

It is not hard to see the reasons for the vehement opposition which global apportionment has aroused in business circles. Its adoption would require TNCs to produce accounts covering their worldwide operations, calculated according to the tax rules of each country requiring them; the tax authorities would then be free to apply to these accounts whatever formula for apportionment they might consider suitable. Overlapping taxation would be the inevitable result of the many possible divergences between national approaches. Differences in both accounting and currency conversion rules would produce a very different tax base (Kopits & Muten, 1984), while variations in the formula used would obviously result in duplicative allocation. Nevertheless, the difficulties can be exaggerated: currency conversion differences and difficulties exist anyway under separate accounting, and international harmonization of accounting rules is itself a desirable goal.[1] Indeed, one of the advantages of moving to a consolidated tax base for international corporate groups would be that taxation could rely more closely on financial accounts, and it would require the countries concerned to agree on consistent currency conversion rules (Vann 1991, p. 159).

The feasibility and desirability of unitary taxation depend on the degree of economic and political integration at the federal, confederal, regional or global level at which its introduction is considered. Increased eonomic integration will undermine the workability of separate accounting in the allocation of income (McLure 1989). Thus, although US states have been obliged to retreat from worldwide unitary taxation, there is no question of abandoning the unitary approach within the US, up to the 'water's edge'. Similarly, within the European Community, the increasing integration of the operations of establishments and subsidiaries within the internal market will lead to pressure to tax integrated corporate groups on a single tax base, probably consolidated accounts rather than the 'combined report' used in the US. Initially, separate national tax systems and rates could be retained, perhaps within an agreed band, but it is only a short step to a single European corporate tax, although it is one that involves more obvious abandonment of national sovereignty.[2] However, although economic integration may undermine taxation based on separate accounts, any move towards a unitary base raises political problems, since it requires explicit agreement on what constitutes a unitary business and, above all, on the apportionment formula.

Although the problems of when and how to apply formula apportionment raise issues of principle, in practice they would need to be resolved *ad hoc* in relation to each firm, and would therefore require a central administrative and

[1] See the criticism by Peggy B. Musgrave of Kopits and Muten in McLure 1984, p. 282; see also Bird 1988.
[2] Commentators are uncertain as to the speed with which such moves are possible: compare Devereux & Pearson 1989, ch. 4, Weiss & Molnar 1988, and Vann 1991, pp. 155, 158–60.

representative body. There is considerable controversy on the test to apply in determining unity: a narrow definition based on the existence of a flow of goods would apply mainly to vertically-integrated firms, while a broader test of interdependence which includes shared costs and synergy advantages would include virtually any corporate group unless limited to 'substantial' interdependence.[1] There would also be problems of legal definition and administrative enforcement, to cope with the evasion of legal ownership rules by concealment of beneficial ownership through secrecy havens, and avoidance of such ownership requirements by the use of contractual relationships. In practice, a joint central body would be needed to decide which firms, and perhaps which parts of firms, should be treated as unitary.

Similarly, the appropriate formula would require adjustment on a case-by-case basis, to take into account wide variations in the labour and capital intensity not only between different types of business but even individual firms, as well as problems of valuing assets for the purpose of the formula (Linde 1977, p. 116; Musgrave 1984, p. 240). Adequate arrangements would be necessary to provide reviewability of these decisions and guarantees of due process for the taxpayer.

The main arguments against formula apportionment have been that international political processes were insufficiently developed to resolve the issues that would be posed. Global apportionment, in particular the need to agree on the formula, would much more directly pose the issue of the basis of entitlement of each state in the allocation of the tax base. The allocation of tax rights under the present treaty system originated (as we have seen in Chapter 1 above) in the debates in the 1920s, which concluded that from both a theoretical and practical perspective tax jurisdiction could not be allocated on the basis of a single principle. The allocation to the state of residence of the investor of the right to tax returns on investment was justified on the grounds that these were 'personal' taxes based on ability to pay; they should therefore be based on personal allegiance, and take into account the investor's worldwide earnings, both to ensure fairness and to discourage choice of investment location based on tax rates. On the other hand, taxation of business profits at source was justified both in practical terms of effectiveness, and because the geographical link with the location of the wealth generated was considered appropriate for 'real' taxes. This distinction between 'personal' and 'real' taxes was undermined in relation to business taxation by the growth of foreign direct investment. Meanwhile, TNCs developed many mechanisms for avoiding the assertion by some of their home countries of the right to tax their worldwide profits, first by taking maximum advantage of tax deferral, and then by locating service functions in low-tax base-havens (Chapter 6 above).

---

[1] See section 2 above, and for arguments for the two perspectives see the papers by J. Hellerstein and C. McLure in McLure (ed.) 1984.

Consolidation of the accounts of an integrated corporate group would at a stroke eliminate most of the problems of characterization and pricing of intrafirm transactions (Vann 1991, pp. 158–9). Global apportionment would also automatically provide greater tax neutrality for investment decisions. At the same time, however, it would bring squarely to the fore the issue of the basis for allocation of tax entitlements between the various 'source' states. The fiction of 'residence' of a corporation could be abandoned, since the factors on which it is based (primarily, location of top management) would simply become one of the corporate functions to be evaluated in allocating tax rights, so that residence taxation would revert to having relevance only for portfolio investment, for states of residence of shareholders.

Difficult questions would remain, however, in quantifying the elements of the formula to be used, which depends also on evaluation of the basis of the state's rights to tax. The taxation of corporate earnings might be considered to be a levy in return for the benefits provided by the state, not merely for infrastructure in the narrow sense, but more broadly, e.g. for reproduction of the labour-force, including housing, transportation, social security, education and training.[1] Alternatively, it could be considered to be a tax on the earnings of capital, which should be allocated according to the location of the use of the capital. The first, it has been suggested, would imply a formula based on value added less profits, plus depreciation of capital, plus margin on sales; whereas the latter would imply as factors the value of fixed and working capital, including the cost of wages (Musgrave & Musgrave 1972). A particular difficulty is that very large differences in costs of production factors would disadvantage underdeveloped as against developed countries. This might be overcome by using actual units rather than monetary values for appropriate factors, such as employees (Harley 1981, p. 382), or by adjusting an asset-based formula to take into account differences in capital/labour ratios (Musgrave 1972, p. 400). More ambitiously, it has been suggested that an internationally-agreed system might provide some redistribution to compensate for unequal resource endowments and per capita income, by applying a schedule of tax rates increasing in inverse relation to per-capita income (Musgrave & Musgrave 1972, p. 74).

Although some aspects of such proposals seem utopian, their advocates argue they are at least as practicable as the alternative, taxation of integrated TNCs on the basis of separate accounts and arm's length prices. There are also broader considerations: Vann states perceptively that separate accounting is defended so vehemently against arguments of principle because 'the debate is the hostage of the bilateral treaty network' (Vann 1991, p. 105), although for him this adds a further reason, in addition to the inflexibility of the treaty network, for a new approach to be made. In fact, some supporters of

[1] Although it might be argued that profits taxation is not appropriate as a benefits charge, user charges can only be approximately correlated to benefits even for utilities, and are difficult to establish for general infrastructure such as labour reproduction costs.

the existing system stress that the important principle is separate accounting, and they accept that a formula approach has a part to play in the arm's length procedure, although a subordinate part.[1] Indeed, as has been pointed out in Chapter 8, business representatives who are otherwise hostile to formula apportionment of profits have argued for formula allocation of fixed costs; while the difficulties of operating the arm's length principle have meant in practice that tax authorities rely on profit-split either as a check or as the primary criterion. The growth of administrative co-operation in taxation of international corporate groups (to be discussed in detail in the next chapter) has facilitated agreed solutions on a case-by-case basis of such allocation issues. What has been lacking, however, is an adequate basis of legitimacy for this process. Hence, the foundation for a transition to formula apportionment has been laid. Still lacking are the all-important elements of legitimacy: openness and fairness of procedures and transparency of criteria.

---

[1] This was the view expressed by Ian Hunter, the UK 'competent authority' (Competent Authorities 1986, p. 594), cited in Chapter 8, section 3.a(ii) above.

10
The Internationalization of Tax Administration

Administrative co-operation has increasingly come to play a key role in the co-ordination of national taxes on international business. As has been shown in previous chapters, governments have preferred to avoid the political problems of trying to agree principles for the definition and allocation of the international tax base, and they have consequently relied on the more pragmatic development of *ad hoc* solutions by administrative processes. When problems of international taxation became prominent again in the 1970s, both policy discussion and practical co-ordination between tax administrators assumed even more importance. International administrative co-operation has been more highly developed in tax matters than in other areas of business regulation, although in a partial and patchy way due to the unevenness of the treaty network. But it has not proved easy to resolve the underlying issues of principle through administrative procedures. Indeed, the problem of legitimacy has also arisen in relation to the procedures themselves, since the lack of adequate substantive criteria has made it harder for governments and officials to accept procedural fairness, while business organizations have opposed proposals for the strengthening of administrative co-operation because of their lack of confidence in the fairness of either the principles or procedures of international taxation.

1. The Development of Administrative Co-operation

The prevention of international double taxation was from the beginning coupled with proposals for administrative co-operation to combat international evasion and avoidance. Due to concern about international capital flight the problem of evasion was specifically included in the brief of the Technical Committee set up by the League of Nations in 1922, which became the Fiscal Committee (see Chapter 1, section 4.a above). However, the overriding aim was to facilitate international capital movements, and the International Chamber of Commerce at its 1922 Congress condemned 'all proposals attacking the freedom of exchange markets or the secrecy of banking operations', although several members of the ICC's Fiscal Commission thought that the problem of evasion should not be ducked (ICC 1925). The preparatory reports and Commentary to the original draft Treaty on Mutual Administrative Assistance in Matters of Taxation of 1928 stressed that the purpose was to ensure not only that incomes were taxed once and once only but also that no one should avoid tax. The combating of fraud would be for the general good, but it was important to avoid the appearance that the international arrangements entailed 'an extension beyond national frontiers of an organised system of fiscal inquisition' or an 'organised plan of attack on the taxpayer' (League of Nations 1927, 1928). Ironically, it was precisely in such terms that, over sixty years later, the multilateral convention for administrative assistance in taxation drawn up through the OECD and the Council of Europe was denounced by business groups and representatives (see below).

In practice, progress on establishing arrangements for administrative co-operation was significantly slower than on agreements for the prevention of double taxation. A study in 1937 for the League by Mitchell Carroll estimated that fewer than half of the bilateral double taxation treaties had been supplemented by provisions for mutual assistance.[1] Asked by the Assembly of the League to study measures against evasion, the Fiscal Committee proposed a general multilateral convention for mutual assistance, but the replies were disappointing. Governments were reluctant to modify their domestic laws, or to require information from their nationals, for the purpose of complying with the needs of foreign administrations;[2] the Committee was therefore reluctantly obliged to accept that assistance would have to be based on the existing legal powers of government, which in view of their diversity ruled out a multilateral convention (PRO file IR40/5703). The two model treaties agreed at the 1928 meeting, for administrative assistance in taxation and for judicial assistance in collection of taxes, were combined into one by the Mexico and London models on the grounds that the type of co-operation necessary was the same for assessment and collection, and that negotiators could easily restrict administrative co-operation to assessment alone, 'as is not infrequently done in bilateral agreements', merely by omitting the provisions on collection (League of Nations 1946, p. 44).

Noting the distrust of mutual assistance arrangements, which had restricted their conclusion to some fifteen countries (mainly neighbouring countries in continental Europe), the Fiscal Committee emphasized the safeguards which

[1] Ten by inclusion of assistance provisions in the treaty and fifteen by means of a separate mutual assistance convention (League of Nations F/Fiscal/99, contained in PRO file IR40/5703).
[2] Report of the eighth session of the Fiscal Committee, 1938, in US Congress 1962a. See also Piatier 1938 for a study of the problems and progress made before the war.

should make such arrangements palatable. In particular, a state could only be required to take actions normally available under its own laws and practices and which could reciprocally be taken by the state requesting the assistance; a state could also refuse a request which would involve a violation of commercial secrecy, or which concerned its own nationals, or which in its opinion would compromise its security or sovereign rights; and the same provisions for confidentiality should apply to information supplied as would apply in the supplying state.[1] Also, the assistance convention was specifically tied to the treaties for prevention of double taxation by direct taxes and death duties, applying only to taxes covered by those treaties.

Despite these safeguards, and despite the rapid spread of tax treaties in the postwar period, very few treaties for mutual assistance were concluded; instead, provisions for co-operation were made in the double taxation prevention treaties themselves. However, the administrative assistance provisions were reduced to a single article on Exchange of Information (Article 26 of the OECD and UN models), and few treaties included a provision for assistance with collection. This tied mutual assistance even more closely to the prevention of double taxation, which not only limited the scope of assistance even between treaty partners, but also meant that states which saw no benefit in negotiating tax treaties need accept no obligations to provide assistance to combat tax avoidance or evasion. In the 1980s, the US authorities have attempted to plug this gap as part of the campaign against tax havens, by using other inducements and pressures to try to obtain specific Tax Information Exchange Agreements, especially with Caribbean countries; however, they have not found it easy to secure agreements containing satisfactory relaxations of bank and commercial secrecy laws without offering a quid pro quo such as US tax exemption for specific offshore business such as insurance (see Chapter 7, section 3 above and section 2.b below).

While the growing network of tax treaties helped to facilitate international capital movements (especially once direct restrictions on such movements began to be lifted after 1958), the emphasis shifted from concern about tax evasion to the large grey area of international avoidance. The increasingly complex structures developed by international business advisors for taking advantage of the differences in national taxation raised difficult questions of legitimacy in the allocation of the international tax base; but, as we have seen in earlier chapters, these were not tackled directly by the tax treaty principles, but to a great extent left for resolution by direct negotiation, often on a case-by-case basis. Hence, the apparently modest tax treaty provisions for administrative assistance took on a great importance, no longer primarily for blatant evasion, but to facilitate a co-ordinated administrative approach to avoidance.

---

[1] Some significant changes have been made in these conditions in the modern treaties, but they remain broadly similar: see below, section 2.b.

Nevertheless, the work in the inter-war period had established a vital principle, without which these issues could not have been confronted at all. This was that the tax authorities of treaty partner states could consult together directly for the purposes of application of the provisions of tax treaties. A general article providing for consultations between the 'competent authorities' of the contracting states to facilitate the application of the treaty, and even its interpretation and adaptation to changing circumstances, was included in the model treaties,[1] originating with the 1928 draft. More specifically, since the Carroll report and the 1935 allocation convention, it had become clear that a procedure to ensure harmony in the application of the treaty principles was necessary: in particular, transfer pricing adjustments to the accounts of a branch or subsidiary by one state might result in double taxation unless a mechanism was established to ensure a corresponding adjustment by the state taxing the related entity. The business lobbies had pressed for a right to an automatic corresponding adjustment and access to international adjudication, but this had been resisted by the state officials, who preferred such adjustments to remain a matter for their discretion and mutual negotiation. Only recently has there been a revival of the possibility of adjudication of corresponding adjustments and other conflicting treaty interpretations (see section 3 below). Although the tax authorities have considered it to be easier to secure the necessary compromises and accommodations by treating the issues as technical matters for resolution by discretionary and secretive administrative processes, this has also to a significant extent undermined legitimacy.

Thus, administrative co-operation through direct contacts between national administrators has been a key factor in the effective operation of international tax arrangements. The authority for these direct contacts is primarily derived from the bilateral tax treaty provisions, especially those for information exchange (Article 26 of the model), corresponding adjustment (Article 9(2)) and mutual agreement (Article 25); in addition, some newer treaty provisions also require administrative co-operation, notably the rules for denial of treaty benefits to ineligible non-residents to prevent treaty-shopping (see Chapter 7, section 3 above). By providing for direct contact between administrators, without the need for communication through diplomatic channels, the tax treaties established a process of administrative internationalization which was, and to a considerable extent remains, unique. Similar arrangements have more recently been developed for co-ordination of other types of economic regulation, notably among bank supervisors (e.g. the Basle Committee of Bank Supervisors, see Chapter 6, section 1.c above) and regulators of markets for financial services, but the administrative co-operation in those areas has so far been confined, formally at least, to information exchange. The tax treaty administrative provisions have gone further than others since they cover not only exchange of information and

---

[1] Article XIX of the London model, see section 3.b below.

policy concertation, but also explicitly provide for co-ordinated enforcement in individual cases, which has also led to establishing procedures for simultaneous examination of related taxpayers (see section 2.c below).

An especially important development was the formation in 1972 of the Group of Four, an informal organization bringing together the tax administrations of France, Germany, the UK and the US. In addition to annual meetings for policy discussions at the highest level of Commissioner or the equivalent, programmes have been developed at staff levels for joint study of specific problems, and it was from these contacts that the simultaneous examination procedures developed. Regarded as an informal arrangement, the proceedings of the Group of Four are confidential and even its existence was treated as secret for some years.[1] Although officials deny that individual cases are dealt with multilaterally within Group of Four meetings, it does seem that these meetings are used at least to select cases and agree procedures, although in principle any substantive discussions about specific taxpayers must be on a bilateral basis. Further, the discussions of particular industries which are an important part of the working level meetings are likely to entail reference both to aggregate data and individual illustrative examples. PATA, the Pacific Association of Tax Administrators, is a Pacific area version of the Group of Four (Australia, Canada, Japan and the US) set up in 1980, which also holds both annual meetings at Commissioner level and regular meetings of working officials, to study and exchange information on specific industries (petroleum, grain, commodities, banking), exchange practical experiences, and even discuss specific cases. Comparable meetings have also been held by a European Group of Six, consisting of Belgium, France, Germany, Luxembourg, the Netherlands and Britain. Other more *ad hoc* groups have exchanged information about and discussed specific industries, such as oil and gas and forestry products.[2]

Some more formal organizations have also facilitated administrative contacts and co-ordination. The importance of the activities of the Committee on Fiscal Affairs of the OECD has been stressed already: its formal work has been confined to policy questions and it is regarded as too large a group to be effective for more specific matters, although its meetings provide a useful occasion for direct personal contact and even camaraderie.

Perhaps surprisingly, the European Community has not yet provided a significant forum for multilateral co-operation, despite the adoption of the Directive on mutual assistance in 1977 (EC Council 1977), which envisaged consultations in a committee of competent authorities of member states plus

[1] Exceptionally, a press release was issued on 3 October 1985 by the German Ministry of Finance on the occasion of the group's meeting in Berlin, briefly describing the aims and organization of the group: Germany, Ministry of Finance 1985. See also UK House of Commons, Written Answers, vol. 939, cols. 269–70 16 November 1977.
[2] Much of my information on these matters derives from interviews with officials involved, in Britain, the USA, France, Germany and Japan.

the Commission (Article 9), and a pooling of experience in the field of transfer pricing and if appropriate the drawing up of rules in this field (Article 10). In the first decade of existence of the Directive these possibilities for multi-lateralization were largely ignored: the main member states preferred to deal with each other bilaterally under their tax treaty provisions,[1] and indeed several member states (Germany, Italy and the UK) were considered by the Commission to be failing in their obligation to implement the Directive in domestic law. However, the extent of co-ordination in enforcement by EC members may increase with the accelerating pace of direct tax harmonization related to completion of the internal market. In particular, the Community has now provided a lead in establishing a procedure for arbitration of claims for corresponding adjustments (EC Council 1990c, see section 3.a(iii) below).

Other bodies have concentrated more on the exchange of experience and training. CIAT (the Inter-American Centre of Tax Administrators) has been in existence since 1967, linking 26 countries in the Americas including Canada and the US, holding annual assemblies which discuss tax administration questions such as planning and control and tax simplification, as well as regular technical conferences which have covered international matters, including the exchange of information under treaties (CIAT 1978), and publishing a regular newsletter and a Review. CATA (the Commonwealth Association of Tax Administrators, based at the Commonwealth Secretariat in London), has held general meetings every three years since its establishment at the 1976 Commonwealth Finance Ministers' meeting, interspersed with technical meetings or seminars discussing matters of common interest such as tax incentives (CATA 1985): it also carried out a survey in the late 1970s of approaches adopted by Commonwealth member states in the taxation of TNCs. There are also close links between the tax administrations of France and her former colonies in Africa; French tax inspectors are seconded to some countries (especially Ivory Coast and Gabon) to provide technical assistance, and an annual meeting is held of senior tax administrators (Tixier & Gest 1985, p. 456). Another potentially important group, whose work has so far been confined to more general discussions, is the Study Group of Asian Tax Administration and Research, including Australia, Japan, Korea, New Zealand and the five ASEAN countries. Regional groups also include the African Association of Tax Administrators (AATA) and the Caribbean Organization of Tax Administrators (COTA).

If in some sense they provide the basis of an embryonic world tax administration, these bodies are as yet heterogeneous, informal and over-secretive about their existence and activities. Clearly, a significant role has

---

[1] In its Note on International Co-operation to the Keith Committee on Revenue Enforcement Powers, the UK Inland Revenue stated in 1981: 'So far no use has been made by the UK Inland Revenue of the 1977 Directive, and little use has been made of it by other member countries. This is because it has been convenient to continue to make exchanges, where they are appropriate, under the double taxation agreements.'

been played by US Treasury and IRS officials, who are present in most of the groups and whose greater experience and resources, as well as the greater difficulties they face, give them a leading role, although neither their opinions nor their policies command automatic acceptance.

International administrative co-operation seems caught in a dilemma: its increasing importance calls for a more comprehensive legal basis clarifying the rights and responsibilities of both tax-gatherer and taxpayer, yet the disparities in national tax laws and practices and the difficulties of reaching agreement on general principles of fairness in defining and allocating the international tax base make it hard to obtain political support for such a comprehensive arrangement. Indeed, considerable opposition has built up, especially within the international business community, to the formalization of mutual assistance in multilateral arrangements. This came to a head over the German legislative proposals to implement the EC mutual assistance directive, and developed into more general opposition to the multilateral Convention on Mutual Administrative Assistance in Tax Matters, drawn up through the OECD and the Council of Europe and opened for signature in January 1988 (Council of Europe 1989). Although this convention essentially establishes on a comprehensive and multilateral basis the legal provisions for information exchange and mutual assistance in assessment and collection along lines familiar since the 1928 model treaties, it was opposed by bodies such as the Business and Industry Advisory Committee (BIAC) of the OECD and the Taxation Commission of the ICC, and strenuously denounced in the press especially the European edition of the *Wall Street Journal*. The objections centred on the lack of adequate safeguards for the taxpayer and the failure to provide a right to double taxation relief, for example by a right of access to arbitration of double taxation claims, as the necessary counterpart to any strengthening of revenue powers (ICC 1985; OECD–BIAC 1985).

As a result, agreement on the text was held up not only by the familiar objections from Switzerland and the other banking centres, but also by the German representatives, who felt constrained by the political opposition of business groups. Once adopted, several key states (Australia, Germany and the UK) announced that they would not sign the Convention, while others, notably France and the US, indicated that they would only adhere to the information exchange provisions and not the provisions on assistance in collection (US Congress 1990b).

It is clearly not possible to overcome the problem of legitimacy of international tax arrangements merely by measures to strengthen powers of co-operation in enforcement. The unwillingness of the tax authorities to accept the application of due process standards to the administrative co-operation arrangements is understandable, as it reflects the difficulties in establishing agreement on the substantive criteria for international taxation. Yet without some measure of agreement on such criteria, as well as procedural safeguards for international administrative arrangements, the legitimacy of international taxation will remain problematic.

2. Obtaining and Exchanging Information

Information is the key to effective enforcement of taxation, as of other regulation. The extent of the powers under national laws to require information, whether from the taxpayer or from third parties, can be hotly contested. Revenue authorities can be very sensitive to accusations that their powers or practices make them the modern equivalent of the Holy Inquisition (although sometimes such protests sound disingenuous). They often prefer, therefore, to cultivate a private relationship with the taxpayer or the taxpayer's professional representatives and advisors, the confidentiality of which aims to encourage trust, negotiation and reasonable accommodation. However, tax planning and avoidance involve the use of a complex maze of corporate structures and transactions, and to track these down tax inspectors require powers, even if they are normally held in reserve, to compel information from the taxpayer, from related entities, and from third parties, especially banks, accountants and lawyers. This is especially the case for international avoidance, which raises the special problem for the tax authorities of obtaining such information from abroad.

2.a Obtaining Information Abroad

Tax authorities rely primarily on informal means of collecting information, including voluntary disclosure, backed by their legal powers. Officials regard the use of formal compulsory procedures as a last resort, and international procedures for assistance have been considered to be particularly laborious and time-consuming; hence, they normally prefer to rely on information or unilateral means of obtaining information about the foreign aspects of a taxpayer's business. Thus, an inquiry may need details of the accounts of a foreign entity doing business in the jurisdiction, or of a foreign branch or subsidiary of a local firm. Such information may be located abroad, but this does not prevent a request for its production; it may even be convenient for the inspector examining a case to travel abroad and request discussions on the spot with the foreign firm's staff or advisors. Inquiries may also be pursued abroad from sources which are public or do not involve any breach of confidentiality, for example by making searches in official registries for company accounts and details of shareholders and directors.

(i) Seeking Information Unilaterally
There is no clear consensus, however, as to how far it is permissible for official inquiries to be pursued abroad unilaterally. The modern state was constituted

as public authorities exercising powers over a geographical area, and it has been a basic principle of public international law that a state cannot perform executive or administrative acts within the territory of another except with the latter's consent (see Chapter 11 below). Provided that such inquiries involve no compulsion or breach of local laws, they may be acceptable. Some states consider that a state official is not barred from making in another state the same inquiries as any private person could make, while others take the view that a foreign official may not exercise any acts ex officio within their territory without prior permission (Akehurst 1972–3, p. 147, fn. 6). For example, the Swiss Penal Code prescribes criminal sanctions, including imprisonment in serious cases, for 'anyone who, without authorization, takes in Switzerland for a foreign state any action which is within the powers of the public authorities'. The US authorities apparently consider that this Swiss prohibition applies to an official inspection of a company's books, even if the company consents (*Gerling v. IRC*, 1988). The US Internal Revenue Service has published a guide to its officials on obtaining information from abroad, which explains the type of information publicly available in each country and differentiates between countries where voluntary and public information may be freely sought and those where such inquiries cannot be made by an IRS agent without prior permission from the relevant local state officials (US Treasury/ IRS 1984c). Normally, a revenue agent making inquiries abroad is required both to request permission from Washington and to inform the local embassy, and the inquiry may be pursued with the assistance of the Revenue Service Representative if there is one; where administrative co-operation with local officials is close, they would also be informed, and might even assist.[1]

Officials may also pursue their inquiries by requesting information from persons within their own territory even if that information is located abroad or is held by a foreign entity. Powers to require production of such information have commonly been enacted, in particular to facilitate the enforcement of provisions against international avoidance such as transfer pricing rules, or

---

[1] On the role of the Revenue Service Representative (RSR) see further below, section 2.b. The IRS Manual states: 'Because the RSR is working outside the territorial jurisdiction of the United States, the procedure that the RSR uses in exploring a particular matter, would depend upon formal and informal understandings with the government of the country in which he or she is operating. Thus, the freedom that the RSR could exercise might depend upon such factors as whether an American citizen is being interviewed, as opposed to a citizen from the country involved, or a citizen of a third country. On some occasions, agents of foreign taxing authorities will assist, collaborate or accompany the RSR on the investigation. In other cases, the scope of permissible action of the RSR may be severely limited. . . . It may also be possible for the district agent conducting the investigation to enter a foreign country, either alone or with OP:I [= Office of the Assistant Commissioner (International)] personnel, for the purpose of directly obtaining desired information. This might be appropriate, for example, in a complicated case under the International Enforcement Program when extensive knowledge of the case is required to interview a witness successfully' (IRS Manual HB 4233, Exhibit 500–5). The reference to 'formal and informal understandings' with the host state seems to imply acceptance that the exercise of such official functions, even if it involves no

laws taxing income sheltered in foreign intermediary companies or trusts. Thus, the British Inland Revenue Board has very broad powers to serve notices requiring information about the transactions of foreign intermediary entities in connection with the provisions against transfer of assets abroad;[1] and to require details of transactions with related entities under the transfer pricing rules,[2] as well as under the Controlled Foreign Corporation provisions to require a UK-resident shareholder to provide details of a foreign company which appears to be a CFC and of any connected or associated company.[3] Where such a notice requires documents of a foreign subsidiary, the taxpayer may apply to the Board for a waiver and may appeal to the Special Commissioners if it is refused.[4]

Without such powers, indeed, international avoidance and evasion would be greatly simplified. Backed by these powers, the Inland Revenue has issued general notices to British resident companies requesting accounts and other details of their foreign subsidiaries (Deutsch 1985). In a reported case, a very general notice was served on the London resident representative of a Bermudan bank requiring details of the formation and management of foreign companies and partnerships for UK clients in eight designated tax havens; the court upheld the notice, rejecting the arguments that this was a general 'fishing expedition' or even 'snooping', and that it was inordinately burdensome: the court considered that the estimate of five months' full-time work to compile the information was greatly exaggerated, and noted that the information required was only that available without making inquiries abroad.[5]

The US Internal Revenue Code generally requires taxpayers to maintain adequate books and records, which must be made accessible to IRS staff for audit; specific requirements were placed on US shareholders of CFCs under Subpart F for records of such corporations, even if kept abroad, to be produced within a reasonable time on demand. The IRS can compel production of

compulsory powers or breaches of local law, requires at least the tacit acceptance of the host state.

[1] ICTA 1988, s.745, previously ICTA 1970, s.481. See *Royal Bank of Canada v. I.R.C.* (1972) upholding the validity of a notice requesting details of suspected 'bond-washing' transactions carried out on behalf of a Bahamas company.

[2] ICTA 1988, s.772, originally FA 1975, s.17.

[3] ICTA 1988, s.755, originally FA 1984, s.90.

[4] The general powers of a tax inspector were in any case greatly extended in 1976 (Taxes Management Act 1970, s.20 as amended by FA 1976, Sch. 6) to require any person to produce documents and particulars relating to that person's liability (s.20(1)) or that of any other person (s.20(3)), covering any documents in the person's possession or power. Although documents may be considered in a person's 'possession or power' even if located abroad, it has been held in civil litigation that this does not include documents held by a foreign related entity, even a wholly-owned subsidiary (*Lonrho v. Shell Petroleum et al.*, 1980); thus, the specific powers relating to international avoidance just mentioned are important in applying unambiguously to documents held by foreign related entities.

[5] *Clinch v. CIR* (1973); on the use of a s.481 notice in the Rossminster investigations, see Tutt 1985, ch. 5.

books and records, from both the taxpayer and third-party record-keepers, as well as testimony under oath, by summons enforceable through a district court, which may impose sanctions for contempt. A summons will be enforced by the courts if the IRS shows 'that the investigation will be conducted pursuant to a legitimate purpose, that the inquiry may be relevant to the purpose, that the information sought is not already within the Commissioner's possession, and that the administrative steps required by the Code have been followed – in particular, that the "Secretary or his delegate", after investigation, has determined the further examination to be necessary and has notified the taxpayer in writing to that effect' (*US v. Powell*, 1964, pp. 57–8).

The test of relevance may also result in modification of a request that is over-broad. If appropriate, these powers may cover documents or information held abroad: '[t]he test for the production of documents is control, not location' (*Marc Rich A.G. v. US*, 1982, p. 667). An alternative to the summons, if civil or criminal proceedings (including a grand jury investigation) have been started, is the subpoena, which has the advantage that it may in an appropriate case be enforced against a US citizen abroad (US Treasury 1981, p. 205).

US courts put a high value on the obtaining of evidence required to establish tax liability, and do not accept that information held by a foreign branch or affiliate is not within a defendant's control. Thus, a foreign-owned US corporation may be required to produce information from its parent: a California district court upheld summonses on the Toyota Motor Corporation of the US, and its Japanese President Mr Isao Makino (who was also Senior Managing Director of the Japanese parent) to produce information on unit selling prices to dealers in Japan for each passenger car model sold by the Japanese company, for comparison with the transfer prices on sales to the US; however, the court refused to enforce another IRS request to Toyota for 'all orders, directives, instructions, commands and regulations issued to the subsidiary by its parent', on the grounds that the information was not identified with sufficient certainty (*US v. Toyota Motor Corp. et al.*, 1983).

The rule has also been applied to require a US bank to produce records held in a foreign branch about a foreign company: in *First National City Bank v. IRS* (1959) the 2nd Circuit Court of Appeals held that records of the bank accounts of a Panamanian corporation held in the Panama branch were in the 'possession, custody or control' of New York's Citibank.[1] It can also extend to requiring a foreign corporation to produce records located abroad. Thus, a district court has upheld a summons against a Panamanian company and its officers to produce its records, which had been requested in an investigation of a US company with which it appeared to be related, and which had been

---

[1] In contrast, British courts have refused to order production of records of transactions with the foreign branch of a British bank: *R. v. Grossman* (1979); *Mackinnon v. Donaldson, Lufkin, & Jenrette* (1986); and they have enjoined a London branch of a US bank from complying with a US subpoena: *X, Y and Z A.G. v. An American Bank* (1983): these cases are discussed below.

removed abroad shortly after the request (*US v. Diefenthal, & Fukaya Trading S.A.*, 1971). An American insurance company has been required to produce the books and accounts of a Swiss reinsurance company which was deemed to be its agent (the two being in substance related): *Gerling v. IRC* (1988). Finally, in *Marc Rich A.G. v. US* (1982), the 2nd Circuit Court of Appeals upheld a summons on a Swiss commodity trading firm, served on its subsidiary Marc Rich International which was doing business in the US, to produce business records relevant to the allegation that there had been a diversion of business profits to the Swiss parent: International had shown a gross loss of over $110 million on sales to US customers of oil 40 per cent of which had been bought from its parent, and the court accepted that there was 'sufficient likelihood that unlawful tax manipulation was taking place between appellant and its wholly-owned subsidiary to . . . require appellant to respond to the grand jury's inquiries'. The Marc Rich case led to a major conflict between the US and Swiss authorities.[1]

Following the IRS/Treasury tax havens report of 1981, a new provision was enacted to encourage production of foreign-based documentation: if normal requests fail, a 'formal document request' may be sent by registered mail to the taxpayer's last known address; unless the taxpayer applies to the district court to quash the request, or produces the documents, the taxpayer may not subsequently rely on the documents.[2] However, the 1988 White Paper found that, although lack of information was a major obstacle to effective enforcement of the transfer pricing rules, IRS agents were reluctant to use either the summons or the formal request procedures, apparently due to the time delay and the need to maintain a good relationship with the taxpayer (US Treasury 1988, p. 16). The White Paper recommended increased use of these procedures. Specific information on intrafirm transactions is required on special forms, and following the Congressional inquiries in 1990 into low tax payments by foreign-owned subsidiaries (see Chapter 8 above), information requirements were strengthened.[3]

The US IRS also makes extensive use of informants, and takes the view that 'there are no restrictions on the development of offshore informants, at least if they are controlled in the US' (US Treasury 1981, pp. 125–6). It also co-operates in joint task forces with criminal law enforcement agencies focusing on financial transactions, in particular money-laundering of the proceeds of crime, especially narcotics.[4] Some of these enforcement activities have

---

[1] See Walter 1985, pp. 52–8; Crinion 1986 and *X, Y and Z A.G. v. An American Bank*, discussed below.
[2] Internal Revenue Code s.982(a), enacted by the TEFRA: Tax Equity and Fiscal Responsibility Act 1982, s.337.
[3] Amendments to the Revenue Code section 6038 were enacted in 1989 reducing to 25 per cent the ownership threshold for corporations required to file details of inter-affiliate transactions; increasing the monetary penalty for non-compliance; in the case of non-compliance giving the government a discretionary power to determine allowable deductions and costs, and requiring that related foreign persons designate US agents for service of process; these were in 1990 made applicable to any taxable year for which the limitations period had not expired.
[4] US Congress 1975; US Congress 1983a Hearings (testimony of Roscoe Egger), pp. 268–70; US Congress 1985, pp. 12–15.

involved undercover operations, including the obtaining of evidence about bank clients in offshore jurisdictions, which involve problems of potential violation of local laws. There have also been allegations of breaches of US laws during IRS investigations: as part of 'Project Haven' in 1972 an IRS informant developed a close relationship with a Bahamian banker, which included arranging a 'date' for him during a visit to Miami, while in his absence the informant entered his hotel room and took a list of bank clients from his briefcase; subsequently a card file containing account details was taken from his office in the Bahamas (Crinion 1986). The evidence obtained by this 'flagrantly illegal search' was nevertheless held admissible by the Supreme Court, since the theft was from a third party and therefore not a violation of the defendant's constitutional rights (*Payner v. US*, 1980). Another IRS operation entailed copying addresses from envelopes of incoming mail from Switzerland to identify and select for audit the holders of Swiss bank accounts: reading envelopes was held not to violate constitutional privacy rights (*US v. Leonard*, 1976).

(ii) Conflict with Foreign Secrecy Laws

A requirement to produce information located abroad may cause difficulties if it creates a conflict with foreign law. An entity is normally free to reveal details of its own business if it wishes, so that compliance by it with the orders of a foreign authority would not normally entail a breach of local law. However, laws prohibiting disclosure of business information contrary to the national interest have become increasingly common in many countries. Such 'blocking statutes' either impose a general prohibition on disclosure of information which may be prejudicial to the national interest, subject to administrative guidance or approval;[1] or empower the government to prohibit compliance with foreign 'extraterritorial' requests or commands if they are considered a threat to economic interests.[2]

A conflict is most likely where information has been requested from a third party: in particular, lawyers, accountants and banks are normally bound by confidentiality in relation to their clients. Here again, however, the nature of the obligation and its enforcement may vary greatly. The basis of the duty of confidentiality is the contractual obligation of the banker or professional to the client.[3] Thus, in the case of bank secrecy the UK and other related common-law jurisdictions apply the often-cited principles laid down in the case of *Tournier v. National Provincial Bank* (1924), which prohibit disclosure except (i) under compulsion of law; (ii) under a duty to the public; (iii) in furtherance of the interests of the banker; and (iv) with the express or implied consent of the

---

[1] E.g. South Africa's Protection of Business Act 1978; and the French Act No. 80–538 of 16 July 1980: see Lowe 1983.
[2] E.g. Britain's Protection of Trading Interests Act 1980, discussed in Picciotto 1983.
[3] In the case of lawyers a different consideration applies, the protection of rights of parties in the legal process.

customer. However, other countries, especially those holding themselves out as financial centres or tax havens, have strengthened the secrecy obligation by statute, usually attaching criminal penalties. Switzerland's bank secrecy law dates back to 1934,[1] although that of other financial centres is more recent: e.g. Panama's Law on Coded Bank Accounts of 1959 (Effros 1982, p. 845); the Cayman Islands' Banks and Trust Companies' Regulation Law of 1966 and Confidential Relationships (Preservation) Law of 1976; the Bahamas' Bank and Trust Companies' Regulation Act 1965; and the Confidential Information Act passed in Montserrat in 1985.

However stringent the secrecy obligation, it may nevertheless be over-ridden, in particular for the purposes of law enforcement, or if the customer can be held to have consented. What has distinguished secrecy jurisdictions is their more restricted view of the circumstances in which this is permitted, and their willingness to enforce obligations of confidentiality against requests for information from foreign authorities. This has led to a series of disputes, in which the use of unilateral powers, especially by US authorities, has created legal conflicts, especially for banks involved in offshore business. Following considerable international pressures, many of the financial centres have accepted arrangements which limit bank secrecy, but these have been confined to the prevention of concealment of criminal activities or the proceeds of crime; they have generally been unwilling to override bank secrecy to help enforce foreign financial regulatory rules and especially to combat tax avoidance.[2]

Switzerland in particular has jealously defended its right to provide a haven for foreigners whose assets may be pursued by their own governments, citing the case of the German Jews. The Swiss banking law of 1934 was passed in response to the banking crisis of 1931 and the collapse of the Banque d'Escompte Suisse; at the time, the Nazi rise to power, and the enactment of Hitler's 'Economic Treason Act' of 1933, under which failure to declare foreign assets was punishable by unlimited imprisonment with hard labour, had led to a renewed outflow of funds to Switzerland.[3] The inclusion of

---

[1] Federal Banking Law of 1934, s.47: see Meyer 1978. Note that Switzerland's commercial confidentiality laws also provide for criminal penalties for an employee who discloses confidential information without authorization, the most notorious case being the imprisonment of Stanley Adams for revealing information about the anti-competitive practices of his firm Hoffman-La Roche to the European Commission.

[2] Chambost 1983 provides a racy and somewhat disorganized survey, including a chronological account, of the attempts of the Algerian government to recover FLN funds which disappeared from a Swiss bank.

[3] Intentional breaches by German citizens entailed a minimum of three years' hard labour with no maximum and loss of civil rights; where mitigating circumstances were present there was a maximum of ten years' imprisonment: Gesetz gegen Verrat der Deutschen Volkswirtschaft, ss.8 and 9; Reichsgesetzblatt 1933–I, p. 360. Since 1918 Germany had attempted to take measures to combat both capital flight (obviously a massive problem during the hyperinflation) and 'tax flight', i.e. tax evasion by transfer of assets abroad either by emigration or transfer to a foreign company or trust such as a Liechtenstein Anstalt, by draconian penalties against German emigrants (Gesetz gegen die Steuerflucht 26 July 1918,

criminal sanctions to reinforce bank secrecy in the 1934 Swiss law was therefore important to hinder collaboration with Gestapo inquiries by Swiss bank staff. Following the war, however, the Allied governments claimed that the same law had been used to conceal the ownership of Nazi assets, many of them looted from the Jews; disputes with the Allies over these assets in the postwar period were resolved only by inter-governmental agreements (Meyer 1978, pp. 40–2).

Subsequently, pressures were put on Switzerland, especially by France and the US, to limit the abuse of bank secrecy for evasion or avoidance of the laws of other countries, including tax laws. Responding to such pressures, but perhaps more from concern to avoid an unsavoury reputation as a haven for the funds of criminals and dictators, Switzerland has agreed to provide assistance, but it has been confined to criminal offences and excludes fiscal matters.[1] Exceptionally, the US–Swiss tax treaty of 1951 allowed for assistance in cases of fiscal fraud, although only after hearings in the US Congress attacking Swiss bank secrecy did the Swiss authorities agree that it could be used to obtain bank records; this was upheld by the Swiss courts, but the information was confined to a summary report not taking the form of evidence for court proceedings.[2]

After a decade of efforts the US also secured a bilateral criminal assistance treaty which includes tax and other economic offences committed in furtherance of the purposes of an organized criminal group.[3] The use of Swiss banks to place orders in US securities markets also led to continuing conflicts over the concealment of violation of securities laws. A partial solution was found by means of a voluntary agreement concluded in 1982 between the Swiss Bankers' Association and the US Securities and Exchange Commission, by which the banks agreed in certain circumstances to provide information about clients' accounts, to enforce the US law against insider dealing; since this arrangement was notified to bank clients it was considered to be incorporated into the contractual relationship and could override the secrecy rule. Linked to this was a 'diligence agreement', under which Swiss banks agreed to vet their clients. These arrangements have largely been superseded by the enactment

Reichsgesetzblatt 1918–I, p. 951), as well as measures begun in 1931 to tax the assets and income of a foreign trust, whether distributed or not, as income of the creator or beneficiary: see Landwehrmann 1974, pp. 265ff., esp. fn. 134.
[1] Since 1981 assistance in criminal cases is available to all states under the Federal Act on International Mutual Assistance in Criminal Matters of 20 March 1981; under these procedures the Swiss authorities have tried to co-operate in appropriate cases, for example by freezing assets of deposed dictators, such as Marcos of the Philippines and Duvalier of Haiti, provided a criminal case has been instituted or is contemplated in the foreign country concerned. The Swiss Federal Office for Police Matters maintains quite close links with some foreign government agencies in such cases.
[2] X and Y-Bank v. Federal Tax Administration (1975), and see the discussion in Meyer 1978, pp. 59–3.
[3] US–Switzerland treaty 1973, effective from 1977; over seven years the US made 200 requests under this treaty, two-thirds involving bank records: see statement of Assistant Attorney-General D. Lowell Jensen in US Congress 1938a, Hearings, p. 217.

by the Swiss Parliament of laws prohibiting both insider dealing and money-laundering. However, a proposal sponsored by the Social Democrats to override bank secrecy for tax evasion was defeated by referendum in 1984; although banks can be required to provide evidence in criminal cases, in the tax area this is limited to tax fraud which entails an overt act such as falsification of documents (Meyer 1978, pp. 32–4), and the Swiss have so far resisted most pressures to co-operate with other states in tax matters.[1]

Increasing international concern about organized crime has led to internationally co-ordinated pressures to make it easier to obtain bank account information and to place obligations on banks to monitor their clients, but in most countries this is kept separate from tax enforcement. An international agreement initiated at the Group of Seven economic summit in Paris in 1989 included undertakings to change bank secrecy laws and create obligations on banks to vet their clients and report suspicious financial movements.[2] However, this was aimed at criminal activities, primarily narcotic drugs trafficking, and did not include tax evasion, without which important financial centres such as Luxembourg, Switzerland, and perhaps even the UK would not co-operate. A major exception is the US, where the IRS is part of the Treasury department, and often operates also in conjunction with other law-enforcement bodies. Nevertheless, it was not until the enactment of the Bank Secrecy Act in 1970 that systematic monitoring arrangements were established to assist in the detection of illegal financial transactions and the movement of the proceeds of crime (referred to as 'money-laundering'). In particular, regulations under this Act require a record of any transmission from or receipt into the US of any sum exceeding $5,000. These and other records are available to the IRS on the Treasury computer system, and following a report by the General Accounting Office in 1979, as well as recommendations in the Gordon Report of 1981, improved use has been made of this information.[3] However, the supervision of financial institutions, including their compliance with the Bank Secrecy Act, is entrusted to agencies primarily concerned with their financial soundness, which may run counter to the need for co-operation with law-enforcement agencies (US President's

---

[1] See the debate in the Swiss Parliament on ratification of the protocols to the European Conventions on Judicial Assistance: a proposal by the Federal Council to accept the obligation to provide assistance in cases of fiscal fraud was rejected by Parliament (Switzerland, National Council 1984). If Switzerland is to maintain or even improve its links with the European Community, it may have to accept a greater obligation; however, stricter EC arrangements for co-operation to combat tax and other economic regulatory avoidance have also been resisted by the financial centres within the EC, in particular Luxembourg and the UK (and sometimes others such as Ireland and Portugal), and the business lobby resisting the development of co-operation between tax authorities is also strong in Germany.

[2] This has been embodied in the European Community by a proposed Directive on Money Laundering, expected to gain approval in 1991, imposing obligations on all financial institutions to monitor their clients and co-operate with the authorities to prevent the laundering of the proceeds of drugs trafficking: see COM (90)593 Final.

[3] US Treasury 1981, pp. 198–204; US Congress 1983a, Hearings: testimony of Roscoe Egger pp. 266–8.

Commission on Organised Crime 1984, p. 20). The dual responsibility of the Treasury may also cause legal difficulties: thus, in *US v. Deak-Perrera* (1983) the courts refused an IRS summons against clients identified as tax evaders from records supplied in reliance on the belief that the purpose of the inquiry was bank supervision.

Not only Switzerland, but most of the 'offshore' financial centres have resisted pressures to relax bank secrecy laws in tax matters. Conflict within the OECD Fiscal Committee for several years on this matter came to a head in July 1985 over the Committee's report 'Taxation and the Abuse of Bank Secrecy', which urged tax authorities in countries with strict bank secrecy laws to stress the importance of amending these laws (OECD 1987a–IV, para. 23). Despite the bold assertion that 'there is no special problem about exchanging bank information' in tax matters (ibid., para. 24), four member states (Austria, Luxembourg, Portugal and Switzerland) rejected this report. Although it correctly pointed out that 'Bank secrecy towards the tax authorities could influence the location of bank deposits only insofar as practices differed among countries',[1] the problem is that such a common standard seems difficult to achieve, and competition between offshore centres makes it hard for any of them to relax the degree of secrecy offered by their laws. Although the UK made no formal objections to the report, the powers of the Inland Revenue to override the privacy of the bank account are more strictly circumscribed than, for example, in France or the US. In the UK an inspector may require from a third party such as a bank only documents which in the inspector's 'reasonable opinion' may contain information about a person's tax liability (Taxes Management Act 1970, s.20(3)). There have been objections to the extension of these powers to include 'random' information, and resistance by British banks to the inclusion of fiscal offences within the ambit of international measures against crime.[2] More seriously, the Inland Revenue itself takes the view that their power to obtain information applies only where there is a UK tax liability, and that they cannot obtain information requested by a foreign state unless there is also a potential British tax liability (although this was extended in 1990 to include a liability to any EC member state, see section 2.b below). Luxembourg in 1989 also passed legislation

---

[1] OECD 1987a–IV, para. 10. This diagnosis is substantially the same as that of the first inter-governmental committee which considered the problem, the Technical Experts appointed by the League of Nations, which concluded (League of Nations 1925, Part III) that the inevitability of capital flight to the least regulated banking environment requires a multilateral solution, although since 'public opinion' was hostile to more stringent international standards, the first step should be to ensure that each state would use its own powers on behalf of others.
[2] See Derek Wheatley, Q.C., 'Murky Waters for the Inland Revenue's "Fishermen" ', *Financial Times*, 16 August 1990. The British Bankers' Association argued that the extension of the Criminal Justice (International Co-operation) Act 1990 to fiscal matters might have serious consequences for the City of London: *Financial Times* 10 September 1990; see also Note in *British Tax Review* [1990] p. 1. Nevertheless, the Act does apply to fiscal offences, although where proceedings have not yet been instituted the Secretary of State must be satisfied that the

imposing a 'diligence' requirement on bankers, and permitting co-operation with foreign authorities in criminal inquiries, but explicitly excluding fiscal matters and reinforcing its long-standing administrative practice of non-response to information requests from abroad relating to tax evasion.

These divergencies have created a tension between the unilateral use of powers by some authorities, especially those of the US, to obtain information abroad, and the defensive use of secrecy and other blocking legislation. Although the US courts have taken the view that, in principle, they will not require a person to perform an act which would violate a foreign law, they require a 'good faith effort' by that person to obtain release from the foreign law obligation.[1] However, US regulatory authorities, including the IRS, have pressed the courts not to allow foreign secrecy laws or blocking statutes to prevent production of information needed to enforce US laws. In response, the US courts have endorsed the position put forward in the American Law Institute's Restatement of the Foreign Relations Law of the United States, that a state may exercise its jurisdiction even if to do so would oblige a person to breach a rule of another state exercising a concurrent jurisdiction. In such circumstances, however, each state is required to moderate the exercise of its enforcement jurisdiction by taking into account relevant factors, notably: (i) the vital interests of each state; (ii) the extent and nature of the hardship caused by the conflicting requirements; (iii) the extent to which action is required in the territory of the foreign state; (iv) the nationality of the person; and (v) the extent to which enforcement would result in compliance. This principle of 'moderation and restraint' in exercising concurrent jurisdiction has also received some endorsement in international bodies, especially the OECD (OECD 1987).

The 'balancing' approach has been criticized as one-sided and tending to over-weight the interests of the jurisdiction being asserted (Maier 1982); it also may lead to a strengthening of the obstacles placed by the foreign jurisdiction, to redress the balance. Such jurisdictional tussles often involve complex legal and diplomatic manoeuvres. There has been much resentment of the activism of the US authorities and their assertion of 'extraterritorial' jurisdiction; this has been countered by US resentment at the unwillingness of others to accept that international comity requires not only respect for the laws of other states, but also a willingness to assist in the enforcement of those laws, or at least not to allow secrecy rules to facilitate international evasion. Nevertheless, even in countries where the bank secrecy obligation is merely contractual and may be overridden for the purposes of enforcement of local law, there has been a refusal to do so in favour of a unilateral foreign court order.

---

conduct would constitute an offence under UK law, unless the request is from a Commonwealth country, or is made under a treaty to which the UK is a party: s.4(3).
[1] *Société Internationale v. Rogers* (1958): this was the 'Interhandel' case, part of the lengthy diplomatic and legal postwar negotiations with Switzerland over German assets – see Meyer 1978.

Thus, third parties such as banks may be caught by conflicting court orders. A notable case involved the Chase Manhattan Bank, which was required by the New York courts to produce records from its Hong Kong branch which the IRS suspected would show that payments made by the Gucci shops and the Gucci family as management charges were in effect transfers of profit overseas.[1] The Southern District Court of New York in making the order was influenced by the lack of any opposition from the Hong Kong government to the request, and by the fact that bank confidentiality in Hong Kong is merely contractual and accepts the exceptions embodied in the *Tournier* principles. Although the Hong Kong company had obtained an interim injunction from the Hong Kong courts enjoining Chase from producing the records, the US court refused to give a counter-order not to pursue the injunction, expressing its 'hope, indeed almost an expectation, that the principles of comity may be seen by the Hong Kong court in the same light as they are viewed here'. Unfortunately for Chase, the Hong Kong Court of Appeal, although sympathetic to the bank's invidious position, took the view that the possibility of its being held in contempt by the New York Court was not relevant to the overriding obligation of Hong Kong courts, since 'All persons opening accounts with banks in Hong Kong, whether foreign or local banks, are entitled to look to the Hong Kong courts to enforce any obligation of secrecy which, by the law of Hong Kong, is implied by virtue of the relationship of banker and customer'.[2] Although the US court was willing to enforce its order with sanctions for contempt (*US v. Chase Manhattan Bank*, 1984), it does not appear that Chase was subjected to sanctions for breach of the injunction of the Hong Kong court.

The British courts are reluctant both to require a bank to produce evidence from its foreign branches, and to permit a UK bank branch to comply with a foreign request. Thus, when a US bank was subpoenaed by the US Department of Justice to produce records from its London branch about a Swiss company, Leggatt J. granted an application by the Swiss client to continue an interim injunction against the bank prohibiting disclosure, holding on the balance of convenience that the bank would be unlikely to be sanctioned for contempt in New York for complying with a British court order in these circumstances.[3] This relied on the availability to the bank in the US of the defence of 'foreign sovereign compulsion', but as the Chase Manhattan Bank case shows, US courts may feel justified to enforce their penalties even where this creates a conflict for the third party caught in the middle.

Influenced by their resentment at 'extraterritorial' orders by US courts, the

[1] *Garpeg and Chase Manhattan Bank v. US* (1984) 583 F. Supp. 789, and other related cases referred to there.
[2] Cited in White 1989, p. 19.
[3] *X, Y and Z A.G. v. A Bank* (1983): although the names of the parties were kept anonymous, from the details provided in the report, it appears that this was part of the long-running investigation by the US authorities of the Marc Rich commodity trading group, discussed in the previous section.

British courts have shown reluctance in the converse situation: notably, when the Inland Revenue requested an order in a criminal tax evasion case against a British bank, Barclays, to produce records from its Isle of Man branch. Barclays had collected cheques on behalf of the Savings and Investment Bank[1] which might provide evidence of payments involving criminal tax evasion (*R. v. Grossman*, 1979). The Inland Revenue had tried to obtain disclosure from the branch under Manx law, but the Isle of Man court (the Deemster) had not only refused to grant an order but had enjoined the bank from disclosure; when the Revenue applied to the British courts for an order against the head office, the Court of Appeal held that the public interest in disclosure was outweighed by other factors. Lord Denning emphasized that a foreign bank branch should be treated as a separate entity subject to foreign law, and conflicts of jurisdiction should be avoided. Oliver and Shaw, LJJ. concurring in the decision, emphasized that orders against third parties should only be made with caution, and the information requested in this case would have been of little help to the Revenue. Similarly, in a civil claim for fraud, Hoffmann, J. held that a subpoena served on the London branch of Citibank to produce records of accounts in New York should not be enforced, since there would be little difficulty in applying directly to the New York courts for the information; only in exceptional circumstances should a British court require a foreign person to reveal information about transactions entered into abroad (*Mackinnon v. Donaldson, Lufkin, & Jenrette*, 1986).

US attempts to enforce information orders against banks in the Caribbean have had mixed results: the outcome has tended to be a tightening up of bank secrecy laws, and a formalization of procedures for international co-operation. But, while offshore financial centres have been willing to concede formal arrangements for assistance in criminal matters, to avoid an unsavoury reputation, these have excluded tax matters, and the negotiation of specific tax information exchange treaties has proved more difficult. This can be seen from the story of US attempts to penetrate bank secrecy in the Bahamas and the Cayman Islands. Cayman laid the legal foundations for its development as a financial centre in its bank and trust laws and foreign exchange regulations of 1966; by 1970 it was well established as a tax haven, apparently with the approval of the British colonial authorities.[2] It received a further boost when the transition of the Bahamas to independence in 1973 created political uncertainty there. Concern by the US authorities at the growing use of Cayman facilities for tax evasion and money-laundering led to close checks on US residents or citizens with connections with the islands. In 1976, as part of joint task force investigations into organized crime, a subpoena was served on

---

[1] The SIB was licensed as a bank in the Isle of Man, but later collapsed, provoking a scandal, and the tightening up of bank supervision on the island: see Chapter 6 above.
[2] The Cayman Islands Report for the years 1966–70 stated that by 1970 over 2,000 companies and trusts were registered and paying fees, and 'The tax haven business, in conjunction with

a Canadian while he was passing through Miami International Airport, to produce records of the Castle Bank and Trust Company of Georgetown, Grand Cayman, of which he was Managing Director, required for investigations into US criminal tax fraud. Although he was resident in Cayman and brought evidence that he could be liable to criminal proceedings there for revealing the records, the summons was upheld (*In re Grand Jury Proceedings, US v. Field*, 1976). The court held that the US interest in violation of its criminal law was overriding; it was also influenced by the consideration that such testimony could be compelled in Cayman to enforce its own laws, and that other countries assert similar powers to compel information from abroad.[1]

The *Field* case resulted in the enactment by Cayman of the Confidential Relationships (Preservation) Law of 1976, which made it a criminal offence to reveal confidential information, unless required in relation to an investigation of a breach of Cayman law or of a foreign law if authorized by the Governor. An amendment of 1979 permitted an application to the courts to request a waiver of confidentiality; but, although the Cayman courts have stated it to be their policy not to allow bank secrecy to permit money-laundering, the Cayman government has restricted the procedure to international requests for criminal judicial assistance which still excludes taxation.[2] Indeed, it was only after further litigation in which US courts imposed fines for contempt on a foreign bank for failure to produce information that Cayman agreed to procedures for criminal judicial assistance. A grand jury investigating tax evasion and narcotic drugs trafficking served a subpoena *duces tecum* on the Miami branch of the Canadian-based Bank of Nova Scotia, initially for records in the Bahamas and Antigua, and subsequently also in the Cayman Islands. The determination of the US courts to enforce their orders, backed by daily fines for contempt, despite repeated pleas by the bank (*In re Grand Jury Proceedings, US v. Bank of Nova Scotia*, 1984), resulted in decisions by the Bahamian government and the Governor of the Cayman Islands authorizing disclosure (Horowitz 1985, pp. 156–61).

The Bahamas courts were nevertheless still inclined to try to block attempts by the US authorities unilaterally to compel production of Bahamas bank records (*Lesser Antilles Trading Co. v. The Bank of Nova Scotia*, 1985); but they were more willing to co-operate with requests for judicial assistance in criminal cases, and to make orders releasing a bank from its duty of confidentiality. Thus, Georges, C.J. held that 'The policy of preserving bank secrecy in the Commonwealth as enshrined in its laws must scrupulously be observed. Of equal importance is the need to ensure that it does not become a

tourism, is therefore considered the main economy of the islands' (UK Foreign and Commonwealth Office 1972, p. 15).

[1] Citing the UK case of *Clinch v. CIR*, which however did not concern information located abroad, as mentioned above.

[2] See the *Interconex* case, involving commercial bribery, in which it proved more difficult to obtain evidence from Cayman than several other offshore centres: US Congress 1983a, Hearings pp. 228–33, and Horowitz 1985, pp. 153–6.

screen for facilitating fraud' (*Royal Bank of Canada v. Apollo Development Ltd*, 1985). Both the Canadian and British governments protested at the 'lack of respect for the rules of international law' involved in the *Nova Scotia* bank case. Nevertheless, the incident was followed by the conclusion first of a 'gentlemen's agreement', quickly followed by the signing of a formal treaty in 1986 between the US and the UK on behalf of the Cayman Islands, for mutual assistance in criminal matters. However, the treaty specifically excludes taxation, except for tax fraud related to the proceeds of crime. The Cayman authorities state that although this treaty resulted in some outflow of funds, it has strengthened the quality of its financial services sector; however, they stress that assistance is available only in respect of activities that are criminal in both Cayman and the US, and confidentiality generally remains essential to the future of Cayman as a financial centre.[1]

Thus, offshore centres such as Cayman have reacted to accusations that the secrecy they offer is a cloak for illegality by moving towards acceptance of formal procedures for criminal judicial assistance, while resisting information exchange agreements for tax matters. In this way they hope to avoid the slur of criminality and strengthen investors' confidence in their facilities, while maintaining the opportunities offered for tax avoidance and evasion. Their agreement to arrangements for assistance in tax matters would require some economic inducement to make up for the inevitable loss of financial business. The US has attempted to offer such inducements to Caribbean countries, but only a limited number of countries have so far negotiated tax information treaties (see Chapter 7, section 3 above and section 2.b below). Although many of the Caribbean havens are still British dependencies[2] Britain can only offer limited inducements to persuade them to replace their offshore financial business, and has concentrated instead on trying to establish adequate supervision to prevent their use for criminal purposes and to safeguard investors (see Chapter 6, section 1.c above).

---

[1] See Tax Notes International, 14 February 1990, speeches of Alan J. Scott, Governor, and Thomas Jefferson, Financial Secretary. The Treaty was not ratified until 1990, although in the meantime a Narcotics Co-operation Agreement was established by exchange of notes between the US and the UK on behalf of its five Caribbean dependencies. The US–UK/Cayman 1990 treaty, which is also to extend to Anguilla, the British Virgin Islands, Montserrat and the Turks and Caicos Islands, in Article 19 explicitly excludes all tax matters, except those involving (i) wilfully or dishonestly making false statements or failing to report income in relation to the unlawful proceeds of a criminal offence, except for those connected with financial transactions (Article 19(3)(e)); and (ii) wilfully or dishonestly defrauding others by false statements regarding tax benefits (Article 19(3)(d)).

[2] For details of the changes in the constitutional status of British territories in the Caribbean, see Chapter 6, note 12 above. The tax 'arrangements' made by the UK with these territories, which were equivalent to a tax treaty and included an information exchange clause, were in many cases terminated: e.g. British Virgin Islands (terminated by UK notice in 1971); Seychelles (1982); Dominica, St Lucia, St Vincent & Grenadines (all in 1986). The UK at present has no formal tax treaty or arrangement with the Bahamas, Bermuda, Cayman Islands, Gibraltar, Liberia, Liechtenstein, the Maldives, Monaco, Nauru, Panama, Tonga, the Turks & Caicos, United Arab Emirates and Vanuatu.

Nevertheless, the strengthening of secrecy laws and the greater sensitivity of foreign jurisdictions to the question of 'extraterritoriality' has led to more caution by US courts in enforcing a summons, especially if it would entail breach of a foreign state's criminal laws, or if the information can be obtained by other means (*In re Sealed Case (Two Cases)*, 1987). Enforcement may also be more cautious where the case does not involve either the proceeds of crime or tax fraud: this was apparently the deciding factor in *US v. First National Bank of Chicago* (1983), in which the 7th Circuit Court of Appeals, applying the 'balancing' approach, declined to enforce a disclosure order which would have entailed breach of the Greek bank secrecy law, because the bank had made a good faith effort to obtain permission from the Greek authorities, the case was a relatively minor one, and the information was needed to assist enforcement not assessment of taxes. Nevertheless, the US courts have also held that use of unilateral powers is not barred where there is a treaty with an information exchange provision, since such treaty procedures are not exclusive: *US v. Vetco* (1981). However, the *Vetco* case involved Swiss subsidiaries of US corporations, and evidence that the Swiss government did not consider it had a strong interest in protecting confidentiality of their records influenced the US court's 'balancing'; the situation might be different if a foreign government insisted that treaty procedures must be used.

2.b Information Exchange under Tax Treaties

The main vehicle for international co-operation between tax authorities has been the bilateral tax treaties' exchange of information provision (the origins of which were discussed in section 1 above).[1] The model treaty article provides for two main types of information exchange: *automatic* and *on request*; in addition, some states authorize the *spontaneous* provision of information. These three categories of information exchange are more formally recognized in the recent measures specifically establishing administrative assistance: the OECD/Council of Europe Convention 1988, the European Community Directive 1990, and the specific assistance treaties concluded by states, especially the US agreements with Caribbean states. Such arrangements permit information exchange in relation to the assessment of tax liability, and therefore establish the potential for much broader co-operation than do procedures enabling information to be obtained abroad for criminal or civil judicial proceedings.

(i) Procedures
Arrangements for automatic annual exchange of specified information were

---

[1] National law may permit the provision of information without a treaty: the new German Fiscal Code of 1977 provided for international assistance on a reciprocal basis without specifying the need for a treaty, but there was disagreement as to the constitutionality of this provision (Bracewell-Milnes in Rotterdam IFS 1979, p. 158; Krabbe 1986); after the

included in the London model treaty of 1946 (Article III). Since the treaty provided for a limitation of withholding tax at source on investment income, it was envisaged that the state of the payer could provide lists of the recipients of payments such as interest, dividends and royalties, to facilitate residence taxation of this income and ensure that the recipient is a bona fide resident of the treaty partner. It was accepted that not all states would have the facilities to provide such information. Indeed, states vary considerably both as to the information they can supply and the form in which they supply it. For example, some countries such as France automatically receive information from banks about interest payments, therefore details of such payments to non-residents can be transmitted to treaty partners; but in others, such as Germany, such information has been confidential and unobtainable. Hence, treaty partners negotiate specific administrative arrangements to suit their mutual circumstances: for example, some states, such as Canada and the USA, have for several years exchanged this information on computer tape. The OECD Committee has established a common form for provision of this material, using standard numerical codes to avoid the need for translation, and use of this form was recommended by the OECD Council in 1981. The sheer volume, amounting to hundreds of thousands of records for some states, makes effective use of such data difficult without a system of agreed taxpayer identification numbers and preferably also fully compatible computerized records, which may develop in time.

The Commentary to the OECD/Council of Europe convention points out that tax compliance would be improved if taxpayers were informed of such arrangements (para. 64), but the normal practice is merely to issue a general statement that such arrangements exist. Concern has been expressed by taxpayers and their advisors that 'there is no mechanism for determining whether information so exchanged is accurate, set in its proper context and does not contain data which could be damaging commercially if confidentiality was breached for any reason' (Arthur Andersen 1985, p. 10).

Provision of information on request is in principle an obligation under most treaty information exchange provisions, although it is subject to significant conditions. A request is normally required to (i) identify the taxpayer and the information requested; (ii) give evidence that it relates to a person or entity subject to a tax covered by information exchange; (iii) show that it is required in good faith to determine a tax liability covered by the treaty; and (iv) state how the information is to be used and if possible where it may be found (Abrutyn & Halphen 1984, A–39). This allows the requested state to screen requests to decide whether to comply, both to protect the taxpayer and to prevent time being wasted on futile or improper requests or 'fishing expeditions'. However, the information request is normally treated as

enactment of the EC Mutual Assistance Law, which laid down more precise conditions, limits have been placed in practice on all assistance: see below.

confidential by the tax authorities and need not be produced to the person from whom information is requested, provided the competent authority certifies that the request falls within the provisions of the treaty (*US v. Bache, Halsey, Stuart,* 1982).

The tax treaty information exchange provision is important in allowing information to be gathered at the investigation stage. In contrast, treaties for judicial assistance aim at the provision of evidence for court proceedings, and in any case not all states accept their application in tax matters. Thus, the Council of Europe Convention for Mutual Assistance in Criminal Matters of 1959 can be explicitly extended to fiscal fraud under the protocol of 1978;[1] while in civil tax cases, the Hague Evidence Convention of 1970 might apply.[2] In practice, judicial assistance treaties have rarely been used in tax matters, presumably because tax authorities usually require information at the earlier stage of investigation. Conversely, some states do not accept that the tax treaty obligation requires them to provide information for use in court proceedings, or in a form which may be so used (i.e. witness depositions, authenticated documents). Hence, it is becoming common to specify that information supplied under a tax treaty may be used in court proceedings[3] and that it should be supplied in the requisite form. In practice, procedures for tax information requests did not become firmly established and regularized between states until the 1970s, when national tax authorities specifically designated the 'competent authority' official through whom such requests would be made. As the use of this procedure has expanded, disagreements have arisen between some states about the extent of the obligation and of the conditions which provide safeguards.

Switzerland, in particular, has a much more restrictive view of the purpose of information exchange, considering that its objective is merely to ensure the correct application of treaty provisions to prevent double taxation. In this light, information exchange is relevant essentially only to secure a corresponding adjustment under the mutual agreement procedure, and to ensure that reduced withholding taxes at source are only provided to bona fide residents of the treaty partner. Hence, Switzerland entered an explicit reservation to Article 26 of the OECD 1977 draft (OECD 1977, p. 188); its treaties contain a

[1] The protocol has not been accepted by all the states party to the Convention: notably, the Swiss Parliament rejected a government proposal to accept the protocol: Switzerland, National Council 1984, see note 28 above. A memorandum on the application of Council of Europe conventions for assistance in penal matters to fiscal offences was submitted to the Colloquy on International Tax Avoidance and Evasion of 1980: see Council of Europe 1981, p. 85.
[2] This was finally confirmed after considerable litigation following applications made under the Convention to the British courts, in connection with a tax case in Norway involving the estate of shipowner Anders Jahre. The British proceedings took the form of a request to take evidence from British directors of the merchant bank, Lazards, which had acted as advisor to a trust the assets of which included the shares of a Panama company; the Norwegian authorities alleged that Jahre was the settlor or controlled the trust so that its assets were liable to tax as part of his estate: *In re Norway's Application (Nos. 1 & 2)* (1990).
[3] Although sometimes only with the permission of the supplying state: OECD Convention Article 22; under this Convention also, information may not be supplied once criminal proceedings have been begun: Explanatory Report para. 56.

restricted version of this article, permitting information exchange only for the purpose of giving effect to the treaty (although the US–Swiss treaty exceptionally covers tax fraud, as mentioned above).

At the other extreme, the United States considers that the purpose of exchange of information is to make a state's enforcement powers available to a treaty partner for enforcement of the latter's taxes. It should therefore apply to 'taxes of every kind imposed by a Contracting State' (Article 26(6) of the US model treaty of 1981) and not only to the taxes covered by the treaty. If accepted by US treaty partners this would permit, for example, exchange of information in relation to local or state taxes and therefore the supply to states within the US of information received from treaty partners, which was one of the conditions agreed for the abandonment by these states of Worldwide Unitary Taxation (see Chapter 9, section 4 above). However, other countries are reluctant to go so far: for example, the new US treaty with Germany signed in 1989 merely provided that the parties might exchange diplomatic notes for information exchange to include taxes other than those covered by the treaty.

Further, the US view is that a treaty partner should have an obligation to use the full extent of its enforcement powers as if the tax being enforced were its own and even if it has no tax interest in the matter. The US courts have interpreted the provision in the OECD model to permit the use of the powers of summons of the IRS even though no US tax liability was at stake, and even if the treaty partner could not go so far (*US v. A. L. Burbank & Co.*, 1975). In taking this view, the court referred to the OECD Commentary on this article, which states that 'types of administrative measures authorised for the purpose of the requested state's tax must be utilised, even though invoked solely to provide information to the other contracting state' (OECD 1977, p. 187, para. 14). The US model treaty makes this explicit, and other instruments such as the EC Directive and the OECD/Council of Europe multilateral convention appear to be intended to have this effect.[1] The US courts have upheld the use of the normal powers available to the IRS in obtaining information in response to treaty requests, extending even to searching for information outside the USA: thus, in response to a Dutch inquiry information was requested from a US stockbroker relating to the Dutch taxpayer's Swiss account, which the Dutch authorities themselves could not have obtained from Switzerland (*US v. Bache, Halsey, Stuart*, 1982). Furthermore, a power may be used in response to a foreign request even though its use in a domestic case might be blocked by other considerations: for example, the administrative powers of the US IRS may not be used when a case has been referred to the Justice Department for possible criminal prosecution, but there is no

[1] The EC Directive Article 2(2) requires the requested state to 'arrange for the conduct of any inquiries necessary to obtain such information'; the OECD/Council of Europe multilateral convention provides in Article 5(2) that if the information requested is not in the files of the requested state it 'shall take all relevant measures', which the commentary (para. 61) explains

requirement to certify that a similar stage has not been reached by the foreign proceedings when using the summons power for a treaty request (*US v. Stuart et al.*, 1989).

However, other states are reluctant to accept such an extensive obligation. In particular, the view of the British Inland Revenue has been that it can and will only supply information already in its files, and cannot use its powers to make inquiries on behalf of a foreign tax authority, unless the request discloses sufficient grounds of possible liability to UK tax. This reluctance has deep roots, apparently linked to fears of damaging the City's position as a financial entrepôt, which were the concerns expressed when it surfaced during the consideration of Britain's first postwar treaty with the US in 1945 (see Chapter 2, section 1.a above). When the EC mutual assistance Directive of 1977 was approved, the UK enabling legislation merely authorized disclosure of information to member states, and even this was hotly debated in Parliament.[1] It was only after pressure from the European Commission that a broader provision was eventually passed, enabling all the powers available to a tax inspector to be used in relation to taxes of other member states (Finance Act 1990, s.125); but an opposition amendment to extend the same arrangements to all treaty partner states was rejected, one MP stating that it was inappropriate to 'allow the Inland Revenue of any banana republic . . . to demand that the Inland Revenue collect information which that republic will be able to use to persecute its own citizens or those of another country'.[2] In 1987 a specific provision was enacted to provide the legal basis to comply with tax treaty obligations which 'may include provisions with respect to the exchange of information necessary for carrying out . . . the laws of the territory to which the arrangements relate'.[3] This could be interpreted broadly enough to authorize the use of powers on behalf of foreign tax authorities even where there is no UK tax interest, especially in the light of the statements in the OECD treaty Commentary mentioned above, but since it considers this to be a matter of some political sensitivity, the Inland Revenue appears unwilling to go so far.[4]

means using 'all relevant measures authorised for the purpose of that state's tax in order to obtain the information'.

[1] Finance Act 1978, s.77, debated in House of Commons Standing Committee A, 21 June 1978, p. 1632.

[2] House of Commons, Standing Committee E, 26 June 1990, p. 418.

[3] Now ICTA 1988, s.788(2); prior to this, the Revenue apparently relied merely on the general provisions empowering double taxation relief by treaty.

[4] Note also that the provision permitting disclosure of information under tax treaties, now ICTA 1988, s.816, lifts the exemption of banks to provide information as to income from securities where the beneficiary is non-resident, in relation to a resident of a treaty partner. In this respect, at least, the Revenue is given powers to obtain and provide information where no UK tax liability is involved. There has certainly been pressure on the Revenue to interpret its powers of assistance more broadly in relation to some countries, notably the US which is anxious for more effective information exchange; thus, the UK is excluded from the list of countries eligible for the supposed benefits of a US Foreign Sales Corporation (see Chapter 5, section 2.c above), because its information exchange provisions are deemed inadequate.

In practice, many requests are likely to be for information already in the files of the requested authority. A request which requires the use of formal compulsory powers is usually a last resort, for example when otherwise unavailable evidence is needed to establish liability for legal purposes. Under most national laws the power of tax authorities to require information relevant to a taxpayer's liability, especially from third parties, is subject to strict conditions and procedures, and a request of this kind made on behalf of a foreign authority will put the taxpayer on notice. This gives an opportunity to object and even resort to the courts, if the request might exceed the treaty obligations, for example if the taxpayer claims commercial secrecy will be violated, or the request entails using powers not available under the laws of the requesting state.[1]

Information already in the files of the requested authority may be supplied without any notification to a concerned taxpayer, although objections have been made to this. In Germany, a campaign by business interest groups against the extension of discretionary assistance came to a head over the law which the government was finally obliged to submit to the Bundesrat to comply with the EC mutual assistance Directive (due to its extension to VAT). Paradoxically, the resulting EC Mutual Assistance Law imposed restrictions on the German tax authorities: the supply of information on request was made subject to the taxpayer being given a right to notification and a hearing (although this right already existed under general tax law); arrangements for automatic exchange are limited to specified areas, and must be agreed by statutory regulations approved by the upper house of the Bundesrat; and only administrative assistance is permitted, so that it is likely that information required for court proceedings for tax fraud would have to be provided under arrangements for judicial assistance, in so far as these exist (Krabbe 1986; Runge 1986). These restrictions created doubts as to whether Germany is in full compliance with the Directive.

On the other hand other countries, such as the US, have considered it inappropriate to alert the taxpayer of a request, especially in potential criminal evasion cases. However, in commenting on the OECD/Council of Europe convention, the US government stated that it intended to adopt an administrative procedure under which an affected taxpayer would be notified of a specific request or of spontaneous exchanges (US Congress 1990b, p. 13). In the UK, the Keith Committee recommended that the Revenue should notify the taxpayer of a request if it might involve disclosure of commercial secrets, and that an appeal should be available to the General Commissioners

Treasury Secretary Brady, in accepting the proposal of the UK and Germany for a multilateral study of transfer pricing problems following the controversy caused by Congressional revelations in July 1990 of low tax payments by foreign TNCs in the US, expressed regret that the UK's extension of assistance powers in respect of EC countries did not apply to the US: see letter of 29 August 1990 in Tax Notes 10 September 1990.
[1] For an account of the US procedures see Bunning 1988 and *US v. Lincoln First Bank N.A.* (1980).

on this point (UK Keith Committee 1983, p. 468). The legislation introduced in the Netherlands formalizing information exchange provides for notification to the taxpayer and a right of appeal.[1] However, even in countries which require notification to the taxpayer of a request received, there is no necessity to notify a taxpayer that a request is being made to a foreign authority for information, although a well-informed taxpayer should be aware of this possibility.

The provision of information to a treaty partner spontaneously, without any specific request, has developed rapidly in recent years, especially with the growth of informal bodies such as the Group of Four. Indeed, the OECD/Council of Europe multilateral convention imposes an obligation to provide information without prior request where there are grounds for supposing that there may be a loss of tax in the other state, as well as in other specified circumstances where there may be tax avoidance (Article 7). While this obligation is not easy to enforce, tax authorities have an interest in developing such mutual assistance on a reciprocal basis, and many have established procedures to encourage inspectors in the field to send relevant information to the appointed competent authority, who can decide if onward transmission is appropriate or desirable, taking into account also the extent of reciprocity from the treaty partner in question.

(ii) Safeguards

Although there are significant safeguards limiting information exchange, they are largely at the discretion of the tax administrations concerned. The second paragraph of the model treaty's Article 26 relieves the requested state from complying with a request either if it would reveal any 'trade, business, industrial, commercial or professional secret',[2] or would entail a disclosure which would be contrary to public policy. This does not authorize a refusal on the grounds, for example, of a professional confidentiality rule that would normally be overridden for tax enforcement purposes. However, a company may consider that details of its business if revealed to a foreign tax authority might leak to a competitor. The OECD Commentary cautions against too wide an interpretation of this provision, which could render the information exchange provisions ineffective, and states that additional exclusions could be specified, 'for example, information protected by provisions on bankers' discretion' (OECD 1977, pp. 187f.), although the more recent OECD report on bank secrecy (discussed in section 2.a above) took a stronger line on the inappropriateness of bank secrecy. The obligation is also limited by the 'lowest common denominator' provision, that there is no obligation to carry out administrative measures at variance with the laws of either state, or to supply information not obtainable under the laws of either state. This is normally

---

[1] Law of 24 April 1986: see *European Taxation*, August 1986, p. 262.
[2] Some treaties also explicitly exclude disclosure of any banking secret: e.g. UK–Switzerland, although this exclusion is not present in the US–Swiss treaty.

interpreted to mean that, provided the measures are available under the laws of both states, the requested state must use them if it could do so to enforce its own taxes (OECD 1977, p. 187, and see above). Thus, a state such as France which has broad powers to obtain details of taxpayers' bank accounts will not normally use them in favour of states such as Belgium or Germany which have much more restricted powers in this respect; on the other hand, those measures which both have in common they will take on behalf of the other.[1] However, the European Commission has put forward a potentially far-reaching proposal, which would oblige a member state to provide information even if it would not normally be obtainable for its own tax purposes, in circumstances where the requesting state can show that a significant transfer of funds has taken place without an appropriate tax declaration.[2]

The main safeguard is as to secrecy: the receiving state is normally required to treat the information as secret in the same way as is usual under its laws, but also specifically to limit disclosure to those involved in enforcement of taxes covered by the convention. Under the OECD bilateral model, this permits use of the information in court proceedings, in which case publication might result; but the OECD/Council of Europe multilateral convention allows the sending state to specify that its permission must be sought before such use is made. Some states cannot offer the same degree of confidentiality: for example, tax information has been available to the exchange control authorities in Italy, and this has restricted the information other states are willing to supply. The secrecy obligation also prevents information being passed on by the recipient to a third state; however, the multilateral arrangements do permit this possibility, although only with the permission of the state originally supplying the information.[3]

There is, therefore, considerable variation between states as to the amount and nature of the information they can give and receive. Even where formal powers exist, some administrations in practice provide little information and are very slow to respond to requests; the Netherlands, for example, has cited shortage of staff as a problem, but there have been natural suspicions that its reluctance to respond may be related to the exemptions of income received from abroad which have made Holland a popular centre for conduit holding companies. Other countries have developed a very active programme to amplify mutual assistance. In particular, both the USA and France have made use of tax administration officials attached to embassies abroad to

[1] Although the requested party may be relieved from the obligation under the exceptions, the information may still be supplied on a discretionary basis, and if so it is subject to the same safeguards.
[2] European Commission 1989. Put forward together with the controversial proposal for a minimum withholding tax on interest payments (see Chapter 3, section 2.b above), this strengthening of administrative co-operation attracted less opposition and even some support: see UK House of Lords 1989; nevertheless, it had not been approved by the end of 1990.
[3] OECD/Council of Europe Convention 1988, Article 22(4), Commentary, para. 217; EC Directive, EC Council 1977, Article 7(4).

facilitate co-operation. The US IRS maintains some fourteen Revenue Service Representatives around the world,[1] each office covering several countries in the region of the embassy where they are stationed. Their justification is partly because federal taxes apply to US citizens even if resident abroad;[2] but they have come to play an increasingly important part in the IRS's international tax programme, especially in mediating the mutual assistance provisions in tax treaties. France also has attachés in several countries,[3] and a number of states have an official at their Washington embassy who is in effect a tax attaché. These fiscal attachés may have delegated 'competent authority' powers (although requests are also channel-led through each country's central authority) and they can play an important part in formulating information requests to the best effect, and developing close links with specific offices and individuals in their host countries.

(iii) Information from Havens

A major problem is the lack of availability of information from offshore financial centres and tax havens, especially those acting as base-havens (see Chapter 6 above), which have no incentive to enter into tax treaties. In some cases, semi-tolerated havens have information exchange arrangements with the state on which they are partially dependent. Thus, the UK concluded inter-governmental agreements equivalent to tax treaties in the period 1947–52 with most of its dependent territories, including Guernsey, Jersey and the Isle of Man (see Simon 1983 – Volume F, and Chapter 6 above), which include a provision similar to the usual tax treaty information exchange provision; but this is of limited usefulness in combating the use of tax havens, since as we have seen the British version extends only to information which each side collects for its own tax purposes, while a tax avoider is likely to be a non-resident of the haven and therefore not taxable there. France has more successfully controlled the use of Monaco as a tax haven by a treaty of 18 May 1963 (see Chapter 6 above). This includes much more extensive assistance arrangements: to permit pursuance of transfer-pricing investigations in the territory of the treaty-partner (Article 19); to supply all information obtainable under the laws of the requested state, and routinely to supply information on holdings of

---

[1] RSRs are currently stationed in Bonn, Caracas, London, Manila, Mexico City, Nassau, Ottawa, Paris, Riyadh, Rome, Singapore, Sao Paulo, Sydney and Tokyo. The RSRs participated in foreign investigations of 303 cases in fiscal year 1985, using information available publicly or with the voluntary co-operation of the taxpayer. In that year also, the US made 170 formal requests for information, from 21 treaty-partners: over half (82) were to Canada, and five others received a substantial number of requests; the remaining fifteen received fewer than five each, of which thirteen received fewer than three, and fourteen treaty partners received no requests. In return, the US received 316 requests. See statement of Stephen E. Shay, Acting Treasury International Tax Counsel, to the Oversight Subcommittee of the House Ways and Means Committee, Hearings on the Caribbean Basin Initiative, 25–7 February 1986, p. 155.

[2] Subject to the foreign earned income exemption: see Chapter 5, section 2.a above.

[3] Belgium, Germany, Italy, the UK and the US.

immovable property, turnover declarations by businesses, and payments on securities (Arts. 20–2), as well as to provide support and assistance in tax collection (Art. 23); however, the benefit of these assistance provisions extends only to France.

The Tax Information Exchange treaties which the US has tried to conclude with actual or potential tax haven countries, especially in the Caribbean, are more effective since they include an explicit obligation to provide any information needed to enforce the treaty partner's tax laws, coupled with the enactment of any necessary amendments to bank and commercial secrecy laws. Specific benefits have been offered in return for such agreements, including duty-free entry into the US for certain products, and US tax deductibility of convention expenses (see Chapter 7, section 3 above). By 1990 eight such agreements had been ratified (with Barbados, Bermuda, Dominica, the Dominican Republic, Grenada, Jamaica and Mexico); while three more had been signed but awaited the necessary action by the treaty partner, including appropriate amendments to domestic laws (Costa Rica, St Lucia, Trinidad and Tobago). Clearly, many offshore centres are reluctant to lose the financial business that the ending of secrecy might entail unless more enticing benefits can be offered. In some cases their caution has resulted in safeguards which the US negotiators have accepted: for example, the US–Bermuda treaty of 1988 specifies that a request for information in a non-criminal tax case must be certified by a designated senior official as relevant and necessary, and if it relates to a non-resident of the requested jurisdiction the relevance and necessity must be demonstrated to the satisfaction of the competent authority of the requested state. This could enable Bermuda to impede the provision of information, especially since the US Congress when ratifying the treaty withdrew the concession exempting Bermudan insurance companies from US tax (see Chapter 7, section 3 above).

The network of bilateral information exchange arrangements clearly leaves many loopholes, especially since the obligation on the receiving state to maintain secrecy of the information received prevents transmission to a third state which may have an interest. Thus, for example, the US treaties with Caribbean havens enable provision of information on third-country residents, but information must not be passed on to third-country tax authorities. However, the multilateral arrangements do open up this possibility: both the EC Directive (Article 7.4) and the OECD/Council of Europe Convention (Article 22(4)) permit transmission to a third party, but only with the permission of the supplying state.

The information exchange provision in tax treaties can be used as the basis not only for the supply of specific information relating to the liability of a particular taxpayer, but also for more general discussions. The tax authorities of the OECD countries have found it useful to develop discussions of industries of particular interest to them, on the basis of industry-wide information exchange. These may be on a bilateral basis, or multilateral, as with the working groups of bodies such as the Group of Four (discussed in section 1 above).

The arrangements for information exchange are at the heart of the international co-ordination of tax administration and enforcement. However, their legal basis remains in many respects ambiguous or obscure, while their operation in practice has been cloaked in secrecy. This has made the international efforts to combat tax avoidance and evasion generally vulnerable to attack.[1] Greater openness about these arrangements would remove many of the objections to them and even facilitate their strengthening.

2.c Simultaneous Examination and Co-operation in Assessment

With the development of information exchange has come an increased frequency of co-operation in assessment especially of related entities. The main form this has taken is the development of programmes for simultaneous examination of related taxpayers, usually members of an international corporate group; these programmes are normally bilateral, but can occur between three or even more states, in appropriate cases. By ensuring close co-ordination from an early stage of assessments, such arrangements can avoid potential double taxation, identify avoidance or evasion, and help to co-ordinate policies on the treatment of transfer pricing issues and other matters of common interest.

Simultaneous examination programmes were initiated by the US, the first one with Canada in 1977; by 1990 the US had a dozen in place (with Canada, the United Kingdom, France, Germany, Italy, Japan, Sweden, Australia, the Philippines, Norway, Korea and Mexico). At the same time, some of these countries, notably the other members of the Group of Four (France, Germany and the UK), had also established such arrangements among themselves. The OECD/Council of Europe multilateral convention also provides for simultaneous examination by agreement between pairs of states. However, the information on these arrangements comes mainly from American sources.[2] Their pattern is broadly similar. Each competent authority may propose cases

---

[1] See, for example, Levine 1988, who complains that the French administrative procedures for mutual assistance take the form of an unpublished internal instruction (p. 30), and no data or other information are published on the extent of information exchange; he goes further, and alleges that much of the administrative practice in this area is against the letter or spirit of the law; although he is unable to provide specific justification for many of his allegations, this inability is itself justified by the secretive attitude of the authorities.

[2] The procedures agreed in each case are published in the IRS Manual; in contrast, the British Inland Revenue has been reluctant to discuss simultaneous examination in any detail. A version of the US–UK Arrangement released in the UK in 1978 (Inland Revenue Press Release, 13 March 1978, published in Newman 1980, p. 183) contains several differences with the version in the IRS Manual: notably, the provision requiring the taxpayer to be advised when an examination is being conducted under the simultaneous examination programme and to be supplied with a copy of the Arrangement on request is omitted.

for simultaneous examination, which the other may reject; an acceptance should be indicated in writing, designating the official responsible for the examination. Subjects must be related taxpayers with connected business activities in both countries, and the criteria for selection of cases normally require tax haven activity, indications of non-compliance, and comparability of tax years. Some arrangements specifically mention the identification of bribes, kickbacks and illegal payments as an additional concern (US–Canada and US–Japan).

The officials will initially co-ordinate their plans, identifying issues and setting target dates, and then separately notify the taxpayers that a simultaneous examination is to take place. Each then conducts a parallel examination in its own territory in the normal way. Information is exchanged where appropriate as the examinations proceed, under the tax treaty provision, and subject to its safeguards. Specific information requests are required to be in writing; the officials may meet at the start or at an appropriate point during the examination, but most contacts are by telephone or letter. Primary responsibility for co-ordination is normally taken by the party with the greater interest in the case: this is usually the country where the parent or base company is located, except where that is a third country.

This procedure has many advantages. Since there is initial agreement by both sides, there is far greater assurance that each will supply relevant information. Co-ordination should ensure that decisions, especially on transfer pricing questions, are harmonious, thus avoiding the need for a subsequent corresponding adjustment claim or mutual agreement procedure; hence, the procedure is seen as having significant advantages also for the taxpayer. The main difficulties are the practical problems arising from differences between national procedures: in particular, not only may tax years differ, but one side may already have concluded examination of the taxpayer for a period which the other wishes to examine. Since such detailed examinations are conducted cyclically and often cover a period of several years for each taxpayer, the simultaneous examination arrangements could develop into a longer-term process of co-ordination of the audit or examination programmes of the major home countries of TNCs.

The co-ordination of assessment may also take other forms. Where the differences in procedure are great, but the interest in co-ordination is also substantial, meetings of inspectors concerned with related taxpayers may be arranged, to exchange information although there is no simultaneous examination. There has also been a move to establish arrangements for officials from one state to be present at the examination of a taxpayer in another. There is no reason in principle why this should not occur without any treaty provision or other formal agreement, but national authorities have adopted a cautious view. The simultaneous examination arrangements specifically exclude any presence by one authority at an examination by the other, and stress that examinations are conducted in parallel by each in its own territory. However, the multilateral instruments (the EC Directive of 1977 and the OECD/Council of Europe Convention 1988) both allow states to agree to authorize the presence of an official of one state, on request, at an examination in the other. This was one of the provisions singled out for criticism by opponents of the multilateral convention, but the US government has indicated that it intends to accept this possibility, although it would permit such presence only with the agreement of the taxpayer concerned (US Congress 1990b, p. 15).

3. Co-ordinating Treaty Interpretation and Application

Although tax treaties are agreements between states, they are exceptional in creating legal rights of an economic character for private persons (individuals and companies), and in establishing an international procedure to try to ensure that those rights are implemented. The treaty rules aim to prevent double taxation, and impose an obligation on the state parties to ensure that their domestic law is in line with those rules (see Chapter 11, section 2 below); and individuals and firms must look primarily to domestic legal procedures to vindicate any claims they have to treaty benefits. However, business representatives from the beginning pressed for a more effective guarantee that the principles agreed in the treaty would in practice be applied by each side in a compatible manner, to ensure the prevention of double taxation. They were concerned especially by the rules embodied in the 1935 Allocation Convention, which empowered states to adjust the accounts of enterprises and branches to comply with the independent enterprise standard: already by that time several states were applying stringent provisions to internationally-operating firms to combat what they perceived as diversion of profits abroad (see Chapter 8 above). Despite pressures for a binding procedure to guarantee the prevention of double taxation, especially by ensuring uniform interpretation of the allocation rules,[1] the 1928 and 1935 model treaties contained only a provision that a dispute arising *between the contracting states* which was not resolved by direct contact between them could be submitted 'with a view to an amicable settlement' to a technical body to be set up by the League Council, with the power to give an 'advisory opinion'.[2]

Continuing pressures on behalf of taxpayers, especially business groups, have gradually forced governments to concede procedures entitling taxpayers to a hearing and resolution of any claims they may have that the divergent application or interpretation of a treaty is resulting in double taxation or

[1] The British National Committee of the ICC in its comments on the 1935 convention proposed that rectification of accounts should be binding on the state of domicile and that a technical body should be set up to resolve disputes: PRO file IR40/5703.
[2] Neither this provision, nor the similar suggestion in the Commentary to the OECD model

denial of a treaty benefit. However, officials have continued to maintain the view that since there can be no perfect harmonization of national tax laws, there can be no firm guarantee that all divergences will be eliminated; the claims of taxpayers must depend on national law, and while states will endeavour to resolve conflicts between themselves, they have been reluctant to concede to an international body the power to take a decision which might restrict national tax jurisdiction. The Mexico and London model treaties gave a taxpayer who had proof that double taxation had resulted from the actions of one of the state parties the right to make a claim with the tax authorities of the country of fiscal domicile or nationality (Art. XVII); but such a claim was to be resolved by consultation between the two competent authorities, and the Commentary stressed that this was 'not a judicial procedure' (League of Nations 1946, p. 32).

The reluctance to accept a binding obligation is linked with hesitations about the extent of the duty to ensure that taxation complies with treaty principles. The OECD and UN models extended the applicability of the competent authority procedure beyond claims of double taxation to any 'taxation not in accordance with the provisions of this Convention'. This makes it clearer that the procedure covers not only juridical but also economic double taxation. It also includes cases where there is no double taxation at all: this may occur for example because, although one state may be taxing contrary to the treaty, the income would be exempt in the other state; or a state may make a transfer price adjustment reallocating income which does not increase the profits but merely reduces the losses of a loss-making subsidiary.[1] However, many treaties limit the mutual agreement procedure to the relief of double taxation.

Particular difficulties are caused by the economic double taxation resulting from transfer price adjustments. Many states have not accepted the second paragraph added by the 1977 OECD model to Article 9, which provides that where one state has adjusted transfer prices in accordance with the 'independent enterprise' criterion of that article, the other 'shall make an appropriate adjustment' and the two competent authorities 'shall if necessary consult each other'.[2] Even for states which accept this commitment to make a 'corresponding adjustment', the obligation is flexible, since it applies only if they accept that the adjustment made by their treaty partner 'is justified both in principle and as regards the amount' (Commentary to Article 9, OECD 1977 p. 88). However, the European Community member states have now by agreement

---

treaty (OECD 1977, p. 182) have apparently ever led to such a request: OECD 1984–I, para. 35.
[1] The motive for such an adjustment might be the effect on loss carry-over, on group relief, or on foreign exchange receipts: Jacob 1985.
[2] Seven OECD members (Belgium, Finland, Germany, Italy, Japan, Portugal and Switzerland) reserved the right not to include it in their conventions. Others also have either omitted or modified paragraph 2: e.g. France (Tixier & Gest 1985, pp. 376–7) and the UK (Davies 1985, para. 14.02).

(EC Council 1990c) established a multilateral obligation and a procedure to eliminate double taxation resulting from transfer price adjustments (see (iii) below). On the other hand, states which do not include Article 9(2) may nevertheless accept that economic double taxation resulting from a transfer price adjustment is 'not in accordance with' at least the spirit of the Convention, and that the mutual agreement procedure applies by virtue of Article 25; although some states prefer to treat corresponding adjustments to relieve economic double taxation as discretionary (OECD 1984–I, paras. 73–9). A corresponding adjustment need not take the form of adjustment of the income and tax liability of the related company, but may be done by accepting the increased tax paid as allowable for an increased foreign tax credit.[1] Even where a state accepts an obligation to make corresponding adjustments to income, it would have a further discretion whether to make or accept 'secondary adjustments', to deal with consequential transactions between the enterprises resulting from the allocation of an increased profit to one, for example an increased dividend (OECD 1977, p. 89). Even more complicated situations can arise where the adjustment affects the capital structure of a TNC, as in thin capitalization cases (OECD 1984–I, p. 13), and this also is likely to make allocation cases into bargains over a sum of money rather than precise readjustments of specific prices.

While states have remained reluctant to give private parties direct rights under a tax treaty which could be enforced other than by domestic procedures, they have recently become more willing to consider a provision for arbitration to resolve competent authority cases which cannot be resolved by mutual agreement. The OECD models provided for competent authority cases which could not be resolved by direct communication between the tax administrations concerned to be referred to a 'mixed commission', which allowed for a hearing and an exchange of views, including the right for the taxpayer's views to be put forward; and this has been commonly included in the treaties of some continental European countries, notably France (e.g. France–Brazil 1972, Art. 25). Nevertheless, it is only recently that some states have begun to accept the possibility of a binding procedure, most importantly in the new treaty signed in 1989 by the US and Germany, and the European Community convention for elimination of double taxation in connection with adjustment of profits of related enterprises (EC 1990c: see (iii) below). However, the OECD/Council of Europe multilateral assistance convention contains no such provision, although it does set up a 'co-ordinating body', which may be requested by a state party to give an opinion in interpretation of the convention, although such opinions are intended to be only advisory (Article 24(4) and Commentary).

[1] This seems to have been the preferred method for the UK. Note that allowance of the additional foreign tax for credit may not provide effective relief if the firm concerned already has an excess of foreign tax credit over its domestic tax liability.

3.a Competent Authority Procedure

Competent authorities have the limited obligation under tax treaties to 'endeavour' to resolve problems caused by divergent interpretation or application of the treaty. As the OECD Commentary admits, this is 'not yet entirely satisfactory from the taxpayer's point of view ... because the competent authorities are required only to seek a solution and are not obliged to find one' (OECD 1977, para. 42, p. 182). The only exception is in deciding the residence of an individual: Article 4 of the treaty models lays down successive tests of residence (permanent home; centre of vital interests; habitual abode; nationality), but if all these fail to resolve the matter, Article 4(2)(d) provides that the competent authorities 'shall settle the question by mutual agreement'.[1] This exception is significant for two reasons: first, the treaty specifies fairly precise criteria of residence which should in most cases avoid the necessity for consultation and facilitate resolution if a doubtful case does arise; and second, failure to resolve the issue of residence would entail juridical and not merely economic double taxation.

The general reluctance of tax authorities to accept a binding procedure to resolve disagreements is not just a matter of 'sovereignty' in the abstract, but in the very real sense that double taxation generally results from divergent perspectives between national systems, frequently in relation to treaty principles which are expressed in general terms. This is especially so for economic double taxation, which makes up the bulk of the cases, the resolution of which depends on the provision which is central to the allocation of the tax base of an international business: the independent enterprise or arm's length criterion. On the other hand, allocation issues are more likely to be resolved by compromise in a bargaining procedure, since the issue is not usually of an all-or-nothing nature. It is therefore not surprising that the majority of individual claims of double taxation referred to the mutual agreement procedure between competent authorities are transfer-price adjustment, or 'allocation' cases.

(i) Specific Cases

Tax treaties have long provided for individual cases of double taxation, raised at the taxpayer's initiative[2] to be resolved, if possible, by mutual agreement between the competent authorities concerned. However, use of this procedure has only become substantial since 1970, when the US authorities established procedural rules for taxpayers to invoke competent authority negotiations, as

[1] The US model treaty has an additional paragraph to Article 4 which also states that the competent authorities 'shall' resolve the question of residence where a person other than an individual or a company is a resident of both states.
[2] The taxpayer should take up a claim with the competent authority of its state of residence, or where the claim relates to the non-discrimination provisions, with the state of nationality. Some states consider that the competent authority can take up an individual case even without a complaint by the taxpayer: thus the US procedure specifies that a competent authority negotiation can be initiated without a taxpayer request, 'to protect US economic interests' (Revenue Procedure 82–29, s.2.05).

a means of attempting to resolve some of the problems of double taxation resulting from the closer scrutiny of transfer pricing and the application of the Section 482 Regulations approved in 1968.[1]

Applications to US treaty partners were further encouraged by a ruling in 1976 which denied a US tax credit for foreign taxes paid on income reallocated as US income by the US authorities, unless all practicable administrative remedies had been pursued with the treaty partner for a corresponding adjustment.[2] Despite the publicity and the encouragement to use the procedure given by US officials, taxpayers were nevertheless reluctant to do so in many cases, since they might have a number of reasons for not wishing to reopen assessments already agreed, and to supply new information to the authorities (Cole, Huston & Weiss 1981, p. 257; Competent Authorities 1986, p. 574); especially as most national authorities would not provide any guarantee that they would not raise new issues in the course or as a result of the procedure which might offset any gains from it (Avery Jones et al. 1979, p. 346). On the other hand, the government position is that no guarantee can be provided that all economic double taxation will be relieved via the competent authority procedure, if only because this would mean that manipulation of transfer pricing would be riskless: in fact, the authorities usually reserve the right to refuse relief where there is evidence of fraud or deliberate manipulation (Competent Authorities 1986, pp. 578, 582). Taxpayers, for their part, have been notably reluctant to pursue a procedure which provided no guarantee of resolution, and which was likely to be lengthy: cases have taken from as little as a few months to as much as five years or more, with an average length of some two to three years (Fogarasi et al. 1989, p. 324). Hence there is a substantial gap between potential corresponding adjustment cases (where a transfer price adjustment has taken place) and the actual number of cases taken up formally through the procedure (Coates and Kanakis, in Competent Authorities 1986, p. 602); although no doubt in some cases the related company accounts can be adjusted informally, if its assessment has not yet been finalized (see Chapter 8, section 2 above).

US treaties since the mid-1960s have usually specified the scope of mutual agreement as including:

(a) the attribution of income, deductions, credits or allowances of an enterprise of a contracting state to its Permanent Establishment situated in the other contracting state;
(b) the allocation of income, deductions, credits, or allowances between persons;
(c) the characterization of particular items of income;
(d) the application of source rules with respect to particular items of income;
(e) the meaning of a term (sometimes only if not otherwise defined in the Convention).[3]

[1] See Chapter 8 above; Revenue Procedure 70–18 for allocation cases, now replaced by Rev. Proc. 82–29, was followed by Rev. Proc. 77–16 for non-allocation cases.
[2] Rev. Ruling 76–508: see Cole 1978, pp. 488–94; Cole, Huston & Weiss 1981, p. 250.
[3] See US Model Treaty 1981, which also contains two additional clauses not always included in actual treaties. The US also prefers to include a provision allowing consultation for the elimination of double taxation in cases not provided for in the Convention, but this is not accepted by some states, in particular the UK: see section 3.b below.

The main published systematic statistics on the mutual agreement procedure are compiled by the US IRS, and they do not provide a breakdown by country. In 1989, the IRS received 90 new claims for treaty relief, and 122 cases were concluded; of the 122, 100 were allocation cases. The total dollar value was $432m. In sixteen years from 1971 to 1987, the US competent authority had received over 1,000 cases, of which some 900 had been concluded, 62 per cent with full relief and a further 7 per cent with partial relief from double taxation; 550 of the 900 cases were allocation cases, and of these 67 per cent resulted in full and a further 7 per cent partial relief.[1] A number of reasons are cited for failure to obtain relief, including procedural or legal barriers and withdrawal by the taxpayer (Fogarasi et al. 1989, p. 324). A handful each year are multilateral cases, presumably involving issues such as a requirement by the country of residence of the parent company of a TNC that it apportion headquarters expenses or other overhead costs to its subsidiaries. Other developed countries deal with between ten and 50 cases per year; for example, Canada has about 30 new cases each year with 70–5 cases active; most are with the US, although the majority of them are initiated by Revenue Canada.[2] Thus, mutual agreement cases are exceptional rather than routine, but are nevertheless significant and entail substantial sums. The increased use of other procedures for administrative co-ordination, such as simultaneous examination, would be likely to reduce the need for resolution of conflicts through the mutual agreement procedure; however, this may be counterbalanced by increased use due to disagreements on transfer pricing rules, in particular resulting from the US 'commensurate with income' standard (Chapter 8, section 3.f above).

An example of a failure to resolve a double taxation issue despite resort to the mutual agreement procedure concerned the orchestra conductor Pierre Boulez. Under a contract with CBS Records, Boulez received payments described as 'royalties' in return for setting up and conducting orchestral performances in the US for recording purposes. The payments were declared as taxable income in Germany, where Boulez was resident, since under the US–German treaty 'royalties' were exempt from tax at source. Upon investigation, however, the US authorities considered that the payments were liable to US tax; and this was upheld by the Tax Court, on the grounds that, although the payments were calculated in relation to the volume of record sales, they were not 'royalties' but payments for personal services, since Boulez had no copyright or other property interest in the recordings which he was capable of selling (*Boulez v. Commissioner*, 1984). Although the issue was taken up through the competent authority procedure, there was apparently a failure to agree; furthermore the IRS reopened his returns for previous years, despite

[1] Statistics prepared by the Office of Tax Treaty and Technical Services, Internal Revenue Service, Dept. of the Treasury.
[2] Avery Jones et al. 1979, p. 21; Calderwood 1989, and in Competent Authorities 1986; interview information.

a compromise apparently reached with the IRS Office of International Operations in the course of the procedure, that he would not be pursued for back taxes; the reopening was also upheld by the courts, since the compromise had not been reduced to writing as required by IRS regulations (*Boulez v. Commissioner*, 1987). However, it has been reported that following the US court decision the German authorities allowed a credit for the US tax paid.[1]

As the *Boulez* case illustrates, the mutual agreement procedure raises delicate questions of interaction with domestic tax law. A claim can be brought to the competent authority at any stage, even when the denial of treaty benefits is only anticipated. The OECD Commentary emphasizes that the competent authority is first obliged to consider whether the complaint is justified and whether the taxation complained of is due to a measure taken by that state; if so, it must itself allow the necessary relief (OECD 1977, p. 178). However, revenue services are reluctant to turn the competent authority into an appeal body from decisions of field officers, and may prefer to pursue a case with the treaty partner even if it is not wholly meritorious (Cole et al. 1981, p. 261).

Taxpayers must therefore carefully consider the interaction between their rights to seek review of an assessment under the ordinary national procedures and under the treaty's mutual agreement procedure. There is no requirement that other domestic remedies should have been exhausted prior to making a competent authority claim, so normally both routes can be pursued. Indeed, it may well be preferable to initiate the procedure before the liability is finally fixed under domestic procedures, to allow flexibility in the negotiations, since it may be easier to reach agreement if there is scope for concession (ibid., pp. 265–6); although in some states it is possible for the competent authority to reach an agreement which has the effect of varying a court decision.[2] Generally, it is best to lodge a domestic appeal in order to safeguard domestic legal rights, while agreeing to a suspension pending the outcome of the competent authority claim; then the taxpayer must decide whether to accept the mutual agreement decision, and if so, withdraw or modify the domestic claim.

Equally, it is important that the tax authorities themselves should ensure that when a decision is being contemplated which may have treaty implications, they notify the taxpayer as soon as possible so that the competent authority procedure may be invoked.[3] In addition to ensuring that flexibility is retained for any compromise which may be necessary in the negotiation, early

---

[1] Goldberg 1986, p. 8. The point is now covered by Art. 12 of the Protocol of the new US–German treaty signed in 1989, which requires a copyrightable interest.

[2] This appears to be possible in Sweden, Switzerland, Japan, the Netherlands, Belgium and Germany: Avery Jones et al. 1979, p. 341. Under British law a competent authority agreement could not overrule or bind a court, although it may influence the court's decision; see *IRC v. Commerzbank* (1990) discussed below. In accordance with this view, the Inland Revenue has invoked Art. 7(3) of the EC Agreement (EC Council 1990c): see section (iii) below.

[3] The procedure must be invoked within three years of first notification of the decision being objected to: model treaty Article 25(1).

notification would help to avoid the difficult procedural problem that the treaty partner state may be unable to grant relief because the limitation period has ended on its related assessment. Although Article 25(2) of the models provides that an agreement reached through the procedure shall be implemented regardless of time-limits in domestic law, not all states are willing to accept this.[1] Early notification of a contemplated decision may also be feared to create unnecessary work (OECD 1984–I, paras. 87–9).

(ii) Advance Approval for Transfer Prices

A further development of the mutual agreement procedure was proposed by the US to its treaty partners in 1990, resulting from its intention to introduce a procedure that would allow companies to obtain advanced approval for their transfer pricing methodology. The proposals for advance rulings on the transfer pricing methodology of TNCs was cautiously welcomed by specialists, although it was likely that only the largest firms would consider it desirable to enter into what would in effect be an advanced audit.[2] The intention of the US authorities that it might also in appropriate cases entail an advance competent authority procedure, perhaps even on a multilateral basis, is ambitious. A full international advance agreement would only be possible between authorities with the power under domestic law to enter into such agreements. However, the taxpayer would in any case have the option, if an advance ruling by one state seemed to raise a potential treaty issue, of deciding whether to raise it through the competent authority procedure.

(iii) Procedural Rights and Arbitration

The major controversy surrounding the competent authority individual case procedure has been the limitation of the taxpayer's procedural and substantive rights, in the name of national fiscal sovereignty. Since the mutual agreement procedure is essentially a negotiation between national state officials, the taxpayer has no right to be present (OECD 1984–I paras. 96–8), and is confined to presenting the facts and arguments beforehand to the appropriate competent authority, which sometimes results in complaints that the agreement has been reached on the basis of an erroneous understanding of the issue (Goldberg 1986, p. 13). The negotiations are normally conducted by correspondence, although in appropriate cases oral discussions may be held, if

---

[1] It would entail an exception to domestic time-limits only for claims which benefit the taxpayer; where however domestic time-limits are long (e.g. six years in the UK) and interpreted flexibly, the problem may not be so acute in practice: Avery Jones et al. 1979, p. 343; Cole et al. 1981, pp. 265–8.

[2] Revenue Procedure 91–22. The draft procedure was unofficially published in Tax Notes, 4 June 1990, pp. 1151 and 1185. The procedure was originally designated an 'advanced determination ruling', but later renamed 'advanced pricing agreement', apparently to prevent disclosure under the Freedom of Information Act. Although the IRS intends that the details of agreements, including documentation submitted by the taxpayer, will be treated as confidential tax return information, it is not clear whether this position will be upheld: see Tax Notes, 6 May 1991.

necessary face-to-face; those states which maintain a fiscal attaché or revenue service representative in their embassy in the treaty partner country may make use of such offices to speed the procedure. Some states provide for the possibility of a mixed commission, where there has been a failure to reach a negotiated settlement; this is usually a more formal procedure and there may be provision for the taxpayer or a representative to appear before the commission.[1]

The emphasis on the character of the mutual agreement procedure as a negotiation between the tax authorities creates suspicions that cases may not be dealt with individually and on their merits by the application of agreed rules or principles, but expeditiously, by bargaining, which may even lead to 'package deals'; the OECD Committee denied that this was the case, but formally stated that each case should be dealt with 'without reference to any balance of the results in other cases' (OECD 1984–I, para. 105). In most countries also, the outcome of specific case mutual agreements is not published, except by notification to the taxpayer (Avery Jones et al. 1979, pp. 345–6). These secret decisions add to the arcana of international tax a further body of practice known only to the practitioners and officials directly involved, and therefore unavailable to guide others, or to undergo public scrutiny (Avery Jones et al. 1979, p. 336).

For these reasons, there have been considerable pressures, dating back to the 1930s, for the introduction of a more judicial procedure. The primary concern of the business representatives who have pressed for such a procedure has been to ensure the certainty of a decision and a reduction of delay (OECD 1984–I, para. 42). Other considerations, in particular the improvement of the legitimacy of allocation decisions by the use of more open and rule-oriented procedures, have been less prominent. The tax authorities have generally resisted any move towards compulsory arbitration, since it would involve treating the treaty provisions as rights enforceable by private parties and overriding other provisions of domestic law. The OECD Committee stated flatly that 'the setting up of such a scheme would involve an unprecedented surrender of fiscal sovereignty' which some members would therefore find quite unacceptable; and it did not consider that existing arrangements were so unsatisfactory that such a radical innovation was required (OECD 1984–I, paras. 55–6). More recently, however, there has been some willingness to make concessions on this point, due perhaps to the continued dissatisfaction expressed by business lobbyists about the lack of fairness in international tax administration generally, notably in the opposition to the OECD/Council of Europe multilateral convention.

The main new initiatives have been the inclusion of an arbitration provision in the new US–German bilateral treaty signed in August 1989; and the

[1] The French procedure provides for a Mixed Commission if necessary: see Ruling 14 F-1-86 of 4 March 1986 discussed in a Note in European Taxation, May 1986, p. 153.

approval by the EC member states in July 1990 of a long-standing proposal for arbitration of transfer price adjustment disputes. The latter was first put forward by the European Commission as a draft Directive in 1976 (EC Commission 1976), and finally agreed in 1990 as a convention between EC member states (EC Council 1990c). During the long period while it remained unapproved, the existence of the proposal nevertheless influenced the debate, and the establishment of the multilateral treaty must now have considerable effects on the practice and procedure of corresponding adjustments.

The US–German provision is rather limited, although it certainly goes beyond what the US negotiators in particular have been willing to concede until now. The mutual agreement article of this treaty provides that 'when it seems advisable in order to reach agreement' the competent authorities shall have an oral exchange of opinions through a commission consisting of official representatives; it further stresses that disagreements regarding interpretation of the convention shall as far as possible be settled by competent authorities, but that if this is not possible a disagreement 'may, if both competent authorities agree, be submitted for arbitration'. The Exchange of Notes which provides details of the arbitration arrangements further specifies that arbitration will not normally be used where tax policy or domestic tax law are concerned, and will only be resorted to after fully exhausting all other procedures, and provided that the taxpayers concerned consent and agree to be bound by the outcome. However, taxpayers are given the right to be represented before the arbitration board, and the decision, which must be provided with an explanation, is to be binding in that case, and should be taken into account in other appropriate cases, especially those involving the same taxpayer and substantially similar facts. It has been pointed out that a similar arbitration procedure is provided in agreements on Social Security 'totalization', but seems to have been rarely, if ever, used (Fogarasi et al. 1989, p. 322). An alternative put forward by tax practitioners is for cases which prove hard to resolve to be referred to a panel drawn from very senior officials of each state; and this could be modified in the direction of the arbitration procedure by including an official from a third state to chair the panel (ibid., p. 324). This proposal aims to ensure resolution of cases, by involving officials sufficiently senior to decide policy questions; but the reluctance to allow an international procedure to override domestic sovereignty cannot be overcome by giving greater power to administrators, however senior: it requires principles and procedures of allocation that can command public acceptance and legitimacy.

The European Community agreement[1] goes much further, although it applies only to transfer price corresponding adjustment or 'allocation' cases, and only in relation to income and corporate income taxes. It therefore begins

---

[1] It is embodied in a treaty between the member states concluded for an initial period of five years in 1990, and due to come into effect two months after all signatories have ratified: EC Council 1990c.

by binding the parties to apply the independent enterprise/arm's length rule, in virtually identical terms to those of articles 7(2) and 9(1) of the OECD model (EC 1990c, Article 4). Where an enterprise considers that these principles have not been observed, it may present the case to its competent authority, which must try to resolve the matter by mutual agreement with any other authority concerned, if it is not itself able to arrive at a satisfactory solution. The competent authority is obliged to reach a decision eliminating the double taxation,[1] subject to three exceptions. First, it is not obliged to take up a case which it does not consider is 'well-founded' (Art. 6(2)). Significantly, since this arrangement was agreed in the form of a treaty between the member states and not as a Directive as originally proposed by the Commission, a decision not to take up a case because it is not considered 'well-founded' might be subject to review by the domestic courts of the state concerned, but not by the European Court of Justice.[2] Second, there is no obligation to initiate the procedure in cases where one of the enterprises concerned has been subjected to a 'serious penalty' by a final ruling in legal or administrative proceedings.[3] The competent authorities are obliged to reach an agreement eliminating the double taxation within two years, failing which they must set up an Advisory Commission, with the help of which the case must be resolved within one further year: six months is allowed for the Commission to deliver its opinion, and a further six months for the authorities to resolve the case. Although they may reach an agreement deviating from the opinion, they must comply with it if they fail to agree (Art. 12). However, there is a third exception (Article 7(3)) which allows exemption from the obligation to set up a commission on the grounds that the domestic law of the state does not permit a competent authority decision to override a court judgment, unless the complainant enterprise has withdrawn any domestic appeal or allowed any applicable time limit to expire. In effect, this allows the enterprise to pursue domestic remedies as well as the mutual agreement procedure (in the normal way) for up to two years, but then requires it to choose between the advisory commission and its domestic remedies; both France and the UK have stated that this provision applies in their cases.

The Advisory Commission consists of two representatives of each competent authority, plus an even number of 'independent persons of standing' chosen by agreement from a list (consisting of five nominees from each member state); these members shall then choose a further person from this list[4] to chair the Commission. The enterprises concerned may (and must if any

---

[1] Under Article 14 this can be done either by allocating the profit so that it is taxable in one state only, or by allowing a full tax credit.

[2] Unlike other treaties between the member states concluded under Article 220 of the Rome Treaty, this convention does not contain a provision giving jurisdiction to the ECJ.

[3] Article 8. What constitutes a 'serious penalty' is variously defined for each state in appended declarations: it generally involves either intentionally or negligently falsifying records or failing to maintain proper accounts.

[4] Who is also required to 'possess the qualifications required for appointment to the highest judicial offices in his country or be a jurisconsult of recognised competence': Art. 9(5).

one of them wishes to) appear or be represented before the Commission. Decisions of the Commission must be based on the independent enterprise criterion as stated in Article 4; may be taken by majority; and may be published, but only by agreement of the competent authorities and subject to the consent of the enterprises concerned. Otherwise, there is a strict obligation on the members of the Commission to keep secret all matters related to its proceedings.

This agreement has gone some way to meet both the two main objectives of the lobbyists, of greater certainty of outcome and reduction of delay. It is less clear that the procedure will provide the improved procedural and substantive due process which is necessary to overcome the sovereignty problem. This would require a stronger combined approach within the Community, for example by activating the provisions of Article 10 of the mutual assistance Directive (EC Council 1977) and drawing up detailed rules on transfer pricing which, together with the publication of decisions of the Advisory Commission, would provide an explicit body of rules which could both command public acceptance and guide those concerned with planning transactions. Alternatively, a more comprehensive solution might be found, by moving to a common definition of the tax base and a system for allocation of profits more akin to formula apportionment.[1]

3.b Treaty Interpretation by Mutual Agreement

Tax treaties have also long included a very general power for the competent authorities to consult together and resolve by agreement problems relating to the convention. The League treaties referred to the taking of required measures in accordance with the spirit of the convention, particularly in cases not explicitly provided for and in the event of substantial changes in the tax laws of either party (League of Nations 1946, pp. 70–1). The OECD model separated this provision into two sentences, the first referring to resolution of 'difficulties or doubts as to the interpretation or application of the convention'; and second adding also 'the elimination of double taxation in cases not provided for in the convention'. In practice, however, the second sentence has frequently been omitted in negotiated treaties (Avery Jones 1979, Pt. II, pp. 14–15), undoubtedly due to the difficulty of obtaining legislative approval for giving tax authorities such a broad discretionary power under domestic law to go beyond the treaty in undefined circumstances.[2]

---

[1] A Committee was set up in December 1990 by Mrs Scrivener, the Commissioner responsible for taxation, to report within a year on whether the Community should prioritize harmonization of direct corporate taxation, and whether to focus on the tax base or rates of tax: see Chapter 3, section 2.b above.

[2] UK practice excludes this second sentence, although remarkably it was included in the 1968 treaty with Luxembourg. In practice it is not always easy to establish whether an agreement is interpretative of the treaty or goes beyond it (the latter is sometimes referred to as a 'legislative' interpretation). Avery Jones et al. (1979, pp. 16–17) could find only two examples

The treaty interpretation provision raises once again some delicate issues of interaction between international and domestic law. From its history, it is clear that it was intended as a means of ensuring that the co-ordination of taxation established by a bilateral treaty should be a continuing matter, so that the treaty provisions should not be outdated or negated by subsequent developments or unforeseen issues or cases. However, as the OECD Commentary acknowledged (OECD 1977, p. 181), the right to interpret treaties under domestic law is often given to other authorities, normally the courts, sometimes exclusively. It may nevertheless be possible for the treaty as incorporated into domestic law to give a power to the competent authority to give authoritative interpretations. The extent to which this is possible will depend on the constitutional law and practice of each state, as well as the extent of the power given to the competent authority. In France, treaties are conceded by courts to be 'actes du gouvernement', which in principle requires courts to refer a term requiring interpretation to the Minister of Foreign Affairs; also, if a competent authority interpretative agreement is published as a treaty in the Official Journal, it would be binding on the courts.[1]

Generally, since treaties are part of domestic law either automatically or by enactment, their interpretation is ultimately a matter for the courts. Although it is unlikely in most cases that the jurisdiction of the courts to interpret the treaty would be ousted, the courts may themselves take into account an interpretative agreement reached by the appropriate administrative authorities. US courts normally give great weight to competent authority interpretative agreements. Thus, in *Great-West Life Assurance Co. v. US* (1982), the Court of Claims accepted an interpretation by the US and Canadian competent authorities of a treaty provision, holding that 'the meaning given a treaty by an appropriate government and government agency is of great weight' (p. 189); and in *Xerox Corp. v. US* (1988), referring to an agreement between the US and UK competent authorities, it said 'Courts have traditionally been reluctant to impinge on the judgments of competent authorities charged by the treaty states with responsibilities of interpretation and implementation'.

of 'legislative' rather than 'interpretative' agreements, and even these could be regarded as providing interpretations. Thus, an agreement between the Netherlands and Germany that diplomats should be regarded as resident in their country of origin rather than that of accreditation is described by Avery Jones et al. as clearly legislative, since it added an exception for diplomats to the normal residence rule; however, the usual residence article defines as a resident anyone liable to tax in a state by reason of domicile or residence, and if diplomats are not normally regarded as liable to tax in a state it seems possible to regard as interpretative an agreement which makes this explicit in the specific case. It is also doubtful that, even where the second sentence is included, the competent authorities would have authority under their own domestic laws to conclude 'legislative' mutual agreements: see Osgood 1984, pp. 266–7.

[1] There has however been a trend towards reviewability under the 'recours pour excès de pouvoir', especially where the treaty provisions have been incorporated into domestic law giving private rights: see Long et al. 1978, pp. 19–20. See also Chapter 11, section 2.a(i) below.

On the other hand, in a subsequent British case (*IRC v. Commerzbank*, 1990), Mummery, J. held that the position in the UK was different, and he gave very little weight to a joint statement issued by the two competent authorities acting under the mutual agreement procedure.

> [T]his joint statement has no authority in the English Courts. It expresses the official view of the Revenue authorities of the two countries. That view may be right or wrong. Although [the mutual agreement article] authorises the competent authorities to communicate with each other directly to implement the provisions of the convention and 'to assure its consistent interpretation and application' it does not confer any binding or authoritative effect on the views or statements of the competent authorities in the English Courts.

Indeed, he went so far as to say that the statement did 'not fall within the description of material to which recourse may be had as an aid to interpretation' of the treaty. This rather extreme statement resulted from the Revenue's difficulty in that case: although the competent authorities' statement reflected what must have been the intention of the drafters of the provision, it was contrary to its clear wording. Another factor was that the mutual agreement provision in question was more limited than usual, only authorizing liaison between the competent authorities in order to 'assure consistent interpretation', while the model treaty provision authorizes them to 'resolve' difficulties or doubts. In particular, the power given to competent authorities in individual cases to 'resolve the case by mutual agreement' could be argued to carry sufficient weight to put the court into the position of reviewing the reasonableness of the competent authorities' view rather than deciding the issue *ab initio*.[1]

Despite the ambiguous legal status of the mutual agreement interpretation provision, it provides an important basis for continuing consultation between the tax authorities, to ensure that the treaty provisions remain relevant and functional. An interpretative agreement between competent authorities may take various forms, involving different degrees of formality both in international and domestic law. At the highest level, it might be embodied in an Exchange of Notes through diplomatic channels, thus becoming a binding protocol to the treaty, which would usually be incorporated into domestic law. More frequently, such agreements take the form of an exchange of letters directly between the tax administrations concerned.[2] Since such agreements are concluded by officials or departments of the central government empowered by the state for the purpose, they must be considered as binding in international law, unless and until subsequently renegotiated or denounced;[3]

---

[1] See generally Avery Jones et al. 1979, p. 346ff.

[2] For an example, see a Norway–Switzerland agreement that offshore areas are not within the territorial scope of the treaty, discussed in Oliver 1990, who argues that it is a 'legislative' mutual agreement.

[3] The Vienna Convention on the Law of Treaties defines as a treaty any written agreement even if contained in more than one instrument (such as an exchange of notes) made by officials with power to represent the state: see also McNair 1961, pp. 15–20. Although the requirement

but in domestic law such agreements may be regarded as incapable of overriding rights created in the treaty itself and incorporated into domestic law.[1] At the lowest level, the interpretation may be expressed in such a way as to be no more than a statement of intention between the administrative authorities, and therefore not binding in international law; while domestically it may take the form of an internal administrative memorandum or circular, frequently unpublished. This would normally have little legal status (for example, would not prevent the administration subsequently taking a different view), and is only a statement of intent or goodwill to the treaty partner. There is no regular form or practice about publication of interpretative agreements, which may range from a press release to an administrative regulation. Regrettably often, information about an agreement emerges unofficially, or official publication takes place in only one state, although this may lead to unofficial publication in the other.[2] In the US such agreements are normally published as Revenue Rulings.

The legal effect of such formally acknowledged agreements on the private rights of parties is a matter of the interaction of international and domestic administrative law. As stated above, a court would normally give some weight to an agreement, although it would not be likely to allow an administrative decision to override a right clearly conferred by a treaty which has been incorporated into domestic law. Also, the administrative authorities may also subsequently wish to change their policy and interpretation. Where the interpretation has clearly taken the form of an agreement rather than a statement of intention, then such a change should entail renegotiation with the treaty partner, or in extreme cases denunciation of the prior agreement. In domestic law, even if the agreement had been published as an administrative regulation or ruling, it may be regarded as merely subsidiary legislation and thus not prevent a contrary position being taken on the governing wording of the treaty or a tax statute; although as a matter of practice, the administration is unlikely to do so save in exceptional circumstances. In some countries, however, an administrative ruling may be binding on the administration.[3]

of an 'agreement' is normally taken to exclude statements of intention or political desirability (such as a communiqué after a summit meeting), it includes an informal agreement such as an exchange of notes or 'memorandum of understanding': see Commentary on the Vienna Convention by the International Law Commission, UN 1966, p. 21. Article 53 of the Vienna Convention permits denunciation of a treaty only if it is established that the parties intended to admit the possibility; since most tax treaties allow termination, usually on six months' notice, it may be presumed that a competent authority mutual agreement is subject to the same notice.

[1] Nevertheless, a domestic court should have regard to such an agreement if it becomes relevant to interpreting an issue before it, and attempt as far as possible to ensure that domestic law is interpreted harmoniously with the international obligations of the state. British courts have been strongly criticized for their failure to give sufficient importance to treaties which have not been incorporated into domestic law: Mann 1986, p. 94.

[2] See the examples listed in Avery Jones et al. 1979, Pt. II, pp. 22–7; virtually all the agreements uncovered by this group of authors seem to have been published in only one of the states, implying that many other agreements must remain unpublished.

[3] This is apparently so in Germany, Belgium, Switzerland and the Netherlands: Avery Jones et al. 1979, p. 352.

The uncertainty surrounding mutual agreements is clearly greatly exacerbated by the haphazard and negative approach to their publication. It is perhaps because they prefer to preserve their freedom of manoeuvre towards taxpayers that tax authorities are so often coy about publishing such agreements. This is a short-sighted view since, as has been repeatedly shown already in this chapter, the lack of openness and due process in international tax administration is a serious hindrance to resolution of many of the substantive problems of international taxation. A more systematic process for regularizing mutual agreement procedures might emerge from the multilateral arrangements, the OECD/Council of Europe multilateral convention and the EC Convention on Elimination of Double Taxation. Thus, the former convention requires parties to notify any interpretative agreements to the Co-ordinating Body, and both these agreements and any advisory opinions rendered by the Co-ordinating Body are to be circulated for information to the state signatories (whether or not they have yet ratified the convention) as part of the role of the Co-ordinating Body to 'encourage the production of uniform solutions' (Commentary, para. 243). Regrettably however, the convention contains no explicit provision for the publication either of agreements or of advisory opinions; and as has been mentioned above, the opinions of the Advisory Commission under the EC Convention are to be published only if all the state and private parties agree.

4. Assistance in Collection

States have been very cautious in the development of arrangements for mutual assistance in the collection of tax. A substantial proportion of the early tax treaties included provisions for such assistance, and there is some evidence that assistance was also provided informally (Surr 1966, p. 221). In the 1980s, following the growing concern about international avoidance and evasion, the issue has been given more attention but has also been controversial, and such arrangements still remain confined to a few states, or to limited circumstances.

4.a General International Law

In general international law, co-operation in the enforcement of fiscal laws has been treated anomalously. On the one hand, courts have frequently taken the firm position that they cannot assist in the enforcement of the revenue laws of another state: this can best be explained as part of the general international law principle that states do not enforce each other's penal or public laws. On the other hand, arrangements for international co-operation in penal or criminal matters, notably for the extradition of alleged offenders, normally exclude fiscal matters, even tax fraud. Hence, in the absence of specific treaty provisions, tax authorities may have little remedy against even a blatant tax evader who is neither present nor has assets in their country; yet governments have proved reluctant to enter into such agreements.

There is nevertheless surprisingly little direct authority for the principle that a court will not enforce the judgment of a court of a foreign state in a tax matter. Consideration of the question often, misleadingly, begins by citing the dictum of Lord Mansfield: 'For no country ever takes notice of the revenue laws of another'.[1] The statement was made in the context of the assertion of the principle that a private contract will be enforced even if it may entail breach of a foreign revenue law; a different view would have provided a convenient exemption from contractual liability for purchasers in an era of high tariffs and widespread smuggling.

Nearly two centuries later, it was applied in quite different circumstances in *Govt. of India v. Taylor* (1955). This case concerned a company incorporated in the UK in 1906, which had conducted an electricity supply and tramway business in Delhi under licence to the municipality, until its business was bought by the government of India in 1947; the purchase payment was immediately remitted to England, only a few weeks before an Act was passed in India imposing a capital gains tax on any sale of a capital asset effected after 31 March 1946. The company went into voluntary liquidation under English law, but the English courts (culminating in some judgments of mixed quality in the House of Lords) held that the Indian government's claim was not a 'liability' which the liquidator was bound to discharge under the Companies Act, since it could not have been enforced in an English court, being essentially a tax claim. The court also cited with approval an unreported contemporaneous decision of an Irish court[2] rejecting the claim of the liquidator of a company against its former main director and 99 per cent shareholder, who had transferred its assets to his Irish bank accounts and had himself left for Ireland, on the grounds that the sole remaining creditor was the Revenue, and although the claim was by the liquidator and for fraud, to enforce it would be indirectly to enforce a Revenue claim. It seems hard to understand how Lord Mansfield's principle, designed to prevent breach of a foreign revenue law from defeating otherwise valid private rights, could be used to justify a refusal to enforce private law because it would entail an indirect enforcement of a foreign revenue claim (Mann 1954; Mann 1955). However, in the more recent case *In re State of Norway's Application* (1990) the British courts did not regard assistance to a foreign revenue authority (to provide evidence in civil proceedings involving a tax claim) as entailing breach of such a strong taboo (see section 2.b above).

In the United States the issue has been more directly considered in a 1979

---

[1] *Holman v. Johnson* (1775) 98 E.R. 1120; see also citations in *Govt. of India v. Taylor* (1955) A.C. 491, at p. 504. Despite criticism of the 'slavish repetition' by others of Lord Mansfield's dictum (Albrecht 1953, p. 461), it has become embedded in the legal subconscious and has come to stand for a far different principle from that intended by its original source.

[2] *Peter Buchanan Ltd v. McVey* (1955). So impressed was the House of Lords with this case that the Irish judgment was then published in the English Law Reports.

case, which seems to be the first time a direct claim has been made by a foreign state to enforce a tax claim in a US court.[1] The court cited with approval the rationale given by Judge Learned Hand for the revenue rule:

> To pass upon the provisions for the public order of another state is, or at any rate should be, beyond the powers of a court; it involves the relations between the states themselves, with which courts are incompetent to deal, and which are intrusted to other authorities. It may commit the domestic state to a position which would seriously embarrass its neighbor. Revenue laws fall within the same reasoning; they affect a state in matters as vital to its existence as its criminal laws. No court ought to undertake an inquiry which it cannot prosecute without determining whether those laws are consonant with its own notions of what is proper.[2]

This reasoning was originally used to justify the non-enforcement of tax claims between US states, a principle subsequently overturned by reference to the 'full faith and credit' clause of the US Constitution (*Milwaukee County v. White Co.*, 1935), and the 1979 court argued there is no similar 'full faith and credit' obligation in international law. The US court might have been willing to accept such an obligation, but for lack of reciprocity on the Canadian side, since in a previous decision the Canadian courts had refused to enforce a US court judgment against a tax fugitive, citing the same reasoning of Judge Learned Hand.[3]

Although the reasoning in these cases is not always sound, and there is little justification for the very wide assertion often made that no case will be entertained which even indirectly entails enforcement of a foreign revenue claim, it seems clear that any arrangements for direct international recovery of taxes must be established by agreement between states.

4.b Treaty Provisions

The reluctance of states to enter into treaty arrangements for recovery of taxes is explicable by the political delicacy of measures to enforce taxation, as well as by the anomalous nature of a tax claim. Tax fraud or evasion is not normally included in international arrangements for extradition or other forms of judicial assistance in criminal cases.[4] Despite the language in statements such as Learned Hand's cited above, a tax liability more closely resembles a civil judgment and could be considered enforceable subject to the usual exception

---

[1] *H.M. The Queen ex rel. Province of British Columbia v. Gilbertson* (1979).
[2] *Moore v. Mitchell* (1929), p. 604. See however the criticism of Learned Hand's reasoning in Mann 1954, pp. 470–1.
[3] *United States v. Harden* (1963), where the Canadian court had itself quoted in explanation the same reasoning of Judge Learned Hand.
[4] However, the Council of Europe conventions for both Extradition and Criminal Judicial Assistance may be extended to fiscal offences by those states which accept the relevant Protocols, European Treaty Series Nos. 98 and 99, adopted in 1978. The Convention on Information and Assistance in Administrative Matters (ETS No. 100) also does not apply to

in cases where such a judgment conflicts with the public policy of the requested state. However, tax judgments have also been commonly excluded from arrangements for mutual enforcement of civil judgments, partly for the political reasons already cited, and partly because a tax liability is often enforced by administrative means rather than as an ordinary civil judgment.

Nevertheless, there are no substantial legal obstacles to the establishment of arrangements for mutual assistance in tax recovery. Their political accept-ability should be facilitated by their inclusion in double taxation treaties, to provide more effective enforcement of tax liability as a quid pro quo for treaty benefits.[1] In practice, however, they have only been concluded between states with especially close relations. The main postwar provisions are: the agreement between Belgium, the Netherlands and Luxembourg in 1952 concluded as part of the establishment of the Benelux economic union; the 1954 treaty between Austria and Germany for legal protection and assistance in tax matters; the provisions in French tax treaties with the francophonic African states (Tixier and Gest 1985, paras. 434–9). The Nordic countries have, since the early 1940s, agreed bilateral collection arrangements, and this culminated in the multilateral convention of 1972 for mutual administrative assistance in tax matters, including collection, between Denmark, Finland, Iceland, Norway and Sweden. A provision for general assistance in recovery was included in some of the first postwar US tax treaties, but when the US Senate indicated its opposition to this provision and deleted it from the proposed treaties with Greece and South Africa in 1951, it was omitted from later treaties; however, the provision remains in the US treaties with France, Denmark, the Netherlands and Sweden.[2] The UK does not seem ever to have negotiated a collection provision.[3] Following the increasing concern with international avoidance and evasion, the OECD committee drew up a

fiscal matters except for those states which on ratification declare that it does, and which may make this subject to reciprocity: Article 1.

[1] This point was made by the then Second Legal Advisor to the UK Foreign Office, Eric Beckett, in a memorandum of 12 April 1943 to the Treasury (PRO file IR40/7463), as part of the campaign to change British policy to international double taxation arrangements, leading to the US–UK treaty of 1945: see Chapter 2, section 1 above. Nevertheless, the US–UK treaty did not contain a recovery assistance clause, and nor had the previous US–Canada treaty of 1942, although the US Treasury gave evidence to the Congress in 1947 that both countries had indicated a willingness to agree to enforcement provisions at such future time as local considerations would permit: see Note 1950, p. 493, fn. 13 and sources there cited.
[2] Abrutyn & Halphen 1984, p. A–45ff. The Netherlands treaty, including the recovery provision, was extended to the Netherlands Antilles, but this has now been abrogated: see Chapter 7 above. The provisions for general assistance in recovery were never adequately activated (see Note 1950); but the US IRS has been more interested in the more limited arrangements for recovery in connection with anti-abuse: see below.
[3] As recounted in Chapter 5, section 1.a above, an attempt was made in 1928 to introduce a provision into British law for enforcement of revenue claims within the British Empire, as a measure against international avoidance; when this failed due to political opposition, no subsequent attempt seems to have made to reintroduce such a provision. In the negotiation of the path-breaking US treaty in 1944–5, the Inland Revenue took the view that the collection

comprehensive model recovery treaty with a Commentary (OECD 1981); and the 1988 OECD/Council of Europe multilateral convention includes a section on recovery.[1] Nevertheless, there has not been any major new movement to participate in such arrangements; due to the orchestrated opposition to the 1988 multilateral convention (discussed above, section 1), even France and the US, which have indicated that they will ratify the remainder of this convention, have excluded the recovery provisions (US Congress 1990b).

Essentially, agreement for assistance in recovery obliges the requested state to use the methods available to it for enforcement, treating the foreign tax claim as if it were its own; except that time-limits are governed by the applicant state's law, and the requested state is not obliged to give the foreign tax claim priority over other creditors.[2] The requested state may refuse if (i) the applicant state has not exhausted the means available within its own territory, unless to do so would entail disproportionate difficulty; (ii) the taxation involved is contrary to international principles or those applicable by treaty between the states concerned; or (iii) to do so would conflict with its public policy. There are two basic safeguards for the taxpayer.[3] First, the liability must have been determined: it is a requirement that the claim must be the subject of an instrument which enables its enforcement; hence, it must be a properly assessed and not a provisional claim. Second, it must be no longer contestable, in other words all appeals must have been exhausted or be out of time; the 1988 multilateral treaty allows an 'uncontested' claim to be enforced provided the taxpayer is a resident of the applicant state: although it would be difficult for the applicant state to show that the claim was uncontested if it were still contestable, there is an obligation to refund any money recovered if the taxpayer subsequently wins an appeal. The requirement that all potential appeals be exhausted could pose a serious limitation, although states may by agreement relax it. It may also be mitigated by the obligation to take conservancy measures for a claim which is not yet finalized; however, the extent to which states are able or may be willing to freeze assets in respect of contested foreign tax claims may be limited.[4] Given these safeguards, there

provision should be omitted, because it would set a precedent for other treaties: see Chapter 2, section 1.a above.
[1] This is essentially a redraft of the OECD 1981 model text, with a commentary largely based on the 1981 commentary in relation to the key principles and provisions.
[2] In many states tax claims rank ahead of most other unsecured creditors, but it is thought unfair to give a foreign tax claim such priority over local creditors: OECD 1981, p. 42.
[3] A third protection which was included in the League models and bilateral treaties excluded assistance if the taxpayer were a citizen of the requested state: in drafting the 1981 model the OECD Committee observed that 'most OECD member countries no longer consider it necessary to refuse assistance in respect of taxes due by their nationals'; the nationality clause is being eliminated in bilateral treaties, having been dropped for example from the more recent French treaties with Algeria (1982) and Madagascar (1983): see Tixier & Gest 1985, p. 453.
[4] Conservancy is apparently not possible in the USA, although provisions for it are included in two US treaties; the US has indicated in reservations to the 1981 OECD model that for constitutional reasons administrative measures cannot be used for collection of a foreign

seems no strong objection to the development on a more widespread basis of arrangements providing for assistance in recovery, although by their nature such procedures are likely to be relatively infrequently used.

More limited provisions for assistance in recovery, designed to prevent the obtaining of treaty benefits by persons regarded as ineligible, have been more actively and even routinely used and included in bilateral treaties. Where dividends or other payments are made to a treaty country, it may not be possible to establish whether the payment is being made to a person genuinely eligible for a reduced withholding tax, for example if the payment is made to a bank which may be acting as nominee for a non-resident (see Chapter 7, section 2.b above). Thus, many US treaties include a provision based on Article 26(4) of the US model, which states that each 'shall endeavour to collect' on behalf of the other such amounts as may be necessary to ensure that treaty relief 'does not enure to the benefit of persons not entitled thereto'.[1] In view of the use of the word 'endeavour', this is less than a watertight obligation; nevertheless such anti-abuse collection arrangements have been operated for many years between a number of developed countries, sometimes even without any treaty provision. Thus, both the UK and Canada have required their residents to make a return of any payments received from the US which have benefited from a reduced or nil withholding tax, and if the recipient is an agent or nominee they must declare this and withhold the appropriate tax, which is then returned to the US Treasury; this arrangement is facilitated by the supply by the US authorities of routine information on payments to residents of the treaty partner states (Abrutyn & Halphen 1984, p. A–47).

A similar procedure has been operated by Switzerland: under its 1962 decree against improper use of tax treaties both federal and cantonal tax authorities may require beneficiaries of tax relief to provide information ensuring that the benefit is one validly claimed under a treaty; they may otherwise refuse certification or recover the withholding tax due to the treaty partner (see Chapter 7, section 2.b above). However, the arrangements for recovery of withholding tax abroad have not been considered fully satisfactory, and it is preferable for the state of the payer to establish a pre-payment control, for example by requiring certification by the paying agent that the payee is entitled to a reduced withholding tax. On the other hand, this might require a more specific definition of those not entitled to treaty benefits (by means of limitation of benefits clauses), as well as stronger information exchange provisions (which would require information from banks); and these provisions have proved hard to agree (see above, Chapter 7, section 2, and section 2.b in this chapter).

country's tax claim in the US, and this would include conservancy measures. Thus, the US can apparently only enforce an actual tax judgment, by judicial means (OECD 1981, p. 36; Abrutyn & Halphen 1984, p. A–51).
[1] This provision is included in the new US–German treaty signed in 1989, Article 26(4).

5. Conclusion

This chapter has shown that, while the international co-ordination of taxation has increasingly relied on administrative co-operation, the basis for this co-operation is still seriously inadequate. First, mutual assistance has only developed actively between a few developed countries. Although developing countries are much more dependent proportionately on corporate taxation, especially of international businesses, for their government revenues (see Chapter 3, section 2.a above), even where treaties with developing countries include exchange of information and mutual agreement clauses, they seem to have been very little used, and developing countries have remained largely uninvolved in the efforts to combat international avoidance. Although this may be partly due to the shortage of skilled revenue staff in those countries, more could be done through bodies such as CATA and CIAT (discussed in section 1); indeed, the development of information exchange would be an important means of improving the effectiveness of their tax administrations.

However, this failure is part of the larger problem, that administrative assistance has been viewed narrowly, as a means of reciprocal resolution of conflicts, rather than more broadly, as a process of collectively reinforcing the effectiveness and harmony of national taxation as applied to international business. The increased use of administrative assistance arrangements has grown as conflicts have been created between major treaty partners by the measures taken by the tax administrations of the main developed countries to improve the effectiveness of their taxation of TNCs (scrutiny of transfer prices, taxation of retained income in intermediary companies by anti-CFC provisions, and disallowance of treaty benefits to treaty-shoppers). The development of active co-operation with developing countries has seemed less justified, since there would be no direct reciprocity, since the flow of investment is largely one-way. However, the benefits to the developing country of access to information might, on the other hand, counterbalance the lack of reciprocity for it in the basic substantive provisions of the tax treaty, with its emphasis on restricting taxation at source.[1]

At the same time, the narrow view of administrative assistance has undermined its effectiveness also for the main developed countries. As they have attempted to strengthen the enforcement of taxes on international business, the extent and type of co-operation they require have greatly expanded, so that tax administrations must in effect take joint decisions on tax enforcement. For example, in combating treaty-shopping by denial of treaty benefits to those who are not bona fide residents of a treaty partner, the source country requires detailed information on the beneficial ownership of companies to ensure they are not conduits, while its treaty partner may wish to

---

[1] This point was made, elliptically, by Gary Hufbauer, at the time an official of the US Treasury Department, to the CIAT Conference in San Salvador in 1976: reprinted in Abrutyn & Halphen 1984, p. B–904.

encourage the formation of holding companies; so that in the many borderline cases, a joint decision must, if possible, be made.

Equally, transfer pricing issues, which account for the large majority of cases under the mutual agreement procedure, require a co-operative approach to the difficult questions of allocation of costs and profits, especially since (as discussed in detail in Chapter 8 above) the arm's length principle provides very little guidance in relation to the highly-integrated businesses which provide the toughest problems. Yet a co-operative approach may be very difficult to achieve if the basis of the procedure is merely a narrow reciprocity, since it will encourage bargaining and override the concern for fairness.

Finally, the failure to achieve the extension and strengthening of co-operation must be largely attributed to the secretive and bureaucratic approach taken to the arrangements. The administrators have been reluctant even to publicize the existence and nature of their practices, let alone to concede minimal provisions for procedural fairness. At the root of this reluctance has been the failure to develop adequate principles for international taxation; the emphasis has been on the national taxation of transnational business, so that international co-ordination has inevitably taken the form of reciprocal bargaining of national interest. Thus, the insistence on national tax sovereignty has been argued to preclude the development of improved international arrangements: for instance, the great reluctance to concede binding arbitration of corresponding adjustment claims, or the unwillingness to publish interpretative mutual agreements and accept them as binding.

Yet, a greater willingness to relax the discretionary powers of national administrators would immeasurably reinforce their attempts to strengthen the basis of mutual assistance. The continued denunciation by business and professional bodies of relatively mild measures such as the OECD/Council of Europe multilateral convention carries force only because the tax authorities have shown such reluctance to seek more open public support for clearly stated substantive rules, as well as procedures providing adequate safeguards for the taxpayer. Little headway has been made in the past by proposals either to establish a general intergovernmental organization for co-operation in taxation ('Intertax': Surr 1966), or for an arbitration commission as an intermediate stage towards an 'international tax court' (Lindencrona & Mattsson 1981). The need of tax administrators for improved international enforcement and the desire of business for more transparency and fairness should be met in combination.

Global Business and International Fiscal Law

1. Tax Jurisdiction, State Sovereignty and International Law

The substance of state sovereignty is jurisdiction: the scope within which the effective and acceptable power of a state can be exercised. The modern state is defined in terms of territory: it consists of public authorities governing a defined territorial space. Thus, in modern international law, sovereignty is defined territorially, as 'the right to exercise (in regard to a portion of the globe) to the exclusion of any other state the functions of a state' (*Island of Palmas, Netherlands v. USA*, 1928, p. 92). However, such exclusive territorial state rights are essentially institutional and formal. Since economic activities and social relations are international or global, the reality of state power is not unlimited exclusive sovereignty, but interrelated and overlapping jurisdictions. It is formally true that the only tax officials who have the right to assess and collect taxes within British territory are those of the British government. However, although other states have no formal right to enforce their taxes by taking official action against persons or assets physically located in Britain, such action may take place either by tacit consent or by formal agreement, as we have seen in the previous chapter. More importantly, even if states exercise only their own exclusive territorial competence, this could produce overlapping and conflicting effects, due to the multiple geographic contacts of individuals and of interrelated economic activities.

From the point of view of formal sovereignty, there is no restriction on a state's right to tax, and it may be exercised without regard to its effects on other states. Thus, many tax and international lawyers have asserted that there is no rule of general international law limiting a state's right to tax, pointing to the lack of any decisions in international or domestic courts or tribunals invalidating or restricting the assertion of such a right (Chrétien 1955; Norr 1962; Knechtle 1979; Tixier & Gest 1985, p. 18). However, even from a formalist viewpoint, it must be conceded that a state cannot claim a right to a tax which could only be collected by action outside its territory (Albrecht 1952, p. 153; Qureshi 1987, p. 21). In opposition to formalism, normative approaches stress the need for a basis of legitimation for state sovereignty, since without such legitimacy state power is ineffective. The scope of such legitimate power and its allocation and co-ordination is normally referred to as jurisdiction (Brilmayer 1989, ch. 1).

Since legitimate state power is normally exercised by legislation, adjudication and administration, these are normally cited as the forms of jurisdiction. It has also become common to distinguish between jurisdiction to prescribe and jurisdiction to enforce: since a state may only exercise its monopoly of legitimate compulsion within its own territory, there is a territorial limitation on enforcement. Thus, official acts of investigation, the service of judicial process, requirements to provide evidence or information, the arrest of individuals or the seizure of assets to enforce an order, cannot be carried out within the jurisdiction of another state except under its authority or by consent. On the other hand, a state's jurisdiction to prescribe is not territorially limited, but may be asserted in relation to persons or transactions having a valid nexus with that state. In the liberal approach expressed most famously in the *Lotus* case (1927), since international law emanates only from the free will of states, they are free to assert any jurisdiction not explicitly prohibited by formal international agreement or a generally agreed positive principle (ibid., at p. 35). Once again, however, those who accept that states, like individuals, exist within a normative framework and are subject to economic and political constraints, look to the bases of legitimacy that can justify a valid assertion of jurisdiction (Martha 1989, ch. 2).

Nevertheless, even the requirement of such a valid nexus necessarily produces a pattern of overlapping and even conflicting jurisdictions, as we have seen quite clearly in relation to taxation. Even if states assert a claim to jurisdiction founded only on territoriality, this justifies taxation both of income which can be defined as having a source within the territory, and of residents on their worldwide income.[1] Thus, the important question in relation to jurisdiction is how far overlapping jurisdiction can be tolerated, and what means can be developed for its co-ordination. International taxation provides a fascinating example of how the political and economic constraints on sovereignty have been expressed in the legal forms developed for the co-ordination of tax jurisdiction.

The first, and perhaps primary means of such co-ordination has been by national limitations of the scope of taxation. Such limitations have resulted from national political pressures, for example from business groups representing international investors; but perhaps more importantly, from the under-

---

[1] See the dictum of Lord Herschell in *Colquhoun v. Brooks* (1889, p. 499), cited in Chapter 2, section 2.d above.

lying economic pressures. The greatest constraint on a state's assertion of its right to tax business stems from the international mobility of capital. Consideration of the tax burden is by no means the only factor taken into account by investors, especially in the case of direct investments made as part of business strategy. Nevertheless, it is a factor, and fear of loss of investment creates a potent pressure on governments, especially in states which have fewer location-specific advantages. Hence, there has been a broad similarity in the patterns of development of national taxes on international business, at least between states with similar levels of development and socio-economic backgrounds.[1] However, significant differences have remained, often motivated by attempts by governments to attract capital in order to develop or support a particular economic sector or social group. In particular, as we have seen in earlier chapters, interest in a financial services sector has led many states to offer facilities which have constrained the effective tax jurisdiction of others, especially by assisting TNCs to develop legal structures enabling them to expand through largely untaxed funds. Although counter-measures in the form of taxation of Controlled Foreign Corporations were taken nationally by states, there have been considerable similarities due to emulation, and the limits of the validity of such measures were generally understood, and later articulated by the OECD Fiscal Committee, so that the potential dangers of excessive jurisdiction were largely avoided, as we have discussed in detail in Chapter 7 above.

The second major means of co-ordination, resulting from international political pressures, has been the development of the network of bilateral tax treaties. The strengths and limitations of the approach developed in these treaties to the allocation of tax rights have been explored in previous chapters, and the next section of this chapter will consider in some detail the interaction of treaty provisions and domestic law. The treaty system has provided a mechanism for the negotiation and definition of national jurisdiction; this has, however, been based on the reciprocal bargaining of what have been perceived as national interests, which has in many ways hindered the emergence of a global perspective on equity in the taxation of international income. Bilateral treaties aim at prevention of international double taxation, and provide no mechanism for ensuring that international investment actually bears a reasonable tax burden. The growth of offshore finance, based on the exploitation of loopholes in the tax treaty network, has created glaring inequities in the taxation of both international portfolio and direct investment.

The measures taken by the tax authorities in response have been increasingly co-ordinated on a multilateral basis, but they have nevertheless remained seriously limited. The lead has been taken by the OECD Fiscal

---

[1] As we have seen in earlier chapters, all states generally tax income at source, while those which assert a right to tax residents or nationals on foreign income have largely accepted exemption (for some, via deferral) for unremitted income (at least if it is from an 'active' business), and allow at least a credit for foreign taxes paid on repatriated income. Thus there has been a significant degree of 'unilateral coherence' (Palmer 1989); although the limits of unilateralism should be clear, much can be done in encouraging greater uniformity of tax laws: Vann 1991, p. 158.

Committee, thus excluding the vast majority of states, not only the poorer underdeveloped countries, but also those with major economies and those attempting rapid economic growth; and yet even the OECD grouping is regarded as too large to deal with sensitive matters, which are confined to even more secretive meetings such as those of the Group of Four. The main difficulty is that international taxation has been regarded as a matter for inter-state co-ordination of national sovereignties. The issues raised by the increasingly wide area of overlapping jurisdictions have thus been treated as technical or administrative matters, while legitimation has been sought purely nationally. While the major TNCs have protested at some aspects of this, notably the lack of taxpayer rights in international tax decisions such as the arbitration of transfer price adjustments, they too have generally resisted the politicization of international tax issues. Yet it has become increasingly clear that a piecemeal and spatchcock approach will prove inadequate.

2. Tax Treaties and Domestic Law

Tax treaties attempt to deal with the problem of overlapping tax jurisdiction by allocating tax rights and granting exemptions which restrict national taxation in a number of respects. In particular, they restrict taxation at source to the business profits of a Permanent Establishment or subsidiary and impose limits on any withholding taxes on dividends, interest and other payments. Further, the non-discrimination clause (Article 24 of the models) requires each state to ensure equivalent tax treatment for nationals of the other state (including entities formed under its laws), as well as for local enterprises and Permanent Establishments owned or controlled by residents of the other state, with its own nationals similarly situated.[1] These rules and restrictions are binding on the state once the treaty is ratified, and will normally be incorporated into domestic law according to the procedures laid down for that purpose in each state. In some states, such as France and the US, ratified treaties are automatically incorporated and become part of domestic law; in others, such as the UK, they are specially incorporated by statute.[2]

[1] See O'Brien 1978 for a discussion of this provision. Investment or commercial treaties may also contain a national treatment clause, which sometimes refers specifically to taxation. This may be important if it is worded differently from or goes beyond the tax treaty, in particular if it covers taxation by political subdivisions, which is often excluded from tax treaties. See *Shell NV v. Graves* (1983), discussed in Chapter 9, section 3 above; that case also illustrates the procedural and substantive difficulties for a foreign firm, especially if operating through a local subsidiary, in showing that a law of general application is discriminatory because it bears more heavily on foreign-owned firms. See also the decision of the International Court of Justice in the case brought by the United States under the US–Italy Treaty of Friendship, Commerce and Navigation, in respect of the requisition by the Mayor of Palermo of a subsidiary of Raytheon: *Elettronica Sicula S.p.A.* (ELSI) (1989).
[2] In the UK, the tax Acts (now ICTA 1988, s.788) provide for each treaty to take effect as an Order in Council after it has been laid before the House of Commons and approved by positive resolution (s.788(10)). Since it is the treaty text itself that is the source of law, this minimizes the 'transformation' problem: see Mann 1986, p. 101. See further subsection (ii) below.

Tax treaties do not create any new liability to tax,[1] but co-ordinate the application of national taxes to international business, in order to prevent international double taxation, as well as evasion and avoidance. The effect of the treaty system is therefore to establish a special tax regime which creates exceptions and grants exemptions under domestic tax law. This has far-reaching implications for national tax laws.

2.a Harmonizing the Interpretation of Treaty and Statute

The limitations on tax jurisdiction embodied in tax treaties in principle entail a restriction on national sovereignty. In practice, states attempt to retain their freedom to change their domestic tax laws, without unreasonably violating treaty obligations. This process of co-ordination varies according to the constitutional procedures in each state governing the interaction between domestic legislation and international treaty obligations. However, as this interaction has become more complex in the area of tax law, the processes of co-ordination have come under greater pressure.

Two principles are generally accepted. First, an incorporated treaty has the status of domestic law, and therefore overrules pre-existing law, so that tax exemptions agreed in a duly incorporated treaty can create exceptions to existing provisions of tax law. Second, courts will wherever possible interpret a domestic legislative provision in such a way as to be compatible with the state's international obligations as expressed in a treaty. Hence, a treaty provision cannot be overridden even by subsequent legislation unless the two are clearly inconsistent. Although some have argued that an intention to override a treaty obligation by statute must be stated explicitly, this has been resisted by governments and legislatures, and courts have generally accepted that a clear domestic statutory provision should take precedence over a prior treaty if the two cannot be reconciled.

(i) Interpretation According to Context and Purpose

Harmonious interpretation of treaty and domestic tax law entails having regard to the character of the treaty as an agreement between states, and to the intentions of the parties, since domestic courts should where possible ensure that the state is not in breach of its international obligations.[2] In French law this is ensured procedurally by the principle that domestic courts are bound by the interpretation of the treaty given by the parties, or in the absence of such an agreed interpretation, by the Minister of Foreign Affairs, as the official responsible for implementation of the obligation. However, the Minister's

---

[1] In some cases, however, the application of a treaty rule may result in a higher tax liability, for example by changing the taxpayer's country of residence: see Avery Jones et al. 1984, p. 17.
[2] Even where this principle is not enshrined in a written constitution, it has been accepted by the courts, e.g. in the UK: see Mann 1986, pp. 102–14, and *Fothergill v. Monarch Airlines* (1981),

interpretation of a term may still leave considerable latitude to the court in applying it to an actual case. For example, in a case where the tax authorities had disallowed deduction of payments made to a Monaco resident for the use of trademarks on the grounds that a dependency relationship existed with the recipient, the Marseille administrative court referred to the Minister the interpretation of the concept of dependency under the France–Monaco treaty; it applied the Minister's reply, that dependency need not be based on ownership but may be contractual, to uphold the denial of deduction; but this was overturned by the Conseil d'Etat, which held that the administration had not shown that a relationship of dependency actually existed.[1]

The principles of interpretation of treaties under international law are codified in the Vienna Convention on Treaties,[2] which provides:

31. (1) A treaty shall be interpreted in good faith in accordance with the ordinary meaning to be given to the terms of the treaty in their context and in the light of its object and purpose.

(2) The context for the purpose of the interpretation of a treaty shall comprise, in addition to the text, including its preamble and annexes: (a) any agreement relating to the treaty which was made between all the parties in connexion with the conclusion of the treaty; (b) any instrument which was made by one or more of the parties in connexion with the conclusion of the treaty and accepted by the other parties as an instrument related to the treaty.

(3) There shall be taken into account, together with the context: (a) any subsequent agreement between the parties regarding the interpretation of the treaty or the application of its provisions; (b) any subsequent practice in the application of the treaty which establishes the agreement of the parties in relation to its interpretation; (c) any relevant rules of international law applicable in the relations between the parties.

(4) A special meaning shall be given to a term if it is established that the parties so intended.

Some special meanings are provided for in tax treaties, both in the Definitions article (Article 3 of the models), and in specific articles.[3] Due to the increasing complexity of treaties, the parties sometimes conclude contemporaneous

---

esp. Lord Diplock at p. 283. For an analysis of approaches to tax treaty interpretation, see 1984 and Avery Jones et al. 1984.

[1] Conseil d'Etat Decisions No. 05.125, 29 March 1978, p. 166. See Tixier & Gest 1985, pp. 215–16. The principle of reference to the Minister has also been limited, first by the refusal of civil courts to concede superiority of a government view except on questions of public international law; second, even administrative courts do not refer a treaty provision if they regard its meaning as clear: ibid., pp. 216–18.

[2] Concluded in 1969 and in force since 1980. Although some states are not parties to the Vienna Convention its rules are considered largely declaratory of modern international law: see e.g. the application of its rules of interpretation in the Canada–France arbitration *La Bretagne* (1986), and by the Inter-American Court of Human Rights in its decision on *Costa Rican Naturalization Laws* (1984).

[3] Especially Art. 4 Residence, Art. 5 Permanent Establishment, Art. 10(3) Dividend, Art. 11(3) Interest, Art. 12(2) Royalties, Art. 14(2) Professional Services, Art. 24(2) Nationals (for the purposes of the non-discrimination provision).

supplementary agreements, which either form part of the treaty as a protocol to it, or constitute related agreements, and are therefore part of the 'context' referred to in Article 31(2)(a).[1]

Since tax treaties are designed to co-ordinate the domestic tax laws of the parties as they apply to international business, the interpretation article normally also includes a clause (Article 3(2) of the models) specifying that, unless the context otherwise requires, any term not otherwise defined shall have the meaning which it has in the domestic law of the taxing state. Essentially, this means that the source state decides whether an item of income is taxable by reference to its own law, while the residence state should give a credit or exemption to an item so taxable.[2] Thus, in a French case, the Conseil d'Etat held that a tax on profit from real property sales was analogous to an income tax, and therefore came within the France–Canada treaty; and since in French law its character was that of a tax on commercial profits rather than a property tax, a Canadian company with no establishment in France could benefit from the treaty's exemption from taxes on business profits (*Min. of Finance v. Société X*, 1975). However, Article 3(2) of the models specifies that a term is given the domestic law meaning 'unless the context otherwise requires', so the priority is given to context.

Hence, the emphasis in treaty interpretation is on context and purpose. It is only where the context of the terms or the intention of the parties clearly require it that either a specific definition, or the domestic law meaning, should be adopted. Giving treaty terms the meaning which will implement the purpose of the treaty also implies the principle of effectiveness (*ut res magis valeat quam pereat*), to ensure that the terms have full and appropriate effect (Cassese 1986, p. 191). Harmonious co-ordination of the tax systems of the parties requires interpretation which implements the intention of the parties in such a way that it does not conflict with a domestic law provision.

Thus, in *Estate of Burghardt v. Commr.* (1983) the US Tax Court gave a sufficiently broad interpretation to a provision of the US–Italy estate tax treaty of 1956 that there was no conflict with a subsequent US statute. The treaty stated that a non-resident alien should be allowed any 'specific exemption' against estate duty which would be allowed to a domiciliary, proportionately to the value of the decedent's property within the state. The court accepted that 'specific exemption' included any method by which small estates are exempt from the estates tax, so that when the method was changed for US citizens and domiciliaries in 1976 from an exemption to a unified credit, a non-resident alien could also get the benefit of the new method.

[1] For example, the US–German treaty signed in 1989 had appended a Protocol containing specific provisions or interpretations of each treaty article, as well as two exchanges of notes, one establishing the procedures for the arbitration of competent authority cases, and one containing a memorandum of understanding giving details of the scope of the limitation of benefits article.

[2] For a discussion of the complications that may arise see Avery Jones et al. 1984–I, pp. 48–54; cf. *American Trust Co. v. Smyth* (1957) discussed in section (ii) below.

The trend of interpretation in UK courts is also towards giving effect to the terms of the treaty in the light of its purposes. Thus, in *I.R.C. v. Exxon Corp.* (1982), the British Inland Revenue had applied a withholding tax to a dividend of £7m paid by Esso Holding Co. UK Inc., a Delaware corporation (which was, however, resident in the UK for UK tax purposes), to its parent, Exxon Corporation of New Jersey. The company claimed exemption under the 1966 protocol to the 1945 US–UK treaty, as incorporated into UK law, which provided that:

> Dividends and interest paid by a corporation of one contracting party shall be exempt from tax by the other contracting party except where the recipient is a citizen, resident, or corporation of that other contracting party. This exemption shall not apply if the corporation paying such dividend or interest is a resident of the other contracting party.

The interpretation clause of the convention excluded any US corporation from the definition of resident of the UK. Although there were strong grounds from the context and the purpose of this particular provision not to apply this definition in either sentence, Goulding, J. felt constrained by precedent to accept that it applied to the first sentence of the provision; however, he applied a purposive interpretation to the second sentence, even though this appeared anomalous.[1] He concluded:

> I think, on a general consideration of the scheme of the Convention that . . . the intended purpose of the second sentence of Article XV can be discerned. Accordingly, although it seems to me that upon the plain meaning of the words used, the expression 'resident of the other contracting party' in that sentence does import the residence definitions . . . I must nevertheless give it a different construction, so that it does not fail of effect. In coming to this conclusion I bear in mind that the words of the Convention are not those of a regular parliamentary draftsman but a text agreed upon by negotiation between the two contracting governments. Although I am thus constrained to do violence to the language of the Convention, I see no reason to inflict a deeper wound than is necessary. In other words, I prefer to depart from the plain meaning of language only in the second sentence of Article XV, and I accept the consequence, strange though it is, that similar words mean different things in the two sentences. [p. 1004.]

The purposive approach of Goulding, J. was followed in *Union Texas Petroleum Corp. v. Critchley* (1988), rejecting a convoluted argument that, although dividends paid to a US corporation from its English subsidiary should be entitled to a tax credit under the US–UK treaty of 1976 equivalent to half the credit to which an individual UK shareholder would be entitled, nevertheless since these payments could not be 'tax credits' as defined in UK

---

[1] The intention of the provision appears to have been to override the US source rule treating dividends and interest paid by a non-US company as US-source if more than half of its income came from business effectively connected with US: Avery Jones 1982. The apparent lack of reciprocity in the provision results from the different residence rules in the UK and the US, so that the court's forced interpretation restored reciprocity: see Osgood 1984, p. 284.

domestic law (which refers to distributions to UK residents) they could not be subject to the deduction of 5 per cent which the US–UK treaty (Article 10(2)(a)) permitted on the aggregate of the dividend and the tax credit paid. Harman, J. said:

> I consider that I should bear in mind that this double tax agreement is an agreement. It is not a taxing statute, although it is an agreement about how taxes should be imposed. On that basis, in my judgment, this agreement should be construed ut res magis valeat quam pereat, as should all agreements. . . . [I]t is plain that the parties are trying in art. 10(2) to provide for the system of imputed tax and tax credits due in respect of dividends due under such a system. If counsel for Corporation's first submission were correct, the parties have referred to some kind of 'tax credit' not otherwise appearing in the United Kingdom tax system. . . . If such a reading of the document results in a provision intended on its face to produce a deduction having no such effect, that is effectively to cause this part of the double tax agreement to 'perish' and the court should lean against such a result. [p. 707.]

However, he accepted the second argument for the corporation, preferring to uphold the plain language of the treaty: since Article 10(2) specified a deduction of 5 per cent on the dividend and credit 'paid', it should be calculated on what was actually paid and not as if the word 'payable' had been used.[1]

A narrower approach was adopted by the Canadian Supreme Court in *The Queen v. Melford Developments Inc.* (1982), rejecting a claim by the Revenue that a guarantee fee of 1 per cent of a loan paid to a German bank was not exempt from withholding tax since it could qualify as 'interest'. The Canadian Income Tax Act of 1974 had introduced a provision specifying that any payment to a non-resident for a loan guarantee should be deemed to be interest; but the Court nevertheless held that this did not expressly overrule the 1956 statute which had incorporated the Canadian–German treaty which exempted the profits of non-residents, and the exclusion of 'interest' from that exemption should be interpreted strictly, and with reference to the laws of Canada in force at the time. This was so despite the treaty's interpretation clause, which included clause 3(2) of the models, specifying that any term not otherwise defined should, unless the context otherwise requires, have the meaning which it has under the laws in force of the relevant state. The court preferred to emphasize the provision of s.3 of the statute incorporating the treaty, which specified that in the event of any inconsistency between the treaty and 'the operation of any other law', the treaty should prevail.

The decision in the *Melford* case assumed that article 3(2) refers in a 'static' way to the domestic law as at the time of the agreements, rather than as from time to time amended; and the court in that case argued strongly that any other view would allow either state unilaterally to amend the agreement by redefining the relevant terms under its domestic law.[2] On the other hand, as

---

[1] This aspect of the decision was overturned prospectively by statute: Finance Act 1989, s.115.
[2] However, the meaning of this article is a separate question from the matter of treaty override: Avery Jones et al. 1984.

shown by the *Burghardt* case above, a static interpretation could deprive the taxpayer of a treaty benefit as a result of changes in domestic law enacted for other reasons. Although various textual arguments can be adduced in favour of both a 'static' and an 'ambulatory' interpretation of article 3(2) (Avery Jones et al. 1984), it seems preferable once again to emphasize the intention of the parties, and to decide whether the changed meaning in domestic law should apply in each case according to the context of the term and the purpose of the provision. Hence, it was regrettable that the Canadian courts appeared to assume that the change in definition of 'interest' was a unilateral measure by Canada, and did not attempt to consider the purpose and intention of the parties. The decision in the *Melford* case resulted in amending legislation requiring tax treaty terms defined by reference to the laws of Canada to be given the meaning which such terms have under the tax laws as amended from time to time.[1] In general, it seems preferable that Article 3(2) should normally be interpreted in this way, unless the context otherwise requires (as it specifies), and provided that the change in domestic law does not affect the balance of the treaty as embodied in the agreement of the parties.[2]

(ii) National Law and the Treaty Regime

The purpose of a tax treaty is to co-ordinate the application of national laws as they apply to international business. This is broader than the conception sometimes put forward, which emphasizes only the prevention of double taxation, and stresses that the treaty merely allocates tax jurisdiction, but cannot itself impose a tax. However, such a narrow approach to interpretation of the treaty tends to prioritize the exemptions it provides from national law, as in the *Melford* case when the exemption given by the treaty was upheld, even against a subsequent domestic law provision, on the ground that a treaty benefit could only be taken away by a very explicit domestic law.

Emphasizing the purpose of co-ordination reflects the historical development of tax treaties as being for the prevention not only of double taxation but also of fiscal evasion. This is illustrated by another case, appealed to the Swedish Supreme Administrative Court, concerning whether a Swedish capital gains tax could be applied to the unremitted gains of a British resident

---

[1] Except to the extent that the context otherwise requires: Income Tax Conventions Interpretation Act 1984, c. 48, s.3. The actual decision in the case was also prospectively overruled, so that 'interest' in a tax treaty includes a bank guarantee, except where the treaty or an agreement between the competent authorities expressly otherwise provides: s.4.

[2] See Tixier & Gest 1985, p. 221; Avery Jones et al. 1984, p. 48. Cf. the phrase used in the US model article 23 providing for credit under US law 'as it may be amended from time to time without changing the general principle thereof'; and Article 2(4) of the models which provides for the continued applicability of the treaty to 'substantially similar' taxes. Although the OECD Commentary to Article 2 does not assist with the meaning of 'substantially similar', the Commentary to Article 25(3) specifies that the Competent Authorities' power of interpretation can help to settle difficulties arising 'where the laws of a state have been changed without impairing the balance or affecting the substance of the Convention': OECD 1977, p. 181.

(who would normally be exempt by treaty from Swedish source taxes). The tax was enacted after the UK–Swedish treaty of 1960 and a 1968 Protocol which provided that where income exempted from tax at source is taxed by the other contracting state only when remitted, the exemption should apply only to the income actually remitted. The question was whether 'income' here applied also to capital gains. The majority of the court considered that the phrase 'income from a source' implied the English concept, which would exclude capital gains, although the Swedish system was schedular and added capital gains as one head of income, and the treaty applied to both types of tax (Avery Jones & Oliver 1988). However, it seems clear that the purpose of this particular provision was not to prevent double taxation, but to ensure that taxation took place somewhere, i.e. 'to prevent double non-taxation' (Sundgren 1990, p. 291), and there seems no reason from the context to prevent its application to capital gains.

More generally, it is becoming harder to maintain, as do some commentators, that the tax treaty is no more than a link between two domestic tax systems, creating special exemptions and a special internal tax regime for international transactions, but in no way substituting a common tax regime governing the international transactions between the contracting states (e.g. Tixier & Gest 1985, p. 187). Generally, treaty provisions are best understood in the context of the interaction of the two systems rather than in the context of the domestic law of one. For example, arrangements for allocation of income and credit between states with different systems of personal and corporate tax integration, such as the provisions for allocating ACT credit between the UK and the US considered in the *Exxon* and *Union Texas* cases discussed above, do essentially create a specific treaty tax regime.[1] Indeed, as we have seen in detail in Chapter 10, this special treaty tax regime has its own apparatus of joint enforcement, through the competent authorities.

The co-ordination of tax systems, as we have seen in earlier chapters, aims to establish international equity for investment, by attempting as far as possible to reconcile the perspectives on equity of the source and residence jurisdictions. In doing so, the contracting states seek approximate reciprocity, or a fair bargain in the revenues surrendered between the governments in order to encourage investment. However, they do so only so far as they consider it necessary in order to remove tax impediments to international investment. Treaties should not, therefore, be interpreted on the assumption either of item-by-item reciprocity (Osgood 1984, pp. 284–6), nor that they aim to produce better tax treatment for reciprocal foreign investment than for equivalent domestic investment. This issue was raised when US trusts claimed exemption under the US–UK treaty of 1945 from US capital gains tax on the fiduciary income, on the grounds that the beneficiaries were resident in the

---

[1] This is also illustrated by a recent US case, in which the Court of Claims held that ACT credit surrendered by a UK company to other UK affiliates did not qualify for a US indirect foreign tax credit: *Xerox Corp. v. US* (1988).

UK and not engaged in US trade or business, while the IRS had denied the exemption on the grounds that under US law the trust was a separate entity and it was resident in the US.[1] In *American Trust Co. v. Smyth* (1957) the 9th Circuit Court of Appeals held:

> We conceive the purpose of the treaty to have been full reciprocity and equality of tax treatment between nationals of the US and the UK. Such being the case, this purpose requires a broad construction of Article XIV, so as to relieve the British beneficiaries from the burden of the capital gains tax to the same extent, in a given situation, as a US beneficiary would be in a similar position in the UK. [p. 152.]

This was so even though the UK did not at that time have a capital gains tax. However, the US Supreme Court took a different view (*Maximov v. US*, 1963). Expressing the unanimous view of the Court, Goldberg, J. found that the plain language of the treaty gave no basis for exempting a US trust from US law, since the term 'person' included a trust as interpreted under US tax law (and under UK law as well), and the trust was clearly resident in the US. He saw no reason to depart from the clear language in the argument that the treaty aimed to produce equality of tax treatment:

> It appears from the relevant materials instructive as to the intent of the parties to the Convention that the general purpose of the treaty was not to assure complete and strict equality of tax treatment – a virtually impossible task in light of the different tax structures of the two nations – but rather, as appears from the preamble to the Convention itself, to facilitate commercial exchange through elimination of double taxation resulting from both countries levying on the same transaction or profit; an additional purpose was the prevention of fiscal evasion [p. 54].

It is perhaps more convincing to use lack of reciprocity as a reason not to impute that a treaty provision requires an exemption from domestic taxes. This was argued in a dissenting judgment in the Court of Claims, on whether interest should be payable on a refund of tax credit, due because the US–UK treaty of 1980 was applied retrospectively to 1975. The US Code provides for interest 'from the date of the overpayment', and the majority surprisingly categorized the back-dated credit as an overpayment refund; while the dissenting judgment pointed out that no interest is paid on refunds in UK law.[2]

The most direct mechanism for ensuring continued harmony in the interpretation of tax treaties between the parties is the mutual agreement provision, which empowers the competent authorities to resolve difficulties or doubts arising as to the application or interpretation of the convention (Article 25(3)). If concluded as formal agreements these instruments are binding on the states (see Chapter 10, section 3.b above), although unless incorporated

---

[1] On the treatment of trusts under tax treaties, see Avery Jones et al. 1989.
[2] Skelton, Circ. J., in *Brown & Williamson Ltd v. US* (1982), at pp. 764–5. Lack of reciprocity also influenced the UK court in *I.R.C. v. Exxon* (1982), discussed above: see however the criticism by Osgood (1984) p. 286.

into domestic law they may not have domestic effect as law. The mutual agreement clause of tax treaties is quite clearly envisaged by Article 31(3)(a) of the Vienna Convention, cited above, which requires account to be taken of any subsequent agreement between the parties regarding interpretation of the treaty or application of its provisions. Even where the competent authorities do not reach a formal interpretative agreement, their contacts may constitute a practice establishing the agreement of the parties, under 31(3)(b).[1] Under this heading also, competent authority decisions in individual cases might be referred to, especially if such decisions are published, as envisaged by the European Community convention (provided that the parties agree: see Chapter 10, section 3.a(iii) above).

Interpretative mutual agreements should therefore be given great weight by courts, whether as agreements or as practice between the parties. Although this has not always been the case, it is partly because of the reluctance of the tax authorities themselves to formalize and publicize competent authority interpretative agreements.[2] Some states do give particular emphasis to such agreements. In French law, as mentioned above, courts are considered bound to apply the interpretation of a treaty agreed by the parties, although to be formally binding such an agreement must be published as such in the Official Journal (Tixier & Gest 1985, p. 228). US courts also give considerable weight to competent authority interpretations, and the US model treaty provides that an interpretation agreed between the competent authorities overrides domestic law (Article 3(2)).

The Commentaries to the model treaties are also generally recognized as important guides to the intentions of the parties. They are formally considered part of the preparatory work, which may be referred to as an aid to understanding the text. The Vienna Convention, and treaty interpretation principles generally, give the preparatory work of the treaty a less important role, as only a supplementary means for resolving ambiguities or avoiding manifestly unreasonable results (Article 32). However, the Commentaries to

---

[1] The US Supreme Court has also given some weight to evidence of a consistent interpretation by one administration which has gone unchallenged by the other party: *O'Connor v. US* (1986), p. 33. See also *Samann v. C.I.R.* (1963) where Treasury regulations, which specified that the treaty exemption for a foreign resident not having a permanent establishment in the US only applied if this was so 'at no time' during the tax year, had been submitted to the treaty partner (Switzerland); the Appeals Court held that since Switzerland had raised no objection, it had tacitly acquiesced in this interpretation by its conduct (at p. 463).

[2] See Chapter 10, section 3.b above, and compare *Great-West Life Ass. Co. v. US* (1982) and *Xerox Corp. v. US* (1988) with *IRC v. Commerzbank* (1990). In the latter case Mummery, J. insisted on adhering to the literal meaning of the text, in contrast also to the approach of Goulding, J. in the *Exxon* case cited above. Nevertheless, it seems that the status of the competent authority interpretative agreement was insufficiently emphasized in the *Commerzbank* case. Although it is clear that, even if it were regarded as an agreement in international law, it was not incorporated into domestic law and thus could not directly override the treaty text as enacted, the mutual agreement must be regarded as either a related agreement or evidence of practice in application of the treaty, in the terms of the Vienna

the texts of the model tax treaties have normally been given considerable weight, since they are themselves agreed by state representatives as members of the relevant committees.[1]

Making use of the Commentaries can also help to ensure harmony in the interpretation of common terms. Courts sometimes also compare a treaty text with a similar text in treaties concluded with other parties, as an aid in showing the broad purpose of that type of provision. Where a similar provision in another treaty is worded differently, the difference may be taken as implying a different intention, or as a clarification. Thus, in the *Burghardt* case, reference was made to a number of treaties with the same provision, in particular the US–Canada treaty, the history of which revealed the origin of the phrase 'specific exemption' as intended to exclude the marital deduction; while a difference in wording in the US–Greece treaty was shown by the legislative history to be intended as a clarification. The harmonious interpretation of similar treaty provisions is clearly desirable where possible, to ensure international equity. It should be borne in mind, however, that such equity may require differences in the regime applicable bilaterally between different states, due to differences in their national tax systems.

(iii) Statute Conflicting with Prior Treaty

The principle that a state should not legislate in breach of its own obligations under international law is sometimes considered to be so strong that even a subsequent statute can only override a treaty provision if it makes specific reference to it. In some states, this is a constitutional principle: thus, in France, Article 55 of the 1958 Constitution provides that a ratified treaty has authority superior to statute, subject to its application by the other party. The OECD Committee's report on Treaty Overrides referred to both France and the Netherlands as systems where a treaty takes precedence over conflicting provisions not only of prior but also of subsequent laws (OECD 1989, p. 8). In practice, however, the French Conseil d'Etat has been reluctant to invalidate a statutory provision on the grounds of conflict with a prior treaty.[2] Nevertheless, such a constitutional provision does create a strong presumption in favour of continued validity of the treaty. In other states, even where treaty and statute are of equal status, there may also be such a presumption, in the

---

Convention, and thus as strong evidence of the intention of the parties (see Avery Jones et al. 1984, pp. 95–6).

[1] Although an argument has been made that this gives them the status of an instrument made between the parties relating to the treaty, this cannot be so, since the discussions leading to the Commentary text are not directly related to the negotiation of any particular treaty: Avery Jones et al. 1984, pp. 92–3. See Chapter 2, section 2.b above, and *Fothergill v. Monarch Airlines* (1981) and *Sun Life Assurance of Canada v. Pearson* (1984).

[2] Tixier & Gest 1985, pp. 182–3. However, the issue now arises most commonly in relation to the interaction of domestic law with that of the European Community, where the overriding integrative purpose is stronger: see the decision of the Conseil d'Etat in Application of M. Boisdet (1990).

absence of a 'clear intention' to override; but this falls short of the requirement of an explicit reference to the specific provision being overridden.

This is essentially the position in the UK, although the starting-point is very different, since a treaty only has effect in British domestic law if, and as, incorporated by statute, and the principle of parliamentary supremacy means that a statute overrules prior inconsistent treaty rights. Tax treaties, however, have normally been incorporated under a section of the tax Acts which specifically provides that they shall have effect 'notwithstanding anything in any enactment', insofar as they provide for the relief of international double taxation.[1] This produces a strong presumption in favour of the treaty; although British courts are unlikely to refuse to give effect to a clear statutory provision on the grounds of a conflict with a prior incorporated treaty, as did the Supreme Court of Canada in *The Queen v. Melford Developments Inc.* (1982), discussed above.

However, this method of treaty incorporation goes a long way towards evading the reluctance of British judges to allow international obligations to limit parliamentary sovereignty. Thus, in *Collco Dealings Ltd v. I.R.C.* (1962), where the treaty exemption as incorporated[2] did not specify that it should apply 'notwithstanding anything in any enactment', Viscount Simonds indignantly asserted that 'neither comity nor rule of international law can be invoked to prevent a sovereign state from taking what steps it thinks fit to protect its own revenue laws from gross abuse, or to save its own citizens from unjust discrimination in favour of foreigners' (p. 19). However, the other judges used more cautious language. Lord Morton pointed out that although a breach of treaty obligations may result in loss to individuals, only the state party to the treaty is properly entitled to complain; and although there is a presumption that Parliament did not intend to infringe the comity of nations,

[1] This phrase was contained in the original provision giving general effect to tax treaties, s.51 of the Finance (No. 2) Act of 1946; the present version is ICTA, s.788(3). This gives effect over other statutory rules in respect of provisions (a) for relief from income or corporation tax; (b) for charging non-residents on income arising, or on gains from disposal of assets taking place, in the UK; (c) for attributing income or gains between non-residents and their UK Permanent Establishments or between UK residents and related entities (transfer pricing); or (d) for conferring on non-residents the right to a tax credit for qualifying distributions by resident companies (ACT). From the context of section 788 (in that part of the Act headed Double Taxation Relief) and the wording of s.788(1), which refers to arrangements made with any foreign territory 'with a view to affording relief from double taxation', it would appear that the treaty provisions can only override conflicting law to the extent necessary to provide relief, and not to create a charge to tax. Thus, for example, the treaty rules on transfer price adjustment (which permit adjustments to income) may apply to corresponding adjustments, giving relief to a taxpayer; whereas an adjustment creating a charge to UK tax must take place under s.770 (which refers to adjustments to the prices of transactions): see Chapter 8, section 1.d above.

[2] Section 349 of the Income Tax Act of 1952. This was an admittedly unmeritorious claim by an Irish company that the measures against dividend-stripping, introduced with the clear but sweeping words of the 1955 Finance Act applying to any 'person entitled under any enactment to an exemption from income tax', should not override the exemption given to Irish residents by the 1926 UK–Eire tax treaty, since to do so would be a breach of the treaty and therefore of international 'comity'.

not every breach of a treaty is necessarily such an infringement, since the action may be a necessary response to changing circumstances and may be accepted as such by the treaty partner. Lord Radcliffe went further in accepting that the apparently wide language of a statute might be interpreted restrictively if it entailed a breach of a treaty. However, he sharply limited this in relation to a tax treaty, which he categorized as a mere inter-governmental agreement[1] 'which by its own terms is subordinated to the approval of the respective legislatures of the countries concerned and persists only so long as those terms are maintained in force by those legislatures' (p. 23). A more balanced approach was taken in a Privy Council appeal from Ceylon, *Woodend Rubber Co. v. C.I.R.* (1971), when Lord Donovan found that the sweeping tax changes introduced in Ceylon in 1959 following the Kaldor report, which included the taxation of remittances of non-resident companies, were clearly intended to be comprehensive and could not be held to exclude payments to a company controlled from and therefore resident in the UK, even though there was no explicit reference in the 1959 Act to overriding the statutory provision giving effect to the UK–Ceylon agreement of 1950. However, for a statutory provision to override a treaty benefit as enacted under the current tax Acts, would now require a specific measure clearly irreconcilable with the benefit, or evidence of a clear intention to override.

In the US, the Supreme Court has stated that 'A treaty will not be deemed to have been abrogated or modified by a later statute unless such purpose on the part of Congress has been clearly expressed'.[2] This entails refusing to uphold a statutory provision which conflicts with a prior treaty obligation if there is no clear indication of a Congressional intention to override: in the *Cook* case, actions of the US Coast Guard in boarding a British vessel and seizing liquor under powers in the 1930 Tariff Act were held invalid as contrary to a US–UK treaty of 1924 which limited US rights to board British vessels beyond the three-mile limit; however, the 1930 Act was a mere re-enactment of identical provisions of the 1922 Act, so the Court held that the 1922 Act remained in force 'with its scope narrowed by the treaty' after re-enactment (p. 120). The requirement of 'clear Congressional intention' falls significantly short of requiring an explicit reference to the prior treaty.[3]

---

[1] In international law however, there can be little doubt that a tax treaty is an agreement between states; the term inter-governmental would imply that the agreement would not bind a subsequent government, which is clearly not the case with tax treaties. See also the criticism of this judgment in Mann 1986, p. 111.

[2] Brandeis, J. in *Cook v. US* 1933, p. 120. More recently the Court has reaffirmed this as a 'firm and obviously sound canon of construction against finding implicit repeal of a treaty in ambiguous Congressional action. . . . Legislative silence is not sufficient to abrogate a treaty' (O'Connor, J. in *Trans-World Airlines v. Franklin Mint Corporation* (1984), p. 252). See also *South African Airways v. Dole* (1987).

[3] Since US courts refer to legislative history as an aid to interpretation, the clear expression of Congressional intention to override could be found in that history, for example in the explanatory reports of the relevant committees. Although this has been derided as providing no basis for conclusions about the intentions of those voting for the measure (Kaplan 1986, p. 213), the notion of legislative 'intention' is a politico-legal fiction, just as much in relation to an obscure clause in a technical Bill.

Hence, the general rule is that a subsequent statute overrides a prior treaty where they are inconsistent: but much depends on the attitude of the courts to the question of inconsistency. Some flexibility is essential, otherwise the powers of national legislatures to enact changes to tax laws affecting international business could be greatly restricted.[1] This necessarily entails some balancing of the principle of parliamentary sovereignty against the view that a legislature should not lightly be taken to have enacted a statute involving a breach of international law.[2] In practice, courts will make the best use they can of canons of construction to try to ensure that a statute does not unreasonably derogate from a prior treaty. In particular, the rule that general words should not be interpreted so as to derogate from specific provisions is important, since the wording of tax treaties is normally very general compared to the detailed provisions of domestic tax law.[3]

What is striking is that there are relatively few court cases invoking a clear inconsistency between a statute imposing a tax burden and a prior treaty granting relief; but that where cases have been brought national courts have normally had little difficulty in finding the claim for exemption from national law unmeritorious. In practice, the basic treaty benefits given to foreign investors by treaties are well-known to the tax authorities; and no doubt if an intended benefit is inadvertently removed by a legislative change, those authorities would normally concede the benefit and seek legislative amendment to restore it. It is when legislation has been deliberately enacted to counteract what the tax authorities or the legislature consider to be the unintended benefits of the tax treaty system, resulting from the increasing complexity of forms taken by international investment, that increasing difficulties have been caused.

2.b Overriding and Renegotiating Treaties

As the interaction between domestic and international tax rules has become more complex, the question of 'treaty overrides' has become more acute. Tax considerations have significant effects on international investment, and this has two major consequences. First, the increasingly ingenious forms devised to minimize taxation by taking advantage of loopholes in the international tax system undermine the equity of national taxation, and have led to counteract-

[1] Osgood 1984, p. 274.
[2] Thus, commenting on a 1968 Swiss Federal Court ruling that national law must be interpreted in conformity with international law, Knechtle states that if national laws could never predominate over prior treaties a serious obstacle would be created for the flexibility of fiscal legislation essential to a modern state, creating legal uncertainty and inequality: Knechtle 1979, p. 173.
[3] Osgood 1984, p. 257. However, an exemption from tax given by treaty may be considered to be a specific benefit not to be lightly taken away by a new general tax: see e.g. Lord Donovan in *Woodend Rubber Co. v. C.I.R.* (1971), although in that case he held that since the statute enacted a comprehensive tax reform, it must have been intended to amend the prior treaty (discussed above).

ing measures. Where such measures entail overriding a treaty, the state enacting them may regard this as removing the unintended consequences of tax treaties. The treaty partner on the other hand, and even more the tax planners who devise avoidance strategies in reliance on treaty terms and the firms who benefit from this avoidance, may take the view that a party to an agreement cannot pick and choose which of its provisions to obey. Second, the increasing difficulty of reconciling national and international tax equity has made the model tax treaty, with its emphasis on crude reciprocity and the bargaining of benefits, an ineffective instrument for international co-ordination of taxation.[1] The treaty system is rigidifying just when it needs to become more flexible. States are reluctant to give up treaty provisions which they perceive as advantageous in influencing investment flows, or unwilling to negotiate changes when domestic tax reform has altered the underlying assumptions of existing treaties.

For a number of reasons, it has been measures taken by the US Congress which have raised the most controversy about treaty overrides. Among the developed countries, the US has been most sharply affected by direct investment flows, first by the rapid postwar expansion abroad of US firms, and subsequently by the equally strong invasion of the US, including the purchase of US businesses by foreign firms. Consequently, professional advisors, officials and politicians have been highly sensitized to the ingenious devices developed to exploit the many disjunctures in the international tax system. As we have seen in previous chapters, the US has led the way in attempts to counteract international avoidance, first in relation to US TNCs (Subpart F and the s.482 transfer price regulations) and then in relation to investment in the US (anti-conduit and treaty-shopping rules; and more recently, disallowance of interest for debt-financed acquisitions).

Although the US has also been active, at least since the mid-1960s, in attempting to ensure international co-ordination of anti-avoidance measures, the domestic political pressures to plug loopholes have created conflicts both with foreign investors and with treaty partners. Firms and their advisors have resented changes in national tax laws depriving them of treaty benefits. Since treaties generally reduce and do not increase tax burdens, the opposition to treaty overrides from the business lobbies can be taken with a grain of salt; but the US government is nevertheless vulnerable to charges of unilateralism and undermining international due process (e.g. Hufbauer et al. 1988, pp. 20–1; Doernberg 1989, p. 210). On the other hand, while its treaty partners may have an apparently strong case against US unilateralism in overriding treaties, they sometimes ignore the underlying problem of inflexibility of the

---

[1] See Vann 1991. A notable example has been the difficulty of agreeing symmetrical treatment of investment flows, specially between the US, which still maintains the 'classical' treatment of separate taxation of corporate taxation and investment income, and its major treaty partners, Canada, France, Germany and the UK, all of which have introduced corporate-personal tax integration in various forms over the past 25 years: see Chapter 2, section 2.d above.

treaty-system, including the difficulties of adapting and renegotiating treaties to plug loopholes. Furthermore, although it has been the US examples that have attracted the most attention and criticism, other states have also enacted provisions deliberately blocking what they consider to be a loophole in the treaty system: an example has already been given above in the Canadian categorization of a bank guarantee as interest, held up by the courts in the *Melford* case but subsequently enforced by statute.[1]

(i) Effects of US Tax Law Changes on Treaties

The dispute over US legislative override of treaties, which was the culmination of these tendencies, came to a head following the massive Tax Reform Act of 1986. The Internal Revenue Code enacted in 1954 contained a provision, s.7852(d), specifically invalidating any of the rules of that Code which conflicted with treaty obligations in effect prior to that date. The original intention of the 1986 reform was to enact a new Code, which would have clarified that pre-1954 treaties prevailed over the rules of the 1954 Code but not over provisions subsequently enacted; but in the event, the 1986 Act merely amended the 1954 Code, leaving s.7852 unchanged.[2]

Tax statutes enacted between 1954 and 1986 adopted several different approaches to existing treaties. The 1962 Revenue Act provided that s.7852 should not apply in respect of amendments made by that Act, thus overriding all treaties. Although the 1962 Act introduced major changes, including Subpart F taxation of the passive income of controlled foreign corporations and the move to a separate foreign tax credit limitation for interest, it was thought at the time that it involved only one minor treaty override, in respect of the Greek estate tax treaty, which the Treasury undertook to renegotiate. Subsequently, however, it was argued that there were other conflicts: specifically, that the separate limitation for the foreign tax credit was in breach of treaties which could be read as requiring the US to retain its previous tax credit arrangements.[3] The Foreign Investors Tax Act of 1966 took the opposite approach: since it was aimed at encouraging portfolio investment into the US, it specifically provided that it should not be read as removing any treaty benefit, nor should any treaty provision be deemed to override any benefit in the Act. A third approach was used in the 1976 Tax Reform Act,

---

[1] See also Vann 1991, p. 109.

[2] For a history of override provisions, with citations from the relevant documentation, see Hufbauer et al. 1988, and US Congress 1988b; Kaplan 1986 mounts an intemperate attack, Forry & Karlin 1987 a more reasoned critique.

[3] Older US treaties, including those with the Netherlands, Germany and Switzerland, required the US to allow as a credit the 'appropriate' amount of the treaty partner's taxes; newer US treaties provide that credit shall be allowed 'in accordance with the provisions and subject to the law of the United States (as it may be amended from time to time without amending the general principle thereof)'. The treaties with the Netherlands, Germany and Switzerland had still not been renegotiated when the 1986 Tax Reform Act once again changed the method of limitation, according to 'separate baskets' of types of income: see Forry & Karlin 1987, p. 795.

which made changes to the foreign tax credit rules, including repealing the option of the per-country method. The explanation of the Bill for the Joint Tax Committee of the Congress stated the understanding that recent treaties did not require the per-country limitation, and that it was the intention of Congress that all existing treaties should be applied in conformity with the overall limitation being enacted. Similarly, the Crude Oil Windfall Profit Tax of 1980, and the provisions on treatment of 'stapled' foreign corporations introduced in the 1984 Tax Reform Act, were accompanied by Committee reports explaining that to the extent that they conflicted with treaties, the statute was intended to override.

Finally, a fourth method was used in the FIRPTA (Foreign Investment in Real Property Tax Act) of 1980, which embodied a change in policy and introduced new rules to tax foreigners on gains from sales of interests in US real property. Such gains are normally taxable under treaty rules in the state where the property is located; but the practice had grown of investing in US real property through foreign-registered companies: by owning shares or other financial instruments instead of the real property directly, a foreign investor could avoid US estate and gift taxes, and perhaps also capital gains tax.[1] This had been tolerated or even encouraged, in order to stimulate investment into the US, but the conviction had grown that such incentives merely produced artificial distortions in capital markets. Since the 1980 Act involved a clear change in policy, it provided that it would not override conflicting tax treaty provisions for five years, until 31 December 1984, during which time it was intended that amendments to the treaties should be negotiated. The FIRPTA also introduced a provision (which became s.897i of the Code) that a foreign corporation holding a US real property interest and which was entitled to non-discriminatory treatment in that respect under a tax treaty, could elect to be treated as a domestic corporation. Only mild objections were made by treaty partners to the changes to the US international tax regime introduced by any of these measures.

The 1986 Tax Reform Act contained far-reaching provisions, many of which affected, and were intended to affect, both US firms investing abroad and foreign investors into the US. The Congress identified a series of conflicts with treaty provisions, in two main areas. First, a number of changes were made to source of income rules, which generally brought the US into line with those of other countries, and which were not objectionable in themselves

---

[1] For a discussion of the changes introduced, not only by the FIRPTA but also subsequently in 1984 and 1986, and an analysis of methods which may still be used to minimize taxation of foreign investment in US real estate, see Langer 1988–, chs. 33 and 34. In *Botai Corp. v. Commr.* (1990) a company incorporated in the Netherlands Antilles (and owned by a Cayman Islands company) attempted to transfer its residence to the UK to avoid US taxation of profits from the sale of interests in Florida real estate, taking advantage of the transitional provisions of the FIRPTA; the Tax Court held that it had not established a bona fide residence in the UK, but since the profits constituted a gain and not ordinary income, they would in any case not be exempt under the US–UK treaty.

(Kaplan 1986, p. 214). The controversy was caused by the committee reports, which stated that these rules were intended to override any conflicting treaty provisions: this applied both to direct conflicts, in case any source rule in a treaty should be found to conflict; as well as indirect conflicts, in that changes in the source rule would reduce the US taxpayer's foreign tax credit (Forry & Karlin 1987, p. 795).[1]

Second, changes were made to the taxation of US branches of foreign companies. The new branch profits tax also was not so much objectionable in itself as in the manner and extent of treaty override involved. It is a flat 30 per cent tax on a foreign corporation's 'dividend equivalent amount', intended to replace the withholding taxes which the US claimed to apply to dividends and interest paid by foreign companies which did over 50 per cent of their business in the US (see Chapter 5, section 2.b above). The 'dividend equivalent amount' is the corporation's earnings and profits effectively connected with the US, adjusted upwards or downwards by decreases or increases in US net equity.[2] A related 30 per cent withholding tax was also applied both to interest paid by the branch, and to the 'excess interest': i.e. the amount by which the interest on borrowings allocated to the US and deductible for US tax purposes exceeds the actual interest paid by it. Foreign companies could benefit from reduction or elimination of these taxes under an applicable treaty, but only if they were 'qualified residents' of the treaty country; a corporation resident in a treaty country could be a 'qualified resident' (i) if over half its stock is owned by individual residents of the treaty country, US citizens or aliens resident in the US *and* less than half of its income is used, even indirectly, to meet liabilities to non-residents of the treaty country or the US; or (ii) its stock is primarily and regularly traded on an established stock exchange of the treaty country. These are essentially benefit limitation provisions of the kind the US had sought since 1981 to introduce to combat treaty-shopping (see Chapter 7, section 3.a); in addition, the Treasury was given authority to grant qualified residence status wherever it considers treaty-shopping is not involved.[3]

Whereas the source of income rule changes were expressly stated to override treaties, the Congress stated that the branch taxes were not intended to do so; but what this meant in practice was not so clear. The legislation explicitly preserved any treaty exemption, but only for bona fide treaty country residents

---

[1] Although the US generally reserves the right in its treaties to tax its own nationals and residents, the reduction of US credit available against foreign taxes could be objectionable to treaty partners: Kaplan 1986, p. 215.
[2] I.R.C., s.884. Part of the intention is to encourage reinvestment of earnings in the US; the vagueness of the rules opens up some avoidance possibilities, although the Treasury is given power to regulate the calculation of US net equity.
[3] This discretion was intended to cover cases where some judgment was involved, e.g. where the company is actively doing business in its state of residence and no special exemption is given there to its US income; or if its US income is used to satisfy liabilities in third countries that are to genuine third parties and do not involve e.g. back-to-back loans: see General Explanation of the 1986 Act prepared for the Joint Committee on Taxation (Bluebook) pp. 1043–5, cited in Hufbauer et al. 1988, p. C–24.

who could satisfy the 'qualified resident' tests.[1] This explicit exclusion from treaty benefits of those who could not show themselves to be bona fide residents of the treaty country was not considered a breach from the US point of view, although (as we have seen in Chapter 7, section 2.b above) others argue that under the basic model treaty provisions in the absence of a more explicit limitation of benefits clause, benefits cannot be so limited. However, the question still remained, whether even a bona fide treaty resident would be exempt: an argument could be made that the treaty non-discrimination provision does not prohibit branch withholding taxes, since they do not treat a foreign company differently from a US corporation transacting the same type of business (Greenberg 1991). However, the main aim of the branch taxes was to prevent tax-free investment in the US through conduit companies formed in treaty havens. For example, a company formed in the Netherlands Antilles could minimize taxation on business profits in the US through deduction of depreciation charges and interest payments and, due to exemption of foreign income and lack of withholding taxes in the Antilles, these profits could be passed tax free to its beneficial owners.[2] Indeed, Netherlands Antilles conduit companies seem to have been one of the prime targets of the branch taxation provisions. The new treaties with the Netherlands Antilles and Aruba which were signed while the 1986 Act was under discussion contained a modified non-discrimination clause which would permit branch taxation, although the parties agreed during the negotiations that they would be reopened to assess the impact of changes in US legislation (Forry & Karlin 1987, p. 797). In the event, the Congress accepted the Treasury opinion that the standard non-discrimination clause would exempt a bona fide treaty country resident.[3] Presumably, the view was taken that since the Netherlands Antilles would in any case not ratify the new treaty once the branch taxes were enacted, the US would be obliged to cancel the existing treaty without replacement.[4]

Thus, the possibility that the new US branch taxes might apply to all foreign corporations notwithstanding tax treaties was eclipsed (although it could be revived by the Congress). Instead, the provisions were aimed at treaty-shoppers.

---

[1] I.R.C., s.884(e). Also, if the treaty permitted a 'second tier' dividend withholding tax, the 1986 Act provided that this tax and not the branch profits tax would apply to all residents of the treaty country; however, this was eliminated by the 1988 Technical Corrections Act, so that treaty-shoppers would be subject to the branch profits tax there also.

[2] This was particularly so for investments in US real estate: although the FIRPTA applied to capital gains, a company could still be exempt on profits having the character of income: see *Botai Corp. v. Commr.* (1990), discussed above.

[3] General Explanation (Bluebook), p. 1043, cited in Hufbauer et al. 1988, p. C–23. The IRS subsequently issued Notice 87–56 which listed 28 countries, including the Netherlands Antilles, whose treaties with the US contained a non-discrimination clause which would provide exemption; and another list of nine, including countries such as France and Canada, whose treaties permit a branch tax, usually subject to a limit.

[4] When the treaty was finally cancelled, the disruptive effects on the Eurobond markets forced the US to announce the continuation in force of Article 8 exempting interest payments from withholding tax: see Chapter 7, section 3.b above.

(ii) Treaty Overrides and Treaty-Shopping

From the point of view of the US legislators, genuine treaty benefits were preserved, and only those who had taken unintended advantage of tax treaties were to be liable to the new taxes. Thus, far from hindering the negotiation of new treaties by the US as alleged by some (e.g. Kaplan 1986), the application of the new branch taxes to those who are not qualified residents of a treaty country would provide an incentive for such negotiations (Greenberg 1991, p. 433). Indeed, after 1986 US tax treaty negotiations experienced renewed urgency and some significant successes. At the same time, the Congress also backed down from other proposals which would have entailed the withdrawal of advantages in treaties with some of its major treaty partners: in particular, a proposed withholding tax on insurance premiums, aimed at foreign insurers (e.g. in the UK or France) which are exempt from the US insurance excise tax, but which allegedly may act as conduits passing on risks to reinsurers based in low-tax havens;[1] and a proposal to allow US corporations a small deduction for dividends with a corresponding withholding tax on foreign shareholders, which would not apply to shareholders resident in a country having a treaty with the US containing adequate treaty-shopping provisions and which granted US shareholders an imputation tax credit equivalent to that granted to domestic shareholders. This latter proposal seemed clearly aimed at Germany, as a spur to satisfactory renegotiation of its treaty with the US (Kaplan 1986, p. 214).

It should also be borne in mind that these events were not the result of the logical development of a unified US policy, but the outcome of interactions between political actors with different positions and powers in the system. US domestic tax changes originate in the House, especially its Ways and Means Committee, which has long had a strong Democrat majority and a protectionist stance in US foreign economic policy; while foreign policy including tax treaty negotiation has been conducted by an executive headed for twenty years by a Republican; although treaty ratification requires consent of the Senate, which has had an intermittent Democrat majority, and more liberal leanings in foreign economic affairs than the House.

[1] See Forry & Karlin 1987, p. 798. US treaties which grant a waiver from the insurance excise tax to foreign firms insuring US risks without a Permanent Establishment in the US have, since the US–French protocol of 1978, included an explicit anti-conduit exclusion of reinsured risks; even where this is not so, as in the UK provision, the US attempts to impose the tax on risks reinsured with a non-exempt third country insurer. This is done by agreement with the foreign insurer, which may be required to post a bond to cover the tax liability on reinsurances, although Lloyd's is the only UK insurance group which is said to have entered into such an agreement (see *Tax Notes*, 21 May 1990). The withholding tax proposal was dropped after lobbying on both sides, but the Treasury was required to produce a report, which appeared in 1990. The Report's view, that the excise tax exemption was justifiable but only subject to anti-conduit provisions, was nevertheless criticized as failing to distinguish between back-to-back reinsurance of specific risks, which might be covered by a general anti-conduit rule as in *Aiken Industries v. Commr.* (1971), and aggregate risk reinsurance, where the primary insurer still bears risk and makes a profit (or loss) and thus has a valid business purpose: Viehe-Naess 1990.

Whether due to US forbearance or pressure from powerful treaty partners, major deliberate conflicts with tax treaties in the 1986 Act were avoided. It was still not clear, however, which of the many new provisions enacted in that Act might conflict with treaty benefits; and since s.7852 had been left unchanged, it left a large area of ambiguity over the interaction of the 1986 Act with treaty provisions. When this came to be addressed as part of the Technical Corrections Act of 1988, the treaty override pot came to the boil. Much effort was devoted, not only by IRS and Treasury officials and Congressional staffers, but also private practitioners, to identifying possible conflicts between the 1986 Act and US tax treaties. As was already clear from the experience of the pre-1986 statutes affecting international taxation, several degrees of conflict were possible. First, there were identified conflicts, in relation to which Congress should indicate whether treaty or statute should prevail. Second, a number of the new statutory rules entailed possible conflicts with treaty rules, and arrangements had to be made for resolving such potential conflicts. Third, there were measures which Congress did not believe conflicted with any treaty rule, but where such a conflict might be argued. Finally, there was the possibility of potential claims that could be made by taxpayers based on treaty provisions creating conflicts not yet identified by Congressional or Treasury staff.

In the end, the 1988 Act specified a treaty override in only one area of clearly identified conflict, the amendments to the foreign tax credit rules (which, as mentioned above, affected only a few, old treaties). In all other cases of identified conflict, Congress allowed treaties to prevail.[1] The controversy was caused, not by explicit overrides, but by the determination of the Congress that the statutory provisions should prevail in unidentified conflicts, as well as over interpretations diverging from the view of treaty provisions taken by the Congress. This was to be ensured by two means: first, a taxpayer would be required to disclose any claim involving exemption from a statutory rule by virtue of a treaty; and second, there would be a residual rule stating that except as otherwise provided in the Act, its provisions should apply notwithstanding any treaty then in force. This 'residual override' provoked a public rebuke in the form of a letter and memorandum from six European Community members to the Treasury Secretary.[2] The issue was also taken up through the

---

[1] There were finally nine such cases, including the taxation of certain fellowships and grants, of some types of transportation income, and of some post-cessation gains from disposal of assets used in a US trade or business: see Hufbauer et al. 1988, pp. C35–8. The taxation of 'excess interest', and the reduction to 25 per cent of the threshold of US income making a branch liable to the 'second tier' withholding tax, which were the only specific examples of override referred to in the letter from the six governments discussed below, were also in the end allowed to yield to treaties.

[2] The letter, dated 16 July 1987, was reprinted in various tax journals, e.g. *Taxes International* of 16 November 1987; it was drafted by the French Ambassador and signed by Belgium, France, Germany, Great Britain, Luxembourg and the Netherlands. Note that it preceded the final version of the 1988 Act and the final Committee explanations in US Congress 1988b and 1988c, which made the specific concessions mentioned in the previous footnote, and revised the residual override.

OECD, resulting in a report by the Fiscal Affairs Committee, and a Council recommendation urging countries both to respond to tax treaty problems with prompt consultations, as well as to refrain from enacting legislation intended to have effects in clear contradiction to treaty obligations (OECD 1989).

As a result of such pressures, the final version of the Act contained further concessions: the taxation of branch 'excess interest' would not override treaty provisions (this was the main specific override to which the letter of the six objected); and the residual override was changed. The final version stated that neither treaty nor law should have preferential status; thus, the later-in-time rule would prevail,[1] subject to the general rules of interpretation, including the initial presumption of harmony (US Congress 1988b, p. 321). However, Congress could not be required to identify every possible conflict between statutory and treaty provisions. Further, it rejected the view that the only way in which treaties could be brought into line with changing domestic tax laws should be by renegotiation, since this would give foreign states an effective veto over US domestic law changes as they apply to international business. This put foreign states on notice that the Congress might be prepared, if necessary, legislatively to remove a treaty benefit which it found unacceptable and which the treaty partner refused to renegotiate. This point was made explicit by a statement by Senator Sarbanes, of the Senate's Foreign Relations Committee during tax treaty hearings in June 1990. These remarks produced complaints from US treaty partners, especially from the Chair of the Bundestag Finance Committee, Hans Gattermann, who said that the delay in ratifying the US–German treaty signed in 1989 was a warning of German impatience with the US Congress's attitude to treaties (*Tax Notes*, 10 December 1990).

In principle, governments concur that solutions should be sought by agreement. The letter of the six stressed their willingness to co-operate with the US to combat treaty-shopping: their objection was not only to unilateral treaty overrides, but also to the imposition of a specific treaty-shopping rule by the 'qualified resident' requirement. They argued that the rule of 50 per cent ownership by local residents and not more than 50 per cent distribution to third-country residents ran counter to their aim in establishing a free capital market in the European Community:

> The pattern of investment relations in Europe is much more complicated than is often the case in an economy of the size of the United States, as companies in Europe often draw their capital from residents of more than one state. Moreover, in some cases, it might be difficult to trace all the shareholders of a given company although its genuine status for tax purposes suffers no doubt.

It is not clear how widely or deeply this objection is shared, since the Protocols signed by the US with Belgium and France in 1988, and the new US–German treaty, all contained anti-shopping provisions substantially compatible with

---

[1] Except that the previous s.7852(d) is retained as a savings clause preserving pre-1954 treaties against provisions of the 1954 Code.

those of the US branch profits tax.[1] In any case, the 'qualified resident' test is also satisfied by a company if its stock is 'primarily and regularly' traded on a recognized stock exchange, a test which is also substantially the same as that in the recent treaties.[2] However, the integration of the European Community's capital markets is likely to require re-evaluation of the residence requirements of tax treaties.

(iii) Treaty Breach, Suspension and Renegotiation

Domestic tax law changes which alter or undermine the operation of a tax treaty raise the question of its suspension or renegotiation. Under the Vienna Convention, a 'material' breach of a treaty entitles the other party to invoke that breach as a ground for termination of the treaty, or its suspension as a whole or in part. Article 60(3) defines a 'material' breach as either a repudiation not sanctioned by the Convention, or the 'violation of a provision essential to the accomplishment of the object or purpose of the treaty'. Even where a state has enacted explicit tax treaty overrides, they have not been accompanied by the repudiation of the treaties concerned; either explicitly or implicitly, the action has been considered either to be compatible with the treaty, or to be justified, for example, on the grounds of change in circumstances. States wishing to abrogate a tax treaty have done so under the article usually included which provides for termination on six-months' notice. The definition of 'material' breach in the Vienna Convention extends to a serious or non-trivial breach, but the word 'fundamental' was rejected by the drafters, so that the breach need not be one affecting the central purpose of the treaty but may relate to any provision which was material in inducing a party to enter into the treaty (UN 1966, p. 83).

Although a treaty override may be considered sufficiently serious to lead the treaty partner to invoke it as grounds for abrogation, the more likely reaction is to protest against the breach. Indeed, states are under a general obligation in international law to seek a negotiated solution to conflicts. Although there is a duty to negotiate in good faith, a state may be justified in taking counter-measures entailing the reciprocal suspension of proportional obligations, provided they are aimed at restoring equality and encouraging resolution of the dispute. Thus, in a dispute over air services when France suspended PanAm flights via London to Paris due to a change of gauge in London, the US proposed arbitration and, receiving no immediate reply, retaliated by issuing

---

[1] The French treaty already contained a 50 per cent ownership rule, and the Protocol added the 'base-erosion' requirement; the Belgian protocol introduced rules substantially similar to those, as did the German treaty: see Chapter 7, section 3.a above.
[2] Recent US agreements (those with Belgium, France and Germany) require 'substantial and regular' trading; the omission of 'primarily' was referred to as a semantic difference in the Explanation of the French Protocol for the Senate Foreign Relations Committee, p. 23. Treasury Regulations under the Branch Tax provisions provide guidelines for the meaning of 'primarily and regularly', which would presumably also be helpful in interpreting the treaty 'substantial and regular' trading requirement.

an order suspending air services by Air France from Los Angeles to Paris for so long as the PanAm flights were barred. The Arbitral Tribunal warned that such countermeasures should be used with moderation and be accompanied by a genuine effort to resolve the dispute, in view of the dangers of retaliation and the sensitivity of the network of air services arrangements; proportionality was difficult to judge, but bearing in mind not only the private loss to PanAm, but also the principled implications of the issue, the countermeasures were not disproportionate in that case (*US–France Arbitration*, 1978). This case has clear parallels with tax treaty overrides.

Until now there has been no formal retaliation or suspension of a tax treaty in such circumstances, although there have been informal retaliations, such as the delay in German ratification of its treaty with the US; and also threats, such as the enactment by the UK Parliament of a power to retaliate against state worldwide unitary taxation by withdrawal of ACT refunds to US corporations.[1] The fact that this threat has not been activated indicates some of the difficulties with such an approach, not least the possibility of counter-retaliation. It has been reported that US treaty partners have raised the question of inclusion in tax treaties of a provision empowering retaliation. This would require some mechanism for agreeing whether a breach has taken place, and a means of identifying an equivalent benefit which could be withdrawn. The difficulties are evident; but the alternatives pose perhaps even greater problems.

3. A New Institutional Framework for International Taxation

International tax arrangements are undoubtedly due for some significant reorganization and rethinking. Already, the OECD Fiscal Committee has begun work on the revision of the 1977 model treaty, a process which, as before, is interacting with the renegotiation of some of the key bilateral treaties, such as the US–Netherlands treaty, following on the US–German agreement signed in 1989. However, both the basic shortcomings of the bilateral treaty model and the inadequacies of the international political framework within which the issues are discussed have become increasingly clear. A strong and persuasive argument has been made by Richard Vann for an international tax institution analogous to the GATT (General Agreement on Tariffs and Trade) (Vann 1991, pp. 156ff.) The GATT itself also resulted from the need to transcend the pattern of trade bargaining based on bilateral reciprocity, but has done so through a relatively loose model of organization;

---

[1] See Chapter 9, section 4 above. Due to the US Senate veto the treaty came into force without the provisions which would have prohibited WUT, so UK withdrawal of ACT refunds would itself constitute breach of the treaty and not a retaliation.

indeed the 'weak' form of the GATT resulted precisely from the failure to obtain national political agreement for a more comprehensive International Trade Organization based on the Havana Charter.

An organization based on the GATT model would allow for (i) a minimal foundation of obligations binding on all members, (ii) a further level of more detailed rules which could be optional or could be varied by agreement between pairs of states, (iii) a framework for adjudication of issues arising from the obligations, and (iv) an organizational basis for regular bilateral and multilateral discussion of policy issues. The minimal obligation should include not only an undertaking to prevent international double taxation, but also to combat fiscal avoidance and evasion and to ensure a minimal level of effective taxation. While this would, initially at least, limit the number of states willing to adhere to such a multilateral agreement by excluding 'havens', it would strengthen the basis of common action against such haven states. The more detailed codes, which might allow for variation, could cover issues such as the definition of 'passive' income and other aspects of CFC taxation; similarly, the parameters for limitation of treaty benefits in anti-conduit rules could be fixed; and guidelines and procedures could be established in relation to the transfer pricing question. Several academic commentators have argued for a radical approach to transfer pricing by moving to a formula approach, while acknowledging the political difficulties (Bird 1988; Vann 1991). However, the analysis in Chapters 8 and 9 above shows that both the separate enterprise and the formula approach require criteria for defining a unitary business and for allocating joint costs and synergy profits, as well as a mechanism for taking decisions on a case-by-case basis. Indeed, the institutional basis for this process has already been gradually established between the major states, by administrative arrangements between the competent authorities. While those involved have been fearful that politicization of these processes might prove fatal, there is no doubt that greater openness and fairness in the procedures and in the substantive criteria would enhance their legitimacy, and strengthen them in the long run. Inclusion of arrangements for co-operation in tax enforcement within such a general institutional framework would provide some insulation against the attacks launched against the OECD/Council of Europe mutual assistance convention.

A move towards a more formalized institutional framework of this type is not a panacea. Whether it takes place or not, much can be done to strengthen the basic mechanisms and principles, as has been indicated in previous chapters. However, what they have also shown is that what has been lacking above all has been an adequate process of legitimation at the international level. While the political difficulties to be overcome in initiating such a development cannot be underestimated, it seems clear that by one means or another, a strengthening of the international institutional basis for international taxation is an urgent necessity.

Appendix: Model Treaties

OECD and United Nations Model
Double Taxation Conventions

{The text given here is based on the 1977 OECD model. Text added in the UN model is given in italics, and text omitted in the UN model is indicated by square brackets; in addition, Article 22 on Taxation of Capital is optional in the UN model and is therefore bracketed in the original, together with references to taxation of capital in Article 1 and elsewhere. Editor's notes are indicated by curly brackets: S.P.}

Title of the Convention
Convention between (State A) and (State B) for the avoidance of double taxation with respect to taxes on income and on capital.

Preamble of the Convention
The Preamble of the Convention shall be drafted in accordance with the constitutional procedure of both Contracting States.

Chapter I: Scope of the Convention

Article 1: Personal Scope

This Convention shall apply to persons who are residents of one or both of the Contracting States.

Article 2: Taxes Covered

1. This Convention shall apply to taxes on income and on capital imposed on behalf of a Contracting State or of its political subdivisions or local authorities, irrespective of the manner in which they are levied.

2. There shall be regarded as taxes on income and on capital all taxes imposed on total income, on total capital, or on elements of income or of capital, including taxes on gains from the alienation of movable or immovable property, taxes on the total amounts of wages or salaries paid by enterprises, as well as taxes on capital appreciation.

3. The existing taxes to which the Convention shall apply are in particular:

    (a) (in State A): . . .

(b) (in State B): . . .

4. The Convention shall [also apply] *apply also* to any identical or substantially similar taxes which are [subsequently] imposed after the date of signature of the Convention in addition to, or in place of, the existing taxes. At the end of each year, the competent authorities of the Contracting States shall notify each other of [any] changes which have been made in their respective taxation laws.

Chapter II: Definitions

Article 3: General Definitions

1. For the purposes of this Convention, unless the context otherwise requires:

(a) the term 'person' includes an individual, a company and any other body of persons;

(b) the term 'company' means any body corporate or any entity which is treated as a body corporate for tax purposes;

(c) the terms 'enterprise of a Contracting State' and 'enterprise of the other Contracting State' mean respectively an enterprise carried on by a resident of a Contracting State and an enterprise carried on by a resident of the other Contracting State;

(d) the term 'international traffic' means any transport by a ship or aircraft operated by an enterprise which has its place of effective management in a Contracting State, except when the ship or aircraft is operated solely between places in the other Contracting State;

(e) the term 'competent authority' means:

(i) (in State A): . . .
(ii) (in State B): . . .

2. As regards the application of the Convention by a Contracting State any term not defined therein shall, unless the context otherwise requires, have the meaning which it has under the law of that State concerning the taxes to which the Convention applies.

Article 4: Resident

1. For the purposes of this Convention, the term 'resident of a Contracting State' means any person who, under the laws of that State, is liable to tax therein by reason of his domicile, residence, place of management or any other criterion of a similar nature. [But this term does not include any person who is liable to tax in that State in respect only of income from sources in that State or capital situated therein.]

2. Where by reason of the provisions of paragraph 1 an individual is a resident of both Contracting States, then his status shall be determined as follows:

(a) He shall be deemed to be a resident of the State in which he has a permanent home available to him; if he has a permanent home available to him in both States, he shall be deemed to be a resident of the State with which his personal and economic relations are closer (centre of vital interests);

(b) If the State in which he has his centre of vital interests cannot be determined, or if he has not a permanent home available to him in either State, he shall be deemed to be a resident of the State in which he has an habitual abode;

(c) If he has an habitual abode in both States or in neither of them, he shall be deemed to be a resident of the State of which he is a national;

(d) If he is a national of both States or of neither of them, the competent authorities of the Contracting States shall settle the question by mutual agreement.

3. Where by reason of the provisions of paragraph 1 a person other than an individual is a resident of both Contracting States, then it shall be deemed to be a resident of the State in which its place of effective management is situated.

Article 5: Permanent Establishment

1. For the purposes of this Convention, the term 'permanent establishment' means a fixed place of business through which the business of an enterprise is wholly or partly carried on.

2. The term 'permanent establishment' includes especially:

(a) a place of management;
(b) a branch;
(c) an office;
(d) a factory;
(e) a workshop; [and]
(f) a mine, an oil or gas well, a quarry or any other place of extraction of natural resources.

3. *The term 'permanent establishment' likewise encompasses*

(a) A building site [or] a construction, *assembly* or installation project [constitutes a permanent establishment only if it lasts more than twelve months.] or *supervisory activities in connexion therewith, but only where such site, project or activities continue for a period of more than six months;*

(b) The furnishing of services, including consultancy services, by an enterprise through employees or other personnel engaged by the enterprise for such purpose, but only where activities of that nature continue (for the same or a connected project) within the country for a period or periods aggregating more than six months within any twelve-month period.

4. Notwithstanding the preceding provisions of this Article, the term 'permanent establishment' shall be deemed not to include:

(a) the use of facilities solely for the purpose of storage, *or* display [or delivery] of goods or merchandise belonging to the enterprise;

(b) the maintenance of a stock of goods or merchandise belonging to the enterprise solely for the purpose of storage, *or* display [or delivery];

(c) the maintenance of a stock of goods or merchandise belonging to the enterprise solely for the purpose of processing by another enterprise;

(d) the maintenance of a fixed place of business solely for the purpose of purchasing goods or merchandise or of collecting information, for the enterprise;

(e) the maintenance of a fixed place of business solely for the purpose of carrying on, for the enterprise, any other activity of a preparatory or auxiliary character;

[(f) the maintenance of a fixed place of business solely for any combination of activities mentioned in sub-paragraphs a) to e), provided that the overall activity of the fixed place of business resulting from this combination is of a preparatory or auxiliary character.]

[5. Notwithstanding the provisions of paragraphs 1 and 2, where a person – other than an agent of an independent status to whom paragraph 6 applies – is acting on behalf of an enterprise and has, and habitually exercises, in a Contracting State an authority to conclude contracts in the name of the enterprise, that enterprise shall be deemed to have a permanent establishment in that State in respect of any activities which that person undertakes for the enterprise, unless the activities of such person are limited to those mentioned in paragraph 4 which, if exercised through a fixed place of business, would not make this fixed place of business a permanent establishment under the provisions of that paragraph.]

5. Notwithstanding the provisions of paragraphs 1 and 2, where a person – other than an agent of an independent status to whom paragraph 7 applies – is acting in a Contracting State on behalf of an enterprise of the other Contracting State, that enterprise shall be deemed to have a permanent establishment in the first-mentioned Contracting State in respect of any activities which that person undertakes for the enterprise, if such person:

(a) has and habitually exercises in that State an authority to conclude contracts in the name of the enterprise, unless the activities of such person are limited to those mentioned in paragraph 4 which, if exercised through a fixed place of business, would not make this fixed place of business a permanent establishment under the provisions of that paragraph; or

(b) has no such authority, but habitually maintains in the first-mentioned State a stock of goods or merchandise from which he regularly delivers goods or merchandise on behalf of the enterprise.

6. Notwithstanding the previous provisions of this article, an insurance enterprise of a Contracting State shall, except in regard to re-insurance, be deemed to have a permanent establishment in the other Contracting State if it collects premiums in the territory of that other State or insures risks situated therein through a person other than an agent of an independent status to whom paragraph 7 applies.

7.[6.] An enterprise *of a Contracting State* shall not be deemed to have a permanent establishment in [a] *the other* Contracting State merely because it carries on business in that State through a broker, general commission agent or any other agent of an independent status, provided that such persons are acting in the ordinary course of their business. *However, when the activities of such an agent are devoted wholly or almost wholly on behalf of that enterprise, he will not be considered an agent of an independent status within the meaning of this paragraph.*

8.[7]. The fact that a company which is a resident of a Contracting State controls or is controlled by a company which is a resident of the other Contracting State, or which carries on business in that other State (whether through a permanent establishment or otherwise), shall not of itself constitute either company a permanent establishment of the other.

Chapter III: Taxation of Income

Article 6: Income from Immovable Property

1. Income derived by a resident of a Contracting State from immovable property

(including income from agriculture or forestry) situated in the other Contracting State may be taxed in that other State.

2. The term 'immovable property' shall have the meaning which it has under the law of the Contracting State in which the property in question is situated. The term shall in any case include property accessory to immovable property, livestock and equipment used in agriculture and forestry, rights to which the provisions of general law respecting landed property apply, usufruct of immovable property and rights to variable or fixed payments as consideration for the working of, or the right to work, mineral deposits, sources and other natural resources; ships, boats and aircraft shall not be regarded as immovable property.

3. The provisions of paragraph 1 shall apply to income derived from the direct use, letting, or use in any other form of immovable property.

4. The provisions of paragraphs 1 and 3 shall also apply to the income from immovable property of an enterprise and to income from immovable property used for the performance of independent personal services.

Article 7: Business Profits

1. The profits of an enterprise of a Contracting State shall be taxable only in that State unless the enterprise carries on business in the other Contracting State through a permanent establishment situated therein. If the enterprise carries on business as aforesaid, the profits of the enterprise may be taxed in the other State but only so much of them as is attributable to *(a)* that permanent establishment; *sales in that other state of goods or merchandise of the same or similar kind as those sold through that permanent establishment; or (c) other business activities carried on in that other State of the same or similar kind as those effected through that permanent establishment.*

2. Subject to the provisions of paragraph 3, where an enterprise of a Contracting State carries on business in the other Contracting State through a permanent establishment situated therein, there shall in each Contracting State be attributed to that permanent establishment the profits which it might be expected to make if it were a distinct and separate enterprise engaged in the same or similar activities under the same or similar conditions and dealing wholly independently with the enterprise of which it is a permanent establishment.

3. In [determining] *the determination of* the profits of a permanent establishment, there shall be allowed as deductions expenses which are incurred for the purposes *of the business* of the permanent establishment, including executive and general administrative expenses so incurred, whether in the State in which the permanent establishment is situated or elsewhere. *However, no such deduction shall be allowed in respect of amounts, if any, paid (otherwise than towards reimbursement of actual expenses) by the permanent establishment to the head office of the enterprise or any of its other offices, by way of royalties, fees or other similar payments in return for the use of patents or other rights, or by way of commission, for specific services performed or for management, or, except in the case of a banking enterprise, by way of interest on moneys lent to the permanent establishment. Likewise, no account shall be taken, in the determination of the profits of a permanent establishment, for amounts charged (otherwise than towards reimbursement of actual expenses), by the permanent establishment to the head office of the enterprise or any of its other offices,*

by way of royalties, fees or other similar payments in return for the use of patents or other rights, or by way of commission for specific services performed or for management, or, except in the case of a banking enterprise, by way of interest on moneys lent to the head office of the enterprise or any of its other offices.

4. Insofar as it has been customary in a Contracting State to determine the profits to be attributed to a permanent establishment on the basis of an apportionment of the total profits of the enterprise to its various parts, nothing in paragraph 2 shall preclude that Contracting State from determining the profits to be taxed by such an apportionment as may be customary; the method of apportionment adopted shall, however, be such that the result shall be in accordance with the principles contained in this Article.

[5. No profits shall be attributed to a permanent establishment by reason of the mere purchase by that permanent establishment of goods or merchandise for the enterprise.] *(Note: the question of whether profits should be attributed to a permanent establishment by reason of the mere purchase by that permanent establishment of goods and merchandise for the enterprise was not resolved. It should therefore be settled in bilateral negotiations.)*

[6.]5. For the purposes of the preceding paragraphs, the profits to be attributed to the permanent establishment shall be determined by the same method year by year unless there is good and sufficient reason to the contrary.

[7]6. Where profits include items of income which are dealt with separately in other Articles of this Convention, then the provisions of those Articles shall not be affected by the provisions of this Article.

Article 8: Shipping, Inland Waterways Transport and Air Transport
Article 8a (Alternative a)

1. Profits from the operation of ships or aircraft in international traffic shall be taxable only in the Contracting State in which the place of effective management of the enterprise is situated.

2. Profits from the operation of boats engaged in inland waterways transport shall be taxable only in the Contracting State in which the place of effective management of the enterprise is situated.

3. If the place of effective management of a shipping enterprise or of an inland waterways transport enterprise is aboard a ship or boat, then it shall be deemed to be situated in the Contracting State in which the home harbour of the ship or boat is situated, or, if there is no such home harbour, in the Contracting State of which the operator of the ship or boat is a resident.

4. The provisions of paragraph 1 shall also apply to profits from the participation in a pool, a joint business or an international operating agency.

Article 8b (Alternative b)

1. Profits from the operation of [] aircraft in international traffic shall be taxable only in the Contracting State in which the place of effective management of the enterprise is situated.

2. Profits from the operation of ships in international traffic shall be taxable only in the Contracting State in which the place of effective management of the enterprise is situated unless the shipping activities arising from such operation in the other Contracting State are more than casual. If such activities are more than casual, such profits may be taxed in that other State. The profits to be taxed in that other State shall be determined on the basis of an appropriate allocation of the overall net profits derived by the enterprise from its shipping operations. The tax computed in accordance with such allocation shall then be reduced by . . . per cent. (The percentage is to be established through bilateral negotiations.)

3. Profits from the operation of boats engaged in inland waterways transport shall be taxable only in the Contracting State in which the place of effective management of the enterprise is situated.

4. If the place of effective management of a shipping enterprise or of an inland waterways transport enterprise is aboard a ship or boat, then it shall be deemed to be situated in the Contracting State in which the home harbour of the ship or boat is situated, or, if there is no such home harbour, in the Contracting State of which the operator of the ship or boat is a resident.

5. The provisions of paragraph 1 *and 2* shall also apply to profits from the participation in a pool, a joint business or an international operating agency.

Article 9: Associated Enterprises

1. Where

(a) an enterprise of a Contracting State participates directly or indirectly in the management, control or capital of an enterprise of the other Contracting State, or

(b) the same persons participate directly or indirectly in the management, control or capital of an enterprise of a Contracting State and an enterprise of the other Contracting State,

and in either case conditions are made or imposed between the two enterprises in their commercial or financial relations which differ from those which would be made between independent enterprises, then any profits which would, but for those conditions, have accrued to one of the enterprises, but, by reason of those conditions, have not so accrued, may be included in the profits of that enterprise and taxed accordingly.

2. Where a Contracting State includes in the profits of an enterprise of that State – and taxes accordingly – profits on which an enterprise of the other Contracting State has been charged to tax in that other State and the profits so included are profits which would have accrued to the enterprise of the first-mentioned State if the conditions made between the two enterprises had been those which would have been made between independent enterprises, then that other State shall make an appropriate adjustment to the amount of the tax charged therein on those profits. In determining such adjustment, due regard shall be had to the other provisions of [this] *the* Convention and the competent authorities of the Contracting States shall if necessary consult each other.

Article 10: Dividends

1. Dividends paid by a company which is a resident of a Contracting State to a resident of the other Contracting State may be taxed in that other State.

2. However, such dividends may also be taxed in the Contracting State of which the company paying the dividends is a resident and according to the laws of that State, but if the recipient is the beneficial owner of the dividends the tax so charged shall not exceed:

(a) [5 per cent] . . . *per cent (the percentage is to be established through bilateral negotiations)* of the gross amount of the dividends if the beneficial owner is a company (other than a partnership) which holds directly at least [25] *10* per cent of the capital of the company paying the dividends;

(b) [15 per cent] . . . *per cent (the percentage is to be established through bilateral negotiations)* of the gross amount of the dividends in all other cases.

The competent authorities of the Contracting States shall by mutual agreement settle the mode of application of these limitations.

This paragraph shall not affect the taxation of the company in respect of the profits out of which the dividends are paid.

3. The term 'dividends' as used in this Article means income from shares, 'jouissance' shares or 'jouissance' rights, mining shares, founders' shares or other rights, not being debt-claims, participating in profits, as well as income from other corporate rights which is subjected to the same taxation treatment as income from shares by the laws of the State of which the company making the distribution is a resident.

4. The provisions of paragraphs 1 and 2 shall not apply if the beneficial owner of the dividends, being a resident of a Contracting State, carries on business in the other Contracting State of which the company paying the dividends is a resident, through a permanent establishment situated therein, or performs in that other State independent personal services from a fixed base situated therein, and the holding in respect of which the dividends are paid is effectively connected with such permanent establishment or fixed base. In such case the provisions of Article 7 or Article 14, as the case may be, shall apply.

5. Where a company which is a resident of a Contracting State derives profits or income from the other Contracting State, that other State may not impose any tax on the dividends paid by the company, except insofar as such dividends are paid to a resident of that other State or insofar as the holding in respect of which the dividends are paid is effectively connected with a permanent establishment or a fixed base situated in that other State, nor subject the company's undistributed profits to a tax on the company's undistributed profits, even if the dividends paid or the undistributed profits consist wholly or partly of profits or income arising in such other State.

Article 11: Interest

1. Interest arising in a Contracting State and paid to a resident of the other Contracting State may be taxed in that other State.

2. However, such interest may also be taxed in the Contracting State in which it arises

and according to the laws of that State, but if the recipient is the beneficial owner of the interest the tax so charged shall not exceed [10 per cent] . . . *per cent (the percentage is to be established through bilateral negotiations)* of the gross amount of the interest. The competent authorities of the Contracting States shall by mutual agreement settle the mode of application of this limitation.

3. The term 'interest' as used in this Article means income from debt-claims of every kind, whether or not secured by mortgage and whether or not carrying a right to participate in the debtor's profits, and in particular, income from government securities and income from bonds or debentures, including premiums and prizes attaching to such securities, bonds or debentures. Penalty charges for late payment shall not be regarded as interest for the purpose of this Article.

4. The provisions of paragraphs 1 and 2 shall not apply if the beneficial owner of the interest, being a resident of a Contracting State, carries on business in the other Contracting State in which the interest arises, through a permanent establishment situated therein, or performs in that other State independent personal services from a fixed base situated therein, and the debt-claim in respect of which the interest is paid is effectively connected with *(a)* such permanent establishment or fixed base, *or with (b) business activities referred to under (c) of paragraph 1 of article 7.* In such case the provisions of Article 7 or Article 14, as the case may be, shall apply.

5. Interest shall be deemed to arise in a Contracting State when the payer is that State itself, a political subdivision, a local authority or a resident of that State. Where, however, the person paying the interest, whether he is a resident of a Contracting State or not, has in a Contracting State a permanent establishment or a fixed base in connection with which the indebtedness on which the interest is paid was incurred, and such interest is borne by such permanent establishment or fixed base, then such interest shall be deemed to arise in the State in which the permanent establishment or fixed base is situated.

6. Where, by reason of a special relationship between the payer and the beneficial owner or between both of them and some other person, the amount of the interest, having regard to the debt-claim for which it is paid, exceeds the amount which would have been agreed upon by the payer and the beneficial owner in the absence of such relationship, the provisions of this Article shall apply only to the last-mentioned amount. In such case, the excess part of the payments shall remain taxable according to the laws of the Contracting State, due regard being had to the other provisions of this Convention.

Article 12: Royalties

1. Royalties arising in a Contracting State and paid to a resident of the other Contracting State [shall be taxable only] *may be taxed* in that other State [if such resident is the beneficial owner of the royalties].

2. *However, such royalties may also be taxed in the Contracting State in which they arise and according to the laws of that State, but if the recipient is the beneficial owner of the royalties, the tax so charged shall not exceed . . . per cent (the percentage is to be established through bilateral negotiations) of the gross amount of the royalties. The competent authorities of the Contracting States shall by mutual agreement settle the mode of application of this limitation.*

[2.]*3*. The term 'royalties' as used in this Article means payments of any kind received as a consideration for the use of, or the right to use, any copyright of literary, artistic or scientific work including cinematograph films, *or films or tapes used for radio or television broadcasting*, any patent, trade mark, design or model, plan, secret formula or process, or for the use of, or the right to use, industrial, commercial, or scientific equipment, or for information concerning industrial, commercial or scientific experience.

[3.]*4*. The provisions of paragraphs 1 *and 2* shall not apply if the beneficial owner of the royalties, being a resident of a Contracting State, carries on business in the other Contracting State in which the royalties arise, through a permanent establishment situated therein, or performs in that other State independent personal services from a fixed base situated therein, and the right or property in respect of which the royalties are paid is effectively connected with *(a)* such permanent establishment or fixed base, *or with (b) business activities referred to under (c) of paragraph 1 of article 7*. In such case the provisions of Article 7 or Article 14, as the case may be, shall apply.

5. Royalties shall be deemed to arise in a Contracting State when the payer is that State itself, a political subdivision, a local authority or a resident of that State. Where, however, the person paying the royalties, whether he is a resident of a Contracting State or not, has in a Contracting State a permanent establishment or fixed base, in connexion with which the liability to pay the royalties was incurred, and such royalties are borne by such permanent establishment or fixed base, then such royalties shall be deemed to arise in the State in which the permanent establishment or fixed base is situated.

[4.]*6*. Where, by reason of a special relationship between the payer and the beneficial owner or between both of them and some other person, the amount of the royalties, having regard to the use, right or information for which they are paid, exceeds the amount which would have been agreed upon by the payer and the beneficial owner in the absence of such relationship, the provisions of this Article shall apply only to the last-mentioned amount. In such case, the excess part of the payments shall remain taxable according to the laws of each Contracting State, due regard being had to the other provisions of this Convention.

Article 13: Capital Gains

1. Gains derived by a resident of a Contracting State from the alienation of immovable property referred to in Article 6 and situated in the other Contracting State may be taxed in that other State.

2. Gains from the alienation of movable property forming part of the business property of a permanent establishment which an enterprise of a Contracting State has in the other Contracting State or of movable property pertaining to a fixed base available to a resident of a Contracting State in the other Contracting State for the purpose of performing independent personal services, including such gains from the alienation of such a permanent establishment (alone or with the whole enterprise) or of such fixed base, may be taxed in that other State.

3. Gains from the alienation of ships or aircraft operated in international traffic, boats engaged in inland waterways transport or movable property pertaining to the operation of such ships, aircraft or boats, shall be taxable only in the Contracting State in which the place of effective management of the enterprise is situated.

4. Gains from the alienation of shares of the capital stock of a company the property of which consists directly or indirectly principally of immovable property situated in a Contracting State may be taxed in that State.

5. Gains from the alienation of shares other than those mentioned in paragraph 4 representing a participation of . . . per cent (the percentage is to be established through bilateral negotiations) in a company which is a resident of a Contracting State may be taxed in that State.

[4]6. Gains from the alienation of any property other than that referred to in paragraphs 1, 2 [and] 3, *4 and 5*, shall be taxable only in the Contracting State of which the alienator is a resident.

Article 14: Independent Personal Services

1. Income derived by a resident of a Contracting State in respect of professional services or other activities of an independent character shall be taxable only in that State [unless he has a fixed base regularly available to him in the other Contracting State for the purpose of performing his activities. If he has such a fixed base, the income may be taxed in the other State but only so much of it as is attributable to that fixed base.] *except in the following circumstances, when such income may also be taxed in the other Contracting State.*

(a) If he has a fixed base regularly available to him in the other Contracting State for the purpose of performing his activities; in that case, only so much of the income as is attributable to that fixed base may be taxed in that other Contracting State; or

(b) if his stay in the other Contracting State is for a period or periods amounting to or exceeding in the aggregate 183 days in the fiscal year concerned; in that case, only so much of the income as is derived from his activities performed in that other State may be taxed in that other State; or

(c) if the remuneration for his activities in the other Contracting State is paid by a resident of that Contracting State and exceeds in the fiscal year . . . (the amount is to be established through bilateral negotiations).

2. The term 'professional services' includes especially independent scientific, literary, artistic, educational or teaching activities as well as the independent activities of physicians, lawyers, engineers, architects, dentists and accountants.

Article 15: Dependent Personal Services

1. Subject to the provisions of Articles 16, 18 and 19, salaries, wages and other similar remuneration derived by a resident of a Contracting State in respect of an employment shall be taxable only in that State unless the employment is exercised in the other Contracting State. If the employment is so exercised, such remuneration as is derived therefrom may be taxed in that other State.

2. Notwithstanding the provisions of paragraph 1, remuneration derived by a resident of a Contracting State in respect of an employment exercised in the other Contracting State shall be taxable only in the first-mentioned State if:

(a) the recipient is present in the other State for a period or periods not exceeding in the aggregate 183 days in the fiscal year concerned, and

(b) the remuneration is paid by, or on behalf of, an employer who is not a resident of the other State, and

(c) the remuneration is not borne by a permanent establishment or a fixed base which the employer has in the other State.

3. Notwithstanding the preceding provisions of this Article, remuneration derived in respect of an employment exercised aboard a ship or aircraft operated in international traffic, or aboard a boat engaged in inland waterways transport may be taxed in the Contracting State in which the place of effective management of the enterprise is situated.

Article 16: Directors' Fees *and Remuneration of Top Level Managerial Officials*

1. Directors' fees and other similar payments derived by a resident of a Contracting State in his capacity as a member of the board of directors of a company which is a resident of the other Contracting State may be taxed in that other State.

2. Salaries, wages and other similar remuneration derived by a resident of a Contracting State in his capacity as an official in a top-level managerial position of a company which is a resident of the other Contracting State may be taxed in that other State.

Article 17: [Artistes] *Income Earned by Entertainers and Athletes*

1. Notwithstanding the provisions of Articles 14 and 15, income derived by a resident of a Contracting State as an entertainer, such as a theatre, motion picture, radio or television artiste, or a musician, or as an athlete, from his personal activities as such exercised in the other Contracting State, may be taxed in that other State.

2. Where income in respect of personal activities exercised by an entertainer or an athlete in his capacity as such accrues not to the entertainer or athlete himself but to another person, that income may, notwithstanding the provisions of Articles 7, 14 and 15, be taxed in the Contracting State in which the activities of the entertainer or athlete are exercised.

Article 18: Pensions *and Social Security Payments*

Article *18a (alternative a)*

1. Subject to the provisions of paragraph 2 of Article 19, pensions and other similar remuneration paid to a resident of a Contracting State in consideration of past employment shall be taxable only in that State.

2. Notwithstanding the provisions of paragraph 1, pensions paid and other payments made under a public scheme which is part of the social security system of a Contracting State or a political subdivision or a local authority thereof shall be taxable only in that State.

Article *18b (Alternative b)*

1. Subject to the provisions of paragraph 2 of Article 19, pensions and other similar remuneration paid to a resident of a Contracting State in consideration of past employment *may be taxed* in that State.

2. However, such pensions and other similar remuneration may also be taxed in the other Contracting State if the payment is made by a resident of that other State or a permanent establishment situated therein.

3. Notwithstanding the provisions of paragraphs 1 and 2, pensions paid and other payments made under a public scheme which is part of the social security system of a Contracting State or a political subdivision or a local authority thereof shall be taxable only in that State.

Article 19: *Remuneration and Pensions in Respect of* Government Service

1. (a) Remuneration, other than a pension, paid by a Contracting State or a political subdivision or a local authority thereof to an individual in respect of services rendered to that State or subdivision or authority shall be taxable only in that State.

(b) However, such remuneration shall be taxable only in the other Contracting State if the services are rendered in that *other* State and the individual is a resident of that State who:

(i) is a national of that State; or

(ii) did not become a resident of that State solely for the purpose of rendering the services.

2. (a) Any pension paid by, or out of funds created by, a Contracting State or a political subdivision or a local authority thereof to an individual in respect of services rendered to that State or subdivision or authority shall be taxable only in that State.

(b) However, such pension shall be taxable only in the other Contracting State if the individual is a resident of, and a national of, that *other* State.

3. The provisions of Articles 15, 16 and 18 shall apply to remuneration and pensions in respect of services rendered in connection with a business carried on by a Contracting State or a political subdivision or a local authority thereof.

Article 20: *Payments Received by* Students *and Apprentices*

1. Payments which a student or business apprentice who is or was immediately before visiting a Contracting State a resident of the other Contracting State and who is present in the first-mentioned State solely for the purpose of his education or training receives for the purpose of his maintenance, education or training shall not be taxed in that State, provided that such payments arise from sources outside that State.

2. In respect of grants, scholarships and remuneration from employment not covered by paragraph 1, a student or business apprentice described in paragraph 1 shall, in addition, be entitled during such education or training to the same exemptions, reliefs or reductions in respect of taxes available to residents of the state which he is visiting.

Article 21: Other Income

1. Items of income of a resident of a Contracting State, wherever arising, not dealt with in the foregoing Articles of this Convention shall be taxable only in that State.

2. The provisions of paragraph 1 shall not apply to income, other than income from

immovable property as defined in paragraph 2 of Article 6, if the recipient of such income, being a resident of a Contracting State, carries on business in the other Contracting State through a permanent establishment situated therein, or performs in that other State independent personal services from a fixed base situated therein, and the right or property in respect of which the income is paid is effectively connected with such permanent establishment or fixed base. In such case the provisions of Article 7 or Article 14, as the case may be, shall apply.

3. Notwithstanding the provisions of paragraphs 1 and 2, items of income of a resident of a Contracting State not dealt with in the foregoing articles of this Convention and arising in the other Contracting State may also be taxed in that other State.

Chapter IV: Taxation of Capital

Article 22: Capital

1. Capital represented by immovable property referred to in Article 6, owned by a resident of a Contracting State and situated in the other Contracting State, may be taxed in that other State.

2. Capital represented by movable property forming part of the business property of a permanent establishment which an enterprise of a contracting State has in the other Contracting State or by movable property pertaining to a fixed base available to a resident of a Contracting State in the other Contracting State for the purpose of performing independent personal services, may be taxed in that other State.

3. Capital represented by ships and aircraft operated in international traffic and by boats engaged in inland waterways transport, and by movable property pertaining to the operation of such ships, aircraft and boats, shall be taxable only in the Contracting State in which the place of effective management of the enterprise is situated.

4. All other elements of capital of a resident of a Contracting State shall be taxable only in that State.

(The Group decided to leave to bilateral negotiations the question of the taxation of the capital represented by immovable property and movable property and of all other elements of capital of a resident of a Contracting State. Should the negotiating parties decide to include in the Convention an article on the taxation of capital, they will have to determine whether to use the wording of paragraph 4 as shown, or wording that leaves taxation to the State in which the capital is located.)

Chapter V: Methods for Elimination of Double Taxation

Article 23a: Exemption Method

1. Where a resident of a Contracting State derives income or owns capital which, in accordance with the provisions of this Convention, may be taxed in the other Contracting State, the first-mentioned State shall, subject to the provisions of paragraphs 2 and 3, exempt such income or capital from tax.

2. Where a resident of a Contracting State derives items of income which, in accordance with the provisions of Articles 10 [and] 11, *and 12* may be taxed in the other

Contracting State, the first-mentioned State shall allow as a deduction from the tax on the income of that resident an amount equal to the tax paid in that other State. Such deduction shall not, however, exceed that part of the tax, as computed before the deduction is given, which is attributable to such items of income derived from that other State.

3. Where in accordance with any provision of [the] *this* Convention income derived or capital owned by a resident of a Contracting State is exempt from tax in that State, such State may nevertheless, in calculating the amount of tax on the remaining income or capital of such resident, take into account the exempted income or capital.

Article 23b: Credit Method

1. Where a resident of a Contracting State derives income or owns capital which, in accordance with the provisions of this Convention, may be taxed in the other Contracting State, the first-mentioned State shall allow[:

(a)] as a deduction from the tax on the income of that resident, an amount equal to the income tax paid in that other State;] *and*
[(b)] as a deduction from the tax on the capital of that resident, an amount equal to the capital tax paid in that other State. Such deduction in either case shall not, however, exceed that part of the income tax or capital tax, as computed before the deduction is given, which is attributable, as the case may be, to the income or the capital which may be taxed in that other State.

2. Where in accordance with any provision of [the] *this* Convention income derived or capital owned by a resident of a Contracting State is exempt from tax in that State, such State may nevertheless, in calculating the amount of tax on the remaining income or capital of such resident, take into account the exempted income or capital.

Chapter VI: Special Provisions

Article 24: Non-discrimination

1. Nationals of a Contracting State shall not be subjected in the other Contracting State to any taxation or any requirement connected therewith, which is other or more burdensome than the taxation and connected requirements to which nationals of that other State in the same circumstances are or may be subjected. This provision shall, notwithstanding the provisions of Article 1, also apply to persons who are not residents of one or both of the Contracting States.

2. The term 'nationals' means:

(a) all individuals possessing the nationality of a Contracting State;
(b) all legal persons, partnerships and associations deriving their status as such from the laws in force in a Contracting State.

3. Stateless persons who are residents of a Contracting State shall not be subjected in either Contracting State to any taxation or any requirement connected therewith, which is other or more burdensome than the taxation and connected requirements to which nationals of the State concerned in the same circumstances are or may be subjected.

4. The taxation on a permanent establishment which an enterprise of a Contracting State has in the other Contracting State shall not be less favourably levied in that other State than the taxation levied on enterprises of that other State carrying on the same activities. This provision shall not be construed as obliging a Contracting State to grant to residents of the other Contracting State any personal allowances, reliefs and reductions for taxation purposes on account of civil status or family responsibilities which it grants to its own residents.

5. Except where the provisions of paragraph 1 of Article 9, paragraph 6 of Article 11, or paragraph [4] 6 of Article 12, apply, interest, royalties and other disbursements paid by an enterprise of a Contracting State to a resident of the other Contracting State shall, for the purpose of determining the taxable profits of such enterprise, be deductible under the same conditions as if they had been paid to a resident of the first-mentioned State. Similarly, any debts of an enterprise of a Contracting State to a resident of the other Contracting State shall, for the purpose of determining the taxable capital of such enterprise, be deductible under the same conditions as if they had been contracted to a resident of the first-mentioned State.

6. Enterprises of a Contracting State, the capital of which is wholly or partly owned or controlled, directly or indirectly, by one or more residents of the other Contracting State, shall not be subjected in the first-mentioned State to any taxation or any requirement connected therewith which is other or more burdensome than the taxation and connected requirements to which other similar enterprises of the first-mentioned State are or may be subjected.

7. The provisions of this Article shall, notwithstanding the provisions of Article 2, apply to taxes of every kind and description.

Article 25: Mutual Agreement Procedure

1. Where a person considers that the actions of one or both of the Contracting States result or will result for him in taxation not in accordance with the provisions of this Convention, he may, irrespective of the remedies provided by the domestic law of those States, present his case to the competent authority of the Contracting State of which he is a resident or, if his case comes under paragraph 1 of Article 24, to that of the Contracting State of which he is a national. The case must be presented within three years from the first notification of the action resulting in taxation not in accordance with the provisions of the Convention.

2. The competent authority shall endeavour, if the objection appears to it to be justified and if it is not itself able to arrive at a satisfactory solution, to resolve the case by mutual agreement with the competent authority of the other Contracting State, with a view to the avoidance of taxation which is not in accordance with [the] *this* Convention. Any agreement reached shall be implemented notwithstanding any time limits in the domestic law of the Contracting States.

3. The competent authorities of the Contracting States shall endeavour to resolve by mutual agreement any difficulties or doubts arising as to the interpretation or application of the Convention. They may also consult together for the elimination of double taxation in cases not provided for in the Convention.

4. The competent authorities of the Contracting States may communicate with each other directly for the purpose of reaching an agreement in the sense of the preceding paragraphs. [When it seems advisable in order to reach agreement to have an oral exchange of opinions, such exchange may take place through a Commission consisting of representatives of the competent authorities of the Contracting States.] *The competent authorities, through consultations, shall develop appropriate bilateral procedures, conditions, methods and techniques for the implementation of the mutual agreement procedure provided for in this article. In addition, a competent authority may devise appropriate unilateral procedures, conditions, methods and techniques to facilitate the above-mentioned bilateral actions and the implementation of the mutual agreement procedure.*

Article 26: Exchange of Information

1. The competent authorities of the Contracting States shall exchange such information as is necessary for carrying out the provisions of this Convention or of the domestic laws of the Contracting States concerning taxes covered by the Convention insofar as the taxation thereunder is not contrary to the Convention *in particular for the prevention of fraud or evasion of such taxes*. The exchange of information is not restricted by Article 1. Any information received by a Contracting State shall be treated as secret in the same manner as information obtained under the domestic laws of that State. *However, if the information is originally regarded as secret in the transmitting State it* [and] shall be disclosed only to persons or authorities (including courts and administrative bodies) involved in the assessment or collection of, the enforcement or prosecution in respect of, or the determination of appeals in relation to, the taxes [covered by] *which are the subject of* the Convention. Such persons or authorities shall use the information only for such purposes[. They] *but* may disclose the information in public court proceedings or in judicial decisions. *The competent authorities shall, through consultations, develop appropriate conditions, methods and techniques concerning the matters in respect of which such exchanges of information shall be made, including, where appropriate, exchanges of information regarding tax avoidance.*

2. In no case shall the provisions of paragraph 1 be construed so as to impose on a Contracting State the obligation:

    (a) to carry out administrative measures at variance with the laws and administrative practice of that or of the other Contracting State;

    (b) to supply information which is not obtainable under the laws or in the normal course of the administration of that or of the other Contracting State;

    (c) to supply information which would disclose any trade, business, industrial, commercial or professional secret or trade process, or information, the disclosure of which would be contrary to public policy (*ordre public*).

Article 27: Diplomatic Agents and Consular Officers

Nothing in this Convention shall affect the fiscal privileges of diplomatic agents or consular officers under the general rules of international law or under the provisions of special agreements.

[Article 28: Territorial Extension

1. This Convention may be extended, either in its entirety or with any necessary modifications {to any part of the territory of (State A) or of (State B) which is specifically excluded from the application of the Convention or}, to any State or territory for whose international relations (State A) or (State B) is responsible, which imposes taxes substantially similar in character to those to which the Convention applies. Any such extension shall take effect from such date and subject to such modifications and conditions, including conditions as to termination, as may be specified and agreed between the Contracting States in notes to be exchanged through diplomatic channels or in any other manner in accordance with their constitutional procedures.

2. Unless otherwise agreed by both Contracting States, the termination of the Convention by one of them under Article 30 shall also terminate, in the manner provided for in that Article, the application of the Convention {to any part of the territory of (State A) or of (State B) or} to any State or territory to which it has been extended under this Article.

Note: The words between brackets { } are of relevance when, by special provision, a part of the territory of a Contracting State is excluded from the application of the Convention.]

Chapter VII: Final Provisions

Article [29] *28*: Entry Into Force

1. This Convention shall be ratified and the instruments of ratification shall be exchanged at . . . as soon as possible.

2. The Convention shall enter into force upon the exchange of instruments of ratification and its provisions shall have effect:

    (a) (in State A): . . .
    (b) (in State B): . . .

Article 30: Termination

This Convention shall remain in force until terminated by a Contracting State. Either Contracting State may terminate the Convention, through diplomatic channels, by giving notice of termination at least six months before the end of any calendar year after the year. . . . In such event, the Convention shall cease to have effect:

    (a) (in State A): . . .
    (b) (in State B): . . .

Terminal clause

Note: The *provisions relating to the entry into force and termination and the* terminal clause concerning the signing *of the Convention* shall be drafted in accordance with the constitutional procedure of both Contracting States.

US Treasury Department's Model Income Tax
Treaty of 16 June 1981

The United States of America and . . . desiring to conclude a convention for the avoidance of double taxation and the prevention of fiscal evasion with respect to taxes on income and capital, have agreed as follows:

Article 1: General Scope

1. This Convention shall apply to persons who are residents of one or both of the Contracting States, except as otherwise provided in the Convention.

2. The Convention shall not restrict in any manner any exclusion, exemption, deduction, credit, or other allowance now or hereafter accorded

(a) by the laws of either Contracting State; or
(b) by any other agreement between the Contracting States.

3. Notwithstanding any provision of the Convention except paragraph 4, a Contracting State may tax its residents (as determined under Article 4 (Residence)), and by reason of citizenship may tax its citizens, as if the Convention had not come into effect. For this purpose, the term 'citizen' shall include a former citizen whose loss of citizenship had as one of its principal purposes the avoidance of income tax, but only for a period of ten years following such loss.

4. The provisions of paragraph 3 shall not affect

(a) the benefits conferred by a Contracting State under paragraph 2 of Article 9 (Associated Enterprises), under paragraphs 1(b) and 4 of Article 18 (Pensions, Annuities, Alimony, and Child Support), and under Articles 23 (Relief From Double Taxation), 24 (Non-Discrimination), and 25 (Mutual Agreement Procedure); and

(b) the benefits conferred by a Contracting State under Articles 19 (Government Service), 20 (Students and Trainees), and 27 (Diplomatic Agents and Consular Officers), upon individuals who are neither citizens of, nor have immigrant status in, that State.

Article 2: Taxes Covered

1. The existing taxes to which this Convention shall apply are

(a) in the United States: the Federal income taxes imposed by the Internal Revenue Code (but excluding the accumulated earnings tax, the personal holding company tax, and social security taxes), and the excise taxes imposed on insurance premiums paid to foreign insurers and with respect to private foundations. The Convention shall, however, apply to the excise taxes imposed on insurance premiums paid to foreign insurers only to the extent that the risks covered by such premiums are not reinsured with a person not entitled to the benefits of this or any other convention which applies to these taxes;

(b) in. . . .

2. The Convention shall apply also to any identical or substantially similar taxes which are imposed after the date of signature of the Convention in addition to, or in place of, the existing taxes. The competent authorities of the Contracting State shall notify each other of any significant changes which have been made in their respective taxation laws and of any official published material concerning the application of the Convention, including explanations, regulations, rulings, or judicial decisions.

Article 3: General Definitions

1. For the purposes of this Convention, unless the context otherwise requires

(a) the term 'person' includes an individual, an estate, a trust, a partnership, a company, and any other body of persons;

(b) the term 'company' means any body corporate or any entity which is treated as a body corporate for tax purposes;

(c) the terms 'enterprise of a Contracting State' and 'enterprise of the other Contracting State' mean respectively an enterprise carried on by a resident of a Contracting State and an enterprise carried on by a resident of the other Contracting State;

(d) the term 'international traffic' means any transport by a ship or aircraft, except when such transport is solely between places in the other Contracting State;

(e) the term 'competent authority' means

(i) in the United States: the Secretary of the Treasury or his delegate; and
(ii) in. . . .

(f) the term 'United States' means the United States of America, but does not include Puerto Rico, the Virgin Islands, Guam, or any other United States possession or territory;

(g) the term . . . means. . . .

2. As regards the application of the Convention by a Contracting State any term not defined therein shall, unless the context otherwise requires or the competent authorities agree to a common meaning pursuant to the provisions of Article 25 (Mutual Agreement Procedure), have the meaning which it has under the laws of that State concerning the taxes to which the Convention applies.

Article 4: Residence

1. For the purposes of this Convention, the term 'resident of a Contracting State' means any person who, under the laws of that State, is liable to tax therein by reason of his domicile, residence, citizenship, place of management, place of incorporation, or any other criterion of a similar nature, provided, however, that

(a) this term does not include any person who is liable to tax in that State in respect only of income from sources in that State or capital situated therein; and

(b) in the case of income derived or paid by a partnership, estate, or trust, this term applies only to the extent that the income derived by such partnership, estate, or trust is subject to tax in that State as the income of a resident, either in its hands or in the hands of its partners or beneficiaries.

2. Where by reason of the provisions of paragraph 1, an individual is a resident of both Contracting States, then his status shall be determined as follows:

(a) he shall be deemed to be a resident of the State in which he has a permanent home available to him; if he has a permanent home available to him in both States, he shall be deemed to be a resident of the State with which his personal and economic relations are closer (center of vital interests);

(b) if the State in which he has his center of vital interests cannot be determined, or if he does not have a permanent home available to him in either State, he shall be deemed to be a resident of the State in which he has an habitual abode;

(c) if he has an habitual abode in both States or in neither of them, he shall be deemed to be a resident of the State of which he is a national;

(d) if he is a national of both States or of neither of them, the competent authorities of the Contracting States shall settle the question by mutual agreement.

3. Where by reason of the provisions of paragraph 1 a company is a resident of both Contracting States, then if it is created under the laws of a Contracting State or a political subdivision thereof, it shall be deemed to be a resident of that State.

4. Where by reason of the provisions of paragraph 1 a person other than an individual or a company is a resident of both Contracting States, the competent authorities of the Contracting States shall settle the question by mutual agreement and determine the mode of application of the Convention to such person.

Article 5: Permanent Establishment

1. For the purposes of this Convention, the term 'permanent establishment' means a fixed place of business through which the business of an enterprise is wholly or partly carried on.

2. The term 'permanent establishment' includes especially

(a) a place of management;
(b) a branch;
(c) an office;
(d) a factory;
(e) a workshop; and
(f) a mine, an oil or gas well, a quarry, or any other place of extraction of natural resources.

3. A building site or construction or installation project, or an installation or drilling rig or ship used for the exploration or exploitation of natural resources, constitutes a permanent establishment only if it lasts more than twelve months.

4. Notwithstanding the preceding provisions of this Article, the term 'permanent establishment' shall be deemed not to include

(a) the use of facilities solely for the purpose of storage, display, or delivery of goods or merchandise belonging to the enterprise;

(b) the maintenance of a stock of goods or merchandise belonging to the enterprise solely for the purpose of storage, display, or delivery;

(c) the maintenance of a stock of goods or merchandise belonging to the enterprise solely for the purpose of processing by another enterprise;

(d) the maintenance of a fixed place of business solely for the purpose of purchasing goods or merchandise, or of collecting information, for the enterprise;

(e) the maintenance of a fixed place of business solely for the purpose of carrying on, for the enterprise, any other activity of a preparatory on auxiliary character;

(f) the maintenance of a fixed place of business solely for any combination of the activities mentioned in subparagraphs (a) to (e).

5. Notwithstanding the provisions of paragraphs 1 and 2, where a person – other than an agent of an independent status to whom paragraph 6 applies – is acting on behalf of an enterprise and has and habitually exercises in a Contracting State an authority to conclude contracts in the name of the enterprise, that enterprise shall be deemed to have a permanent establishment in that State in respect of any activities which that person undertakes for the enterprise, unless the activities of such person are limited to those mentioned in paragraph 4 which, if exercised through a fixed place of business, would not make this fixed place of business a permanent establishment under the provisions of that paragraph.

6. An enterprise shall not be deemed to have a permanent establishment in a Contracting State merely because it carries on business in that State through a broker, general commission agent, or any other agent of an independent status, provided that such persons are acting in the ordinary course of their business.

7. The fact that a company which is a resident of a Contracting State controls or is controlled by a company which is a resident of the other Contracting State, or which carries on business in that other State (whether through a permanent establishment or otherwise), shall not of itself constitute either company a permanent establishment of the other.

Article 6: Income from Real Property (Immovable Property)

1. Income derived by a resident of a Contracting State from real property (including income from agriculture or forestry) situated in the other Contracting State may be taxed in that other State.

2. The term 'real property' shall have the meaning which it has under the law of the Contracting State in which the property in question is situated.

3. The provisions of paragraph 1 shall apply to income derived from the direct use, letting, or use in any other form of real property.

4. The provisions of paragraphs 1 and 3 shall also apply to the income from real property of an enterprise and to income from real property used for the performance of independent personal services.

5. A resident of a Contracting State who is liable to tax in the other Contracting State on income from real property situated in the other Contracting State may elect for any taxable year to compute the tax on such income on a net basis as if such income were attributable to a permanent establishment in such other State. Any such election shall be binding for the taxable year of the election and all subsequent taxable years unless the competent authorities of the Contracting States, pursuant to a request by the taxpayer made to the competent authority of the Contracting State in which the taxpayer is a resident, agree to terminate the election.

Article 7: Business Profits

1. The business profits of an enterprise of a Contracting State shall be taxable only in that State unless the enterprise carries on business in the other Contracting State through a permanent establishment situated therein. If the enterprise carries on business as aforesaid, the business profits of the enterprise may be taxed in the other State but only so much of them as is attributable to that permanent establishment.

2. Subject to the provisions of paragraph 3, where an enterprise of a Contracting State carries on business in the other Contracting State through a permanent establishment situated therein, there shall in each Contracting State be attributed to that permanent establishment the business profits which it might be expected to make if it were a distinct and independent enterprise engaged in the same or similar activities under the same or similar conditions.

3. In determining the business profits of a permanent establishment, there shall be allowed as deductions expenses which are incurred for the purposes of the permanent establishment, including a reasonable allocation of executive and general administrative expenses, research and development expenses, interest, and other expenses incurred for the purposes of the enterprise as a whole (or the part thereof which includes the permanent establishment), whether incurred in the State in which the permanent establishment is situated or elsewhere.

4. No business profits shall be attributed to a permanent establishment by reason of the mere purchase by that permanent establishment of goods or merchandise for the enterprise.

5. For the purposes of this Convention, the business profits to be attributed to the permanent establishment shall include only the profits derived from the assets or activities of the permanent establishment and shall be determined by the same method year by year unless there is good and sufficient reason to the contrary.

6. Where business profits include items of income which are dealt with separately in other Articles of the Convention, then the provisions of those Articles shall not be affected by the provisions of this Article.

7. For the purposes of the Convention, the term 'business profits' means income derived from any trade or business, including the rental of tangible personal property and the rental or licensing of cinematographic films or films or tapes used for radio or television broadcasting.

Article 8: Shipping and Air Transport

1. Profits of an enterprise of a Contracting State from the operation of ships or aircraft in international traffic shall be taxable only in that State.

2. For the purposes of this Article, profits from the operation of ships or aircraft in international traffic include profits derived from the rental of ships or aircraft if such ships or aircraft are operated in international traffic by the lessee or if such rental profits are incidental to other profits described in paragraph 1.

3. Profits of an enterprise of a Contracting State from the use, maintenance, or rental of

containers (including trailers barges, and related equipment for the transport of containers) used in international traffic shall be taxable only in that State.

4. The provisions of paragraphs 1 and 3 shall also apply to profits from participation in a pool, a joint business, or an international operating agency.

Article 9: Associated Enterprises

1. Where

(a) an enterprise of a Contracting State participates directly or indirectly in the management, control or capital of an enterprise of the other Contracting State: or

(b) the same persons participate directly or indirectly in the management, control, or capital of an enterprise of a Contracting State and an enterprise of the other Contracting State, and in either case conditions are made or imposed between the two enterprises in their commercial or financial relations which differ from those which would be made between independent enterprises, then any profits which, but for those conditions would have accrued to one of the enterprises, but by reason of those conditions have not so accrued, may be included in the profits of that enterprise and taxed accordingly.

2. Where a Contracting State includes in the profits of an enterprise of that State, and taxes accordingly, profits on which an enterprise of the other Contracting State has been charged to tax in that other State, and the profits so included are profits which would have accrued to the enterprise of the first-mentioned State if the conditions made between the two enterprises had been those which would have been made between independent enterprises, then that other State shall make an appropriate adjustment to the amount of the tax charged therein on those profits. In determining such adjustment due regard shall be paid to the other provisions of this Convention and the competent authorities of the Contracting States shall if necessary consult each other.

3. The provisions of paragraph 1 shall not limit any provisions of the law of either Contracting State which permit the distribution, apportionment, or allocation of income, deductions, credits, or allowances between persons, whether or not residents of a Contracting State, owned or controlled directly or indirectly by the same interests when necessary in order to prevent evasion of taxes or clearly to reflect the income of any of such persons.

Article 10: Dividends

1. Dividends paid by a company which is a resident of a Contracting State to a resident of the other Contracting State may be taxed in that other State.

2. However, such dividends may also be taxed in the Contracting State of which the company paying the dividends is a resident, and according to the laws of that State, but if the beneficial owner of the dividends is a resident of the other Contracting State, the tax so charged shall not exceed.

(a) 5 per cent of the gross amount of the dividends if the beneficial owner is a company which owns at least 10 per cent of the voting stock of the company paying the dividends;

(b) 15 per cent of the gross amount of the dividends in all other cases. This paragraph shall not affect the taxation of the company in respect of the profits out of which the dividends are paid.

3. The term 'dividends' as used in this Article means income from shares or other rights, not being debt-claims, participating in profits, as well as income from other corporate rights which is subjected to the same taxation treatment as income from shares by the laws of the State of which the company making the distribution is a resident.

4. The provisions of paragraph 2 shall not apply if the beneficial owner of the dividends, being a resident of a Contracting State, carries on business in the other Contracting State, of which the company paying the dividends is a resident, through a permanent establishment situated therein, or performs in that other State independent personal services from a fixed base situated therein, and the dividends are attributable to such permanent establishment or fixed base. In such case the provisions of Article 7 (Business Profits) or Article 14 (Independent Personal Services), as the case may be, shall apply.

5. A Contracting State may not impose any tax on dividends paid by a company which is not a resident of that State, except insofar as

(a) the dividends are paid to a resident of that State,
(b) the dividends are attributable to a permanent establishment or a fixed base situated in that State, or
(c) the dividends are paid out of profits attributable to one or more permanent establishments of such company in that State, provided that the gross income of the company attributable to such permanent establishment constituted at least 50 per cent of the company's gross income from all sources. Where subparagraph (c) applies and subparagraphs (a) and (b) do not apply, the tax shall be subject to the limitations of paragraph 2.

Article 11: Interest

1. Interest derived and beneficially owned by a resident of a Contracting State shall be taxable only in that State.

2. The term 'interest' as used in this Convention means income from debt-claims of every kind, whether or not secured by mortgage, and whether or not carrying a right to participate in the debtor's profits, and in particular, income from government securities, and income from bonds or debentures, including premiums or prizes attaching to such securities, bonds, or debentures. Penalty charges for late payment shall not be regarded as interest for the purposes of the Convention.

3. The provisions of paragraph 1 shall not apply if the beneficial owner of the interest, being a resident of a Contracting State, carries on business in the other Contracting State, in which the interest arises, through a permanent establishment situated therein, or performs in that other State independent personal services from a fixed base situated therein, and the interest is attributable to such permanent establishment or fixed base. In such case the provisions of Article 7 (Business Profits) or Article 14 (Independent Personal Services), as the case may be, shall apply.

4. Interest shall be deemed to arise in a Contracting State when the payer is that State itself or a political subdivision, local authority, or resident of that State. Where, however, the person paying the interest, whether he is a resident of a Contracting State or not, has in a Contracting State a permanent establishment or a fixed base in connection with which the indebtedness on which the interest is paid was incurred, and such interest is borne by such permanent establishment or fixed base, then such interest shall be deemed to arise in the State in which the permanent establishment or fixed base is situated.

5. Where, by reason of a special relationship between the payer and the beneficial owner or between both of them and some other person, the amount of the interest, having regard to the debt-claim for which it is aid, exceeds the amount which would have been agreed upon by the payer and the beneficial owner in the absence of such relationship, the provisions of this Article shall apply only to the last-mentioned amount. In such case the excess part of the payments shall remain taxable according to the laws of each Contracting State, due regard being had to the other provisions of the Convention.

6. A Contracting State may not impose any tax on interest paid by a resident of the other Contracting State, except insofar as

    (a) the interest is paid to a resident of the first-mentioned State;

    (b) the interest is attributable to a permanent establishment or a fixed base situated in the first-mentioned State; or

    (c) the interest arises in the first-mentioned State and is not paid to a resident of the other State.

Article 12: Royalties

1. Royalties derived and beneficially owned by a resident of a Contracting State shall be taxable only in that State.

2. The term 'royalties' as used in this Convention means payments of any kind received as a consideration for the use of, or the right to use, any copyright of literary, artistic, or scientific work (but not including cinematographic films or films used for radio or television broadcasting), any patent, trademark, design or model, plan, secret formula or process, or other like right or property, or for information concerning industrial, commercial, or scientific experience. The term 'royalties' also includes gains derived from the alienation of any such right or property which are contingent on the productivity, use, or disposition thereof.

3. The provisions of paragraph 1 shall not apply if the beneficial owner of the royalties, being a resident of a Contracting State carries on business in the other Contracting State, in which the royalties arise, through a permanent establishment situated therein, or performs in that other State independent personal services from a fixed base situated therein, and the royalties are attributable to such permanent establishment or fixed base. In such case the provisions of Article 7 (Business Profits) or Article 14 (Independent Personal Services), as the case may be, shall apply.

4. Where, by reason of a special relationship between the payer and the beneficial owner or between both of them and some other person, the amount of the royalties,

having regard to the use, right, or information for which they are paid, exceeds the amount which would have been agreed upon by the payer and the beneficial owner in the absence of such relationship, the provisions of this Article shall apply only to the last-mentioned amount. In such case the excess part of the payments shall remain taxable according to the laws of each Contracting State, due regard being had to the other provisions of the Convention.

Article 13: Gains

1. Gains derived by a resident of a Contracting State from the alienation of real property referred to in Article 6 (Income from Real Property (Immovable Property)) and situated in the other Contracting State may be taxed in that other State.
2. Gains from the alienation of

(a) shares of the stock of a company (whether or not a resident of a Contracting State) the property of which consists principally of real property situated in a Contracting State; or
(b) an interest in a partnership, trust, or estate (whether or not a resident of a Contracting State) to the extent attributable to real property situated in a Contracting State may be taxed in that State. For the purposes of this paragraph, the term 'real property' includes the shares of a company referred to in subparagraph (a) or an interest in a partnership, trust, or estate referred to in subparagraph (b).

3. Gains from the alienation of personal property which are attributable to a permanent establishment which an enterprise of a Contracting State has in the other Contracting State, or which are attributable to a fixed base available to a resident of a Contracting State in the other Contracting State for the purpose of performing independent personal services, and gains from the alienation of such a permanent establishment (alone or with the whole enterprise) or such a fixed base, may be taxed in that other State.

4. Gains derived by an enterprise of a Contracting state from the alienation of ships, aircraft, or containers operated in international traffic shall be taxable only in that State.

5. Gains described in Article 12 (Royalties) shall be taxable only in accordance with the provisions of Article 12.

6. Gains from the alienation of any property other than property referred to in paragraphs 1 through 5 shall be taxable only in the Contracting State of which the alienator is a resident.

Article 14: Independent Personal Services

Income derived by an individual who is a resident of a Contracting State from the performance of personal services in an independent capacity shall be taxable only in that State, unless such services are performed in the other Contracting State and the income is attributable to a fixed base regularly available to the individual in that other State for the purpose of performing his activities.

Article 15: Dependent Personal Services

1. Subject to the provisions of Articles 18 (Pensions, Annuities, Alimony, and Child Support) and 19 (Government Service), salaries, wages, and other similar remuneration derived by a resident of a Contracting State in respect of an employment shall be taxable only in that State unless the employment is exercised in the other Contracting State. If the employment is so exercised, such remuneration as is derived therefrom may be taxed in that other State.

2. Notwithstanding the provisions of paragraph 1, remuneration derived by a resident of a Contracting State in respect of an employment exercised in the other Contracting State shall be taxable only in the first-mentioned State if

(a) the recipient is present in the other State for a period or periods not exceeding in the aggregate 183 days in the taxable year concerned;

(b) the remuneration is paid by, or on behalf of, an employer who is not a resident of the other State; and

(c) the remuneration is not borne by a permanent establishment or a fixed base which the employer has in the other State.

3. Notwithstanding the preceding provisions of this Article, remuneration derived by a resident of a Contracting State in respect of an employment as a member of the regular complement of a ship or aircraft operated in international traffic may be taxed only in that State.

Article 16: Limitation on Benefits

1. A person (other than an individual) which is a resident of a Contracting State shall not be entitled under this Convention to relief from taxation in the other Contracting State unless

(a) more than 75 per cent of the beneficial interest in such person is owned, directly or indirectly, by one or more individual residents of the first-mentioned Contracting State; and

(b) the income of such person is not used in substantial part, directly or indirectly, to meet liabilities (including liabilities for interest or royalties) to persons who are residents of a State other than a Contracting State and who are not citizens of the United States.

For the purposes of subparagraph (a), a company that has substantial trading in its stock on a recognized exchange in a Contracting State is presumed to be owned by individual residents of that Contracting State.

2. Paragraph 1 shall not apply if it is determined that the acquisition or maintenance of such person and the conduct of its operations did not have as a principal purpose obtaining benefits under the Convention.

3. Any relief from tax provided by a Contracting State to a resident of the other Contracting State under the Convention shall be inapplicable to the extent that, under the law in force in that other State, the income to which the relief relates bears significantly lower tax than similar income arising within that other State derived by residents of that other State.

Article 17: Artistes and Athletes

1. Notwithstanding the provisions of Articles 14 (Independent Personal Services) and 15 (Dependent Personal Services), income derived by a resident of a Contracting State as an entertainer, such as a theatre, motion picture, radio, or television artiste, or a musician, or as an athlete, from his personal activities as such exercised in the other Contracting State, may be taxed in that other State, except where the amount of the gross receipts derived by such entertainer or athlete, including expenses reimbursed to him or borne on his behalf, from such activities does not exceed twenty thousand United States dollars ($20,000) or its equivalent in . . . for the taxable year concerned.

2. Where income in respect of activities exercised by an entertainer or an athlete in his capacity as such accrues not to the entertainer or athlete but to another person, that income of that other person may, notwithstanding the provisions of Articles 7 (Business Profits) and 14 (Independent Personal Services), be taxed in the Contracting State in which the activities of the entertainer or athlete are exercised, unless it is established that neither the entertainer or athlete nor persons related thereto participated directly or indirectly in the profits of that other person in any manner, including the receipt of deferred remuneration, bonuses, fees, dividends, partnership distributions, or other distributions.

Article 18: Pensions, Annuities, Alimony and Child Support

1. Subject to the provisions of Article 19 (Government Service)

(a) pensions and other similar remuneration derived and beneficially owed by a resident of a Contracting State in consideration of past employment shall be taxable only in that State; and

(b) social security benefits and other public pensions paid by a Contracting State to a resident of the other Contracting State or a citizen of the United States shall be taxable only in the first-mentioned State.

2. Annuities derived and beneficially owned by a resident of a Contracting State shall be taxable only in that State. The term 'annuities' as used in this paragraph means a stated sum paid periodically at stated times during a specified number of years, under an obligation to make the payments in return for adequate and full consideration (other than services rendered).

3. Alimony paid to a resident of a Contracting State shall be taxable only in that State. The term 'alimony' as used in this paragraph means periodic payments made pursuant to a written separation agreement or a decree of divorce, separate maintenance, or compulsory support, which payments are taxable to the recipient under the laws of the State of which he is a resident.

4. Periodic payments for the support of a minor child made pursuant to a written separation agreement or a decree of divorce, separate maintenance, or compulsory support paid by a resident of a Contracting State to a resident of the other Contracting State, shall be taxable only in the first-mentioned State.

Article 19: Government Service

Remuneration, including a pension, paid from the public funds of a Contracting State or a political subdivision or local authority thereof to a citizen of that State in respect of services rendered in the discharge of functions of a governmental nature shall be taxable only in that State. However, the provisions of Article 14 (Independent Personal Services), Article 15 (Dependent Personal Services) or Article 17 (Artistes and Athletes), as the case may be, shall apply, and the preceding sentences shall not apply, to remuneration paid in respect of services rendered in connection with a business carried on by a Contracting State or a political subdivision or local authority thereof.

Article 20: Students and Trainees

Payments received for the purpose of maintenance, education, or training by a student, apprentice, or business trainee who is or was immediately before visiting a Contracting State a resident of the other Contracting State and who is present in the first-mentioned State for the purpose of his full-time education or training shall not be taxed in that State, provided that such payments arise outside that State.

Article 21: Other Income

1. Items of income of a resident of a Contracting State, wherever arising not dealt with in the foregoing Articles of this Convention shall be taxable only in that State.

2. The provisions of paragraph 1 shall not apply to income, other than income from real property as defined in paragraph 2 of Article 6 (Income from Real Property (Immovable Property)), if the beneficial owner of the income, being a resident of a Contracting State, carries on business in the other Contracting State through a permanent establishment situated therein, or performs in that other State independent personal services from a fixed base situated therein, and the income is attributable to such permanent establishment or fixed base. In such case the provisions of Article 7 (Business Profits) or Article 14 (Independent Personal Services), as the case may be, shall apply.

Article 22: Capital

1. Capital represented by real property referred to in Article 6 (Income from Real Property (Immovable Property)), owned by a resident of a Contracting State and situated in the other Contracting State, may be taxed in that other State.

2. Capital represented by personal property forming part of the business property of a permanent establishment which an enterprise of a Contracting State has in the other Contracting State, or by personal property pertaining to a fixed base available to a resident of a Contracting State in the other Contracting State for the purpose of performing independent personal services, may be taxed in that other State.

3. Capital represented by ships, aircraft, and containers owned by a resident of a Contracting State and operated in international traffic, and by personal property pertaining to the operation of such ships, aircraft, and containers shall be taxable only in that State.

4. All other elements of capital of a resident of a Contracting State shall be taxable only in that State.

Article 23: Relief from Double Taxation

1. In accordance with the provisions and subject to the limitations of the law of the United States (as it may be amended from time to time without changing the general principle hereof); the United States shall allow to a resident or citizen of the United States as a credit against the United States tax on income

(a) the income tax paid to . . . by or on behalf of such citizen or resident; and

(b) in the case of a United States company owning at least 10 per cent of the voting stock of a company which is a resident of . . . and from which the United States company receives dividends, the income tax paid to . . . by or on behalf of the distributing company with respect to the profits out of which the dividends are paid.

For the purposes of this paragraph, the taxes referred to in paragraphs 1(b) and 2 of Article 2 (Taxes Covered) shall be considered income taxes. Credits allowed solely by reason of the preceding sentence, when added to otherwise allowable credits for taxes referred to in paragraphs 1(b) and 2 of Article 2, shall not in any taxable year exceed that proportion of the United States tax on income which taxable income arising in . . . bears to total taxable income.

2. In accordance with the provisions and subject to the limitations of the law of . . . (as it may be amended from time to time without amending the general principle thereof) . . . shall allow to a resident or citizen of . . . as a credit against the . . . tax on income. . . .

3. For the purposes of allowing relief from double taxation pursuant to this Article, income shall be deemed to arise exclusively as follows

(a) income derived by a resident of a Contracting State which may be taxed in the other Contracting State in accordance with this Convention (other than solely by reason of citizenship in accordance with paragraph 2 of Article 1 (General Scope)) shall be deemed to arise in that other State;

(b) income derived by a resident of a Contracting State which may not be taxed in the other Contracting State in accordance with the Convention shall be deemed to arise in the first-mentioned State. The rules of this paragraph shall not apply in determining credits against United States tax for foreign taxes other than the taxes referred to in paragraphs 1(b) and 2 of Article 2 (Taxes Covered).

Article 24: Non-discrimination

1. Nationals of a Contracting State shall not be subjected in the other Contracting State to any taxation or any requirement connected therewith which is other or more burdensome than the taxation and connected requirements to which nationals of that other State in the same circumstances are or may be subjected. This provision shall apply to persons who are not residents of one or both of the Contracting States. However, for the purposes of United States tax, a United States national who is not a resident of the United States and a . . . national who is not a resident of the United States are not in the same circumstances.

2. For the purposes of this Convention, the term 'nationals' means

(a) in relation to . . . .; and
(b) in relation to the United States, United States citizens.

3. The taxation on a permanent establishment which an enterprise of a Contracting State has in the other Contracting State shall not be less favourably levied in that other State than the taxation levied on enterprises of that other State carrying on the same activities. This provision shall not be construed as obliging a Contracting State to grant to residents of the other Contracting State any personal allowances, relief, and reductions for taxation purposes on account of civil status or family responsibilities which it grants to its own residents.

4. Except where the provisions of paragraph 1 of Article 9 (Associated Enterprises), paragraph 5 of Article 11 (Interest), or paragraph 4 of Article 12 (Royalties) apply, interest, royalties, and other disbursements paid by a resident of a Contracting State to a resident of the other Contracting State shall, for the purposes of determining the taxable profits of the first-mentioned resident, be deductible under the same conditions as if they had been paid to a resident of the first-mentioned State. Similarly, any debts of a resident of a Contracting State to a resident of the other Contracting State shall, for the purposes of determining the taxable capital of the first-mentioned resident, be deductible under the same conditions as if they had been contracted to a resident of the first-mentioned State.

5. Enterprises of a Contracting State, the capital of which is wholly or partly owned or controlled, directly or indirectly, by one or more residents of the other Contracting State, shall not be subjected in the first-mentioned State to any taxation or any requirement connected therewith which is other or more burdensome than the taxation and connected requirements to which other similar enterprises of the first-mentioned State are or may be subjected.

6. The provisions of this Article shall, notwithstanding the provisions of Article 2 (Taxes Covered), apply to taxes of every kind and description imposed by a Contracting State or a political subdivision or local authority thereof.

Article 25: Mutual Agreement Procedure

1. Where a person considers that the actions of one or both of the Contracting States result or will result for him in taxation not in accordance with the provisions of this Convention, he may, irrespective of the remedies provided by the domestic law of those States, present his case to the competent authority of the Contracting State of which he is a resident or national.

2. The competent authority shall endeavour, if the objection appears to it to be justified and if it is not itself able to arrive at a satisfactory solution, to resolve the case by mutual agreement with the competent authority of the other Contracting State, with a view to the avoidance of taxation which is not in accordance with the Convention. Any agreement reached shall be implemented notwithstanding any time-limits or other procedural limitations in the domestic law of the Contracting States.

3. The competent authorities of the Contracting States shall endeavour to resolve by mutual agreement any difficulties or doubts arising as to the interpretation or

application of the Convention. In particular the competent authorities of the Contracting States may agree

(a) to the same attribution of income, deductions, credits, or allowances of an enterprise of a Contracting State to its permanent establishment situated in the other Contracting State;

(b) to the same allocation of income, deductions, credits, or allowances between persons;

(c) to the same characterization of particular items of income;

(d) to the same application of source rules with respect to particular items of income;

(e) to a common meaning of a term;

(f) to increases in any specific amounts referred to in the Convention to reflect economic or monetary developments; and

(g) to the application of the provisions of domestic law regarding penalties, fines, and interest in a manner consistent with the purposes of the Convention.

They may also consult together for the elimination of double taxation in cases not provided for in the Convention.

4. The competent authorities of the Contracting States may communicate with each other directly for the purpose of reaching an agreement in the sense of the preceding paragraphs.

Article 26: Exchange of Information and Administrative Assistance

1. The competent authorities of the Contracting States shall exchange such information as is necessary for carrying out the provisions of this Convention or of the domestic laws of the Contracting States concerning taxes covered by the Convention insofar as the taxation thereunder is not contrary to the Convention. The exchange of information is not restricted by Article 1 (General Scope). Any information received by a Contracting State shall be treated as secret in the same manner as information obtained under the domestic laws of that State and shall be disclosed only to persons or authorities (including courts and administrative bodies) involved in the assessment, collection, or administration of, the enforcement or prosecution in respect of, or the determination of appeals in relation to, the taxes covered by the Convention. Such persons or authorities shall use the information only for such purposes. They may disclose the information in public court proceedings or in judicial decisions.

2. In no case shall the provisions of paragraph 1 be construed so as to impose on a Contracting State the obligation

(a) to carry out administrative measures at variance with the laws and administrative practice of that or of the other Contracting State;

(b) to supply information which is not obtainable under the laws or in the normal course of the administration of that or of the other Contracting State;

(c) to supply information which would disclose any trade, business, industrial, commercial, or professional secret or trade process, or information the disclosure of which would be contrary to public policy (*ordre public*).

3. If information is requested by a Contracting State in accordance with this Article, the other Contracting State shall obtain the information to which the request relates in

the same manner and to the same extent as if the tax of the first-mentioned State were the tax of that other State and were being imposed by that other State. If specifically requested by the competent authority of a Contracting State, the competent authority of the other Contracting State shall provide information under this Article in the form of depositions of witnesses and authenticated copies of unedited original documents (including books, papers, statements, records, accounts, and writings), to the same extent such depositions and documents can be obtained under the laws and administrative practices of that other State with respect to its own taxes.

4. Each of the Contracting States shall endeavour to collect on behalf of the other Contracting State such amounts as may be necessary to ensure that relief granted by the Convention from taxation imposed by that other State does not enure to the benefit of persons not entitled thereto.

5. Paragraph 4 of this Article shall not impose upon either of the Contracting States the obligation to carry out administrative measures which are of a different nature from those used in the collection of its own taxes, or which would be contrary to its sovereignty, security, or public policy.

6. For the purposes of this Article, the Convention shall apply, notwithstanding the provisions of Article 2 (Taxes Covered), to taxes of every kind imposed by a Contracting State.

Article 27: Diplomatic Agents and Consular Officers

Nothing in this Convention shall affect the fiscal privileges of diplomatic agents or consular officers under the general rules of international law or under the provisions of special agreements.

Article 28: Entry into Force

1. This Convention shall be subject to ratification in accordance with the applicable procedures of each Contracting State and instruments of ratification shall be exchanged at . . . as soon as possible.

2. The Convention shall enter into force upon the exchange of instruments of ratification and its provisions shall have effect

(a) in respect of taxes withheld at source, for amounts paid or credited on or after the first day of the second month next following the date on which the Convention enters into force;

(b) in respect of other taxes, for taxable periods beginning on or after the first day of January next following the date on which the Convention enters into force.

Article 29: Termination

1. This Convention shall remain in force until terminated by a Contracting State. Either Contracting State may terminate the Convention at any time after five years from the date on which the Convention enters into force, provided that at least six months' prior notice of termination has been given through diplomatic channels. In such event, the Convention shall cease to have effect

(a) in respect of taxes withheld at source, for amounts paid or credited on or after the first day of January next following the expiration of the six months' period;

(b) in respect of other taxes, for taxable periods beginning on or after the first day of January next following the expiration of the six months' period.

DONE at . . . in duplicate, in the English and . . . languages, the two texts having equal authenticity, this . . . day of . . . . 19 . . .
FOR THE UNITED STATES OF AMERICA
FOR. . . .

Note

An alternative draft of Article 16 was published by press release on 23 December 1981. It has not been reproduced here, since treaty practice has continued to evolve, and the limitation on benefits provisions in particular have been subject to further change following negotiations with US treaty partners.

Bibliography

A. Articles and Books

Abrutyn, Michael & Halphen, Christine (1984) *Income Tax Treaties – Administrative and Competent Authority Aspects, Tax Management, Portfolio 402-2nd*, Bureau of National Affairs, Washington DC.

Adams, J. D. R. & Whalley, J. (1977) *The International Taxation of Multinational Enterprises in Developed Countries*, Institute for Fiscal Studies, Associated Business Programmes, London; Greenwood Press, USA.

Akehurst, M. (1972–3) 'Jurisdiction in International Law', XLVI *British Yearbook of International Law*, 145–257.

Aland, Robert B. (1981) 'The Treasury Report on Tax Havens – a Response', *Taxes*, 993–1030.

Albrecht, A. R. (1952) 'The Taxation of Aliens under International Law', XXIX *British Yearbook of International Law*, 145.

Albrecht, A. R. (1953) 'The Enforcement of Taxation under International Law', XXX *British Yearbook of International Law*, 454.

Allen, B. A. & Ward, C. S. (1985) *The United States, Transnational Business and the Law*, Oceana, New York.

Alworth, Julian S. (1988) *The Finance, Investment and Taxation Decisions of Multinationals*, Basil Blackwell, Oxford.

Amico, Joseph C. (1989) 'Brazil: Developing and Implementing Tax Treaty Policy: The Tax Sparing Clause', *Bulletin for International Fiscal Documentation*, 39–42.

Arnold, Brian J. (1985) 'The Taxation of Controlled Foreign Corporations: Defining and Designating Tax Havens', *British Tax Review*, 286–305; 362–76.

Arnold, Brian J. (1986) *The Taxation of Controlled Foreign Corporations: An International Comparison*, Canadian Tax Paper no. 78, Canadian Tax Foundation, Toronto.

Arthur Andersen & Co. (1985) Revenue Exchanges of Information.

Ashton, R. K. (1981) *Anti-Avoidance Legislation*, Butterworths, London.

Ashton, R. K. (1988) 'The Ramsay Saga – Is there Now Light at the End of the Tunnel?' *British Tax Review*, 482–98.

Atchabahian, A. (1975) *Fiscal Harmonization in the Andean Countries*, International Bureau of Fiscal Documentation, Amsterdam.

Auerbach A. J. (1983) *Corporate Taxation in the US*, Brookings Papers on Economic Activity no. 2, Washington DC.

Ault, H. J. (1978) 'International Issues in Corporate Tax Integration', 10 *Law & Policy in International Business*, 461.

Avery Jones J. F. (1974) *Tax Havens and Measures against Tax Evasion and Avoidance in the EEC*, Associated Business Programmes, London.

Avery Jones, J. F. et al. (1979) 'The Legal Nature of the Mutual Agreement Procedure under the OECD Model Convention', *British Tax Review*, 333–53, 1980, 12–27.

Avery Jones J. F. (1981) 'Dual Residence', *British Tax Review*, 15, 104.

Avery Jones, J. F. et al. (1984) 'The Interpretation of Tax Treaties with Particular Reference to Article 3(2) of the OECD Model', *British Tax Review*, 14–54, 90–108.

Avery Jones, J. F. (1982) 'The Context Otherwise Requires: *I.R.C. v. Exxon Corporation*', *British Tax Review*, 187–90.

Avery Jones, J. F. & Oliver, J. D. B. (1988) 'How Others See Us', *British Tax Review*, 437–40.

Avery Jones, J. F. et al. (1989) 'The Treatment of Trusts under the OECD Model Convention', *British Tax Review*, 41–60, 65–102.

Barlow E. R. & Wender Ira T. (1955) *Foreign Investment and Taxation*, Harvard Law School International Program in Taxation, Harvard College.

Bartlett, Christopher A. & Ghoshal, Sumantra (1989) *Managing Across Borders. The Transnational Solution*, Harvard Business School Press, Boston; Hutchinson, London.

Bartlett, Sarah (1981) 'Transnational Banking: a Case of Transfer Parking with Money', in Murray (1981), 96–115.

Bennett, Mary (1991) 'The US–Netherlands Tax Treaty Negotiations: A US Perspective', *Bulletin for International Fiscal Documentation*, 3–9.

Bird, Richard M. (1988) 'Shaping a New International Tax Order', *Bulletin for International Fiscal Documentation*, 292–9.

Bird, Richard M, & Head, John G. (eds.) (1972) *Modern Fiscal Issues. Essays in Honour of Carl S. Shoup*, University of Toronto Press.

Birnbaum, Jeffrey H. & Murray, Alan S. (1987) *Showdown at Gucci Gulch. Lawmakers, Lobbyists and the Unlikely Triumph of Tax Reform*, Random House, New York.

Bischel, Jon E. (1973) 'Tax Allocations Concerning Inter-Company Transactions in Foreign Operations: A Reappraisal', 13 *Virginia Journal of International Law*, 490–515.

Blum, Richard H. (1984) *Offshore Haven Banks, Trusts and Companies. The Business of Crime in the Euromarkets*, Praeger, New York.

Booth, Neil D. (1986) *Residence, Domicile and UK Taxation*, Butterworths, London.

Bowe, Michael (1988) *Eurobonds*, Square Mile Books/Dow Jones-Irwin, London.

Bracewell-Milnes, Barry (1980) *The Economics of International Tax Avoidance. Political Power versus Economic Law*, no. 4 in the International Series of the Rotterdam Institute for Fiscal Studies, Erasmus University; Kluwer, Deventer.

Bracewell-Milnes, Barry (1971) 'Overseas Development and British Taxation', in Peter Ady (ed.) *Private Foreign Investment and the Developing World*, Praeger, New York & London.

Briffett, Richard (1990) 'Leverage and the Changing Concept of Adequate Capitalisation', *British Tax Review*, 12–35.

Brilmayer, Lea (1989) *Justifying International Acts*, Cornell University Press, Ithaca & London.

Brownlee, W. Elliot (1989) 'Taxation for a Strong and Virtuous Republic', *Tax Notes*, 25 December, 1613–20.

Buckley, P. J. & Roberts, B. R. (1982) *European Direct Investment in the USA Before World War I*, Macmillan, Basingstoke.

Bunning, David (1988) 'IRS Third-Party Recordkeeper Summonses Issued at the

Request of a Treaty Partner: A Practical and Theoretical Approach', *The International Lawyer*, 989–1015.

Burns, Jane O. (1980) 'How IRS applies the intercompany pricing rules of Section 482: a corporate survey', *The Journal of Taxation*, 308–14.

Caccamise William C. (1988) 'US Countermeasures against Tax Haven Countries', *Columbia Journal of Transnational Law*, 555–71.

Calderwood, John A. (1989) 'Pricing for Intangibles, Goods and Services under a Superroyalty: a Canadian View', *Intertax*, 93–104. Reprinted in De Hosson (ed.) (1989).

Carlson, George N., Fogarasi, Andre P. & Gordon, Richard A. (1988) 'The S.482 White Paper: Highlights and Implications', *Tax Notes*, 31 October, 547–56.

Carroll, Mitchell B. (1939) *The Prevention of Double Taxation and Fiscal Evasion. Two Decades of Progress under the League of Nations*, League of Nations no. 1939 II A 8, F/Fiscal/ 111, Geneva.

Carroll, Mitchell B. (1944) 'International Double Taxation', in Harriet Eager Davies (ed.) *Pioneers in World Order. An American Appraisal of the League of Nations*, Columbia University Press, New York.

Carroll, Mitchell B. (1951) 'Report on the meeting of the UN Fiscal Commission, Lake Success, 7–17 May 1951', V *Bulletin for International Fiscal Documentation*, 309.

Carroll, Mitchell B. (1952) 'Action on tax treatment of foreign income at session of UN Fiscal Commission', VII, *Bulletin for International Fiscal Documentation*, 183.

Carroll, Mitchell B. (1965) 'International Tax Law. Benefits for American Investors and Enterprises Abroad', 2 *The International Lawyer*, 692–728.

Carroll, Mitchell B. (1978) 'The Historical Development of Tax Treaties', in Jon. E. Bischel (ed.) *Income Tax Treaties*, Practising Law Institute, New York.

Cassese, Antonio (1986) *International Law in a Divided World*, Clarendon Press, Oxford.

Casson, Mark (1983) *The Growth of International Business*, Allen & Unwin, London.

Chambost, Eduard (1983) *Bank Accounts. A World Guide to Confidentiality*, John Wiley, Chichester.

Chambost, Eduard (1989) *Guide des Paradis Fiscaux face à 1992*, Sand, Paris.

Chandler, A. D. (1962) *Strategy and Structure: The History of American Industrial Enterprise*, MIT Press, Cambridge, Mass.

Chrétien, Maxime (1954) 'Contribution à l'étude du droit international fiscal actuel: Le rôle des organisations internationales dans le règlement des questions d'impôts entre les divers états', 86–II *Recueil des Cours de Droit International*, The Hague, 5–116.

Chrétien, Maxime (1955) *A la Recherche du Droit International Fiscal Commun*, Sirey, Paris.

Citizens for Tax Justice (1985) *Corporate Taxpayers and Corporate Freeloaders*, Washington DC.

Cnossen, Sijbren (1983) 'Harmonization of Indirect Taxes in the EEC', *British Tax Review*, 232–53.

Cnossen, Sijbren (ed.) (1987) *Tax Coordination in the European Community*, Kluwer, Deventer.

Cole, Robert T. (1978) 'Administrative Provisions of Income Tax Treaties', in Bischel (ed.) *Income Tax Treaties*, Practising Law Institute, New York.

Cole, Robert T., Huston, John & Weiss, Stanley (1981) 'United States', LXVIa *Studies on International Fiscal Law, Mutual Agreement – Procedure and Practice*, International Fiscal Association; Kluwer, Netherlands.

Competent Authorities (1986) 'International Taxation: Competent Authorities Share Their Concerns', *Tax Notes*, 11 August, 573–605.

Cooper, George (1980) 'The Avoidance Dynamic', 80 *Columbia Law Review*, 1553–1622.

Cooper, George (1985) 'The Taming of the Shrew: Identifying and Controlling Income Tax Avoidance', 85 *Columbia Law Review*, 657.

Court, J.-F. (1985) 'La France et les Conventions Fiscales', 1 *Journal du Droit des Affaires Internationales*, 31–90.

Cowell, F. A. (1988) 'Tax Sheltering and the Cost of Evasion', ESRC Programme in Taxation Incentives and Distribution of Income, Disc. Paper TIDI/119.

Cox, Robert W. (1981) 'Social Forces, States and World Orders: Beyond International Relations Theory', 10 *Millenium*, 126–55; revised version in R. O. Keohane (ed.) *Neorealism and its Critics*, Col. U.P. New York, 1986.

Crinion, Gregory P. (1986) 'Information Gathering on Tax Evasion in Tax Haven Countries', 20 *International Lawyer*, 1209.

Curtin, Dennis D. (1986) 'Exchange of Information under US International Tax Treaties', 12 *Brooklyn Journal of International Law*, 35–72.

Dale, Richard (1984) *The Regulation of International Banking*, Woodhead-Faulkner, London.

Davidson, Ann J. (1986) 'US Signs New Treaty with Neths. Antilles and Aruba', *Tax Notes*, 8 October, 631–2.

Davies, Harriet Eager (ed.) (1944) *Pioneers in World Order. An American Appraisal of the League of Nations*, Columbia U.P., New York.

Davies, David R. (1985) *Principles of International Double Taxation Relief*, Sweet & Maxwell, London.

De Hosson, Fred (ed.) (1989) *Transfer Pricing for Intangibles*, Kluwer, Deventer.

Deutsch, Robert L. (1985) 'International Taxation: Extending the UK Revenue Network', 7 *The Company Lawyer*, 3–9.

Devereux, M. (1987) 'On the growth of corporation tax revenues', 8 *Fiscal Studies*, 77–85.

Devereux, M. & Pearson, M. (1989) *Corporate Tax Harmonization and Economic Efficiency*, Report series no. 3, Institute for Fiscal Studies, London.

Dewhurst (1984) 'Getting the Measure of s.482', *British Tax Review*, 282.

Dexter (1985) 'Comment on the Unitary Taxation Working Group', *Tax Notes*, 28 October, 419.

Diamond, Walter H. & Diamond, Dorothy B. (1974–) *Tax Havens of the World* (vol. 3, 1990).

Donnelly, David P. (1986) 'Eliminating Uncertainty in Dealing with Section 482', 12 *The International Tax Journal*, 213–27.

Doernberg, Richard L. (1989) 'Legislative Override of Income Tax Treaties: the Branch Profits Tax and Congressional Arrogation of Authority', 42 *Tax Lawyer*, 173–210.

Dunning, John H. (1988) *Explaining International Production*, Unwin Hyman, London.

Easson A. J. (1980) *Tax Law and Policy in the EEC*, Sweet & Maxwell, London.

Easson, A. J. (1988) 'The Evolution of Canada's Tax Treaty Policy since the Royal Commission of Taxation', 26 *Osgoode Hall Law Journal*, 495–536.

Eccles, Robert G. (1985) *The Transfer Price Problem. A Theory for Practice*, Lexington Books, Mass.

Edwardes-Ker (1987) (looseleaf), *The International Tax Treaties Service*.

Effros, Robert C. (1982) *Emerging Financial Centres*, International Monetary Fund, Washington DC.

Einaudi, Luigi (1928) 'La Cooperation Internationale en Matière Fiscale', 25 *Académie de Droit International*, La Haye, Receuil des Cours, 1–123.

Engler R. (1961) *The Politics of Oil*, Macmillan, New York.

Ernst & Young (1991) Study for the Institute of International Bankers on the tax issues related to cross-border trading of financial instruments by international banks. *Tax Notes*, 13 May.

Fogarasi, A., Gordon, R., Venuti, J. & Renfroe, D. (1989) 'Current Status of US Tax Treaties', a regular feature published in *Tax Management International*.

Fogarasi, A., Gordon, R. & Venuti, J. (1989) 'Use of International Arbitration to Resolve Double Taxation Cases', 18 *Tax Management International Journal*, 319–27.

Fordham Corporate Law Institute (1976) *International Taxation and Transfer Pricing*, E. Yorio (ed.), Mathew Bender, New York.

Forry, John I. & Karlin, Michael (1987) '1986 Act: Overrides, Conflicts and Interactions with US Income Tax Treaties', *Tax Notes*, 25 May, 793–801.

Franko, L. G. (1976) *The European Multinationals*, Harper & Row, NY and London.

Freeman & Kirshner (1946) 'An Ounce of Prevention. A Study in Corporate Tax Avoidance', 46 *Columbia Law Review*, 951–74.

Freud, Nicholas S. & Gurwitz, Michael L. (1985) 'Exchange of Information Agreements under the CBI Program: the Monroe Doctrine Revisited?' *Tax Management International Journal*, 111–16.

Fuller, James P. (1988) 'The IRS Section 482 White Paper', *Tax Notes*, 655–64.

Gallant, Peter (1988) *The Eurobond Market*, Woodhead-Faulkner, London.

Gammie, Malcolm & Robinson, Bill (1989) *Beyond 1992: A European Tax System*, Institute for Fiscal Studies, London.

Ganiatsos, Tom (1981) 'The Control of Transfer Pricing in Greece: A Progress Report', in Murray (1981), 286–303.

Gibbons, William J. (1956) 'Tax Effects of Basing International Business Abroad', 69 *Harvard Law Review*, 1206–49.

Gifford, William C. & Owens, Elizabeth A. (1982) *International Aspects of US Income Taxation: Cases and Materials*, Vol. II, Harvard Law School International Tax Program.

Goldberg, Sandford H. (1986) 'How and Does the Competent Authority Work? A Multinational Analysis', *The Tax Executive*, 5–44.

Governor of the Bank of England (1973) 'Multinational Enterprises'. Text of an address given at the Colloquium organized by the Société Universitaire Européenne de Recherches Financières, 13 *Bank of England Quarterly Bulletin*, 184–92.

Granwell A. W., Hirsch B. & Milton D. R. (1986) 'Worldwide Unitary Tax: Is it Valid Under Treaties of Friendship, Commerce and Navigation?' 18 *Law & Policy in International Business*, 695–748.

Greenberg, Jonathan A. (1991) 'Section 884 and Congressional "Override" of Tax Treaties: a Reply to Professor Doernberg', 10 *Virginia Tax Review*, 425.

Gregg, Sir Cornelius (1947) 'Double Taxation', 33 *Grotius Society Transactions*, 77.

Hammer, R. M. (1973) 'The Foreign Tax Credit in the United States and the United Kingdom', *British Tax Review*, 107–25.

Harley, Geoffrey John (1981) *International Division of the Income Tax Base of Multinational Enterprise*, Multistate Tax Commission, Boulder Colorado.

Harvey, Charles & Press, Jon (1990) 'The City and International Mining', 32 *Business History*, 98–107.

Hellerstein, Jerome R. (1982) 'Allocation and Apportionment of Dividends and the Delineation of the Unitary Business', *Tax Notes*, vol. 14, no. 4, 25 January, 160.

Herndon J. G. (1932) *Relief from International Income Taxation*, Callaghan, Chicago.

Hines, James R. & Hubbard, R. Glenn (1989) 'Coming Home to America: Dividend Repatriation by US Multinationals', Working Paper no. 2931, National Bureau of Economic Research, Cambridge, Mass. Reprinted in Razin & Slemrod (1990).

Hirschleifer, Jack (1956) 'On the Economics of Transfer Pricing', 29 *Journal of Business*, 172–84.

Höppner, H.-D. (1983) 'German Regulations on Transfer Pricing: A Tax Administrator's Point of View', *Intertax*, 208–23.

Horowitz, Jeffrey I. (1985) 'Piercing Offshore Bank Secrecy Laws Used to Launder Illegal Narcotics Profits: The Cayman Islands Example', *Texas International Law Journal*, 133–65.

Hufbauer, Gary & Foster, David (1977) 'US Taxation of the Undistributed Income of Controlled Foreign Corporations', in US Treasury, *Essays in International Taxation*, Washington DC.

Hufbauer, Gary, Elliott, Kimberley and Maldonado, Eduardo (1988) *Tax Treaties and American Interests. A report to the National Foreign Trade Council*, New York and Washington DC.

Hymer, Stephen (1960/1976) *The International Operations of National Firms: A Study of Direct Investment*, Ph.D. thesis, MIT; published by MIT Press in 1976.

Institute of Economic Affairs (1979) *Tax Avoision*, IEA, London.

Institute for Fiscal Studies (1982) *Report of the Working Party on Company Residence, Tax Havens and Upstream Loans*, IFS Reports Series, no. 3, London.

International Bureau of Fiscal Documentation 1987– (looseleaf), *Tax Treatment of Transfer Pricing*, with Introduction and concluding Analysis and Comparison by Maurice H. Collins, IBFD, Amsterdam.

Intriago, Charles A. (1991) *International Money Laundering*, Eurostudy publishing, London.

ICC (International Chamber of Commerce) (1921) *Double Taxation. Report of Select Committee to First Congress*, Brochure no. 11, ICC, Paris.

ICC (International Chamber of Commerce) (1925) *Report of 3rd Congress (Brussels), Group Meetings*, Brochure no. 43, ICC, Paris.

ICC (International Chamber of Commerce) (1985) *ICC Statement on OECD/Council of Europe Draft Multilateral Convention on Mutual Administrative Assistance in Tax Matters*, Document no. 180/261 Rev.

IFA (International Fiscal Association) (1983) *Tax Avoidance/Tax Evasion*, Cahiers de Droit Fiscal International, Kluwer, Netherlands.

IFA (International Fiscal Association) (1989) *The Disregard of a Legal Entity for Tax Purposes*, LXXIVa Cahiers de Droit Fiscal International, Kluwer, Netherlands.

Ireland, Paddy (1984) 'The Rise of the Limited Liability Company', 12 *International Journal of the Sociology of Law*, 239.

Irish, Charles R. (1974) 'International Double Taxation Agreements and Double Taxation at Source', 23 *International & Comparative Law Quarterly*, 292–316.

Jacob, F. (1985) 'Corresponding Adjustments in Loss Situations: Economic Double Taxation a Prerequisite?' *European Taxation*, November, 311–13.

Jacob, F. (1986) 'German Federal Government Replies to Comprehensive Question in Parliament on International Tax Evasion', *European Taxation*, July, 219–23.

Johns R. A. (1983) *Tax Havens and Offshore Finance. A Study of Transnational Economic Development*, Frances Pinter, London.

Kaldor N. (1980) 'A New Look at the Expenditure Tax', in *Reports on Taxation I, Collected Economic Essays, vol. 7*, Duckworth, London.

Kaplan, Philip T. (1986) 'Reasons, Old and New, for the Erosion of US Tax Treaties', *British Tax Review*, 211–27

Karzon A. U. (1983) 'International Tax Evasion: Spawned in the US and Nurtured in Secrecy Havens', 16 *Vanderbilt Journal of Transnational Law*, 757–832.

Kay J. A. (1979) 'The Economics of Tax Avoidance', *British Tax Review*, 354–65.

Kelman, Mark (1987) *A Guide to Critical Legal Studies*, Harvard U.P., Cambridge, Mass.

Kennedy, Duncan (1976) 'Form and Substance in Private Law Adjudication', 89 *Harvard Law Review*, 1685–1778.

Kindleberger, C. (1969) *American Business Abroad – Six Lectures on Direct Investment*, Yale U.P., New Haven & London.

Kingson, Charles I. (1981) 'The Coherence of International Taxation', 81 *Columbia Law Review*, 1151–1288.

Knechtle, A. A. (1979) *Basic Problems in International Fiscal Law*, Kluwer, The Netherlands.

Kopits, George & Muten, Leif (1984) 'The Relevance of the Unitary Approach for Developing Countries', in McLure (ed.) (1984), 268–80.

Krabbe, Helmut (1986) 'Das EG-Amtshilfe-Gesetz', 2 *Recht der Internationalen Wirtschaft*, 126–33.

Krever, Rick (1989) 'Australia: New International Tax Regime', *Bulletin for International Fiscal Documentation*, 327–33.

Lamoreaux W. R. (1985) *The Great Merger Movement in American Business 1895–1904*, Cambridge University Press, Cambridge.

Landwehrmann, Friedrich (1974) 'Legislative Development of International Corporate Taxation in Germany: Lessons for the United States', 15 *Harvard International Law Journal*, 238–97.

Langbein, Stanley I. (1986) 'The Unitary Method and the Myth of Arm's Length', *Tax Notes* 17 February, 625–81.

Langbein, Stanley I. (1989) 'Transaction Cost, Production Cost, and Tax Transfer Pricing', *Tax Notes* 18 September, 1391–1413.

Langer, Marshall J. (1978) 'The Need for Reform in the Tax Treaty Area', in Jon E. Bischel (ed.) *Income Tax Treaties*, Practising Law Institute, New York.

Langer, Marshall J. (1988–) *Practical International Tax Planning*, 3rd edn., Practising Law Institute, New York.

Leegstra, Eager & Stolte (1988) 'The California Water's Edge Election', 14 *International Tax Journal*, 101–63.

Leftwich, Robert B. (1974) 'US Multinational Companies: Profitability, Financial Leverage, and Effective Income Tax Rates', *Survey of Current Business*, May, 27–36, US Dept. of Commerce, Washington DC.

Leite, Eduardo de Cerqueira (1991) 'Transfer Pricing in Brazil', *Bulletin for International Fiscal Documentation*, 76–9.

Lessard, Donald R. (1979) 'Transfer Prices, Taxes and Financial Markets: Implications of International Financial Transfers within the Multinational Corporation', in

Robert G. Hawkins (ed.), *The Economic Effects of Multinational Corporations*, Vol. 1 of *Research in International Business and Finance*, JAI Press, Greenwich, Conn.

Lessard, Donald R. & Williamson, John (1987) *Capital Flight and Third World Debt*, Institute for International Economics, Washington DC.

Levine, Pierre (1988) *La Lutte contre l'Evasion Fiscale de Caractère International en l'Absence et en Présence de Conventions Internationales*, Pichon & Durand-Auzias, Paris.

Liang, Tan Wee (1989) 'Tax Avoidance and Section 33 of the Income Tax Act', 31 *Malaya Law Review*, 78–111.

Liénard J.-L. (1985) 'Présent et avenir des modèles de convention de double imposition', 4 *Journal de Droit des Affaires Internationales*, 91–102.

Linde, Stephen A. (1977) 'Regulation of Transfer Pricing in Multinational Corporations: an International Perspective', 10 New York University Journal of International Law and Politics, 67–123.

Lindencrona, G. & Mattsson, N. (1981) *Arbitration in Taxation*, Kluwer, Deventer.

Loebenstein, Edwin (1972) *International Mutual Assistance in Administrative Matters*, Springer, Vienna, New York.

Long, M., Weil, P. & Braibant, G. (1978) *Les Grands Arrêts de la Jurisprudence Administrative*, Sirey, Paris.

Lowe, A. V. (1983) *Extraterritorial Jurisdiction. An annotated collection of legal materials*, Grotius, Cambridge.

Maier H. G. (1982) 'Extraterritorial jurisdiction at a Crossroads: an Intersection between Public and Private International Law', 76 *American Journal of International Law*, 280–320.

Mann, F. A. (1986) *Foreign Affairs in English Courts*, Clarendon Press, Oxford.

Mann, M. (1954) 'Foreign Revenue Laws and the English Conflict of Laws', 3 *International and Comparative Law Quarterly*, 465–78.

Mann, M. (1955) 'The House of Lords and Foreign Revenue Laws', 4 *International and Comparative Law Quarterly*, 564–7.

Mansfield G. (1989) 'The "New Approach" to Tax Avoidance: First Circular, then Linear, Now Narrower', *British Tax Review*, 5–19.

Martha, Rutsel Silvestre J. (1989) *The Jurisdiction to Tax in International Law*, Kluwer, Deventer.

Mathews, R. C. O., Feinstein, C. H. & Odling-Smee, J. C. (1982) *British Economic Growth 1856–1973*, Clarendon Press, Oxford.

Mathewson, G. F. & Quirin, G. D. (1979) *Fiscal Transfer Pricing in Multinational Corporations*, University of Toronto Press for the Ontario Economic Council.

Mattson, R. N. (1986) 'Setting Straight the Unitary Working Group Record', *Tax Notes*, vol. 30, no. 1, 57–61.

McBarnet D. (1984) 'Law and Capital in the Role of Legal Form and Legal Action', 12 *International Journal of the Sociology of Law*, 233.

McDaniel, Paul R. & Ault, Hugh J. (1989) *Introduction to United States International Taxation*, 3rd edn., Kluwer, Deventer and Boston.

McLure, Charles E. (ed.) (1984) *The State Corporation Income Tax. Issues in Worldwide Unitary Combination*, Hoover Institution Press, Stanford California.

McLure, Charles A. (1986a) 'State Exemption of Foreign-Source Dividends and Disallowance of International Expenses', *Tax Notes*, vol. 30, no. 1, 55–6.

McLure, Charles A. (1986b) 'State Taxation of Foreign-Source Dividends – Starting from First Principles', *Tax Notes*, vol. 30, no. 10, 975–89.

McLure, Charles A. (1989) 'European Integration and Taxation of Corporate Income at Source: Lessons from the US', in Gammie & Robinson (1989); also in *European Taxation*, August, 243–50.

McNair, Lord (1961) *The Law of Treaties*, Oxford University Press, Oxford & London.

Meade, J. E. (1978) *The Structure and Reform of Direct Taxation*, Allen & Unwin for the Institute of Fiscal Studies, London.

Mendelsohn M. S. (1980) *Money on the Move. The Modern International Capital Market*, McGraw-Hill, New York.

Mentz, J. Roger, Carlisle, Linda E. & Nevas, Susan R. (1990) 'Leveraged Buyouts: A Washington Perspective of 1989 Legislation and Prospects for 1990', *Tax Notes* 26 February, 1047–53.

Meyer, Bernhard F. (1978) 'Swiss Bank Secrecy and its Legal Implications in the United States', 14 *New England Law Review*, 18–81.

Miller, Benjamin F. (1984) 'Worldwide Unitary Combination: The California Practice', in McLure (ed.) (1984), 132–66.

Millett, P. (1986) 'Artificial Tax Avoidance. The English and American Approaches', *British Tax Review*, 327–39.

Murray, Robin (1981) *Multinationals Beyond the Market. Intra-Firm Trade and the Control of Transfer Pricing*, Harvester, Brighton.

Musgrave, Peggy B. (1972) 'International Tax Base Division and the Multinational Corporation', 27 *Public Finance*, 394–413.

Musgrave, Peggy B. (1978) 'The UK Treaty Debate: Some Lessons for the Future', *Tax Notes*, 10 July.

Musgrave, Peggy B. (1975) 'The OECD Model Tax Treaty: Problems and Prospects', 10 *Columbia Journal of World Business*, 29.

Musgrave, Peggy B. (1984) 'Principles for Deriving the State Corporate Tax Base', in McLure (ed.) (1984), 228–46.

Musgrave, Peggy B. & Musgrave, Richard A. (1972) 'Inter-Nation Equity', in Bird & Head (1972).

Musgrave, Peggy B. & Musgrave, Richard A. (1984) *Public Finance Theory and Practice*, 4th edn., McGraw Hill, NY & London.

Naylor, R. T. (1987) *Hot Money and the Politics of Debt*, Unwin Hyman, London.

Newbery, David & Stern, Nicholas (1987) *The Theory of Taxation for Developing Countries*, Oxford University Press for the World Bank, New York, Oxford, London.

Newcity, Michael (1990) 'Perestroika, Private Enterprise and Soviet Tax Policy', 28 *Columbia Journal of Transnational Law*, 225–52.

Newman, John A. (1980) *US/UK Double Tax Treaty on Income and Capital Gains*, Butterworths, London.

New York University (1978) *Tax Treaties and Competent Authority*, Institute on Tax and Business Planning, edited by V. di Francesco & N. Liakas.

New York State Bar Association Tax Section (1986) 'The Proposed Foreign Corporation Branch Level Tax', *Tax Notes*, 21 July, 247–54.

Norr, Martin (1962) 'Jurisdiction to Tax and National Income', 17 *Tax Law Review*, 431–63.

Note (1950) 'International Enforcement of Tax Claims', *Columbia Law Review*, 50, 490–504.

Note (1984) 'Standing Under Commercial Treaties: Foreign Holding Companies and the Unitary Tax', 97 *Harvard Law Review*, 1894–1911.

Oborudu, Margaret T. (1987) 'Legal Measures against Tax Evasion and Avoidance. The Nigerian Experience', 13 *International Tax Journal*, 129–56.

O'Brien, James G. (1978) 'The Non-Discrimination Article in Tax Treaties', 10 *Law and Policy in International Business*, 545–612.

Odell, Peter R. (1986) *Oil and World Power*, 8th edn., Penguin Books, Harmondsworth, Middlesex.

Oldman, Oliver & Surrey, Stanley S. (1972) 'Technical Assistance in Taxation in Developing Countries', in Bird & Head (1972), 278–91.

Oliva, Robert R. (1984) 'The Treasury's Twenty-Year Battle with Treaty-Shopping: Article 16 of the 1977 US Model Teaty', 14 *Georgia Journal International & Comparative Law*, 293–324.

Oliver, J. D. B. (1990) 'Some Aspects of the Territorial Scope of Tax Treaties', *British Tax Review*, 303–12.

Olmstead, Dennis J. & DeJean, Niels (1989) 'Belgium–US and France–US Protocols: Highlighting US Tax Treaty Concerns', *Bulletin for International Fiscal Documentation*, 3–8.

Osborn, John E. (1982) 'Renegotiation of the US–British Virgin Islands Tax Convention – A Prelude to the End of Treaty-Shopping?' 22 *Virginia Journal of International Law*, 381–412.

Osgood, Russell K. (1984) 'Interpreting Tax Treaties in Canada, the US and the UK', 17 *Cornell International Law Journal*, 255–97.

Owens, Elizabeth A. (1980) *International Aspects of US Income Taxation: Cases and Materials*, Vols I & III, Harvard Law School International Tax Program (see also Gifford & Owens).

Owens, Jeffrey (1987) 'Tax Reform: What are the Main Issues?' *OECD Observer*, June–July, 29–31.

Palmer, Robert W. (1989) 'Towards Unilateral Coherence in Determining Jurisdiction to Tax Income', 30 *Harvard International Law Journal*, 1–64.

Patrick, Robert J. (1978) 'A Comparison of the US and the OECD Model Income Tax Conventions', 10 *Law & Policy in International Business*, 613–718.

Piatier, André (1938) *L'Evasion Fiscale et l'Assistance Administrative entre Etats*, Sirey, Paris.

Picciotto, Sol (1979) 'The Theory of the State, Class Struggle and the Rule of Law', in Fine, Kinsey, Lea, Picciotto & Young (eds.), *Capitalism and the Rule of Law*, Hutchinson, London. Also printed in Beirne & Quinney (eds.) *Marxism and the Law*.

Picciotto, Sol (1983) 'Jurisdictional Conflicts, International Law and the International State System', 11 *International Journal of the Sociology of Law*, 11–40.

Picciotto, Sol (1991) 'The Internationalization of the State', *Capital & Class* no. 43 (Joint Special Issue with *Review of Radical Political Economics*), 43–63.

Plambeck, Charles T. (1990) 'The Taxation Implications of Global Trading', *Tax Notes*, 27 August.

Plant, Philip M., Miller, Benjamin F. & Crawford, Roy E. (1989) 'California Unitary Taxation and Water's Edge Election', *European Taxation*, July, 211–24.

Plasschaert, Sylvain (1980) *Transfer Pricing and Multinational Corporations. An Overview of mechanisms and regulations*, Gower, Aldershot.

Pocock, H. R. S. (1975) *The Memoirs of Lord Coutanche. A Jerseyman looks back*, Phillimore, London & Chichester.

Qureshi (1987) 'The Freedom of a State to Legislate in Fiscal Matters under General

International Law', *Bulletin for International Fiscal Documentation*, 14–21.

Rädler, A. & Jacob, F. (1984) *German Transfer Pricing/Prix de Transfert en Allemagne*, Kluwer, Deventer.

Rappako, Annamaria (1987) *Base Companies in Multinational Corporate Structures. A Comparative Study of Anti-Avoidance Legislation and its Impact on Investment*, Helsinki.

Razin, A. & Slemrod J. (1990) *Taxation in the Global Economy*, University of Chicago Press, Chicago & London.

Regan, Donald T. (1988) *For the Record. From Wall Street to Washington*, Hutchinson, London.

Rosenbloom, H. David & Langbein, Stanley I. (1981) 'United States Tax Treaty Policy: An Overview', 19 *Columbia Journal of Transnational Law*, 359–406.

Rosenbloom, H. David (1983) 'Tax Treaty Abuse: Policies and Issues', 15 *Law and Policy in International Business*, 763–831.

Rotterdam Institute for Fiscal Studies (1978) *International Tax Avoidance, Volume B, Country Reports*, Kluwer, Deventer.

Rotterdam Institute for Fiscal Studies (1979) *International Tax Avoidance, Volume A, General and Conceptual Material*, Kluwer, Deventer.

Rugman, Alan M. (ed.) (1982) *New Theories of the Multinational Enterprise*, Croom Helm, London & Canberra.

Rugman, A. M. (1979) *International Diversification and the Multinational Enterprise*, Lexington Books, Lexington, Mass.

Rugman, Alan M. & Eden, Lorraine (1985) *Multinationals and Transfer Pricing*, Croom Helm, London.

Runge, B. (1986) 'The Mutual Assistance by the German Tax Administration in the Field of Direct Taxation', 25 *European Taxation*, 163–8.

Sabine, B. E. V. (1966) *A History of Income Tax*, Allen & Unwin.

Saunders, M. Roy (1989) 'Transfer Pricing and Multinational Enterprise', *European Taxation*, August, 251–62.

Saunders, M. Roy (1990–) *International Tax Systems and Planning Techniques*, Oyez Longman, London.

Seligman, Edwin R. A. (1928) *Double Taxation and International Fiscal Cooperation. Being the text of the lectures delivered at the Hague Academy of International Law*, Macmillan, New York.

Seligman, Edwin R. A. (1927) 'La Double Imposition et la Coopération Fiscale', 20 *Académie de Droit International de la Haye, Receuil des Cours*, 463–603.

Selter, A., Godfrey, K. & Atkinson B.(1990) 'The UK Taxation of Interest Rate and Currency Swaps', *European Taxation*, 35–41.

Sharp, William M. & Steele, Betty K. (1985) 'The Caribbean Basin Exchange of Information Draft Agreement – a Technical Analysis', 19 *The International Lawyer*, 949–72.

Shay, Stephen E. & Bok, Geoffrey R. (1988) 'Section 864(e) and the allocation and apportionment of interest expense under the proposed regulations', 17 *Tax Management International Journal*, 51–69.

Shenfield, A. A. (1968) *The Political Economy of Tax Avoidance*, Institute of Economic Affairs, London.

Sheridan, Denis (1990) 'The Residence of Companies for Taxation Purposes', *British Tax Review*, 78–112.

Simon, (1983–) *Simon's Taxes*, Revised 3rd edn. (loose-leaf, with updating service), Butterworths, London.

Sloan, Alfred G. (1965) *My Years with General Motors*, Sidgwick & Jackson, London.

Smith, Andrew M. C. (1991) 'The Implications of the Commissioner's Statement on s.99', 45 *Bulletin of International Fiscal Documentation*, 60–6.

Smith, Kent W. & Kinsey, Karyl L. (1987) 'Understanding Taxpayer Behaviour. A Conceptual Framework with Implications for Research', 21 *Law & Society Review*, 639–63.

Spall, Hugh (1981) 'International Tax Evasion and Tax Fraud: Typical Schemes and the Legal Issues Raised by their Detection and Prosecution', 13 *Lawyer of the Americas*, 325–59.

Spitz, Barry (1990–) *Tax Havens Encyclopaedia*, Butterworths, London.

Stamp, Josiah (1921) *Principles of Taxation*, Macmillan, London.

Stopforth, David (1987) 'The Background to the Anti-Avoidance Provisions Concerning Settlements by Parents on their Minor Children', *British Tax Review*, 417–33.

Strobl, Jakob (1975) 'Tax Treatment in the Federal Republic of Germany of International Transactions Between Affiliated Companies', *British Tax Review*, 219–31; 312–23.

Sumption, A. (1982) *Taxation of Overseas Income and Gains*, 4th edn., Butterworths, London.

Sundgren, Peter (1990) 'Interpretation of Tax Treaties – A Case Study', *British Tax Review*, 286–301.

Surr, John V. (1966) 'Intertax: Intergovernmental Cooperation in Taxation', 7 *Harvard International Law Journal*, 179–237.

Surrey, Stanley S. (1956) 'Current Issues in the Taxation of Corporate Foreign Investment', 56 *Columbia Law Review*, 815.

Surrey, Stanley S. (1969) 'Complexity and the Internal Revenue Code: the Problem of the Management of Tax Detail', 34 *Law & Contemporary Problems*, 673–710.

Surrey, Stanley S. & Tillinghast, D. (1971) 'General Report'. in *56b Cahiers de Droit International Fiscal, Criteria for the Allocation of Items of Income and Expense between Related Corporations in Different States*.

Surrey, Stanley S. (1978a) 'Reflections on the Allocation of Income and Expenses Among National Tax Jurisdictions', 10 *Law & Policy in International Business* 409–60.

Surrey, Stanley S. (1978b) 'The UN Group of Experts and the Guidelines for Tax Treaties between Developed and Developing Countries', 19 *Harvard International Law Journal*, 1–220.

Surrey, Stanley S. (1980) *UN Model Convention for Tax Treaties between Developed and Developing Countries. A Description and Analysis*, International Bureau of Fiscal Documentation, Amsterdam.

Tang, Roger Y. W. (1981) *Multinational Transfer Pricing, Canadian and British Perspectives*, Butterworths, Toronto.

Tanzi, Vito (1988) 'Trends in Tax Policy as Revealed by Recent Developments in Research', *Bulletin for International Fiscal Documentation*, 97–103.

Tax Institute (1960) *Taxation and Operations Abroad*, Symposium conducted at the Tax Institute, Princeton, New Jersey.

Terr, Leonard B. (1989) 'Treaty-Routing vs. Treaty-Shopping: Planning for Multi-country Investment Flows under Modern Limitation on Benefits Articles', *Intertax*, 521–30.

Terra, Ben & Kajus, Julie (1990) 'The Elimination of Tax Borders within the EC: Recent Developments Regarding VAT', *Bulletin for International Fiscal Documentation*, 311–20.

Tiley, John (1988a) 'Judicial Anti-Avoidance Doctrines', *British Tax Review*, 63–103; 108–45.

Tiley, John (1988b) 'Judicial Anti-Avoidance Doctrines: the US Alternatives', *British Tax Review*, 180–97; 220–44.

Tillinghast, David R. (1979) 'Taxing the Multinationals: Where is the US Headed?' 20 *Harvard International Law Journal*, 253–75.

Tixier, Gilbert & Gest, Guy (1985) *Droit Fiscal International*, PUF, Paris.

Tomsett, Eric (1989) *Tax Planning for Multinational Companies*, Woodhead-Faulkner, London.

Tutt, Nigel (1985) *The Tax Raiders. The Rossminster Affair*, Financial Training, London.

Vann, Richard J. (1991) 'A Model Tax Treaty for the Asian-Pacific Region?' *Bulletin for International Fiscal Documentation*, 99–111; 151–63.

van Raad, Kees (1983) *Model Income Tax Treaties. A comparative presentation of the texts of the model double taxation conventions on income and capital of the OECD (1963 and 1977), the United Nations (1980) and the United States (1981)*, Kluwer, Deventer.

van Raad, Kees (1990) *1963 and 1977 OECD Model Income Tax Treaties and Commentaries*, 2nd edn., Kluwer, Deventer.

Vernon, Raymond (1966) 'International Investment and International Trade in the Product Cycle', 80 *Quarterly Journal of Economics*, 190–207.

Viehe-Naess, Brenda R. (1990) 'Critique of Insurance Excise Tax Anti-Conduit Rule', *Tax Notes*, 24 December.

Walter, Ingo (1985) *Secret Money. The Shadowy World of Tax Evasion, Capital Flight and Fraud*, Allen & Unwin, London, Boston & Sydney.

Ward, David A. et al. (1985) 'The Business Purpose Test and Abuse of Rights', *British Tax Review*, 68–123.

Ward, David A. et al. (1988) 'The Other Income Article of Income Tax Treaties', *British Tax Review*, 352–84.

Weber-Fas, Rudolf (1968) 'Corporate Residence Rules for International Tax Jurisdiction: A Study of American and German Law', 5 *Harvard Journal on Legislation*, 175–251.

Weber-Fas, Rudolf (1973) *Internationale Steuerrechtsprechung. Die Entscheidungen des Reichsfinanzhofs und Bundesfinanzhofs zum Recht der Deutschen Doppelbesteuerungsabkommen*, Carl Haymanns Verlag, Köln.

Weiss, Arnold H. & Molnar, Ferenc F. (1988) 'International Co-operation *Is* Possible', in Herbert Stein (ed.), *Tax Policy in the Twenty-First Century*, John Wiley, New York.

Wheatcroft, G. S. A. (1955) 'The Attitude of the Courts to Tax Avoidance', 18 *Modern Law Review*, 209.

Whichard, Obie G. (1981) 'Trends in the US Direct Investment Position Abroad 1950–79', *Survey of Current Business*, US Dept. of Commerce, February, 39–56.

White, John J. (1989) 'Principles of Confidentiality in Cross-Border Banking', in R. Cranston (ed.) *Legal Issues of Cross-Border Banking*, Bankers' Books Ltd, London.

White, Roger (1979) 'Section 485 – the Law', *British Tax Review*, 85–95.

Wilkins, Mira (1970) *The Emergence of International Enterprise*, Harvard U.P., Cambridge, Mass.

Williamson, Oliver (1985) *The Economic Institutions of Capitalism*, Collier-Macmillan, NY, London.

Wills, John (1990) 'Transfer Pricing and Currency Risk', *Tax Notes*, 29 October.

Witte, Ann Dryden & Chipty, Tasneem (1990) 'Some Thoughts on Transfer Pricing', *Tax Notes*, 26 November.

Woodard, Percy P. (1988) 'The IRS Redirects its International Programme', *Tax Notes*, 24 October, 455–9.

Yerbury, Paul D. (1991) 'Tax Developments: United Kingdom', *International Business Lawyer*, January, 32.

Zagaris, Bruce (1989) 'The Caribbean Basin Tax Information Agreements Program of the United States: Eat Softly and Carry a Big Stick', 1 *Caribbean Law & Business*, 94–7.

B. Official Documents and Reports

1. National Governments

Germany (Federal Republic)

German Government (1964) *Tax Havens Report*, Report of the Federal German Government on Distortions of Competition resulting from Changes of Domicile to Foreign Countries, (Translation) Supplementary service to European Taxation, no. 12.

German-French memorandum (1974) 'Tax Evasion/Avoidance on the International Level', 14 *European Taxation* 136–42.

Ministry of Finance (1985) 'Senior Executives Representing the Finance Administrations of France, the United Kingdom, the United States of America, and the Federal Republic of Germany Meet in Berlin', Press Release, 3 October; reprinted in *European Taxation* 3 December 1985, 375.

Deutscher Bundestag (1986) *Antwort der Bundesregierung auf die grosse Anfrage der Abgeordneten Dr Apel . . . und der Fraktion der SPD*, Drucksache 10/5562, 28 May 1986.

Italy

Ministry of Finance (1980) Transfer Prices in the computation of taxable income of enterprises subject to foreign control. Circular letter No. 9.2267 of 22 September. Unofficial English translation in *Transfer Pricing – the Italian Experience*, Kluwer 1981, reprinted in *International Bureau of Fiscal Documentation* (1987–).

Japan

Ministry of Finance (1985) *An Outline of Japanese Taxes*.

Switzerland

Federal Council (1962) Decree concerning measures against the improper use of tax conventions, 14 December, English translation printed in Avery Jones (1974), 117–21.

National Council (1984) 'Conseil de l'Europe. Protocoles additionnels (entr'aide judiciaire)', *Bulletin officiel de l'Assemblée fédérale*. Session d'été, 4e session de la 42e législature, 4 juin.

United Kingdom

Board of Inland Revenue (1980) *The Transfer Pricing of Multinational Enterprises.*

Board of Inland Revenue (1981a) *Company Residence. A Consultative Document.*

Board of Inland Revenue (1981b) *Tax Havens and the Corporate Sector. A Consultative Document.*

Board of Inland Revenue (1981c) *International Tax Avoidance. I Company Residence. II Tax Havens and the Corporate Sector. III Upstream Loans.*

Board of Inland Revenue (1982) *Taxation of International Business*, London.

Board of Inland Revenue (1988) *Management Planning*, 3 vols.

Foreign and Commonwealth Office (1972) *Report of the Cayman Islands for the Years 1966–72*, HMSO, London.

Gallagher Report (1990) *Report of Mr Rodney Gallagher of Coopers and Lybrand on the Survey of Offshore Finance Sectors in the Caribbean Dependent Territories*, House of Commons, 1989–90, no. 121.

House of Commons (1971–2) Public Accounts Committee, First Report.

House of Lords (1989) *Withholding Tax*. Report of Select Committee on the European Communities 13 June, HL paper 55.

Keith Committee (1983) *Report of the Committee on the Enforcement Powers of Revenue Departments*, Vols. 1 & 2 Cmnd. 8822; vols. 3 & 4 Cmnd. 9120.

Monopolies Commission (1973) *Chlordiazepoxide and Diazepam.*

Parliamentary Commissioner for Administration (1989) *The Barlow Clowes Affair*, House of Commons paper HC 76, 19 December.

PRO: Public Records Office; references are to the PRO's file numbers.

Royal Commission on Income Taxation (1919–20) Minutes of Evidence and Final Report, CMD 615.

Royal Commission on the Taxation of Profits and Income (1953) First Report, CMD 8761, HMSO, London.

Royal Commission on the Taxation of Profits and Income (1955) Final Report, CMD 9474, HMSO, London.

United States

Commerce Department (1988) *The Caribbean Basin Initiative*, 1989 Guidebook.

Conference Board (1972) 'Tax Allocations and International Business: Corporate Experience with Section 482 of the Internal Revenue Code', Report no. 555.

Congress (1938) Report of Joint Committee on Tax Evasion and Avoidance.

Congress (1962a) *Legislative History of US Tax Conventions*, prepared by staff of the Joint Committee on Taxation, 4 volumes.

Congress (1962b) House Committee on Ways & Means, Revenue Act of 1962, to accompany HR 10650.

Congress (1973) House Committee of Ways and Means, *General Tax Reform*, Panel Discussion, Taxation of Foreign Income (Pt. 11 of 11) 28 February, 93rd Congress 2nd Session.

Congress (1975) *Oversight Hearings into the Operations of the IRS (Operation Tradewinds, Project Haven, and Narcotics Traffickers Tax Program)*, Subcommittee on Commerce, Consumer and Monetary Affairs of the House Committee on Government Operations, Hearings.

Congress (1976) Senate Judiciary Committee, *The Petroleum Industry*, Hearings, 94th Congress, 1st Session.

Congress (1979) *International Tax Treaties*, Hearing before the Committee on Foreign Relations of the US Senate, 96th Congress, 1st Session, 6 June 1979, US GPO Washington DC.

Congress (1983a) Senate Committee on Governmental Affairs, Permanent Sub-committee on Investigations, *Crime & Secrecy: the Use of Offshore banks and Companies*, Staff Study, S. Print 98–21; Hearings March & May 1983 S-Hrg. 98–151.

Congress (1983b) House Committee on Government Operations, Hearings before a Subcommittee, *Tax Evasion through the Netherlands Antilles and other Tax Haven Countries*, 12–13 April.

Congress (1984a) *Study of 1983 Effective Tax Rates of Selected Large US Corporations*, Staff of the Joint Committee on Taxation.

Congress (1984b) House Committee on Government Operations, Hearings before a Subcommittee, *Tax Evasion through the Use of False Foreign Addresses*, 28 February.

Congress (1985) *Drug Money Laundering*. Hearing before the Committee on Banking, Housing and Urban Affairs of the Senate. 28 January. S.Hrg. 99–8; 43–487 O.

Congress (1987) Office of Technology Assessment, *International Competition in Services*, OTA-ITE-328, US GPO, Washington DC.

Congress (1988a) Senate Committee on Foreign Relations, *Report on the Tax Convention with the United Kingdom (on behalf of Bermuda)*, Exec. Rpt. 100–23.

Congress (1988b) *Technical Corrections Act of 1988*. Report of Committee on Finance, US Senate, to accompany Resolution S.2238. 3 August.

Congress (1988c) Conference Report to accompany HR 4333, *Technical and Miscellaneous Revenue Act of 1988*, vol. II. 21 October.

Congress (1989) *Drugs, Law Enforcement and Foreign Policy*. Report prepared by the Subcommittee on Terrorism, Narcotics and International Operations of the Senate Committee on Foreign Relations. S100–165, December 1988. US GPO, 1989.

Congress (1990a) *Background and Issues Relating to the Taxation of Foreign Investment in the United States*. Joint Committee on Taxation (JCS-1-90) 23 January.

Congress (1990b) *Explanation of Proposed Convention on Mutual Administrative Assistance in Tax Matters*. Joint Committee on Taxation (JCS-14-90) 13 June.

Congress (1990c) *Present Law and Certain Issues Relating to Transfer Pricing* (Code sec. 482), Joint Committee on Taxation (JCS-22-90) 28 June.

General Accounting Office (1980) *The Foreign Tax Credit and US Energy Policy*. Report of the Comptroller-General to the Congress, EMD-80–86.

General Accounting Office (1981) *IRS Could Better Protect US Tax Interests in Determining the Income of Multinational Corporations*. Report of the Comptroller-General to the Chairman, House Committee of Ways and Means GGD-81-81.

Internal Revenue Service (1984) *Sources of Information from Abroad*, Doc. 6743 (Rev. 4–84) T22.2 IN 3.

Internal Revenue Service (1984) *Study of International Cases involving S.482 of the Tax Code*, Report to the Associate Commissioner (Operations) by the Assistant Commissioner (Examination), Pub. 1243 4–84.

Justice Department (1983) Criminal Division Narcotics and Dangerous Drugs Section, *Investigation and Prosecution of Illegal Money Laundering: A Guide to the Bank Secrecy Act*, October. T.22.19/2:IN 8.

President's Commission on Organized Crime (1984) *The Cash Connection. Organized Crime, Financial Institutions and Money-Laundering*. Interim Report to the President and the Attorney-General, October.

Tax Havens Study Group (1981) *A Study to Quantify the Use of Tax Havens for a Report Submitted by Richard A. Gordon*, US Govt. mimeo.

Treasury (1973) *Summary Study of International Cases Involving s.482 of the Internal Revenue Code*. Also reprinted in Murray (1981).

Treasury (1981) *Tax Havens and their Use by United States Taxpayers – An Overview* (Gordon Report), A report by Richard A. Gordon, the Special Counsel for International Taxation, to the Commissioner of Internal Revenue, the Assistant Attorney-General (Tax Division) and the Assistant Secretary of the Treasury (Tax Policy).

Treasury (1984a) Regan Report: *Worldwide Unitary Taxation Working Group, Final Report: Chairman's Report and Supplementary Views*.

Treasury (1984b) *Tax Havens in the Caribbean Basin*.

Treasury & IRS (1984c) *Sources of Information from Abroad*, Document 6743 (Rev. 4–84), T22.2.In3.

Treasury & IRS (1988) *A Study of Intercompany Pricing, Discussion draft* (The White Paper), October 1988.

B. International Organizations
CATA (Commonwealth Association of Tax Administrators)
CATA (1985) Report of 5th Technical Conference, 6–12 September 1984, Apia, W. Samoa.

Commonwealth Secretariat
n.d. (1987?) 'Taxation of Multinational Companies. Follow-up Commentaries based on a Commonwealth-wide Survey'.

CIAT (Centro Interamericano de Administratores Tributarios)
CIAT (1978) *The Exchange of Information under Tax Treaties*, International Bureau of Fiscal Documentation, Amsterdam.

Council of Europe
Parliamentary Assembly (1981) *Colloquy on International Tax Avoidance and Evasion*, 5–7 March 1980, International Bureau of Fiscal Documentation, Amsterdam.

Committee on Legal Cooperation (1984) Report of the Committee of Experts on Fiscal Law on the Proposed Convention on Mutual Administrative Assistance in Tax Matters, 20 December.

Council of Europe (1989) *Explanatory Report on the Convention on Mutual Administrative Assistance in Tax Matters (together with text of the Convention)*, Strasbourg.

European Communities
Commission (1973) Report on the Tax Arrangements Applying to Holding Companies, COM (73) 1008 EEC. Reprinted in Avery-Jones (1974) 109–16.

Commission (1975) Proposal for a Directive of the Council concerning the Harmonization of Company Taxation and of Withholding Taxes on Dividends, Official Journal C 253, 5 November.

Commission (1976) Proposal for a Council Directive on the elimination of double taxation in connection with the adjustment of transfers of profits between associated enterprises (arbitration procedure), Official Journal C 301/4, 21 December.

Commission (1984) Community Action to Combat International Tax Evasion and

Avoidance, Communication to the Council and the European Parliament, COM(84)603 Final.

Commission (1989) The Taxation of Savings, Communication to the Council and to the European Parliament, COM(89)60 Final, Official Journal, 7 June, C/141.

Commission (1991a) Proposal for a Council Directive on a Common System of Taxation Applicable to Interest and Royalty Payments made between Parent Companies and Subsidiaries in Different Member States, 24 January 1991, COM(90) 571 Final.

Commission (1991b) Proposal for a Council Directive Concerning Arrangements for the Taking into account by Enterprises of the Losses of their Permanent Enterprises Situated in other Member States, 24 January 1991, COM(90) 595 Final.

Council (1977) Directive on Mutual Administrative Assistance in Direct Taxation, Directive 77/799 of 19 December. Official Journal L366/15; extended to VAT in 1979, Dir. 79/1070.

Council (1990a) Directive on the Common System of Taxation Applicable to Mergers, Divisions, Transfers of Assets and Exchanges of Shares Concerning Companies of Different Member States, Directive of 23 July, 90/434/EEC, Official Journal L 225, 1.

Council (1990b) Directive on the Common System of Taxation Applicable in the Case of Parent Companies and Subsidiaries of Different States, Directive of 23 July, 90/435/EEC Official Journal L 225, 6.

Council (1990c) Convention on the Elimination of Double Taxation in Connection with the Adjustment of Profits of Associated Enterprises, 90/436/EEC, Official Journal L 225, 10.

Economic & Social Committee (1989) Opinion on the proposal for a Council Directive on a common system of withholding tax on interest income, and the proposal for a Council Directive amending Directive 77/799/EEC concerning mutual assistance by the competent authorities of the member states in the field of direct taxation and value added tax, Official Journal C 221/29.

IBRD (International Bank for Reconstruction and Development/The World Bank)
IBRD (1988) *World Development Report.*

IMF (International Monetary Fund)
IMF (1990) *International Capital Markets. Developments and Prospects*, By a staff team from the Exchange and Trade Relations and Research Departments.

League of Nations
League of Nations (1923) Economic and Financial Commission. Report on Double Taxation Submitted to the Financial Committee, 5 April. Document EFS.73.F.19. Reprinted in US Congress (1962a) vol. 4.

League of Nations (1925) Double Taxation and Tax Evasion. Report and Resolutions submitted by the Technical Experts to the Financial Committee, 7 February, Document F.212. Reprinted in US Congress 1962a.

League of Nations (1927) Double Taxation and Tax Evasion. Report by the Committee of Technical Experts, April, Document C.216.M.85. 1927II. Reprinted in US Congress 1962a.

League of Nations (1928) Double Taxation and Tax Evasion. Report by the General Meeting of Governmental Experts on Double Taxation and Fiscal Evasion, Geneva, October, Document C.562.M.178. 1928II. Reprinted in US Congress 1962a.

League of Nations (1932) *Taxation of Foreign and National Enterprises*. A study of the tax systems and the methods of allocation of the profits of enterprises operating in more than one country. Volume 1 (France, Germany, Spain, the UK and the USA), no.C.73.M.38, 1932 II A 3, Geneva.

League of Nations (1933) *Taxation of Foreign and National Enterprises*, Vols. II and III, and Methods of Allocating Taxable Income Vol. IV; Allocation Accounting for the Taxable Income of Industrial Enterprises by Ralph C. Jones; Doc. no. C.425.M.217 1933 II A 18, Geneva.

League of Nations (1946) London and Mexico Model Tax Conventions, Commentary and Text, Doc. no. C.88.M.88. 1946 IIA, Geneva.

OECD (Organization for Economic Cooperation & Development; formerly OEEC: Organization for European Economic Cooperation)

Fiscal Committee (1958) First Report.

Fiscal Committee (1959) Second Report.

Fiscal Committee (1960) Third Report.

Fiscal Committee (1961) Fourth Report.

Committee on Fiscal Affairs (1963) *Draft Double Taxation Convention on Income and Capital*.

Committee on Fiscal Affairs (1977) *Model Double Taxation Convention on Income and Capital (with Commentary)*.

Committee on Fiscal Affairs (1979) *Transfer Pricing and Multinational Enterprises*.

Committee on Fiscal Affairs (1981) *Model Convention for Mutual Administrative Assistance in the Recovery of Tax Claims (with Commentary)*.

Committee on Fiscal Affairs (1984) *Transfer Pricing and Multinational Enterprises. Three Taxation Issues*. I Transfer Pricing, Corresponding Adjustments and the Mutual Agreement Procedure; II. The Taxation of Multinational Banking Enterprises; III. The Allocation of Central Management and Service Costs.

BIAC (Business and Industry Advisory Committee) (1985a) 'Comments on Draft OECD/Council of Europe Convention on Mutual Administrative Assistance in Tax Matters'.

Committee on Fiscal Affairs (1985b) *Trends in International Taxation*. I Leasing; II Containers; III International Labour Hiring.

Committee on Fiscal Affairs (1987a) *International Tax Avoidance and Evasion. Four Related Studies*, Issues in International Taxation No. 1. I. 'Tax Havens: Measures to Prevent Abuse by Taxpayers'; II. 'Double Taxation Conventions and the Use of Base Companies'; III. 'Double Taxation Conventions and the Use of Conduit Companies'; IV. 'Taxation and the Abuse of Bank Secrecy', Paris.

Committee on Fiscal Affairs (1987b) *Taxation in Developed Countries*, Paris.

Committee on Fiscal Affairs (1987c) *Issues in International Taxation no. 2*. I 'Thin Capitalisation'; II 'Taxation of Entertainers, Artistes and Sportsmen', Paris.

OECD (1987d) *Minimizing Conflicting Requirements. Approaches of 'moderation and restraint'*, OECD, Paris.

Committee on Fiscal Affairs (1988) *Issues in International Taxation no. 3*. 'Tax Consequences of Foreign Exchange Gains and Losses'. Paris.

Committee on Fiscal Affairs (1989) Tax Treaty Override, (Mimeo), Paris.

United Nations

UN (1948–) Dept. of Economic and Social Affairs. *International Tax Agreements*, Vols. 1–9 Doc. E/CN.8/30; ST/ECA/Ser.C. Vol. 9 (1958) has been updated by regular Supplements (Supp. No. 50 issued in 1989).

UN (1953) Dept. of Economic & Social Affairs. *US Income Taxation of Private US Investment in Latin America*, by Stanley Surrey, Dan Throop Smith & Ira T. Wender, ST/ECA/18.

UN (1954) Technical Assistance Administration. *Taxes and Fiscal Policy in Underdeveloped Countries*.

UN (1966) International Law Commission. Commentary on the Draft Vienna Convention on the Law of Treaties. General Assembly Official Records, 21st session, Supp. 9.

UN (1970) Dept. of Economic & Social Affairs. Tax Treaties between developed and developing countries. Second Report (including report of the Secretary-General to the Group of Experts) ST/ECA/137.

UN (1972) Dept. of Economic & Social Affairs. Tax Treaties between developed and developing countries. Third Report, ST/ECA/166.

UN (1973) Dept. of Economic & Social Affairs. Tax Treaties between developed and developing countries. Fourth Report, ST/ECA/188.

UN (1974a) Dept. of Economic & Social Affairs. *The Impact of Multinational Corporations on Development and International Relations*, ST/ESA/6.

UN (1974b) Dept. of Economic & Social Affairs, *Guidelines for Tax Treaties between Developed and Developing Countries*, ST/ESA/14.

UN (1975) Dept. of Economic & Social Affairs, Tax Treaties between developed and developing countries. Fifth Report, ST/ESA/18.

UN (1976) Dept. of Economic & Social Affairs, Tax Treaties between developed and developing countries. Sixth Report, ST/ESA/42.

UN (1978a) Conference on Trade and Development (UNCTAD) The Control of Transfer Pricing in Greece TD/B/C6/32, 31 August.

UN (1978b) Conference on Trade and Development. Dominant Positions of Market Power of Transnational Corporations; Use of the Transfer Price Mechanism, New York.

UN (1978c) Dept. of Economic and Social Affairs. Tax Treaties betwen developed and developing countries. Seventh Report, ST/ESA/79.

UN (1979) Dept. of International Economic and Social Affairs. *Manual for the Negotiation of Bilateral Tax Treaties between Developed and Developing Countries*, ST/ESA/94.

UN (1980) Dept. of International Economic and Social Affairs. Tax Treaties betwen developed and developing countries. Eighth Report, ST/ESA/101.

UN (1984) Department of International Economic & Social Affairs. International Cooperation in Tax Matters, ST/ESA/142.

UN (1988a) Commission on Transnational Corporations, *Transnational Corporations in World Development. Trends and Prospects*, New York, ST/CTC/89.

UN (1988b) Department of International Economic and Social Affairs. Contributions to International Co-operation in Tax Matters. Treaty Shopping; Thin Capitalization; Co-operation between Tax Authorities; Resolving International Tax Disputes, ST/ESA/203.

UN (1988c) Commission on Transnational Corporations. International Income Taxation and Developing Countries, ST/CTC/56.

Treaties

Belgium–Netherlands–Luxembourg (1952) Agreement Concerning Reciprocal Assistance in the Collection of Taxes, 15 April, UNTS vol. 256, no. 3619, p. 3.

Council of Europe (1978) Mutual Assistance in Criminal Matters (Additional Protocol), European Treaty Series no. 99.

Council of Europe (1988) Convention on Mutual Administrative Assistance in Tax Matters, European Treaty Series no. 127.

France–Brazil (1972) Income Tax Treaty, 10 April, UNTS vol. 857, no. 12290-I, 3.

France–Monaco (1963) Income Tax Treaty, 18 May, UNTS vol. 658; no. 9438-I, 393.

Nordic Countries: Sweden–Denmark–Finland–Iceland–Norway (1972) Agreement Concerning Reciprocal Administrative Assistance in Matters of Taxation, 9 November, UNTS vol. 956, no. I-13695, 97.

OECD/Council of Europe (1988) Convention on Mutual Administrative Assistance in Tax Matters (see Council of Europe (1988)).

UK–Barbados (1970) Convention for the Avoidance of Double Taxation and the Prevention of Fiscal Evasion with Respect to Taxes on Income and Capital Gains, UK Treaty Series 93/1970; CMND 4496; S.I. 1970/952.

UK–Ghana (1977) Convention for the Avoidance of Double Taxation and the Prevention of Fiscal Evasion with Respect to Taxes on Income and Capital Gains. UK Treaty Series 89/1979; CMND 7717; S.I.1978/785. [This treaty was apparently not ratified by Ghana, and thus did not enter into force, although it was treated as being in force by the UK until 1991: see [1991] *British Tax Review* 3.]

United States–Bermuda (1986) Convention between the Government of the USA and the Government of the UK (on behalf of Bermuda) Relating to the Taxation of Insurance Enterprises and Mutual Assistance in Tax Matters, with a related exchange of notes, signed at Washington on 11 July 1986.

United States–Germany (1989) Convention for the Avoidance of Double Taxation and the Prevention of Fiscal Evasion with Respect to Taxes on Income and Capital and to Certain Other Taxes. Signed in Bonn 29 August, together with Protocol, Exchange of Notes on Arbitration Procedure, and Exchange of Notes with Understandings on the Scope of the Limitation of Benefits Article. Published as a Special Supplement to the Bulletin of International Fiscal Documentation.

United States–United Kingdom (1957) Agreement Relating to the Application of the Income Tax Convention to Specified British Territories, 19 August 1957, 9 UST 1459; TIAS no. 4141; UK Treaty Series no. xxx.

United States–United Kingdom (1990) Treaty between the USA and the UK of Great Britain and Northern Ireland Concerning the Cayman Islands Relating to Mutual Legal Assistance in Criminal Matters. Signed 3 July 1986. Ratified 19 March 1990. UK Treaty Series no. 82(1990), CM 1316.

United States–Switzerland (1973) Treaty on Mutual Assistance in Criminal Matters. Bern, 25 May; entered into force 23 January 1977. 27 UST 2019, TIAS no. 8302; (1973) 12 International Legal Materials 916. See also Exchange of Letters of 1975, in (1976) 15 *International Legal Materials*, 283.

Tax Treaty Collections

International Bureau of Fiscal Documentation (1988–) Tax Treaties Data-base on

CD-ROM. A collection of virtually all the world's treaties on avoidance of double taxation on income and capital, and a large selection of bilateral estate, death and gift tax treaties. Updated each six months.

United Nations (1948–) International Tax Agreements. Vols. 1–9. Doc. E/CN.8/30; ST/ECA/Ser.C. Vol. 9 (1958) has been updated by regular Supplements (Supp. No. 50 issued in 1989). Continuation of series begun by the League of Nations.

TABLE OF CASES CITED

INDEX